Modern Public Economics

In almost all economies, the government plays an important role in the allocation and distribution of resources, as well as the regulation of economic activity. A proper study of public economics is therefore central to understanding modern economics.

Modern Public Economics covers all aspects of state intervention in the marketplace. Part I is a detailed study of classical theories of welfare economics and also explains key concepts in consumer demand theory. Part II analyses the theory of public expenditure, paying particular attention to pure public goods. Part III is an extremely detailed account of the theory of taxation. Subjects covered include the incentive effects of taxation on labour supply, investment and risk-taking; static and dynamic tax incidence; commodity taxation; optimal income taxation and tax reform. Part IV assesses applied problems in public economics and deals with issues such as public sector pricing, international taxation and cost-benefit analysis. Part V deals with key issues in fiscal federalism.

Modern Public Economics is a comprehensive text for advanced undergraduates and postgraduates which will also be very useful for academics and policy-makers who are interested in the latest developments in public economics.

Raghbendra Jha is Professor of Economics at Indira Gandhi Institute of Development Research, Bombay, India. He has taught previously at Columbia University, USA Queen's University, Canada and the University of Warwick, England. He is the author of twelve books, including *Macroeconomics for Developing Countries* (Routledge, 1994). He is an adviser to the Fiscal Affairs Division of the IMF.

Modern Public Economics

Raghbendra Jha

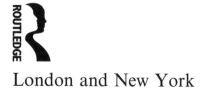

London and New York

First published 1998 by Routledge
11 New Fetter Lane, London EC4P 4EE

Simultaneously published in the USA and Canada
by Routledge
29 West 35th Street, New York, NY 10001

© 1998 Raghbendra Jha

Typeset in Times by Pure Tech India Ltd, Pondicherry
Printed and bound in Great Britain by
TJ International Ltd, Padstow, Cornwall

British Library Cataloguing in Publication Data
A catalogue record for this book is available from the
British Library

Library of Congress Cataloging in Publication Data
A catalogue record for this book has been requested.

ISBN 0–415–14314–4 (hbk)
ISBN 0–415–14315–2 (pbk)

To Mataji

Contents

Preface

Public economics, loosely defined as the study of government intervention in the marketplace, is a rapidly growing area of research. Until a few years ago, public economics could be thought of as being applied micro theory. Not any more. Branches of economics, which were, just a decade ago, thought to have little connection with public finance, have intruded into the domain of public economics. For example, the theory of regulation which has traditionally been an area of concern for the economics of regulation, is now actively researched by scholars working in public economics. The worldwide attention given to issues of the burden of the public debt has led to considerable refinement of the macroeconomic side of public sector behavior. With increasing integration in international trade and commerce, the international aspects of government behavior are becoming increasingly important. Examples like this can be multiplied considerably.

We who study public economics live in exciting and, sometimes, trying times. From time to time a need is felt to provide a sense of perspective on the state of the art – particularly at its frontiers – from which both practitioners as well as students can benefit. This is what courses and texts are supposed to do.

In writing this book I have tried to provide such a sense of perspective. This book develops the foundations of public economics and explores, in considerable detail, research being done at the frontiers. It is written with upper level undergraduates and postgraduate students of economics as audience. With this objective in mind, key arguments are carefully developed and mathematical proofs are carefully worked out so that there are no 'missing steps' for students to fill in. It has been my experience while teaching public economics to students in three countries – Queen's University, Canada, University of Warwick, UK, and IGIDR and Delhi School of Economics in India – that students find it very hard to work through the missing steps in proofs of papers published in scientific journals or, for that matter, advanced texts. This has the predictable result that teachers have to provide considerable background notes. The present book should help to ameliorate this difficulty. I have made a conscious effort to provide complete proofs which should be easy to follow without the need for any background notes. This book should also be useful to academics and policy planners who want a complete account of recent developments in the field of public economics.

The book is organized as follows. Part I is entitled 'Welfare Economics' and consists of three chapters. In Chapter 1 I have developed key concepts in consumer demand theory which are heavily used in public economics. The topics covered include direct and indirect utility functions, expenditure functions, compensation, Roy's identity, Slutsky equation and the like. This chapter is quite self-contained so students will not have to appeal to a microeconomic text to learn these concepts. In Chapter 2, the distinction between reaching the Pareto frontier and choosing any point on the frontier is spelt out. This chapter deals with the efficiency question of devising mechanisms under ideal conditions to reach the Pareto frontier. The question of choosing a point on the frontier is developed in Chapter 3. In this context the issue of democratic aggregation of preferences is taken up. The Arrow Impossibility Theorem, Gibbard's Oligarchy Theorem and Sen's Impossibility of a Paretian Liberal Theorem are all proved to emphasize the difficulties involved in democratic aggregation of preferences. At this point the information content of the Arrow framework is explored and it is shown that possibility results emerge when one admits interpersonal comparisons of utility. The utilitarian, neo-utilitarian, Rawlsian and Atkinson's measures of social welfare are all explained in this chapter since these welfare functions have been used extensively in applied and theoretical work.

Part II of the book is entitled 'The Theory of Public Expenditure' and consists of three chapters. In Chapter 4, the presence of externalities as a basic rationale for public expenditure is explored. Solutions to the problems of various types of external effects are explained and assessed. Chapter 5 concerns itself almost exclusively with pure public goods. Various forms of the Samuelson condition for Pareto optimal supply of a pure public good are derived. The free rider problem and attempts at its solution are also discussed here. There is also a brief discussion of voting models of public goods. Chapter 6 takes up some issues of interest in the theory of public goods. We study the theory of clubs and the Tiebout process, the financing of public goods with distortionary taxation and asymmetric information in the theory of public goods.

Part III is entitled 'The Theory of Taxation' and consists of ten chapters. Chapters 7, 8, 9 and 10 deal with the incentive effects of taxes. Chapter 7 deals with effects of taxes on savings, Chapter 8 with labor supply, Chapter 9 with investment behavior and Chapter 10 with taxation and risk-taking. Chapter 11 deals with static tax incidence. The static two-sector general equilibrium model of tax incidence is studied. Then we move to incidence analysis with involuntary unemployment and incidence analysis in the presence of regulation. In Chapter 12 we study tax incidence in some dynamic models. Tax incidence is studied in the basic Solow model as well as in the

Diamond life-cycle model. The notion of balanced growth path tax incidence is also developed. Tax incidence in the Blanchard-Yaari life cycle model is also discussed as well as the issue of tax versus debt finance of government expenditure. Some issues relating to Ricardian equivalence are also dealt with here. We also study tax incidence in monetary growth models. In Chapter 13 we study commodity taxation. We examine the standard elasticity formulae as well as the issue of the limits to redistribution with commodity taxation. Chapter 14 discusses optimal income taxation – linear as well as non-linear. We also study the problem of optimal taxation with incomplete information. In Chapter 15 we study four topics in the theory of income taxation: optimal taxation in a model of endogenous growth, the problem of income tax indexation in an inflationary economy, the problem of time consistency and, briefly, some models of tax compliance. Chapter 16 discusses some aspects of tax reform.

Part IV of the book is entitled 'Applied Problems in Public Economics' and consists of three chapters. Chapter 17 is a fairly detailed analysis of issues related to public sector pricing. Marginal cost and efficient and redistributive second-best pricing, non-linear pricing, pricing of joint products and related issues are considered in this chapter. Chapter 18 deals with some issues in international taxation and Chapter 19 has a brief overview of cost benefit analysis.

Part V of the book is entitled 'Fiscal Federalism' and consists of two chapters. Chapter 20 deals with key issues in federalism such as the optimal degree of decentralization. Chapter 21 discusses the delegation of grants and taxes within a federal framework. There is an extensive bibliography at the end of the book to help plan further reading.

In writing this book I have run up a long list of acknowledgments. First, I have benefited enormously from my association with Robin Boadway at Queen's University, Kingston, Canada, during my two spells as visiting faculty. I learnt a great deal from Robin in conversations as well as during my coauthorship with him. Dan Usher was a source of intellectual stimulation while I was at Queen's as were Isao Horiba (then visiting Queen's from Tokyo), and Bagala Biswal (then a graduate student at Queen's). Thanks are also due to two friends and occasional coauthors: Balbir Sahni of Concordia University and Anandi Sahu of Oakland University for their constant encouragement. Throughout the long years over which this book was conceived and written, I benefited greatly from the comments of my students in Queen's University, Canada, University of Warwick, UK and Indira Gandhi Institute of Development Research (IGIDR) and Delhi School of Economics in India. The students' evaluation of my class lectures has served as a critical input into this book. I would like to thank each of them individually but they are far too many to mention.

The book in its final form has been written at the University of Warwick. The economics department at Warwick has provided an excellent environment for my work. I owe a great debt of gratitude to Norman Ireland for making my stay here so pleasant and intellectually stimulating. Tony Addison, Jeff Round, John Whalley, Chris Heady and Mike Waterson also deserve heartfelt thanks from me. I would also like to take this (statistically improbable) opportunity to thank Edmund Phelps who, as my PhD guide twenty years ago, introduced me to the exciting area of public economics. At IGIDR, Bombay, I would like to thank Kirit Parikh for his constant help, support and encouragement. Mudit Kulshreshtha, Nibedita Das and especially Santanu Gupta, all graduate students at IGIDR, have helped with the diagrams. Without Santanu's help the figures would not have been possible.

I have also benefited greatly from the help and support of the economics section at Routledge. Alison Kirk, economics editor, provided consistent and unflinching support. The extremely thoughtful comments of anonymous referees helped considerably in bringing the manuscript to its present form. I am grateful to all these people for their help, patience and friendship. Given these, the task of writing this book was never a chore.

My greatest debt of gratitude is to my family – my wife Alka and our son Abhay. It would be impossible, indeed presumptuous, for me even to begin thanking them.

Raghbendra Jha
Coventry, UK

November 1996

Part I
Welfare economics

Introduction to Part I

Part I consists of three chapters and sets the stage for the analysis in the rest of the book. Elements of consumer demand theory are used fairly extensively in public economics because efficiency and welfare implications of public policy changes have to be evaluated and this can only be done in terms of a calculus of individual welfare.

Modern microeconomic theory usually articulates individual consumer behavior in terms of preference orderings or utility functions. In Chapter 1 we study the underpinnings of the theory of consumer behavior. We begin by specifying the basic properties of an ordering such as convexity, continuity, completeness and rationality. We then detail the link between preference orderings and consumer utility functions. Properties of utility functions are then discussed. The Slutsky equation is derived as are the properties of Marshallian and Hicksian demand functions. Constructs such as the indirect utility function and the expenditure function are discussed, as are important results such as Roy's identity, the envelope theorem and compensating and equivalent variations. Throughout the emphasis is on familiarizing the students with the basic results. Hence some complex proofs are eschewed.

In Chapter 2 a survey of Paretian welfare economics is undertaken. We begin by developing the notions of the Pareto criteria and Pareto optimality. The two classical theorems of welfare economics are proved using the notion of consumer orderings and consumer utility functions as (alternative) bases. The point is made that the Paretian criterion cannot help us choose any particular welfare optimum. We then extend the proof of the second optimality theorem to the case of uncertainty. Both the Debreu contingent commodity market solution as well as the security market solution are discussed. The difficulty of extending these results to the case of production economies is considered. There is also a discussion of the theory of second best.

In Chapter 3 we study the problem of making social choice through means other than the Paretian criterion since the latter is not adequate for social choice. Scitovsky indifference curves are derived and the compensation criteria of Kaldor, Hicks and Scitovsky are examined. We then broach the thorny question of aggregating individual preference to make social choice. The impossibility result of Arrow, Gibbard's oligarchy Theorem and Sen's impossiblity of a Paretian liberal are all discussed here. We then consider the problem of informational scarcity in the Arrowian framework and show that it is possible to aggregate individual preference to make reasonable social choice. The possibility results of Strasnick and Hammond are looked at here. Finally some forms of the social welfare function used in applied work are discussed.

1 A quick primer on consumer demand

Key concepts: preference ordering; transitivity, quasi-transitivity and acyclicity of preferences; continuity and convexity of orderings; utility functions: direct and indirect, concave and quasi-concave utility functions; compensated and uncompensated demand functions; expenditure functions; Slutsky equation, consumer's surplus, equivalent and compensating variations; Roy's identity; excess burden of a tax; the Envelope theorem.

1.1 INTRODUCTION

In public economics some key results from consumer demand theory are often used. In some instances, students would have picked up these results in micro theory. However, for the sake of completeness these results are provided here. This review is not meant to be exhaustive but should be viewed as a necessary prelude to studying some aspects of public economics. This chapter, then, is an entry point to the study of public economics, not public economics proper.

We begin this chapter with the definitions of some basic notions in consumer demand theory. Later we derive key concepts that will be useful in our study of tax and expenditure policies.

1.2 SOME KEY DEFINITIONS

Definition 1.1 (weak preference relation or ordering)

In the classical theory of consumer demand the basic weak preference relation for any consumer i is written as R_i (read as 'at least as good as'). Thus if x and y are two consumption baskets available to individual i and if it is discovered that xR_iy then it follows that commodity bundle x is considered by individual i to be at least as good as commodity bundle y. (Sometimes, R_i is also called an ordering.) If, at the same time, y is not R_ix then we say that commodity bundle x is strictly preferred by individual i to commodity bundle y. This is written as xP_iy. If, however, xR_iy **and** yR_ix

then individual i is indifferent between commodity bundles x and y; this is written as xI_iy. The consumer is assumed to have a consumption set X_i from which all choices of consumption baskets must be made. The weak preference relation R_i is defined over this consumption set.

Definition 1.2 (rational weak preference relation)

The weak preference relation R_i defined on X_i is rational if it possesses the following properties.

(i) Completeness

This requires that the ordering R_i be defined over all pairs of consumption baskets in X_i; i.e. for all consumption baskets $a, b \in X_i$ we must have either aR_ib, bR_ia or both. (Clearly, aR_ia. This property is referred to as **reflexivity**). Sometimes, but not necessarily, this requirement is coupled with the additional requirement of **binariness** or **independence of irrelevant alternatives**. This requires that, when comparing two alternatives a and b, it is not necessary to appeal to any third alternative c.

(ii) Forms of transitivity and rationality

These refer to relations between three alternatives. The simplest form is **full transitivity** which requires that if aR_ib, and bR_ic then aR_ic. Typically, to consider an ordering to be rational we usually require that transitivity hold.

Rarely, but not insignificantly, we will meet a weaker form of transitivity called **quasi-transitivity**. This requires that the strict preference relation is transitive (and is silent on the transitivity of the weak preference relation). Thus, if gP_ih, and hP_ij then gP_ij.

A still weaker requirement is that of **acyclicity**. P_i is acyclic if there does not exist a sequence of consumption baskets $a, b, \ldots, l$ such that $aP_ib \,\& \, bP_ic \,\& \ldots \& \, kP_il$ and lP_ia.

Another desirable requirement is that of **non-satiation**, i.e., more is always at least as good as less. In other words, if aR_ib and $b \in X_i$, then $a \in X_i$. A stronger requirement is that of **local non-satiation**. If $a \in X_i$ then there exists another consumption basket, u, with $|u - a| < \epsilon$ with ϵ arbitrarily small such that uP_ia. Standard utility analysis always assumes local non-satuation. See Figure 1.1.

(iii) Convexity

(This is not a requirement for rationality of preferences.) The ordering R_i on X_i is convex if for every $a \in X_i$ the upper contour set is convex. In other words for $a, b, c \in X_i$ if aR_ic and bR_ic then $[\alpha a + (1 - \alpha)b]R_ic$ for $0 \leqslant \alpha \leqslant 1$. We can define the analogous concept of **strong convexity**. For

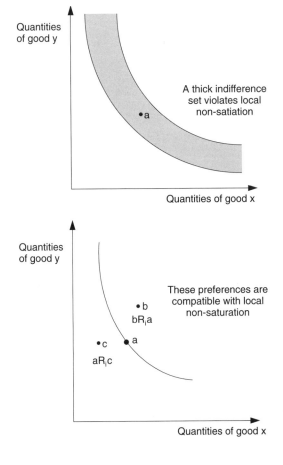

Figure 1.1

$a, b, c \in X_i$ if $aR_i b$, and $bR_i c$ then $[\alpha a + (1 - \alpha)b] P_i c$ for $0 \leqslant \alpha \leqslant 1$. Indifference curves of the 'standard' type satisfy strong convexity. (See Figure 1.2.)

From the primitive notion of an ordering as defined above, it is a short, but eventful, step to reach utility functions. Orderings which are **continuous** can be represented by a utility function.

Definition 1.3 (continuity)

The ordering R_i on X_i is continuous if it is preserved under limits, i.e, for any sequence of pairs $\{(x^n, y^n)\}_{n=1}^{\infty}$ with $x^n R_i y^n$ for all n, $x = \lim_{n \to \infty} x^n$, and $y = \lim_{n \to \infty} y^n$, we have $xR_i y$.

As mentioned above, when an ordering is continuous it can be represented by a real valued utility function such that when $xR_i y$ then

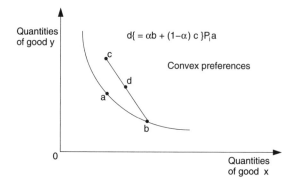

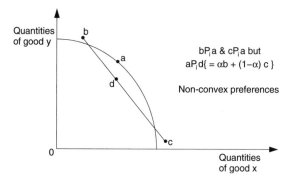

Figure 1.2

$U(x) \geq U(y)$ where $U(.)$ is the real valued utility function. To be perfectly precise, however, we should mention Cantor's theorem.

Cantor's theorem

There is a real valued function $U(.)$ on X_i such that for all $x, x' \in X_i$, xR_ix' implies $U(x) \geq U(y)$ if and only if R is an ordering on X_i and there exists a countable subset of X_i that is P order dense in X_i (for a proof see Luce and Suppes, 1965).

When an ordering is **lexicographic**, for example, then it cannot be represented by a utility function. This is a celebrated exception to the rule that orderings can be represented by real valued functions. Suppose we take a consumption set that is uncountably infinite. Suppose a consumer loves fish very much. Indeed she loves it so much that given any amount of fish more rice would make her better off, but if you gave her a little bit more fish she would be better off than with the old consumption basket irrespective of the amount of rice in that basket. Thus, an infinite number of real numbers is exhausted in calculating utility values associated with just one quantity of fish.

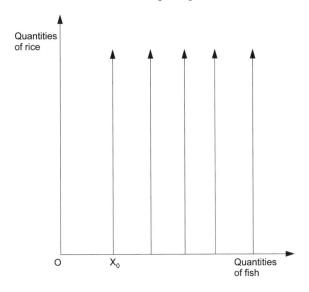

Figure 1.3

This is illustrated in Figure 1.3. In this diagram with x_0 amount of fish, utility increases along the vertical line through x_0 but the very next highest amount of fish gives higher utility than any point on the vertical line through x_0. So, intuitively speaking, we run out of real numbers.

1.3 UTILITY FUNCTIONS

We now assume that there is in existence a real valued utility function. For analytical purposes, it is also convenient to assume that the consumer's utility function is differentiable. Most of the time we require that the utility function be **twice continuously differentiable**. From the property of convexity of weak preferences we can deduce that $U(.)$ is **quasiconcave** [and, similarly, strict convexity of weak preference implies **strict quasiconcavity** of $U(.)$]. The utility function $U(.)$ is said to be quasiconcave if the set $\{y \in R_+^N$ (where R_+^N covers the set of N goods in the positive quadrant) is such that $U(y) \geqslant U(x)\}$ is convex for all x or, equivalently, if $U(\alpha x + (1-\alpha)y) \geqslant \text{Min}\{U(x), U(y)\}$ for any x, y and all $\alpha \in [0,1]$. (If the inequality is strict for for all $x \neq y$ and $\alpha \in (0,1)$ then $U(.)$ is strictly quasiconcave). Note, however, that convexity of R_i does **not** imply the stronger property that $U(.)$ is concave: $\{U(\alpha x + (1-\alpha)y) R_i\{\alpha U(x) + (1-\alpha)U(y)\}$ for any x, y and for $\alpha \in [0,1]$.

We now state another property of utility functions:
A continuous R_i on $X = R_+^N$ is **homothetic** if it admits a utility function $U(x)$ that is **homogeneous of degree one** (i.e., such that $U(\alpha x) = \alpha U(x)$ for all $\alpha \in [0,1]$).

1.4   THE CONSUMER'S UTILITY MAXIMIZATION PROBLEM

We now turn to the consumer's choice problem. We assume throughout that the consumer has a rational, continuous, and locally non-satiated weak preference. We take this utility function U(x) to be a twice continuously differentiable, quasi-concave function. We can now state the following result.

Proposition

If prices and wealth are strictly positive and wealth is (w) then the utility maximization problem:

$$\text{Max } U(x) \text{ s.t. } p.x \leqslant w$$
$$x \geqslant 0$$

has a solution. The proof follows immediately from the fact that a continuous function always has a maximum value on any compact set.

Marshallian demand – *un compensated or ordinary*

The rule that assigns the set of optimal consumption vectors in the utility maximization problem to each price–wealth situation (p, w) is denoted by $x(p, w) \in R_+^N$ and is known as the **Marshallian** demand function. It will variously be referred to also as the **uncompensated** or **ordinary** demand function. This demand function possesses the following properties (stated without proof):

(i) **Homogeneity of degree zero in (p, w)**. This means that $x(\alpha p, \alpha w) = x(p, w)$ for any p, w and any scalar $\alpha > 0$.
(ii) **Walras' Law**: $p.x = w$ for all $x \in x(p, w)$.
(iii) **Convexity/uniqueness**. If R_i is convex, so that U(.) is quasi-concave, then x (p, w) is a convex set. Moreover, if R_i is strictly convex, so that U(.) is strictly quasi-concave, then x (p, w) consists of a single element.

If, as has been assumed here, U(.) is continuously differentiable, an optimal consumption bundle $x^* \in x(p, w)$ can be characterized in a very useful manner by means of first-order conditions. The **Kuhn-Tucker (necessary) conditions** say that if $x^* = x(p, w)$ is a solution to the utility maximization problem, then there exists a Lagrange multiplier $\lambda \geqslant 0$, such that for all $k = 1, \ldots, N$ (where k indexes commodities):

$$\partial U(x^*)/\partial x_k \leqslant \lambda p_k \tag{1.1}$$

with equality if $x_k^* > 0$.
In matrix notation we can proceed as follows. Let $\nabla U(x^*) = [\partial U(x)/\partial x_1, \ldots, \partial U(x)/\partial x_N]$ denote the gradient vector of U(.) at x, we can then write equation (1.1) in matrix notation as:

$$\nabla U(x^*) \leqslant \lambda p \tag{1.2}$$

$$\text{and} \quad x^*[\nabla U(x^*) - \lambda p] = 0. \tag{1.3}$$

Thus, if we are at an interior optimum (if $x^* > 0$), it must be the case that:

$$\nabla U(x^*) = \lambda p. \tag{1.4}$$

We denote some solutions to the utility maximization problem in the case of two commodities in Figure 1.4. If we have an interior solution then it must be the case that for any two goods r, and t:

$$MRS = \frac{\partial U(x^*)/\partial x_r}{\partial U(x^*)/\partial x_t} = p_r/p_t. \tag{1.5}$$

The expression on the lefthand side is the marginal rate of substitution (mrs) of good r for good t.

The Lagrange multiplier, λ, in the first-order conditions (1.2) and (1.3) gives the marginal or shadow value of relaxing the constraint in the utility maximization. It therefore equals the consumer's marginal utility of wealth at the optimum.

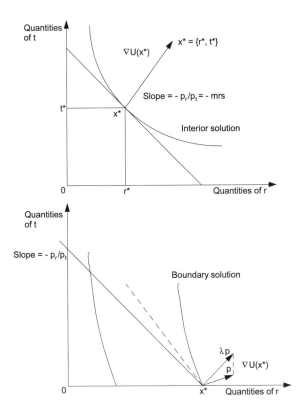

Figure 1.4

The indirect utility function

For each $(p, w) > 0$, the utility value of the utility maximization problem is denoted as $V(p, w) \in R$. It is equal to $U(x^*)$ for any $x^* \in x(p, w)$. The function V (p, w) is called the **indirect utility function** and, in public economics, tends to be a very useful analytical tool. With regard to the indirect utility function we state, without proof, the following proposition.

Proposition 1.1

Suppose that $U(.)$ is a continuous utility function representing a locally non-satiated preference relation R_i defined on the consumption set $X = R_+^N$. The indirect utility function $V(p, w)$ is:

(i) homogeneous of degree zero;
(ii) strictly increasing in w and non-increasing in p_k for any commodity k;
(iii) quasiconvex, i.e., the set $\{(p, w) : V(p, w) \leqslant \bar{V}\}$ is convex for any $\bar{V}$;
(iv) continuous in p and w.

We can now proceed to the **expenditure minimization problem**. This is defined as follows.
For $p > 0$ and $\bar{U} > 0$
$\text{Min}_{x \geqslant 0}$ p.x subject to $U(.) \geqslant \bar{U}$. This problem then calculates the minimum level of wealth required to reach the level of utility $\bar{U}$. The expenditure minimization problem is the dual to the utility maximization problem. We state without proof the following important proposition.

Proposition 1.2

Suppose that $U(.)$ is a continuous utility function representing a locally non-satiated weak preference relation R_i defined on the consumption set $X = R_+^N$ and that the price vector $p > 0$. We have

(i) If x^* is optimal in the utility maximization problem when wealth is $w > 0$, then x^* is optimal in the expenditure minimization problem when the required utility level is $U(x^*)$. Moreover, the minimized expenditure level in this expenditure minimization problem is exactly w.
(ii) If x^* is optimal in the expenditure minimization problem when the required utility level is $\bar{U} > U(0)$, then x^* is optimal in the utility maximization problem when wealth is p.x*. Moreover, the maximized utility level in this utility maximization problem is exactly $\bar{U}$.

The expenditure function

Given prices, $p > 0$, and required utility level $\bar{U} > U(0)$, the value of the expenditure minimization problem is denoted $e(p, \bar{U})$. The function $e(p, \bar{U})$

is called the expenditure function. With respect to this expenditure function we state, without proof, the following proposition.

Proposition 1.3

Suppose that $U(.)$ is a continuous utility function representing a locally non-satiated weak preference relation R_i defined on the consumption set $X = R_+^N$. The expenditure function $e(p, U)$ is:

(i) homogeneous of degree one in p;
(ii) strictly increasing in U and nondecreasing in p_k for any k;
(iii) concave in p;
(iv) continuous in p and U.

In addition, we have an important relation between the expenditure function and the indirect utility function. For any $p > 0, w > 0$, and $\bar{U} > U(0)$ it must be the case that:

$$e(p, V(p, w)) = w \quad \text{and that} \quad V(p, e(p, \bar{U})) = \bar{U}.$$

This will be useful in defining the equivalence between the compensating variation and the equivalent variation of a price change to be considered later. We now turn to compensated demand functions.

The Hicksian (or compensated) demand function

The set of optimal commodity vectors in the expenditure minimization problem is denoted $h(p, \bar{U}) \subset R_+^N$ and is known as Hicksian or compensated demand function. The basic properties of the Hicksian demand function are reported in the following proposition.

Proposition 1.4

Suppose that $U(.)$ is a continuous utility function representing a locally non-satiated weak preference relation R_i defined on the consumption set $X = R_+^N$. Then for $p > 0$ the Hicksian demand function possesses the following properties:

(i) Homogeneity of degree zero in p : $h(\alpha p, U) = h(p, U)$ for any p, U and $\alpha > 0$.
(ii) No excess utility: for any $x \in h(p, U), U(x) = U$.
(iii) Convexity/uniqueness: if R_i is convex, then $h(p, U)$ is a convex set; and if R_i is strictly convex, so that $U(.)$ is strictly quasi-concave, then there is a unique element in $h(p, U)$.

Using proposition 1.4 we can relate the Hicksian and Marshallian demand functions as follows:

$$h(p, U) = x(p, e(p, U)) \quad \text{and} \quad x(p, w) = h(p, V(p, w)).$$

Hicksian demand and the direction of substitution effects

Suppose that U(.) is a continuous utility function representing a locally non-satiated weak preference relation R_i and that $h(p,U)$ consists of a single element for $p > 0$. Then along the Hicksian demand function demand changes in the opposite direction of the price change. In other words for all p', p'':

$$(p'' - p')[h(p'', \bar{U}) - h(p', \bar{U})] \leqslant 0.$$

The compensated demand function is intimately related to an important relation in consumer demand theory known as the Slutsky equation. Since this equation is so important to several results in public economics, we shall derive it from first steps for the case of two commodities. The case of many commodities is a straightforward generalization.

Derivation of the Slutsky equation

Consider the following utility maximization problem:

$$\max_{x_1, x_2} U(x_1, x_2) \quad \text{subject to} \quad p_1 x_1 + p_2 x_2 = w.$$

Set up the Lagrangean:

$$\Lambda = U(x_1, x_2) + \lambda[w - p_1 x_1 - p_2 x_2]. \tag{1.6}$$

First-order conditions for an internal maximum are that:

$$U_1 - \lambda p_1 = 0 \tag{1.7a}$$
$$U_2 - \lambda p_2 = 0 \tag{1.7b}$$
$$w - p_1 x_1 - p_2 x_2 = 0 \tag{1.7c}$$

where $U_1 \equiv \partial U / \partial x_1$ and $U_2 \equiv \partial U / \partial x_2$.

Totally differentiating these first-order conditions and denoting partial derivatives by subscripts we have that:

$$U_{11} dx_1 + U_{12} dx_2 - \lambda dp_1 - p_1 d\lambda = 0 \tag{1.8a}$$
$$U_{21} dx_1 + U_{22} dx_2 - \lambda dp_2 - p_2 d\lambda = 0 \tag{1.8b}$$
$$dw - p_1 dx_1 - x_1 dp_1 - p_2 dx_2 - x_2 dp_2 = 0 \tag{1.8c}$$

We can write these equations in matrix form with dx_1, dx_2 and $d\lambda$ as the endogenous variables as:

$$\begin{bmatrix} U_{11} & U_{12} & -p_1 \\ U_{21} & U_{22} & -p_2 \\ -p_1 & -p_2 & 0 \end{bmatrix} \begin{bmatrix} dx_1 \\ dx_2 \\ d\lambda \end{bmatrix} = \begin{bmatrix} \lambda dp_1 \\ \lambda dp_2 \\ C \end{bmatrix} \tag{1.9}$$

where $C = -dw + x_1 dp_1 + x_2 dp_2$.

By Cramer's rule we can solve:

$$dx_1 = [\lambda dp_1 D_{11} + \lambda dp_2 D_{21} + C D_{31}]/D \tag{1.10}$$

and

$$dx_2 = [\lambda dp_1 D_{12} + \lambda dp_2 D_{22} + CD_{32}]/D \qquad (1.11)$$

where D_{ij} is the cofactor of the ijth element in the matrix on the lefthand side of equation (1.9) and D is the determinant of the matrix on the left-hand side of equation (1.9). The price effect of p_1 on x_1 (along the Marshallian demand function) is given by setting $dp_2 = dw = 0$ in equation (1.10) to get:

$$\partial x_1/\partial p_1 = \lambda D_{11}/D + x_1 D_{31}/D. \qquad (1.12)$$

It can easily be checked that $\partial x_1/\partial w = -D_{31}/D$ so that:

$$\partial x_1/\partial p_1 = \lambda D_{11}/D - x_1 \partial x_1/\partial w. \qquad (1.13)$$

Now, when $dU = 0$ we know that $U_1 dx_1 + U_2 dx_2 = 0$. We also know from (1.8a, b) that $U_1/U_2 = p_1/p_2$. Thence from (1.8c) we get $-dw + x_1 dp_1 + x_2 dp_2 = 0$ from which we have:

$$[\partial x_1/\partial p_1]_{dU=0} = [D_{11}/D]\lambda. \qquad (1.14)$$

Substituting in equation (1.13) we have:

$$\partial x_1/\partial p_1 = [\partial x_1/\partial p_1]_{dU=0} - x_1 \partial x_1/\partial w. \qquad (1.15)$$

This is known as the Slutsky equation. In general for any two goods *i* and *j*:

$$\partial x_i/\partial p_j = [\partial x_i/\partial p_j]_{dU=0} - x_j \partial x_i/\partial w. \qquad (1.16)$$

Total price effect (along the Marshallian demand function) = substitution effect (along the Hicksian demand function) – income effect.

1.5 SOME OTHER USEFUL RELATIONS IN DEMAND THEORY

Suppose that U(.) is a continuous utility function representing a locally non-satiated and strictly convex weak preference relation R_i defined on the consumption set R_+^N. For all p and U, the **Hicksian demand** h(p,U) is the derivative vector of the expenditure function with respect to prices:

$$h(p, U) = \nabla_p e(p, U). \qquad (1.17)$$

In other words, $h_k(p, U) = \partial e(p, U)/\partial p_k$ for all goods $k = 1, \ldots, N$.

Envelope theorem

Consider the value function $\phi(\beta)$ of the constrained minimization problem:

$$\underset{x}{M}\text{in } f(x, \beta) \text{ subject to } g(x, \beta) = 0.$$

If $x^*(\beta)$ is the (differentiable) solution to this problem as a function of the parameter β then the envelope theorem assures us that at any β_0

$$\partial\phi(\beta_0)/\partial\beta = \partial\phi(x^*(\beta_0), \beta_0)/\partial\beta - \lambda[\partial g(x^*(\beta_0), \beta_0)/\partial\beta] \qquad (1.18)$$

where λ is the Lagrange multiplier associated with the constraint.

Roy's identity

Suppose that $U(.)$ is a continuous utility function representing a locally non-satiated and strictly convex weak preference relation R_i defined on the consumption set $X = R_+^N$. Suppose that the indirect utility function is differentiable at some $(p_0, w_0) > 0$. Then, for goods $k = 1, \ldots, N$:

$$x_k(p_0, w_0) = -[\partial V(p_0, w_0)/\partial p_k]/[\partial V(p_0, w_0)/\partial w] \qquad (1.19)$$

where $x_k = \partial x/\partial p_k$.

1.6   CONSUMER'S SURPLUS AND MEASUREMENT OF WELFARE CHANGES

We now move to the area of measuring welfare changes in response to a price change for individual consumers. Suppose that we know the consumer's weak preference relation R_i. In this case, it is straightforward to articulate the effect of the price change on the welfare of the consumer. If $V(p, w)$ is any indirect utility function derived from R_i, the consumer is worse off with the price change from p_0 to p_1 iff $V(p_1, w) - V(p_0, w) < 0$.

One class of indirect utility functions is specially amenable for making welfare comparisons because it leads to measurement of welfare changes expressed in units of money. Start from any indirect utility function $V(.)$, choose an arbitrary price vector $\bar{p} > 0$ and consider the function $e(\bar{p}, V(p, w))$. This function gives the wealth required to reach utility level $V(p, w)$ when prices are $\bar{p}$. Clearly this measure is strictly increasing as a function of the level $V(p, w)$. Hence, viewed as a function of (p, w), $e(\bar{p}, V(p, w))$ is itself an indirect utility function for R_i, and $e(\bar{p}, V(p_1, w)) - e(\bar{p}, V(p_0, w))$ provides a measure of welfare changes expressed in units of money. Two natural choices for the price vector $\bar{p}$ are the initial price vector p_i and the final price vector p_f. These two choices lead to two well-known measures of welfare changes: the equivalent variation (EV) and the compensating variation (CV). Let $U^i = V(p_i, w)$ and $U^f = V(p_f, w)$ and note that $e(p_i, U_i) = e(p_f, U_f) = w$.
Now define:

$$EV(p_i, p_f, w) = e(p_i, U^f) - e(p_i, U^i) = e(p_i, U^f) - w \qquad (1.20)$$

and

$$CV(p_i, p_f, w) = e(p_f, U^f) - e(p_f, U^0) = w - e(p_f, U^0). \qquad (1.21)$$

The equivalent variation can be thought of as the amount of money that the consumer would be willing to accept when the price change occurs and still be as well-off as before the price change. Thus it must be the case that $V(p_i, w + EV) = U^f$. The compensating variation is the negative of the amount that the consumer would be just willing to accept from the planner

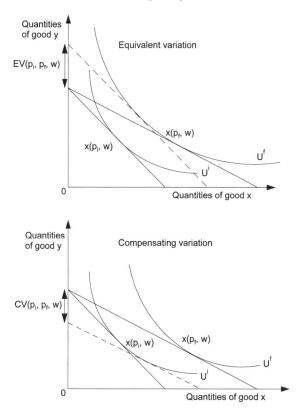

Figure 1.5

to permit the price change to happen. Thus, $V(p_f, w - CV) = U^i$. We depict the equivalent and compensating variations in Figure 1.5.

An important application of the concepts of equivalent and compensating variations is in the area of measuring the excess burden of a tax change. We discuss this concept in its simplest form in Figure 1.6. This diagram shows the demand and supply functions of a single commodity. When a tax is imposed on this commodity, the supply curve shifts up and the price rises from p_0 to p_1. The shaded area represents the revenue from the tax. But the loss in consumer's surplus exceeds the government revenue by the extent of the triangle ABC. This is the so-called 'excess burden' or 'deadweight loss' of the tax in its simplest terms. The supply curve is drawn as horizontal in Figure 1.6. Had the supply curve been upward sloping, there would have been a loss of producer's surplus in addition to the loss in consumer's surplus.

What we have in Figure 1.6 is the Marshallian demand curve. This is not very useful in determining excess burden. The reason for this is that this measure has the serious flaw of path dependence: the measure of consumer

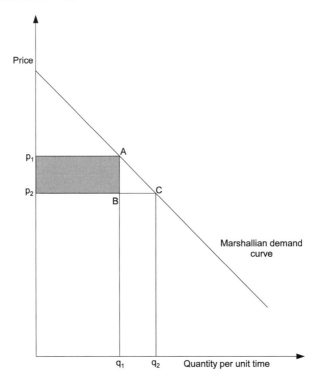

Figure 1.6

surplus depends upon the sequence of price changes. It is quite easy to demonstrate this. Let x^j and p^j be the quantity demanded and the price in the jth. market the sum of individual changes in consumers' surplus, ΔS^j, i.e., the line integral:

$$\Delta S = \sum_j \Delta S^j = -\int_{p^i}^{p^f} \sum_j x^j(.)dp^j. \tag{1.22}$$

This takes on different values according to the path of integration from the initial price vector p^i to the final price vector p^f. To see this consider a simple example with two markets. In the following p_1^f should be read as the price in the market for commodity 1 **after** the price change. If we change the price in market 1 first the change in surplus is:

$$\Delta S_1 = -\int_{p_1^i}^{p_1^f} x^1(p^1, p_2^i)dp^1 - \int_{p_2^i}^{p_2^f} x^2(p_1^f, p^2)dp^2. \tag{1.23}$$

However, if we change the price in market 2 first we will get:

$$\Delta S_2 = -\int_{p_1^i}^{p_1^f} x^1(p^1, p_2^f) dp^1 - \int_{p_2^i}^{p_2^f} x^2(p_1^i, p^2) dp^2. \tag{1.24}$$

The difference between ΔS_2 and ΔS_1 will, in general, not be zero. For small changes in price we can write:

$$\Delta S_2 - \Delta S_1 = [\partial x^2(p_1^i, p_2^f)/\partial p^1] dp^1 dp^2 - [\partial x^1(p_1^i, p_2^i)/\partial p^2] dp^1 dp^2 \tag{1.25}$$

which equals zero only if the cross-partial derivatives are zero. This property is true of Hicksian (compensated) demand curves and not Marshallian demand curves. In other words, when price changes are small equivalent variation and compensated variation provide path-independent measures of the excess burden of the tax.

By the envelope theorem (already discussed) the derivative of the expenditure function with respect to an individual price p^i is the Hicksian or compensated demand function for that good $h^i(p, \bar{U})$. Thus either of the Hicksian variations may be expressed (for the appropriate value of $\bar{U}$) as:

$$e(p^f, \bar{U}) - e(p^i, \bar{U}) = \int_{p^i}^{p^f} \frac{de(p, \bar{U})}{dp} dp = \int_{p^i}^{p^f} h^i(p, \bar{U}) dp. \tag{1.26}$$

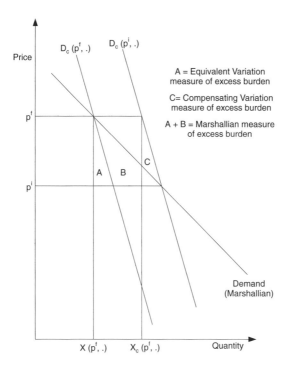

Figure 1.7

The various definitions of excess burden for our special case are shown in Figure 1.7.

1.7 CONCLUSIONS

In this chapter we have discussed some key concepts in consumer demand theory that are used in public economics. We started out with some basic definitions which serve as the building blocks of consumer demand. We discussed both the 'ordering' as well as the 'utility' approach to the consumer's utility maximization problem and pointed out the link between the two. We then developed important notions such as the measurement of welfare changes through compensating and equivalent variations as well as compensated and uncompensated demand functions, Roy's identity and the like. The discussion here is by no means exhaustive nor complete. However, it does provide a basis for the discussion that is to follow later in this book. This becomes evident in Chapter 2 where we begin our examination of the building blocks of welfare economics.

ADDITIONAL READING

The subject matter of this chapter is treated at length in graduate texts on microeconomic theory. Examples are Mas-Colell *et al.* (1995) and Kreps (1990).

2 Perfect competition and Pareto optimality

Key concepts: weak and strong Pareto optimality; the Pareto criterion; Edgeworth boxes of production and consumption; point and situation utility possibility frontiers; the classical theorems of welfare economics; the expected utility Theorem; contingent markets; the theorem of Second-best and Piecemeal policy.

2.1 INTRODUCTION

Public economics is intimately concerned about the welfare implications of governmental intervention in the marketplace. Traditionally, it has been split up into an analysis of the 'positive' question of efficiency and the 'normative' question of choosing the right distribution of welfare among individuals. In this chapter we will study the foundations of the positive question. In Chapter 3 we will consider the vexed issue of distribution among individuals – the 'normative' question.

In the literature the notion of efficiency has invariably used the concept of Pareto optimality as a bench mark. Pareto optimality has occupied a central place in modern welfare economics. Paretian principles are guides to ordering (in terms of social welfare) of social states and do not necessarily have anything to do with the market mechanism. However, as we will see below, the correspondence between perfect competition and Pareto optimality is central to what are called the classical theorems of welfare economics.

2.2 PARETIAN RANKING OF SOCIAL STATES

Consider a two-person world where utility is ordinally measurable and we are interested in discovering which allocations of utilities among these two people are 'better' than others. The Paretian principle gives us one method of ranking these alternative distributions. On the x-axis of Figure 2.1 we measure the utility of individual I and on the y-axis of individual II.

The Weak Pareto Criterion (WPC) says that an allocation a_1 is superior to another allocation a_2 if and only if (iff) both individuals I and II are

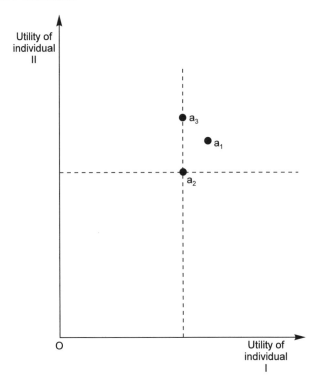

Figure 2.1

better off at a_1 than at a_2. In Figure 2.1 since a_1 lies to the north-east of a_2 it (a_1) is weakly preferred (in the Pareto sense) to a_2.

According to the Strict Pareto Criterion (SPC) an allocation a_3 is preferred to a_2 iff everyone is at least as well off at a_3 as at a_2 and at least one person is strictly better off. In Figure 2.1 both a_1 and a_3 are strictly preferred to a_2 but a_3 is **not** weakly preferred to a_2.

The Pareto criterion gives us one method of ranking social alternatives. This method has the advantage of being non-controversial and, when applicable, quite satisfying. The major difficulty with the Paretian criterion is that it is silent over vast ranges of social choices. In particular, we are given no clue whatsoever about ranking social states in which one person's utility has decreased and the other's increased. As would be expected, many people have tried to get around this difficulty. The efforts have not met with considerable or unqualified success.

2.3   PARETO OPTIMALITY

The Pareto criterion as outlined above, is concerned with ordering arbitrary social states such as a_1, a_2, a_3 etc. in Figure 2.1. The notion of Pareto optimality focuses attention on the 'best' among those social states that is feasible. Let us study this concept in the simplest model of general equilibrium.

Consider a two-person, two-commodity, two-factor of production model. Each consumer in society has strictly quasi-concave, twice continuously differentiable utility functions. The production of the two commodities is carried on under conditions of constant returns to scale and diminishing returns to each factor of production. Both factors of production (say labor, L and capital, K) are substitutable for each other and full employment is continuously maintained. Static equilibrium in this economy is best visualized diagrammatically.

Figure 2.2(a) shows an Edgeworth box diagram depicting production of two goods A (apples) and B (blankets) by capital and labor inputs. The availability of capital and labor defines the size of the box and the southwest and the north-east corners of the box define are the origins for measuring the outputs of A and B respectively. Plotted inside the box are the isoquants of A and B. Output of A increases as we move toward O_B and vice versa. This contract curve is mapped as the production possibility frontier in Figure 2.2 (b).

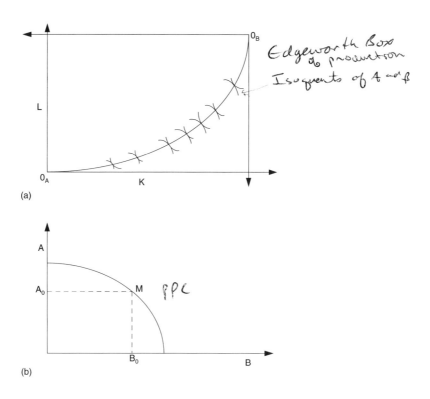

(a)

(b)

Figure 2.2

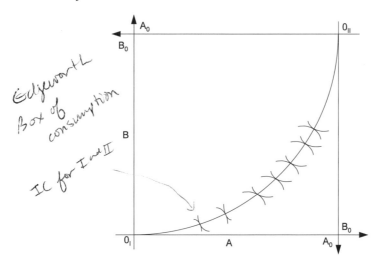

Figure 2.3

Let us now move to the problem of distribution. Take any combination of outputs of *A* and *B*, say point *M* in Figure 2.2(b). This basket of goods can be distributed in an infinite number of ways between individuals I and II. Let us chart the possibilities in Figure 2.3.

Figure 2.3 depicts an Edgeworth box of consumption. The amounts of *A* and *B* available at point *M* in Figure 2.2(b) define the size of this box. The origin of individual II is the north-east corner of the box and the south-west corner is the origin for individual I. Plotted inside the box are indifference curves for individuals I and II. Individual I's utility increases as we move towards O_{II} and II's utility increases as we move toward O_I. The points of tangencies of the two sets of indifference curves (called the contract curve of consumption) gives the highest level of utility individual I can attain given the utility of individual II.

In Figure 2.4 we plot the utilities of the two individuals on the two axes. Line $M_1 M_1$ maps the contract curve of Figure 2.3 onto utility space. This is called a Point Utility Possibility Frontier (PUPF). It is a point frontier since it is generated by alternative distributions of one basket of goods – one point on the production possibility frontier.

However, there is nothing sacrosanct about the output combination denoted by *M* and, indeed, it is possible to study the distribution of each basket of goods on the production possibility frontier. We may plot the resultant PUPFs in Figure 2.5. Clearly there is an infinite number of possible PUPFs. If we wish to summarize the utility tradeoffs for all points on the production possibility frontier we should take an outer envelope of all such PUPFs. The resulting envelope is called a Situation Utility Possibility Frontier (SUPF) or Global Utility Possibility Frontier (GUPF). It is depicted in Figure 2.6.

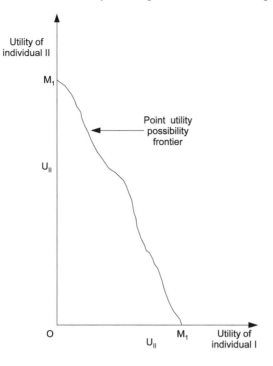

Figure 2.4

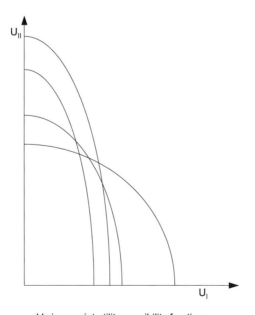

Various point utility possibility frontiers

Figure 2.5

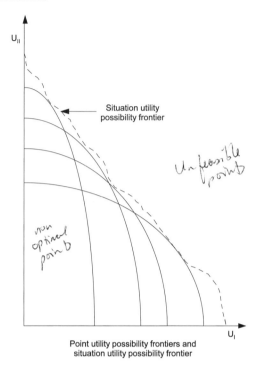

Point utility possibility frontiers and
situation utility possibility frontier

Figure 2.6

By definition (or construction) every point on the SUPF has a PUPF tangent to it. This SUPF depicts the utility tradeoffs that are feasible given the fullest utilization of society's resources. Hence, any discussion of social choice must be restricted to points on this frontier. Points outside the frontier are infeasible – given resources and technology – and any point within the frontier is inferior and Pareto dominated by some point on the frontier.

In this social utility possibility set a feasible point b_1 is weakly Pareto optimal iff there does not exist a feasible point b_2 where both I and II are strictly better off; b_1 is strictly Pareto optimal if there does not exist another feasible allocation b_3 such that everyone is at least as well off at b_3 as she was at b_1 and at least one individual is strictly better off.

In Figures 2.7(a) and 2.7(b) all points on both SUPFs are weakly Pareto optimal. All points on the SUPF in 2.7 (a) are also strictly Pareto optimal whereas only points along the segment ZZ are strictly Pareto optimal in Figure 2.7 (b).

Some authors have criticized the use of the Paretian criterion in modern welfare economics on the ground that it is opposed to redistribution. This criticism is misplaced. The trouble with the Pareto criterion is not that it says too much but that it says too little. It does tell us to be on the SUPF

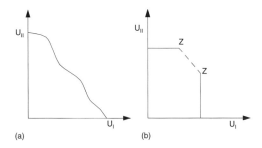

Figure 2.7

but cannot narrow down the range any further. We will study this in Chapter 3. Our principal concern in this chapter is to establish the two classical theorems of welfare economics. We will first consider the case of certainty and then move on to the case of uncertainty. We will also discover that fairly stringent conditions have to be satisfied to reach Pareto optimality using the market mechanism.

2.4 THE CLASSICAL THEOREMS OF WELFARE ECONOMICS

These deal with the equivalence between Pareto optimality and the perfectly competitive market mechanism. We will first prove Theorems 1 and 2 for the general case in which we do not presume the existence of utility or production functions. The existence of preference orderings and production sets is all that is assumed. Before we can prove these theorems, however, a few definitions are in order.

Definition 2.1

An economy E is characterized by:

(i) N commodities.
(ii) m consumers (indexed by i) with consumption sets $X_i \in R^N_+$ for all i.
(iii) n producers (indexed by j) with production sets $Y_j \leqslant R^N_+$ for all j.

From this very general economy we construct a more interesting subset.

Definition 2.2

A private enterprise economy $\hat{E}$ is E with the following additional specifications:

(a) Each consumer has an initial endowment bundle $(w_i \in R^N_+)$ and the sum of the initial endowment bundles is w $(w = \sum_{i=1}^m w_i)$.
(b) In a private enterprise economy, all firms are owned by private individuals (consumers). Let $\theta_{ij}(\theta_{ij} \geqslant 0)$ be the share of the jth firm owned

by the ith consumer. Clearly $\sum_{i=1}^{m} \theta_{ij} = 1$; i.e., each firm is completely owned by its shareholders. We have now explicitly brought in ownership.

(c) An allocation a for this economy is an $(m + n)$ tuple of points in R^N specifying a consumption plan for each consumer and a production plan for each producer.

$$a = \{x_1, \ldots, x_m; y_1, \ldots, y_n\}.$$

This allocation is attainable if (i) $x_i \in X_i$ for all i; (ii) $y_j \in Y_j$; and (iii) $\sum_i x_i = w + \sum_j y_j$. So each consumption plan must lie in the appropriate consumption set, each production plan lies in the appropriate production set and aggregate consumption cannot exceed aggregate production plus initial endowments. Now we can define a perfectly competitive equilibrium for this economy.

Definition 2.3

A perfectly competitive equilibrium is an ordered pair $< \bar{a}, \bar{p} >$ such that:

(a) $\bar{a}$ is attainable.
(b) for all i, $\bar{x}_i$ is the R_i greatest bundle (utility maximizing bundle) in $\{x_i \in X_i : \bar{p}x_i \leqslant \bar{p}w_i + \sum_j \bar{p}\theta_{ij}\bar{y}_j\}$. At the price vector $\bar{p}$, the lefthand side of this inequality is the value of the consumer's consumption bundle; and the righthand side is the value of the consumer's initial endowment bundle and her earnings from various firms.
(c) for all j, $\bar{p}\bar{y}_j \geq \bar{p}y_j$, i.e., profit when producing the output basket in the perfectly competitive equilibrium must be at least as large as the profit when producing any other basket in the production set at the price vector prevailing in the perfectly competitive equilibrium.
(d) Each producer and each consumer take the perfectly competitive price vector to be parametrically given.

Now we can prove **the classical theorems of welfare economics**.

Theorem 2.1

Let $\hat{E}$ be a private enterprise economy where every consumer satisfies the property of local non-saturation. Let $< \bar{a}, \bar{p} >$ be a perfectly competitive equilibrium for $\hat{E}$; then $< \bar{a}, \bar{p} >$ is Pareto optimal.

Proof

Deny the theorem; then there exists an allocation a such that a is attainable and $x_i R_i \bar{x}_i$ for all consumers and for some consumer h we have $x_h P_h \bar{x}_h$. This implies that either $xI\bar{x}$ or $xP\bar{x}$. We shall show that if $x_i I_i \bar{x}_i$ then $px_i \geqslant \bar{p}\bar{x}_i$. Deny this; then $\bar{p}x_i < \bar{p}\bar{x}_i$ and $x_i I_i \bar{x}_i$. Now, since the consumer satisfies the

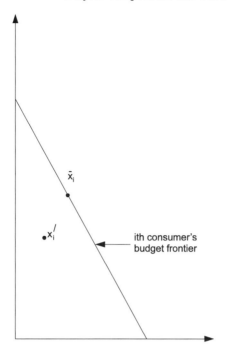

Figure 2.8

property of local non-saturation, in Figure 2.8 we can find a consumption bundle x_i' arbitrarily close to $\bar{x}_i$ (and hence below the budget line) so that $x_i' P_i x_i$ and, by transitivity, $x_i' P_i \bar{x}_i$. But this is a contradiction since, by definition, $\bar{x}_i$ is R_i greatest bundle in the consumer's budget set. Thus if $x_i I_i \bar{x}_i$ then $\bar{p} x_i \geqslant \overline{px}_i$. Analogously it is easy to show that if $x_h P_h \bar{x}_h$ then $\overline{px}_h > \overline{px}_h$. Adding these two results we get the conclusion that $\bar{p} x > \overline{px}$ which means that $\sum_j \bar{p} y_j > \sum_j \overline{py}_j$ but this is a contradiction of the statement for a perfectly competitive equilibrium which is that $\bar{p}_j \bar{y}_j \geqslant \bar{p} y_j$ for all $y_j \in Y_j$. Hence the theorem is proved.

It should be understood that theorem 2.1 is rather trivial. It says that if a perfectly competitive equilibrium exists, then it is Pareto optimal. Thus it sidesteps the question of whether the perfectly competitive equilibrium exists. There may be several reasons (for example, presence of public goods) why establishing a perfectly competitive equilibrium may be quite difficult. Theorem 2.2 makes the circumstances under which a perfectly competitive equilibrium may exist quite explicit.

Theorem 2.2

Let $\bar{a}$ be a Pareto optimal allocation for economy E. Let:

(a) for every i, X_i be convex,

(b) for every i, R_i be convex,
(c) for every j, Y_j be convex,
(d) for every i, R_i satisfy continuity,
(e) for some i, $\bar{x}_i$ (the consumption basket chosen in the Pareto optimal allocation) satisfy local non-saturation. Then there exists a non-trivial price vector $\bar{p}$ such that if $x_i R_i \bar{x}_i$ then $\bar{p} x_i \geqslant \bar{p} \bar{x}_i$. Now, if at this price vector $\bar{p}$ there exist a consumption bundle x_i' (for all i) such that $\bar{p} x_i' < \bar{p} \bar{x}_i$ then $< \bar{a}, \bar{p} >$ constitutes a perfectly competitive equilibrium for some private enterprise economy $\hat{E}$ that can be constructed out of E.

This theorem says that, under certain conditions, any Pareto optimal allocation can be reached by a perfectly competitive mechanism. We will present a calculus proof (which presumes the existence of twice continuously differentiable utility and production functions) after the more general proof to which we now turn.

Proof

The proof of this theorem needs two lemmas. Suppose $\hat{x}_i \in X_i$ is a consumption basket in individual i's consumption set. With reference to $\hat{x}_i$ we define the following two sets:

(i) NW $(\hat{x}_i)$ The not-worse than $\hat{x}_i$ set: $\{x_i \in X_i$, such that $x_i R_i \hat{x}_i\}$.
(ii) B$(\hat{x}_i)$ The better than $\hat{x}_i$ set: $\{x_i \in X_i$, such that $x_i P_i \hat{x}_i\}$.

Then we have:

Lemma 2.1a

NW$(\hat{x}_i)$ and B $(\hat{x}_i)$ are convex sets for all $\hat{x}_i \in X_i$.

Lemma 2.1b

Let x_i, x_i' and $x_i'' \in x_i$ and let $x_i' R_i x_i$ and $x_i'' P_i x_i$. Then every consumption basket in the closed interval (x_i', x_i'') is strictly preferred to x_i.

Proof of Lemma 2.1a

Take NW $(\hat{x}_i)$. Let $x_i' R_i \hat{x}_i$ and $x_i'' R_i \hat{x}_i$ (for x_i' and $x_i'' \in X_i$). We have to show that $\{\alpha x_i' + (1 - \alpha)x_i''\} R_i \hat{x}_i$ for $1 \geqslant \alpha \geqslant 0$. Deny this. Then there exist some point along the closed interval (x_i', x_i'') such that $\hat{x}_i$ is preferred to them (by transitivity). Let there be just two such points: x_i^a and x_i^b. Thus $\hat{x}_i P_i x_i^a$ and $\hat{x}_i P_i x_i^b$. By transitivity of R_i we must have $x_i' P_i x_i^a$, $x_i' P_i x_i^b$, $x_i'' P_i x_i^a$ and $x_i'' P_i x_i^b$. By convexity and continuity of R_i all points along the segment x_i' to x_i^b are preferred to x_i^b and, hence, $x_i^a P_i x_i^b$. By a similar argument, $x_i^b P_i x_i^a$. This, of course, is a nonsensical result. Suppose there is only one such point. But this immediately violates the conditions of continuity placed on R_i. Hence $NW(\hat{x}_i)$ must be convex. We now turn our attention to the $B(\hat{x}_i)$ set. We have that x'_i, $x''_i \in X_i$ and $x'_i P_i \hat{x}_i$ and $x''_i P_i \hat{x}_i$. We have to show that $x^e_i = \{\alpha x'_i + (1 - \alpha)x''_i\}P_i\hat{x}_i$. Deny this. Then either $\hat{x}_i P_i x^e_i$ or $\hat{x}_i I_i x^e_i$. Now, the first conclusion cannot hold since both x'_i and x''_i belong to the $NW(\hat{x}_i)$ set. The second conclusion can be shown to wrong by an argument exactly analogous to the proof of the first part of lemma 2.1a.

Proof of Lemma 2.1b

Let x_i, x'_i, $x''_i \in X_i$ and $x'_i R_i x_i$ and $x''_i P_i x_i$. We have to prove that: $x^e_i = [\alpha x'_i + (1 - \alpha)x''_i]P_i x_i$. Now if $x'_i P_i x_i$ then x^e_i belongs to the $B(x_i)$ set which we know to be convex. If $x'_i I_i x_i$ then, by transitivity, $x''_i P_i x'_i$. Then, all points along the segment x'_i to x''_i are preferred to x'_i (or x_i) by continuity. Hence $x^e_i P_i x'_i$.

We will state the second lemma without proof. For a proof see Debreu (1959).

Lemma 2.2

Two non-empty, convex and non-intersecting sets in R^N_+ can be separated by a hyperplane.

Proof of Theorem 2.2

The proof of the theorem is split up into five parts:

(a) Define two sets G and H satisfying Lemma 2.2. The normal $\bar{p}$ is the price vector in the Pareto theorem.
(b) The aggregate consumption bundle specified in the Pareto optimal allocation lies on the hyperplane itself.
(c) Given $\bar{p}$, every producer maximizes profits if he produces $\bar{a}$.
(d) Given $\bar{p}$, if $x_i R_i \bar{x}_i$ then $\bar{p} x_i \geqslant \bar{p} \bar{x}_i$ for every i.
(e) There exists another bundle $x^h_i \in X_i$ such that $\bar{p} x^h_i < \bar{p} \bar{x}_i$.

We will prove each part in turn.

(a) Define $G = \{x(x = \sum_i x_i, x_i \in X_i)$ such that for all i $x_i R_i \bar{x}_i$ and for some consumer u, it is the case that $x_u P_u \bar{x}_u.\}$
Define $H = \{h (h = w + \sum_j y_j, y_j \in Y_j)$ for all $j\}$.
To show that G is non-empty. We have assumed that in Pareto optimum at least one consumer is not satiated. Without loss of generality, let this be consumer 1. Define a new consumption basket

$$\hat{x} = x_1 + \sum_{i=2}^{m} \bar{x}_i \quad \text{and} \quad x_1 P_1 \bar{x}_1. \text{ Thus set } G \text{ is non-empty.}$$

To show that G is convex. Consider x', $x'' \in G$. Define $\hat{x}$ as:
$\hat{x} = \alpha(x'_1 + x'_2 + \ldots + x'_m) + (1 - \alpha)(x''_1 + x''_2 + \ldots + x''_m)$
$= \hat{x}_1 + \hat{x}_2 + \ldots + \hat{x}_m$. We know that $\hat{x}_1 P_1 \bar{x}_1$ and that $\hat{x}_i R_i \bar{x}_i$ for $i = 2, \ldots, m$. Hence by Lemma 2.1, G is convex.

Now we show that the set H is non-empty. We know that for all producers, j, $y_j \in Y_j$. Hence set H is non-empty. We can now prove that H is convex. Choose two points h', and $h'' \in H$. We have to show that $\hat{h} = \{\alpha h' + (1 - \alpha)h''\} \in H$. $(1 \geqslant \alpha \geqslant 0)$. Now, $\hat{h}$ can be written as: $\hat{h} = \alpha y'_1 + (1 - \alpha)y''_1 + \ldots + \alpha y'_n + (1 - \alpha)y''_n = \hat{y}_1 + \ldots + \hat{y}_n$. By convexity of Y_j we have $\hat{y}_j \in Y_j$ for all j. Hence the set H is convex. We now want to show that the sets G and H are non-intersecting. Let G and H intersect. Hence, we have found a set of consumption and production plans that match and are, hence, attainable. Hence any element of this set is Pareto superior to $\bar{a}$ and hence $\bar{a}$ is not Pareto optimal – which gives us a contradiction.

Hence, we have found two sets that satisfy all the conditions of Lemma 2.2. Hence, by Lemma 2.2, there must be a hyperplane separating them.

(b) We now show that $\bar{a}$ lies on the hyperplane itself. Deny this; then $\bar{a}$ can lie below the hyperplane or above it. Take the case where $\bar{a}$ lies above the hyperplane. Since $\bar{a}$ is attainable, it follows that $\bar{x} = (w + \sum_j y_j) = h$. However, $h \in H$; hence we have a contradiction. Let $\bar{x}$ lie below the hyperplane. Consider $x \in G$ and take a convex combination $\hat{x} = \alpha\bar{x} + (1 - \alpha)x$ as in Figure 2.9a. Let α become larger and closer to one. $\hat{x}$, by Lemma 2.1, is preferred to $\bar{x}$. Hence we have found a consumption basket that is feasible and is preferred to $\bar{x}$. This is a contradiction. Hence, it must be the case that $\bar{x}$ will lie on the hyperplane itself.

(c) We now show that profit is maximized (relative to $\bar{p}$) if producers produce $\bar{h}$. Now, aggregate demand is $\bar{p}\bar{x}$ and aggregate supply is $\bar{p}w + \sum_j \bar{p}\bar{y}_j$. We also know that $\overline{px}$ is greater in value than any bundle on the hyperplane or below it. Hence, $\overline{px} > \bar{p}h$ (for all $h \notin \bar{h}$).

(d) To show that, given $\bar{p}$, if $x_i R_i \bar{x}_i$ then $\bar{p}x_i \geqslant \overline{px}_i$ for all i. Deny this, then, we have $\bar{p}x_i < \overline{px}_i$ and $x_i R_i \bar{x}_i$. Fix up $\bar{x}_2, \ldots, \bar{x}_m$ and take a convex combination of x_1 and a point (x'_1) in the set G as in Figure 2.9b: $\hat{x}_1 = \alpha x_1 + (1 - \alpha)x'_1$ and let α tend to 1. Then $\hat{x}_1$ would be feasible and preferred to $\bar{x}_1$. This, of course, is a contradiction.

(e) We now show that $\bar{x}_i$ is R_i greatest bundle in the budget set: $\{x_i \in X_i : \bar{p}x_i \leqslant \bar{p}w_i + \bar{p}\sum_j \theta_{ij}\bar{y}_j\}$; in other words in: $\{x_i \in X_i : \bar{p}x_i \leqslant \overline{px}_i\}$. Divide this set into two groups: $\{x_i : \bar{p}x_i < \overline{px}_i\}$ and $\{x_i : \bar{p}x_i = \overline{px}_i\}$. In the case of the first set, from stage (d) of the proof, it follows that $\bar{x}_i$ is the R_i greatest bundle.

Now consider the second set in Figure 2.9c. Consider x_i which lies below the hyperplane and $\hat{x}_i$ which is another point on the hyperplane. Take a sequence $\alpha x_i + (1 - \alpha)\hat{x}_i$ and let $\alpha \to 0$. By continuity it immediately follows that $\bar{x}_i R_i \hat{x}_i$. Hence $\bar{x}_i$ is the R_i greatest bundle.

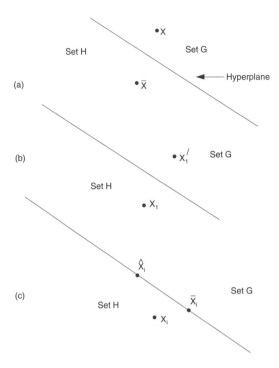

Figure 2.9

Remarks

1 This theorem is truly fundamental. Although it is not stated explicitly, the theorem is dropping a strong hint to the effect that the question of reaching any Pareto optimal allocation can be separated from the question of which Pareto optimal allocation society should attain. Thus the 'normative' question of which distribution to aim for is separated from the 'positive' question of how to reach such a distribution. This distinction is absolutely vital for a whole line of welfare theorists such as Hayek, Buchanan, and Friedman. Dobb (1937) has criticized this distinction as being 'artificial'. Graaf (1957), and Koopmans (1957) examine the foundations of this distinction quite closely.
2 The fact that any Pareto optimal allocation can be reached by the market mechanism means that, in principle, a case can be made for non-interference by the government in the marketplace. The market is efficient, indeed perfect, and an economical and proper user of information.
3 Stated this way one may tend to get a little complacent about the actual choice of a distribution. It is important to remember that the market

cannot do that and the Pareto criterion is of no help either. We will consider these issues in later chapters of this book. For now, we detail a calculus proof of Theorem 2.2 and consider an extension of it.

Calculus version of Theorem 2.2

Since we have already proved Theorem 2.2 in a general form we will take up a simple case for the calculus proof. Consider a society consisting of m consumers. Each consumer has a utility function defined over N goods: $U_i(x_{1i}, \ldots, x_{Ni})$ where x_{1i} is the amount of commodity x_1 consumed by individual i and so on. Consider an exchange economy such that the amounts of the various goods are given. The Pareto problem can be written as max $U_1(x_{11}, \ldots, x_{N1})$ subject to $U_i(.) = \bar{U}_i$ $(i = 2, \ldots, m)$ and $\bar{x}_t = \sum_{i=1}^{m} x_{ti}$ $(t = 1, \ldots, N)$ and $\bar{x}_t$ is the fixed amount of commodity x_t. The Lagrangean for this problem can be written as:

$$\Lambda = U_1(.) + \sum_{i=2}^{m} \mu_i(U_i - \bar{U}_i) + \sum_{t=1}^{N} \lambda_t \left(\bar{x}_t - \sum_{i=1}^{m} x_{ti}\right) \tag{2.1}$$

Some first-order conditions for an internal maximum are:

$$\partial U_1/\partial x_{1t} - \lambda_t = 0 \quad (t = 1, \ldots, N) \tag{2.2a}$$

$$\mu_i \partial U_i/\partial x_{it} - \lambda_t = 0 \quad (i = 2, \ldots, m; \; t = 1, \ldots, N). \tag{2.2b}$$

From these two we get the crucial condition that in Pareto optimum the marginal rate of substitution (mrs) between any pair of goods should be the same for all consumers. Realize that this will be true in perfectly competitive equilibrium. The price ratio between every pair of goods is given parametrically to the consumer. Utility maximization requires that the consumer equates her *mrs* to this price ratio. This is sometimes referred to as the condition for **efficiency in exchange** (Boadway and Bruce 1984; Boadway and Wildasin 1984).

We can now proceed to the case of efficiency in production. To simplify the algebra, and without any loss of generality, let us suppose that there are only two commodities: x_1 and x_2. Each is produced according to smooth neoclassical production functions with capital (K) and labor (L) as inputs. The total amounts of capital and labor in the economy are assumed fixed at $\bar{L}$ and $\bar{K}$ respectively. Production functions are written as:

$$x_1 = x_1(K_1, L_1) \tag{2.3a}$$

$$x_2 = x_2(K_2, L_2). \tag{2.3b}$$

Suppose producers of x_1 and x_2 take the prices of their goods as well as the prices of factors of production as being parametrically fixed. Profit $(\prod_j)$ for producers of commodity x_j $(j = 1, 2)$ can be written as:

$$\Pi_j = p_j x_j(K_j, L_j) - wL_j - rK_j. \tag{2.4}$$

Firms can choose the amounts of capital and labor they will employ. This will define output from the production function. Factor and output prices are all parametrically given. (w is the price of labor and r is the price of capital).

Differentiating with respect to each factor and rearranging, we get the relation that:

$$\partial x_j / \partial K_j = r/p_j \tag{2.5a}$$

$$\partial x_j / \partial L_j = w/p_j. \tag{2.5b}$$

In other words, the marginal product of each factor is equated to its 'real' price. We can rewrite equation (2.5) as:

$$\frac{\partial x_j / \partial K_j}{\partial x_j / \partial L_j} = r/w. \tag{2.6}$$

In other words, the rate of technical substitution between the two factors of production (the lefthand side) is equal to the factor price ratio. This is referred to as the **condition for production efficiency**. This is true in perfectly competitive equilibrium as Figure 2.10 shows. The rate of technical substitution is equal to the slope of the isoquant in the Edgeworth box of production. This is equated, in competitive equilibrium, for each industry.

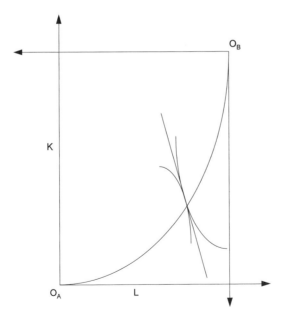

Figure 2.10

Finally, we have the condition for **overall efficiency**. This defines a relation between the rate at which goods can be transformed in consumption and the rate at which they can be transformed in production. We know that in consumption the rate of transformation between two goods is given by their *mrs*. One can define a similar construct for production. From the production functions for the two goods we have upon total differentiation:

$$dx_1 = [\partial x_1/\partial K_1]dK_1 + [\partial x_1/\partial L_1]dL_1 \tag{2.7a}$$

$$dx_2 = [\partial x_2/\partial K_2]dK_2 + [\partial x_2/\partial L_2]dL_2. \tag{2.7b}$$

When total capital and total labor are fixed in supply it must be the case that $dK_2 = -dK_1$ and $dL_2 = -dL_1$. Thus we can rewrite equation (2.7) as:

$$dx_1 = [\partial x_1/\partial K_1]dK_1 + [\partial x_1/\partial L_1]dL_1 \tag{2.7c}$$

$$-dx_2 = [\partial x_2/\partial K_2]dK_1 + [\partial x_2/\partial L_2]dL_1. \tag{2.7d}$$

Now the ratio of the lefthand sides of equations (2.7c) and (2.7d) is the marginal rate of transformation (mrt) in production (slope of the production possibility frontier) between the two goods which, in equilibrium, equals the price ratio (Figure 2.11). We know that the price ratio is also equated to the *mrs* in consumption. So the condition for **overall efficiency** is that the *mrt* in production must equal the *mrs* in consumption. This is clearly satisfied in competitive equilibrium.

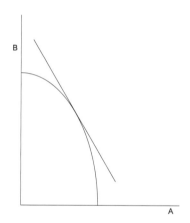

Figure 2.11

2.5   AN EXTENSION TO THE CASE OF UNCERTAINTY

We have examined the circumstances under which the classical theorems of welfare economics are valid. The assumptions of the theorem are quite rarefied and may not hold under a wide variety of circumstances. One direction in which the theorems can be generalized is that of uncertainty. Proving the results would take us too far afield, in any case, they are available elsewhere (Debreu 1959; Arrow and Hahn 1971). We will state the principal results for an exchange economy and note why an extension to a production economy is not easy.

Debreu argues that the problem of uncertainty is essentially one of non-existence of markets. He argues that if the existence of markets can be assured, then the classical theorems should go through. Usually, a commodity is defined with respect to three characteristics – a certain physical homogeneity, date and place. Thus, red grapefruit from the 1995 harvest in Florida is one commodity and distinct from white grapefruit from the 1993 season in Florida. Debreu adds a fourth dimension to commodities: state of the world. An umbrella is one commodity if it rains and another commodity if it does not rain. So, the definition of a commodity (as usually articulated) is contingent upon the state of the world that obtains.

Debreu then goes on to argue that the essential reason why the classical theorems do not go through in the case of uncertainty is that there are no markets (or incomplete markets) for contingent commodities. If complete contingent markets can be made to exist, then uncertainty (at least in an exchange economy) will not pose a problem for the welfare theorems to go through. Let us formalize this a little.

In any time period $l(\geq 1)$ any of the following $E^* = (s_1, \ldots, s_k)$ states of the world is possible. We shall assume that E^* is finite. This is known as an event tree.

An **event tree** is a finite sequence $< \rho_0, \ldots, \rho_f >$ satisfying the following conditions.

(i) $\rho_0 = E^*$.
(ii) For every time period t $(1 \leq t \leq f)$ there exists exactly one partition ρ_t in the sequence $< \rho_0, \rho_1, \ldots, \rho_f >$; the non-empty elements of ρ_t are called events and are indexed by e_t going from l_t to g_t.
(iii) Every element at f is a singleton.
(iv) Every element at $(t + 1)$ is a subset of some element at t.

We can then define a **path**. Consider any event e_f at time f. Let:

$$\rho = < l_1, 2_1, \ldots, g_1, \ldots, 1_f, \ldots, g_f >$$

then the path from l_0 to e_f is defined as $\rho(e_f)$ and is derived by dropping from ρ all events of which e_f is not a subset.

Following Debreu we now reinterpret consumption sets, production sets, and orderings. Thus given e_f we can define a production set $Y_j(e_f)$. A production plan $y_j(e_f)$ is feasible if it belongs to $Y_j(e_f)$. The production set is one thing if it rains and quite another thing if it does not rain. Similarly, a consumption set is defined as $X_i(e_f)$ and a feasible consumption plan is $x_i(e_f) \in X_i(e_f)$.

Orderings are now defined over the consumption set. But the convexity of R_i implies that the individual is risk averse. In a formal sense, then, the second optimality theorem will go through.

Arrow's security market theorem

Arrow's work, discussed exhaustively in Arrow and Hahn (1971), is a further refinement of this result of Debreu. The main innovation of Arrow is to provide a mechanism whereby we do not have to think in terms of contingent commodities. To study the Arrow mechanism first we have to consider the expected utility theorem.

Axioms of the expected utility theorem

Let $\Omega(\theta)$ be the (finite) set of all possible outcomes and let $\Omega(\alpha)$ be the (finite) set of all possible actions. Action can then be looked upon as a function σ from $\Omega(\theta)$, i.e., $\theta_i = \alpha(s)$ the outcome depends on the action and state of the world (i.e. if I take action α and state of the world s is realized then the outcome is θ_i). It also follows that any outcome that was not visualized does not affect my action. Suppose an event $e \subseteq \sigma$ is given to me. Then if I take action α', then I define a probability distribution over all the θ_i's. Let this probability distribution be designated as $\square\,(e, \alpha')$. A special case of this is when there is no information whatsoever and we have to deal with the entire σ. (See Figure 2.12.)

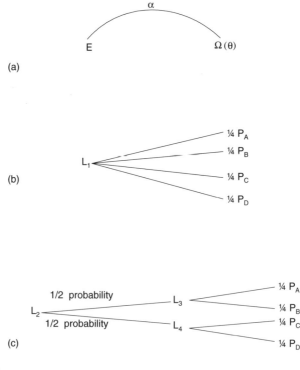

Figure 2.12

We can then state the axioms of the von Neumann–Morgenstern expected utility theorem.

1 Conditional ordering: given any event e, the agent has a conditional ordering R_e defined over $\Omega(\alpha)$ such that for $\alpha, \alpha' \in \Omega(\alpha)$ if $\alpha'(s) = \alpha''(s)$ for all $s \in e$ then $\alpha' I_e \alpha''$.

2 Probabilistic belief: given any event e any two actions α', α'' if $\square(e, \alpha') = \square(e, \alpha'')$ then $\alpha' I_e \alpha''$. This means that all that matters for choice is the probability distribution.

3 Axiom of continuity: Let α', α'' and $\alpha''' \in \Omega(\alpha)$ and let e be the given event such that $\alpha' P_e \alpha''$. Then there exists a neighborhood of $\square(e, \alpha')$ such that if $\square(e, \alpha''')$ lies in that neighborhood then $\alpha''' P_e \alpha''$. Also there exists a neighborhood of $\square(e, \alpha'')$ such that if $\square(e, \alpha''')$ lies in this, then $\alpha' P_e \alpha'''$.

Then we have:

Expected utility theorem

Let the agent satisfy the axioms mentioned above, then there exists a continuous real valued utility function, U, defined over $\Omega(\alpha)$ such that:

(a) for all $\alpha', \alpha'' \in \Omega(\alpha)$, $\alpha' R_e \alpha''$ iff $U(\alpha') \geq U(\alpha'')$.

(b) for all $\alpha' \in \Omega(\alpha)$; $U(\alpha') = \Sigma_i \tau_i U(\theta_i)$ where τ_i is the probability of θ_i, given α' and $U(\theta_i)$ is the utility number assigned to θ_i, per se, irrespective of its being realized.

Arrow then introduces a security market into his model. Unlike the case in Debreu's model where there is contingent delivery of goods, in Arrow's framework prices are contingent – to be paid when the state of the world is realized. There are m consumers (indexed by i), N ordinarily defined goods (indexed by k), S unit securities (one for each state of the world), S states of the world (indexed by s), γ prices for the goods (there are NS such prices).

Unlike in Debreu's world where prices are paid and there is contingent delivery of the goods, in Arrow's framework prices are contingent – to be paid when the state of the world is realized. q_s is the price of the sth type of security – this is to be paid now. S such prices exist. x_i is, as before, the consumer's commodity bundle; x_{is} is the vector of x_i referring to state s; d_{is} is the amount of securities corresponding to state of the world s that consumer i purchases. Thus consumer i's vector of securities is:

$$(d_{i1}, d_{i2}, \ldots, d_{is}) = d_i.$$

Moreover, we define $(d_1, \ldots, d_m)$ as b; γ_{ks} is the price prevailing for physically defined good k in state of the world s. The interpretation of allocation, economy etc. remain the same as in Theorem 2.2.

Definition 2.4

Let E_u be a private ownership, pure exchange economy where contingent markets for commodities do not exist but security markets exist. Suppose every consumer in this economy satisfies the assumption of conditional ordering. A Pareto optimal equilibrium for E_u is an ordered pair $< (\bar{a}, \bar{b}), (\bar{\gamma}, \bar{q}) >$ such that:

(i) $\bar{a}$ is an attainable allocation.

(ii) $\Sigma_{s=1}^{S} q_s = 1$ (cash is a composite unit consisting of one of each type of security). If $\Sigma_{s=1}^{S} q_s > 1$ then people would move into securities and this certainly would not be an equilibrium situation.

(iii) $\Sigma_{s=1}^{S} q_s d_{is} = w_i$ for all i. The agent has to, by definition, exhaust his cash. Even if he does not actually physically do so, he has exhausted his cash since cash is, by definition, a composite bundle of securities.

(iv) $\Sigma_i d_{is} = \Sigma_i w_i = w$ (for all s, i.e., when state of the world s has been realized, then people get back the same amount of cash. This is a market clearing equation.

(va) $\bar{\gamma}_s \bar{x}_{is} \leq d_{is}$ for all s and all i. This is the consumer's budget constraint.

(vb) There does not exist d_i and $x_i \in X_i$ such that $\Sigma_s q_s d_{is} = w_i$ and for all s, $\bar{\gamma}_s x_{is} \leq d_{is}$ and $x_i P_i \bar{x}_i$.

(vi) For all i and all s, $\bar{x}_{is}$ is R_{is} greatest bundle in:

$$\{x_{is} \in X_{is} : \gamma_s x_{is} \leq d_{is}\}.$$

We are now in a position to address the central point. Can this Pareto optimal allocation be reached by a perfectly competitive mechanism. In other words, can this Pareto optimal allocation be thought of as a perfectly competitive equilibrium for some private enterprise economy that can be constructed out of E_u?

Arrow's security market theorem states that under the following conditions this equivalence can be established.

Condition 1: X_i is convex for every i.

Condition 2: Every consumer satisfies the axioms of conditional ordering, probabilistic belief, continuity, and dominance. Hence for each consumer i, there exists a von Neumann–Morgenstern utility function, U_i, such that for all $x_i \in X_i$, $U_i(x_i) = \Sigma_s \delta_{is} U_i(x_{is})$ where δ_{is} is the probability i sets for state of the world s and $U_i(x_{is})$ is the utility number attached to a bundle where for each state of the world, s, the consumption bundle is x_{is}.

Condition 3: For every i, R_i is convex.

Condition 4: non-saturation (strict monotonicity): For every consumer i, if $x_i, x_i' \in X_i$ if $x_i' > x_i$ then $x_i' P_i x_i$. Then there exist $(\bar{\gamma}, \bar{q}) \neq 0$ such that for all $x_i \in X_i$, if $x_i R_i \bar{x}_i$ then:

$$\sum_{s=1}^{S} \sum_{k=1}^{N} \bar{q}_s \bar{\gamma}_{ks} x_{iks} \geq \sum_{s=1}^{S} \sum_{k=1}^{N} \bar{q}_s \bar{\gamma}_{ks} \bar{x}_{iks}$$

and if, at this $(\bar{\gamma}, \bar{q})$ there exists $\tilde{x}_i \in X_i$ such that:

$$\sum_{s=1}^{S} \sum_{k=1}^{N} \bar{q}_s \bar{\gamma}_{ks} \tilde{x}_{iks} < \sum_{s=1}^{S} \sum_{k=1}^{N} \bar{q}_s \bar{\gamma}_{ks} \bar{x}_{iks}$$

then for some $\bar{b}$ it must be the case that $< (\bar{a}, \bar{b}), (\bar{\gamma}, \bar{q}) >$ will be a perfectly competitive equilibrium for some $\bar{E}_u$ that can be constructed out of E_u.

The proof of this proposition is fairly involved and proceeds along the lines of the proof of Theorem 2.2 and takes six steps. This follows below.

Proof of Stage 1

To the Debreu type framework, we add a fourth dimension-contingency. No security markets nor securities exist but markets for contingent commodities do exist. Thus for this system we are assured that there exists a price vector $\bar{p} \neq 0$ such that if $x_i R_i \bar{x}_i$ $(x_i \in X_i)$ then $\bar{p} x_i \geqslant \bar{p} \bar{x}_i$ and, if at $\bar{p}$ there exist a consumption bundle $\tilde{x}_i$ such that $\bar{p} \bar{x}_i > \bar{p} \tilde{x}_i$ then $(\bar{a}, \bar{p})$ constitutes a perfectly competitive equilibrium for some $\bar{E}_u$ that can be constructed out of E_u.

In the remaining stages of the proof of the theorem we shall construct a market for securities so that any Pareto optimal allocation can be reached as a result of the perfectly competitive process working through the goods and securities markets.

Stage 2

Define:

$$\bar{q}_s = \sum_{i=1}^{m} \bar{p}_s \bar{x}_{is} / (\bar{w}) \text{ for all s and where } \bar{w} = \sum w_i.$$

Also define $\bar{\gamma}_{ks} = \bar{p}_{ks} / (\bar{q}_s)$ for all k and all s, and $\bar{d}_{is} = \bar{\gamma}_s \bar{x}_{is}$ for all s where $\bar{\gamma}_s = (\gamma_{1s}, \ldots, \gamma_{Ns})$ is the vector of commodity prices in state of the world s.

To avoid triviality we assume $\bar{w} > 0$ so that $\bar{x}_{is}$ is non-negative. Furthermore, since we have strict monotonicity $\bar{p}_s > 0$. Hence, $\Sigma_{i=1}^{m} \bar{p}_s \bar{x}_{is} \geqslant 0$ for all s. Hence, $\bar{q}_s \geqslant 0$; but since $\bar{x}_{is} > 0$ for some i, it must be the case that $\bar{q}_s > 0$.

Now, we have defined $\bar{\gamma}_{ks} = \bar{p}_{ks} / \bar{q}_s$ for all k and all s, hence we must have $\bar{\gamma}_{ks} > 0$. Moreover, $\bar{d}_{is}$ $(= \bar{\gamma}_s \bar{x}_{is})$ is strictly positive and, hence, $\bar{b}$ is strictly positive.

We have now defined the characteristics of the 'chosen' Pareto optimal allocation for a free enterprise economy with uncertainty in which markets for contingent commodities do not exist but security markets do exist to cover all states of the world. We will now show that $< (\bar{a}, \bar{b}), (\bar{\gamma}, \bar{q}) >$ is a competitive equilibrium for this free enterprise economy. Let us show, first, that $< (\bar{a}, \bar{b}), (\bar{\gamma}, \bar{q}) >$ satisfies all the conditions for a competitive economy.

(i) To show that $\bar{a}$ is attainable. This is obvious since $\bar{a}$ is a Pareto optimal allocation.

(ii) To show $\Sigma_{s=1}^{S} \bar{q}_s = 1$. By definition,

$$\sum_{s=1}^{S} \bar{q}_s = \sum_s \sum_i \bar{p}_s \bar{x}_{is} / \bar{w} = (1/\bar{w}) \sum_i \bar{p}\bar{x}_i \quad \text{where} \quad \sum_i \bar{p}\,\bar{x}_i \quad \text{is the total}$$

expenditure of the ith. consumer in the Debreu model.

Now, since each consumer satisfies strict monotonicity, he would exhaust initial endowment in purchases.

$$\sum_s \bar{q}_s = (1/\bar{w}) \left(\sum_i \bar{p}\,\bar{x}_i \right) = \sum_i w_i / \bar{w} = \bar{w}/\bar{w} = 1.$$

(iii) To show that $\sum_s \bar{q}_s \bar{d}_{is} = w_i$.

Substitute for $\bar{d}_{is}$ in the lefthand side of the above expression to get $\Sigma_s \bar{q}_s \bar{\gamma}_s \bar{x}_{is}$ (remember that $\bar{\gamma}_s$ is a vector with $\bar{\gamma}_{ks}$ as a typical element and q_s is a scalar). Now, substitute for $\bar{\gamma}_{ks} = \bar{p}_{ks} / \bar{q}_s$ in the above expression to get

$$\sum_s \bar{p}_s \bar{x}_{is} = \bar{p}\bar{x}_i = w_i \quad \text{(by strict monotonicity)}.$$

(iv) To show that the security market clears, i.e., $\Sigma_i \bar{d}_{is} = \bar{w}$ for all s.

Now $\Sigma_i \bar{d}_{is} = \Sigma_i \bar{\gamma}_s \bar{x}_{is}$. Moreover, $\bar{\gamma}_{ks} = \bar{p}_{ks} / \bar{q}_s$ or $\bar{\gamma}_s = \bar{p}_s / \bar{q}_s$.

Hence $\Sigma_i \bar{d}_{is} = \Sigma_i (\bar{p}_s / \bar{q}_s) \bar{x}_{is} = (1/\bar{q}_s) \Sigma_i \bar{p}_s \bar{x}_{is} = (1/\bar{q}_s) \bar{p}_s \Sigma_i \bar{x}_{is} = (1/\bar{q}_s) \bar{w} \bar{q}_s = \bar{w}$.

(v) This stage has two parts:

(a) $\bar{d}_{is} \geqslant \bar{\gamma}_s \bar{x}_{is}$ for all i and all s.

(b) For no i does there exist a d_i and x_i such that $\Sigma_s \bar{q}_s d_{is} = w_i$ for all s and $x_i \in X_i$ and $\bar{\gamma}_s x_{is} \leqslant d_{is}$ for all s and $x_i P_i \bar{x}_i$. In other words, no feasible bundle is preferred to the Pareto optimal bundle.

Take part (a) first. Deny this result then we have to show that this leads to a contradiction. Let $d_{is} \geqslant \bar{\gamma}_s x_{is}$ for all s. Multiply both sides of this inequality by $\bar{q}_s$ to get:

$$\bar{q}_s d_{is} \geqslant \bar{q}_s \bar{\gamma}_s x_{is} \text{ for all } s \text{ so } \sum \bar{q}_s d_{is} \geqslant \sum \bar{q}_s \bar{\gamma}_s x_{is}.$$

By assumption:

$$\sum_s \bar{q}_s d_{is} = w_i \text{ so that } w_i \geqslant \sum_s \bar{q}_s \bar{\gamma}_s x_{is} = \sum_s \bar{p}_s x_{is} = \bar{p}x_i.$$

Hence, the budget constraint is satisfied. Now, $x_i P_i \bar{x}_i$. Hence, it is Pareto improving to move from $\bar{x}_i$ to x_i. Hence, $\bar{x}_i$ cannot be Pareto optimal. This gives us the required contradiction. Part (b) is trivial and left as an exercise for the reader.

(vi) We finally have to show that for all i and all s, $\bar{x}_{is}$ is the R_{is} greatest element in

$\{x_{il} \in X_{il} / \bar{\gamma}_i x_i \leqslant \bar{d}_{il}\}$ where we have chosen s = 1, without any loss of generality. If this is not true, then there must exist a commodity bundle $x_{il} \in X_{il}$, such that $\bar{\gamma}_1 x_{il} \leqslant \bar{d}_{il}$ and $x_{il} P_1 \bar{x}_{il}$.

Construct $\tilde{x}_i \in X_i$ such that for all $s \neq 1$, $\tilde{x}_{is} = \bar{x}_{is}$ for all i and $\tilde{x}_{il} = x_{il}$ for s = 1. Consider:

$$U_i(\bar{x}_i) = \delta_{il} U_i(\bar{x}_{il}) + \sum_{s=2}^{S} \delta_{is} U_i(\bar{x}_{is})$$

and

$$U_i(\tilde{x}_i) = \delta_{il} U_i(x_{il}) + \sum_{s=2}^{S} \delta_{is} U_i(\bar{x}_{is}).$$

Now, to avoid triviality $\delta_{il} > 0$.
Hence,

$$\delta_{il} U_i(x_{il}) > \delta_{il} U_i(\bar{x}_{il})$$

which implies that $U_i(\tilde{x}_i) > U_i(\bar{x}_i)$.

Hence $x_i P_i \bar{x}_i$. This contradicts the proof in part (v). Hence, the original supposition must have been wrong so that $\bar{x}_{il}$ must be the R_i greatest bundle in $\{x_{il} \in X_{il} / \gamma_1 \bar{x}_{il} \leqslant \bar{d}_{il}\}$. This completes the proof of the Arrow securities markets theorem.

Remarks

This theorem can be formally extended to a production economy without involving considerations such as probabilistic profits. Let us take an example. Suppose a producer is planning for state of the world 1. The price vector in this state of the world is given by $\gamma_1 = (2, 3)$. Output plan, y_{jt}, by producer j for state of the world 1 is to use 5 units of inputs to produce 6 units of output, i.e., $y_{jt} = (-5, 6)$. Hence his profit is 8 so that today he can sell 18 securities for state of the world $s = 1$. Therefore, today he gets $18q_1$ and will have net $8q_1$. Hence, he has to choose his production plan in such a way that he gets maximum net cash flow. This is a perfectly objective consideration and does not involve consideration of probabilistic profit at any stage.

However, although our theorem is going through, we might occasionally encounter problems from some unexpected quarters. To take an example, let us suppose we have, in the absence of uncertainty, a fixed coefficients technology and, hence, constant returns to scale. This, of course, is essential for a perfectly competitive equilibrium. In the presence of uncertainty, this fixed coefficients technology might show increasing returns.

Suppose one machine and one man hour of labor give us 24 units of output. Now let us use two machines and two man hours of labor so that, with certainty, we would get 48 units of output. We introduce uncertainty by supposing that each machine has 1/2 probability of breaking down. Initially, we have 2 machines and 1 man hour. Then we double both inputs.

If no machines work, we get zero output. If one or both machines work we get 24 units of output. Probability of both machines failing is 1/4. Hence, expected output is:

$$1/4\ (0) + 3/4(24) = 18.$$

In the new situation, with no machines working we get zero output, one machine with one man-hour produces 24 units of output, two machines and two man hours produce 48 units of output.

The probability that no machine works is 1/16. The probability that 1 machine works is $(4 \times 1)/(2 \times 8) = 1/4$. The probability that more than one machine works is:

$$1 - 1/16 - 1/4 = 11/16.$$

Hence, expected output is:

$$0 \times (1/16) + (1/4) \times 24 + 11/16 \times (48) = 39.$$

Hence, doubling input use more than doubles output. The assumption of convex production sets becomes hard to defend. Many other assumptions of Theorem 2.2 are hard to defend. We take up these issues in later chapters.

2.6   THE THEOREM OF SECOND BEST

A Pareto optimal allocation is often referred to as a first-best solution. Consider an economy without uncertainty and external effects (the subject matter of Chapter 4). We know what the Pareto optimum or first-best conditions are here. What happens when all these conditions cannot be satisfied simultaneously. A natural temptation would be to suggest that these conditions should be satisfied in all the sectors where they can be satisfied. Lipsey and Lancaster (1957), however, argue that this need not get us to our second best optimum. This could arise because of several reasons – say a monopoly in one sector or increasing returns to scale somewhere, or something else. Lipsey and Lancaster proved the following simple but powerful theorem.

The general theorem of second best

(i) If all the conditions for Pareto optimality cannot be met then it is not necessarily second best to satisfy a subset of these conditions;

(ii) in general, to attain the second-best optimum it is necessary to violate all the conditions of Pareto optimality.

Let us study a simple proof of this proposition. Suppose we are trying to maximize an objective function $F(x_1, \ldots, x_n)$ subject to the constraints

$G(x_1, \ldots, x_n) = 0$. If we had no other restrictions to worry about, the first-order condition would simply be:

$$F_i/F_n = G_i/G_n \quad (i = 1, \ldots, n-1)$$

where a subscript denotes a partial derivative. When the second optimality theorem is valid, this would simply be equated to the price ratio between commodity *i* and commodity *n* and that would guarantee first-best optimality.

But now let us say that in just one sector this condition cannot be met. To be more specific, let us say that we have an additional constraint: $F_1/F_n = kG_1/G_n \quad k \neq 1$.

If we now try to maximize F (.) we will form the Lagrangean:

$$\Lambda = F(x_1, \ldots, x_n) + \lambda_1[G(x_1, \ldots, x_n)] + \lambda_2[(F_1/F_n) - k(G_1/G_n)]$$

and the first-order conditions are:

$$\partial\Lambda/\partial x_i = F_i + \lambda_1 G_i + \lambda_2\{[(F_n F_{1i} - F_1 F_{ni})/(F_n^2)] -$$
$$k[(G_n G_{1i} - G_1 G_{ni})/(G_n^2)]\} = 0$$
$$(i = 1, \ldots, n-1)$$
$$\partial\Lambda/\partial\lambda_1 = \partial\Lambda/\partial\lambda_2 = 0 \quad \text{where} \quad F_{1i} = \partial F_1/\partial x_i \quad \text{etc.}$$

We see that the single incongruity $F_1/F_n \neq G_1/G_n$ pervades all first-order conditions. Unless the cross-effects are zero, all the first-order conditions are changed. All the first-best conditions may have to be violated to reach second-best optimum. If there is more than one second-best constraint removing one of them may raise or lower welfare. It is hard to be definitive about this, a priori.

A problem with the Lipsey–Lancaster formulation is in the interpretation of the second-best constraint. The particular second-best constraint studied above is interpreted by them to mean that some output distortion in the market for good 1 forbids the equality between *mrs* and *mrt* of that industry with respect to the numeraire good *n*. As early as 1958 McManus pointed out the inadequacy of this interpretation and concluded that good *n* cannot be interpreted as the numeraire.

The actual source of the second-best constraint and why it should be taken seriously are both important issues. In some cases, problems arise because of say a 'natural monopoly' or because lump-sum taxes are infeasible or because some distortion has to be maintained for historical reasons. In practice, the most important reason is that decision-making about public works is often done in isolation of tax policy. No grand coordination of public policy measures is attempted or, it may be argued, is even feasible.

A question that naturally arises at this point is: when is it appropriate to satisfy the Pareto optimum conditions in one sector of the economy irrespective of whether such conditions are satisfied elsewhere. This is the question of when **piecemeal** policy is appropriate. The answer to this question is: quite rarely. See Boadway and Harris (1977) and Boadway and Bruce (1984).

We can, however, attempt a related question. This has been called the **second-better** or **nth best** approach. This approach considers only marginal changes in some distortion and evaluates the welfare consequences of these changes. This method has three practical advantages. First, since only small changes are being evaluated, only local rather than global information is required. Second, there is no need to derive complicated conditions for optimality as in a formal second-best exercise. Third, since only incremental changes are being considered it is possible to derive necessary and sufficient conditions.

2.7   CONCLUSIONS

Pareto theorems constitute the foundations of efficiency questions in modern welfare economics. In this chapter we have carefully delineated the conditions when they are valid under conditions of certainty. We have also examined the fragility of the theorems when we move to situations of uncertainty. The fact that the conditions imposed by the theorems are very strong has also been emphasized. If even one condition for Pareto optimality is violated we can get into all sorts of difficulties.

Assuming that we can reach the Pareto frontier – no trivial task in itself – the next question to tackle is: which point on this frontier do we want to choose. This is the issue of **social choice** to which we turn in the next chapter.

ADDITIONAL READING

A classic in the area of welfare economics is Graaf (1957). Another lucid account can be found in Arrow and Hahn (1971). This contains many of the formal proofs including the proof of Debreu's result. The original proof of Debreu's result can be found in Debreu (1959). A more recent statement can be found in Boadway and Bruce (1984). Other useful readings are Hayek (1960), Baumol (1965), Friedman and Friedman (1980), Just et al. (1982), and Murray (1988).

3 Forms of the social welfare function

Normative - what should be aspects

Key concepts: Bergson–Samuelson social welfare function; Scitovsky indifference curves; Kaldor, Hicks, Scitovsky compensation criteria; Arrow's general possibility theorem; Gibbard's oligarchy theorem; Sen's impossibility of a Paretian liberal; interpersonal comparison of utility and the Arrow theorem; utilitarian, neo-utilitarian and Rawlsian justice.

3.1 INTRODUCTION

We have learnt in Chapter 2 that under certain conditions the market mechanism is a good allocator of resources in the sense that it can reach any Pareto optimal allocation that may be desired. The principal difficulty remaining was that the range of choices was quite large. Pareto optimal allocations are silent over the question of distribution. In this chapter we will consider some efforts that have been made to define more sharply the particular Pareto optimal allocations that society may want. Two broad approaches to this issue can be thought of – one is the imposition of certain welfare norms on society (a **social welfare function**) and the second would be to arrive at social preferences by aggregating individual preferences. We will begin by considering some early forms of the social welfare function and then move on to aggregation of individual preferences, sometimes called social choice theory. A host of 'impossibility' results are proved. We then realize that the difficulty in aggregating preferences comes from the information requirements of the theory. Once the information set is expanded 'possibility' results emerge. We study some social welfare functions – some of which have been used in applied work – in this context.

3.2 EARLY ATTEMPTS AT FORMULATING AN APPROACH TO DISTRIBUTION

In their classic formulations, Bergson and Samuelson had given some coherence to the idea of social choice. Their approach was that of formulating a social welfare function (SWF). Suppose we have a set of social alternatives x, y, z, w, etc. These may be different rates of unemployment and inflation and/or various distributions of income in society, and the like. This set of social alternatives may be infinite but the more important aspects may be captured in a set of variables $\alpha_1, \alpha_2, \ldots, \alpha_n$. Social welfare $W(\alpha_1, \ldots, \alpha_n)$ is a function of these variables. The domain of this SWF is the set of αs whereas the range of this function is the set of real numbers. In this manner we articulate the notion of social welfare.

But to fix a form of $W(.)$ we need to weight the αs but to weight the αs we need value judgments. We need to express clearly how society values different alternatives and this cannot be done except by explicitly introducing value judgments. Bergson and Samuelson were not prepared to commit themselves to any specific set of value judgments. We now show a geometric interpretation of this idea which was popularized by Scitovsky. The innovation is often called **Scitovsky social indifference curve** or, simply, **social indifference curve** and has been used extensively in the area of international trade theory.

Used in int'l trade theory

Take a two-person, two-commodity economy in which individual utilities are fixed at prespecified levels and the supply of one good is fixed. What is the minimum amount of the other commodity that is needed to sustain utilities at the prespecified levels? This, clearly, is a Pareto optimizing exercise. The problem can be formally defined as Min: $x_1^1 + x_2^1$ subject to:

(i) $U_1(x_1^1 + x_1^2) - \bar{U}_1 = 0$
(ii) $U_2(x_2^1 + x_2^2) - \bar{U}_2 = 0$
and
(iii) $x_1^2 + x_2^2 = x^{-2}$; where x_j^i is the amount of the ith commodity going to the jth individual and $\bar{x}^2$ is the fixed supply of commodity 2, etc. Setting up the Lagrangean we have:

$$\Lambda = x_1^1 + x_2^1 + \lambda_1[U_1(x_1^1 + x_1^2) - \bar{U}_1] + \lambda_2[U_2(x_2^1 + x_2^2) - \bar{U}^2]$$
$$+ \lambda_3[\bar{x}^2 - x_1^2 - x_2^2].$$

The minimum quantity of x^1 is determinate. For each value of $\bar{x}^2$, a different value (x^1*) of x^1 can be found. The locus of all such $(x^1*, \bar{x}^2)$ points for given values of U_1 and U_2 forms a Scitovsky indifference curve.

If the indifference curves of the individuals are convex to the origin, the Scitovsky contours will also be convex. But it is immediately obvious that if we change the specified values of U_1 and U_2 we will get a different Scitovsky indifference curve. To realize this, look at point P in Figure 3.1. P belongs to the Scitovsky indifference curve S_1 and corresponds to utility levels $\bar{U}_1$ and $\bar{U}_2$ for the two individuals. But the quantities of x^1 and x^2 could also be distributed differently and that would result in different utility levels for the two individuals. The Scitovsky indifference curve S_2 for these utility levels will pass through P but there is no reason whatsoever why S_1

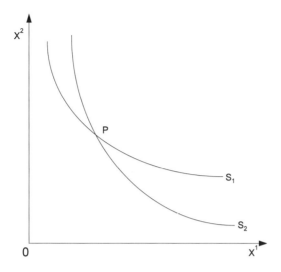

Figure 3.1

and S_2 should coincide. Thus, social indifference curves are very sensitive to distribution and can intersect, even though individual indifference curves do not intersect.

We can eliminate intersecting social indifference curves in the manner depicted in Figure 3.2. Suppose we define a Bergson social welfare function $W(U_1, U_2)$ and consider the various U_1, U_2 combinations which give a prespecified value W^0 of the Bergson social welfare function. Four such Scitovsky indifference curves are depicted as S_1, S_2, S_3 and S_4 in Figure 3.2. Now, take the lower envelope JJ of all such Scitovsky indifference curves. JJ is called a Bergson contour and depicts the minimum $x^2(x^1)$ needed to sustain Bergson welfare level W^0 given the value of $x^1(x^2)$. Formal optimization gives us this leeway, but we do know that we need value judgments to fix the form of the Bergson social welfare function.

Other early attempts

Kaldor (1939) tried to say something about the vast ranges of the SUPF where the Pareto criterion is silent. Actually Kaldor himself announced this criterion solely for production efficiency but the 'Kaldor criterion' has been used as a welfare norm. The Kaldor criterion says the following. Social state x is better than social state y if the gainers in the transition from y to x can more than adequately compensate the losers for their loss and yet remain better off.

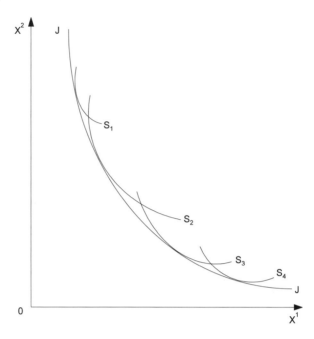

Figure 3.2

It is important to point out that the criterion does not say that compensation actually takes place. The possibility of adequate compensation is sufficient. A problem with this criterion is that it is two-term inconsistent, i.e., we can simultaneously have social state x being Kaldor preferred to social state y and social state y preferred to social state x. In Figure 3.3 two PUPFs are drawn and are labelled a_1a_1 and a_2a_2. According to the Kaldor mechanism individual I can 'potentially' move along a_1a_1 from x and come to a point north-east of y. Hence, x is Kaldor-preferred to y. At the same time, individual II can 'potentially' move from y along a_2a_2 and come to a point north-east of x. Hence, y is Kaldor-preferred to x.

Hicks advocated the 'dual' of the Kaldor compensation criterion and argued that social state x is preferred to social state y if the losers in the move from y to x cannot adequately bribe the gainers not to affect the change and still remain better off. The Hicks criterion also involves hypothetical, not actual, transfers and, like the Kaldor criterion, can be shown to be two-term inconsistent.

The Scitovsky criterion combines the Kaldor and Hicks criteria to say that social state x is preferred to social state y if the gainers in the movement from y to x can adequately compensate the losers and still remain better off and the losers cannot bribe the gainers not to make the change and still remain better off. This criterion again calls for hypothetical transfers. The Scitovsky criterion is also not free of internal contradictions.

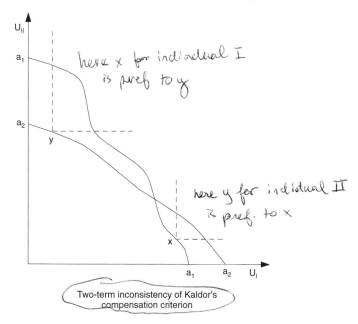

here x for individual I is pref to y

here y for individual II is pref. to x

Two-term inconsistency of Kaldor's compensation criterion

Figure 3.3

In Figure 3.4 four PUPFs are drawn. In terms of the Scitovsky criterion the movement from *x* to *y*, *y* to *z*, *z* to *w*, and *w* to *x* are all preferred. Thus we get our preference cycle.

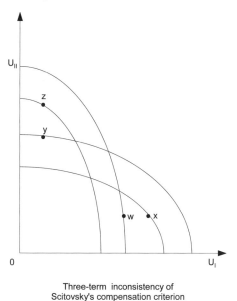

Three-term inconsistency of Scitovsky's compensation criterion

Figure 3.4

3.3   AGGREGATING INDIVIDUAL PREFERENCES TO ARRIVE AT SOCIAL CHOICE

We know that the principal problem with the Bergson–Samuelson formulation is that without specific value judgments, it is not possible to nail down a specific form of this function. In one of the truly pioneering contributions to modern welfare economics Arrow (1963 a,b) tried to confront this problem head-on. He posed the following problem: suppose we start with individual preference functions, try to aggregate these into social preference functions and make this social preference function obey some meaningful and appealing norms. How far, asked Arrow, can we go without encountering some absurd results? The answer is not very far at all. Before we study Arrow's result we need some notation. To this we now turn.

Notation

The set of all conceivable alternatives is S. There are N individuals in society. At any point in time, a non-empty subset of S is feasible and is called the issue B. The basic value judgment that Arrow makes is that social choice is based on individual preference relations.

Each individual, i, is supposed to have a binary weak preference relation R_i defined over S (or, B, if we so please). Any given N tuple of individual weak preference relations $(R_1, \ldots, R_N)$ is called a situation s. We then define:

A **Group Decision Rule (GDR)** is a functional relation, f, which for every possible situation, s, specifies exactly one social weak preference relation R defined over S. Thus, $R = f(s)$. We define a preference relation, P, as xPy iff xRy and not yRx. The indifference relation is defined as xIy iff xRy and yRx. A GDR satisfies some elementary properties such as: (i) **reflexivity** (xRx, for all alternatives x), an alternative is at least as good as itself; (ii) **connectedness** (for any two alternatives x and y we must have either xRy or yRx or both.

Before we examine Arrow's result, a little background work is necessary. Our weightage of the individual R_i's will fix the form of $f(.)$ and, hence, determine R. We will call R a **binary GDR** if, when considering the preference between two alternatives x and y we do not have to appeal to other alternatives z, w, etc. R is **transitive** iff xRy and yRz implies xRz for all x,y,z in S. R is **quasi-transitive** iff xPy and yPz implies xPz for all x,y,z $\in$ S. This does not say anything about the weak preference relation R. P is **acyclic** over S iff there does not exist an integer m such that $x_1 P x_2$ & $x_2 P x_3$ & $\ldots$ & $x_{m-1} P x_m$ and $x_m P x_1$ for $x_1, \ldots, x_m \in S$. P is **founded** over S iff there does not exist a long descending chain such that $\infty \ldots$, and $x_3 P x_2$ and $x_2 P x_1$ where $x_1, x_2, \ldots \infty \in S$.

We can then prove:

Lemma 3.1

(a) If R is transitive, it is also quasi-transitive but the converse is not necessarily true.

(b) If R is quasi-transitive, P is acyclic but the converse is not necessarily true.

(c) If P is founded, it is also acyclic but the converse is not necessarily true.

(d) If S is finite then foundedness of P and acyclicity of P are equivalent statements.

Proof

(a) Suppose R is transitive and not quasi-transitive. This means that xPy and yPz and not xPz. Now, xPy $\rightarrow$ xRy and yPz $\rightarrow$ yRz. But R is not quasi-transitive so that not xPz. But not xPz means not xRz. But this contradicts the transitivity of R. Hence transitivity of R implies quasi-transitivity of R.

To show that quasi-transitivity of R does not necessarily imply transitivity consider the following example: aIb and xPy and xIa and yIa. This clearly violates transitivity of R but quasi-transitivity is not violated because the preference relation is defined only over two elements.

(b) Suppose that quasi-transitivity of R does not imply acyclicity of P. Then there exists an integer m such that x_1Px_2 & x_2Px_3 &...& $x_{m-1}Px_m$ and x_mPx_1. If R is quasi-transitive then x_1Px_m. Hence we have x_1Px_m and x_mPx_1 – which is absurd. Hence, we have a contradiction and the result is proved. To show that acyclicity of P does not necessarily imply quasi-transitivity of R consider the following example xPy and yPz and xIz. P is acyclic but R is not quasi-transitive.

(c) To show that foundedness of P implies acyclicity of P. Deny this, then there exists an m such that:

x_1Px_2 and ... $x_{m-1}Px_m$ and x_mPx_1. Extend this chain indefinitely. Here we immediately violate foundedness of P. To show that acyclicity of P does not necessarily imply foundedness of P consider an infinite number of alternatives in the interval $]x, y[$. We stipulate that for all a, b $\in]x, y[$ we have aRb iff $a \geqslant b$. Here R is an ordering but we have an infinite number of points in $]x, y[$ so P is not founded.

(d) We have already shown that there exists an infinite chain:

∞ ... and ... x_3Px_2 and x_2Px_1. If $x_1 = x_2$ then the result is proved. If $x_1 \neq x_2$ but $x_2 = x_3$ then, again, there is a P cycle. Hence, the preference chain consists of distinct elements to avoid violation of acyclicity of P. But since S is finite, a cycle is established.

Definition 3.1

Let f be any GDR. Let s and s' be any two situations. Let $R = f(s)$ and $R' = f(s')$. We define the following properties of R.

(i) **Rationality Condition 1**: [RC(1)] R is an ordering for every possible situation, i.e., R is reflexive, connected and transitive.
(ii) **Rationality Condition 2**: [RC (2)] R is reflexive, connected, and quasi-transitive.
(iii) **Rationality Condition 3**: [RC (3)] R is reflexive and connected and P is acyclic.
(iv) **Binariness**: for all x, y $\in$ S if $[(xR_i y$ iff $xR'_i y)$ and $(yR_i x$ iff $yR'_i x)]$ for all i then $[(xRy$ iff $xR'y)$ and $(yRx$ iff $yR'x)]$, i.e., when comparing x and y we do not have to appeal to any other alternatives z, w, etc.
(v) **Weak Pareto criterion** (WP): for all x, y $\in$ S if $xP_i y$ for all i then xPy.
(vi) **Strict Pareto criterion** (SP): for all x, y $\in$ S if $xR_i y$ for all i and $xP_j y$ for some j, then xPy.
(vii) **Non-dictatorship** (ND): there does not exist any individual i such that for all x, y $\in$ S and for all situations s:

$$xP_i y \rightarrow xPy.$$

We can now state and prove Arrow's fundamental result.

3.4 ARROW'S GENERAL POSSIBILITY AND OTHER IMPOSSIBILITY THEOREMS

Ironically, Arrow's impossibility theorem is called a general possibility theorem. We are in a position to prove it now. Let S have at least three distinct alternatives x, y and z. Then there does not exist a GDR satisfying binariness, WP, RC(1), and ND. These absolutely innocuous-looking value judgments are inconsistent with each other!

The proof of this theorem needs a lemma. We need some notation for this lemma. Let L be the set of individuals in society and let L' be a non-empty subset of it. Define two subsets: L' (**nearly decisive set**) is the set of individuals i such that for all x, y $\in$ S and $L' \subseteq L$ and $x \neq y$ and for every situation s if $xP_i y$ for all $i \in L'$ and for all $j \in L - L'$, $yP_j x$, then xPy. Hence if everyone in L' prefers x to y and L' is nearly decisive. This is written as $xD_{L'}y$. We also define a **fully decisive set**. L'' is fully decisive over alternatives x and y if $xP_i y$ (for all $i \in L'$ and $x \neq y$) implies that xPy. This is a stronger requirement than near-decisiveness since it holds irrespective of the preferences of the people in $L - L''$. Full decisiveness is written as $x\bar{D}_{L''}y$. Now, we can state our lemma.

Lemma 3.2

Let S have at least three distinct alternatives and the GDR satisfy binariness, WP and RC(2) (these conditions are weaker than those in Arrow's theorem). Let $L' \subseteq L$. Then if $xD_{L'}y$ for some x, y $\in$ S then $a\bar{D}_{L'}$ b for all a, b $\in$ S. In other words, if L' is nearly decisive over some pair of alternatives and the GDR satisfies RC(2), binariness, and WP then this set is fully decisive over every pair of alternatives.

Proof

We are given $xD_{L'}y$. Let z be an alternative distinct from x and y. We prove the lemma in two stages:

  I We first prove it for a, b $\in$ {x, y, z}.
 II We next generalize it to all a, b $\in$ S.

I. Consider a situation s such that for all $i \in L'$ we have xP_iyP_iz and for all $j \in L - L'$ we have yP_jx and yP_jz. This does not imply anything, yet, about the relation between x and z. From the fact that xP_iy for $i \in L'$ and yP_jx for all $j \in L - L'$ and the fact that L' is nearly decisive over x and y, it follows that xPy. Now, everyone prefers y to z. Hence, by WP it must be the case that yPz. Hence, from quasi-transitivity of R, it follows that xPz. Now, xP_iz for $i \in L'$ and xPz irrespective of the preferences of individuals in the group $L - L'$. Hence, by binariness, we have:

$$xD_{L'}y \rightarrow x\bar{D}_{L'}z.$$

II. Consider a situation s such that for all i in L' we have
zP_ixP_iy and for all $j \in (L - L')$ we have yP_jx and zP_jx.
Now, given $xD_{L'}y$ we have xPy. By WP we have zPx. Hence, by RC (2) we have zPy. By using binariness we have:

$$xD_{L'}y \rightarrow z\bar{D}_{L'}y.$$

Now, there is nothing special about x, y, z and we can interchange them. We write two purely hypothetical relations and interchange y and z in them. These relations are:

$$xD_{L'}y \rightarrow x\bar{D}_{L'}z \tag{3.1}$$

$$xD_{L'}y \rightarrow z\bar{D}_{L'}y. \tag{3.2}$$

Interchanging y and z in (3.1) and (3.2) we get:

$$xD_{L'}z \rightarrow x\bar{D}_{L'}y \tag{3.1'}$$

$$xD_{L'}z \rightarrow y\bar{D}_{L'}z. \tag{3.2'}$$

Combine (3.1') and (3.1) to get:

$$xD_{L'}y \rightarrow x\bar{D}_{L'}y. \tag{3.3}$$

Combine (3.2') and (3.2) to get:

$$xD_{L'}y \rightarrow y\bar{D}_{L'}z. \tag{3.4}$$

In (3.1) interchange x and z to get:

$$zD_{L'}y \rightarrow z\bar{D}_{L'}x. \tag{3.1''}$$

Combine (3.2) and (3.1″) to get:

$$xD_{L'}y \rightarrow z\bar{D}_{L'}x. \tag{3.5}$$

In equation (3.5) interchange y and z to get:

$$xD_{L'}z \rightarrow y\bar{D}_{L'}x. \tag{3.5'}$$

Combine (3.5′) and (3.1) to get:

$$xD_{L'}y \rightarrow x\bar{D}_{L'}z \rightarrow x\bar{D}_{L'}z \rightarrow y\bar{D}_{L'}x$$

and, hence:

$$xD_{L'}y \rightarrow y\bar{D}_{L'}x. \tag{3.6}$$

All of these statements are 'if then' statements. Now assert what we know to be true, i.e., $xD_{L'}y$, from which we get:

$$x\bar{D}_{L'}z \text{ and } z\bar{D}_{L'}y \text{ and } x\bar{D}_{L'}y \text{ and } y\bar{D}_{L'}z \text{ and } z\bar{D}_{L'}x \text{ and } y\bar{D}_{L'}x.$$

Hence, the first part of the lemma is proved. Let us have a generalization, i.e., we have to show that $a\bar{D}_L$, b for all *a*, *b* in S. We have the following possibilities of choosing *a* and *b*.

(1) $a \in \{x, y, z\}$ and $b \in \{x, y, z\}$. This we have already done.
(2) $a \notin \{x, y, z\}$ and $b \in \{x, y, z\}$
(3) $a \in \{x, y, z\}$ and $b \notin \{x, y, z\}$

Cases (2) and (3) are entirely symmetric and hence we need to consider only one.

(4) $a \notin \{x, y, z\}$ and $b \notin \{x, y, z\}$.

Consider case (2). Since x, y, z are all distinct there must be two alternatives in x, y, z distinct from b. Suppose $b = x$. Hence, $b\bar{D}_{L'} z$ (by first step) with $a = y$, i.e., the triple (b, a, z). The earlier proof is applicable in a straightforward manner.

Consider case 4. We know $y\bar{D}_{L'} z$. Consider $\{a,y,z\}$. We know $a\bar{D}_{L'}y$.

Consider $\{a,y,b\}$. L' is fully decisive for *a* against *y*. Hence it is nearly decisive for *a* against *y* and, hence, fully decisive for any alternative against any other alternative. Hence $a\bar{D}_{L'}b$. This proves the lemma. With this lemma proved the proof of Arrow's general possibility theorem is a relatively simple matter.

Proof of Arrow's general possibility theorem

The conditions of Arrow's general possibility theorem are stronger than those of the lemma we have just proved. Hence, the lemma is valid. Since WP is satisfied there exists a set which is nearly decisive for some alternative against some other alternative. In other words, given WP for all $x, y \in S$, if $x \neq y$, then there exists a set of people L' such that $xD_{L'}y$. Consider distinct

$x, y, z \in S$. There exists at least one L' such that $x D_{L'} y$. In general, we cannot rule out the possibility of more than one such group existing. Similarly for y and z. Out of these nearly decisive sets pick up the one with the fewest members, L'. Assume without loss of generality that L' is nearly decisive for x against y.

Now consider an individual k who belongs to this nearly decisive set L'. Construct a situation s such that:

$$x P_k y P_k z$$
$$y P_i z P_i x \text{ for all i in } L - L'$$
$$z P_j x P_j y \text{ for all j in } L' - k.$$

Consider the choice between x and y. We know $x D_{L'} y$. We know from the situation constructed that all members of L' prefer x to y whereas everyone else prefers y to x. So we must have $x P y$.

Now consider the choice between y and z. Within the set L' only individual k prefers y to z everyone else prefers z to y. We know that L' is the smallest nearly decisive set. Therefore, we cannot have $z P y$. By connectedness we have $y R z$. Combining $x P y$ and $y R z$ by transitivity we get $x P z$.

Now k is the only person who prefers x to z. Everyone, including other members of L' prefer z to x. Hence k is nearly decisive in the choice between x and z. By Lemma 3.2 k is fully decisive in all choices, i.e.,

$x D_k z \rightarrow a \bar{D}_k b$ for all a, b $\in S$. Thus, k is a dictator. Since the GDR satisfies binariness, WP, and RC(1) it violates ND.

This, of course, is an eminently important as well as a profoundly disturbing result. Unfortunately, it is not possible to get around this difficulty in a simple way. A whole new area of welfare economics (social choice theory) has developed around Arrow's result. Economists have tried every conceivable method to get around Arrow's difficulty. But so long as they stuck to the basic Arrowian framework, they found that all they managed to do was to come up with some new absurdity. To give readers an idea of such results, we present two important theorems, Gibbard's oligarchy theorem and Sen's impossibility of a Paretian liberal.

Gibbard's oligarchy theorem

Gibbard relaxed RC(1) to RC(2) and came up with a powerful oligarchy instead of a dictator. Before we prove this theorem, we need a lemma.

Lemma 3.3

Let S have at least three distinct alternatives and let the GDR satisfy RC(2), WP and binariness. If for some a, b, a', $b' \in S$ and for some subsets L_1 and L_2 we have

$aD_{L_1}b$ and $a'D_{L_2}b'$ then for all distinct x, $y \in S$ it must be the case that $x\bar{D}_{L_1 \cap L_2}y$. Thus if one set of people is nearly decisive over two alternatives and another set of people is nearly decisive over two other alternatives then the intersection of these two sets is fully decisive over all alternatives.

Proof

Let L_1, L_2, a, b, a', b' exist. Partition the set of individuals into four subsets: $L_1 \cap L_2$, $L_1 - L_2$, $L_2 - L_1$, $L - L_1 \cup L_2$ as in Figure 3.5. Consider three distinct alternatives x, y, z in S. Assign preference orderings as:

$$xP_iyP_iz \text{ for all } i \in L_1 \cap L_2$$
$$yP_izP_ix \text{ for all } i \in L_2 - L_1$$
$$zP_ixP_iy \text{ for all } i \in L_1 - L_2$$
$$zP_iyP_ix \text{ for all } i \in \{L - (L_1 \cup L_2)\}.$$

Everyone in L_1 prefers x to y and everyone opposes this choice. By near decisiveness we have xPy. Everyone in L_2 prefers y to z and everyone else opposes it. By near decisiveness we have yPz. By RC(2) we must have xPz. But only people in $L_1 \cap L_2$ prefer x to z; everyone else opposes this choice. Hence the set $L_1 \cap L_2$ is nearly decisive between the alternatives x and z. By Lemma 3.2 it is fully decisive over any pair of alternatives in S. This proves the lemma.

Statement and proof of Gibbard's oligarchy theorem

Let S have at least three alternatives and let the GDR satisfy RC(2), WP, and binariness. Then there exists a unique, non-empty subset $L^* \subseteq L$ such that for all x, y in S:

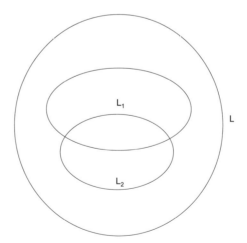

Figure 3.5

(i) if xP$_i$y for all i in L* then xPy.
(ii) if yP$_j$x for some j ∈ L* then yRx.

Hence there exists a strong oligarchy. With consensus within the oligarchy, the views of rest of society do not matter at all. If even one person prefers one option to another society irrespective of the preferences of all others (including other members of L*) must consider the first option to be at least as good as the second.

Since the GDR satisfies WP, there exists some group of individuals which is nearly decisive for some alternative x against another alternative y. Pick out the smallest such set L*. We now show that L* is the group referred to in Gibbard's theorem.

Now, if x = y then the theorem is trivially true since the antecedent is false. Consider the case where x ≠ y. We know that aD$_{L^*}$b implies that for a′, b′ ∈ S it must be the case that a′$\bar{D}_{L^*}$b′. Hence the first part of Gibbard's theorem is proved. We now show that if yP$_j$x for some j ∈ L*, it must be the case that yRx. The proof proceeds by contradiction. Suppose not yRx. By connectedness we know xRy. Putting these together we get xPy. Now partition L into three groups: L$_a$ = {i ∈ L/xP$_i$y}, L$_b$ = {i ∈ L/xI$_i$y}, L$_c$ = {i ∈ L/yP$_i$x}. j belongs to L$_c$. Construct a situation s′ such that:

$$zP'_i xP'_i y \text{ for all i in } L_a$$
$$zP'_i xI'_i y \text{ for all i in } L_b$$
$$yP'_i zP'_i x \text{ for all i in } L_c.$$

Between x and y the individual preferences have remained unchanged. So we must have xP′y. Now, compare z and x. Everyone prefers z to x so by WP it must be the case that zP′x. By RC(2), we have zP′y. Now realize that zP$_i$y for all i ∈ L$_a$ and zP$_i$y for all i ∈ L$_b$ whereas all others prefer y to z. Thus zD$_{L_a \cup L_b}$y. We also know that the set L* is nearly decisive for some alternative against some other alternative. By Lemma 3.3 it must be the case that the set L$_a$ ∪ L$_b$ ∩ L* is fully decisive for every pair of distinct alternatives in S.

This leads to a contradiction. The intersection of two sets has to be a proper subset of both sets. We know that j ∈ L$_c$, i.e., j ∉ L$_a$ ∪ L$_b$. Hence, L* ∩ {L$_a$ ∪ L$_b$} must be a proper subset of L*. But L* is the smallest nearly decisive set. Hence we have the required contradiction. Hence if yP$_j$x then it must be the case that yRx.

To show that L* is unique. Let L** be another such set. By assumption L* ≠ L**. Then we must have either:

(i) there is some k in L* who is not a member of L**; or
(ii) there is some l in L** who is not a member of L*.

Consider case (i). Construct a situation s″ such that xP″$_i$y for all i ∈ L** and yP″$_i$x for all i ∈ L*. The first relation gives us xPy whereas the second gives us yPx which is, of course, a contradiction. The proof for case (ii) is entirely symmetric. This completes the proof of Gibbard's theorem.

Sen's impossibility of a Paretian liberal

Now we give up both binariness as well as RC(2) but we run up against another difficulty: the Pareto criterion conflicts with some basic principles of liberalism. In a society that claims to be liberal, people are allowed some basic freedoms. It is in this spirit that we define:

Minimal Federalism (MF)

There exist two non-empty disjoint subsets L_d and L_e such that for some pairs (a,b), (c,d) of distinct alternatives, if aP_ib for all $i \in L_d$ then aPb; and if bP_i a for all $i \in L_d$ then bPa. Similarly, if cP_id for all $i \in L_e$ then cPd; and if dP_ic for all $i \in L_e$ then dPc. It is hard to object to this requirement because different groups stay in society only if they can retain a certain individuality of their own. Two groups of people are given decisive say over just one pair of alternatives each. Think, for example, of a multi-ethnic society. Society is liberal and allows an ethnic group the freedom, for example, to send their children to secular or religious school. The choices could be even more innocuous. Then the consequence is Sen's theorem.

Sen's theorem

There does not exist a GDR which satisfies RC(3), WP and MF. Binariness is not involved here.

Proof

Since MF is being satisfied, there exist two non-empty disjoint subsets: L_d and L_e satisfying MF. Realize that if a = c and b = d then each of these sets is decisive over the same pair of alternatives. Consider a situation such that aP_ib for all $i \in L_d$ so that aPb and dP_ic for all $i \in L_e$ so that bPa. This is, of course, a contradiction. Hence, there are two alternatives now:

(i) a, b, c, d are all distinct.
(ii) (a,b) ∩ (c,d) is a singleton.

Consider case (i). Consider a situation such that:

$$dP_jaP_jbP_jc \quad \text{for all } j \in L_d$$
$$bP_kcP_kdP_ka \quad \text{for all } k \in L_e$$
$$dP_ha \text{ and } bP_hc \text{ for all } h \in L - L_d - L_e$$

By MF we get aPb and cPd. By WP we get bPc. Hence we should have aPd but by WP again we get dPa. Hence we have a P cycle and RC(3) is violated.

Consider case (ii) now. Without loss of generality assume that d = c and construct a situation such that:

$$dP_jaP_jb \quad \text{for all } j \in L_d$$
$$bP_kdP_ka \quad \text{for all } k \in L_e$$
$$dP_ha \quad \text{for all } h \in L - L_d - L_e$$

By MF we have aPb and bPd. So that we should have aPd. However, by WP we get dPa. Hence, we have a *P* cycle and RC(3) is violated. Sen accepts RC(3), so we have a conflict between MF and WP. Hence, the impossibility of a Paretian liberal.

3.5 BEYOND THE ARROW FRAMEWORK

There is no easy escape from the Arrow dilemma. Various methods have been tried but without any significant success. The list of impossibility theorems is very long. The interested reader is referred to Kelly (1976) for an early survey, and Sen (1979b) for a relatively recent one.

Just when the string of impossibility theorems made it appear that the death knell had been sounded for social choice theory, a completely different line of inquiry began. Some people began wondering whether the Arrow dilemma had been rendered inevitable by the way in which the question was posed. This point needs some amplification. To this we now turn.

Welfare economics, in the classical tradition, always postulated individual utility as being cardinal and further postulated that it was possible to compare the utilities of different people. This was done both for expounding the theory of consumer behavior as well as for making pronouncements on social welfare. This methodology was perceived as being archaic and a monumental attack on this line of reasoning was initiated by Hicks (1939). Hicks convincingly argued that for, among other things, demand theory and welfare (as the classical theorists interpreted it) we need neither cardinal utility nor interpersonal comparison of utility. Ordinal ranking expressed in the form of consumer indifference maps was sufficient for demand theory and Paretian welfare economics. So, in the interest of scientific refinement, the 'cumbersome' and value-loaded notions of cardinality and interpersonal comparisons of utility were abandoned. Later refinements, as we know, realized that even an ordinal utility function was unnecessarily demanding. An ordering was all that was required to obtain the results.

Some economists, however, have linked the Arrowian paradox to this advancement. Cardinality is not really important since cardinal utility functions do not rescue us from this dilemma. But interpersonal comparison of utility is important. Fresh ground in this direction was broken by Steven Strasnick and Peter Hammond who, in separate papers, showed that if interpersonal comparison of utility is allowed then one can get social decision rules or social welfare functions that satisfy all of Arrow's conditions and more. It was shown that Rawls' maximin criterion satisfied Arrow's conditions with even the Strict Pareto criterion substituted for the Weak Pareto criterion. Moreover, if indifference curves were 'thick' in the sense that the consumer did not always satisfy the axiom of local non-satiation, then the utilitarian criterion was also capable of resolving the Arrowian dilemma, provided of course, in both cases, that interpersonal comparisons of utility is allowed. Interpersonal comparison of utility is visualized in the following manner. A person i compares her well-being in state x with person j in state y. Thus, an individual ordering is defined over the ordered pair (x,i). Hence, (x,i) R_i (y,j) is read person i considers herself in state x at least as well-off as person j in state y. The Group Decision Rule is an aggregation of such R_i. Hammond showed that the maximin criterion satisfied all of Arrow's conditions and more. Strasnick showed the same thing. Ng demonstrated the result with thick indifference curves and the utilitarian criterion.

As such results began to trickle in, the suspicion began to grow that the Arrowian dilemma results from the fact that its framework starves itself of information. Sen's 1979b paper formally demonstrated this to be the case.

Sen's interpretation of information in the Arrowian framework

Sen shows that within the Arrow framework a GDR which satisfies Binariness, WP and RC(1) and Universality of Domain (i.e. a GDR is defined for every constellation of individual R_i's) is necessarily dictatorial. In other words, the restrictions on information are so severe that a GDR which satisfies these criteria has to be dictatorial.

Recall Lemma 3.2. This lemma said that if the GDR satisfies Binariness, WP, and RC(2) then if there exists a group that is nearly decisive over any pair of alternatives, then this group is necessarily fully decisive over all pairs of alternatives. Thus, for this group, opposition is irrelevant. Along the same lines one can prove the following result.

Lemma 3.4　Irrelevance of support

This lemma enables one continuously to reduce the size of the nearly decisive (or decisive) set. Suppose, there are three distinct alternatives x, y and z and suppose that a set L_f is decisive between alternatives x and y. Suppose further that the GDR satisfies binariness, WP and RC (1). Partition L_f into two subset $L_{f'}$, and $L_{f''}$ Construct a situation s such that:

$$xP_iyP_iz \quad \text{for all } i \in L_{f'}$$
$$yP_izP_ix \quad \text{for all } i \in L_{f''}$$
$$zP_ixP_iy \quad \text{for all } i \in L - L_f.$$

By Lemma 3.2 we must have yPz. Now we must have either yPx (in which case $L_{f''}$ is nearly decisive between y and x and, by Lemma 3.2, between every pair of alternatives) or xRy. In the latter case, since we have yPz if the GDR satisfies RC(1) we must have xPz. This would make $L_{f'}$ nearly decisive between x and z and, by Lemma 3.2, fully decisive over every pair of alternatives. Thus, no matter what the size of the decisive set, it is always possible to reduce it. The logical conclusion is the Arrowian dictator.

Hence, a reconstruction of the proof of Arrow's theorem would read something like the following. By WP, the entire population (at least) is nearly decisive between some pair of alternatives. By Lemma 3.2 it is also fully decisive. By Lemma 3.4, it is always possible to keep cutting down the size of this set. Since the number of people is finite, we have the lone dictator as the logical outcome of restricting the information set. The Arrowian dictator is, after all, inevitable.

When Sen's results are juxtaposed with those of Hammond and Strasnick one starts interpreting GDRs in a different manner. By confining ourselves to individual orderings we also neglect or discard information, say on interpersonal comparison of utility, which is really a waste. The restrictions on the GDR constructed by aggregating individual orderings makes the Arrowian dilemma a logical inevitability. The only way to escape such problems is to expand the information set.

3.6 FORMS OF THE SOCIAL WELFARE FUNCTION (SWF)

For some time before the advent of social choice theory economists have tried to get a straightforward and acceptable measure of social welfare. We know that Bergson and Samuelson were hesitant to make value judgments to fix a form of the SWF. But writers in this earlier tradition have never hesitated to make value judgments to justify their measure of social welfare. We discuss some popular SWFs used in the literature.

Classical utilitarianism Mill, Bentham

This is one of the oldest forms of the SWF and can be traced to the writings of John Stuart Mill, Bentham and even earlier. To utilitarians individual utility is measured in cardinal terms and society's welfare is measured as the sum of the utilities of everyone in society. Thus if $U_1, U_2, \ldots, U_n$ are the individual utility functions and these individuals get consumption baskets $x_1, x_2, \ldots, x_n$ respectively so that individual i's utility is, simply $U_i(x_i)$, then society's welfare is, simply:

$$\sum_{i=1}^{n} U_i(x_i).$$

Social policy should be geared to maximize this welfare. This means that optimal policy equates marginal utility across the population. In other words,

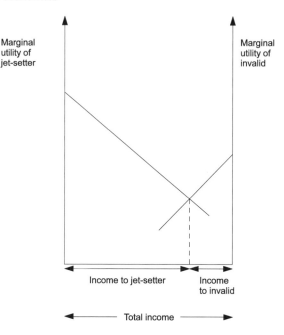

Figure 3.6

resources are distributed in such a way that everyone has the same marginal utility. If everyone has the same utility function then this amounts to an egalitarian distribution of income. But if this is not the case then the utilitarian criterion can exacerbate existing inequalities. Examine, for example, Figure 3.6 which considers the problem of distributing a fixed basket of goods between two persons – one of whom is an invalid with very limited capacity to enjoy himself and the other is a jet-setter with a very high marginal utility schedule. A utilitarian would give the lion's share to the jet-setter.

Realizing this difficulty, some authors have toyed with the idea of making the utilitarian social welfare function concave. Suppose, for example, instead of adding up utilities we added up natural logs of utilities. This would reduce the significance of the problem in Figure 3.6.

Sen has proposed another axiom to make the utilitarian function more equitable. He calls it the **weak equity axiom**. This says the following. Suppose individual *i* always has lower utility than individual *j* for every distribution of income between them. Then every distribution of income between them must give individual *i* higher income than individual *j*.

Neo-Utilitarianism   *Vickery + Harsanyi*

This theme is developed in papers by Vickrey and Harsanyi. Uncertainty is specifically built into this formulation. Everyone is uncertain about their position in the next time period. It is then argued that if society is to be fair people must be ethically impartial between alternative social states between who they are going to be in the next time period. Thus you have to be impartial between being in the shoes of a Bill Gates or a beggar. This can be accomplished only if each of us had the same chance of being any person in society. We assume that the probability of being in different states is known so that I define a von Neumann–Morgenstern utility function by adding up the products of different utilities and the associated probabilities. As a rational agent, I maximize $\sum_i \pi_i U_i$ where U_i is the utility of being in individual i's shoes and π_i is the associated probability. Thus each possibility gets an adequate weightage and, in this sense, I am impartial between different alternatives. π_i is the same for you as it is for me.

There are three quite serious problems with this approach. Let us suppose that you and I have the same probability (1/2) of winning \$100 in a lottery. Compare this with a situation where we know that person j is sure to win the lottery and each of us has the same probability (1/2) of being in person j's shoes. From the perspective of the neo-utilitarians these two would be equivalent statements. But from a moral point of view they are clearly not equivalent statements.

Second, people with different degrees of risk aversion will not rank social states in a similar manner. Moreover, quite apart from risk aversion, different people have different ethical perceptions about different states of the world. Such differences may have nothing to do with differences in risk perceptions.

Rawls (1971) raises another point. The π_i that I assign to state i depends upon the number of people in that state. Thus, solely the number of people in a particular state determine the weight given to that particular state of the world. Morally, this is rather arbitrary.

Maximin – Rawls

The major expositor of this approach is John Rawls. In this conception of justice people make choices behind 'a veil of ignorance'. They do not know who they are going to be in the next time period. People are also risk averse. Rawls argues that under such conditions a just society would opt for the following two-part constitution.

(a) The same amount of basic liberty is available to all. No matter whose shoes you land yourself in you get the same amount of basic protection from criminals, say.

(b) Since each individual is assumed to be risk averse she would like to protect herself in case she lands in the shoes of the least well-off person. Thus, she would like social arrangements to be made in such a manner so as to maximize the welfare of the least well-off person.

Hence, this criterion of justice is called maximin justice or Rawlsian justice. Rawls orders states according to the principle of **lexical difference**. Just as a chain is as strong as its weakest link, a society is as well-off as its least well-off member. State x is better than state y only if the least well-off person in the former is better off than the least well-off person in the latter. State z is maximin optimal or Rawls optimal if the least well-off person in state z is at least well-off as any other state.

Several objections have been raised against the Rawlsian society. Some people have argued that if there is non-zero probability of my not being the least well-off person then I may not act so conservatively. Others have asked how the maximin criterion can be used across federal states. When states in a federation are such that there is considerable inequality between them, if the (national) maximin criterion calls for equalizing the welfare of the least well-off person(s) across states, then does this not conflict with the principle of federalism? Arrow has raised another criticism against the maximin criterion. Suppose we apply the maximin criterion across time, when do we not get a directive to arrest economic growth? Because if the utility of future generations rises then we would have been unfair to earlier generations. Calvo, however, argues that it is easy to get around this difficulty. Suppose the utility function of a typical person of generation 1 is $U_1(C_1, U_2)$; i.e., it depends upon his own consumption and the utility of his children. The utility of his children would, in turn, depend upon their own consumption and the utility of their generation. Thus, if the utility of future generations goes up so does the utility of the present generation. The maximin criterion is not anti-growth.

Atkinson's social welfare function

A social welfare function proposed by Anthony Atkinson in a celebrated paper (1970) has proved to be quite popular in applied work in public economics. For the sake of simplicity let there be two groups in society rich (r) and poor (p). Let the indirect utility function of the rich be V^r and that of the poor V^p. Atkinson's measure of social welfare is defined as:

$$W = \frac{1}{1 - \epsilon} \sum_{h=p}^{r} [(V^h)^{1-\epsilon}]. \tag{3.7}$$

ϵ is interpreted as 'an inequality-aversion' parameter. The larger is ϵ, the greater the weight that is placed on the welfare of the poor and the more inequality averse is society.

3.7   CONCLUDING REMARKS

This chapter has examined the problem of narrowing down the range of choices on the Pareto optimal frontier. We began by examining early approaches aimed at formulating 'social indifference curves'. We then examined the problem of aggregating individual preferences to reach social preferences. Several problems were encountered in this process and some of these, for example, Arrow's impossibility theorem, Gibbard's oligarchy theorem and Sen's impossibility of a Paretian liberal were proved. We then realized that the principal reason for these impossibility results was our working within the confines of traditional utility theory where inter-personal comparisons of utility are not permitted. Once this assumption was dropped we discovered 'possibility' theorems. This led directly to a discussion of the major social welfare functions for which these possibility results can be derived as well as those that have been popular in applied work in public economics.

ADDITIONAL READING

An excellent treatment of various types of social welfare functions can be found in Boadway and Bruce (1984). Sen (1979b) is an excellent survey. Atkinson (1970) and Atkinson and Stiglitz (1980) also provide lucid discussions.

Part II
The theory of public expenditure

Introduction to Part II

[handwritten annotations: "Public Expenditures"; "Looks at perceived mkt. failure and proposed solutions for state intervention"]

Part II deals with the theory of public expenditure. As shown in Table II.1 public expenditure has grown very significantly in major countries of the world.

Table II.1 Government expenditure as a percentage of GDP

Year	Sweden	Japan	Canada	USA	UK	Germany
1900	6.5		4.9	2.8	15.6	
1910	7.0		5.7	2.1	13.2	
1920	7.5		9.5	7.2	29.1	
1930	8.1	11.2	7.7	12.2	27.1	
1940	10.7	14.9	28.5	20.3	31.8	37.9
1950	16.8	16.0	22.0	24.4	39.2	28.6
1960	26.8	13.0	25.1	26.6	29.5	28.1
1970	35.9	13.9	28.5	31.3	33.5	34.0
1980	56.9	25.0	37.5	32.6	41.5	43.1
1990	59.1	26.2	44.0	34.6	38.1	42.6

Sources: For 1960–1990, *OECD Historical Statistics*, OECD Economic Outlook, Paris. Thelma Liesner, *One Hundred Years of Economic Statistics*, The Economist, 1989

In every country in the sample shown in Table II.1 government expenditure has grown steadily. If the goods produced by the public sector were to be treated on par with private goods then, since incomes have grown steadily during the period of the sample, one would have to conclude that the income elasticity of goods produced in the public sector is quite high. This factor gets emphasized still more because there is some evidence to suggest that the unit cost of supplying goods by the public sector has risen relative to goods produced in the private sector.

It is here that the analogy of goods produced in the public sector with those produced in the private sector breaks down. It is now realized that most of the expansion in the public sector has taken place in areas where government exercises coercive authority, albeit with the sanction of the political process behind it. For example, if we look at the 1995–6 budget of the UK we realize that over 71 per cent of total government expenditures were made by the central government. The main items of central government expenditure (accounting for more than two-thirds of the total) were social security, health and defense. Local governments spent most of their budgets on school education, personal social services, housing and the police.

Thus there appear to be two broad categories of government expenditure – redistributive and social services and public goods. The first category of expenditure has grown mainly in response to the rise of the welfare state in the postwar era. The second category, which is of concern to us in this part, has arisen because of the perceived failure of the market in providing certain essential goods such as police services, defense and the like.

Part II, then, discusses aspects of market failure and the proposed solutions that state intervention in the market may provide. In Chapter 4 we introduce the concept of an externality and discuss the reasons why the second optimality theorem of welfare economics may fail to hold in the presence of external effects. We then discuss proposed solutions to this problem, for example, the Coase solution, Pigovian taxation/subsidization and the design of liability laws. We demonstrate Arrow's important result that the Coase solution would fail to hold under conditions of uncertainty. We then examine an example of dealing with external effects – pricing of education when education has substantial external economies. Finally, we examine the question of common property resources and the important distinction between bilateral and multilateral external effects.

In Chapter 5 we examine an extreme form of externalities – pure public goods. We begin by spelling out the Samuelson conditions for Pareto optimality in the presence of pure public goods when these goods are (alternately) pure consumption goods and pure producer goods. We then amend the Samuelson conditions in case only distortionary taxation is available to finance the public good. The free rider problem is studied at this point. The Lindahl, Groves-Loeb, Groves–Ledyard and Groves–Vickrey–Clarke solutions are discussed. Hurwicz's result that it is not possible to design mechanisms for demand revelation of a public good which simultaneously satisfy Pareto optimality, incentive compatibility and a balanced budget is discussed. This leads to the conclusion that there will always be some degree of arbitrariness in the supply of a pure public good. There is a section on voting models of public goods as well as some aspects of democratic decision-making in regard to public goods.

In Chapter 6 we discuss some related topics. Various aspects of the theory of clubs are discussed. The Tiebout hypothesis as well as the problems associated with it are also examined. The marginal cost of public funds is considered again. We also study a simplified model of public goods supply with asymmetric information. Then we turn our attention to rent-seeking behavior on the part of bureaucrats and others. We study the original rent-seeking model due to Krueger (1974) as well as some more recent refinements of the theory.

4 External effects and the market mechanism

Key concepts: externalities; market failure; the Coase solution; Pigovian taxation and subsidization; conditional perfect price discrimination; conditional perfect internalization; common property resources; multilateral externalities

4.1 INTRODUCTION

In Part I we have examined the circumstances under which the market mechanism works efficiently. More specifically the second classical theorem of welfare economics, which was proved in Chapter 2, delineates these conditions. If such conditions did indeed obtain there would be no reason for government intervention in the working of the market mechanism.

We realize, of course, that the conditions of this theorem are very stringent. In this chapter we relax one of these conditions and examine the implications for public policy. It has been implicit in our analysis so far that the preference ordering of any consumer is defined over her own consumption set. Similarly it has been assumed that the production set of any producer is independent of the production sets of other producers and consumption sets of consumers. In real life these assumptions are often violated and we have interdependence between production and/or consumption sets. When this occurs, an **externality** is said to exist. Formally, then, an externality is a **commodity** which is produced during the production and/or consumption of other goods and which affects other producers/consumers. When a paper mill dumps toxic waste into a river, thus contaminating the fish downstream, it affects the production sets of fishermen living downstream. When your neighbor plays loud music late at night when you are trying to sleep, he affects your consumption set and welfare. When a firm trains workers in a new skill and other firms step in to hire the newly trained workers, the first firm has positively helped the production sets of the other firms.

A moment's introspection will tell us that externalities are much more than abundant in real life. Some are positive like the firm which trains the workers or the lighthouse on the seashore which guide ships into the harbor

Must an externality be a commodity?

at night, many are negative. In each case, however, a new commodity is produced: skills in the labor force, sludge in the river and so on.

A basic difficulty with these commodities, called externalities, is that they are hard to price because it is difficult to establish a market in such cases. Why is it problematic to establish a market for an externality? Three reasons can be advanced in general. Specific cases will involve specific reasons in addition to these.

1 **Information costs**. Suppose a honey producer keeps his bees next to an apple orchard. The bees take the nectar (the externality) from the apple flowers. The apple producer would find it impossible to ascertain how much nectar the bees have taken from the flowers. For an ordinary commodity, this condition is necessarily satisfied. There is no problem in finding out how many chocolates you ate yesterday.

2 **Excludability**. Even if information costs are not a stumbling block, excludability often is. How is the apple producer going to prevent the entry of bees into his orchard? How are the owners of the lighthouse to prevent ships that do not pay for being guided from using its services. In the case of ordinary goods, there is no problem. If I cannot pay the price of a Rolls-Royce then I cannot have a Rolls-Royce.

3 **Non-competitive behavior**. Even if excludability and information costs are not serious problems, non-competitive behavior almost always obtains in the case of externalities. In the market for apples and the market for honey, there is a large number of buyers and sellers and competitive or 'price-taking' behavior prevails. But no such statements can be made about the nectar from apple flowers. This commodity is defined only between two people – one of whom is the 'buyer' and the other the 'seller'. Hence, there is no guarantee that competitive behavior will prevail. Externalities are, undoubtedly, a fundamental problem for the market mechanism. In this chapter we examine various aspects of the problem of externalities. We begin with a discussion of the results of external effects and then proceed to solutions in the case of certainty as well as uncertainty. Some of these solutions involve public expenditure. Then we discuss an applied problem of devising optimal public expenditure policies in the presence of externalities. We also discuss common property resources as well as the problem of multilateral externalities.

4.2   EFFECTS OF EXTERNALITIES

Let us see, in an extremely simple set-up, the effects of externalities. Consider an exchange economy in which there are two consumers (1 and 2) consuming two goods x_1 and x_2. Each consumer causes an externality for the other while consuming either commodity. This is an exchange economy so that the total quantities of both goods are fixed (at x^1 and x^2 respectively). The notation is as follows. U^i is utility of individual i; x_{ik} is individual i's consumption of commodity k; and x_{ikj} is individual i's consumption of commodity k affecting individual j (i, j, k = 1,2). Now, $x_{11} + x_{21} = x^1$ and $x_{12} + x_{22} = x^2$. Also $x_{11} = x_{112}$; $x_{12} = x_{122}$; $x_{21} = x_{211}$; $x_{22} = x_{221}$ for the sake of convenience and without loss of generality. Now, let us conduct the Pareto optimizing exercise of maximizing individual 1's utility subject to individual 2's utility being at a particular level $\bar{U}^2$. Setting up the Lagrangean, we have:

$$\Lambda = U^1(x_{11}, x_{12}, x_{211}, x_{221}) + \lambda_1 [U^2(x_{21}, x_{22}, x_{112}, x_{122}) - \bar{U}^2]$$
$$+ \lambda_2[x_{11} - x_{112}] + \lambda_3[x_{12} - x_{122}] + \lambda_4[x_{21} - x_{211}] \qquad (4.1)$$
$$+ \lambda_5[x_{22} - x_{221}] + \lambda_6[x^1 - x_{11} - x_{21}] + \lambda_7[x^2 - x_{12} - x_{22}].$$

First-order conditions for an internal maximum are:

$$\partial\Lambda/\partial x_{11} = (\partial U^1/\partial x_{11}) + \lambda_2 - \lambda_6 = 0 \qquad (4.2a)$$

$$\partial\Lambda/\partial x_{12} = (\partial U^1/\partial x_{12}) + \lambda_3 - \lambda_7 = 0 \qquad (4.2b)$$

$$\partial\Lambda/\partial x_{211} = (\partial U^1/\partial x_{211}) - \lambda_4 = 0 \qquad (4.2c)$$

$$\partial\Lambda/\partial x_{221} = (\partial U^1/\partial x_{221} - \lambda_5 = 0 \qquad (4.2d)$$

$$\partial\Lambda/\partial x_{21} = \lambda_1(\partial U^2/\partial x_{21}) + \lambda_4 - \lambda_6 = 0 \qquad (4.2e)$$

$$\partial\Lambda/\partial x_{22} = \lambda_1(\partial U^2/\partial x_{22}) + \lambda_5 - \lambda_7 = 0 \qquad (4.2f)$$

$$\partial\Lambda/\partial x_{112} = \lambda_1(\partial U^2/\partial x_{112}) - \lambda_2 = 0 \qquad (4.2g)$$

$$\partial\Lambda/\partial x_{122} = \lambda_1(\partial U^2/\partial x_{122}) - \lambda_3 = 0 \qquad (4.2h)$$

$$\partial\Lambda/\partial\lambda_i = 0 \ (i = 1, \cdots, 7). \qquad (4.2i)$$

If any allocative mechanism (including the market mechanism) wants to reach Pareto optimum it must satisfy these conditions. But can the market mechanism satisfy these conditions? If there are no external effects, Lagrange multipliers λ_2 through λ_5 disappear and we get the usual condition that the *mrs* between two goods must be the same for both individuals. In a competitive set-up both consumers will look at the price ratio between the two goods and find it individually rational to equate their *mrs* to this price ratio. Thus, through this price ratio the *mrs* of the two individuals get equated. With externalities, the individuals may still behave in the same manner, but the difficulty is that the Pareto optimum conditions are different now. In fact the 'prices' λ_2 through λ_5, which figure in the Pareto optimum conditions, do not exist. So there is no point in talking about any automatic equivalence between the market mechanism and Pareto optimality. What we have here is a case of market failure.

How can we reach Pareto optimum in the presence of externalities? In Figure 4.1 we display some basic solutions. In this example person 1 consumes a commodity R which causes an external diseconomy (a bad) for individual 2. This commodity is available at a fixed marginal cost (MC_R) to individual 1. So, left to himself, this individual would consume

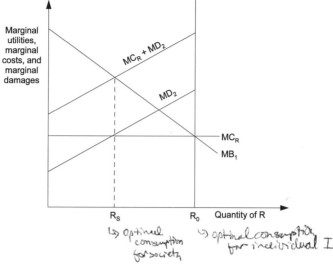

Figure 4.1

the amount R_0 (by equating his marginal benefit from the commodity to the marginal cost) and, in the process, cause an external diseconomy for individual 2 which is measured by going up to individual 2's marginal damage schedule (MD_2). We make the reasonable assumption that as individual 1's consumption of this commodity increases, the marginal damage to individual 2 rises along MD_2. True or social marginal cost of this commodity is the private marginal cost to individual 1 plus the consequent marginal damage to individual 2 ($MC_R + MD_2$). Optimal consumption of this commodity, therefore, is at R_S where individual 1 would equate his marginal benefit to the true social cost. How can we persuade this individual to move from R_0 to R_S? We will discuss some simple methods that have been used to address this problem.

(i) The Coase solution

Coase would rely upon the market mechanism. He argues that the essential reason why the market mechanism is failing here is because there are no incentives for individual 1 to move from R_0 to R_S. Suppose individual 1 is given **property rights** over the consumption of this commodity. It is now up to individual 2 to persuade 1 to reduce consumption of this commodity. At the margin, individual 2 would be willing to offer individual 1 an amount equal to MD_2 to reduce consumption by one unit. So long as MD_2 exceeds the net gain to individual 1 from consuming this commodity ($MB_1 - MC_R$) individual 1 would be willing to reduce consumption.

This process of offering inducement to reduce consumption will go on until $MD_2 = MB_1 - MC_R$ (i.e. where $MB_1 = MD_2 + MC_R$). At this point individual 2 will not be able to persuade individual 1 to reduce his consumption of this commodity any further. Thus, through a process of mutual bargaining and **without state intervention**, the two parties reach a solution which is Pareto optimal. Please note that this process involves transfer of resources from individual 2 to individual 1.

(ii) Pigovian taxation *- Requires state intervention   Lump Sum Tax*

Suppose individual 1 could be taxed **in a lump-sum manner** an amount equal to MD_2. Effectively, then, the private marginal cost for individual 1 becomes $MD_2 + MC_R$. He will equate his marginal benefit to this and, thus, arrive at a Pareto optimal situation. This situation requires state intervention. It also requires the tax on individual 1 to be of a lump-sum nature. If the tax was distortionary then it would impose its own dead-weight loss on individual 1 and a first-best solution would be precluded. Realize, once again, that there is a transfer of resources from individual 1 to the government.

(iii) Pigovian subsidization

A direct parallel to method (ii) is to subsidize (in a lump-sum manner) reduction of individual 1's consumption of the commodity to the extent of MD_2. This would raise the opportunity cost of consuming to $(MC_R + MD_2)$. Individual 1 would then find it optimal to reduce consumption to the socially optimal level. Once again, the distribution of resources has to be changed in order to reach the Pareto optimum position.

(iv) Liability laws

Individual 1 could be made liable to individual 2 for the damages that he inflicts upon him. This will raise the cost of consumption to him and ensure that the socially optimal amount of the commodity gets consumed.

An important aspect of the solutions listed above is that the distribution of resources is altered to reach the Pareto optimal allocation. Hence, the independence of the allocative mechanism from the desired Pareto optimal allocation is compromised. The distinction between the goal and the means to reach it, so important in classical welfare theory, is no longer possible to make. Another relevant point is that whereas other methods rely on government intervention, the Coase solution in particular is able to function without any state intervention apart from fixing property rights. This attribute has, of course, made the Coase solution the subject of considerable research.

Arrow (1977), for example, argues that the optimality of the Coase solution cannot be taken for granted when we have uncertainty. He considers an extreme form of externalities with non-rivalrous consumption (a pure public good, considered in Chapter 5) in an exchange economy. There are two goods in this economy: a public good (G) and a private good (x)

Arrow says w/ uncertainty Coase solution may not be optimal.

and two consumers 1 and 2. It is costless to transfer the public good into the private good and vice versa. In this case the conditions for Pareto-optimal allocation will turn out to be that the sum of the *mrs* for the two goods by the two individuals should turn out to be equal to the mrt (= 1).

$$\text{mrs}^1_{G,x_1} + \text{mrs}^2_{G,x_2} = 1 \tag{4.3}$$

where x_i is consumption of the private good by individual *i* and mrs^i is person *i*'s marginal rate of substitution. Total wealth in this economy is *w* so that:

$$x_1 + x_2 + G = w. \tag{4.4}$$

We would like to pursue the Coase method of finding a Pareto optimal solution for this economy. We will assume that both *x* and *G* are normal goods in the preferences of both individuals so that if there is no agreement about the production of the public good and each individual is forced to consume his initial endowment (w_i) as the private good then utility is lowered. In other words:

$$U^i(x_i, G) \geqslant U^i(w_i, 0). \tag{4.5}$$

The two individuals are free to choose any allocation they like (without state intervention), but if they fail to reach agreement then there is zero production of the public good and each individual consumes his initial endowment as the private good.

Suppose individual 1 makes an offer to 2 which 2 can either accept or reject. If we are operating in the world of certainty so that utility functions are known 1's optimal strategy would be to maximize his own utility subject to:

$$x_1 + x_2 + G = w \text{ and } U^2(x_2, G) \geqslant U^2(w_2, 0). \tag{4.6}$$

This is precisely a Pareto optimizing exercise and we would expect a Pareto optimum outcome. So the Coase solution is optimal in this case.

Now, let us bring uncertainty into the picture. For the sake of simplicity, let us suppose that uncertainty enters the picture through lack of knowledge about utility functions. In particular, individual 1 knows that individual 2 has utility function U^2_a with probability π_a and utility function U^2_f with probability π_b with $\pi_a + \pi_b = 1$. There are three feasible offers that individual 1 can now make:

Offer 1: Individual 1 offers $A^* = (x_1^*, x_2^*, G)$ so as to max $U^1(x_1, G)$ subject to $x_1 + x_2 + G = w$ and $U^2_a(x_2, G) \geqslant U^2_a(w_2, 0)$ and $U^2_b(x_2, G) \geqslant U^2_b(w_2, 0)$.

Offer 2: Individual 1 offers $A^a = (x_1^a, x_2^a.G)$ so as to max $U^1(x_1, G)$ subject to $x_1 + x_2 + G = w$ and $U^2_a(x_2, G) \geqslant U^2_a(w_2, 0)$.

Offer 3: Individual 1 offers $A^b = (x_1^b, x_2^b, G)$ so as to max $U^1(x_1, G)$ subject to $x_1 + x_2 + G = w$ and $U^2_b(x_2, G) \geqslant U^2_b(w_2, 0)$.

Offer 1 has all the chances of being accepted by individual 2. But it is suboptimal because individual 2's utility function is either U^2_a or U^2_b, not both.

Hence, there is an additional constraint here which will reduce welfare. Offer 2 will be rejected with probability π_b and Offer 3 with probability π_a. Hence, the Coase solution will no longer guarantee Pareto optimality.

4.3 A POLICY EXAMPLE: THE PRICING OF EDUCATION

Let us study the problems associated in dealing with externalities in the case of education. Suppose education, apart from imparting earning capability to students, also has external effects. An educated person might, for example, be considered a role model for others. The importance of this kind of external effect might be more for the disadvantaged groups of society but it is probably non-negative for almost all strata of society. Given this fact, what kind of price policy for education should be adopted? The analysis here is based on the seminal work of Ordover and Willig (1979) and others.

We start out by making some simplifying assumptions. Assume that we can carry out a partial equilibrium exercise, i.e., the externality producing activity we are considering has no implications for the rest of the economy. Similarly what is happening in the rest of the economy does not affect the education sector. We will further assume that (private) benefits and external effect can be measured in the same units (money). We will assume that the joint distribution of people over private benefits and external effects is known.

By getting educated a person derives private benefits B and generates external effects E. The social marginal cost of education, c, is constant. Society and, sometimes, the individuals themselves, are imperfectly informed about their benefits and external effects from education but the joint distribution $\phi(B,E)$ of people over B and E is common knowledge. Thus, high-school education may mean different things to different people. A poor student may seek a job immediately after graduation whereas her richer classmates may opt for more education. However, the poor girl also comes from a poor neighborhood where her success is a source of inspiration to her disadvantaged friends. The rich student lives in a neighborhood where almost everyone is highly educated so that the external effects generated by her education may be quite limited. We can think of the following types of pricing rules for education.

Pure price subsidy

Suppose there is a common fee for all students. Each prospective student will have a reservation price for education, i.e., if education costs more than the student's reservation price it will not be worthwhile for her to pursue studies.

The government recognizes this and also realizes that students are generating external effects that benefit society but which the individuals are in no position to realize as personal gain. It is in society's collective interest to encourage education, particularly of the less advantaged sections who are generating the most significant externalities. Suppose the government decides to do this by introducing a uniform subsidy for all students. What is the effect of this policy and what are its merits and demerits? To these questions we now turn.

The optimal uniform subsidy is determined by maximizing:

$$W = \int_p^\infty \int_0^\infty (B + E - c)\phi(B, E) \, dB \, dE \qquad (4.7)$$

where p is the price of education. ϕ (B,E) is a continuous distribution over B and E so that $(B + E - c)$ is the net social gain from this person getting educated. The private benefit will range from the price charged (p) to ∞ whereas the external effects from any particular student could range from 0 to ∞. The fixed marginal cost to society is c. Society would choose p to maximize the expression in equation (4.7).

Performing this maximization we have:

$$\partial W/\partial p = -\int_0^\infty (B + E - c)\phi(B, E)dE = 0$$

which implies:

$$p^* + \gamma(E/p^*) = c \qquad (4.8)$$

where p^* is the optimal price, $\gamma(E/p^*)$ is the average externality generated when the price is p^*. Remember that there is only one price for everyone. Thus students having a B level higher than p^* will get educated. The average externality generated from these students is $\gamma(E/p^*)$. The lefthand side of equation (4.8) is the marginal social gain from education whereas the righthand side represents the marginal cost. Optimum occurs, not surprisingly, when social marginal gain equals marginal cost. As a single price rule, equation (4.8) makes eminent sense.

But a single price rule is not necessarily the best possible rule available to the government. We see this in Figure 4.2.

In Figure 4.2 we have drawn the $B + E = c$ line which shows various combinations of B and E which give the same marginal cost c. We have also drawn the optimal price line p^* and a 45° ray along which $B = E$. Above the $B + E = c$ line we have $B + E > c$ and below it we must have $B + E < c$. The p^* line divides the population into two interesting sets. One is $K_1 K_2 K_5$ (the set of people for whom $B + E < c$ but since their $B > p^*$ they go to school) and the other is $K_2 K_3 K_4$ (for whom $B + E > c$ but since $B < p^*$ they do not go to school). Roughly speaking, the first set of people consists of 'rich' students with low external effects and the latter of 'poor' students with high external effects. A single price rule, therefore, errs in both direction. It excludes people with high social benefits and includes people with low social benefits. This naturally leads us to consider screening mechanisms that depend on self-selection.

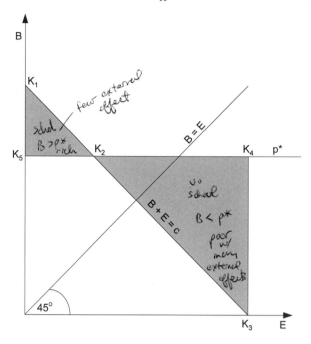

Figure 4.2

Screening mechanisms

Instead of a single price, suppose we can adopt a dual price system. Suppose that we can distinguish between two broad classes of students – those with annual parental income smaller than $40,000 and those with greater parental income. The former group is said to have characteristic α and has a joint distribution over B and E labelled ϕ^α (B,E) whereas the latter group has the distribution $\bar{\phi}^\alpha$. It is assumed that both these distributions are known. We can now define aggregate welfare as the sum of that arising from these two groups.

Students with characteristic α have to subject themselves to a test to determine whether they truly belong to this group. The test costs s. Students who do not belong to this group do not have an incentive to cheat because they have to pay the testing fees and, if they are caught, go back to paying the higher fees plus penalties. Social welfare can now be written as:

$$W = \int_p^\infty \int_0^\infty (B + E - c)\bar{\phi}^\alpha(B, E) \, dB \, dE + \int_{p_\alpha}^\infty \int_0^\infty (B + E - C - B)\phi^\alpha(B, E) \, dB \, dE. \quad (4.9)$$

Presumably, students with characteristic α pay a lower fee. Optimal prices for the two groups will satisfy:

(for the non-α group)

$$p^* + \gamma(E/p^*) = c \qquad \gamma = avg\ externalities \qquad (4.10)$$

(for the α group)

$$p_\alpha^* + \gamma^\alpha(E/p_\alpha^*) = c + s \qquad (4.11)$$

where p^* is the price charged to the non-α group whereas p_α^* is the price charged to the α group. γ and γ^α are, respectively, the average externality levels for the non-α and the α groups.

This set of prices clearly improves upon the earlier single price policy. The higher price for the non-α group excludes some students with high Bs and low Es whereas the lower price for the α group includes some students with high Es but low Bs.

This has the gov't value judg't held for the benefit of the ed.

It is, in principle, possible to classify the population into several different characteristics and have a real multiplicity of prices. But imagine the administrative difficulties! This policy retains its attractiveness only if the number of criteria as per which we classify the population is relatively small. We should, therefore, look at other methods if we wish to improve upon the performance of the pricing system. We discuss some of these now.

Conditional perfect price discrimination (cppd)

This is a policy which can usefully be appended to any price program. Suppose students know their Bs and Es but the government does not. Under this program students can get their Bs and Es tested for a small fee f (the cost of screening). Screening will be carried out only if $B + E > c + f$. If this criterion is met, the student gets back his fee and is offered a price just below his measured B so as to ensure that he will opt for education. Once again, there is no room for adverse selection. If a student cheats he can be detected. Not only will he not get the lower price but his application fee will also not be returned. Thus adverse selection is ruled out, by assumption – practically.

To who? Not the rich

This system of personalized prices is clearly a desirable improvement. In fact, $B + E \geq c + f$ is the first-best method of allocating fees among the students. Obviously, with a large population it will be hard to institute a program of cppd as the only pricing mechanism. It is more likely that cppd will be added on to an existing program of price subsidy.

Conditional perfect internalization (cpi)

This policy is particularly useful in cases where the Es are very high, but the measured Bs are low. An example might help. Let us compare two hypothetical adult education groups. One is a bunch of highly motivated social workers with low salaries. The other is sponsored by a large business house which gets tax write-offs for the amount it spends on this group. Both groups have high Es but the second group has high Bs as well. The problem for the policy-maker is to determine how to supply education material to the two groups. Here we may want to screen people only by their Es.

The policy-maker announces an *E* verification test for people with *E*s equal to some prespecified value. The cost of verifying *E*, say *e*, is less than the *f*, cost of verifying *B* as well as *E*. Those with a particular value of *E* say $\hat{E}$ are offered a special price $p(\hat{E})$. Social welfare from this group is:

$$W(\hat{E}) = \int_{p(\hat{E})}^{\infty} (B + \hat{E} - c - e)\phi(B, E)dB. \qquad (4.12)$$

Maximization with respect to p ( ) yields the following optimal pricing rule:

$$p^*(\hat{E}) = \begin{cases} (c + e) - \hat{E} & \text{if } \hat{E} < c + e \\ 0 & \text{if } \hat{E} \geqslant c + e \end{cases}$$

People with $E = \hat{E}$ will participate in the program if their *B* is larger than $p^*(\hat{E})$. Since it is assumed that the *E* of an individual can be measured accurately, adverse selection is ruled out, by assumption.

This process yields a perfect allocation relative to the information cost *e*. If $\hat{E} \geqslant c + e$ then the agents are all desirable and it is only appropriate that they face a zero price. For those with $B \geqslant c + e - \hat{E}$ the imposition of $p^*(.)$ implies that $B + E \geqslant c + e$ and this is only appropriate.

One can visualize the consequences of *cpi* with the help of Figure 4.3. In this diagram we are screening on the externality level $\hat{E}$. The line $B + E = c + f$ is drawn parallel to and above the line $B + E = c + e$, since screening costs under *cppd* are larger than under *cpi*. *p* is the optimal price under the pure price subsidy scheme (drawn for purposes of reference).

People having *E* levels equal to $\hat{E}$ have *B* levels ranging from 0 to *N*. People who lie on the segment MZ_1 will switch from *cppd* to *cpi* (since they will now have to pay a lower price) and will save society (f-e) in screening costs (per person). People who lie on the segment Z_1Z_2 were excluded from the *cppd* (because their $B + E < c + f$) but can now participate in the program and thus generate external effects. People on the segment $Z_2\hat{E}$ are excluded even from *cpi*. These are the plus points of *cpi*. However, with *cpi* people on the segment MN who could have paid a higher price end up paying a lower price. Remember that in *cpi* everybody with the same $\hat{E}$ gets a lower price and the Bs are not particularly relevant. The net usefulness of *cpi* then depends on which effects are stronger, i.e., on the distribution of agents along $\hat{E}N$. Moreover, for *cpi* to be useful *E* levels have to be quite high. It would be wasteful to try *cpi* at a low *E* level.

4.4 COMMON PROPERTY RESOURCES

We now study another example of external effects. This has been referred to in the literature as **common property resources** or the **tragedy of the commons**.

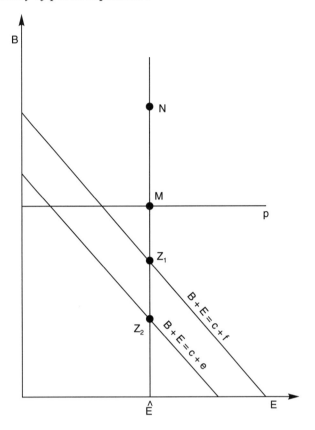

Figure 4.3

Suppose that production in an industry takes place as per a standard neoclassical production function:

$$x = x(L, F) \tag{4.13}$$

where x is the output of this industry, L is the labor employed and F is the quantity of some fixed factor of production. This latter factor of production is available free of cost. The classic example is grazing land for cattle.

Suppose, initially, that this land is owned by one producer who realizes the necessity of upkeep of the land. The only input that this producer actually has to pay for is labor. Labor is available in a competitive labor market at a wage of w. This producer is a perfect competitor in the market for his product and, therefore, takes the product price (p) as given. The marginal cost of the product is, therefore:

$$MC = wdL/dx = w/MP_L \tag{4.14}$$

where MP_L is the marginal product of labor. In equilibrium, therefore:

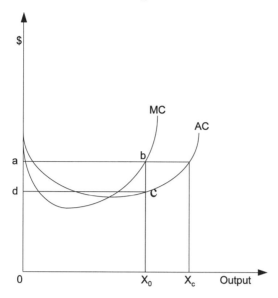

Figure 4.4

$$p = MC. \tag{4.15}$$

This equilibrium is depicted in Figure 4.4. Profits labelled *abcd* are not actual profits because they are used for the upkeep of the unpriced factor of production. Optimal production is at X_0.

Suppose, now, that this resource is not owned by a single producer but is freely available to all. Producers will now no longer recognize the necessity of the upkeep of the land. The area *abcd* in Figure 4.4 will be recognized not as an amount necessary for the upkeep of the land but as 'profits'. The 'no-profit' competitive equilibrium occurs at X_c where no provision will be made for the upkeep of the land and the land will decay in quality. Hence, the tragedy of the commons.

The solution to the tragedy of the commons lies in either entrusting this land to one producer or imposing a tax on competitive producers of the amount *abcd* which will force them to produce at X_0 and the proceeds of the tax could go towards the maintenance of the property. For practical reasons, the former line of action is likely to be more attractive.

4.5 MULTILATERAL EXTERNALITIES

In many cases externalities are generated and affect several persons at the same time. Examples are industrial pollution, smog caused by traffic, noise pollution by airplanes near an airport and so on.

In the case of such multilateral externalities a distinction can be made between **depletable** (or **private** or **rivalrous**) multilateral externalities and **non-depletable** (or **public** or **non-rivalrous**) multilateral externalities. For example, if someone dumps litter on someone else's property then he has that much less litter to dump on some other person's property. This is an example of a depletable externality. The amount of air pollution experienced by a resident of Los Angeles is not reduced by the fact that so many other residents of that city are also experiencing this pollution. This is an example of a non-depletable externality.

We shall assume that agents who create multilateral externalities are different from those who suffer from it (although this assumption is not essential).[1] It is possible to show that market solutions may work reasonably well for depletable multilateral externalities but will not work for non-depletable externalities. We proceed to do so now.

There are n goods produced by N producers indexed by j; there are M consumers indexed by i. Let the private price vector of these n goods be p. Let the level of externalities generated by the jth producer be e_j and let us write the profit of the jth producer as a function of e_j as $\pi_j(e_j)$. Let the externality experienced by the ith consumer[2] be h_i and her utility as a function of the amount of externality she experiences be $\phi_i(h_i)$. We will assume that $\phi_i' < 0$ and that $\pi_j'' < 0$ and $\phi_i'' < 0$. (A prime ($'$) denotes a partial derivative.)

Depletable externalities

From our earlier discussion we know that the market mechanism will lead to a non-Pareto optimal allocation. We can write the Pareto optimizing exercise for this problem as one of maximizing total utility and total profits as a function of the amount of externalities generated. Thus we write:

$$\operatorname*{Max}_{\substack{(e_1,\ldots,e_N)\,\geqslant\,0 \\ (h_1,\ldots,h_M)\,\geqslant\,0}} \quad \sum_{i=1}^{M} \phi_i(h_i) + \sum_{j=1}^{N} \pi_j(e_j) \tag{4.16}$$

subject to:

$$\sum_{i=1}^{M} h_i = \sum_{j=1}^{N} e_j. \tag{4.17}$$

Equation (4.17) expresses the fact that the externality being considered is depletable. The total amount of externality generated by firms must equal the total amount of externality experienced by consumers. If we let λ be the Lagrange multiplier on this constraint the first-order conditions can be written as:

$$\phi_i'(h_i^*) \leqslant \lambda \text{ with equality if } h_i^* > 0 \quad (i = 1,\ldots,M) \tag{4.18a}$$
$$-\pi_j'(e_j^*) \geqslant \lambda \text{ with equality if } e_j^* > 0 \quad (j = 1,\ldots,N) \tag{4.18b}$$

where a star (*) refers to an optimum value. Equation (4.18a) and (4.18b) characterize the optimum for this economy. If h_i^* and e_j^* are both positive then these two equations say that the marginal 'gain' to the consumer (ϕ_i') should be equal to the marginal 'loss' to the producer ($-\pi_j'$). From what we know of the Coase solution we can say that if property rights were well defined and there were a large number of producers as well as consumers,[3] then the market would lead us to the optimal solution depicted by equation (4.18).

Non-depletable externalities

Suppose now that externalities are not depletable. To make things concrete assume that each consumer experiences the total amount of externalities ($\sum_j e_j$) generated by the producers. The Pareto optimum exercise can now be written as:

$$\max_{(e_1,\ldots,e_N)} \sum_{i=1}^{M} \phi_i \left(\sum_{j=1}^{N}\right) e_j + \sum_{j=1}^{N} \pi_j(e_j). \tag{4.19}$$

The first-order conditions for Pareto optimality can now be written as:

$$\sum_{i=1}^{M} \phi_i' \left(\sum_{j=1}^{N}\right) e_j \leq -\pi_j'(e_j) \text{ for all } j \text{ and with equality if } e_j^* > 0. \tag{4.20}$$

This is exactly parallel to the Pareto optimum conditions for a public good derived and discussed in detail in Chapters 5 and 6.[4] Apart from the relevance of the optimality conditions derived in these two chapters another factor that will become relevant[5] is that under private production too much of the private bad will be produced.[6]

Hence, with multilateral externalities of the non-depletable kind we move inexorably to a study of non-rivalrous behaviour which is the hallmark of public goods.[7] In such cases, it would become important for the government to intervene in the operation of the market mechanism. If there was complete information[8] then the government could design mechanisms that would satisfy equation (4.20). In any event, even in the absence of complete information, the government is likely to do a better job of regulating non-depletable multilateral externalities than the private mechanism.

4.6 CONCLUSIONS

In this chapter we have studied various aspects of the theory of external effects. We have tried to understand the cases in which the market fails to allocate resources efficiently and what can be done to correct this. We have also tried to highlight situations where the market may not work at all. In such cases the government might be able to do a better job provided the costs of government intervention do not outweigh the benefits.

Another problem with externalities[9] is that sometimes the presence of external effects leads to non-convexities. Suppose a firm's production function (without a beneficial external effect) displays constant returns to scale. With the beneficial external effect, increasing returns might set in and the assumption of convex production sets might be belied. This has serious implications for the very existence of a competitive equilibrium as noted by Arrow and Hahn (1971). One way of getting around this (in the context of public sector pricing) is discussed in Chapter 17.

In the next chapter we discuss an extreme case of externalities – public goods. Consumption of such goods is non-competitive or less competitive than that of private goods.

NOTES

1 Throughout we will concentrate on negative (harmful) externalities.
2 We will assume that each consumer has a quasi-linear utility function with respect to a numeraire ordinary good.
3 So that price taking is guaranteed.
4 The only difference here is that we have a public 'bad' as opposed to the public good as discussed in Chapters 5 and 6.
5 Also discussed in Chapter 5.
6 As discussed in Chapter 5 with private production too little of a public good is produced.
7 Or public bads.
8 A tall assumption indeed.
9 One which we have not broached in this chapter.

ADDITIONAL READING

Boadway and Bruce (1984) and Boadway and Wildasin (1984) provide excellent treatment of external effects. More advanced treatment can be found in Green (1973). See also Buchanan (1968), Mishan (1971) and Head (1974).

5 The theory of pure public goods

Key concepts: pure public goods; Samuelson conditions for optimality; intermediate public goods; distortionary taxation and public goods; the free-rider problem; Lindahl–Wicksell, Groves–Loeb, Groves–Ledyard and Groves–Clarke–Vickrey mechanisms; private provision of public goods; median voting theorem and single-peaked preferences; logrolling.

5.1 INTRODUCTION

Public goods are an extreme form of externalities. Their consumption is non-competitive. The entire amount of your consumption of a pure public good enters my utility function. If the local store has six loaves of bread and I buy two of them, then there are only four left for you. Your consumption and mine are competitive. But, if the Air Force adds another squadron of fighter planes, then that means additional protection for both you as well as me. Our consumptions are non-competitive. Defense is a public good, whereas bread is a private good.

Public goods can be of various types: pure public goods like defense services, impure or crowdable public goods such as a neighborhood park, local public goods such as the sewerage system of a town and so on. Some problems associated with public goods are common to all of them whereas others are peculiar to particular types of public goods. We shall discuss some of these problems in this chapter. We begin, however, with a reworking of the conditions for Pareto optimality in an economy with pure public goods. We consider two cases: when the public good is an item of final consumption and when it is an intermediate good. This analysis assumes that public goods are provided by imposing lump-sum taxes. We later relax this assumption to derive the Pareto optimal supply of a public good when the public good is financed with distortionary taxation. Since the consumption of public goods is non-conflicting, it follows that people will have an incentive to understate their true preferences for the public good. This is the so-called 'free-rider' problem. This problem is studied here and efforts to get around this difficulty are examined. We also (briefly) explore voting models of public goods as well as the theory of private provision of public goods. The analysis in this chapter follows the work of Boadway and Wildasin (1984) and Oakland (1987).

5.2   PARETO OPTIMALITY WITH PURE PUBLIC GOODS

Suppose we have two goods in an economy – a private good x and a pure public good G. Suppose, further, that both are consumption goods and produced as per a standard transformation function (production possibility curve) $F(x, G) = 0$. There are two consumers in this economy – 1 and 2. What are the conditions for Pareto optimality in this economy? Let us analyze this problem diagrammatically in a manner portrayed by Samuelson (1954, 1956). We depict this in Figure 5.1. In the upper panel of this figure we draw the production possibility curve PP′. To conduct a Pareto optimum exercise we keep the utility of individual 2 fixed at $\bar{U}^2$ (depicted as an indifference curve in the upper panel of Figure 5.1. Individual 1 has available to him the excess of production over what is given to individual 2. Remember now that both consumers consume the full amount of the public

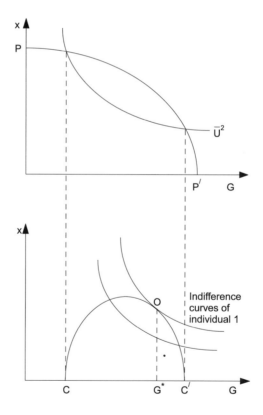

Figure 5.1

good. Hence we obtain the consumption possibilities available to individual 1 by vertically subtracting consumption levels of commodity x for individual 2 along $\bar{U}^2$ from the production possibility frontier. This is the consumption possibility set for individual 1 and is depicted as COC' in the lower panel of Figure 5.1.

Also drawn in the lower panel of Figure 5.1 are the indifference curves of individual 1. To conduct a Pareto optimum exercise we maximize individual 1's utility subject to this consumption possibility set. Optimum occurs at point O where an indifference curve is tangent to the consumption possibility frontier.

Now, at O, the slope of the consumption possibility frontier is equated with the slope of the indifference curve. Since the consumption possibility set is obtained by vertically subtracting the indifference curve $\bar{U}^2$ from the production possibility frontier, its slope is equal to the slope of the production possibility frontier less the slope of individual 2's indifference curve: $(\mathrm{mrt}_{x,G} - \mathrm{mrs}^2_{x,G})$. Thus, in equilibrium, we have:

$$\mathrm{mrt}_{x,G} - \mathrm{mrs}^2_{x,G} = \mathrm{mrs}^1_{x,G} \text{ or } \mathrm{mrs}^1_{x,G} + \mathrm{mrs}^2_{x,G} = \mathrm{mrt}_{x,G}. \tag{5.1}$$

In other words, the sum of the *mrs* should equal the *mrt*. This condition cannot be satisfied in the case of the market economy because each consumer would equate his own *mrs* to the *mrt*.

Mathematically, this derivation proceeds as follows. The two utility functions are written as: $U^1(x_1, G)$ and $U^2(x_2, G)$. The production possibility frontier is written as: $F(x_1 + x_2, G) = 0$. To conduct a Pareto optimum exercise we wish to maximize individual 1's utility while keeping individual 2's utility at a fixed level $\bar{U}^2$. Forming the Lagrangean, we have:

$$\Lambda = U^1(x_1, G) + \lambda_1[U^2(x_2, G) - \bar{U}^2] + \lambda_2[F(x_1 + x_2, G)]. \tag{5.2}$$

First-order conditions are:

$$\partial\Lambda/\partial x_1 = \partial U^1/\partial x_1 + \lambda_2 F_1 = 0 \tag{5.3a}$$

$$\partial\Lambda/\partial x_2 = \lambda_1\partial U^2/\partial x_2 + \lambda_2 F_1 = 0 \tag{5.3b}$$

$$\partial\Lambda/\partial G = \partial U^1/\partial G + \lambda_1\partial U^2/\partial G + \lambda_2 F_2 = 0 \tag{5.3c}$$

$$\partial\Lambda/\partial\lambda_1 = \partial\Lambda/\partial\lambda_2 = 0. \tag{5.3d}$$

From equation (5.3c) we get: $\partial U^1/\partial G + \lambda_1\partial U^2/\partial G = -\lambda_2 F_2$ so that:

$$[\partial U^1/\partial G + \lambda_1\partial U^2/\partial G]/F_2 = -\lambda_2.$$

From (5.3a) and (5.3b) we get:

$$[\partial U^1/\partial x_1]/F_1 = [\lambda_1\partial U^2/\partial x_2]/F_1 = [\partial U^1/\partial G + \lambda_1\partial U^2/\partial G]/F_2.$$

Cross-multiplying and rearranging, we have:

$$F_2/F_1 = [\partial U^1/\partial G]/[\partial U^1/\partial x_1] + [\partial U^2/\partial G]/[\partial U^2/\partial x_2]. \tag{5.4}$$

In other words, *mrt* = sum of *mrs*.

Pure public goods as intermediate goods

It is easy to derive the conditions for Pareto optimum supply of a public good when it is an intermediate good. We work with the example discussed by Oakland (1987). Consider an economy of N individuals, and R firms. Each firm produces the same private good, x, using labor input L, and an intermediate public good G. This public good has the property that its use by one firm does not reduce its availability to other firms. Thus the production function of the jth firm can be written as:

$$x_j = x_j(L_j, G) \qquad (5.5)$$
$$j = 1, \ldots, R$$

The production function for the public good can be written as:

$$G = G(L_G) \qquad (5.6)$$

where L_G is the amount of labor used in the production of the public good. We will assume that $G' > 0$ and $G'' < 0$. In addition, the sum of the labor demands for the production of x and G must add up to labor supply.

$$\sum_j L_j + L_G = \sum_i L_i \qquad (5.7)$$

where L_j is the labor demand of the jth firm and L_i is the labor supply of the ith individual. The utility functions of the individuals are written as functions of the private good consumed and the amount of labor supplied: $U^i(x_i, L_i)$ $(i = 1, \ldots, N)$.

To find the Pareto optimum condition we form the Lagrangean:

$$\Lambda = U^1(x_1, L_1) + \sum_{i=2}^{N} \lambda_i(U^i(x_i, L_i) - \bar{U}^i) + \mu[\sum_{j=1}^{R} L_j + L_G - \sum_{i=1}^{N} L_i]$$

$$+ \psi[\sum_{j=1}^{R} x_j - \sum_{i=1}^{N} x_i] + \sum_{j=1}^{R} \beta_j(x_j - x_j(L_j, G(L_G))). \qquad (5.8)$$

The first-order conditions are as follows:

$$\partial\Lambda/\partial x_1 = \partial U^1/\partial x_1 - \psi = 0 \qquad (5.9a)$$

$$\partial\Lambda/\partial L_1 = \partial U^1/\partial L_1 - \mu = 0 \qquad (5.9b)$$

$$\partial\Lambda/\partial x_i = \lambda_i\partial U^i/\partial x_i - \psi = 0 \ (i = 2, \ldots, N) \qquad (5.9c)$$

$$\partial\Lambda/\partial L_i = \lambda_i\partial U^i/\partial L_i - \mu = 0 \ (i = 2, \ldots, N) \qquad (5.9d)$$

$$\partial\Lambda/\partial L_j = -\beta_j\partial x_j/\partial L_j + \mu = 0 \ (j = 1, \ldots, R) \qquad (5.9e)$$

$$\partial\Lambda/\partial x_j = \beta_j + \psi = 0 \qquad (j = 1, \ldots, R) \qquad (5.9f)$$

$$\partial\Lambda/\partial L_G = -\sum_{j=1}^{R} \beta_j(\partial x_j/\partial_G)(\partial G/\partial L_G) + \mu = 0. \qquad (5.9g)$$

We can rearrange the above first-order conditions in the following more convenient form:

(i) $\quad -(\partial U^i/\partial L_i)/(\partial U^i/\partial x_j) = -(\partial U^k/\partial L_k)/(\partial U^k/\partial x_j) = \partial x_j/\partial L_s$ (5.10)
$$(i,\, k = 1,\ldots,N,$$
$$j, s = 1,\ldots,R)$$

(ii) $\quad \displaystyle\sum_{j=1}^{R} \partial x_j/\partial G = (\partial x_j/\partial L_j)/(\partial G/\partial L_G) \quad (j = 1,\ldots,R).$ (5.11)

Equations (5.10) state that the marginal valuation of work must be the same for all individuals and also be equal to the marginal productivity of labor in the production of private goods. The second condition is the Samuelson condition in case the public good is an intermediate good. It states that the aggregate marginal product of the public good input should be equal to the amount of private good forgone by producing the marginal unit of the public good. Thus, in place of adding the *mrs* of various consumers we add the marginal valuations of different firms using the public good input. Since the use of the public good by firms is non-competitive, it also follows that price exclusion for the public good input may be undesirable and even infeasible. Finance of the public good input must take place from some other revenue sources.

5.3 PUBLIC GOODS WITH DISTORTIONARY TAXATION

In the analysis above, it has been implicitly assumed that the financing of the public good creates no distortions of its own, in other words, the public good is financed by a lump-sum tax. In the real world, this is rarely the case. Hence, it is more realistic to assume that the public good is financed by a distortionary taxation. Clearly, then, the Samuelson rule will imply a greater than optimal production of the public good and a new rule for the supply of the public good must be derived. We proceed to do this now.

We take the simple case where only labor is necessary for the production of the private as well as the public good. Labor is paid its marginal product (measured in terms of the private good), Ω. If there are N workers, the production possibilities of this economy are adequately defined by:

$$N\Omega L = pG + Nx \tag{5.12}$$

where L represents labor supply by the representative worker, and p is the cost of the public good in terms of the private good whose price has been normalized to unity.

Suppose now that the public good is financed by a tax of rate t on private goods. Then we must have as the government's budget equation:

$$txN = pG \tag{5.13}$$

if the private good is sold at its marginal cost.

The representative individual will behave so as to maximize:

$$U = U(x, L, G) \tag{5.14}$$
$$+ - +$$

where a sign below an argument denotes the sign of the corresponding partial derivative. The budget constraint for this consumer is:

$$x = [\Omega/(1+t)]L = \omega L. \tag{5.15}$$

The amount of public good is taken as given by the individual. Setting up the Lagrangean for the individual we have:

$$\Lambda = U(x, L, G) + \lambda[\omega L - x] \tag{5.16}$$

so that the first-order conditions imply:

$$\partial U/\partial x = \lambda \tag{5.17a}$$

$$\partial U/\partial L = -\lambda\omega. \tag{5.17b}$$

This would yield a labor supply function of the form:

$$L = L(\omega, G). \tag{5.18}$$

To arrive at the social optimum for this economy we should maximize $NU(\omega L, L, G)$ subject to:

$$(\Omega - \omega)NL = pG \tag{5.19}$$

which yields as first-order conditions:

$$N[(\partial U/\partial G)/(\partial U/\partial x)] = (N\mu/\lambda)[p - Nt\omega(\partial L/\partial x)] \tag{5.20}$$

$$\text{and} \quad \mu/\lambda = 1/(1 - t\epsilon) \tag{5.21}$$

where $\epsilon = (\partial L/\partial\omega)(\omega/L)$ is the elasticity of the supply of labor with respect to the real wage and μ is the Lagrange multiplier associated with the constraint (5.19). The Samuelson rule, $N[(\partial U/\partial G)/(\partial U/\partial x)] = p$ holds only if labor supply is invariant with respect to tax rates, i.e., $\epsilon = 0$. Thus, if labor supply rises with the real wage then satisfying the Samuelson condition would lead to an oversupply of the public good.

5.4   THE FREE-RIDER PROBLEM

One very significant problem with public goods and externalities in general and pure public goods, in particular, is that of **incentive compatibility**. It is best to study this problem in the context of pure public goods where it is most vivid. When consumption is not competitive, it follows, in particular, that one cannot use prices to prevent consumers from consuming the public good. Whether you pay your taxes or not, the Air Force will protect you from foreign aggression. From this, it is a short step to suggest that, as atomistic agents, individual consumers would have a tendency to understate their demand for the public good in order to avoid paying for it. Hence, there will be a shortage of funds to pay for the public good and there will be drastic underproduction. How do we get over this difficulty? It turns out that overcoming it is not an easy problem at all. This problem has also, sometimes, been called the **free-rider** problem. So far as the public good is concerned, every consumer wants to have a free ride.

Revealing true demand for public goods is a problem, hence financing the public good is a problem. Ideally, we would like to devise a non-cooperative game such that the Nash solution is one where (a) the supply of the public good is Pareto optimal; (b) everyone finds it in his self-interest to tell the truth; given that we do not want allocative repercussions on the rest of the economy (c) the public goods budget is balanced.

We will discuss some important attempts to solve the free-rider problem. Unfortunately none of them is truly satisfactory. Let us discuss these attempts seriatim.

The Lindahl–Wicksell mechanism

The Lindahl–Wicksell mechanism may, at only marginal risk of oversimplification, be called the market's solution to the problem of public goods. We will study this and some other mechanisms within a very simple context since our aim is to focus on the incentive structure rather than complication for the sake of complication.

We have an N person exchange economy in which there is one commodity which can be used either as a private good or (costlessly transformed) into a public good. Hence, the marginal rate of transformation between the private and the public good is 1 and the conditions for Pareto optimum supply of the public good is that the sum of the *mrs* between the private and the public good be equal to 1. We, once again, assume that the individual's utility function is separable in the public good (G) and the private good (x). and takes the form:

$$U^i(G, x_i) = V_i(G) + x_i \text{ for individual } i.$$

Each individual $V_i(.)$ function is assumed to be concave so that we can graphically depict it as in Figure 5.2.

If the individual consumers were to act on their own, then the free-rider problem will ensure that the public good does not get produced. Now, let us suppose that each individual has to pay a tax T_i to pay for the public good so that the ith individual's budget constraint is:

$$x_i + T_i = w_i \qquad i = 1, \ldots, N \tag{5.22}$$

where w_i is the initial endowment of this individual.

Along with Lindahl and Wicksell we assume that the tax is linear so that:

$$T_i = t_i G \qquad i = 1, \ldots, N \tag{5.23}$$

and, naturally:

$$\sum_{i=1}^{N} t_i = 1. \tag{5.24}$$

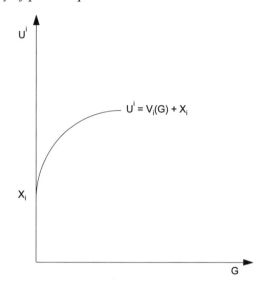

$$U^i = V_i(G) + X_i$$

Figure 5.2

Let us look at this individual's maximization problem under these condi-tions. Individual i maximizes $V_i(G) + x_i$ subject to $x_i + T_i = w_i$. In other words, she wants to maximize $V_i(G) + w_i - T_i$ (since $x_i = w_i - T_i$). The first-order condition for a maximum is that: $(dV_i(G)/dG) - (dT_i/dG) = 0$, or that the marginal utility from the public good equals the marginal (and average) tax rate. Diagrammatically, in Figure 5.3 the consumer's optimum occurs when the slope of the $V_i(.)$ schedule equals t_i or, in other words, when the gap between the V_i and T_i schedules is the largest.

In Figure 5.3 the line OA with slope t_i measures tax liability. To find i's tax liability, for any G, we refer to the schedule OA. If the individual had a choice she would demand G^* amount of the public good. The line Z_1Z_1 is parallel to OA.

Lindahl and Wicksell are after such a tax structure, but with the follow-ing additional specifications:

(a) The supply of the public goods must be Pareto optimal, i.e,. $\Sigma_{i=1}^{N} V_i' = 1$ where V_i' is the first derivative of the V_i schedule.
(b) The tax liability of any person should be linked, in the interest of fairness, to the amount of benefits she receives from the public good.

Now, by the condition for utility maximization by the individual con-sumer $V_i' = T_i' = t_i$ so $\Sigma_i V_i' = \Sigma_i t_i = 1$ so that the Lindahl–Wicksell mechan-ism automatically satisfies stipulation (a) above.

In satisfying stipulation (b) we have the following problem. I, with a strong preference for the public good, might want G^* units of the public good, whereas you with a weaker preference for the public good might want

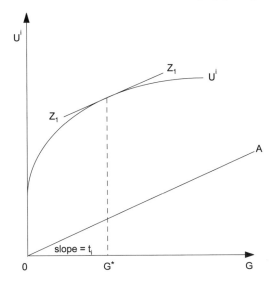

Figure 5.3

(at the same tax rate) a smaller amount of the public good G^{**}. But, by the very nature of a public good, you and I must consume all of the public good.

Lindahl and Wicksell propose an iterative algorithm to solve this problem and link this method with stipulation (b). The tax shares, t_i, are interpreted as 'prices'. Let us begin, without any loss of generality, with $t_i = 1/N$ for all i. Some people may want less of the public good and some may want more. Then the iterative mechanism works as follows. Increase the tax share for those who want more of the public good and reduce the tax shares of those who want less of the public good. The demand of the former group should fall and the latter group increase. This process can be repeated until there is convergence. Lindahl and Wicksell assume that such convergence will be forthcoming.

Formally, then, a **Lindahl equilibrium**, is a set of personalized tax rates $t_1, \ldots, t_N$ and an amount $(\hat{G})$ of the public good such that

(i) each individual wants the same amount $(\hat{G})$ of the public good.
(ii) $\hat{G}$ is a Pareto optimal supply of the public good.

However, although the Lindahl–Wicksell logic is powerful and simple there is a couple of very serious flaws with it.

(i) The Lindahl–Wicksell mechanism is not solving the free-rider problem – it is merely wishing it away. It is supposing that an individual faced with a tax rate t_i will honestly reveal her 'true' preference for the public good. But the crux of the free-rider problem is that the the individual finds it strategically profitable to misrepresent preferences for the public good.

(ii) There is nothing to guarantee that the iterative process suggested by Lindahl and Wicksell will converge. If this algorithm does not converge then the Lindahl–Wicksell mechanism collapses.

The Groves–Loeb mechanism

Groves and Loeb have, in a number of articles, spoken of a very different method of dealing with the free-rider problem. Below we discuss the main features of their arrangement. There are points of detail which we purposely avoid. We study the Groves–Loeb mechanism within the same structure as that of Lindahl–Wicksell. However, the important difference is that there is a serious attempt to confront the free-rider problem.

In the Groves–Loeb mechanism a public goods board is entrusted with the task of supplying the public good. This board asks the people for their V_i schedules. At this stage there is no presumption that this V_i schedule is true. The public goods board also lets it be known that person i's tax liability will be decided by the rule:

$$T_i = \hat{G} - \sum_{j \neq i} V_j(\hat{G}) \qquad (5.25)$$

where $\hat{G}$ is the amount of the public good supplied. Thus, my tax liability is the amount of the public good supplied less the sum of utilities (from the public good) of everyone except me.

Let us for a moment suppose that everyone is telling the truth about their preferences. We will see that under the Groves–Loeb mechanism no one will have an incentive to lie.

On obtaining information about the $V_i(.)$ schedules the public goods board decides on the optimal supply of the public good by solving equation (5.26) for $\hat{G}$:

$$\sum_{i=1}^{N} V_i'(\hat{G}) = 1. \qquad (5.26)$$

This is one equation in one variable and can easily be solved. We are also assured that if people tell the truth about their $V_i(.)$ schedules, then the public goods board is assuring a Pareto optimal supply of the public good.

How does individual i decide which V_i schedule to report? This, of course, is the product of a rational utility maximizing exercise. Consumer i maximizes $U^i = V_i(\hat{G}) + x_i$ subject to $x_i + T_i = w_i$ which is tantamount to maximizing $V_i(\hat{G}) + w_i - T_i$ or, effectively, $V_i(\hat{G}) - T_i$ since w_i is a constant and will vanish upon differentiation. Substituting for T_i from equation (5.25) we have that the individual consumer is trying to maximize $V_i(\hat{G}) - [\hat{G} - \sum_{j \neq i} V_j(\hat{G})]$. In other words, if everyone is telling the truth then this individual is trying to maximize the net surplus from the public good: $[\sum_{i=1}^{N} V_i(\hat{G}) - \hat{G}]$.

The public goods board could attempt to maximize this sum as well and yet attain Pareto optimality. If the public goods board maximizes $[\sum_i V_i(\hat{G}) - \hat{G}]$ with respect to $\hat{G}$ the first order condition will yield precisely the Pareto optimum condition: $\sum_{i=1}^{N} V_i'(\hat{G}) = 1$. Hence, under these conditions, each individual consumer and the public goods board are maximizing the same objective function. If any consumer were to misrepresent his preferences, his 'true' welfare will be lowered. Hence, it is in everyone's interest to tell the truth about his preferences for the public good.

This is an ingenious solution to the free-rider problem. But, unfortunately, it does not mean that the problem has been solved. Although we have an incentive compatible structure, and a Pareto optimal supply of the public good, there is still one basic problem that is quite damaging for the Groves–Loeb mechanism.

In the Groves–Loeb mechanism, nothing assures us that the public good board's budget will be balanced. Nothing in this set-up ensures us that $\sum_{i=1}^{N} T_i = \hat{G}$. Remember that we are doing a partial equilibrium exercise and cannot appeal to the rest of the economy to bail us out. That equilibrium cannot be upset without causing incalculable damage. The solution to this problem must come from the public goods sector itself.

If we have a deficit in the budget of the public good then we do not have the Pareto optimum supply of the public good. A different class of problems arises if there is a surplus. This surplus will either have to be given back to the consumers (in which case the tax mechanism is different from that visualized in the Groves–Loeb scheme and, therefore, has different incentive implications) or thrown away (in which case it involves waste and cannot be optimal).

The Groves–Ledyard mechanism

This scheme is quite similar to the Groves–Loeb mechanism. In the present case, people are asked to state not their V_i schedules but only their desired increment (Δ_i) in the quantity supplied of the public good. Hence, people might express their views about the nation's Air Force (a public good) by saying that they want three more planes or five less.

For this mechanism to work well it is clear that initially we must have mutually consistent desired increments or there must be an iterative procedure which converges fairly quickly) to make consistent initially inconsistent proposals by members of the public. This is a problem with the Groves–Ledyard mechanism.

Turning now to the operational side of the story, the public goods board decides on the amount of the public good, by summing up the desired increments of various people:

$$\hat{G} = \sum_{i=1}^{N} \Delta_i. \tag{5.27}$$

The public goods board sets taxes according to the rule:

$$T_i = (\hat{G}/N) + (\gamma/2)[\{(N-1)/N\}(\Delta_i - A_i)^2 - \sum_{j \neq i}\{1/(N-2)\}(\Delta_j - A_i)^2] \tag{5.28}$$

where

$$A_i = \{1/(N-1)\}\sum_{j \neq i}\Delta_j = \{1/(N-1)\}(\hat{G} - \Delta_i) \tag{5.29}$$

and where γ is some positive number. The first term in T_i $(\hat{G}/N)$ allocates an equal share of the cost of the public good to everyone. A_i is the mean of the desired increments of the other $(N-1)$ people and so long as Δ_i does not depend on Δ_j, A_i is independent of Δ_i. Thus it is being assumed that individual i takes Δ_j as a parameter when making an announcement of his desired increment (Δ_i). This is a Cournot–Nash type of assumption.

Having discussed the decision-making process of the public goods board we proceed to a discussion of how individuals decide upon the Δ_i message to send to it. A representative individual chooses Δ_i to maximize $V_i(G) + x_i$ subject to $x_i + T_i = w_i$ as before. In other words he wishes to maximize $V_i(.) - T_i$.

Substituting for T_i from equations (5.28) and (5.29) we have as the individual's problem:

$$\begin{align} \max_{\Delta_i} V_i\left(\Delta_i + \sum_{j \neq i}\Delta_j\right) &- (1/N)\left(\Delta_i + \sum_{j \neq i}\Delta_j\right) - (\gamma/2)[\{(N-1)/N\}(\Delta_i - A_i)^2 \\ &- \sum_{j \neq i}(\Delta_j - A_i)^2/(N-2)]. \end{align} \tag{5.30}$$

Differentiating with respect to Δ_i, setting the derivative equal to zero and rearranging we have:

$$V_i'(\Delta_i + \sum_{j \neq i}\Delta_j) = (1/N) + \{\gamma(N-1)/N\}\{\Delta_i - A_i\}. \tag{5.31}$$

Thus, person i chooses the Δ_i that solves equation (5.31). This choice has certain very desirable properties. Summing up the righthand side and the lefthand side of equation (5.31) we get:

$$\sum_{i=1}^{N} V_i'\left(\Delta_i + \sum_{j \neq i}\Delta_j\right) = \sum_{i=1}^{N}[(1/N) + \{\gamma(N-1)/N\}(\Delta_i - A_i)]$$

or

$$\sum_{i=1}^{N} V'_i(\Delta_i) = 1 + \{\gamma(N-1)/N\} \sum_{i=1}^{N} (\Delta_i - A_i). \tag{5.32}$$

The last term on the righthand side is the sum of deviations from the mean and must, therefore, sum up to zero. Hence in the Groves–Ledyard framework the supply of the public good is Pareto optimal. Moreover, in the tax formula the constant γ can always be chosen such that $\sum_{i=1}^{N} T_i = \hat{G}$ and, therefore, that the budget of the public goods sector is always balanced.

Hence, the Groves–Ledyard mechanism produces a Pareto optimal supply of the public good, is incentive compatible and invariably manages to balance the budget. However, we must necessarily temper our enthusiasm for the Groves–Ledyard mechanism. The apparent success of this mechanism rests on the Cournot–Nash assumption that Δ_i does not affect Δ_j. But suppose that individual i (or a proper subset of individuals forming a coalition) decides to exploit the fact that he knows the public goods supply rule. Then Δ_i would depend on Δ_j and the same first-order conditions for utility maximization will not apply. Pareto optimality is no longer assured. If more and more people recognize their mutual interdependence, the model will break down. Certain equilibria may exist but there is no reason to suppose that they will involve a Pareto optimal supply of the public good or that they should be incentive compatible. In the face of enlightened strategic behavior the Groves–Ledyard scheme breaks down. This scheme requires people to be rational in a very narrow sense.

The Clarke–Groves–Vickrey mechanism

This is another quite ingenious way of approaching the free-rider problem. An outline of this mechanism is sketched below. We follow the exposition in Oakland (1987).

The public goods board asks people for information on their utility schedules just as in the Groves–Loeb mechanism. The announced utility schedules are called $\tilde{V}_i(.)$ whereas the true utility schedules are $V_i(.)$. The public goods board then collects all the $\tilde{V}_i$ schedules adds them up: $(\sum_i \tilde{V}_i(\hat{G}))$ and subtracts from them the cost of providing the public good say $C(\hat{G})$.

The tax of agent i is stated as T_i where:

$$T_i = C(\hat{G})/N + \{F_i - \sum_{j \neq i} [\tilde{V}_j(\hat{G}) - C(\hat{G})/N]\}. \tag{5.33}$$

Then F_i is defined as:

$$F_i = \sum_{j \neq i} (\tilde{V}_j(\bar{G}) - C(\bar{G})/N) \tag{5.34}$$

where $\bar{G}$ is the public good board's chosen level of public activity when agent i fails to submit his $V_i(.)$ function. Thus, $\bar{G}$ maximizes $\sum_{j \neq i} (\tilde{V}_j(G) -$

$C(G)/N$. Thus F_i is the social surplus earned by all citizens other than i when i does not submit a $V_i(.)$ schedule. When i does submit a $V_i(.)$ schedule, the surplus of everyone except individual i is $\sum_{j\neq i}[\tilde{V}_j(\hat{G}) - C(\hat{G})/N]$. Thus T_i, the tax liability of individual i consists of two components: (i) i's equal share of the total cost: $C(\hat{G})/N$; (ii) the difference between the social benefits earned by everyone except i when i does not announce a $V_i(.)$ schedule and the surplus for everyone except i when i does announce his $V_i(.)$ schedule.

Now, every individual i knows that the public goods board will choose the level of public activity to maximize net social benefit defined as $\sum_{i=1}^{N}[\tilde{V}_i(G) - \frac{C(G)}{N}]$ which can also be written as:

$$\bar{V}_i(G) - C(G)/N + \sum_{j\neq i}[\tilde{V}_j(G) - C(G)/N].$$

Individual i will manipulate his message $V_i(G)$ so that the public goods board provides i's preferred level of the public good. We get this level by maximizing i's own true net benefits:

$$V_i(G) - T_i = V_i(G) - C(\hat{G})/N - \{F_i - \sum_{j\neq i}[V_j(\hat{G}) - C(\hat{G})/N]\} \quad (5.35)$$

which can be rewritten as:

$$V_i(G) - C(G)/N + \sum_{j\neq i}[\tilde{V}_j(\hat{G}) - C(\hat{G})/N] - F_i. \quad (5.35a)$$

Now, this specification of the individual's objective function corresponds to the rewritten version of the objective function of the public goods board except that: (i) $V_i(G)$ need not equal $\hat{V}_i(G)$; (ii) $\hat{G}$ need not equal G; (iii) there is the term F_i in the individual's maximand. However, from the point of the individual the term F_i is fixed since it depends upon the messages of other agents. It is, therefore, irrelevant to individual i's decision problem of whether to send his correct message or not.

The difference between V_i and $\tilde{V}_i$ is important. However, realize that just as in the Groves–Loeb mechanism, it will not pay for the individual to lie about his true preferences. If he does not lie, then the objective function of the public goods board and that of the individual consumer coincide and this would only benefit the individual. Misrepresenting his preferences would mean that individual i is **not maximizing** utility.

So does the Vickrey–Groves–Clark mechanism solve the free-rider problem? The answer is a definite no. There are three reasons for this:

(i) It is assumed that the $V_i(.)$ does not depend upon the amount of the private goods consumed. This assumption is not satisfied in practice.
(ii) If groups of agents form coalitions then they can improve their (joint) utility position as shown by Bennett and Conn (1976).
(iii) The Vickrey–Groves–Clark mechanism will always run a budget surplus.

This mechanism raises revenue to cover production costs and also imposes a tax on the 'externality' effect of each agent's message to the public goods board. This externality tax will cause the budget surplus. If this surplus is returned to the agents then the incentives are completely changed and incentive compatibility cannot be assured. If it is thrown away then it is a waste and cannot be Pareto optimal.

These results make us think about a deeper problem. Is it possible at all to solve the free-rider problem so as to ensure Pareto optimality, incentive compatibility and a balanced budget. Hurwicz (1979) and Laffont (1987) argue that it is inherently impossible to do so. It may, therefore, be better to give up the requirement of Pareto optimality altogether and recognize incentive-compatibility as an additional constraint. This would then enable us to recognize the free-rider problem essentially as a problem in second best. This is the way in which current models treat the twin problems of supply of a public good and optimal taxation. See Stiglitz (1982, 1987), Boadway and Keen (1993) and Boadway et al. (1996).

5.5 PRIVATE PROVISION OF PUBLIC GOODS

This is sometimes also called **voluntary provision of a public good**. The idea here is to investigate how, in the absence of governmental intervention, private markets would provide for public goods. The result would depend upon a number of things, among them possibilities for exclusion, the number of individuals deriving utility from the public good and so on. In most cases, it is the fact that there will be an undersupply of public goods. In others, the market may do reasonably well. Hence, we need to distinguish between some cases. We examine a version of the example considered in Oakland (1987).

(i) No exclusion, small number of participants

Suppose there is a neighborhood occupied by two households (for convenience call them 1 and 2). The neighborhood has very poor drainage and good drainage is a public good in the sense that draining away of stagnant water undertaken by anyone benefits the other. Let G_i be the extent of drainage undertaken by households $i (= 1, 2)$.

Utility functions are $U^i(G_1 + G_2, x_i)$ where x_i is the amount of a private good consumed by the two households. Resources are limited by initial endowments w_i:

$$G_i + x_i = w_i. \tag{5.36}$$

To begin with suppose that each household takes the amount of drainage available as a datum. In that case each household will, upon maximizing utility, satisfy the condition (a subscript denotes a partial derivative with respect to that argument: $U^i_x = \partial U^i / \partial x$):

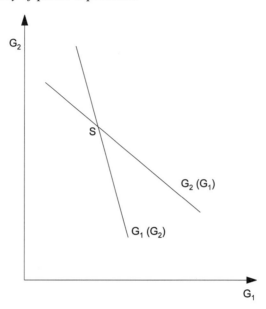

Figure 5.4

$$U^i_G / U^i_x = 1 \quad (i = 1, 2). \tag{5.37}$$

Solving equation (5.37) for households 1 and 2 we get the reaction functions $G_1 = G_1(G_2)$ and $G_2 = G_2(G_1)$. These functions are depicted in Figure 5.4. The equilibrium amount of drainage established is the 'non-cooperative' amount S. Now, S would be Pareto optimal only if a pair of indifference curves for both households is tangent at S. Typically points of tangency between the two indifference curves will lie as in Figure 5.5. Choosing a point on the contract curve CC would be superior to S. Both protagonists would, of course, argue over the exact position on CC. Individual i gains as we move along CC toward his axis. What is clear, however, is that at S the total amount of drainage would be less than optimal. In general, then, there will be an undersupply of public goods, if these are provided privately. Several other cases can be cited. As an example consider adoption of population control practices in overpopulated, poor countries. Given, the extent of population control practiced by others, it would pay any one family not to limit drastically the number of children because the larger the number of children, the greater the number of working hands in the family. If everybody cooperates and limits family size, society would gain as children could go to school and not have to work. With cooperation the amount of public goods produced would be greater.

In the literature, the essence of the problem of the failure of two (more generally 'few') individuals to cooperate even when cooperation is in their joint interest, has been labelled the **Prisoner's Dilemma**. Consider two

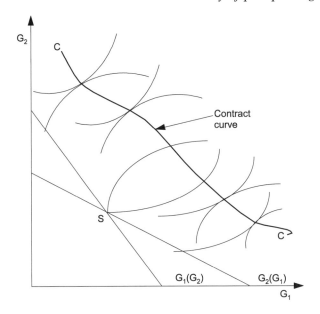

G₂ axis labeled, with C at top, "Contract curve" pointing to curve, S point, G₁(G₂) and G₂(G₁) curves, G₁ axis.

Figure 5.5

individuals who are pondering the issue of whether they should produce a public good. The public good, when produced, yields a benefit of $9 but costs a total of $11 to produce. The two agents can cooperate (strategy C) or not cooperate (NC). No communication or precontracting is allowed. Since the commodity being produced is a public good, once it is provided the benefits are enjoyed by both parties.

We can display the pay-offs to the two individuals as follows:

Individual 1

	C	NC
(1)	$3.50	$9
(2)	$3.50	−$2

Individual 2

	C	NC
(1)	−$2	$0
(2)	$9	$0

In the above pay-off matrix a figure in parenthesis means a pay-off to that individual. Thus if both individuals cooperate and share costs each will benefit to the extent of $9-11/2 = 3.50$. If one person cooperates and the other does not, the latter will gain $9 but lose $11 for a net loss of $2. If neither cooperates then the commodity does not get produced and there is no gain or loss. This is what is portrayed in the above pay-off matrix. Notice that under non-cooperative conditions, the optimal strategy for each individual is to not cooperate. Thus for individual 1 if individual 2 does not cooperate NC is best since C gets him a loss of $2. If individual cooperates then the optimal strategy for him is to NC since then he will gain $9 as opposed to $3.50 for the cooperation case. Similarly for individual 2. Thus, in this case, neither individual cooperates and no amount of the public good gets produced.

The essential reason for the collapse reported in the Prisoner's Dilemma is that there is non-cooperative behavior among the participants. If we are interested in state intervention as a last resort then the appropriate question to ask at this stage is: is it possible to ensure cooperation voluntarily among the participants.

The Prisoner's Dilemma game reported above was played once among the participants so there was no point in trusting your opponent. Suppose, however, that the number of times this game is played is finite and is known in advance to both participants. Then, if the game is repeated n times, then at the beginning of the nth iteration both players would be back in the position of the one-shot game since each knows that the nth. iteration is the last one.

Axelrod (1981) drops the restriction that the finite Prisoner's Dilemma game has a known number of iterations and permits each player to be uncertain that the next play will be the last. The question Axelrod asks at this stage is: will cooperative behavior emerge in this uncertain setting. The answer to this question is yes provided that after each play there is a sufficiently large probability that the next play will not be the last. The argument then proceeds in two stages. First, it is shown that if the probability that the game will continue is high enough, then there is no best strategy against all strategies that your opponent may play (unlike the one-shot Prisoner's Dilemma game). In particular, the non-cooperative strategy is no longer the dominant strategy.

In the second stage, Axelrod proves that a cooperative strategy which punishes non-cooperators (the tit-for-tat strategy) is potentially stable in the sense that it will tend to dominate the pure non-cooperative strategy. With the tit-for-tat strategy, each player plays cooperatively until his opponent acts non-cooperatively, and then he plays one round non-cooperatively in retaliation. With everyone playing tit-for-tat and everyone uncertain about the duration of the game, cooperative behavior emerges. Radner (1980) and Smale (1980) have discussed other methods of inducing cooperative behavior.

While the analyses of Axelrod, Radner, and Smale suggest some methods of getting around the problem of non-cooperation in the Prisoner's Dilemma game, their solutions are to be looked upon as theoretical possibilities rather than as practical solutions to the problem of non-cooperation in the voluntary production of public goods. It is rather hard to escape the conclusion that enforced cooperation through an institution such as the state may well lead us from non-cooperation to cooperative behavior.

(ii) No exclusion, large number of participants

The inefficiency that arises in the previous case is because of the fact that very few parties are involved. Similar problems would arise even in the case of private goods if we had, for example, a bilateral monopoly. If the number of people involved rises in the case of private goods then we would approximate the efficiency outcome of perfect competition. However, in the case of public goods even if the number of parties increases arbitrarily, efficiency would not result.

If there is a large number of parties involved, then each person would take decisions independently of others. Hence, instead of equation (5.37) first-order condition for individual i would be characterized by:

$$U_G^i/U_x^i \leqslant 1 \qquad (5.38)$$

with the inequality holding in the case of the agent who devotes no resources to drainage. This would be the case when the person involved considers the cost of drainage to be large in comparison to the benefits he receives from this activity. Let us assume that equation (5.38) holds for $J < N$ agents then it must be the case that:

$$\sum_{i=1}^{N} U_G^i/U_x^i \geqslant J. \qquad (5.39)$$

It should be appreciated here that no matter what the size of J there would be serious underproduction of public goods in this case as in the previous case because no single individual could afford some types of public goods but the aggregate advantage of an Air Force, for example, would vastly exceed the costs. There would, in any case, be a drastic undersupply of public goods and public bads such as that the arms race would be controlled to a less than optimal extent.

(iii) Exclusion possible: large number of participants

In this case as Oakland (1974) and others have argued it is possible to obtain efficient amounts of the public good in the private sector. But there are two problems with the mechanism proposed. First, by assuming that exclusion is costless, it assumes that demand revelation for the public good is not a problem, which we know is far from being the case. Second, the equilibrium achieved in the case above is not Pareto optimal for reasons outlined below.

We now describe the procedure. Suppose each firm produces one unit of the public good and the number of firms producing this commodity is large. Here, we are implicitly assuming that economies of scale in the production of the public good are low so that it is feasible to have a large number of private producers.

If the firm serves n consumers and charges them a price p each, total revenue will pn. If total cost is c then it must be the case that for no profit no loss we must have:

$$p = c/n. \tag{5.40}$$

Thus the price of a particular unit will vary inversely with the number of individuals consuming it.

If people have different demand functions for this commodity, then at the lowest possible price given by c/n firms will produce enough output to satisfy the consumer with the lowest demand. Consumers with higher demand will have to pay higher prices for the public good. For example, if the demands of all consumers are distinct, then at the price $[c/(n-1)]$ firms will produce sufficient output to satisfy the demand of the person with the second lowest demand and so on. The price for the person with the highest demand would be c. Moreover, this individual will consume the entire industry output. For this person then:

$$mrs = c \tag{5.41}$$

so that:

$$\sum mrs > c. \tag{5.42}$$

Hence, Pareto optimality is violated. We have already noted some other problems associated with private provision.

We can extend this analysis to cover the case where there is exclusion in the supply of public goods. But if there is exclusion then the commodity does not remain a pure public good. It becomes an impure or a crowdable public good which we will cover in the next chapter.

5.6   VOTING MODELS OF PUBLIC GOODS

A reading of the above should convince us that decisions about public goods are hard to make. In all likelihood, therefore, decisions about public goods would be made through the political process. In democratic societies such decisions are more often than not likely to take place through the voting process. The study of decision-making through the voting process is a rich and varied area of economic research and is generally collected under the rubric of 'public choice theory' as opposed to 'public economics' which is the subject matter of this book. Interested readers are referred to the work of Inman (1987) and Mueller (1995).

In this chapter we want to mention a few of the principal results. The first result worth mentioning is the **median voting theorem**. This theorem states that if individual preferences are single peaked, and if voters vote on the amount of the public good they want then, under majority voting, the preferences of the median voter shall triumph.

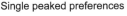

Single peaked preferences

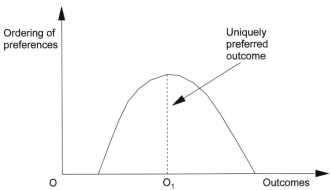

Non-single peaked preferences

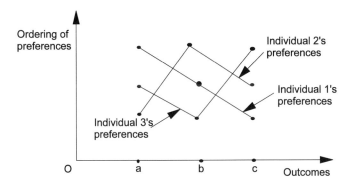

Figure 5.6

We depict single and non-single-peaked preferences in Figure 5.6. Essentially, when a voter has single-peaked preferences then he has a unique most preferred amount of the public good. We show the process of voting in Figure 5.7 with seven consumers $1, \ldots, 7$. O_1 is the most preferred outcome of individual 1 and so on. Society votes on each of these possible outcomes $O_1, \ldots, O_7$ one outcome at a time and votes are counted by the majority voting rule. We can tally the votes as shown in Table 5.1.

Under majority voting, O_4 the outcome most desired by the median voter wins. Thus, majority voting for amounts of the public good has some desirable characteristics.

The absence of single-peaked preferences may give rise to a well-known problem in voting theory known as **Condorcet's Paradox**. This problem is that of cyclical majorities. Consider a society that has three voters and three alternatives to choose from. The preferences of the three individuals (1,2,3) over three alternatives (a,b,c) are as follows.

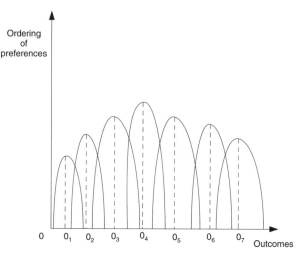

Figure 5.7

Table 5.1 Tally of votes

	Votes in favor	*Votes against*
O_1	1	6
O_2	2	5
O_3	3	4
O_4	4	3
O_5	3	4
O_6	2	5
O_7	1	6

aP_1bP_1c
bP_2cP_2a
cP_3aP_3b

Now between *a* and *b*, 2 persons prefer *a* to *b*; so we must have aPb. Between *b* and *c*, 2 persons prefer *b* to *c* so we must have bPc. Between *c* and *a*, 2 persons prefer *c* to *a*; so we have cPa. Hence we get a P-cycle.

Logrolling

Under majority voting it is possible to adopt policies that are actually opposed by a majority of voters. The process by which this may happen is known as **logrolling**. Suppose there are three alternatives *a, b, c* and three voters 1,2,3. Each alternative is actually preferred only by one voter and opposed by the remaining two. The preference patterns are as described in Table 5.2.

Table 5.2 Preference patterns

Voters	a	b	c
1	+200	−100	−120
2	−100	+250	−80
3	−40	−100	+300
Total net effect	+60	+50	+100

Individual 1 prefers alternative *a* and the monetary equivalent of this alternative occurring is +$200. Individual 1 will lose $100 if alternative *b* occurs, and so on. If the three alternatives are put to vote no alternative would get enough votes. Suppose, however, that individual 1 proposes to individual 3 that he (1) will vote for *c* if 3 votes for *a*. Now *a* and *c* will win. In the case of this particular example, society as a whole will gain. However, if the numbers were different society could easily have lost. Thus logrolling may or may not be efficient. It is often said that logrolling in a situation where alternatives supported by a minority group are opposed by sections of the majority would be useful in a multi-ethnic society. The minority group may propose support for some options supported by sections of the majority group in order to get the support of these majority groups for causes of interest to the minorities.

An important question that arises at this stage is whether voters will vote for policies that are efficient, i.e., for policies whose total benefits exceed their costs. So far as any particular voter, say voter *A*, is concerned, a policy may benefit her and have total benefits larger than total cost or it may benefit her and have total benefits less than total costs. In the first case the policy is efficient whereas in the second case the policy would be inefficient.

Empirical evidence has it that there are no inherent tendencies for voters to support efficient government policies. Domestic producers can be expected to favor import tariffs (even though free trade is in the best interest of the country); workers in declining industries may favor tariffs on competing imports, and so on.

In practice voters rarely have the opportunity to express their preference on a single policy issue. Instead they must choose among candidates having different views on matters of interest to voters. Textile workers, for example, are likely to vote for a candidate who will press for an increase in the import duty on textiles. These voters may rationalize their choice by saying that what is in their interest is also in the best interest of the country. (Recall the statement that 'What is good for General Motors is also good for America'.) However, the fact is that usually voters are not very well informed about public decision-making – certainly not as well as concerning private decisions in the marketplace. This phenomenon has come to be known as **rational voter ignorance**. It can easily be seen in terms of a comparison of a private health insurance policy and a national health insurance policy. When one is buying a private health insurance policy one is very careful about assessing the costs and benefits of this policy because one is directly affected by them. Consider, however, the issue of voting for or against a national health insurance policy. A voter would have to collect a very large amount of information about the implications of the national insurance policy, particularly for herself and her family, before she could make an informed judgment about it. The cost of collecting such information is likely to be prohibitive. Hence it may be rational for the voter to remain ignorant about the implications of the national health insurance policy. It should be repeated, however, that this ignorance is rational.

So far as politicians are concerned, there is a school of thought which argues that they play a role similar to businesspersons in private markets. Just as businesspersons are the moving force in private markets, successful politicians set the agenda in administrative and public policy areas.

However, the analogy between businesspersons and politicians can go only so far. A businessman cannot force someone to consume his product – so he has to rely on advertising. However, a politician in power has the coercive power of the state at his command. Nevertheless the politician also has to seek re-election so that he may risk voter preferences only at his peril. All other things remaining the same, politicians will tend to favor policies that have higher perceived total benefits than perceived total costs. However, all other things do not necessarily remain the same and politicians tend to take up sectarian positions at times favoring one group of people over another.

Apart from politicians, the total supply of public goods in society is also affected by the actions of bureaucrats. It is not very clear what bureaucrats have as their objective function. In Chapter 21 the view that bureaucrats want to maximize the size of the public sector budget in order to maximize their influence is considered. In trying to increase the size of the public sector budget the bureaucrats have an informational advantage over politicians. Bureaucrats are more likely to know of the true costs of a project than politicians. Hence cost figures can be exaggerated without the politicians knowing it. Thus the legislative authority may not be able to rein in costs and reduce the size of the public budget.

Another important group of actors in the process of decision-making about public goods is pressure groups and lobbyists. Olson (1968) developed a theory to explain the existence of lobbying in a large number of settings. Sometimes lobby groups can be formed to further some non-public good type of interest. Workers, for example, pay union dues. Unions, in turn, lobby for additional jobs and other non-public goods. Lobbies often play significant roles during the process of rent-seeking by bureaucrats. This is discussed in Chapter 6.

5.8 CONCLUDING REMARKS

In this chapter we have examined salient aspects of the theory of pure public goods. We derived conditions for Pareto optimality but realized that there is a prior problem of demand revelation. We studied various approaches to solving this problem and discovered that it is very hard to design satisfactory mechanisms for revealing the true demand of a pure public good. We studied some voting models of public goods as well as the inefficiency of their private supply. An essential message from this chapter is that pure public goods will almost invariably be publicly supplied and there will be an element of arbitrariness in such supply.

Our brief brush with public choice theory has recognized the implication of occasional government failure. Thus if we evaluate the consequences of market failure when dealing with externalities or public goods we must understand that government intervention may not always improve matters. Both the market and the political process are to be seen as mechanisms for allocating resources, each with their own promises and pitfalls. The fact that the market is inefficient may not imply that government intervention will make matters any better. Indeed, this may make a bad situation worse. Similarly, simply because the government is not performing very well in a particular area does not mean that the market will perform better. For example, just because there is waste in the supply of national defense does not mean that defense services should be handed over to the private sector. In making an informed decision about which allocative mechanism to use – government or the market – one must take all implications of this choice into consideration. Considerably more research needs to be done on this subject.

Public choice theory also highlights the fact that government decisions depend upon procedures and institutions in the political process. These are not written in stone and can be altered better to serve the needs of the public. Thus a reform of the political system always remains on the agenda. Similarly the market may be better monitored and regulated.

In this chapter we have not discussed issues concerning public goods that are not pure. This and some other topics are considered in the next chapter.

ADDITIONAL READING

The classic in the theory of public goods is Samuelson (1956). Excellent introductory references include Boadway and Bruce (1984) Boadway and Wildasin (1984). A good survey is Oakland (1987) and Inman (1987). See also Buchanan (1968) and Cornes and Sandler (1986). Good surveys of public choice theory are available in McNutt (1996) and Pardo and Schneider (1996).

6 Topics in the theory of public goods

Key concepts: the theory of clubs; the Tiebout hypothesis; principal–agent model; rent seeking with public goods

6.1 INTRODUCTION

The public goods that we studied in Chapter 5 satisfy two important criteria:

- There is no congestion or crowding out in the sense that no matter what the population a public good caters to, everybody enjoys all of it.
- The population that the public good is catering to is not variable.

These two criteria are satisfied by pure public goods only.

Many goods do not satisfy these criteria but are still public goods in some important sense of the term. We will study the characteristics of some of these goods in this chapter. Since some public goods are crowdable, there will be an incentive for groups of people to come together to enjoy and exclude others. This is the **theory of clubs** which we will study here. One way of analyzing local public goods is to think of the consuming public shopping around for the local jurisdiction that supplies a preferred local public goods/local tax package. This is the subject of the **Tiebout hypothesis** which we will also study here. This chapter also examines impure and crowdable public goods as well as public goods production with **distortionary taxation** and under conditions of **asymmetric information**. Finally, we recognize since there remains an element of arbitrariness in public goods supply and also because public goods are inherently desirable, there will be a tendency by residents to lobby for locating public goods in their locality. This is related to the phenomenon of **rent seeking** which we will consider here. Thus a whole host of issues has to be discussed to which we now turn.

6.2 THE THEORY OF CLUBS

Buchanan (1965) began a line of inquiry which gave rise to the idea of a **club**. Suppose there is a public good whose services are crowdable in the following sense. As the number of persons enjoying the public good increases the use value of this commodity to those already enjoying it (members of the club) decreases, e.g. a neighborhood park. However, those in the club recognize that an additional member will also lower the per person cost of the public good enjoyed by the club. Hence the fact of congestion would tend to make the club size smaller but an additional member would also lower per person cost. This would make the club size larger. The optimal club is a balance between these two forces. Let us formalize this somewhat.

A representative individual's utility depends upon two things – a private good x and a crowdable public good G. A person's actual consumption of the public good is G^* where $G^* = G/\alpha(n)$ where n is the size of the population enjoying the public good and α is an increasing function of n. The individual's utility function is written as:

$$U(G^*, x) \quad \text{where} \quad x = w - T(G)$$

and $T(.)$ is a tax function that defines the tax liability of this individual as a function of the amount of the public good consumed by him and w is the initial endowment. To keep things simple, suppose that an equal sharing arrangement is in effect, i.e., $T = (pG)/n = (\alpha(n)pG^*)/n$ where n is, as noted, the size of the club and p is the cost of the public good in terms of the private good. Setting up the consumer's utility maximization problem we have:

$$\Lambda = U(G^*, x) + \lambda[x - w - \alpha(n)pG^*/n] \tag{6.1}$$

where λ is a Lagrange multiplier.

First-order conditions yield:

$$U_{G^*}/U_x = \alpha(n)p/n \tag{6.2}$$

(where a subscript denotes a partial derivative). This is known in the literature as the adapted Samuelson condition (for Pareto optimal supply of a 'crowdable' public good).

Denote the tax price $\alpha(n)p/n$ by p^* and differentiate this tax price with respect to n to get:

$$dp^*/dn = (n\alpha'p - \alpha p)/n^2$$

where $\alpha' = \partial\alpha/\partial n$.

The club has two objectives. First, it wants to ensure that each member satisfies the amended Samuelson conditions for Pareto optimal supply of the public good. This we have already done. Second, it wants to minimize the 'effective' price paid by each club member. We achieve this by setting $dp^*/dn = 0$ to get:

$$[\alpha p/n^2][\delta - 1] = 0 \quad \text{or}$$
$$\delta = 1 \tag{6.3}$$

where $\delta = (n/\alpha)(\partial\alpha/\partial n)$ is the elasticity of α with respect to n. Equation (6.3) then determines the optimal size of the club.

This is Buchanan's fundamental result. We could state it somewhat differently. There is some fixed factor – say, land. People have to share this. The community has to be larger than 1. Every new entrant into the community automatically satisfies the amended Samuelson condition. He reduces the tax burden of everyone in the community which is a plus point. The negative point, of course, is that he also adds to congestion. Buchanan then defines the optimal club as one where the marginal decrease in tax liability is just balanced by the marginal increase in congestion. This occurs when $\delta = 1$, i.e., when the elasticity of α with respect to n is equal to 1.

One should note a few facts about this result.

1 Since individuals are identical in every respect in this conceptualization and lump-sum taxes are being used, it follows that there are no distortions and everybody shares the cost of the public good equally. If people are non-identical and/or taxes are distortionary (we have an income or commodity tax, for example) then optimal club size need not be determined by this relation.

2 Since n is a determinant of tax liability, the same public service can be priced differently in different communities. Tax obligations are minimized when p^* takes its optimal value. If a public good that is optimally supplied for n individuals is suddenly supplied centrally, tax obligations will rise and, hence, G^* will be lower unless the price elasticity of demand is zero.

3 Implicit in our discussion so far has been the assumption that the benefits of the public good are confined to members of the club. But no club is an island, so to speak, and there may be external effects from one club to another.

The analysis so far has concerned itself with a club that is a mutual benefit club. As an illustration, let us take the case where the club is profit maximizing. Suppose that a public good G is provided to a club membership n from a club facility of capacity $\bar{G}$. Thus we define $G = G(\bar{G}, n)$. Clearly, $G_{\bar{G}} > 0$ and $G_n < 0$. Let us assume that facilities are provided at a fee of p per unit time. We further assume the $G(.)$ function to be strictly convex so that we can invert and write:

$$\bar{G} = \bar{G}(n, G) \qquad (6.4)$$

with $\bar{G}_n > 0$ and $\bar{G}_{nn} > 0$.

Let us further posit a demand function of the form:

$$G = D(p).$$

The revenue for the club is:

$$R(G, n) = npG = nD^{-1}(G)G. \qquad (6.5)$$

If we define π as the constant marginal (and average) cost of supplying the commodity then we can write the cost of the club as:

$$\pi\bar{G}(G, n)$$

so that the profit of the club is:

$$nD^{-1}(G)G - \pi\bar{G}(G, n).$$

We can maximize this profit with respect to G and n. Maximizing with respect to G we have:

$$np + Gn(\partial p/\partial G) - \pi(\partial\bar{G}/\partial G) = 0 \qquad (6.6)$$

which can be manipulated to yield:

$$np(1 + 1/\beta) - (\pi\bar{G}/G)\varepsilon = 0 \qquad (6.7)$$

where β is the elasticity of demand and ε is the elasticity of $\bar{G}$ with respect to G.

Maximizing profit with respect to n we have:

$$pG - \pi(\partial\bar{G}/\partial n) = 0 \qquad (6.8)$$

which can be rewritten as:

$$npG - \pi(n/\bar{G})(\partial\bar{G}/\partial n)\bar{G} = 0$$

or, as $$n[pG - \pi\bar{G}\eta] = 0 \qquad (6.9)$$

where η is the elasticity of $\bar{G}$ with respect to n.

If other factors are treated as parameters, equations (6.7) and (6.9) can be used to solve for optimal p and optimal G. As would be obvious it is easy to establish a one-to-one relationship between the n derived from this model and the benefit-maximizing club's n.

The theory of clubs has been used to explain a wide variety of situations. See, for example, Biswal (1996).

6.3 THE TIEBOUT HYPOTHESIS

The theory of clubs has implicitly assumed that individuals are identical. It then proceeds to solve for the optimal size of the club when this choice is constrained only by the beneficial aspects of the public good in question and by the possibility of congestion. However, an important reason why people live in different towns or neighborhoods is because they have different tastes. Thus, we find middle-income families averse to living in poor neighborhoods. Zoning laws are drawn with care in many localities. One would find very few, if any, poor families in the rich suburbs of New York and Chicago. Whereas Buchanan (1965) emphasized the discretionary powers of groups, nine years earlier Tiebout (1956) had emphasized the role of the individual in defining a neighborhood. His intriguing result, popularly known as the **Tiebout hypothesis**, is a central result in the theory of public goods.

Tiebout starts by noting that most public goods are local (and not national) in character. Most of these local public goods (sanitation, police, etc.) are provided by local governments. Let us suppose that these local governments are small in size but large in number. Moreover, any individual who is contemplating settling down, knows (costlessly) the public goods package offered by each government as well as the tax liabilities associated with each public goods package.

Individuals are mobile and there are zero transport costs. Tiebout's consumers are all rentiers so their decision to locate is not bound by any place of work. There are no external effects between jurisdictions. There are fixed factors of production (say, land) and each jurisdiction has a U-shaped cost curve. Zoning laws prevent population of any jurisdiction from exceeding that given by the minimum point of the community's U-shaped cost curve.

Now, the greater the number of jurisdictions and the greater the variance among their (local public goods) characteristics, the greater the chance that any individual will be able to settle down in the jurisdiction of his choice. Thus the rich can live with the rich, people who like pets can live with people who like pets, people who dislike pets can live with people who dislike pets, and so on. In Tiebout's scheme of things, a community gets defined by its members and not, loosely speaking, the other way around. As in markets for private goods, the mobile individual is a price taker and quantity adjuster. It is implicit that taxes are lump sum (non-distortionary), otherwise we would have to worry afresh about the welfare properties of the Tiebout equilibrium.

The Tiebout hypothesis is very important because of the intriguing nature of the solution offered. As would have been expected, it raised considerable controversy. Samuelson thought that people liked variety and would be willing to incur some welfare costs to live in heterogeneous communities. Mueller raised a more practical issue. Tiebout claims that the larger the number of communities and the greater the variance of their attributes, the greater is the chance that an individual would be satisfied. Mueller argues that the number of communities would have to be very large if considerable variety in tastes have to be satisfied. He considers the case where a town has an open space which can be filled with tulip plants and trees. Some people may not want tulips at all, some may want 100 per cent tulips and so on. Once we add trees the complications become even greater. In Mueller's particular example $(101)^2$ clubs would be required. Theoretically, this would be satisfactory except for the fact that in the case of, say, produced public goods, such heterogeneity may not be able to sustain production at minimum cost. In other words, if the cost conditions for the public good are summarized by a U-shaped cost curve, it is implied that a certain minimum rate of production must take place in order to ensure that production is taking place in the most cost-efficient manner. If, on the other hand, the requirements of the Tiebout model are such that very few people belong to this community then it would not be able to exercise enough demand to make production at minimum cost a meaningful operation.

Oates has launched another fundamental attack on the Tiebout process. Individuals, he argues, are members of two communities at the same time. One is the local community and the other is the larger national community. The national government is the legislatively superior government and has the authority to create and curtail powers of local governments. Suppose the national government functions according to a simple majority rule. The majority may find it necessary, in order to maximize its benefits, to curtail the activities of local governments. A major national highway may go through land earmarked for a park for residents of a nearby community. Hence, there is no reason to suppose that automatically homogeneous communities will emerge. The national government may also curtail the powers of the local governments to collect taxes and affect their incentives to invest by changing the formulae for fiscal devolution from national to local governments.

Another serious attack on the Tiebout process comes from a number of sources: Buchanan and Wagner (1970); Buchanan and Goetz (1972); Flatters *et al.* (1974), Boadway (1979) and Atkinson and Stiglitz (1980). These contributions argue that free movement between communities may not be Pareto optimal. The argument is put forward in the following manner. Suppose there are two communities A and B. They are identical in every respect except that A is larger in area. Both A and B are producing the same local public good. Migration is costless. Since labor has more land to work within region A, its marginal product (and, under competitive conditions, its remuneration) will be higher in A than in B. This will induce a movement of labor from B to A which, of course, is efficient. This migration will go on until factor rewards are equalized across the two regions.

Because of larger population now, total income and, therefore, total tax collection are higher in A than in B. Hence, for the same public goods package, tax liability per person can be lower in region A than in region B. Therefore, people in region A will have larger consumers' surplus which the residents of B will recognize and this will, in turn, induce a second round of migration from B to A. This migration is, clearly, Pareto non-optimal.

This is a powerful criticism of the Tiebout process. However, under one condition, this criticism loses considerable force. In the long run, if land and property constitute the tax base and capital is mobile, the fact of higher consumer surplus in A would be reflected in higher land prices in region A relative to B as the difference in consumer surplus gets capitalized. Any individual would eventually attempt to optimize the joint price of land and public goods. Once, this joint price is equalized across regions A and B, the Pareto non-optimal allocation will automatically stop.

Despite all this, the important criticisms against the Tiebout hypothesis remain. Some have tried to gather empirical evidence in support of it. But these attempts have, at best, been only partially successful. Thus, although no one is suggesting that people are not sensitive to local fiscal variables when making a decision to settle down, the Tiebout hypothesis seems to be a rather extreme proposition.

An important deficiency of the Tiebout hypothesis is that it cannot explain the presence of heterogeneous communities. This is most likely to happen when we abandon the assumption of a rentier society and consider workers. It is relatively straightforward to show along the lines of Berglas (1976) and others that if people work and vary in skills as well as in taste, and if workers of different skills are imperfect substitutes for each other, then heterogeneous communities will result.

Consider a simple proof of this proposition. In a society we have two types of individuals: skilled (s) and unskilled (n). Each group is homogeneous within itself with respect to both skills as well as tastes. There are n_s individuals of type s and n_n individuals of type n. There is a local public good G and a private good x and individual utility functions (for a representative individual of each type) have the form: $U^s(G, x_s)$ and $U^n(G, x_n)$ where x_s and x_n are amounts of the private good consumed by a typical member of each group. Total consumption of the private good is $x = n_s x_s + n_n x_n$ and production conditions for the private good are defined by:

$$x = x(n_x, s_x) \qquad (6.10)$$

where n_x and s_x refer to the number of unskilled and skilled workers in the production of x. We assume $x_n > 0$, $x_s > 0$, sign $x_{nn} =$ sign $x_{ss} < 0$ and $x(n, 0) = x(0, s) = 0$. Hence marginal products are positive and diminishing and each type of labor is essential for the production of x.

In the production of the public good the private good and labor are inputs. Here, however, it does not matter whether labor is of type n or s. The production function is:

$$G = G(x_G, n_G + s_G) \qquad (6.11)$$

where x_G is the amount of the private good used in the production of the public good and n_G and s_G are the amounts of the unskilled and skilled labor force enjoying the public good. Equation (6.11) makes it explicit that the two types of labor are perfect substitutes for each other. However, production of G by labor here has to be understood in terms of crowding. The larger the size of the population enjoying the public good, the smaller its effective supply. For a given level of production of G an increase in the population requires more of the private good x to maintain that level of G. In other words:

$$[\partial x_G / \partial (n_G + s_G)]|_{G \text{ constant}} > 0. \qquad (6.12)$$

Apart from the congestion argument advanced above, one can interpret the production relation as saying that as population increases, the costs of servicing it increase as would reasonably be the case with, say, police protection and fire services.

Let us first look at the Pareto optimum for this community. We maximize the utility of type n individuals subject to the utility of type s individuals being at a particular level and the production relations for goods G and x. We will here make the realistic and simplifying assumption that the number of people of each type who are producing the private good are the same as the number of people enjoying the public good. Hence we set $n_n = n_x = n_G = n_n$ (say) and and $n_s = s_x = s_G = n_s$ (say). Setting up the Lagrangean we have:

$$\Lambda = U^n(x_n\, G) + \lambda_1(\bar{U}^s - U^s(x_s,\, G)) + \lambda_2[x_G + n_s x_s + n_n x_n \\ - x(n_n,\, n_s)] + \lambda_3[G(x_G,\, n_n + n_s) - G]. \tag{6.13}$$

First-order conditions for an internal maximum are:

$$U_G^n - \lambda_1 U_G^s - \lambda_3 = 0 \tag{6.14a}$$

$$\lambda_2[x_s - x_{n_s}] + \lambda_3[G_n] = 0 \tag{6.14b}$$

$$\lambda_2[x_n - x_{n_n}] + \lambda_3(G_n) = 0 \tag{6.14c}$$

$$\lambda_2 + \lambda_3 G_{x_G} = 0 \tag{6.14d}$$

with a subscript denoting the corresponding partial derivative. From (6.14d) we derive $\lambda_2 = -\lambda_3 G_{x_G}$ and then substituting this for λ_2 in equations (6.14b) and (6.14c) we will have:

$$x_s - x_{n_s} = -G_n/G_{x_G} = x_n - x_{n_n}. \tag{6.15}$$

$x_s - x_{n_s}$ is the net contribution of a skilled worker (marginal product less congestion) and $x_n - x_{n_n}$ is the net contribution of an unskilled worker. These are equated to each other (so that we have an optimal mix of skilled and unskilled workers) and to the social marginal cost $(-G_n/G_{x_G})$. These and other first order conditions will also yield:

$$n_s(U_G^s/U_x^s) + n_n(U_G^n/U_x^n) = 1/G_{x_G} \tag{6.16}$$

which is the Samuelson condition for Pareto optimality under these conditions, i.e., the sum of the mrs equals the mrt.

The Pareto optimum condition defined here is relative to $\bar{U}^s$. As we parametrically change U^s, U^n will change. As a consequence, the mix of the community, its size, and consumption of the two groups will change. The direction of change will depend on the relative preferences for the public good by the two types of individuals. But that we need heterogeneous communities is clear from the very specification of the production relations.

Suppose there exist a U^{s^*} for which the optimal population mix is $n_s^*/n_n^* = S^*/N^*$ where S^* is the total number of skilled people in the country and N^* is the total number of unskilled people in the country. Then the

Pareto optimum allocation from the point of view of the whole country would be to distribute the population of skilled and unskilled people in the above exact ratio among $N^*/n_n^* = S^*/n_s^*$ identical communities across the country.

Let us suppose that with such a population mix, one community starts taxing people of type s more heavily. Then the skilled workers in this community will have a lower return and the unskilled workers a higher return. Migration across communities will ensure that the returns to both groups of workers get equalized across communities.

Hence, no matter how people shop for communities, heterogeneity will result. In this stipulation there are two opposing forces. The crowding of public goods might make for homogeneity whereas the fact that both types of workers are needed for production necessitates heterogeneity.

The above proposition can be shown to be a little more general. By keeping the group small and homogeneous, agreement on the amount of public good and congestion is facilitated. On the other hand, small groups require increased outlay for the public good because of the need for more clubs.

The problem is similar to that posed by monopolistic competition where firms have a fixed set-up cost. The larger the number of firms, the closer the configuration of output matches tastes, but the greater the aggregate fixed costs. The presence of fixed set-up cost introduces a non-convexity into the analysis. The resulting analysis is necessarily complex but it is clear that heterogeneity will prevail.

6.4   MULTI-PRODUCT CLUBS

An important problem in the theory of clubs is the following. Suppose the size of the population is N and a typical club has n members so that there are N/n clubs. If N/n is an integer then the entire population would have been absorbed in clubs. If, however, N/n is not an integer then it would follow that there would be some people who would not be members of any club. They could then be interested in forming clubs of their own so that the existing structure of clubs would not be stable. This is known as the **integer problem** in the theory of clubs. In general, then, one has to consider the dynamics of many clubs existing simultaneously. It is also possible to consider multi-product clubs as Cornes and Sandler (1986) and Sandler and Tschirhart (1993) have shown. In actual practice single-product clubs are the exception and multi-product clubs are the rule. A sports club, for example, may offer tennis, swimming and other facilities – not just one of these.

Suppose, to take the simplest example, each club provides two services. Each member of each club makes one visit to the club so that crowding depends only upon membership size – not on the number of visits that each club member may make.[1]

Because only one visit per member is permitted only equal membership fees are charged. It is also assumed that there are no barriers to entry for potential clubs. We can now examine whether this club structure is sustainable.

The society consists of homogeneous individuals and we deal with the simplest possible case where there are two clubs providing two services each. Congestion of any club service depends only upon the number of members and we write:

$$c^i = c^i(n) \tag{6.17}$$

where c^i is the congestion function of club service $i (i = 1, 2)$.

For a typical club member utility U^m is written in the following linear form:

$$U^m = Y - p + f - c^1(n) - c^2(n) \tag{6.18}$$

where Y is exogenously given income, p is the price of club services,[2] f is the utility equivalent of gross benefits received from joining the club and $c^i(.)$ is congestion of service i. If the individual does not join any club then his utility would be:

$$U^0 = Y. \tag{6.19}$$

Hence, a representative individual would like to join a club only if:

$$U^m - U^0 = -p + f - c^1 - c^2 \geq 0. \tag{6.20}$$

This can be written in the equivalent form:

$$f \geq p + c^1 + c^2 \tag{6.21}$$

that is, the benefits from joining the club must not be outweighed by the costs. If equation (6.21) holds as a strict inequality then people will be willing to join clubs until it does become an equality.

If equation (6.21) holds as an equality then we can write club size as a function of the price:

$$n = n(p). \tag{6.22}$$

It is natural to presume that $dn/dp = n' < 0$ for $p_l \leq p \leq p_h$. If $p < p_l$ then there are too many people in the club and crowding is so high that no one else wants to join in. If $p > p_h$ then the price is so high that no one wants to join in. For the intermediate range as price rises, club size should fall.

The cost function of the club consists of two elements – a fixed cost and a variable cost. If $C(S)$ is this cost function then we write:

$$C(S) = S_1 + S_2 + F(1, 2) \tag{6.23}$$

where S_i is the level of service of type i provided and $F(1,2)$ is the fixed cost function of providing these two services.

Since equation (6.22) is single signed it is possible to invert it to write the price function applicable to the club: $p = p(n)$. Hence the profit (π^m) of a typical club can be written as:

$$\pi^m = p(n)n - S_1 - S_2 - F(1, 2). \qquad (6.24)$$

If we assume that variable costs do not depend upon the number of people enjoying the service then we can maximize profits with respect to n in equation (6.24) to get:

$$p'(n)n + p(n) = 0 \qquad (6.25)$$

where a prime $(')$ denotes the first derivative. Equation (6.25) implies that marginal revenue equals zero. This follows from the fact that production cost is independent of club size and congestion is reflected on the demand side by $p(n)$.

We now define Average Cost per club member as:

$$AC(n) = [S_1 + S_2 + F(1, 2)]/n. \qquad (6.26)$$

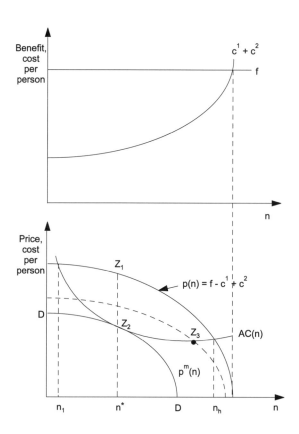

Figure 6.1

Equilibrium for the profit-maximizing club is denoted in Figure 6.1. Clearly the club will make profits; break even; incur losses as $p(n) > AC(n)$; $p(n) = AC(n)$; $p(n) < AC(n)$.

Realize that $AC(n)$ is a declining function of n. This is depicted in the lower panel of Figure 6.1. In fact since the numerator of equation (6.26) does not depend on n, it might well be a rectangular hyperbola. In the lower panel of this figure we also denote condition (6.21) as an equality $(p(n) = f - c^1 - c^2)$. Profit is maximized when the vertical distance between $p(n)$ and $AC(n)$ is the maximum, i.e., at point Z_1 which would also imply the satisfaction of equation (6.25) at n^*. In the upper panel of Figure 6.1 we draw the f and c schedules. The vertical difference between these two appears as the $p(n)$ schedule in the lower panel. It is assumed that the interior solution (n^*) is feasible. The upper and lower limits of n (n_h and n_l) are also denoted in the diagram.

If this club was member owned then the profit motive would disappear. The relevant $p(n)$ schedule is now drawn as $p^m(n)$ and this is the $p(n)$ schedule vertically lower by the amount of profit earned at Z_1. To break even, the membership club would choose Z_2 with a lower price but the same club size as the profit-maximizing club.

Given this result an important question at this stage is whether the profit-maximizing club is sustainable? The answer to this question is a clear no if free entry is allowed. Potential clubs would recognize the profits being made and enter the market. This would shift the $p(n)$ schedule down in the lower panel of Figure 6.1 until zero profits are being made. Thus, in order to be sustainable, a club must make zero profits.

Furthermore, if entry is unrestricted into this market then the incumbent club must minimize the gross price to each member. This gross price is defined as:

$$p + c^1 + c^2.$$

An incumbent club must then solve the problem:

$$\min_{p,n} p + c^1 + c^2 \text{ subject to } p = C(S)/n.$$

This can be shown clearly from Figure 6.1. Any club charging a fee higher than AC is non-sustainable. However, this is not sufficient for sustainability. At Z_3 profits are zero for a non-efficient club but positive for an efficient club for which we can draw the p schedule given by DD. Thus at this point, an incumbent club will be vulnerable to potential entrants.

So far we have been assuming that each service gets charged the same price. Suppose the club is free to charge different prices for different services. Sandler and Tschirhart (1993) call this an **unrestricted club**. The club charges price p_i for service i whereas the cost structure is the same as before. Profits for this club are written as:

$$\pi = \sum_{i=1}^{m}(p_i n_i - S_i) - F(S_1, \ldots, S_m) \tag{6.27}$$

where n_i is the size of the membership enjoying service i and there are m such services. The congestion function is now written as:

$c^i(n_i, n_{i-1})$ where n_{i-1} is the number of people enjoying facilities other than i. The utility function of a representative individual is written as:

$$U = Y - \sum p_i + f - \sum c^i(.) \qquad (6.28)$$

Hence this unrestricted club must minimize $\Sigma(p_i + c^i)$ in order to be sustainable.

Also it must be the case that if the solution n_i^* for the unrestricted club case is different from the n in the case where a uniform price had to be charged then it would be clear that the latter would not be sustainable. The possibility of charging different prices for different services is open only in the case of unrestricted clubs and this would only improve their sustainability. However, since the unrestricted club also faces potential entrants, it must produce at least cost.

Competition from single-product clubs

It might be the case that price for some services within a multi-product club may be raised in order for prices of other services to be lowered. This is the phenomenon of **cross-subsidization**. In this case there might be an incentive for single-product[3] clubs to emerge for the services that are doing the cross-subsidization. An important problem for this club to recognize, then, is that such clubs do not emerge. This is the problem of designing cross-subsidy free prices and is discussed in detail in Chapter 17.

6.5   FINANCING PURE PUBLIC GOODS WITH DISTORTIONARY TAXES

Very rarely is it possible to finance public goods with non-distortionary (lump-sum) taxes. In this section we wish to study the supply of public goods when we have only distortionary taxes at our disposal. We first study this in the case of certainty and then consider a simplified version of a model of public goods provision under conditions of asymmetric information.

The analysis of public goods provision with distortionary taxation under conditions of full certainty has been considered in a paper by Mikami (1993) who builds up on the earlier work of Hatta (1979) and others. Consider an economy consisting of $(n + 2)$ goods. One good is leisure, another is a pure public good and there are n private goods. Welfare changes are evaluated in terms of the utility of a representative consumers[4] which is written as:

$$U(l, d, G)$$

where *l* is leisure, *d* is a column vector of *n* private goods and *G* is the public good. Let the consumer price vector be denoted by *p* and the producer price vector by *q*. This consumer's budget constraint can then be written as:

$$p_l l + \sum_{i=1}^{n} p_i d_i = 0 \tag{6.29}$$

where p_l is the after tax wage rate. Demand functions for the private goods can be written as $d_i(p_1, p, G)$, if there is no lump-sum income.

The indirect utility function for this individual can now be defined by *V* where:[5]

$$U \equiv V(l, p, G). \tag{6.30}$$

We will assume that the public good is produced using labor alone and the labor requirement of the public good is given by $\phi(G)$. We take the pre-tax wage as the numeraire. The production of private goods is characterized by constant cost technology. Without loss of generality it can be assumed that these costs of production are the same and equal to 1. Further, units can be chosen so that the tax on leisure is zero and the producer as well as the consumer price of leisure are both equal to 1.

We can then write:

$$q_1 = 1$$
$$q_i = 1 + t_i, i = 1, \ldots n$$

where t_i is the specific tax on commodity *i*.

Denote supplies by s_i. In equilibrium, the supply and demand for each good must be equal and the production constraint for this economy can be written as:

$$l(p, G) + \sum_{i=1}^{n} q_i d_i(p, G) + \phi(G) = 0. \tag{6.31}$$

First, upon differentiating the indirect utility function with respect to the vector *t* and the scalar *G* and using Roy's identity we derive:

$$(dU/dG)/\alpha = V_G - (\partial d/\partial t)(dt/dG) \tag{6.32}$$

where α is the marginal utility of income. Now since all tax revenue is assumed to be spent for the production of the public good we can write the government's budget constraint as:

$$\sum_{i=1}^{n} t_i d_i = \phi(G) \text{ or } t'd(p, G) = \phi(G) \tag{6.33}$$

(where a prime (') denotes a transpose).
Totally differentiating (6.33) we have:

$$(d' + t'\partial d/\partial t)(dt/dG) = \phi_G - t'd_G. \tag{6.34}$$

We will assume that expression (6.34) is positive. At issue now is the following: is expression (6.32) positive when equation (6.34) is satisfied? If that is the case then it would follow that a balanced budget increase in the supply of the public good will increase welfare.

Mikami (1993) shows that the answer to the above question depends on two factors:

(i) ways of changing tax rates that meet the increased public expenditure;
(ii) the substitutability/complementarity relation that may exist between the public good and private goods.

To see point (i) above index commodities such that $t_1 < t_2 < \ldots < t_n$. Clearly this involves no loss of generality. Consider the following rule for changing taxes in order to finance the additional units of the public good: we raise low tax rates and keep high tax rates unchanged.

Thus $dt_i/dG = \delta > 0$, for $i = 1, \ldots, m$ and $dt_i/dG = 0$ for $i = m+1, \ldots, n$. Substitute this for dt/dG in expression (6.34) and solve for δ to get:

$$\delta = (\phi_G - t'd_G)/\sum_{i=1}^{m}(d_i + t'\partial d/\partial t_i). \tag{6.35}$$

Assume that the first m commodity tax rates are the same and equal to a value t_I. Using the Slutsky equation and some results due to Hatta (1979), Mikami (1993) shows that expression (6.32) can be written as:

$$(dU/dG)/\alpha = mb - [mc - t'(\partial d/\partial G)]/[1 + (\Omega - t'(\partial d/\partial Y)] \tag{6.36}$$

where mb = marginal benefit of the public good, mc = the marginal cost and:

$$\Omega = \left[\sum_{i=1}^{m}\sum_{j=0}^{n}(t_j - t_I)c_{ji}/[(1 + t_I)\sum_{i=1}^{m}d_i]\right] \tag{6.37}$$

where c_{ji} is the partial derivative of the compensated demand function of the jth commodity with respect to the ith price.

When the public good is financed by lump-sum taxes all $t_i = 0$ and expression (6.36) will reduce to $[(dU/dG)/\alpha = mb - mc]$. Hence if mb > mc then it would be worthwhile to increase the supply of the public good.

If, however, we do not have lump-sum taxes and have to rely upon commodity taxes to finance the public good then the marginal financing cost of the public good is affected by the tax change (represented by the term $\Omega - t'(\partial d/\partial Y)$) and by the change in public goods supply (represented by $-t'(\partial d/\partial G)$).

The first term $(\Omega - t'(\partial d/\partial Y))$ consists of two effects. The substitution effect will, at constant utility, reduce the distortion because of the gap between the higher and lower taxes. Hatta (1986) and Fukushima and Hatta (1989) show that the second-best optimum involves almost complete uniformity between commodity tax rates. Hence, this should reduce the mc and Ω should be negative.

However, an increase in commodity tax rates will involve a decline in income so that the income effect should increase the mc of the public good. Hence, the impact of this particular type of commodity tax reform on the mc would depend on the relative strengths of these two effects.[6]

We can now examine the effect of the term $(t'\partial d/\partial G)$ on the mc. Clearly, if the utility function is separable[7] in the public and private goods this term will be zero. If the utility function is weakly separable in commodities, from leisure and the public good, then the utility function can be written as:

$$U(l, d, G) = U(l, f(d), G)$$

so that commodity functions can be written as:

$$d_i[p_1, p,\ Y - l(p_1, p, G)].$$

Differentiating these demand functions with respect to G would yield:

$$
\begin{aligned}
(\partial d_i/\partial G) &= (\partial d_i/\partial Y) - (\partial l/\partial G)\,)\ \text{so that} \\
-t'(\partial d/\partial G) &= t'(\partial d/\partial Y)(\partial l/\partial G).
\end{aligned}
\tag{6.38}
$$

From equation (6.38) we find that if leisure is substitutable for (complementary with) the public good, then the term $(-t'(\partial d/\partial G)\,)$ is negative (positive) and decreases (increases) the marginal cost of the public good.

The intuition for this result goes as follows. If commodity tax rates are higher than the tax on leisure, then leisure is consumed more than it would be under the lump-sum tax. Hence, when leisure is substitutable for the public good the increased consumption of leisure is discouraged when we increase the supply of the public good. Conversely, when leisure is complementary with the public good an increase in the supply of the public good would increase the consumption of leisure.

6.6 PUBLIC GOODS PROVISION WITH ASYMMETRIC INFORMATION

The analysis that we have considered so far has made no distinction between the agent responsible for funding the public good and that responsible for actually producing it. This, of course, is at variance with reality, especially in the case of local public goods. These are often provided by agencies that are not responsible for their funding. Examples would include hospital and education services. Furthermore, since most of these services are provided free of cost or with only nominal user charges, the normal disciplines of the market do not operate and there is no reason to suppose that the agencies providing them will minimize costs.

The existence of such a problem has potential implications both for the granting formula as well as for the optimal amount of the public service to provide. Ideally, the granting formula would relate the amount of funding to the level of service provided, would screen out the low-cost agencies from the high-cost agencies as well as induce high effort from producing agencies when such effort is an additional variable in order to reduce costs. The difficulty, of course, is that agencies have private information about their cost structure which the funding agency does not. Thus this problem takes the form of a signaling problem, or a moral hazard problem, or both.

The optimal design of the granting formula under such situations has been considered in a paper by Boadway *et al.* (1996). We will consider here a simplified version of this model and only for the problem of signaling.

There are three types of decision-makers in the economy: the government which makes the grant to an agency in order to get the local public good produced; agencies producing the local public good;[8] and a representative individual whose welfare the government is interested in maximizing.

The utility of the representative individual is written as the following quasi-linear function:[9]

$$U(L, X, G) = u(L) + X + b(G) \tag{6.39}$$

where L is labor, X is a composite consumption good and G is the amount of a public good provided. The wage rate that this individual is given, and the choice of G is made by the actions of the government and the public goods producing agencies. $b(.)$ is the utility from the public good. The consumer, therefore, takes G as given and maximizes utility with respect to X and L. However, these are related by the relation: $X = (w - t)L$ where w is the wage rate and t is the tax rate on labor supplied.[10] Hence the consumer has only one choice variable – say L.

The consumer then maximizes the above utility subject to $X = (w - t)L$, using L as the choice variable. This leads to a labor supply function which can be written as:

$$L = L(w - t). \tag{6.40}$$

It is easy to show that:

$$L' = -1/(u'') > 0$$

(where a prime $(')$ denotes a first derivative, a double prime $('')$ a second derivative and so on. This should cause no confusion since we are not dealing with any vectors in this section).

The consumer's indirect utility function is, therefore:

$$V(w - t, G) \equiv u(L(w - t)) + (w - t)L(w - t) + b(G).$$

From the envelope theorem we will get:

$$\partial V / \partial t = -L(w - t) < 0 \text{ and } (\partial V / \partial G) = b' > 0.$$

Revenue from the taxation of labor is used to finance the provision of the public good. Hence the amount of subsidy is S where:

$$S = tL(w - t) \equiv S(t). \tag{6.41}$$

By inverting this function we can obtain $t(S) = S^{-1}(t)$ where:

$$t'(S) = 1/[L(w - t) - tL'(w - t)]. \tag{6.42}$$

We will assume that this expression is positive.

We can then write the indirect utility of the individual as:

$$V(S, G) = V(w - t(S), G) \tag{6.43}$$

where it is clear that

$$V_S = (\partial V/\partial t)t'(S) = -L/(L - tL') \tag{6.44a}$$

and

$$V_G = (\partial V/\partial G) = b'(G) > 0 \tag{6.44b}$$

(where a subscript denotes a partial derivative).

Totally differentiating equation (6.43) we can write the slope of an indifference curve in (S, G) space as:

$$(dS/dG)|_{V=\bar{V}} = -V_G/V_S = (L - tL')b'/L = (1 + \epsilon)b' > 0 \tag{6.45}$$

where ϵ is the elasticity of supply of labor with respect to the tax rate. This indifference curve is upward sloping because G is desirable whereas an increase in the subsidy implies an increase in the tax rate and is, therefore, undesirable.

The public good is provided by the local agency. It can have two levels of costs – high or low. We write the cost function of type i as:

$$C^i = F^i + c^i G^i \tag{6.46}$$

where C^i is the total cost, F^i the fixed cost, c^i the marginal cost and G^i the production level of agency of type $i(i = l, h)$. We will examine two cases: (i) where variable costs differ across agencies $c^l < c^h$ with $F^l = F^h = F$. In this case the so-called single-crossing property holds.[11] (ii) where the single-crossing property does not hold, i.e. $c^l = c^h = c$ and $F^l < F^h$. The profit of agency of type i is:

$$\pi^i = S - C^i(G) \quad \text{with} \quad dS/dG|_{\pi=\bar{\pi}} = c^i.$$

The government does not know which agency is of which type but knows the probability Φ^i of the agency being of type i. The government's problem is, therefore, to maximize the expected utility of the representative individual $\sum_{i=l,h} [\Phi^i V(S^i, G^i)]$ subject to two constraints.

(a) A participation constraint on the part of the agency. An agency will participate in the public goods production program only if it makes non-negative profits. In other words:

$$S^i - C^i(G^i) \geqslant 0 \text{ for } i = l, h. \tag{6.47}$$

(b) A second constraint will be that no agency would like to mimic the behavior of the other agency. In other words, the high-(low-) cost agency would reveal itself to be the high-(low-) cost agency. This is known as the self-selection constraint and is written as:

$$S^i - C^i(G^i) - S^j + C^i(G^j) \geqslant 0, \quad i,j = l,h. \tag{6.48}$$

The government's problem is then a standard **principal–agent problem**. If there had been no problem of asymmetric information the self-selection constraint would not have been relevant and the Lagrangean for the government would have been written as:

$$\wedge(S^i, G^i, \lambda^i) = V(S^i, G^i) + \lambda^i(S^i - C^i(G^i)) \tag{6.49}$$

where λ^i is the Lagrange multiplier for the ith type agent.
The first-order conditions would be:

$$-V^i_G/V^i_S = C^{i'}(G^i) = c^i.$$

Using equation (6.45) this becomes:

$$b'(G^i) = C'_i(G^i)L^i/(L^i - tL^i) = C'_i(G^i)/(1 + e^i). \tag{6.50}$$

The lefthand side of this expression is the marginal benefit of the public good. On the righthand side we have the marginal cost. This consists of two elements – the technical marginal cost $(C^{i'})$ and the excess burden of the additional taxation required to finance the marginal unit of the public good. This is represented by the term $(1 + e^i)$. If the public good was financed by lump-sum taxes then e^i would be zero and we would be back with the Samuelson rule – marginal benefit equals marginal cost.

Optimal grants with differences in marginal cost

We now abandon the full information case and assume that the only difference between the two types of agencies lies with respect to their variable (marginal) costs. In this case it can be shown[12] that the low-cost agency will earn a pure profit whereas the high-cost agency will just break even. Similarly it can be shown that the self-selection constraint will not be binding on the high-cost agency. Then the Lagrangean of the government can be written as:

$$\begin{aligned} \Lambda &= \Phi^l V(S^l, G^l) + \Phi^h V(S^h, G^h) + \lambda^h(S^h - C^h(G^h)) \\ &+ \lambda^{lh}(S^l - C^l(G^l) - S^h + C^l(G^h)). \end{aligned} \tag{6.51}$$

The first-order conditions are as follows:

$$\Phi^l V^l_S + \lambda^{lh} = 0 \tag{6.52a}$$

$$\Phi^l V^l_G - \lambda^{lh} C^{l'}(G^l) = 0 \tag{6.52b}$$

$$\Phi^h V^h_S + \lambda^h - \lambda^{lh} = 0 \tag{6.52c}$$

$$\Phi^h V^h_G - \lambda^h C^{h'}(G^h) + \lambda^{lh} C'_l(G^h) = 0. \tag{6.52d}$$

From (6.52a) and (6.52b) we have:

$$-V_G{}^l/V_S{}^l = C^{l'}(G^l)$$

which means that

$$b'(G^l) = C^{l'}(G^l)/(1 + \varepsilon^l). \tag{6.53}$$

In other words, optimality conditions of the type given by equation (6.50) will be satisfied for the low-cost agency.

For the high-cost agency from equations (6.52c) and (6.52d) we will get:

$$\begin{aligned} -V_G{}^l/V_S{}^h &= [\lambda^h C^{h'}(G^h) - \lambda^{lh} C^{l'}(G^h)]/(\lambda^h - \lambda^{lh}) \\ &= C^{h'}(G^h) + [C^{h'}(G^h) - C^{l'}(G^h)]\lambda^{lh}/(\lambda^h - \lambda^{lh}). \end{aligned} \tag{6.54}$$

It is the case that $\lambda^{lh} > 0$ (by equation (6.52a)) and $(\lambda^h - \lambda^{lh}) > 0$ (by equation (6.52c)). Hence the second term on the righthand side of equation (6.54) is positive indicating that for the high-cost agency mrs of the public good for transfers exceed the marginal cost of provision. The difference is the cost of signaling. Hence the supply of the public good in the high-cost case will be lower than that given by equation (6.50). The cost of signaling, or the cost of information being private, is further illustrated by the fact that, while the profit of the high-cost agency is zero, that of the low-cost agency is positive. The government is precluded by the self-selection constraint from reducing the profits of the low-cost agency to zero.

Now, substituting from (6.52a) and (6.52c) into (6.54) we will get:

$$\begin{aligned} b'(G^h) &= C^{h'}(G^h)/(1 + \epsilon^h) + (\Phi^l/\Phi^h)[C^{h'}(G^h) - C^{l'}(G^h)]/(1 + \epsilon^l) \\ &> C^{h'}(G^h)/(1 + \epsilon^h). \end{aligned} \tag{6.55}$$

This clearly shows that the marginal cost of public funds for the high-cost agency exceeds the value given by the standard expression. The difference is greater the larger is the difference in marginal costs, the larger the probability of the agency being low cost and and the smaller is ϵ^l.

The solution to the asymmetric information case is compared with that for the full information case in Figure 6.2. For the asymmetric information case, the levels of public services and grants are labeled A^l and A^h for the low- and high-cost agencies. We also label the full information case with o so that G^{ho}, for example, stands for the supply of the public good by the high-cost agency in the full information case. From Figure 6.2 we can see that $G^h < G^{ho}$ where G^h is the public goods supply in the asymmetric information case. Further, $S^h < S^{ho}$. Also while $S^l > S^{lo}$, G^l could be larger or smaller than G^{lo}.

Optimal policy when the single-crossing property does not hold

Consider now the case when the agencies differ only in their fixed costs and have the same marginal cost. In this case the iso-profit curves will be

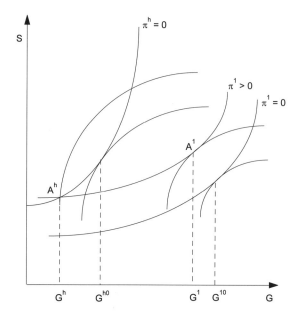

Figure 6.2

parallel and not cross each other. It is easy to show that the optimal policy under asymmetric information will be a **pooling equilibrium**. Furthermore the participation constraint of the high-cost agency will be binding, while that of the low-cost agency will not be binding ($\lambda^l = 0$). The proof is relatively straightforward and is left as an exercise for the reader. In any case it is available in Boadway *et al.* (1996).

The problem of the government is to choose a common transfer level S and quantity of public good G for the agency to supply regardless of its costs. The government will wish to maximize expected utility subject to a non-negative profit constraint on the high-cost agency. In this case, the household obtains the same utility regardless of the cost type of the agency. Hence the Lagrangean of the government can be written as:

$$\Lambda = V(S, G) + \lambda^h(S - C^h(G^h)). \tag{6.56}$$

First-order conditions are:

$$(\partial L/\partial S) = V_S + \lambda^h = 0 \tag{6.57a}$$

$$(\partial L/\partial G) = V_G - \lambda^h C^{h'}(G) = 0. \tag{6.57b}$$

Eliminating λ^h and using equations (6.44a) and (6.44b) we have:

$$b'(G) = [C^{h'}(G)L]/[L - tL'] = C^{h'}(G)/(1 + \epsilon) \tag{6.58}$$

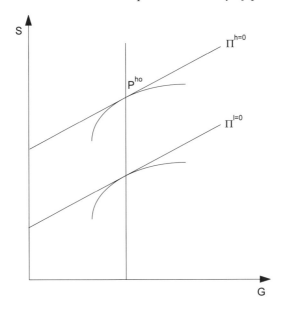

Figure 6.3

where $\epsilon = -tL'/L < 0$ is the elasticity of the labor supply with respect to the tax rate in the pooling equilibrium. Equation (6.58) is the standard expression for the marginal cost of public funds when public goods are financed using a distortionary linear tax.

We compare the equilibrium here with that in the full information case in Figure 6.3. With full information S^i and G^i will satisfy equation (6.50). A^{ho} is the optimal policy combination in the high-cost case and A^{lo} in the low-cost case. With full information $S^{ho} > S^{lo}$. However, G^{ho} could be greater or lower than G^{lo} as before. The consumer is better off in the low-cost case.

With asymmetric information the pooling equilibrium is at p^{ho} in Figure 6.3. The government must transfer more funds to the low-cost agency than is required to cover costs. The cost that the asymmetric information imposes on the government is the unobservable level of profits earned by the low-cost agency. The structure of grants consists of announced levels of s^h and G^h which are common to both types of agencies.

It is possible to extend this analysis to consider cases where costs depend on the level of effort put in by agents. This is the **moral hazard** version of the model. Results are discussed in detail in Boadway *et al.* (1996).

6.7 RENT SEEKING

Another topic in the theory of public goods that has been quite popular is **rent seeking**. Our work so far should have convinced us that there are no perfect guidelines for allocation in the presence of public goods. Since this is the case and since public goods are inherently desired by people, it would follow that groups of people would like to influence government policy toward public goods. For example, groups of people would like to have a public park located near their homes. Others would like to ensure that a potentially busy highway does not run too close to their neighborhood. Other groups might lobby for defense facilities to be located close to them in the expectation that such facilities would help generate local jobs, and so on. At the very least, it is likely that there will be intense competition among groups of people about the location of public goods facilities.

Given that this is the case, then people would be willing to lobby for these services. This is the phenomenon of **rent seeking**. This notion has actually come from international trade theory where authors were trying to understand the flow of resources into lobbying for quotas on imports. Pioneering works in this area include Krueger (1974) who coined the phrase 'rent seeking' and Bhagwati (1982) who preferred the term 'directly unproductive activities'. To understand the basic idea involved we present below a stylized version of the Krueger analysis.

Consider a country producing one commodity X_1[13] whose amounts are denoted by x_1. The output of this commodity depends upon the input of labor into the production process.

$$x_1 = g(L_1), \quad \text{with} \quad g' > 0 \quad \text{and} \quad g'' < 0 \tag{6.59}$$

(where a prime (') denotes as before, a first derivative and so on).

This country, however, consumes two goods X_1 (which it also exports) and X_2 which it imports. International trade, however, involves the expending of resources.[14] Resources spent here are called 'distributive output' (D) and, to keep things simple, the amount of imports is set equal to D, i.e:

$$D = x_2. \tag{6.60}$$

One unit of D entails exchanging one unit of imports for food with the agricultural sector at the domestic terms of trade and exporting the food in exchange for imports at the international terms of trade. In the distribution activity we assume that labor required is a fixed fraction of output:

$$L_D = \gamma D, \ \gamma \text{ constant} \tag{6.61}$$

If imports are available internationally at price $p = 1$ (in terms of food)[15] then domestically their price (p_2) has to be higher in order to cover the costs of distributive activity. Thus:

$$p_2 = 1 + p_D.$$

Society's demands for imports are written as:

$$x_2 = f(p_2, x_1) \tag{6.62}$$

x_1 is a scale variable as it is an index of national output. Clearly, $(\partial f / \partial p_2) < 0$ and $(\partial f / \partial x_1) > 0$.

Since the international terms of trade between x_1 and x_2 have been set equal to 1 we can write food consumption F as:

$$F = x_1 - x_2. \tag{6.63}$$

The total labor available in this economy is given by $\bar{L}$ so that there is an aggregate labor constraint:

$$\bar{L} = L_A + L_D + L_R \tag{6.64}$$

where L_R is the amount of labor engaged in rent seeking.

The algebra of the solution for equilibrium of this economy is relatively straightforward but it is more revealing to look at the solution diagrammatically. In Figure 6.4 we depict the free trade solution for this economy. If all labor is engaged in the production of food the maximum output that is possible is OF. If there were no distribution costs, society could choose along the line FA. However, since society wants both goods, labor has to be withdrawn from agriculture. Every unit of food can be exchanged for one unit of the imported good in the international market. However, to get imports one has to expend labor in the distribution activity. With diminishing marginal product of labor in agriculture, the domestic cost of additional imports in terms of food rises. Hence the consumption possibility set for this economy looks like FB. International trading opportunities are given by the locus BB$_1$. We have also drawn a social indifference curve I_0. The economy comes to an equilibrium such that it consumes ON$_1$ units of food and transfers labor that would have produced N$_1$F units of food to distribution activity to get imports amounting to N$_1$C. The slope of I_0 at C

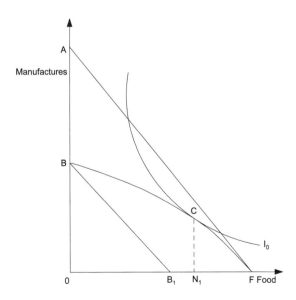

Figure 6.4

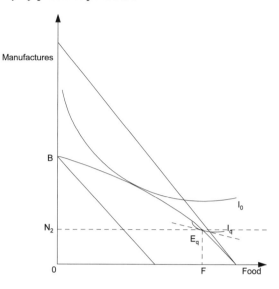

Figure 6.5

shows the domestic rate of transformation of X_1 and X_2 in equilibrium. It shows that one would have to give up more than one unit of food to get one unit of the import even though the international relative price is 1.

Let us now look at the consequences of restricting imports to a maximum of N_2O as shown in Figure 6.5. A quota has been imposed. This quota creates an excess demand for imports and its domestic price (in terms of food) rises. This would mean that importers who import at the relative price of 1 would be able to make considerable profits at home. We further assume that there is no lobbying (rent seeking). Equilibrium occurs at the point E_q. Society can come only to a lower indifference curve I_q. (We have also drawn in the free trade social indifference curve I_0). But the fact that all labor is being used up in the production of food and distribution means that the consumption possibility frontier remains unaltered.

Let us now permit rent-seeking activity. People realize that there are extra-normal profits to be made from selling imports and they lobby for rights to this quota. Resources are spent in rent seeking. Since labor is the only factor of production in this model, from equation (6.64) we get the result that the amount of labor in the production of food and distribution is reduced. In other words, the consumption possibility frontier **shrinks**.

With reference to Figure 6.6 with a quota equal to N_2O and rent seeking we are at the point E_r within the consumption possibility frontier. The domestic relative price will change as is shown in the diagram. The no rent-seeking quota equilibrium (E_q) and the free trade equilibrium (E_f) are also shown in the diagram. Rent seeking lowers welfare and leads to a wastage of resources.

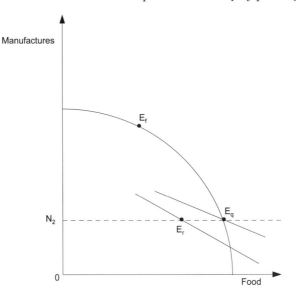

Figure 6.6

In the case of public goods, rent seeking is an important phenomenon. The literature on rent seeking has a long and important history. See, for example, Buchanan (1980), Bhagwati (1982), Becker (1983), van Winden (1983), Bates (1988), van Velthoven (1989) and Pedersen (1995). The analysis here will follow, in the main, the work of Pedersen (1995).

Suppose a bureaucrat b has been put in charge of the distribution of tax burden associated with a public good. There are three types of individuals in society. People of type k and w can influence the allocation of tax burden, whereas people of type o have no influence whatsoever. The bureaucrat, implicitly or explicitly, tries to maximize a weighted average of the welfare of people of types 1 and 2. For these two types of consumers the budget constraint is written as:

$$C_i = Y_i - B_i - T_i (i = 1, 2) \tag{6.65}$$

where C_i is consumption, Y_i is income, B_i is the amount spent on rent seeking (bribes paid), and T_i is the tax paid by individual of type i. The utility of a consumer of type i takes the simple form:

$$U_i = \ln C_i. \tag{6.66}$$

Since the amount of the public good produced has already been decided this appears as a constant and is omitted from the utility function without any loss of generality. The significant issue here is the distribution of the tax burden – not the amount of the public good produced.

Y_i is exogenous but taxes can be lowered by paying bribes. Hence, in optimum, it must be the case that individual i will pay bribes such that:

$$dC_i/dB_i = -dT_i/dB_i - 1 = 0. \tag{6.67}$$

When determining how much resources to spend on rent seeking, each agent considers the amount on rent seeking by the other type of person as being given. Hence, we can define a reaction function for each type of agent and compute the Nash equilibrium.

Without loss of generality, it is assumed that the utility of the private person o, who does not have any influence, is kept fixed at some level $\bar{U}_o$. Taxes paid by this agent are, simply, $Y_o - C_o$.

Aggregate private production GDP_p can be written as:

$$GDP_p = (Y_1 - B_1) + (Y_2 - B_2) + Y_o \tag{6.68}$$

whereas maximum (GDP_m, when no resources are wasted on rent seeking) is:

$$GDP_m = Y_1 + Y_2 + Y_0. \tag{6.69}$$

The bureaucrat tries to maximize a social welfare function which is a weighted average of the utility of people of types k and w. This is written as:

$$SW = \beta_1 \ln C_1^e + \beta_2 \ln C_2^e \tag{6.70}$$

where $\beta_i (> 0)$ is the weight given to the utility of the ith individual and C_i^e is the consumption of the ith individual as perceived by the bureaucrat. It is assumed that the bureaucrat has been instructed not to accept the agents' perception of their consumption. From the point of view of the bureaucrat we assume that a one-unit increase in B_i causes a reduction of private consumption by b_i units:

$$C_i^e = Y_i - T_i - b_i B_i. \tag{6.71}$$

If rent seeking is entirely of the unproductive variety then $b_i = 1$. In general it would be less than one.

The public sector's budget equation is written as:

$$T_1 + T_2 + T_0 = E \tag{6.72}$$

where E is the amount of expenditure on the public good which, without loss of generality, may be set equal to zero.

The bureaucrat now maximizes the social welfare function (6.70) with respect to T_1 and T_2, subject to the budget relation (6.72) and the weights β_1 and β_2. T_o is determined as a residual.

The resulting tax functions are:

$$T_1 = \beta_2 [Y_1 - b_1 B_1] - \beta_1 [T_0 + (Y_2 - b_2 B_2)] \tag{6.73a}$$
$$T_2 = \beta_1 [Y_2 - b_2 B_2] - \beta_2 [T_0 + (Y_1 - b_1 B_1)]. \tag{6.73b}$$

Agent 2's weight in the welfare function, β_2, can be thought of as the marginal tax rate on individual 1 and vice versa. The bureaucrat's perception of the consumption of the two agents is:

$$C_1^e = \beta_1[(Y_1 - b_1B_1) + (Y_2 - b_2B_2) + T_0] \qquad (6.74a)$$
$$C_2^e = \beta_2[(Y_1 - b_1B_1) + (Y_2 - b_2B_2) + T_0]. \qquad (6.74b)$$

The term $[(Y_1 - b_1B_1) + (Y_2 - b_2B_2) + T_0]$ may be thought of as the bureaucrat's perception of the total income and consumption that can be distributed between agents 1 and 2.

Given these results, it would obviously be in the interest of both agents to try to influence the weights (βs) that are assigned to them. Pedersen uses some results of Becker (1983) to try to endogenize the βs. He writes:

$$\beta_1 = I_1/(I_1 + I_2) \qquad (6.75a)$$
$$\beta_2 = I_2/(I_1 + I_2) \qquad (6.75b)$$

where I_i is the amount of 'influence' that agent i has. This could include, for example, as index of the number of legislators who can lobby for him, the size of his private army and so on. Let B_i^x be some exogenous political capital or goodwill that agent i enjoys. Then, I_i would depend on B_i^x plus the amount spent on bribes. Hence, we can write:

$$I_1 = \delta_1(B_1^x + B_1) \text{ with } B_1^x \geqslant 0 \text{ and } \delta_1 > 0 \text{ and}$$
$$I_2 = \delta_2(B_2^x + B_2) \text{ with } B_2^x \geqslant 0 \text{ and } \delta_2 > 0.$$

Agent o with no political influence has $\delta_o = 0$. δ is a response function of the bureaucrat to the agent's rent-seeking behavior.

We look now at an example where $\Delta = \delta_2/\delta_1 > 1$ and $B_2^x > B_1^x$. In this case, agent 1 would have to spend more on bribery[16] in order to get the same political influence as agent 2. This is demonstrated in Figure 6.7. This figure illustrates how β_1 and β_2 vary with the extent of agent 1's rent-seeking behavior. This diagram is drawn under the assumption that the amount of rent seeking engaged in by agent 2 is given at $\bar{B}_2$ and that there is no exogenous political capital for any agent, i.e., $\beta_1^x = \beta_2^x = 0$.[17] Political reform taking the form of an increase in β_1^x and/or a reduction of Δ will lead to an upward shift of the β_1 schedule and a downward shift of the β_2 schedule.

We can now write:

$$dT_1/dB_1 = -\beta_2b_1 - (\partial\beta_1/\partial B_1)[(Y_1 - b_1B_1) + (Y_2 - b_2B_2) + T_0] < 0 \qquad (6.76a)$$
$$dT_2/dB_2 = -\beta_1b_2 - (\partial\beta_2/\partial B_2)[(Y_1 - b_1B_1) + (Y_2 - b_2B_2) + T_0] < 0 \qquad (6.76b)$$

with

$$(\partial\beta_1/\partial B_1) = \delta_1I_2/(I_1 + I_2)^2 > 0 \qquad (6.77a)$$
$$(\partial\beta_2/\partial B_2) = \delta_2I_1/(I_1 + I_2)^2 > 0. \qquad (6.77b)$$

Equations (6.76) can be interpreted in the following manner. When determining the extent of rent seeking (B_i) agent i perceives two types of benefits. For a given level of δ_i, so long as $b_i > 0$, there is a tax reduction

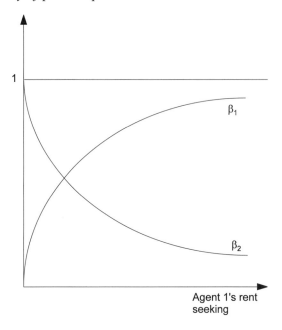

Figure 6.7

caused by a decline in agent i's tax base when B_i is increased. In the polar case when $b_i = 1$, there is one-dollar reduction in the tax base for every dollar spent on rent seeking. In addition, from equation (6.77) since δ_i increases with rent seeking, agent i is able to capture a larger part of total income.

Now, using equations (6.76) and (6.77) the quantity of resources used in rent-seeking activities (B_1 and B_2) by agent i ($i = 1, 2$) can be calculated. Their weights in the welfare function β_1 and β_2 can then be computed from equation (6.75). The distribution of tax burden will be given by equations (6.73). Consumption levels for the two individuals are then obtained as residuals from equation (6.65).

Pedersen then does comparative static analysis of this model and also solves it for two special cases: (i) $b_1 = b_2 = 1$; (ii) $b_1 = b_2 = 0$.

6.8   CONCLUSIONS

This has been a long and complex chapter. Several issues in the theory of public goods have been considered in order to give students an idea of the range of issues that has been discussed in the literature. Results have been hard to come by and seem to be applicable in special cases. This is as we would expect of an area that is inherently so difficult and so much in the center of active research. We have considered the theory of single and multi-product clubs, the Tiebout hypothesis, public goods supply with distortionary taxation and asymmetric information and the theory of risk taking.

The range of issues considered in this chapter, although large, is by no means an exhaustive list of the work being done in the theory of public goods. However, it should equip students to venture out in the world of journals and read the work being done at the frontiers.

NOTES

1 Sandler and Tschirhart (1993) show that the results here can be extended to cover the case when the number of visits is another variable.
2 We assume that club members are price takers with regard to this price.
3 These may be single-product clubs or subsets of the number of services m.
4 Hence redistributive considerations are eschewed.
5 If there was a lump sum payment Y then this would also enter the indirect utility function.
6 If the additional unit of the public good was financed by increasing taxes so as to increase the dispersion of taxes then the substitution and income effects would work in the same direction and the mc of the public good will unambiguously go up.
7 In other words the utility function is written as $U(l, d, G) = U^1(l, d) + U^2(G)$.
8 Such agencies can be of two types: high cost or low cost.
9 This is done for analytical convenience. Getting qualitative results with general utility functions is not possible.
10 Tax is modeled in this fashion in order to minimize the algebra. It is easy to see that a regular wage tax could easily have been accommodated.
11 See, for example, Laffont and Tirole (1993).
12 For a proof see Boadway *et al.* (1996).
13 Call this food.
14 These could be thought of as resources spent in collecting and processing orders for exports as well as imports.
15 The domestic price of food is assumed to be equal to its international price.
16 If there is no rent seeking then the βs depend upon political endowments alone. $\beta_1 = B_1^x/(B_1^x + \Delta B_2^x)$ and $\beta_2 = B_2^x/(B_1^x + \Delta B_2^x)$.
17 Otherwise, the β schedules would have an intercept.

ADDITIONAL READING

The theory of public goods is well discussed in Oakland (1987) and Inman (1987). Also useful are Mueller (1979) and Musgrave and Musgrave (1982). For a good treatment of the theory of clubs see Cornes and Sandler (1986) and Brueckner and Lee (1991).

Part III
The theory of taxation

Introduction to Part III

This is the largest section of the book and contains ten chapters. Various aspects of the theory of taxation are considered. There are several broad areas of concern in the theory of taxation: incentive effects of taxes; tax incidence; optimal taxation and mix of direct and indirect taxation; tax reform and international aspects of taxation. All these facets of the theory of taxation are considered here.

Chapter 7 considers the incentive effects of taxation on savings behavior. We begin with the effects of wage taxation in the two-period, life-cycle model of savings and labor supply. The conflict between the income and substitution effects in various contexts is worked out. This leads to the prediction that the elasticity of tax with respect to the after-tax interest rate is small. We then consider the incentive effects of taxation on savings when there are capital market distortions. We then examine broader models of savings and taxation – in particular the work of Summers who argues that the interest elasticity of savings is much higher in more complex life-cycle models (and reality) than the two-period one. This result leads to the question of whether expenditure taxes would be more suitable than income taxes. This issue is considered in detail here. The chapter also discusses the links between saving and social security as well as computable models of effects of taxation on savings. A review of the empirical evidence on savings and taxation is also provided.

Chapter 8 deals with the effects of taxation on labor supply. We begin by considering the basic one-period model of labor supply and detail the conflict between the income and substitution effects of an increase in the wage tax on labor supply. The effects of various tax structures – lump sum, proportional, progressive – are also compared. The effect of an income tax in affecting the decision to enter the labor market is also discussed. The chapter also examines the effect of tax progression on aggregate labor supply and closes with a review of the empirical evidence on the effects of taxation on labor supply.

In Chapter 10 we consider the effects of taxation on investment behavior. We begin with a discussion of the Fisherian and neoclassical approaches to the determination of investment. Then we proceed to model the effects of corporate taxation, depreciation allowance and the investment tax credit on investment behavior by the firm. We compare the stimulative effects of an increase in the investment tax credit and a cut in the corporate tax rate. The effects of inflation in distorting the incentive to invest are also considered. We then move to analyze some simple financial theories of investment and the role that personal taxes play in this. There is, in this context, a preliminary discussion of the Modigliani–Miller theorem. Measures of the effective rate of tax due to King–Fullerton and others are also discussed and these are extended to cover an open economy.

Chapter 10 considers the effects of taxation on risk taking. We begin by proving Sandmo's classic result that the elasticity of the amount of a consumer's wealth in the risky asset depends only upon the tax rate and not upon the return on the risky asset or the form of the utility function. We then prove the Modigliani–Miller theorem and consider some cases when it may not hold exactly. The chapter closes with an analysis of the effects of increasing progression on risk taking.

Chapters 11 and 12 are concerned with tax incidence analysis. In Chapter 11 we examine tax incidence in three models of static general equilibrium. We consider the static two-sector general equilibrium model with full employment and derive, in considerable detail, the factor substitution and output effects of various taxes. We then look at a model of tax incidence in a general equilibrium model with involuntary unemployment. Finally we consider tax incidence in a model with one sector operating under conditions of a rate of return regulation.

In Chapter 12 we consider tax incidence in growing economies. We develop the standard Solow model of economic growth and examine the effects of various taxes on steady state growth. Bonds are introduced into this model and the notion of balanced growth path incidence – one that leaves the capital/labor ratio unchanged – is developed. We also develop the two-period Diamond life-cycle model and discuss balanced growth path incidence as well as the incidence of redistributive taxation. Tax incidence in more general life-cycle models like those of Blanchard and Yaari is also discussed. Finally, two questions of lasting interest in dynamic tax incidence theory are taken up. First, is the question of the incidence of a tax on land and the second is the question of choice of fiscal instrument. Given that government expenditure is to go up, how should it be financed – by issuing bonds or by taxation?

In Chapter 13 we consider aspects of commodity taxation. We begin by proving three important 'elasticity' type results in the theory of commodity taxation: those relating to compensated and uncompensated elasticities of demand as well as the Corlett–Hague result. These three results refer to efficiency in commodity taxation. We then delineate the cases under which uniform commodity taxation is optimal. Redistributive commodity taxation is also considered. We try to understand how much redistribution is possible through commodity taxation and realize that this extent is quite limited.

There is also a discussion of the popular value added tax (VAT) and the experience that some countries have had with it.

Chapter 14 considers optimal income taxation. We begin by deriving the properties of an optimal redistributive linear income tax. We then consider Ramsey–Mirrlees type optimal non-linear taxation with one as well as many goods. Then optimal taxation with imperfect information about worker skills is considered. We consider both cases – when the elasticity of substitution between labor types is (alternately) infinite and finite. We then examine optimal intra- as well as inter-generational taxation in a dynamic model. The old direct versus indirect tax debate is also taken up. The literature has typically emphasized the superiority of direct taxes. Recent work which says that under uncertainty we require a mix of direct and indirect taxes – not just direct taxes – is also discussed.

Chapter 15 discusses three important topics in tax theory. The first deals with tax policy in a model of endogenous growth where expenditures on research and development determine the rate of technological progress and, therefore, the rate of growth of the economy. We then study models of income tax indexation in an inflationary economy. This chapter also provides an introduction to the recent theories of time inconsistency in dynamic tax policy models. We develop notions of time-consistent and time-inconsistent equilibria and illustrate these notions in the context of a popular model due to Stanley Fischer. The chapter also illustrates some problems associated with tax evasion. Tax evasion by firms and households is analyzed and the role of borrowing constraints is also discussed.

Chapter 16 is concerned with tax reform. The basic elements of recent tax reforms in various countries are discussed. Tax reform in the Diamond–Mirrlees framework is examined. There is then some discussion of tax reform in a dynamic context. These reforms are studied with respect both to balanced and unbalanced government budgets. Finally we discuss the marginal approach to tax reform when tax reforms are guided by calculations of marginal costs and benefits of public funds that are associated with such reforms.

7 The effects of taxes on savings

Key concepts: life cycle models of taxation and savings; aggregate effects of taxation and savings; expenditure taxation; Blanchard–Yaari model of consumption; social security, pensions and benefits.

7.1 INTRODUCTION

With this chapter we begin our analysis of the incentive effects of taxation. In later chapters we consider labor supply, investment behavior, and risk taking.

The issue of how taxes affect savings is important for several reasons, most of which deal with the importance of additional investment and, therefore, savings for higher economic growth. This is crucial, for obvious reasons, for developing countries but is also relevant for richer nations where sagging rates of savings have aroused concern and led to examination of the role of taxation in the determination of savings.

We will first study models which may be called traditional in the sense that they present the tax (and therefore interest) elasticity of savings as the resolution of an income effect – substitution effect conflict. One effect tends to make savings go up when the after-tax interest rate goes up and the other tends to lower it. This branch of the literature then suggests a relatively low interest elasticity of savings. We will then extend this somewhat by bringing in variable labor supply and present a more modern version of the life-cycle hypothesis where the interest elasticity of savings can be much higher than the standard life-cycle models. We also consider some models of savings for retirement as well as the effects of expenditure taxes on savings. We finally review some empirical evidence on the effects of taxes on savings.

7.2 THE ELEMENTARY LIFE-CYCLE MODEL OF SAVING

In the simplest version of this model a consumer lives for two time periods (1 and 2). In the first time period she works, consumes and saves and in the second time period she is retired and consumes her savings. The duration of the working and the retirement phase are perfectly known, as is the time of death. There is only one rate of interest which is applied to her savings and she is paid principal and interest at the beginning of the second period. In the simplest version of the model, labor supply is contractually fixed and there are no opportunities for work in the second time period.

The consumer's utility function is written as $U(c_1, c_2)$ where c_i is consumption in period i $(i = 1, 2)$ and her life-time budget constraint is $c_1 + c_2/(1 + r) = w$ where r is the interest rate and w is the income earned by the consumer in the first time period. With a tax t_r on interest income and t_w on wage income the budget constraint can be written as:

$$c_1 + c_2/(1 + r(1 - t_r)) = w(1 - t_w) \qquad (7.1)$$

Two points are worth observing about equation (7.1). The imposition of the wage tax should be looked upon here as a lump-sum or non-distortionary tax. A wage tax does not alter the choice between the present and the future. Moreover, since the supply of labor is fixed, all that the wage tax does is to reduce lifetime wealth and, therefore, both c_1 and c_2. An interest tax, on the other hand, does alter the choice between the present and future. It lowers the opportunity cost of present consumption (the substitution effect). This, in itself, should increase present consumption and lower savings. However, the income effect of a reduction in the net rate of interest would tend to lower current consumption (increase savings). This is the essential conflict between the substitution effect and the income effect which is portrayed in Figure 7.1. In this figure we have traced the effects of a reduction in the net rate of interest on the consumer. In case (a) savings rise after a drop in the net rate of interest (the income effect dominates); in case (b) savings fall, which implies that the substitution effect dominates.

Let us write $p = 1/(1 + r)$ as the price of consumption in the second period in terms of first-period consumption so that the budget constraint is written as:

$$c_1 + pc_2 = w.$$

We can write the Slutsky equations for changes in p as:

$$\partial c_1/\partial p = \partial c_1/\partial p|_{dU=0} - c_2 \partial c_1/\partial w. \qquad (7.2)$$

The first term of this expression is the substitution effect which goes to increase first-period consumption, whereas the second term is the income effect which tends to decrease first-period consumption. If we write the Slutsky equation for c_2 and assume c_2 to be a normal good, we will come to the conclusion that a drop in the rate of interest will unambiguously reduce second-period consumption as both the income as well as the substitution effects work in the same direction.

We can now define the elasticity of substitution between first- and second-period consumption as:

$$\sigma = \frac{d\ln(c_2/c_1)}{d\ln(1 + r)}\bigg|_{dU=0} = [\partial \ln c_1/\partial \ln p]|_{dU=0} - [\partial \ln c_2/\partial \ln p]|_{dU=0}. \qquad (7.3)$$

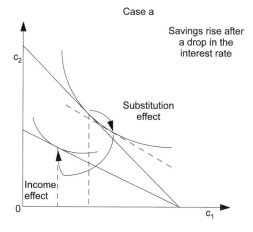

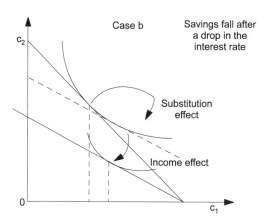

Figure 7.1

From the fact that the expenditure function is homogeneous of degree one in prices (see Chapter 1) we know that:

$$\partial c_1/\partial \ln p|_{dU=0} + p\partial c_2/\partial \ln p|_{dU=0} = 0. \tag{7.4}$$

Substituting equations (7.3) and (7.4) into the Slutsky equation for c_1 we get:

$$\partial \ln c_1/\partial p = s(\sigma - \delta) \tag{7.5}$$

where s is the rate of savings $(pc_2/(c_1 + pc_2))$ and δ is the wealth elasticity of first-period consumption. Thus, for example, if the utility function is of the Cobb–Douglas form:
$U = c_1^\alpha c_2^\beta$; with $1 \geqslant \alpha \geqslant 0, 1 \geqslant \beta \geqslant 0$ then $\sigma = 1$ and if the income elasticity of consumption also equals one, then, the substitution effect and the

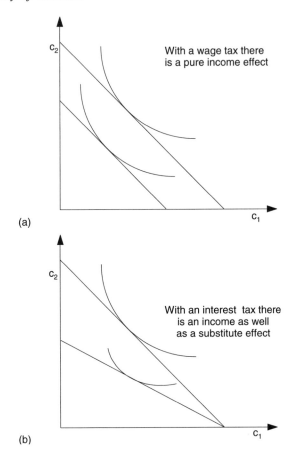

Figure 7.2

income effect will exactly cancel each other out and there will be no change in savings following a drop in the after-tax interest rate.

So long as the supply of labor is fixed, a wage tax will not have anything but a wealth effect, irrespective of whether the consumer earns non-wage income or income in the second period. In such cases, the analysis of the effects of a wage tax will be as in Figure 7.2a and that of an interest tax as in Figure 7.2b. In Figure 7.2a a wage tax causes a parallel shifting-in of the individual's budget line reducing both c_1 and c_2. If the utility function is homothetic, then the consumption of both will, in post-tax equilibrium, be in the same proportion as in the pre-tax equilibrium. In Figure 7.2b the relative price of first-period consumption changes and there are the usual substitution and income effects.

A remarkable change to this analysis occurs if labor is variable, rather than being contractually fixed. Suppose the utility function is now written as $U(c_1, c_2, L)$ where L is leisure. The total amount of time available to the individual is H so that time worked is H-L. The budget constraint of the individual can be written as:

$$c_1 + c_2/(1+r) = w(H-L) + I \qquad (7.6)$$

where I is non-wage income.

Performing the maximization of the utility function with respect to c_1, c_2 and L subject to the budget constraint in equation (7.6) we will obtain from the first-order conditions: (U_i is the partial derivative of the utility function with respect to the ith argument. All three goods – first-period consumption, second-period consumption and leisure are desirable).

$$U_2/U_1 = 1/(1+r) \rightarrow U_2 = U_1/(1+r) \qquad (7.7a)$$
$$U_3/U_1 = w \qquad \rightarrow U_3 = U_1 w \qquad (7.7b)$$

From this we easily derive:

$$U_3/U_2 = w(1+r). \qquad (7.7c)$$

Hence, we now have three commodities and essentially only two relative prices. We can assume that the income effects are positive as before. Since all three goods are assumed normal an increase in income would, ceteris paribus, increase demand for all three goods. As far as substitution effects are concerned, we can safely assume that 'own' effects are negative. An increase in the interest rate, with utility held constant will raise the relative price of first-period consumption and, therefore, increase second-period consumption (savings). Thus: $(\partial c_2/\partial r)|_{dU=0} > 0$. Again, an increase in the wage rate, with utility held constant, will raise the price of leisure and, therefore, reduce leisure: $(\partial L/\partial w)|_{dU=0} < 0$.

For a constant utility level the interest rate must satisfy:

$$U_1(\partial c_1/\partial r)|_{dU=0} + U_2(\partial c_2/\partial r)|_{dU=0} + U_3(\partial L/\partial r)|_{dU=0} = 0.$$

Substituting from the second parts of equations (7.7a) and (7.7b) we have:

$$(\partial c_1/\partial r)|_{dU=0} + [1/(1+r)][\partial c_2/\partial r]|_{dU=0} + w(\partial L/\partial r)|_{dU=0} = 0. \qquad (7.8)$$

From equations (7.7a) and (7.7b) it is not possible to deduce the sign of the first term on the lefthand side of equation (7.8). If labor is fixed then the last term on the lefthand side of (7.8) is zero and we know that the second term is positive so that the first term must be negative. However, in the present case leisure and c_2 can be Hicksian substitutes so that c_1 and c_2 could end up being complements so that c_1 could be positively related to the interest rate along the Hicksian demand curve. Hence the substitution term for c_1 (the first term on the lefthand side of equation (7.8)) is not unambiguously negative. It will be so only if leisure and c_2 are Hicksian complements. This is an important result. The impact of interest and, for that matter since labor is variable, a wage tax depends upon the exact relations, along Hicksian demand, between c_1, c_2 and L.

We can easily extend the model to consider other cases. Under a general income tax the consumer's budget constraint can be written as:

$$c_1 + c_2/(1 + r(1 - t)) = w(1 - t)(H - L) + I(1 - t). \qquad (7.9)$$

This is the usual Haig–Simons definition of an income tax with all forms of income: interest, wage and other non-wage income taxed at the common rate t. This will clearly have both income and substitution effects. If labor is variable then substitution and income effects will apply to both wage and interest taxation. If labor is fixed in supply, then the substitution effect will apply only to the interest tax and the wage tax will have a pure income effect.

A general expenditure tax or an indirect tax at rate τ will change the budget constraint as:

$$(1 + \tau)c_1 + [(1 + \tau)/(1 + r)][c_2] = w(H - L) + I. \qquad (7.10)$$

Dividing through by $(1 + \tau)$ we have:

$$c_1 + c_2/(1 + r) = [w/(1 + \tau)][H - L] + I/(1 + \tau). \qquad (7.11)$$

So an expenditure tax is like an income tax with interest income exempt. Hence, if labor is fixed, an expenditure tax will have only an income effect. If, however, labor is variable, then an expenditure tax will have a substitution as well as an income effect.

From equation (7.11) it is clear that the imposition of the indirect tax or the expenditure tax has effects equivalent to a reduction of the wage rate and the non-wage income, leaving the net rate of interest unchanged. One might be tempted, on this basis, to say that the income tax by distorting the interest rate is more discriminatory toward saving. But one has to be careful about the basis of comparison. If one uses constant utility as the basis for comparison then the interest rate is higher under indirect or expenditure taxation but the net wage must be lower. What is involved is a comparison of two cross-substitution effects on present consumption, and the outcome of this cannot be decided on a priori grounds.

There is another important aspect which we should discuss – the optimal tax treatment of savings. This is explored in a series of papers: e.g. Ordover (1976), Ordover and Phelps (1979), Atkinson and Sandmo (1980) and M. King (1980). We pick up this theme in Chapter 14. In Table 7.1 we compress our principal results on the effects of taxes.

7.3   CAPITAL MARKET IMPERFECTIONS AND THE LIFE-CYCLE MODEL

In this section we try to study a simple model of imperfections in the capital market along the lines of Jaffee and Russell (1976), Stiglitz and Weiss (1979), Atkinson and Stiglitz (1980), Sandmo (1987a). This problem is studied in Figure 7.3.

Table 7.1 Comparative static properties of alternative life-cycle models

Fixed labor supply model

$$U = U(c_1, c_2); c_1 + c_2/(1 + r) = w + I$$

	Decision variable	
Parameter increasing	c_1	c_2
w or I	+	+
r (compensated)	−	+

Variable labor supply model

$$U = U(c_1, c_2, L); c_1 + c_2/(1 + r) = w(H - L) + I$$

	Decision variable		
Parameter increasing	c_1	c_2	L
I	+	+	+
r (compensated)	?	+	?
w (compensated)	?	?	−

Suppose the consumer earns income w_1 in the first time period and w_2 in the second. Let us denote lifetime earnings as $E = w_1 + w_2/(1 + r)$. In Figure 7.3 AA^1 is the budget line under the assumption that capital markets are perfect – the borrowing and lending rates of interest are the same and the consumer is free to lend and borrow any amount at this rate of interest – and no taxation of interest income. We will denote by $p = (1/(1 + r))$ the relative price of consumption, as before. Equilibrium in the absence of taxation occurs at *P*.

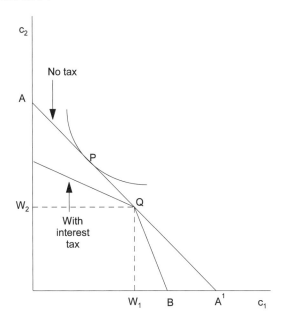

Figure 7.3

If we have a tax on interest income the budget line to the north-west of the no-borrowing, no-lending point Q will tilt anti-clockwise denoting the fact that the after-tax rate of return on savings (lendings) has fallen. If the consumer is a borrower in the first time period and if interest payments are tax deductible, then the budget constraint south-east of Q remains QA^1. If interest payments are not tax deductible, however, then the budget line will have a kink at Q and the portion south-east of Q will shrink to QB.

As before the Slutsky equation for this problem can be written as:

$$\partial c_i / \partial p = \partial c_i / \partial p_{|dU=0} - (c_2 - w_2)\partial c_i / \partial E.$$

If c_2 is nearly equal to w_2 then the substitution effect will dominate and the imposition of the tax will lower savings.

If there is no deductibility of tax paid on interest then people to the right of Q (net borrowers) are unaffected by the tax. If the borrowing and lending rates (r_b and r_1) are different, typically $r_b > r_1$, then, under certain conditions, people will neither borrow nor lend. Atkinson and Stiglitz (1980) study the following constant elasticity utility function:

$$U^{1-(1/\sigma)} = c_1^{1-(1/\sigma)} + [1/(1+\delta)]c_2^{1-(1/\sigma)}$$

where δ is the 'subjective' discount factor. This utility function is maximized subject to the following budget constraint:

$$c_1 + c_2/(1+r) = w_1 + w_2/(1+r)$$

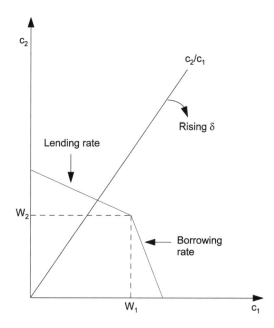

Figure 7.4

where $r = r_b$ (if the consumer is a borrower) and $r = r_1$ (if the consumer is a lender).

The optimal consumption plan will satisfy:

$$[c_2/c_1] = [(1+r)/(1+\delta)]^\sigma.$$

As can be seen from Figure 7.4 as we consider larger values of δ the chosen point moves toward the kink. Let us suppose that people have different discount rates (δ_1 for lenders and δ_2 for borrowers). At some values of δ_1 and δ_2 we will have:

$$[(1+r_1)/(1+\delta_1)]^\sigma = w_2/w_1 = [(1+r_b)/(1+\delta_2)]^\sigma.$$

w_2 and w_1 are assumed to be the same for both borrowers as well as lenders. Hence, individuals with δ in the range $\delta_1 \leqslant \delta \leqslant \delta_2$ will choose to be neither borrowers nor lenders. This is a well-known result of Stiglitz and Weiss (1979) that in imperfect capital markets, some consumers would choose neither to lend nor borrow.

7.4 BROADER LIFE-CYCLE MODELS OF SAVINGS AND TAXES

It is a relatively straightforward matter to extend the analysis to a multi-period framework. Suppose that an individual expects to live for T time periods.[1] Thus he is interested in maximizing his utility $U(c_1, \ldots, c_T)$. The wage income in period t is w_t. If the interest rate in period t is r then the individual consumer's budget constraint can be written as:

$$\frac{\sum_{t=1}^{T} w_t}{\sum_{t=1}^{T}(1+r)^{t-1}} = \frac{\sum_{t=1}^{T} c_t}{\sum_{t=1}^{T}(1+r)^{t-1}}. \tag{7.12}$$

This framework can easily be extended to include bequests received (B_0) and bequests left behind (B_T). Both get included in the budget constraint whereas the latter will also have to figure in the consumer's utility function. The problem can then be written as: Max $U(c_1, \ldots, c_T, B_T)$ by choosing $c_1, \ldots, c_T, B_T$ subject to:

$$\sum_{t=1}^{T} w_t/(1+r)^{t-1} + B_0 = \sum_{t=1}^{T} c_t/(1+r)^{t-1} + B_T/(1+r)^T \tag{7.13}$$

Any pair of taxes (t_1, t_2) that affect the lefthand side and righthand side of the budget constraint in the same manner are equivalent in their effects on consumer choice. Thus a proportional tax t_1 on wage income plus inheritance reduces net resources and alters the budget constraint to read:

$$\left[\sum_{t=1}^{T} w_t/(1+r)^{t-1} + B_0\right](1-t_1) = \sum_{t=1}^{T} c_t/(1+r)^{t-1} + B_T/(1+r)^T. \tag{7.14}$$

A proportional tax at rate t_2 on consumption plus bequests would increase gross expenditure and the budget constraint would read:

$$\sum_{t=1}^{T} w_t/(1+r)^{t-1} + B_0 = \left[\sum_{t=1}^{T} c_t/(1+r)^{t-1} + B_T/(1+r)^T\right](1+t_2) \quad (7.15)$$

If the nominal effects of the two taxes are the same (i.e. if the imposition of t_1 reduces receipts by the same amount as the imposition of t_2 increases gross expenditure) then the two sets of taxes have equivalent effects on the consumer's equilibrium. In a completely analogous manner one can speak of other pairs of equivalent taxes, e.g., taxes only on bequests and inheritances or on wage income and consumption, etc. It should be remembered, however, that the assumption of perfect capital markets is central to this analysis. Imperfect capital markets will disturb this equilibrium in a profound manner (see, for instance, Jha 1986).

It would be a relatively simple manner to extend the analysis to consider variable labor supply. Suppose the consumer works for l time periods $l < T$. With variable labor supply, the consumer's utility function can be written as:

$$U(c_1,\ldots,c_T;L_1,\ldots L_l,B_T)$$

and his budget constraint is written as:

$$\sum_{t=1}^{T} c_t/(1+r)^{t-1} + B_T = \sum_{t=1}^{l}(H_t - L_t)w_t/(1+r)^{t-1} + B_0.$$

7.5   AGGREGATE SAVINGS AND TAXATION

The analysis that we have conducted so far would generally tend to predict a low elasticity of savings with respect to the interest rate. However, there are good reasons why the life-cycle models detailed above may be inappropriate for analyzing the behavior of savings in the aggregate. This problem was addressed in an important paper by Summers (1981).

Summers argues that the standard two-period formulation of the savings decision obscures two important points. First, savings are carried on to finance future consumption. Eventually each saver will dissave all his savings. Positive savings arise because the young who save are more numerous and more affluent than the old who are dissaving. Second, the standard model does not have a good treatment of future labor earnings – in particular it does not recognize the fact that in a growing economy the future earnings of the individual are going to increase steadily.

Individuals choose a consumption plan to maximize an intertemporal utility function, subject to a lifetime budget constraint.

$$max \int_0^T U(c_t)e^{-\delta t}dt \quad \text{subject to} \quad \int_0^T C_t e^{-rt}dt = \int_0^V w_t e^{-rt}dt \quad (7.16)$$

where δ is the individual's discount rate, r is the rate of interest, V is the age of retirement and T is the life span of the individual. The analysis is carried out with a constant elasticity utility function so that the Lagrangean for the individual can be written as:

$$
\begin{aligned}
\Lambda &= \int_0^T c_t^\gamma e^{-\delta t} dt - \lambda \left[\int_0^T c_t e^{-rt} dt - \int_0^V w_0 e^{gt} e^{-rt} dt \right] \text{ if } \gamma \neq 0 \\
&= \int_0^T \ln c_t e^{-\delta t} dt - \lambda \left[\int_0^T c_t e^{-rt} dt - \int_0^V w_0 e^{gt} e^{-rt} dt \right] \text{ if } \gamma = 0
\end{aligned}
\tag{7.17}
$$

where γ is the elasticity of the marginal utility function. The expression $1/(1 - \gamma)$ corresponds to the intertemporal elasticity of substitution. It is assumed that the economy is in steady-state equilibrium and growing at a constant rate. Now, it is a well-known result that in a neoclassical growth model the only kind of neutral technical progress that is consistent with steady-state growth is Harrod neutral or labor-augmenting technical progress (see, for example, Burmeister and Dobell 1970). Such technical progress amounts to a growth in labor productivity and therefore, under competitive conditions, a rise in the wage rate at a rate equal to the rate of labor augmenting technical progress. In the case above, labor augmenting technical progress is assumed to occur at the rate g. Hence, wages are assumed to be growing in steady state at the rate g.

First-order conditions are:

$$
\partial \Lambda / \partial c_t = \int_0^T \gamma c_t^{\gamma-1} e^{-\delta t} dt - \lambda \left[\int_0^T e^{-rt} dt \right] = 0
\tag{7.17a}
$$

which implies that

$$
c_t^{\gamma-1} = [\lambda e^{-rt}]/[\gamma e^{-\delta t}] \quad \text{or that} \quad c_t = [\gamma/\lambda]^{1/(1-\gamma)} e^{(r-\delta)/(1-\gamma)t}
$$

so that

$$
c_t = c_0 e^{(r-\delta)/(1-\gamma)t}.
\tag{7.18}
$$

Upon differentiating the Lagrangean with respect to λ we get: $\partial \Lambda / \partial \lambda = 0$ which implies that $\int_0^T c_t e^{-rt} dt = \int_0^V w_0 e^{(g-r)t} dt$.

Substituting for c_t from equation (7.18) and integrating on both sides we have:

$$
\left[c_0 \frac{e^{\{(r-\delta)/(1-\gamma)-r\}t}}{\{(r-\delta)/(1-\gamma)-r\}} \right]_0^T = \left[w_0 \frac{e^{(g-r)t}}{(g-r)} \right]_0^V
$$

or,

$$
c_0 \frac{e^{\{(r-\delta)/(1-\gamma)T} - e^0}{\{(r-\delta)/(1-\gamma)-r\}} = w_0 \frac{e^{(g-r)V} - e^0}{(g-r)}
$$

where $e^0 = [\gamma/\lambda]^{1/(1-\gamma)}$

so that:

$$c_0 = \frac{w_0\{e^{(g-r)V} - 1\}\{[(r-\delta)/(1-\gamma)] - r\}}{\{e^{\{[(r-\delta)/(1-\gamma)]-r\}T} - 1\}(g-r)}$$ (7.19)

Hence we get the final value for c_t by substituting for c_0 from equation (7.19) in equation (7.18).

Now, in the aggregate, we can write savings, S, as:

$$S = \text{wage income} + \text{capital income} - \text{consumption}$$
$$= wL + rK - C$$

where K is aggregate consumption and C is aggregate consumption. Since savings are added to the capital stock we have:

$$S = (n+g)K$$ (7.20)

where n is the rate of growth of the population.

Thus, $(n+g)K = wL + rK - C$, or $K = (wL - C)/(n+g-r)$.

Hence aggregate savings as a percentage of wage income is:

$$[S/(wL)] = (n+g)K/(wL) = [(n+g)/(wL)][(wL - C)/(n+g-r)]$$
$$= (n+g)[\{C/(wL)\} - 1]/(r-n-g).$$ (7.21)

Substituting for C/wL from equations (7.18) and (7.19) we get the aggregate savings rate:

$$S/(wL) =$$

$$\frac{[(r-\delta)/(1-\gamma) - r][e^{(g-r)V} - 1][e^{([(r-\delta)/(1-\gamma)]-g-n)T} - 1]n(n+g)}{[[(r-\delta)/(1-\gamma)] - n - g][g - r][e^{[(r-\delta)/(1-\gamma)-r]T} - 1](1 - e^{-nV})(r-n-g)}$$
$$- (n+g)/(r-n-g).$$

(7.22)

Equation (7.22) shows that the life-cycle hypothesis gives rise to a steady-state aggregate savings function which may be represented as zero propensity to save out of capital income and variable propensity to save out of labor income. Summers then goes on to demonstrate that with this savings function and plausible values of the parameters γ, δ, T and V the elasticity of savings with respect to the interest rate is quite high. The following general conclusions are warranted from Summers' numerical calculations:

 (i) For given γ the economy saves more at higher interest rates.
 (ii) Higher taxes on savings would reduce effective rate of return to saving which, in turn, would result in a decline in the propensity to save.
(iii) For a given γ the higher the rate of interest, the greater would be the saving by younger people and older people would dissave more.

It would thus appear that an important instrument to improve the savings rate would be the net rate of return on savings. Thus lower interest tax rates would be advised if the objective were to improve rates of saving and investment and, ultimately, the rate of economic growth.

At this point, then, it becomes natural to ask whether complete exemption of savings taxation would be a useful policy option. This is possible, as we have seen, by a substitution of the income tax by a consumption tax. We turn to some issues of the desirability and feasibility of the consumption tax.

7.6 A CONSUMPTION/EXPENDITURE TAX

We now proceed to a detailed comparison of the income, consumption and expenditure tax. We will also have opportunity to comment on the administrative feasibility of the expenditure tax. We follow the work of Kay (1991).

Suppose that an individual lives and works for T years and spends income at the rate of c_t. His assets at time t are written as A_t and, in the absence of bequests, assets at the beginning and end of one's life span are zero. $A_0 = A_T = 0$. The individual earns a wage w per time period and the rate of interest is r per time period. Hence asset accumulation ($\dot{A}$) (a dot (.) above a variable represents a derivative with respect to time) can be written (on dropping time subscripts which just clutter up the notation without adding any insight) as:

$$\dot{A} = w + rA - c \qquad (7.23)$$

so that assets at time t are:

$$A_t = \int_t^T (c - w)e^{-r(\tau - t)}d\tau \int_0^t (w - c)e^{r(t - \tau)}d\tau \qquad (7.24)$$

where the integration over time is written as τ. Let us call a labor tax t_l and a consumption tax t_c. Now, it can easily be seen that a labor tax and a consumption tax are identical if $t_l = t_c/(1 + t_c)$.

To see this realize that with a tax on labor income equation (7.23) can be written as:

$$\dot{A} = (1 - t_l)w + rA - c \qquad (7.25a)$$

whereas with a consumption or a consumption tax we will have:

$$\dot{A} = w + rA - (1 + t_c)c. \qquad (7.25b)$$

With a tax on labor income a consumption plan c_t is feasible if:

$$\int_0^T [(1 - t_l)w + rA - c - \dot{A}]e^{-rt}dt \geqslant 0 \qquad (7.26)$$

i.e., if

$$\int_0^T (1 - t_l)\, we^{-rt}dt \geqslant \int_0^T c_t e^{-rt}dt \qquad (7.27)$$

since $A_0 = A_T = 0$.

With a consumption tax c_t is feasible only if:

$$\int_0^T [w + rA - (1 + t_c)c - \dot{A}]e^{-rt}dt \geq 0 \qquad (7.26a)$$

which amounts as above to saying:

$$\int_0^T [we^{-rt}dt] \geq \int_0^T c_t e^{-rt}dt. \qquad (7.27a)$$

Hence the two sets of taxes are identical only if:

$$(1 - t_l) = 1/(1 + t_c) \text{ so that } t_l = t_c/(1 + t_c).$$

If this condition holds then the same consumption plan will be chosen under both tax regimes. It can further be shown that the tax collections under the two cases will be the same. The present value of tax revenue under the labor income tax is:

$$t_l \int_0^T we^{-rt}dt$$

while under the consumption tax the present value of tax revenue will be:

$$t_c \int_0^T ce^{-rt}dt = t_c/(1 + t_c) \int_0^T we^{-rt}dt.$$

Hence, if $t_l = t_c/(1 + t_c)$ then the two taxes yield the same present value of tax revenue.

Let us now study the case of a comprehensive income tax (t_y) wherein both wage and interest incomes are taxed. With such a tax asset accumulation will be given by:

$$\dot{A} = (1 - t_y)[w + rA] - c. \qquad (7.28)$$

Suppose the pattern of labor earnings over one's lifetime is fixed. Then tax revenue from the income tax is:

$$R_y = \int_0^T t_y(w + rA)e^{-rt}dt$$

whereas under the labor tax it is

$$R_l = \int_0^T t_l we^{-rt}dt.$$

So if the present discounted value of assets $(\int_0^T Ae^{-rt}dt)$ is greater than zero then an income tax applied at the same rate as the consumption tax will yield higher revenue. The value of $(\int_0^T Ae^{-rt}dt)$ denotes how late in lifetime an individual chooses to consume his assets given that he starts out with zero assets and dies without leaving bequests. The later an individual runs down his assets, the greater will be the income tax on him.

We can then define a consumption plan c_{1t} to be later than an alternative c_{2t} if

$$\int_0^T c_{1t}e^r(\tau - t)dt \leqslant \int_0^T c_{2t}e^{r(\tau - t)}dt$$

for some τ_0 and all $\tau \leqslant \tau_0$. This definition is intuitively plausible. Discounted value of consumption under c_1 is lower than that under c_2 over some horizon τ_0.

It is straightforward, then, to prove the intuitively plausible result that an individual with a later consumption plan would pay a higher tax and have a lower present value of lifetime consumption under an income tax as opposed to a consumption tax.

With an income tax, asset accumulation will be given by:

$$\dot{A} = (1 - t_y)(w + rA) - c. \tag{7.29}$$

If w is fixed, then, it must be the case that the difference between asset accumulation along the later plan (1) and the earlier plan (2) at any point in time will be governed by:

$$\dot{A}_1 - \dot{A}_2 = (1 - t_y)r(A_1 - A_2) - (c_1 - c_2). \tag{7.30}$$

Hence over any two points in time T_1 and T_2 it must be the case that:

$$\int_{T_1}^{T_2} (\dot{A}_1 - \dot{A}_2)e^{-rt}dt = (1 - t_y)r\int_{T_1}^{T_2} (A_1 - A_2)e^{-rt}dt - \int_{T_1}^{T_2} (c_1 - c_2)e^{-rt}dt$$

so that

$$[(A_1 - A_2)e^{-rt}]_{T_1}^{T_2} = -t_yr\int_{T_1}^{T_2} (A_1 - A_2)e^{-rt}dt - \int_{T_1}^{T_2} (c_1 - c_2)e^{-rt}dt. \tag{7.31}$$

We can show that the consumption path c_2 cannot cross c_1 as in Figure 7.5. The proof proceeds by contradiction. Suppose there is some T^c such that:

$$\int_0^{T^c} (c_1 - c_2)e^{r(T^c - t)}dt = 0. \tag{7.32}$$

Then by setting $T_2 = T^c$ and $T_1 = 0$ in equation (7.31) we have:

$$[A_1 - A_2]e^{-rT^c} = -t_yr\int_{T^c}^T (A_1 - A_2)e^{-rt}dt. \tag{7.33}$$

and also by setting $T_2 = T$ and $T_1 = T_c$ in equation (7.31) we will have $-[A_1 - A_2]e^{-rT^c} \leqslant -t_yr\int_{T_c}^T (A_1 - A_2)e^{-rt}\,dt$.
Hence, we must have:

$$\int_0^T (A_1 - A_2)e^{-rt}dt \leqslant 0. \tag{7.34}$$

If we set $T_2 = T$ and $T_1 = 0$ in equation (7.31) we will get:

$$t_yr\int_0^T (A_1 - A_2)e^{-rt}dt = \int_{T_1}^{T_2} (c_2 - c_1)e^{-rt}dt \tag{7.35}$$

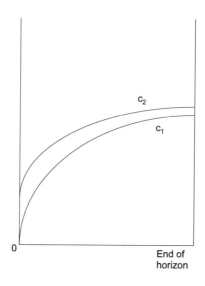

Figure 7.5

which leads to:

$$\int_{T_1}^{T_2} c_2 e^{-rt} dt > \int_{T_1}^{T_2} c_1 e^{-rt} dt. \qquad (7.36)$$

Thus in Figure 7.5 we need only consider cases where:

$$\int_0^\tau (c_1 - c_2) e^{-rt} dt < 0 \quad \text{for all} \quad \tau \in (0, T).$$

If we now set $T_1 = 0$ and $T_2 = T$ in equation (7.31) we will immediately realize that c_2 involves a higher present value of lifetime consumption and a lower present value of lifetime tax payment. Thus our claim is proved.

Differences in earnings profiles

We can now work with different earnings profiles. Early and late earnings profiles can be defined in essentially the same manner as early and late consumption profiles. We will say that an earnings profile w_{1t} is earlier than an alternative w_{2t} if:

$$\int_0^\sigma w_1 e^{-r(\sigma-t)} dt \leqslant \int_0^\sigma w_2 e^{-r(\sigma-t)} dt \text{ for some } \sigma_0 \text{ and all } \sigma < \sigma_0.$$

The income tax penalizes early earners among those with the same pattern of lifetime consumption. We can prove this much like the proposition about differences in consumption patterns. We start with:

$$\dot{A}_1 = (1 - t_y)(w + rA) - c \text{ with } c \text{ being fixed.}$$

Hence, we have:

$$(\dot{A}_1 - \dot{A}_2) = (1 - t_y)(w_1 - w_2) + r(A_1 - A_2) \tag{7.37}$$

so that:

$$[(A_1 - A_2)e^{-rt}]_{T_1}^{T_2} = (1 - t_y) \int_{T_1}^{T_2} (w_1 - w_2)e^{-rt}dt - t_y r \int_{T_1}^{T_2} (A_1 - A_2)e^{-rt}dt.$$

$$\tag{7.38}$$

Hence the result is proved.

Some straightforward extensions of these results are possible. Suppose we have inheritances (I) as well as bequests (B). Then it can be shown that a tax on labor income and inheritances at rate t_l is equivalent to a tax (t_c) on consumption if $t_1 = t_c/(1 + t_c)$. The consumer's budget constraint under the income tax can be written as:

$$(1 - t_l)I + \int_0^T (1 - t_l)we^{-rt}dt \geqslant \int_0^T c_t e^{-rt}dt + B. \tag{7.39}$$

With the consumption tax the budget constraint of the consumer can be written as:

$$I + \int_0^T we^{-rt}dt \geqslant \int_0^T (1 + t_c)c_t e^{-rt}dt + (1 + t_c)B. \tag{7.40}$$

Hence it is clear that the two sets of taxes will have identical effects if $t_l = t_c/(1 + t_c)$. It can also be shown that the revenue will be the same under the two taxes.

Thus it is seen that there is a large number of equivalence results for the income and the consumption/expenditure tax. Some of these propositions extend to the case of uncertainty as well. However, it is to be remembered that these equivalence results do not hinge upon utility comparisons but are done only for the case of budget constraints. This is not as important however as the fact that expenditure taxes are notoriously hard to administer. We discuss some of these difficulties below.

Difficulties in measuring the base of an expenditure tax

(a)   The direct method

How does one calculate directly the base of the expenditure tax? How does one determine how much an individual has spent during a certain period of time? In this electronic age credit cards and data processing can be used to manage the vast problems of direct calculation of individual period expenditure. One would have to replace 'anonymous' money (banknotes and coins) with individualized money (that which is held in the forms of accounts only) and to assign a personal number to any resident of the country. In that case no economic transactions should be paid for by cash. One must use credit cards, checks and other similar devices. All objects of economic transactions may then be classified easily and earmarked as to whether they are liable to an expenditure tax or not. All other administrative problems then get reduced to a matter of electronic data processing.

An objection to this method is that the state will have access to a considerable amount of information about the individual and privacy could be at stake. Another disadvantage is that the administrative requirements would be beyond the realms of possibility for less developed countries. Third, any use of cash for purposes of expenditure would paralyze the system.

(b)   An indirect method: the cash-flow approach

In this method expenditure during a period is computed as period income from all sources less gross savings plus all dissavings. The administration of an expenditure using this method would require the keeping of meticulous asset registers by all taxpayers to control for current consumption financed by dissaving. Otherwise, it would be possible to evade taxes altogether by saving all of current income and financing current consumption by dissaving. Under this cash-flow method registers are kept in nominal terms. This means that the cash-flow method takes into account only realized capital gains or windfall gains in the very period that they are realized.

(c)   The wealth-accrual method of expenditure tax administration

This method of expenditure tax administration is essentially the same as the cash-flow method but requires that asset registers be kept in constant rather than current prices. This would mean that it requires rather complicated revaluations of all taxpayers' wealth at any time period. This also implies a periodic reassessment of the market value of all firms. Because of this rather formidable amount of computation most proposals for an expenditure tax advocate the use of the cash-flow method.

However, notice that neither the cash-flow method nor the wealth accrual method of calculating the base of an expenditure tax can afford to avoid meticulous accounting and adequate control by tax inspectors in order to prevent untaxed flow of funds or commodities in kind from businesses to shareholders.

(d)   Business-cash-flows-cum-wages method of expenditure tax

This method is inspired by considerations of national income accounting. Let Y represent GNP, I investment, C consumption and W labor income. Then, since

$$Y - I = C$$

it must be the case that

$$(Y - I - W) + W = C.$$

This suggests that consumption can be taxed equally as well by taxing business cash flows and wages.

As macroeconomic identities hardly ever translate immediately into individual tax bases the above argument is of dubious quality. Everything will go well so long as wage earners consume all income and only entrepreneurs possibly save. In this case $(Y-I-W)$ is roughly equivalent to that part of the profits which is consumed by the entrepreneurs. But when a wage earner saves part of her income, her tax burden is not reduced, as should properly be done under an expenditure tax. Rather the tax burden of the enterprise into which her savings were invested would be reduced and it is up to this individual to negotiate with this enterprise a tax reduction for herself.

The treatment of consumer durables – the most significant drawback

The greatest administrative complication of a consumption tax under any method of base calculation is the treatment of consumer durables. This is similar to the problem of treatment of depreciation under the income tax. Consumer goods are bought in one time period but they create a consumption stream spreading over many time periods. This would imply an exorbitant burden under the expenditure tax.

Several methods have been proposed to gear the periods of the virtual consumption stream to the time pattern of taxation.

(i) **Tax averaging**. All consumer durables are taxed in the period of acquisition. A tax-averaging method is put in place to remove fluctuations in taxation due to irregular acquisition of consumer durables as in Vickrey (1947: Ch.6). Using this methods, however, it is not possible to eliminate the systematic bias inherent in consumer durables, as the period of acquisition precedes the periods representing the greater part of the consumption stream.

(ii) **Depreciation method**. This method allows the taxpayer to spread the amount expended on consumer durables over a greater number of periods. The number of periods is chosen either at the discretion of the taxpayer or following some guidelines issued by the tax authorities.

(iii) **User charges**. For very expensive durables such as housing and consumer durables not subject to wear and tear such as jewelry, an annual user charge could serve to capture the consumption stream of a period and should form part of the period expenditure.

One should state however that consumer durables create problems for an income tax as well and we shall discuss these in a later chapter. Suffice it to say here that whenever a consumer durable is acquired a consumption stream extending into the future is implied. The individual will acquire the consumer durable only if its present value is non-negative. But in order for it to be treated consistent with capital goods, the interest associated with the future consumption streams of consumer durables should also be taxed under an income tax. Otherwise, an income tax will be distortive as well as inequitable.

However, it should be noted that although consumer durables plague an income tax as well, the problem is less severe in this case because it is only the 'interest' that calls for an appropriate treatment and not the 'capital' itself, as is the case with the expenditure tax.

7.7   SAVINGS BY FIRMS

We now leave our discussion of firms to return to the main theme of savings. Corporations save in the form of retained earnings. There are at least two views on how to treat this. One view taken by Feldstein (1973, 1978) called the 'Keynesian' view argues that retained earnings of corporations should be included in the disposable income of the household sector since households themselves will take inadequate notice of this. A second view with origins in Fisher (1930) argues that households see through the 'corporate veil' and adjust savings to incorporate the effects of retained earnings by corporations. The *flow* of capital income has no effect on personal saving. This view is also taken by modern life-cycle theories. Empirical work on US data sets by Bhatia (1979) give qualified support to the Fisherian view.

7.8   SOCIAL SECURITY, PENSIONS AND SAVINGS

Social security and public and private pensions should be regarded as forms of compulsory saving. In return for contributions to social security and pensions the individual gets an income stream in old age. Suppose such a pension or social security scheme is imposed in a situation where consumers have already made their optimal consumption plans. What effect may this be expected to have on the total volume of savings?

The answer to this question depends upon what use the government makes of the amount collected. If the government uses this amount for current consumption then, clearly, the total volume of savings will fall. If, however, the proceeds are left in a fund to accumulate then the rate of saving should stay constant or even rise. It may rise for two reasons. First, there may be some external effects in savings mobilization which are overlooked by individual savers. Second, given the large amounts collected by the government these may be invested in properly diversified portfolios and thereby earn a larger rate of return.

To analyze these we go back to the simple life-cycle model of savings. Let S be social security benefits received in period 2 (the retirement period) and let α be the contribution paid in period 1. If the contribution is paid in a lump-sum manner then the consumer's budget constraint is:

$$c_1 + c_2/(1+r) = w_1 + w_2/(1+r) - \alpha + S/(1+r) \qquad (7.41)$$

where we are assuming that the individual earns w_i in period $i, i = 1, 2$.

We now assume that S is calculated as a multiple of some reference contribution α_0. If the multiplicative factor is $(1 + \rho)$ then we can write: $S = (1 + \rho)\alpha_0$ and rewrite the budget constraint as:

$$c_1 + c_2/(1+r) = w_1 + w_2/(1+r) - \alpha\{1 - [(1+\rho)/(1+r)][\alpha_0/\alpha]\}. \quad (7.42)$$

From this we may conclude the following:

(i) If $\alpha_0 = \alpha$ and $\rho = r$ then the social security scheme will have no effect on aggregate savings. Thus personal savings will fall by an amount exactly equal to the rise in public savings.

(ii) If $\alpha_0 = \alpha$ and $\rho \neq r$ then there is an income effect on consumption in both periods which is positive or negative depending on whether $\rho > r$ or $\rho < r$. If marginal propensities to save are positive and less than one, savings will change in the same direction as consumption.

(iii) If $\rho = r$ and $\alpha \neq \alpha_0$ then we would have similar types of income effects. In some countries benefits increase less than proportionately with contributions, so that there may be positive income effects for low-income savers.

(iv) Feldstein (1976) has argued that the assumptions on which this model is based are very restrictive. He argues, for example, that the date of retirement is a choice variable for the individual and leisure belongs in the utility function. If there is a pension plan then individuals might be tempted to save more today and prepone the date of retirement in order to enjoy more leisure. This would come in addition to the 'replacement effect' in point (i) and would tend to make the net effect indeterminate.

(v) The yield on social security might be more certain because the government can have a properly diversified investment portfolio.

(vi) Suppose that each generation cares about its descendants. The next generation does so too. In effect, then, each person behaves as if he was infinitely lived. This is the 'Ricardian equivalence' argument of Barro (1974) and others. Suppose now an unfunded pension scheme is introduced with the immediate effect of reducing private savings. The current generation will realize that when they are old there will be an additional burden on the young of the next generation to fulfill the second-period consumption plans of their predecessors. This increased liability will be reflected in the calculations of the generation today and private savings will go up as a consequence.

(vii) The formula in equation (7.42) assumes that social security payments are financed through lump-sum taxes. If distortionary taxes are used then this may affect, for example, the net rate if interest and savings.

Feldstein (1977) has used international cross-section data to study the effects of social security on private savings. He confirms the existence of a negative relation and interprets this as evidence that the replacement effect outweighs the induced retirement effect. Kurz (1981) used a much more representative sample of households and concluded that there is no effect of social security on private savings. On the other hand, he finds that private pension plans do have effects on saving, but that these are rather complex. Other work confirming complex and often conflicting relations between social security and saving have been reported by Green (1981), Browning (1982), Hemming and Harvey (1983) and Dicks-Mireaux and King (1984).

From a purely theoretical point of view the relation between saving and social security becomes increasingly complex as we move from the simple life-cycle framework discussed above. It is not surprising, therefore, that clear cut econometric evidence should not be forthcoming.

7.9   THE EXTENDED LIFE-CYCLE MODELS OF SAVINGS

Scarf's algorithm (1973) for computable general equilibrium models had a particularly invigorating influence on research on the effects of taxes on savings. A particularly useful example of this is the computable dynamic general equilibrium which was studied, among others, by Auerbach (1987). Auerbach's model encompasses economy-wide computation. We wish to outline here the life-cycle model of savings that is embedded in his work.

A representative consumer starts planning at a young age. He expects to live and work for the next 55 years. His utility function is specified as:

$$U(c,l) = [1/(1-\gamma)] \sum_{t=1}^{55} (1 + \delta^{-(t-1)})[c_t^{(1-1/\rho)} + \alpha l_t^{(1-1/\rho)}]^{(1-1/\gamma)/(1-1/\rho)}$$

(7.43)

where c is consumption, l is leisure, δ is the discount rate, α is the intensity parameter of leisure (the higher is α the greater is the preference for leisure, ceteris paribus, γ is the elasticity of substitution between consumption in different time periods, and ρ is the elasticity of substitution between consumption and leisure in any time period. Students will recognize equation (7.43) as a Constant Elasticity of Substitution (CES) form of utility function.

The budget constraint of this individual is written as:

$$\sum_{t=1}^{55} \left\{ \prod_{s=2}^{t} [1 + r_s(1 - \bar{\tau}_{ys})] \right\}^{-1} (1 - \bar{\tau}_{yt}) w_t e_t (1 - l_t) \geqslant$$

$$\sum_{t=1}^{55} \left\{ \prod_{s=2}^{t} [1 + r_s(1 - \bar{\tau}_{ys})] \right\}^{-1} c_t. \tag{7.44}$$

This budget constraint allows for changes in the interest rate, the wage rate as well as general non-proportional taxes different for savings and wage incomes. r_s is the gross interest rate in period s, w_t is the wage in period t (in output units), $\bar{\tau}_{ys}$ is the average tax rate faced by the household. The e_t terms are included to reflect the accumulation of human capital. These terms describe how many units of 'standard' labor the household supplies per unit of leisure foregone in any given year. Thus $w_t e_t$ may be interpreted as the individual's gross wage rate. The human capital profile is the same for all individuals. Auerbach considers a particular form of the profile. Labor supplied by different generations, after adjustment for efficiency, is homogeneous. Hence the same assumption of Harrod-neutral or labor-augmenting technical progress is being made here as in the Summers model.

The following constraint is imposed on the model:

$$l_t \leqslant 1 \text{ for all } t.$$

First-order conditions for an internal maximum are:

$$(1 + \delta)^{-(t-1)} \Omega_t c_t^{-1/\rho} = \lambda \left\{ \prod_{s=2}^{t} [1 + r_s(1 - \bar{\tau}_{ys})] \right\}^{-1} \theta_t \tag{7.45a}$$

$$(1 + \delta)^{-(t-1)} \Omega_t \alpha l_t^{-1/\rho} = \lambda \left\{ \prod_{s=2}^{t} [1 + r_s(1 - \bar{\tau}_{ys})] \right\}^{-1} w_t^* \theta_t \tag{7.45b}$$

where

$$\Omega_t = [c_t^{(1-1/\rho)} + \alpha l_t^{(1-1/\rho)}]^{(1/\rho - 1/\gamma)/(1-1/\rho)} \tag{7.46}$$

$$\theta_t = \prod_{s=t+1}^{55} \{[1 + r_s(1 - \tau_{ys})]/[1 + r_s(1 - \bar{\tau}_{ys})]\} \tag{7.47}$$

$$w_t^* = w_t e_t(1 - \tau_{yt}) + \mu_t \tag{7.48}$$

where μ_t is the Lagrange multiplier for the period t labor supply constraint and τ_{yt} is the marginal tax rate.

From equations (7.45a) and (7.45b) we have:

$$l_t = [w_t^*/\alpha]^{-\rho} c_t \tag{7.49}$$

Substitute into equation (7.46) and solve for Ω_t in terms of c_t and then substitute back into (7.45a) to get the transition equation:

$$c_t = \{[1 + r_t(1 - \tau_{yt})]/(1 + \delta)\}^{\gamma} [v_t/v_{t-1}] c_{t-1} \tag{7.50}$$

where

$$v_t = \left[1 + \alpha\rho w_t^{*(1-\rho)}\right]^{(\rho-\gamma)/(1-\rho)}. \tag{7.51}$$

Similarly,

$$l_t = \{[1 + r_t(1 - \tau_{yt})]/(1 + \delta)\}^\gamma (v_t/v_{t-1})(w_t^*/w_{t-1}^*)^{-\rho}l_{t-1}. \tag{7.52}$$

The production sector

One single output is produced with a constant elasticity of substitution (CES) production function:

$$Y_t = A[\epsilon K_t^{(1-1/\sigma)} + (1 - \epsilon)L_t^{(1-1/\sigma)}]^{(1/(1-1/\sigma))} \tag{7.53}$$

where Y_t, K_t and L_t are output, aggregate capital, and aggregate effective labor. A is a scaling constant, ϵ is the capital intensity parameter (Auerbach assumes it to be 0.25), σ is the elasticity of substitution between capital and labor. K_t is deduced by a recursive equation that dictates that the current capital stock equals the inherited capital stock plus current private savings.

Perfect competition in the output and factor markets assures that:

$$w_t/r_t = [(1 - \epsilon)/\epsilon][K_t/L_t]^{1/\sigma} \tag{7.54}$$

(wage–rental ratio equals mrt).

Further, because we have perfect competition and a constant returns to scale production relation, it must be the case that (from the Euler equation)

$$r_t K_t + w_t L_t = Y_t. \tag{7.55}$$

The government sector

The government finances a stream of public expenditure G_t that grows at the same rate as the population. Aside from various taxes, the government uses one-period debt to help finance current expenditure. If D_t is defined as the value of the government's debt, government tax revenue at the end of period t is:

$$R_t = \bar{\tau}_{yt}[w_t L_t + r_t(K_t + D_t)] + \bar{\tau}_{ct}C_t + \bar{\tau}_{wt}L_t \tag{7.56}$$

where $\bar{\tau}_{yt}$, $\bar{\tau}_{ct}$, and $\bar{\tau}_{wt}$ are aggregate average tax rates on income, consumption and wages respectively and D_t is depreciation.

The intertemporal budget constraint of the government is, therefore:

$$\sum_{t=0}^{\infty}[\prod_{s=0}^{t}(1 + r_s)]^{-1}R_t = \sum_{t=0}^{\infty}[\prod_{s=0}^{t}(1 + r_s)]^{-1}G_t + D_0. \tag{7.57}$$

Auerbach solves this model by first solving for the initial steady state. This steady state is perturbed by a tax or taxes. Then the path of adjustment to the new steady state is worked out. Values of the parameters $\delta, \gamma, \rho, \alpha, A$ and the human capital vector e are fixed exogenously.

7.10 EMPIRICAL EVIDENCE ON EFFECTS OF TAXES ON SAVINGS

To estimate the effects of taxes on savings, one often looks at the aggregate consumption function but the effects of taxation on savings are postulated in terms of individual not aggregate behavior. We know from theory that the conditions for perfect aggregation of demand relationships are extremely stringent. Essentially we require that all consumers have identical homothetic utility functions. If this is satisfied then, clearly, any redistribution of resources between consumers will leave aggregate consumption unchanged. This also requires that we assume that all consumers face the same vector of prices. This is a reasonable assumption for atemporal consumer choice, but not for intertemporal choice which involves forming expectations of future inflation and interest rates. For example, with progressive taxation, richer individuals will face lower effective interest rates than poorer ones. Moreover, different types of individuals may face different types of quantitative constraints in the labor and credit markets. Under such circumstances, aggregation of individual consumption demands is an exercise fraught with considerable danger.

Despite these difficulties the estimation of the consumption function has been an active area of empirical research. Wright (1969) neglected the aggregation problem and provided evidence of a significant negative substitution effect of the interest rate on present consumption. He calculated the compensated elasticity (for the USA) to be around -0.03. Wright emphasized that this result had significant implications both for the Keynesian view of effectiveness of monetary policy (a change in the money supply would change the interest rate which would then go on to affect saving and, hence, aggregate demand by the above amount) as well as the calculation of the excess burden of taxation.[2] Blinder (1975), working again with US data, explicitly took the distribution of income into account and found the value of the compensated elasticity to be much lower – only about a tenth of that calculated by Wright. However, Blinder did not take into account the effect of the tax on the net rate of interest. He further found that an equalization of incomes would lower aggregate consumption expenditure.[3] From this we may surmise that the presumed equivalence between tax changes on the one hand and interest rate changes on the other should be treated with caution. The distribution of the income effects across the population may be very different for changes in the rate of interest and for changes in taxation.

We have already discussed Summers' (1981) result where he claims that a proper treatment of the life cycle will lead to higher values for the interest elasticity of savings. The work of Boskin (1978) and Boskin and Lau (1978) also seems to agree with Summers. Their preferred value of the saving elasticity for the USA is 0.4 which corresponds to a consumption elasticity of around −0.3 which is ten times the value estimated by Wright. Later work of Boskin and Lau extended the theoretical model to an integrated model of savings and labor supply. They found significant cross-effects of interest and wage changes on labor supply and consumption.

At this point it should be stated that much of the evidence for tax substitution effects on consumption and savings is indirect because these are inferred from the estimated interest rate effects using as base their equivalence from the theoretical models. Ideally one would like to see a direct test which, so far, has not been forthcoming. One should recognize that there is disagreement about the measure of the rate of interest to use. Earlier studies have used nominal before-tax interest rates; the increases in both the rate of inflation as well as the marginal tax rate have led more recent work to use the real after-tax interest rate. The relation between the two could be quite complex as has been pointed out by Jha *et al.* (1990).

Another important measurement problem concerns the choice of the appropriate nominal interest rate. In the real world we observe different borrowing and lending rates and borrowers having different degrees of access to capital markets. There is disagreement about which interest rate to use. Blinder, for example, chooses a weighted average of rates paid on time deposits by financial institutions. Boskin (1973) and Christensen and Lau (1973) compute rates of return to the household sector, computed as income from assets divided by asset value. However, all these rates of return are annual. In the case of the life-cycle model it would be more appropriate to have a measure of a long-run rate of interest. We know, for instance, that when the results are used to comment on the move from an income to an expenditure tax the purpose is to forecast the effect of a long-run shift in the real after-tax rate of return.

Another popular area of empirical work on the effects of taxation on saving has been the influence of social security and pensions. Feldstein (1974) found that for the USA during the period 1929 to 1971 social security reduced private saving by about 40 per cent. However, if one takes the postwar period (1947–71) this conclusion is far less clear. Feldstein (1977) has used international cross-section data to study the effect of social security on savings. The results confirm the negative association noted for time series data for the USA. However, this conclusion has not been universally accepted. Munnell (1976) found a negative association, but Kotlikoff (1979) found the results to be mixed. Kurz (1981) concludes that there is no effect of social security on private saving. Private pension plans affect saving in complex ways with differences between men and women, and so on.

Barro and MacDonald (1979) re-examined the international evidence on a basis of mixed cross-section and time series data for sixteen OECD countries for the period 1951 to 1960. Again the results are inconclusive. Dicks-Mireaux and King (1984) have studied cross-section data for Canadian households for 1977. They conclude that there is a small negative effect. Using time series evidence for the UK, Browning (1982) found that public pensions tend to increase consumption.

With this as background, we realize that firm conclusions from the empirical work are hard to draw. It seems to be the case that the relative price effects are quite substantial and the consequences of taxation for saving incentives go beyond those of a reduction in real disposable income. Nevertheless, it should be emphasized, yet again, that conclusive statements must await the availability of much better data sets and estimation techniques.

7.9 CONCLUSIONS

This is the first chapter in this book on the incentive effects of taxes. We recognize that the decision to save is essentially an intertemporal decision. We considered various models of savings supply. We began with the simplest life-cycle model and then integrated labor supply decisions. The effects of capital market imperfections were also examined. We also considered Summers' argument that in all such models there is a tendency to understate the importance of the effects of the interest rate on the supply of savings. We also outlined the more complex life-cycle model proposed by Kautlikoff and others as well as some empirical evidence on the effects of taxes on savings supply.

Our principal conclusions are that taxes do affect savings significantly. Moreover, the effects of taxes are more complex than a simple reduction of income as postulated in the theoretical models. Considerable work remains to be done to refine both the theoretical approach, particularly in light of measurement problems, as well as developing better data sets.

NOTES

1 Yaari (1964) considers the continuous time analog of this problem where T is stochastic, i.e., the individual is uncertain about his longevity. He proves the following important result. Suppose the probability of death causing events is well described by a poisson process with parameter λ. If the consumer is maximizing a utility function with stochastic T and discount rate δ, then the individual is actually maximizing utility over an infinite horizon with discount rate $\delta + \lambda$. This assumption of death causing events being described by a Poisson distribution is, strictly speaking, valid only for young people. More recent work on this area include Blanchard (1985) and Blanchard and Fischer (1991).
2 This is discussed in some detail in Chapters 13, 14 and 15.
3 The traditional Keynesian argument has been that this would raise aggregate demand since (less affluent) workers, presumably, have higher propensities to consume than (affluent) capitalists.

ADDITIONAL READING

A good treatment of the expenditure taxation can be found in Ahsan (1976). See also Boadway and Wildasin (1984), Auerbach and Kotlikoff (1987), Mintz and Purvis (1987), Dardanoni (1988). For social security Feldstein (1974 a,b), Feldstein *et al.* (1983) King and Fullerton (1984) Giovannini *et al.* (1993), and Breyer and Straub (1993) are useful. Additional useful texts include Mieszkowski (1978), Bosworth (1984), Boskin (1988), and Slemrod (1990b), Fullerton and Rogers (1993).

8 Taxation and labor supply

Key concepts: income and substitution effects of a wage tax; reservation wage; tax progression and labor supply; optimal income tax; taxation and aggregate labor supply; commodity taxation and labor supply.

8.1 INTRODUCTION

We have already examined some effects of taxes on labor supply in the context of the life-cycle model of Chapter 7. In this chapter we want to examine the effects of taxes on labor supply in models that are not necessarily intertemporal. We begin, however, with the basic model of labor supply in the absence of taxes. Next we compare the effects of lump sum and proportional taxes on labor supply and the effect of taxation on the decision to enter the labor market. We then examine the effects of increasing progression on labor supply and then present a summary of the empirical results on the effects of taxation on labor supply.

8.2 THE BASIC MODEL OF LABOR SUPPLY

Consider a consumer-worker who is making a decision about how much labor to supply during a particular time period. She has non-wage income (I) and the wage rate is w per hour of work. Her utility function is U(c,L) where c is consumption and L is hours worked. Total time available is H so that (H−L) is leisure. The consumer derives utility from consumption and leisure but more consumption can be had only by sacrificing additional leisure. We assume that the worker is free to choose hours of work. The consumer good is the *numeraire* and its price is set equal to one for convenience, and without loss of generality.

We depict the consumer's equilibrium in Figure 8.1. On the horizontal axis we measure leisure. At the maximum she can enjoy H units of leisure when her income and consumption will be equal to her non-wage income I. As she sacrifices an additional hour of leisure she earns w and is entitled to consume w units of the consumption good. Hence, the vertical axis measures the amount of the consumption good or income. The slope of the

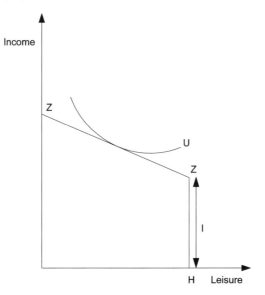

Figure 8.1

budget line ZZ is *w*. As the wage rate changes, say due to an imposition of a tax, this budget line is going to change. A wage tax will spare non-wage income and twist the budget line as in Figure 8.2a. The consumer's budget constraint would then look like: $w(1 - t_w)L + I = c$ where t_w is the proportional tax rate on wages. With an income tax both the wage as well the non-wage incomes are lowered and the consumer's budget constraint will look like: $[wL + I](1 - t_i) = c$ where t_i is the rate of the income tax. This is shown in Figure 8.2b.

In both Figures 8.2a and 8.2b we realize that the tax has two effects. One is the substitution effect. If the after-tax wage falls, then the opportunity cost of leisure will go down and the substitution effect will make the consumer consume, at constant utility, more of leisure (supply of labor would fall). However, the income effect would make the consumer work harder to earn more to protect consumption and, on this count, labor supply should rise. As in Section 7.2, the income and substitution effects work in opposite directions. The alert reader would have noticed that since there are only two commodities in the consumer's utility function, the substitution effect is decidedly negative. What determines whether the labor supply curve is upward sloping (the substitution effect dominates)?

We study this problem in the case of a simplified utility function. Suppose the consumer's utility function is separable in consumption and leisure:

$$U = U_1(wL + I) + U_2(H - L). \tag{8.1}$$

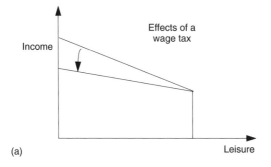

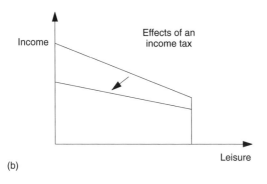

Figure 8.2

Differentiating with respect to w we have (with a prime ($'$) denoting a first derivative and a double prime ($''$) denoting a second derivative and so on, we have (for optimality):

$$U' = wU_1'(wL + I) - U_2'(L) = 0. \tag{8.2}$$

Differentiating once again with respect to w we have:

$$wU_1'' [L + w(\partial L/\partial w)] + U_1'(wL + I) + U_2''(\partial L/\partial w) = 0, \text{ or}$$
$$[\partial L/\partial w][w^2 U_1'' + U_2''] = -U_1' - wLU_1''.$$

Taking w/L common on the lefthand side (in order to define the elasticity of labor supply with respect to the wage rate):

$$[w/L][\partial L/\partial w]\{wU_1'' L + U_2'' L/w\} = \\ - U_1'[1 - \{wL/(wL + I)\}]\{-U_1''(wL + I)/U_1'\}. \tag{8.3}$$

If the utility function is well behaved, which we assume to be the case, then the term in the curly bracket {.} on the lefthand side of equation (8.3) is negative. The sign of the (uncompensated) elasticity of labor supply with respect to the wage rate (we know from the Slutsky equation that the compensated elasticity is negative) would depend on the sign of the right-hand side.

On the righthand side $wL/(wL + I)$ is share of wages in total income, whereas the term $[-U_1''(wL + I)/U_1'] = \epsilon_1$ the elasticity of marginal utility of income. Hence, we come to the conclusion that the elasticity of labor supply with respect to the after-tax wage rate is positive or negative as ϵ_1 times the share of labor income in total income is less than or greater than unity. Thus if $\epsilon_1 = 1$ (U_1 is logarithmic) then the labor supply curve is upward sloping provided $I > 0$ (there is some non-wage income). Remember, however, that this result is valid only for the separable utility function assumed here. If the utility function is not separable then the marginal utility of consumption would depend on leisure and vice versa and the above derivation would be inappropriate.

8.3   COMPARISON OF THE EFFECTS OF VARIOUS TYPES OF TAXES

In this section we compare the effects of a lump-sum tax and a proportional income tax. One has first to make the basis of comparison clear. Some authors have argued in favor of using a utility calculus, i.e., we compare taxes that reduce utility to the same extent. The tax that yields the higher revenue for the government is, then, the better tax. Others have argued that one should not make an unobservable such as utility the basis for comparing taxes. They would prefer to compare taxes that yield the same revenue.

In Figure 8.3 we present a case where either of these criteria would yield equivalent results. The budget line for the consumer is AA' before any tax.

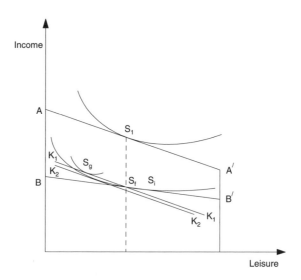

Figure 8.3

The consumer comes to equilibrium at a point like S_1. After a proportional income tax, the budget line is BB' and the consumer comes to equilibrium at S_i. The amount of revenue collected is the difference between pre and post income at S_1, i.e., the vertical difference between AA' and BB' (say S_1S_f). A lump-sum tax with the same tax collection would not have distorted the choice between leisure and consumption. Hence the budget constraint of the consumer under an equal yield lump-sum tax would be parallel to AA' and go through S_f (this is the line K_1K_1 in Figure 8.3). With this budget line the consumer could have attained a higher level of utility (indifference curve passing through S_g) than in the case of the income tax (indifference curve passing through S_i). Alternatively, if we reduced consumer utility to the indifference curve passing through S_i but imposed a lump-sum tax to collect revenue, then the amount of revenue collected would have been higher by the vertical distance between K_1K_1 and K_2K_2. Thus, no matter what basis of comparison we use – utility or revenue – a lump-sum tax is better than a distortionary tax. With equal revenue, the difference in utility between the lump-sum tax case and the distortionary tax case can be thought of as another measure of the 'excess burden' or the 'deadweight loss' associated with the tax.

8.4 TAXATION AND THE DECISION TO ENTER THE LABOR MARKET

So far we have focused on the decision about the number of hours worked by an individual worker. It may be the case that a tax affects the decision of the worker to enter the labor market. We will study two cases here – one dealing with the decision of an individual worker and the other with the decision of a family to send an additional member into the labor force.

Consider a situation in which work hours are not open to choice. You either work at least 40 hours a week or not at all; 40 hours is the usual work week. If a person works longer than that then he gets overtime wages. This is the usual situation in the labor market. One does not have much freedom about the hours worked.

Consider the situation depicted in Figure 8.4 The individual has to work a minimum of HM hours. The indifference curve F_1F_1 goes through through the point where the individual does not work at all and the point T on the individual's budget line when the individual works HM hours and faces a wage rate w_1. Clearly, then, if the market wage rate is w_1 the individual will be indifferent between working and not working. w_1 is the individual's **reservation wage**. Only for wages higher than w_1 will the individual consider working.

A tax on wages will lower the returns from working. If the tax rate is t_i then the wage rate will have to be at least w_2 to induce the individual to work where $(w_2 + I)(1 - t_i) = w_1 + I$ or $w_2 = (w_1 + I)/(1 - t_i) - I > w_1$ becomes the new reservation wage. Thus, when labor is not truly variable,

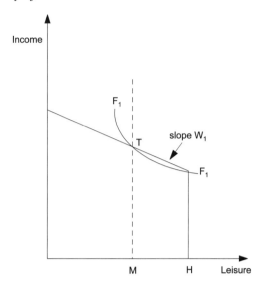

Figure 8.4

as is the case here, then the tax rate has the effect of increasing the reservation wage. Hence, the income tax here will reduce participation in the labor market.

An income tax will also affect decisions on the amount of overtime. We analyze this case in Figure 8.5 which starts off as being a replication of Figure 8.4. The current after tax wage rate is w_3 where the individual works HM hours at this wage (point T' on the budget line).

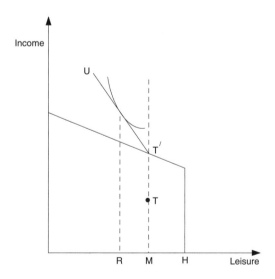

Figure 8.5

If the individual is to work still more the net wage will have to be higher. The individual faces the budget line T'U (which is equal to the after-tax overtime wage rate) and chooses to work an additional MR hours. We are making the realistic assumption that one is free to choose the amount of overtime work. Clearly as the tax rate rises, the substitution effect will make the amount of overtime work decline. The income effect will make overtime rise. However, since the amount of leisure sacrificed here is already quite high, it could well be the case that the substitution effect will dominate unambiguously.

Let us now consider the family (rather than the individual) as the decision-making unit. Let us suppose that one member of the family (member 1) is already in the workforce. The family is debating whether a second member (member 2) should also enter the workforce. Thus, the husband may be in the labor force and the family may be debating whether the wife should also enter the labor force.

The utility of the family may be written as a function of the net total income earned by husband and wife and the leisure time available to each. We will make the simplifying assumption that this utility function is separable. Thus we write:

$$U = U_a[(1 - t_i)(w_1 L_1 + w_2 L_2)] + U_b(H - L_1) + U_c(H - L_2) \qquad (8.4)$$

U_a is utility from family income which, in turn, is $(1 - t_i)(w_1 L_1 + w_2 L_2)$. U_b and U_c are, respectively, the utility from leisure of the husband and the wife.

The first-order condition for the choice of L_2 is that:

$$(1 - t_i)w_2 U_a' \leqslant U_c' \qquad (8.5)$$

with $L_2 = 0$ when the strict inequality holds. From this we can see the effect of income taxation on the participation decision. Suppose that, in the absence of taxation, only the primary worker has a job and that the hours of work are fixed. The effect of the tax on the lefthand side of (8.5) may be seen by differentiating with respect to t_i taking account of the fact that U_a' depends on t_i.

$$\text{If } -w_2 U_a' - w_2(1 - t_i)L_1 U_a'' > 0 \qquad (8.6)$$

then the lefthand side of equation (8.5) increases with t_i. Dividing (8.6) by $w_2 U_a'$ and rearranging we get as the condition for the lefthand side of (8.5) to rise:

$$-(1 - t_i)w_1 L_1 U_a''/U_a' > 1$$

or, that, $\epsilon_a > 1$ where ϵ_a is the elasticity of the marginal utility of family income. If this is greater than one then an increase in the tax rate will induce the second member of the household to join the labor force.

This result makes eminent sense. If family income is valued highly ($\epsilon_a > 1$) then the family will supply more labor (the second member of the household will decide to enter the labor force). If ϵ_a is low then the family will reduce labor supply (the second member of the household will not enter the labor force). The fact that the family utility function is separable in the three arguments implies that this decision is independent of the leisure of the primary worker. This would be a good assumption to make if work hours are fixed so that leisure can essentially be taken as a constant.

8.5   EFFECTS OF A PROGRESSIVE TAX ON LABOR SUPPLY

Let us now look at the case of a progressive tax. There are various definitions of a progressive tax, but the following are quite commonly used.

(i) a linear progressive tax: in this case, the marginal rate of tax is constant although the average rate rises with income. This is shown in Figure 8.6. The tax liability T(Y) of an individual with income Y can be written as:

$$T(Y) = \beta(Y - G) \tag{8.7}$$

where $G(> 0)$ is an exemption limit of the tax. β is the marginal rate of the tax (dT/dY) and is a constant whereas the average rate of the tax is $\beta(Y - G)/Y = \beta - G/Y$ which clearly rises as income rises.

(ii) general non-linear income tax: here the tax schedule can be written as T(Y) with $T' > 0$ and $T'' > 0$ for a progressive tax. This is also shown in Figure 8.6.

(iii) Particular forms of the general non-linear tax are:

(a) rising average rate of taxation $d(T/Y)dY > 0$ (this is one form of the progressive linear income tax).

(b) rising marginal rate of taxation $T'' > 0$ (already discussed)

(c) liability progression: $(d/dY) [T' / (T/Y)]$, i.e., the behavior of the ratio of the marginal rate of tax to the average rate of tax as income rises.

(d) residual income progression, i.e., the behavior of the ratio $[(1 - T')/(1 - T(Y)/Y)]$

We now compare a progressive and a proportional income tax yielding the same revenue. This is done in Figure 8.7. We make the simplifying assumption that there is no non-wage income. In Figure 8.7, AA′ is the pre-tax budget line with a slope equal to the wage rate. The consumer comes to equilibrium at point *d* on the indifference curve I_0.

With a linear progressive tax, there is an exemption limit of A′B and then the tax has to be paid. Hence, the budget line with the tax is: A′BC. The consumer comes to an equilibrium at point *e* on the indifference curve I_1. The vertical distance between the budget lines without the tax and with the linear progressive tax (ef) represents the revenue collected from the progressive tax. Let us draw the line JJ′ parallel to AA′ but passing through

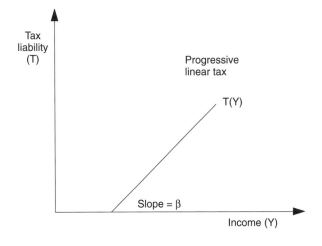

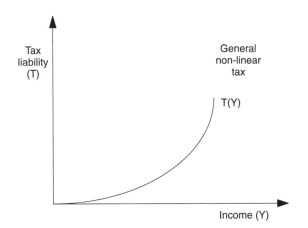

Figure 8.6

point *e*. Thus all points along JJ′ denote the same revenue as that from the progressive linear income tax.

In Figure 8.7 we have also drawn the price consumption curve (PCC) A′P for changes in the wage rate. As the wage rate (alone) changes, say due to a proportional wage tax, the consumer equilibrium would move along this PCC. With a proportional tax which yields the same revenue (ef) as the progressive income tax we would be at the point *z* on the indifference curve I_p. Thus it would appear that, for the same revenue collected, a progressive tax would involve a greater loss in utility.

We should be careful about reading too much into this result. The idea of a representative consumer is alien to a progressive tax system whose main

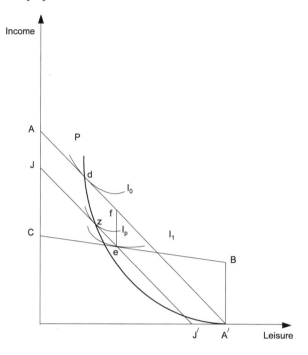

Figure 8.7

purpose is to differentiate between consumers. The income tax seeks to reduce inequalities of income and, hence, must necessarily not deal with any notion of a 'representative' consumer.

Effects of progression on labor supply

We now want to confront the question of whether increased progression leads to a drop in labor supply? This question was addressed in an important paper by Sandmo (1983) and here we follow his work. Sandmo extends the above analysis by recognizing that the role of the income tax is to be redistributive so that a representative agent model is hardly satisfactory. He also tries to articulate within this context the notion of an **optimal income tax** (something which we will analyze at considerable length later on) and its impact on labor supply.

There are H individuals in society indexed by $h = 1, \ldots, H$ and each individual's utility function can be written as:

$$U_h = U_h(C_h, l_h) \tag{8.8}$$

where C_h is consumption and l_h is leisure with L_h being labor. There is a progressive linear income tax in place so that the tax liability of the individual can be written as:

$$T_h = tw_h L_h - I_0 \tag{8.9}$$

where w_h is the wage rate (determined by marginal product of labor), t is the marginal tax rate and I_0 is the exemption limit of the linear tax. Hence, the average tax rate is rising and the tax structure is progressive. Clearly:

$$L_h + l_h = 1. \tag{8.10}$$

The consumer's budget constraint is, therefore,

$$C_h = w_h L_h - T_h = (1 - t)w_h(1 - l_h) + I_0.$$

Setting up the Lagrangean for utility maximization we have:

$$\Lambda = U_h(C_h, l_h) - \lambda_h[C_h - (1 - t)w_h(1 - l_h) - I_0] \tag{8.11}$$

where λ_h is the Lagrange multiplier.

Differentiating the Lagrangean with respect to C_h and l_h we have:

$$(\partial U_h/\partial C_h) - \lambda_h = 0 \tag{8.12a}$$
$$-(\partial U_h/\partial l_h) + \lambda_h(1 - t)w_h = 0. \tag{8.12b}$$

From these first-order conditions we can derive the labor supply function:

$$L_h = L_h[(1 - t)w_h, I_0] \tag{8.13}$$

and the indirect utility function

$$V_h = V_h((1 - t)w_h, I_0). \tag{8.14}$$

The Slutsky equation for a change in the tax rate is:

$$(\partial L_h/\partial t) = (\partial L_h/\partial t)|_{dU=0} - w_h L_h(\partial L_h/\partial I_0). \tag{8.15}$$

It might well be argued that the Slutsky term (the first term on the lefthand side of equation (8.15) will definitely show that an increase in tax progressivity lowers the supply of labor. But it should be remembered that an increase in the tax rate t in equation (8.15) amounts to a simultaneous increase in the marginal as well as the average rate of the tax. So the basis for comparison is not clear.

Some methods have been devised to get around this difficulty. One is to increase progression while leaving the utility of the individual unchanged. Thus when the marginal rate of tax is increased, the individual is compensated for the income loss by an increase in the exemption limit of the tax. This is depicted in Figure 8.8. The original budget line is 1aa′, and with increased progression it changes to 1bb′. The movement in the optimum from A to B will imply a decrease in the labor supply which is simply the substitution term in equation (8.15).

Constant utility may be a difficult standard to effect in practice. Another method to isolate the pure effect of an increase in progression would be to consider an increase in progression that leaves total government revenue from the tax unchanged. This is demonstrated in Figure 8.9.

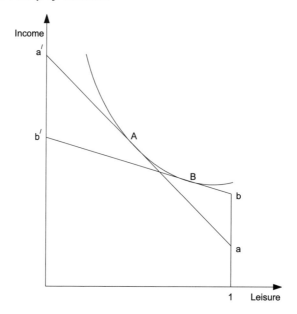

Figure 8.8

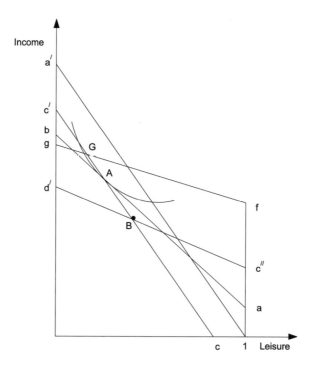

Figure 8.9

In Figure 8.9 the no tax budget line is 1a'. With a linear income tax the budget line becomes 1ab and the consumer comes to an equilibrium at point A. The line cAc' is parallel to 1a' and goes through point A – hence it is the locus of all points giving the same tax revenue as the income tax represented by the line 1ab. Suppose we now move to a more progressive income tax represented by the budget line 1c"d'. At point B on this line we get the same amount of tax revenue as at point A with the less progressive tax. At point B, once again, labor supply is lower. Increased progressivity and equal tax revenue could also make us move to a point like G on budget line 1fg involving higher tax progressivity. At G labor has increased but it can be checked; at G we are treating leisure as a Giffen good.

Whereas the constant tax revenue does make the effect of an increase in tax progression more ambiguous, it is the single consumer framework that makes the analysis of the effects of an increase in tax progressivity that is unsatisfactory. Hence, we move to the effects of the tax on aggregate labor supply.

Effects of increased progression on aggregate labor supply

Two methods of aggregating labor supply could be used. One is to add unweighted hours worked by different people. The other is to weight labor by wages (an index of productivity) to arrive at a more effective measure of aggregate labor supply. Sandmo uses the latter. Aggregate labor supply could then be written as:

$$J = \sum_{h=1}^{H} w_h L_h. \tag{8.16}$$

Totally differentiating this we have:

$$dJ = \sum_h w_h (\partial L_h / \partial t) dt + \sum_h w_h (\partial L_h / \partial I_0) dI_0. \tag{8.17}$$

Equation (8.17) makes clear the fact that a change in hours worked could come from changes in the marginal rate of tax as well as a change in the exemption limit of the tax.

The government requires an amount T_0 in tax revenue:

$$T_0 = t \sum_h w_h L_h - H I_0. \tag{8.18}$$

If tax rates are to be changed subject to the amount of tax revenue being held constant then, upon totally differentiating equation (8.18), we must get:

$$dT_0 = t \sum_h w_h (\partial L_h / \partial t) dt + \sum_h w_h L_h dt + t \sum_h w_h (\partial L_h / \partial I_0) dI_0 - H dI_0 = 0. \tag{8.19}$$

Solving for dI_0/dt we get:

$$dI_0/dt = \left[t\sum_h w_h(\partial L_h/\partial t) + \sum_h w_h L_h\right] / \left[H - t\sum_h w_h(\partial L_h/\partial I_0)\right]. \quad (8.20)$$

Substitute this for the second term on the righthand side of equation (8.17) and divide through by dt to get in a situation where tax revenues are constant:

$$(dJ/dt)|_{dT=0} = \sum_h w_h(\partial L_h/\partial t) + \sum_h w_h(\partial L_h/\partial I_0)[\sum_h w_h L_h$$
$$+ t\sum_h w_h(\partial L_h/\partial t)]/[H - t\sum_h w_h(\partial L_h/\partial I_0)]. \quad (8.21)$$

An increase in the progression of the tax would lower work effort only if equation (8.21) is negative. Multiplying through by $[H - t\sum_h w_h(\partial L_h/\partial I_0)]$ and rearranging terms this requires that:

$$H\sum_h w_h(\partial L_h/\partial t) + \sum_h w_h(\partial L_h/\partial I_0)\sum_h w_h L_h \text{ be negative.}$$

Substitute for $(\partial L_h/\partial t)$ from the Slutsky equation (8.15) to get:

$$H\sum_h w_h\{(\partial L_h/\partial t)|_{dU=0} - w_h L_h(\partial L_h/\partial I_0)\} + \sum_h w_h(\partial L_h/\partial I_0)\sum_h w_h L_h < 0$$

or, collecting terms, that:

$$H\sum_h w_h(\partial L_h/\partial t)|_{dU=0} - H\sum_h (w_h)^2(\partial L_h/\partial I_0)$$
$$+ \sum_h w_h(\partial L_h/\partial I_0)\sum_h w_h L_h < 0.$$

On dividing this through by H^2 we can rewrite this expression as:

$$\{1/H\}\sum_h w_h(\partial L_h/\partial t)|_{dU=0} - \text{cov}[w_h(\partial L_h/\partial I_0), w_h I_h] < 0.$$

The first term on the lefthand side is the weighted mean of the substitution effect across all workers and 'cov' stands for covariance. Hence, we can write: an increase in the progression of the tax with constant tax revenue decreases labor supply if and only if:

$$\text{cov}[w_h(\partial L_h/\partial I_0), w_h L_h] > \overline{w_h(\partial L_h/\partial t)}|_{dU=0} \quad (8.22)$$

where the bar (-) stands for arithmetic mean. The righthand side of inequality (8.22) is the mean substitution effect. By the earlier reasoning, this must be negative. Hence, a sufficient condition for the labor supply to fall is that the cov term be non-negative. With an increase in progression with total tax revenue held constant, everyone faces a higher marginal tax rate. The substitution effect from this will make everyone work less. However, the average tax rate falls for people with low incomes and rises for people with high incomes. The income effect will make the less well-off work less (consume more leisure) and the more well-off will work more. If this positive income effect on the more well-off outweighs the negative income effect on the less well-off as well as the negative substitution effect for everyone, the supply of labor in the economy will actually rise.

8.6 A SUMMARY OF THE EMPIRICAL EVIDENCE ON EFFECTS OF LOWER TAXES ON LABOR SUPPLY

Income taxes, progressive or not, normally tax only income from market activities and thus do not tax leisure directly, though consumption taxes might tax activities complementary to leisure more heavily, for instance, vacations.[1] To focus on the income tax, let us assume that this is not the case. In this situation the substitution and income effects work in opposite directions. Empirical studies on which effect dominates have been summarized in Break (1974), Atkinson and Stiglitz (1980) and Stiglitz (1986). The consensus seems to be that these two effects tend to cancel each other out. Moreover, a zero effect on labor is to be expected for the widely used logarithmic utility function for work and leisure (Atkinson and Stiglitz 1980: 36). As has been discussed in this chapter, however, tax rates may influence the decision of spouses to enter the labor market. In addition, it is likely that with lower tax rates labor will flow from the underground economy to the regular economy. Illegal transactions in labor will decline. It would appear that these labor increasing effects of lower taxation (women and workers in the underground sector) will be most likely in the service sector where wages are quite low. At the same time a less progressive tax schedule (with the same average tax rate) when applied to the lower wage section of the wage distribution will probably imply higher taxation in this segment. This would tend to reduce supply of labor in the service industry.

Some substitution of an intertemporal nature is also possible. Ippolito (1985) argues that higher tax progressivity may stimulate workers to postpone retirement and enjoy additional leisure during work life. Moreover, it is possible that highly paid managerial staff may work longer at yet higher wages. Moreover, overtime labor supply may rise with a drop in the marginal tax rate.

In this section we will examine some of the empirical results on the effects of taxes on labor supply. Consider, first, income taxation and income support. Econometric analysis here would begin with a sample of individuals. For example, we may be interested in asking the question whether individuals in a particular sample change their supply of labor when fiscal variables change. If individuals cannot react then policy changes become easier to understand. The larger the change in the individuals' behavior, the more difficult it becomes to analyze the effects of policy. Changing the structure of a non-linear tax and benefit scheme will only produce behavioral responses if individuals are not constrained. Hence, it is important to assess the importance of constraints in a market for which policy is being formulated.

As Brown *et al.* (1986) and Ham (1986) show, constraints on short-run behavior are quite evident in the labor market. An econometric model must, therefore, describe the way in which these constraints operate and cannot be based purely on the assumptions of the theoretical model. Hence, many researchers focus on groups of individuals for whom significant response to policy changes is possible. In the case of the labor market an obvious group for such analysis is 'married women'. There are several reasons for this. First, this group tends to move in and out of the labor force (for obvious reasons). Second, these women make up the bulk of those in part-time employment and thus face the most complex portions of the income tax regulations as well as the income support systems. Even so, it is unlikely that these individuals can choose exactly the hours they want to work or can move in and out of the workforce at will. In such cases one often estimates a labor supply function by married women as:

$$L* = \beta_0 + \beta_1 Y^i + \beta_2 W^i + \beta_3 Z \tag{8.23}$$

where $L*$ is desired hours of work, Y^i is the net income, W^i is the marginal wage (part-time workers are often paid differently; often there might be overtime work), and Z is a set of characteristics such as level of education, the number of children, and so on. The βs are parameters to be estimated.

Despite its simplicity equation (8.23) provides a suitable model for illustrating the econometric issues involved. Indeed, it was used in the pioneering works of Heckman (1974) and Hausman (1979). The first important point to be thought about here is the specification of the error term in equation (8.23). The error term could enter in one of two ways. It might be the case that one or more of the parameters – the βs – may vary randomly across the population reflecting heterogeneity in tastes. If we take the βs to be constant then we will get biased estimates. Alternatively, we may argue that actual hours of work (L) may differ from desired hours of work, $L*$. This second specification of the error term was used by studies on US micro data by Hausman (1978), and on Swedish and British micro data by Blomquist (1983) and Zabalza and Arrufat (1986). The first specification of the error term has been used by, among others, Ham (1982, 1986) and Blundell and Walker (1986). Hausman (1985) provides a useful summary of the models applying the two types of error terms.

To get a feel for some of the results we refer to the work of Blundell and Walker (1986). They show that labor force participation of married women is quite sensitive to the net wage. Moreover, their labor supply is far more elastic than men's. Elasticity of labor supply rises with age of the women and reaches a peak at age 35–40 before dropping off again. It would, therefore, appear that the labor supply of this control group is quite sensitive to changes in direct tax rates.

Commodity tax rates and labor supply

We will now consider the interaction between commodity demands and labor supply. The relationship between any commodity and non-market time in the household is crucial in any evaluation of the mix of direct and indirect taxation. In empirical work care has to be exercised not to over-restrict behavior or to precondition optimality results. A good example of this would be the Stone–Geary utility function which yields the linear expenditure system. Although this utility function has several desirable properties, it assumes direct separability between goods and leisure and is, therefore, inappropriate. A specification for empirical application must be chosen that does not restrict itself to additivity and allows for secondary workers.

In principle relaxing additivity is quite straightforward. Under additivity wage rates affect all commodity demand in the same manner. Under non-separability there will be a differential effect as some commodities will be substitutes for and others complements with leisure. Under additivity or separability all commodities become substitutes for non-labor market time.

The linear expenditure system is generated from Stone–Geary preferences in which households are assumed to have Cobb–Douglas utility functions defined over 'uncommitted' consumption or consumption in excess of 'minimum requirement'. In other words if X_i represents the consumption of good i (be it leisure time or commodity consumption) and if γ_i is the necessary level of precommitted consumption (this may be zero), then utility is defined over $(X_i - \gamma_i)$. Given total income I and prices P_i expenditures are defined by:

$$p_i X_i = \gamma_i p_i + \delta_i \left(I - \sum_j \gamma_j P_j \right) \qquad (8.24)$$

for $i = 1, \ldots, n$ goods and where δ_i is the marginal income effect for commodity i. Including time allocations among the X_i simply leads to an interpretation of the corresponding prices as wages. One should note from equation (8.24) that if X_i and X_j are commodities and and X_n is leisure, the wage rate (p_n) will affect X_i and X_j in the same way. The household's indirect utility function in the Stone–Geary case (see Deaton and Muellbaure 1980: 165) is simply:

$$V = \left(I - \sum_j \gamma_j P_j \right) / (\pi_j P_j^{\delta_j}) \qquad (8.25)$$

Since all goods enter preferences symmetrically, it is straightforward to incorporate secondary workers. Utility-based decisions are cast in terms of non-market time so that hours of work can be calculated by subtracting this measure from the total time available. Income, I, in equation (8.25) is, therefore, defined as 'full income'.

Atkinson and Stern (1980) extend the Stone–Geary preferences by assuming that each commodity is consumed with a given amount of 'leisure time'. Since they use a single labor supply or time allocation decision, defining t_j to be the time component for consumption of the jth good implies a marginal cost of consuming of the jth good equal to $P_j + t_j P_n$ (the nth good is leisure). The indirect utility function in this case relaces P_j by $(P_j + t_j P_n)$ in equation (8.25) to get:

$$V = \left(I - \sum_j \gamma_j (P_j + t_j P_n) \right) / [\pi_j (P_j + t_j P_n)^{\delta_j}] \qquad (8.26)$$

where $t_n = 0$.

In an extreme form of this model, pure leisure is assumed to have no separate value and leisure enters utility only through the parameters, t_j. Atkinson and Stern use this assumption in their application of the model to male labor supply and disaggregated commodity demand in the UK. For female non-market time, 'pure leisure' has considerable separate value in, for example, looking after young children and could not be modeled using the Atkinson–Stern approach. Nonetheless, the idea of associating demand for time with the time spent in consumption is an attractive one.

The commodity expenditures associated with equation (8.26) are:

$$P_i X_i = P_i \gamma_i + \delta_i^* \left(I - \sum_j \gamma_j (P_j + t_j P_n) \right) \qquad (8.27)$$

where $\delta_i^* = \delta_i P_i / (P_i + t_i P_n)$ for $i = 1, \ldots, n-1$.

The factors $t_i P_n$ represent the 'time price' for consumption of commodity i and would be negative if the commodity is time saving (e.g. certain durables, such as vaccuum cleaners, microwave ovens, etc.). In the estimation of Atkinson and Stern (1980) durables and transportation have negative time prices. The only negative parameter that is significant is that associated with services. A significant t_i parameter is sufficient to reject the additive Stone–Geary utility function and, therefore, the optimality of uniform commodity taxation.[2] The results of Atkinson and Stern refer to a sample of 1,600 households drawn from the 1973 UK Family Expenditure Survey. In this survey detailed records of household consumption expenditures are kept. In Table 8.1 we report some of the results of Atkinson and Stern.

Table 8.1 shows the results of a simulated percentage change in expenditure on selected commodity groups that would result from a 10 percentage point rise in indirect tax rates (VAT) for a household with wage rate a little above average but with otherwise average characteristics. The real wage drop of 5 per cent brought about by the indirect tax increase has only a small (but positive) effect on males' hours of work.

Blundell and Walker (1982) extend the Atkinson–Stern study to include the labor supply of married women. They do not have commodity specific time price coefficients but the marginal wage of both husband and wife is

Table 8.1 The effect of indirect taxation on expenditure

Commodity group	Percentage change in expenditure	Percentage rise in price
Food	0.2	1.2
Tobacco	7.7	9.0
Clothing and footwear	1.7	8.3
Transport and vehicles	−0.1	3.3
Services	−2.0	5.2
Labor supply (hours)	0.06	−5.0

Source: Atkinson and Stern, 1980, Table 5

allowed to have a separate effect on each of the commodity expenditures. This permits them to test for additive separability as well as the complementarity/substitutiability of each good with respect to time. The last two goods n and n-1 refer to female and male non-market time respectively. The indirect utility function is written as:

$$V = \left(I \sum_j \gamma_j^* P_j \right) \Big/ \left(\prod_j P_j^{\delta_j} \right) \qquad (8.28)$$

where $\gamma_j^* = \gamma_j$ for $j = 1, \ldots, n - 2$ and

$$\gamma_{n-1}^* = \gamma_{n-1} \prod_j^{n-2} P_j^{\beta_{1j}} \quad \text{and} \quad \gamma_n^* = \gamma_n \prod_j^{n-2} P_j^{\beta_{2j}}.$$

In this case P_n and P_{n-1} represent the wage rates for female and male workers respectively and the Stone–Geary model is generated by the restriction $\beta_{1j} = \beta_{2j} = 0$ for all $j = 1, \ldots, n - 2$. Commodity expenditures then have the form:

$$P_i X_i = P_i \gamma_i + \gamma_{n-1} \beta_{1i} P_{n-1} + \gamma_n \beta_{2i} P_n + \delta_i \left(I - \sum_j \gamma_j^* P_j \right) \qquad (8.29)$$

for $i = 1, \ldots, n - 2$. β_{1i} and β_{2i} represent the commodity-specific time effects of the husband and wife respectively. A strongly negative β_{2i} denotes complimentarity whereas a positive β_{2i} denotes substitutability between the ith good and female time.

The parameter estimates of the model indicate that a number of $\gamma_{n-1} \beta_{1i}$ and $\gamma_n \beta_2$ terms differ significantly from zero. Thus services are a significant complement to female time whereas clothing is a substitute.

In any estimation of commodity demands from survey data some further econometric complexities arise. For example, if the survey has a short duration then we may record 'no purchase' for some consumer durables. Kay *et al.* (1984) discuss the estimation of the linear expenditure system with infrequency of purchase and Keen (1986) presents a useful instrumental variable estimator.

At a more disaggregated level, zero expenditures may arise as a result of corner solutions whereby at given prices a household decides not to consume one or more commodities. Although this problem is easy to tackle at a theoretical level, there are severe problems at the empirical level (see Lee and Pitt 1986). Along similar lines Deaton and Irish (1984) provide a useful way of dealing with commodities (such as alcohol and cigarettes) whose demand is typically under-reported.

Blundell and Ray (1984) have proposed a system of demand equations which allows for testing for non-linear Engle curves as well as non-separable preferences. They write the expenditure function as

$$E(p, U)^\alpha = a(p, \alpha) + b(p, \alpha)U \qquad (0 < \alpha \leqslant 1) \qquad (8.30)$$

where p is a vector of prices, α represents a one parameter generalization of the standard expenditure function and U is the level of utility. Clearly a(.) and b(.) are homogeneous of degree α in prices. The forms chosen by Blundell and Ray are:

$$a(p, \alpha) = \sum_i \sum_j \gamma_{ji} p_i^{\alpha/2} p_j^{\alpha/2} \qquad (8.31)$$

$$b(p, \alpha) = \prod_i p_i^{\beta_i \alpha} \qquad \sum \beta_i = 1. \qquad (8.32)$$

If $\alpha = 1$ and $\gamma_{ji} = 0$ we will get back to the standard demand form. However, in the case of Blundell and Ray these are propositions to be tested. They discover in the case of both time series as well as pooled cross-section and time series data that linearity of Engel functions as well as separbility of preferences are decisively rejected by the data.

8.7 CONCLUSIONS

In this chapter we have examined various aspects of the effects of taxation on labor supply. We began with the simple atemporal model of representative consumer behavior. In this context we studied the effects of lump sum, proportional and progressive taxes. We then developed models where taxation affects decision to enter the labor market and the extent of overtime put in. We also studied the effects of increased progression in the tax structure on labor supply in a model where the notion of a representative consumer is eschewed. We discussed some empirical models that tend to quantify the effects of taxation on labor supply. Some ideas for further research are also advanced.

NOTES

1 We must keep in mind, however, the drawbacks of the consumption tax. These are discussed in Chapter 7.

2 In Chapter 13 it is explained that if the utility function is additive separable a uniform commodity tax may be optimal. This is a result due to Atkinson and Stiglitz (1976).

ADDITIONAL READING

Allan (1971) provides a useful framework for analyzing the incentive effects of taxes, as do Atkinson and Harrison (1978). Cowell (1981, 1985) provides useful reviews of effects of taxation on labor supply under uncertainty.

APPENDIX

In this appendix we discuss an additional aspect of Sandmo's model of effects of increased progression of taxation on labor supply. He considers the incentive implications of the income tax when set optimally. Suppose taxes are set by a social planner to maximize a utilitarian social welfare function:

$$W = \sum_h U_h = \sum_h V_h \qquad (A8.1)$$

where V_h is the indirect utility function. This is maximized subject to the government budget constraint (equation 8.18) and an exogenously given tax requirement T_0. The Lagrangean for the social planner is:

$$\Lambda = \sum_h V_h((1-t)w_h, I_0) + \mu \left[t \sum_h w_h L_h - HI_0 \right]. \qquad (A8.2)$$

Maximizing this with respect to I_0 and t we get:

$$\sum_h (\partial V_h / \partial I_0) + \mu \left[t \sum_h w_h (\partial L_h / \partial I_0) - H \right] = 0 \qquad (A8.3)$$

and

$$\sum_h (\partial V_h / \partial t) + \mu \left[\sum_h w_h L_h + t \sum_h w_h (\partial L_h / \partial t) \right] = 0. \qquad (A8.4)$$

From the properties of the indirect utility function we have that:

$$(\partial V_h / \partial I_0) = \lambda_h \qquad (A8.3a)$$
$$(\partial V_h / \partial t) = -\lambda_h w_h L_h \qquad (A8.4a)$$

where λ_h is the Lagrange multiplier in the consumer utility maximization problem discussed in equation (8.11). Substituting in equations (A8.3) and (A8.4) we have:

$$\sum_h \lambda_h + \mu [t \sum_h w_h (\partial L_h / \partial I_0) - H] = 0 \qquad (A8.3b)$$

$$-\sum_h \lambda_h w_h L_h + \mu [\sum_h w_h L_h + t \sum_h w_h (\partial L_h / \partial t)] = 0. \qquad (A8.4b)$$

Now substitute the Slutsky equation for $(\partial L_h/\partial t)$, multiply equation (A8.3b) by $\sum_h w_h L_h/H^2$ and divide (A8.4b) by H. Then add the two equations to get:

$$-\text{cov}(\lambda_h, w_h L_h) + \mu t[\overline{w_h(\partial L_h/\partial t)}|_{dU=0} - \text{cov}(w_h(\partial L_h/\partial I_0), w_h L_h)] = 0 \tag{A8.5}$$

so that we can solve for the optimal tax rate (t^*) to get:

$$t^* = \text{cov}(\lambda_h, w_h L_h)/[\mu\{\overline{w_h(\partial L_h/\partial t)}|_{dU=0} - \text{cov}(w_h(\partial L_h/\partial I_0), w_h L_h)\}]. \tag{A8.6}$$

Hence, the marginal tax rate is positive only if the numerator as well as the denominator in equation (A8.6) have the same sign.

It can be shown that if the consumer's utility function is twice continuously differentiable and strictly concave (not just quasi-concave) and if consumer and leisure are both normal goods, then it is the case that $\text{cov}(\lambda_h, w_h L_h) < 0$. Hence it would follow that if the optimal tax rate is positive, then progression is pushed to the point where it reduces labor supply in the aggregate.

An interpretation of this result could proceed as follows. If the social welfare function is inequality averse then the marginal tax rate is positive only if condition (8.22) holds. Given this and the government revenue requirement, it can be shown that $I_0 \geqslant 0$ as well.

9 The effects of taxes on investment behavior

Key concepts: Fisherian and neoclassical views of investment; the Penrose effect; economic and technological rate of depreciation; neutral corporate tax; effects of inflation; the Modigliani–Miller theorem.

9.1 INTRODUCTION

In this chapter we discuss the effects of taxation on investment behavior. The first point to be understood about investment is that it is always an intertemporal decision. A firm sets aside resources for future use in order to derive more profits later.

In the literature two approaches to investment have been discussed. One is the Fisherian **general equilibrium** approach after the work of Irving Fisher (1930). The essence of this view is to build up models of 'representative' consumer and firm behavior and then analyze the ways in which taxes impinge upon these decisions.

The second is the **aggregate** approach which tries to build models of representative firms and then aggregate these decisions to get a macro model of investment and the movement in the capital stock. Both approaches serve very useful purposes in understanding investment behavior as well as the effects of taxes on investment. Needless to say, the two approaches are not necessarily in conflict with each other. We begin this chapter with an examination of them. Then we study two specific examples – the Keynesian and Jorgenson models of investment behavior. A number of related issues are taken up here, for example, the incentive effects of taxes on investment behavior and the notion of 'effective tax on capital'.

9.2 THE FISHERIAN MODEL

This model lays emphasis on three factors:

(i) the role of technology in transforming current resources into future resources;
(ii) the role of tastes, particularly the rate of time preference, in determining the amounts of resources to be transformed to future uses;

(iii) the role of capital markets in facilitating borrowing and lending. Capital markets are seen as intermediaries between lenders (the savers) and borrowers (firms and businesses).

The technology is represented by a production possibility curve between present and future goods as depicted in Figure 9.1. Total production in each period is given by a production function that involves inputs of capital and labor and a productivity shock. Thus, in period 1 the output can be written as:

$$Q_1 = F(K_1, L, \gamma_1) \qquad (9.1)$$

where Q_1, K_1, and L are, respectively, output, capital and labor in period 1. γ_1 is the realization of a productivity shock for period 1. F is a standard neoclassical production function with positive but falling marginal products.

In period 1 capital is given exogenously. Investment decisions in period 1 will affect the availability of capital in period 2. A part of output in period 1 is saved (and invested): $Q_1 = C_1 + I_1$ where C_1 is consumption in period 1 and I_1 is gross investment since it is assumed that a fraction δ of the

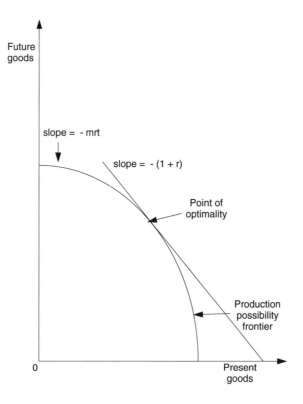

Figure 9.1

capital depreciates each time period. Hence, the capital stock in period 2 can be written as:

$$K_2 = K_1(1 - \delta) + I_1. \tag{9.2}$$

In the simplest version of the intertemporal model period 2 is thought of as the future. Hence, time ceases to be an important factor after period 2 and all capital in period 2 will be consumed. Hence, we can write second period consumption, C_2 as:

$$C_2 = Q_2 = F(K_2, L, \gamma_2) + (1 - \delta)K_2. \tag{9.3}$$

Consumption in period 2 is equal to production plus the undepreciated portion of the capital stock.

In Figure 9.1 the absolute value of the slope of the production possibility frontier reflects the rate at which present goods can be transformed at the margin into future goods (the marginal rate of transformation or *mrt*). Now:

$$mrt = -dQ_2/dQ_1 = (\partial F/\partial K_2) + 1 - \delta = 1 + (\partial F/\partial K_2 - \delta). \tag{9.4}$$

On the righthand side of equation (9.4) the only variable is the marginal product of capital in period 2. As we produce more in period 2 (given that labor is unchanged) more capital must be used which means that the marginal product of capital must fall. Hence the *mrt* must fall. Let us now look at the optimization problem of a representative firm.

The representative firm maximizes the present value of cash flows. Hence the firm chooses the level of investment to maximize:

$$V = (Q_1 - w_1 L - I) + (Q_2 - w_2 L)/(1 + r). \tag{9.5}$$

The first term on the righthand side is the value of cash flow to the firm in the first time period. L is labor supply and r is the rate of interest. In the second period, there is no investment to be made. Cash flow is $(Q_2 - w_2 L)$ which has to be discounted at the going rate of interest in order to make it comparable with the cash flow of the first time period. w_1 and w_2 are the wage rates of labor in periods 1 and 2 respectively. Furthermore Q_1 is fixed by initial conditions and Q_2 is given by equation (9.3). Performing the maximization of V we get the first-order condition:

$$\partial F/\partial K_2 = (\delta + r) \tag{9.6}$$

or, as

$$(\partial F/\partial K_2) - \delta = r.$$

In other words the net rate of return to capital (marginal product less the rate of depreciation) in period 2 is set equal to the interest rate. This simple rule will be encountered on other occasions in this chapter and has a rather intuitive appeal. The net rate of return to capital is what the entrepreneur earns from the marginal unit of capital. The rate of interest is the marginal cost of borrowing capital or, more generally, the opportunity cost of using capital as investment in this firm. So long as the net rate of return to capital is larger than the interest rate, the yield from the investment in this firm would be more profitable at the margin and, hence, more investment in this firm is warranted. As more investment is made, the marginal product of capital falls and the gap between the net rate of return from investing in this firm and the opportunity cost of such investment, is reduced. Optimal investment is clearly given by equation (9.6).

So far as tastes are concerned, the analysis proceeds exactly along the lines of the discussion in Section 7.2 (without the taxes). An individual has a utility function $U(C_1, C_2)$ defined over consumption in the two time periods whereas his budget constraint is simply that the discounted sum of consumption equals the discounted sum of earnings (where the rate of discount is the interest rate r). We write the budget constraint as:

$$C_1 + C_2/(1 + r) = Y_1 + Y_2/(1 + r) \text{ where } Y_i \text{ is income in period } i(i = 1, 2).$$

The condition for optimality is that the *mrs* (which is the negative of the ratio of the marginal utility of first-period consumption and that of second-period consumption) should equal 1 plus the interest rate. This is shown, even at the risk of being repetitive in Figure 9.2 by the tangency of the indifference curve to the budget line at the point Z.

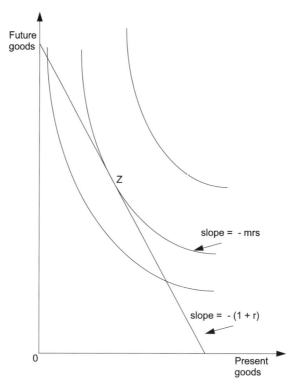

Figure 9.2

$$-U_1/U_2 = \text{mrs} = (1+r). \tag{9.6a}$$

The way the Fisherian model is set up, the household is indifferent between the time pattern of income receipts – all that matters is the present value of such receipts. This supposes that this economy has a well-organized capital market where individual agents who have a surplus of current consumption can lend to individuals who wish to borrow in the current period in order to consume in excess of first-period resources. In the next period, consumption goods are repaid to the individual who made the loans in the first period. The ratio of the quantity of future goods repaid to current goods lent is one plus the rate of interest, that is, $(1+r)$.

General equilibrium in the Fisherian model

Suppose now that there is a large number of firms and households those whose behavior is as we have characterized above. Equation (9.6) describes aggregate investment behavior and equation (9.6a) consumption behavior. In each period households receive income from the sale of labor services as well as from investment income (dividends). Hence, the present value of household earnings is:

$$(w_1 L) + (w_2 L/(1+r)) + (Q_1 - w_1 L - I) + (Q_2 - w_2 L)/(1+r) = \\ Q_1 - I + Q_2/(1+r). \tag{9.7}$$

Market clearing requires that $C_1 = Q_1 - I$ and $C_2 = Q_2$ and this is shown in Figure 9.3. The optimal allocation will be jointly determined by the technology of transforming current into future output and by tastes as represented by the indifference map of the representative consumer. Pareto optimality is achieved when the rate at which current production can be transformed into future consumption is equal to the rate at which consumers are willing to substitute current for future consumption, i.e., when the *mrt* in production equals the *mrs* in consumption.

If the *mrt* > *mrs* then a reduction in consumption today would yield a return in terms of future consumption that would exceed the amount required to compensate consumers for the loss of consumption. Hence the economy should allocate more resources to investment and less to first-period consumption. Conversely, if the *mrt* < *mrs* then the economy is investing too much and should consume more at the margin.

9.3   THE AGGREGATE APPROACH

The aggregate approach stresses the stock-flow dynamics that flow out of the interaction between the demand to own the capital stock and the flow supply of newly produced investment goods. The focus is on the determination of gross and net investment. Two examples of this are studied here – the Keynesian and the neoclassical approaches.

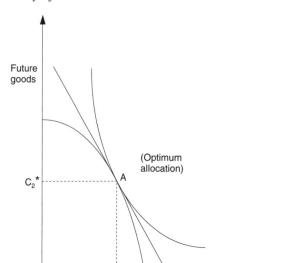

Figure 9.3

To Keynes in the *General Theory* the fundamental determinant of investment is what he calls the 'marginal efficiency of capital' (MEC). The MEC is the rate of discount which, when applied to the stream of returns from an investment, will make the present value (so computed) of these yields just equal to the present value of cost of investment (computed using the interest rate as the rate of discount). Keynes then argues that investment is a declining function of the MEC. Moreover, optimizing the rate of investment calls for equating the MEC with the rate of interest. Hence, the rate of investment is a declining function of the rate of interest.[1] Keynes explained this relationship in terms of a rising supply curve of capital goods. As the rate of investment rises, the price of capital goods rises since the capital goods industry has an upward-sloping supply schedule. Hence, cost of investment rises. But, given the nominal stream of returns from the investment, the MEC must be lower to equate the present value of returns to the present value of costs. Since the MEC is set equal to the rate of interest, the rate of investment is a declining function of the rate of interest.

This, by way of an opening remark, helps keep a potential source of confusion at bay. We will do well to remember this when we start thinking of the channels of effects of taxes on investment.

The starting point of the **neoclassical theory of investment** is an aggregate demand for capital equation, derived as an aggregate representation of the Jorgenson cost of capital relation for the individual firm. We proceed to discuss this now.

We have to make a number of assumptions. Certain assumptions are specific to the particular model being studied and they are best listed there. The more general assumptions are enumerated here. Almost throughout, we work within a partial equilibrium framework. We assume that firms are perfectly competitive and, therefore, that when studying the problems of investment, we will find it sufficient to study the behavior of a 'representative' firm. Moreover, by and large, we will concentrate on a world with certainty. We make the standard neoclassical assumption of a frictionless world. Armed even with this kit of assumptions, the going is tough.

The neoclassical theory of investment is available in two forms: Jorgenson's model and Tobin's **q** theory. The two are equivalent under a wide variety of conditions. The second approach places emphasis on financial markets whereas the first has a more product market orientation.

The neoclassical model recognizes the fact that difficulties exist both at the level of predicting the future and that of adjusting to new capital.[2] The firm must predict the future stream of costs and returns associated with an investment. Investment thus invariably involves prediction of future events – or at least intelligent guesses about them. What we assume about the telescopic faculty of the entrepreneur has an important bearing on the type of investment function we end up with. Usually the assumption of long-run perfect foresight has been made and we will essentially confine ourselves to this case.

Even within the relatively simple framework with which we are working, the nature of investment matters for the results we get. Thus, we could have investment with zero or positive adjustment/installation costs. Investment could involve adjustment within the firm and it matters whether these costs of adjustment are convex or concave, separable or non-separable from the cost of output. It matters whether investment is of the putty-putty, putty-clay, or clay-clay type.[3] In this chapter we attempt to accommodate various types of costs. We start with the simplest version of the Jorgenson model with taxation.

Consider the decision problem of an investing firm which has perfect foresight. Capital equipment, once installed, has two types of costs. One is an external cost – the price of the capital good, for example. The second is an internal cost of adjustment to the higher capital stock. The latter is known as the **Penrose effect** after Edith Penrose (1963) who introduced it into the investment literature. We capture both these costs through a cost of investment function C (I) with C', and C'' both positive. We define the cash flow (without taxation) of a firm at time t as:

$$R_t = [p_t Q_t - w_t L_t](1 - t_\pi) - (1 - \alpha - t_\pi x_t)C(I_t) \qquad (9.8)$$

where R_t is cash flow at time t, and p_t, Q_t, w_t, L_t and I_t are, respectively, the price of output, the quantity of output produced, the wage rate of labor, the quantity of labor hired, and the quantity of investment undertaken. t_π is the corporate profit tax rate, α is the fraction of C(I) that is paid back to the firm as investment tax credit. We further suppose that for one unit of capital aged n the government allows D(n) as depreciation allowance. The firm is visualized as having capital of different vintages and they fetch depreciation allowance as per the form of the function D(n). The present value of such deductions is x_t where:

$$x_t = \int_0^t D(s)e^{rs}ds. \qquad (9.9)$$

At time t, x_t is a constant.

Hence the total cash inflow due to depreciation is $x t_\pi C(I)$. Hence, there is a net outflow because of capital cost which is equal to total investment cost less investment tax credit and depreciation allowance. The net cash outflow of the firm, on account of investment, is therefore $(1 - \alpha - t_\pi x_t)C(I)$.

The firm wants to maximize the discounted sum of this R_t over an infinite horizon. It knows, with full certainty, the values of p_t, and w_t for all time. This discounted sum can be written as:

$$V = \int_0^\infty R_t e^{-rt}dt$$

where r is the exogenously determined rate of discount.[4] The constraint on this optimization is as follows:

$$\dot{K} = I - \delta K \qquad (9.10)$$

Net addition to the capital stock ($\dot{K}$) equals gross investment (I) less depreciation (exponential rate of depreciation (δ) multiplied by the capital stock (K)). A dot ($\cdot$) over a variable denotes a derivative with respect to time.

We define output to be given by a production function of the type F(L, K) = Q which is assumed to be of the constant returns to scale variety and satisfies all regularity conditions including twice continuous differentiability and quasi-concavity. We define θ as a costate variable the Hamiltonian:

$$H = \{R_t + \theta(I - \delta K)\}. \qquad (9.11)$$

We now work through the first-order conditions:

$$\partial H/\partial I = -(1 - \alpha - t_\pi x_t)C'(I) + \theta = 0. \qquad (9.12a)$$

This means that:

$$C'(I) = \theta/[1 - \alpha - t_\pi x_t]. \tag{9.12b}$$

The righthand side of equation (9.5b) is Tobin's **q** – the ratio of the shadow price of installed capital (θ) to the tax-adjusted cost of replacement. Hence, marginal cost of investment, in optimum, is equated to (marginal) q. Furthermore, since $C'(I) > 0$ it follows that investment is an increasing function of q.

We can then proceed to get:

$$\partial H/\partial L = (p_t\partial F/\partial L - w_t)(1 - t_\pi) = 0 \tag{9.12c}$$

so that

$$\partial F/\partial L = w_t/p_t$$

(marginal product of labor equals the real wage rate).

K is a state variable in the model and the canonical equation for θ is:

$$\dot\theta = r\theta - \partial H/\partial K = r\theta - \{p_t[\partial F/\partial K](1 - t_\pi) - \theta\delta\} = \theta(r + \delta)$$
$$- p_t[\partial F/\partial K](1 - t_\pi) \tag{9.13}$$

so that

$$\partial F/\partial K = \{\theta(r + \delta) - \dot\theta\}/[p_t(1 - t_\pi)]. \tag{9.14}$$

This is the crucial equation of the Jorgenson model of investment. It states that the marginal product of capital (the lefthand side) is equal to the real user cost of capital. The term in the numerator of the righthand side is the nominal user cost [interest plus depreciation evaluated at the shadow price of investment $(\theta(r + \delta))$ less the capital gain, $\dot\theta$]. The term in the denominator of the righthand side is the after-tax (or net) price of a unit of the capital good.

There are two dynamical equations for this model. One is the equation (9.13) for the behavior of the costate variable. The other from equation (9.10) is the equation for the behavior of the state variable. From the latter we can write:

$$\dot K = C'^{-1}[\theta/(1 - \alpha - t_\pi x_t)] - \delta K. \tag{9.15}$$

In steady state $\dot\theta = \dot K = 0$ so that steady state θ is:

$$\theta = p_t[(\partial F/\partial K)][1 - t_\pi]/(r + \delta). \tag{9.16}$$

For given values of other parameters this is a declining function of K since the marginal product of capital falls as the amount of capital rises.

Steady state K from equation (9.15) is (upon setting $\dot K = 0$):

$$K = C'^{-1}[\theta/(1 - \alpha - t_\pi)]/\delta. \tag{9.17}$$

Since $C' > 0$ steady state K is an increasing function of θ. We draw equations (9.16) and (9.17) in the phase diagram in Figure 9.4. The steady state

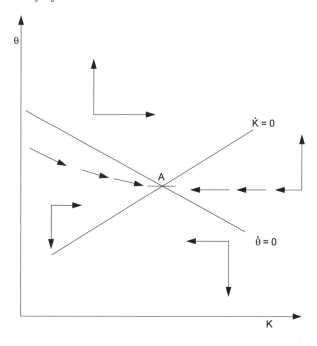

Figure 9.4

A is a saddle path stable equilibrium. K* (given by the intersection of $\dot{k} = 0$ and $\dot{\theta} = 0$ schedules) is the optimal capital stock. Whenever the actual capital stock is lower than the optimal capital stock, investment will occur. If the actual capital stock equals the optimal capital stock, investment will be zero. Changes in any of the parameters (in particular the tax parameters t_π and α) will change the optimal capital stock and the pattern of investment.

An alternative interpretation

We do not need the notion of adjustment to new capital to derive the Jorgenson rule for investment or the user cost formula. Suppose, for the sake of simplicity, that output depends upon capital alone. The production function is $F(K_t)$ and the cost of investment goods is z_t. The firm's maximand is, then:

$$W = \int_0^\infty e^{-rt}\{p_t F(K_t) - z_t I_t\}dt \tag{9.18}$$

which is maximized subject to the relation:

$$\dot{K}_t = I_t - \delta K_t.$$

Substituting for I_t in equation (9.18) we have:

$$W = \int_0^\infty e^{-rt}\{p_t F(K_t) - z_t(\dot{K}_t + \delta K_t)\}dt. \qquad (9.19)$$

The Euler–Lagrange condition for a maximum is:
with a prime $(')$ denoting a partial derivative:

$$p_t F' - z_t \delta - z_t r + \dot{z}_t = 0 \qquad (9.20)$$

so that the marginal product of capital (F') is such that:

$$F' = (z_t/p_t)[r + \delta - \dot{z}/z]. \qquad (9.21)$$

The righthand side is the familiar real user cost of capital. We can derive an alternative interpretation for the above condition by substracting and adding the current rate of inflation $(\dot{p}/p)$ to the term within the square brackets on the righthand side to get:

$$F' = (z_t/p_t)[r - (\dot{p}_t/p_t) + \delta - \{d/dt((z_t/p_t))/(z_t/p_t)\}]. \qquad (9.22)$$

An interpretation of equation (9.22) is as follows. In output units, the total earnings at date t from an investment are $(p_t/z_t)F'$ (the gross marginal product of capital) plus the real change in asset value: $-\{\delta - [d/dt][z_t/p_t]/(z_t/p_t)\}$. These must equal the **real** interest rate $(r - \dot{p}/p)$. The term $\{\delta - [d/dt][z_t/p_t]/(z_t/p_t)\}$ is the **economic rate of depreciation** as opposed to the **technological rate of depreciation**, δ. The economic rate of depreciation takes account of changing relative prices. If capital goods are expected to rise in price relative to output, this represents a capital gain that will oppose the effect of depreciation in lowering the asset's value.

Effects of taxes

We look now at the effects of various taxes. There is a single corporate tax assessed at rate t_π on cash flow $(p_t F(K_t))$ less depreciation allowance on existing capital. In addition, let us suppose that there is an investment tax credit at the rate α on new capital goods purchases. We ignore the additional complication of personal taxes and the special treatment of debt. Thus we are thinking of the representative firm as being a self-financed entrepreneur.

Letting D_t be the depreciation allowance given to a unit of capital originally purchased for a dollar, we obtain the following value for the firm's maximand:

$$V = \int_0^\infty e^{-rt}\{(1 - t_\pi)p_t F(K_t) - z_t(1 - \alpha - t_\pi x_t)I_t\}dt. \qquad (9.23)$$

In equation (9.23) we are making the harmless assumption that the firm began operation at time zero. Otherwise we would have to add a constant to the righthand side of equation (9.23) denoting depreciation provisions between $(-\infty)$ and zero. At time zero this is a constant and can be ignored without changing any of the results.

Solving the Euler equation we have:

$$F' = (z_t/p_t)\{r - (\dot{p}_t/p_t) + [\delta - [(d/dt)(z_t/p_t)]/(z_t/p_t)](1 - \alpha - t_\pi x_t)/(1 - t_\pi)\}. \quad (9.24)$$

The two factors $(\alpha + x_t t_\pi)$ and t_π represent the extent to which the effective purchase price of capital is lowered by the investment credit and depreciation allowance and the extent to which future cash flows are lowered by the corporate tax. If $\alpha + x_t t_\pi = t_\pi$ or $t_\pi = \alpha/(1 - x_t)$ then the incentive to invest is unaffected by the tax. This may be called a **neutral corporate tax**.

We can think of an alternative condition for the optimum capital tax. A marginal product is one for which the marginal product of capital equals the user cost (say c_t). Hence the gross return from such a project t years after purchase will be $c_t e^{-\delta t}$ in units of output or $p_t c_t e^{-\delta t}$ dollars per unit of capital. Hence the discount rate ρ that results in the project's gross flows having a zero net present value (the project's **internal rate of return**) is defined implicitly by the equation:

$$z_0 = \int_0^\infty e^{-\rho t} p_t c_t e^{-\delta t} dt. \quad (9.25)$$

Substituting for c_t from the righthand side of equation (9.24) we have:

$$\rho = [r - (\dot{p}_t/p_t) + \{\delta - (d/dt)(z_t/p_t)/(z_t/p_t)\}](1 - \alpha - x_t t_\pi)/(1 - t_\pi)$$
$$- [\delta - (d/dt)(z_t/p_t)/(z_t/p_t)] + \dot{p}_t/p_t. \quad (9.26)$$

Since ρ is determined by the nominal cash flows, it is the nominal cost of capital. The real cost of capital would express the return in constant dollars multiplying them in the expression for z_0 by the initial price p_0, rather than the actual price p_t. This would yield a discount rate of $\rho - (\dot{p}_t/p_t)$.

Equation (9.26) can now be interpreted to read to say that the real before tax return $(\rho - (\dot{p}_t/p_t))$ plus economic depreciation $[\delta - (d/dt)(z_t/p_t)/(z_t/p_t)]$ must equal the cash flow net of tax: $\{[r - (\dot{p}_t/p_t) + (\delta - (d/dt)(z_t/p_t)/(z_t/p_t)]$ adjusted by the term $(1 - \alpha - t_\pi x_t)/(1 - t_\pi)$ which accounts for the tax$\}$. This is another useful interpretation of the optimum capital stock condition.

For the simple case where inflation is zero and depreciation allowances do follow economic depreciation $(x_t = \delta/(r + \delta))$, the cost of capital ρ is constant only if the investment tax credit satisfies $\alpha = \alpha_0(1 - \delta/(r + \delta))$ where α_0 is the credit that applies to assets for which $\delta = 0$. This requires a tax credit that increases with the productive life of the asset (decreases with δ).

Effects of inflation

Let us now extend this analysis to cover inflation. Since nominal depreciation allowances typically do not change with the price level, there is decline in real value during inflationary periods. In other words, there is an increase in the effective taxation[5] of capital income and in the cost of capital. To see this, suppose that economic depreciation is not indexed for inflation. Hence, assuming that all prices rise at the same rate $\mu (= \dot{z}_t/z_t = \dot{p}_t/p_t)$, and the price of capital goods at time t is $z_t = e^{\mu t}z_0$, then the economic depreciation of an asset purchased at time zero for z_0 can be written as:

$$z_t \delta e^{-\delta t} = z_0 e^{\mu t} \delta e^{-\delta t}.$$

The present value (x_e) of economic depreciation per dollar of assets purchased at time zero is:

$$x_e = (1/z_0) \int_0^\infty e^{-rt}z_0 e^{\mu t} \delta e^{-\delta t} dt = \delta/(r - \mu + \delta). \tag{9.27}$$

With depreciation allowances based on prices in the year of purchase, the present value of depreciation allowance is:

$$V_f = (1/z_0) \int_0^\infty e^{-rt}z_0 \delta e^{-\delta t} dt = \delta/(r + \delta). \tag{9.28}$$

Thus, for a fixed real discount rate $(r - \mu)$, x_e is fixed but x_f declines with inflation. An interesting question is what happens to $(r - \mu)$ when μ rises. This could go either way (see Jha *et al.* 1990).

Personal taxes

Most countries do not have integrated corporate and personal tax structures. There are several reasons for this:

(i) Personal income taxes have progressive rate structures whereas corporate taxes typically do not.
(ii) Capital gains are taxed (if at all) at a lower rate than dividends and that too on realization rather than on accrual.
(iii) Corporations can deduct interest payments for tax purposes but not dividends paid out.
(iv) No price level adjustments are made to account for the fact that nominal interest payments and capital gains include inflation premia that do not represent real income to the receiver.

Let us consider some implications for the cost of capital in a discrete time framework.

Let us define gross profits (S_t) as value of output minus cost of variable inputs (say labor):

$$S_t = p_t F - w_t L_t. \tag{9.29}$$

New bond issues are $(B_{t+1} - B_t)$ where B_t denotes bonds outstanding at the beginning of t. New equity issues are $(E_{t+1} - E_t)$ where E_t denotes equities outstanding at time t.

The corporation pays out dividends (D_t) and interest payments to bond holders (rB_t). Investment expenditure is I_t. Revenues must equal disbursements so that:

$$S_t + B_{t+1} - B_t + E_{t+1} - E_t = D_t + I_t + rB_t \qquad (9.30)$$

(in other words, gross profits plus additional resource gathered through bond and equity issue must equal all disbursements toward dividends, investment and payments to bond holders).

Let us define retained earnings (RE_t) as:

$$RE_t = S_t - rB_t - D_t \qquad (9.31)$$

that is, profits not distributed as interest or dividend. Hence, it follows that:

$$I_t = RE_t + (B_{t+1} - B_t) + (E_{t+1} - E_t) \qquad (9.32)$$

that is, investment is financed by retained earnings, borrowings, or new issues.

In the absence of taxation, the net financial flow from the corporation to the personal sector is:

$$Y_t = D_t + rB_t - (B_{t+1} - B_t) - (E_{t+1} - E_t). \qquad (9.33)$$

This is equal to $S_t - I_t$. In other words, net flow is determined by $S_t - I_t$ and does not depend upon the financial policy of the firm. This is the so-called **Modiglani–Miller theorem**: in the absence of taxation and bankruptcy, corporate financial policy is irrelevant and has no effect on the value of the firm. We discuss this theorem briefly again in Section 9.5 and in some detail in Chapter 10.

We now introduce a tax system with the following provisions:

(a) corporate profits are taxed at the rate t_π;
(b) interest payments by corporations are deductible for tax purposes;
(c) interest payments by individuals are deductible at the personal tax rate t_p;
(d) dividends and interest received by individuals are taxable at the rate t_p;
(e) capital gains are taxed at the effective rate $t_g (t_g < t_p)$.

We can now write down the following financial identity:

$$S_t(1 - t_\pi) + (B_{t+1} - B_t) + (E_{t+1} - E_t) = D_t + I_t + r(1 - t_\pi)B_t. \qquad (9.34)$$

For the personal sector, there is liability for income tax and capital gains tax so that the net financial flow after tax is:

$$Y_t = (D_t + rB_t)(1 - t_p) - (B_{t+1} - B_t) - (E_{t+1} - E_t)$$
$$- \text{ capital gains tax liability} \qquad (9.35)$$

Let us consider a simple perturbation. Suppose that the firm reduces both D_t and $(E_{t+1} - E_t)$ by \$1. The former costs the personal sector $\$(1 - t_p)$ whereas the effect of the latter depends upon the capital gains tax and can be seen to be $\$(1 - t_g)$. Since $t_g < t_p$ this represents a net gain to shareholders and bond holders are no worse off. A question that naturally arises here is: Why pay dividends?

Consider now a perturbation of financial policy such that the firm increases dividends by \$1 in period 1 financed by borrowing, with the interest and principal being repaid in period 2 by a reduction in dividends. The reduction in dividends in period 2 is $(1 + r(1 - t_\pi))$. If initially we assume that t_g is zero, then the change in wealth is as described in Table 9.1.

Table 9.1

	Shareholders	*Bondholders*
Period 1	$+(1 - t_p)$ (dividend)	-1 (lending)
Period 2	$-(1 - t_p)[1 + r(1 - t_p)]$ (dividend)	$+1 + r(1 - t_p)$ (repayment of principal and interest)

The effect on the individual depends on his rate of discount or the opportunity cost of funds which we write $r(1 - \tau)$. If he reduces his borrowing on receiving $\$(1 - t_p)$ in dividends or if he increases his lending then $\tau = t_p$. If he increases his saving in a tax-exempt medium (e.g. pension funds) then $\tau = 0$. For the shareholder, the increase in borrowing is desirable when:

$$(1 - t_p)[1 + r(1 - \tau)] \geqslant (1 - t_p)[1 + r(1 - t_\pi)]. \tag{9.36}$$

The condition is simply, therefore, that $t_\pi \geqslant \tau$. Essentially, the individual is substituting corporate borrowing for personal borrowing since interest is deductible. Whether this is desirable depends on where tax savings are greatest.

9.4 COMPARING THE EFFECTS OF AN INVESTMENT TAX CREDIT VERSUS A CORPORATE TAX CUT: A COBB–DOUGLAS EXAMPLE

Suppose we are interested in finding out the relative effects of an investment tax credit and a corporate tax cut in stimulating investment. In making this comparison we shall work with the Jorgenson model with a Cobb–Douglas production function.

Let t_{π_1} and t_{π_2} be the corporate profits tax rates before and after the corporate tax cut, and α_1 and α_2 be the investment tax credit before and after the tax credit increase. Now define R_π as $R_\pi = $ tax collection at new tax rate $-$ investment tax credit paid at old rate. Thus:

$$R_\pi = t_{\pi_2} \int_0^\infty p(\partial Q/\partial K)\,K\,e^{-rt}dt - (\alpha_1 + t_{\pi_2}x) \int_0^\infty C(I)e^{-rt}dt. \qquad (9.37)$$

If we take $Q = L^\alpha K^{1-\alpha}$ we will have:

$$(\partial Q/\partial K) = (1-\alpha)L^\alpha K^{-\alpha} = (1-\alpha)(L/K)^\alpha. \qquad (9.38)$$

From the first-order conditions we get:

$$MPL = w/p = \alpha L^{\alpha-1}K^{1-\alpha}$$

or,

$$(L/K) = (w/\alpha p)^{1/(\alpha-1)}. \qquad (9.39)$$

Substituting into equation (9.31) and then into dQ/dK we have:

$$R_\pi = t_{\pi_2} \int_0^\infty p(1-\alpha)(w/\alpha p)^{\alpha/(\alpha-1)}\,K\,e^{-rt}dt - (\alpha_1 + xt_{\pi_2}) \int_0^\infty C(I)e^{-rt}dt.$$
$$(9.40)$$

Along similar lines we define R_α as government revenue before tax credit change minus the amount paid out as tax credit and derive for a change in the investment tax credit:

$$R_\alpha = t_{\pi_1} \int_0^\infty p(1-\alpha)(w/\alpha p)^{\alpha/(\alpha-1)}Ke^{-rt}dt - (\alpha_2 + t_{\pi_1}x) \int_0^\infty C(I)e^{-rt}dt.$$
$$(9.41)$$

Hence:

$$R_\alpha - R_\pi = (t_{\pi_1} - t_{\pi_2}) \int_0^\infty (1-\alpha)p(w/\alpha p)^{\alpha/(\alpha-1)}Ke^{-rt}dt$$
$$- \{(\alpha_2 + t_{\pi_1}x) - (\alpha_1 + t_{\pi_2}x)\} \int_0^\infty C(I)e^{-rt}dt. \qquad (9.42)$$

We need a basis for comparing the loss in tax revenue in the two cases. The simplest and most appealing case is where the capital stocks are the same in the two cases. This will be the case when:

$$(1-t_{\pi_1})/(1-\alpha_2 - xt_{\pi_1}) = (1-t_{\pi_2})/(1-\alpha_1 - xt_{\pi_2})$$

or, when,

$$(\alpha_2 + xt_{\pi_1}) - (\alpha_1 + xt_{\pi_2}) = (t_{\pi_1} - t_{\pi_2})[1 - (\alpha_2 + xt_{\pi_1})].$$

Substituting in equation (9.42) we have:

$$R_\alpha - R_\pi = [(t_{\pi_1} - t_{\pi_2})/(1-t_{\pi_1})]\{\int_0^\infty (1-t_{\pi_1})(1-\alpha)p(w/\alpha p)^{\alpha/(\alpha-1)}$$
$$Ke^{-rt}dt - (1 - (\alpha_2 + xt_{\pi_1})) \int_0^\infty C(I)e^{-rt}dt\}. \qquad (9.43)$$

Realize that the expression inside braces ($\{\cdot\}$) is the maximized present value of cash flow under investment tax credit increase. Let us denote this by V^α. Further $V^\alpha > 0$; thus:

$$R_\alpha - R_\pi = (t_{\pi_1} - t_{\pi_2})/(1 - t_{\pi_1})V^\alpha > 0 \text{ since } 1 > t_{\pi_1} > t_{\pi_2} > 0.$$

Thus, with an increase in investment tax credit the government loses less revenues than an equivalent corporate tax cut. We can, therefore, conclude that a permanent increase in the investment tax credit is better than a permanent reduction in the corporate tax rate.

9.5   DECISIONS ON THE FINANCING OF INVESTMENT EXPENDITURE

Unlike the real theory of investment, which we have just gone through, the financial theory is essentially static. Only very recently have efforts been made to extend it to cover dynamic situations. (Merton 1982, for example). From a general viewpoint, one may well argue that it is probably better to study the real theory of investment and its financing at the same time.

The separation of the investment and the financing decisions, which we have implicitly been making, is a reflection of the Modigliani–Miller theorem, henceforth known as MM (see Modigliani and Miller 1958) which argued that financial policy is irrelevant to determining the present value of the firm's earnings. Since then two strands of the literature have grown up – one that supports the MM result and the other which shows that it does not hold in more general situations.

The Modigliani–Miller theorem

When financing investment, firms have three sources: retained earnings, debt and new equity. The first is referred to as an internal source whereas the latter two are called external sources. Finer classification is possible, for example, long debt and short debt but we will ignore these.

The MM theorem makes a number of assumptions that make a straightforward application of the Jorgenson model untenable. These assumptions and the MM theorem are discussed in detail in Chapter 10.

9.6   THE EFFECTIVE RATE OF TAXATION AND THE COST OF FINANCE

In assessing the implications of the tax structure for investment, the notion of an **effective rate of tax** is often used. In this section we develop the notion and also comment on how it could be measured in practice.

A typical derivation of the effective rate of taxation on capital (see Boadway *et al.* 1986) starts off with the neoclassical theory of the investing firm as discussed earlier in this chapter. This firm formulates expectations about the future and then adjusts its capital stock, perhaps subject to adjustment costs. The typical analysis assumes that the tax structure is expected to be unchanging over time. The taxes usually considered are corporate and personal taxes, as has already been done in this chapter. Other taxes that have been considered are resource taxes and commodity taxes.

The firm maximizes the market value of its equity or, alternatively, the present value of cash flow which is equal to the total value of equity plus debt. As we have seen earlier, the optimal capital stock is characterized by the equality of the marginal product of capital and the real user cost of capital – suitably adjusted. We have seen modifications due to costs of adjustment. We can also incorporate additional modifications due to the characteristics of the tax structure. Several approaches have been tried in the literature. These include those by King and Fullerton (1983), Boadway *et al.* (1986) and Gerard (1994). The approach taken here is suggestive of their work.

We concentrate on firms that have an infinite horizon, and use only one factor of production – capital. We further assume that the firm is initially unlevered, that there is no uncertainty and that firms are owned by households who are residents, i.e, firms are not owned by foreigners. We shall relax this last assumption subsequently.

Let r_p be the before-tax return and before payment for financial liabilities (interest payments, dividends, etc.) on a marginal investment project, after accounting for depreciation. We also let σ' be the post-tax real rate of return to the dominant shareholders in the firm and σ'' the post-tax real rate of return to the supplier of funds (this may also be the dominant shareholders). Then the marginal effective tax rate (t_e) can be defined as:

$$t_e = [r_p - \sigma' - \sigma'']/r_p. \tag{9.44}$$

Here the effective tax rate is defined as the difference between the pre-tax rate of return and the sum of the after-tax rate of return to dominant shareholders and financiers. If $t_e = 0$ then all taxes on returns from this project are absorbed by dominant shareholders and financiers. This is one definition of the effective tax rate. There are others as well. Boadway *et al.* (1986), for example, define the effective tax rate as the difference between the rate of return paid out by the firm and the rate of return received by households.

It seems natural to require that:

$$\sigma' \geqslant 0 \tag{9.45}$$

since a dominant shareholder will not invest in the project unless he makes no losses. Similarly, it can be assumed that:

$$\sigma'' \geqslant (1 - t_i)(r + \mu) - \mu \tag{9.46}$$

where t_i is the tax rate on interest income μ, as before, is the rate of inflation and r is here the real rate of interest. $(r + \mu)$ is then the nominal rate of interest and the first term on the righthand side of equation (9.46) denotes the after-tax rate of return on savings. The value of this gets eroded because of inflation so that the righthand side of equation (9.46) is the after-tax real rate of return on savings. If financiers are to fund the project in question then they should get a rate of return from the project equal to at least the real after-tax return from savings. In competitive equilibrium, it is possible that people would be indifferent between putting their money in this project and ordinary savings accounts because (9.46) may hold as an equation rather than a weak inequality.

Value of a marginal project

The value of a marginal project is the difference between the discounted flow of benefits that the project generates for both the owners of the firm as well as the creditors. For every dollar invested, the marginal value of the project can be written as:

$$MV = (1 - t_d) \left[\int_0^\infty (1 - t_\pi)(r_p + \delta)e^{-(\rho + \delta - \mu)t} dt + S - F \right] + R - 1 \quad (9.47)$$

or, upon performing the integration:

$$MV = (1 - t_d)[\{(1 - t_\pi)(\rho + \delta)/(\rho + \delta - \mu)\} + S - F] + R - 1 \quad (9.48)$$

where ρ = rate of discount,
$\quad t_\pi$ = the corporate tax rate (as before),
$\quad S$ = present value of tax shields,
$\quad R$ = Present value of net income for the supplier of funds;
$\quad F$ = present value of net corporate liabilities.
$\quad t_d$ = the personal tax rate on dividend defined by

$$(1 - t_d) = [(1 - t_i)(1 - t_\pi + yt_\pi)d/(1 - t_\pi)] + (1 - t_c)(1 - v)$$

where t_i = marginal personal income tax rate on interest income,
$\quad y$ = imputation ratio, $0 \leqslant y \leqslant 1$,
$\quad v$ = pay-out ratio,
$\quad t_c$ = tax rate on accrued capital gains.

Due to the definition of the value of a project that we have utilized we can rewrite equation (9.48) as:

$$MV = [(\sigma' + \sigma'' + \mu)/\rho - 1] \quad (9.49)$$

so that:

$$\sigma' = (1 - t_d)[\{(1 - t_\pi)(r_p + \delta)/(\rho + \delta - \mu)\}\rho + \rho(S - F)] \quad (9.50)$$

and:

$$\sigma'' = \pi R - \mu. \quad (9.51)$$

Clearly, there is a link between F and R which depends on the way the project has been financed and the arbitrage equation ((9.46)).

Let us now consider three alternative ways of financing the project: by issuing new shares, by issuing new debt, and by retained earnings.

New shares

In case of the issue of new shares the return to the saver will be characterized by:

$$\rho R = (1 - t_d)\rho F. \tag{9.52}$$

Hence using equations (9.51) and (9.49) (interpreted as an equality) we can write:

$$\rho F = (1 - t_i)(1 - t_d)(r + \mu) = i/\Lambda \tag{9.53}$$

where i is the nominal interest rate and:

$$\Lambda = (1 - t_\pi + y t_\pi) v/(1 - t_\pi) + (1 - t_c)(1 - v)/(1 - t_i). \tag{9.54}$$

In the classical tax system (Haig–Simons definition) capital gains are taxed at the same rate as any other income. Furthermore, $y = 0$ and $t_c = t_i$ so that $\Lambda = 1$ and $\rho F = i$. Several countries have tried combinations of these tax rules. For instance, in Germany $t_c = 0$. It turns out that one way to render F independent of v is to set $y = 0$ and $t_c = t_i$. In this case we will get back to the 'irrelevance' of dividend policy discussed by the Modigliani–Miller theorem.

New debt issue

Suppose the marginal project is financed by new debt rather than new equity issue. Since interest liabilities are usually deductible against the corporate tax base, we will have:

$$\rho R = [(1 - t_i)/(1 - t_\pi)]\rho F \tag{9.55}$$

and by equations (9.51) and (9.49) again:

$$\rho F = i(1 - t_\pi). \tag{9.56}$$

It is well known that under a cash flow tax system, equation (9.56) becomes $\rho F = i$ as interest is no longer deductible against the corporate tax base. Thus, a classical tax system provides neutrality with respect to equity and debt finance under conditions of full distribution.

Using retained earnings

Now consider the case where retained earnings are used to finance the marginal project. This financing policy enables the supplier of funds (now also the owner of the firm) to avoid taxation on distributed profits and capital gains at the personal level. Then:

$$\rho R = (1 - t_d)\rho F \qquad (9.57)$$

but as the sacrifice is $(1 - t_d)$ rather than 1, the arbitrage condition will imply that:

$$\rho R = (1 - t_d)(1 - t_i)i \qquad (9.58)$$

and

$$\rho F = (1 - t_i)i. \qquad (9.59)$$

Once again, $t_i = t_\pi$ might be a condition of tax neutrality with respect to corporate financing policies.

Return to a project and the marginal effective tax rate

As a result of the optimality conditions under different financing methods depicted by equations (9.53), (9.54) and (9.56) the return from a project to the owner of the corporation can be written as:

$$\sigma'_j = (1 - t_d)[\{(1 - t_\pi)(\delta + \rho)/(\rho + \delta - \mu)\}\rho + \rho S - \eta_j i] \qquad (9.60)$$

where

$$\eta_j = \begin{bmatrix} 1/\Lambda \text{ for } j = 1, & \text{financing by new shares,} \\ 1 - t_\pi \text{ for } j = 2, & \text{financing by new debt,} \\ 1 - t_i \text{ for } j = 3, & \text{financing by retained earnings} \end{bmatrix}$$

whereas for the supplier of funds the return is:

$$\sigma'' = (1 - t_i)i - \mu \qquad (9.61)$$

which is, clearly, independent of the mode of financing the marginal project. Now, from the fact $\sigma' \geqslant 0$ we have:

$$r_p \geqslant [\eta_j i/\rho - S][\rho + \delta - \mu](1 - t_\pi) - \delta. \qquad (9.62)$$

Equations (9.60), (9.61) and (9.62) are central to the analysis of marginal effective tax rates. In view of equation (9.44) the marginal effective tax rate also depends upon the method of financing and can be written as:

$$t_e = 1 - (1 - t_d)[\{(1 - t_\pi)(\rho + \delta)/(\rho + \delta - \mu)\}\rho + \rho S - \eta_j i]/r_p \qquad (9.63)$$
$$\quad - [(1 - t_i)i - \mu]r_p.$$

This is the generalized version of the marginal effective rate of taxation.

The King–Fullerton method of measuring marginal effective tax rates assumes that, at the margin, the project gives no returns to the owner. In that case $\sigma' = 0$ for all methods of financing. With this substitution equation (9.62) becomes the strict equality:

$$r_p = [(\eta_j i/\rho) - S][(\rho + \delta - \mu)/(1 - t_\pi)] - \delta \qquad (9.64)$$

so that the King–Fullerton measure of marginal effective rate of taxation becomes:

$$t_e^{KF} = 1 - [(1 - t_i)i - \mu]/r_p \tag{9.65}$$

where r_p is given by equation (9.64).

Extension to an open economy

Let i_w be the highest net of tax nominal interest rate that is available anywhere in the world (called country w) to a domestic saver. In that case, the domestic interest rate (ignoring exchange rate fluctuations) should be such that:

$$(1 - t_i)i = i_w. \tag{9.66}$$

In order to be competitive, the net of tax interest rate at home must be equal to the best interest rate available abroad. If the tax rate on interest income in country w is t_i^w then the gross of tax interest rate must be i_w^g where:

$$i_w^g(1 - t_i^w) = i_w. \tag{9.67}$$

Hence, the domestic interest rate is:

$$i = i_w^g(1 - t_i^w)/(1 - t_i) \tag{9.68}$$

so that the domestic interest rate has become a predetermined variable. Hence, equation (9.46) will become:

$$\sigma'' = i_w^g(1 - t_w) - \mu. \tag{9.69}$$

Costs of transnational investment

Consider a prospective dominant shareholder who is a resident of the home country. He considers investing in country s. The investor has to provide the supplier of the funds with a return equal to $(1 - t_i^w)i_w$ which is the best rate of return available. Let us consider the same three alternative sources of finances: equity finance, debt finance and retained earnings.

With new shares we will have:

$$\rho F = i_w^g/\Lambda^S \tag{9.70}$$

with

$$\Lambda^s = [(1 - t_d^s)/(1 - t_i^w)]v + (1 - t_c^s)/(1 - t_i^w)(1 - v) \tag{9.71}$$

where t_d^s is the withholding tax rate on dividend in country s and t_c^s is the withholding rate on capital gains on accrual basis.

With new debt we will have:

$$\rho F = (1 - t_\pi^S)\{(1 - t_i^w)/(1 - t_i^s)\}i_w^g \tag{9.72}$$

where t_π^s and t_i^s stand for the corporate tax rate and the withholding tax on interest income in country s.

With retained earnings, the investor will take into account his own net sacrifice in terms of unpaid dividend or immediate capital gain. However, unlike the saver, he cannot avoid personal income tax in either his country of business or his country of residence. Hence his net sacrifice per unit of capital is $(1 - t_r^s)$ where t_r^s is the repatriation tax rate on dividend and capital gains paid in country s and taxed possibly both in the country of origin, s, and the country of residence of the shareholder. This rate is a statistic encompassing relevant provisions of the tax treaty between the home country and country s. Hence, we will have:

$$\rho F = (1 - t_w) i_w^g. \tag{9.73}$$

As a consequence of equations (9.70) to (9.73) we can write the return on a project in country s with the owner resident in the home country as:

$$\sigma_j' = (1 - t_r^s)[\{(1 - t_\pi)(r_p + \delta)/(\rho + \delta - \mu)\}\rho + \rho S^s - \eta_j^s i_w^g] \tag{9.74}$$

with

$$\eta_j^s = \begin{bmatrix} 1/\Lambda^s & \text{for } j = 1 \,(\text{equity finance}) \\ (1 - t_\pi^s)(1 - t_i^w)/(1 - t_i^s) & \text{for } j = 2 \,(\text{debt finance}) \\ 1 - t_i^w & \text{for } j = 3 \,(\text{retained earnings}). \end{bmatrix}$$

Thus, in view of equation (9.45) we must have:

$$r_p \geqslant [(\eta_j^s i_w^g/\rho) - S^s](\rho + \delta - \mu)/(1 - t_\pi^s) - \delta \tag{9.75}$$

so that the marginal effective tax rate on transnational investment now becomes:

$$t_e = 1 - (1 - t_r^s)[\{(1 - t_\pi^s)(r_p + \delta)/(\rho + \delta - \mu)\}\rho + \rho S^s - \eta_j^s i_w^g]/r_p$$
$$- [i(1 - t_i^w) - \mu]/r_p \tag{9.76}$$

which can be compared to the effective tax rate in a closed economy derived in equation (9.63) and the effective tax rate of the King–Fullerton variety derived in equation (9.65).

In the case of the open economy the King–Fullerton measure of effective tax rate will become:

$$t_e^{KF} = 1 - [i_w^g(1 - t_i^w) - \mu]/r_p^* \tag{9.77}$$

where

$$r_p^* = \{(\eta_j^s i_w/\rho) - S^s\}(\rho + \delta - \mu)/(1 - t_\pi^s) - \delta. \tag{9.78}$$

An interesting aspect of the King–Fullerton result is that the arbitrage condition means that the repatriation tax drops out of the formula for the effective tax rate.

9.7   CONCLUSIONS

The effects of taxes on the rate of investment is an exceedingly complex topic. In this chapter we have tried to understand some aspects of this problem. We began by detailing the dominant theories of investment – the Fisherian model and the related Jorgenson model. We modeled extant aspects of tax policy such as corporate tax, investment tax credit, and historical depreciation allowance. We then examined the effects of changing some of these instruments on the incentive to invest or, for stationary capital stock, on the amount of government revenue from the tax. We also discussed the financial aspects of investment. The Modigliani–Miller theorem was cited in support of separating financial from real decisions. However, some exceptions were considered. We also developed the notion of an effective rate of tax on capital.

The discussion in this chapter is only indicative of the type of research being done in the general area of the effects of taxation on capital investment. Much of the literature suggests that the process of capital formation is quite sensitive to tax rules. There has been considerable work on the effects of the capital gains tax – particularly the decision to realize the capital gain.[6] Work has also been done (see Auerbach and Hines 1987, for example) on the process of forming expectations about tax changes and the effects of such changes. International aspects of taxation and effects on investment at home and abroad are increasingly important (see Giovanni *et al.* 1993). Calculations of effective tax rates and their effects on investment also abound.

NOTES

1 Recall that in standard textbook exposition the MEC is a declining function of the rate of investment because the marginal product of capital falls with addition to the capital stock. However, current investment is too miniscule a fraction of the capital stock for this to serve as an adequate explanation for the aforementioned relation.
2 See, for instance, Lucas (1976) or Abel (1978) Merton (1978).
3 Putty-putty means capital/labor ratio can be changed before and after the investment. Putty-clay means the capital/labor ratio is alterable before investment – not after it and clay-clay means the capital/labor ratio is fixed both before and after investment.
4 We have more to say on this discount rate later in the chapter.
5 For a discussion on the notion of 'an effective rate of tax' see Section 9.7.
6 There is some disagreement about whether capital gains should be taxed on realization or on actual accrual. If one uses the realization criterion then it might be the case that many people would face liquidity crises in the process of paying the tax. Think of a house owner whose asset value goes up because of inflation or some other reason. If he had to pay capital gains tax every year (even though he retained the house) he would find the going difficult. If, however, capital gains are taxed on realization, then there might be a tendency to postpone indefinitely the sale of an asset – merely in order to avoid having to pay the capital gains tax.

ADDITIONAL READING

The survey by Mintz and Purvis (1987) is very useful. Boadway *et al.* (1986) provide an excellent example of the use of the theory for policy purposes. See also King and Fullerton (1984) and Gordon (1985).

10 Taxation and Risk Taking

Key concepts: Modigliani–Miller theorem; taxation and the MM theorem; tax progression and risk taking

10.1 INTRODUCTION

In this chapter we discuss the effects of taxation on the taking of risk. Does the tax system discourage risk taking and the supply of funds to finance it? Taxation may influence risk taking at two levels. It may affect portfolio decisions by households or institutions and, hence, the availability of funds or it may affect real investment decisions made by firms.

Needless to say, there are several dimensions to the effects of taxation on risk taking. In this chapter we study these effects in some simple models of portfolio choice. We then proceed to prove the Modigliani–Miller theorem on the irrlevance of capital structure at the level of the firm. If the capital structure of the firm is irrelevant then taxation may not affect its financing decisions. This naturally leads to a consideration of the set of conditions under which the Modigliani–Miller result would not hold. In particular we pay attention to the effects of uncertainty and the presence of non-linear corporate tax structures. The chapter closes with some concluding comments.

10.2 EFFECTS OF TAXATION ON RISK TAKING BY HOUSEHOLDS

To start consider a simple example due to Sandmo (1987). Suppose there are two types of assets: a safe asset with zero return (say cash) and a risky asset with return x. Initial wealth is A_0. The individual wants to maximize terminal wealth: $A = A_0(1 + ax)$ where a is the fraction of wealth in the risky asset. Suppose that, as per the individual's calculations, the optimal fraction is a^*.

Suppose now that we introduce a proportional wealth tax at the rate of t_h. Let us suppose that losses can be offset against taxes so that after tax return is $x(1 - t_h)$ where x can be positive or negative. To get the same terminal wealth as in the no-tax case the individual needs to increase the proportion of wealth in the risky asset to â where:

$$â = a^*/(1 - t_h). \tag{10.1}$$

In this example private risk taking as measured by the net of tax risk $[â(1 - t_h)]$ is the same as before, however, social risk taking has increased because the proportion of wealth in the risky asset has risen.

In this version of the model there is a simple result due to Sandmo (1987a) and others which can be easily derived. Suppose individuals have a utility function U(W) defined over terminal wealth. Initial wealth W_0 can be split up into the amount held in the riskless asset money (m) and the risky asset (a) so that the budget constraint of the individual is:

$$m + a = W_0. \tag{10.2}$$

Final wealth of this wealth-holder is:

$$W = a[1 + x(1 - t_w)] + m \tag{10.3}$$

assuming that money pays no interest nor does it depreciate in value due to inflation. We will assume that x is continuously distributed on the interval $[-1, \infty)$ so that expected utility is:

$$E(U(W)) = \int_{-1}^{\infty} U\{a[1 + x(1 - t_w)] + m\}f(x)dx \tag{10.4}$$

where $f(x)$ is the (known) distribution of returns from the risky asset. Upon substituting from equation (10.2) we have:

$$E(U(W)) = \int_{-1}^{\infty} U(W_0 + ax(1 - t_w))f(x)dx. \tag{10.5}$$

The wealth-holder chooses a to maximize the above utility function for which the first-order condition will be:

$$E(U'(W_0 + ax(1 - t_w))x(1 - t_w)) = 0. \tag{10.6}$$

If the utility function is concave, the second-order condition for an internal maximum will be satisfied. Arrow (1970) has shown that $a > 0$ only if $E(x) > 0$. If we are to proceed further, we will have to assume that this is the case.

We would now like to find out how the investor would react to changes in the tax rate t_w. To do this we will have to differentiate the first-order condition (10.6) with respect to t_w. Performing this we have:

$$E[U''(W)\{(\partial a/\partial t_w)x(1 - t_w) - ax\}x(1 - t_w) - U'(W)x] = 0. \tag{10.7}$$

In view of equation (10.6) the last term in this expression is zero, in optimum. Hence, we must have:

$$(\partial a/\partial t_w)x(1 - t_w) = ax$$

or, that

$$(\partial a/\partial t_w) = a/(1 - t_w) \text{ or that} (t_w/a)(\partial a/\partial t_w) = t_w/(1 - t_w). \quad (10.8)$$

In other words, the elasticity of the amount of wealth in the risky asset depends only on the tax rate in the manner shown in equation (10.8). In particular, this is independent of both the return on the risky asset (x) and the form of the utility function.

The rule in equation (10.8) has a simple interpretation. The individual is interested in keeping the value of final wealth constant at the level given by equation (10.6). Hence, when the tax rate rises, the individual will invest more in the risky asset in order to compensate for the loss in wealth because of taxation.

There is a couple of quite strong assumptions associated with the analysis so far. We mention two here: first, that money carries no interest; second, that the size of savings is not affected by an increase in taxes.

Suppose we abandon the first assumption and allow money to carry an interest of r. Clearly, a rational wealth-holder will hold wealth in the risky asset only if $E(x) > r$.

We will assume that this is the case. It is easy then to extend the previous analysis to cover a positive interest rate on money. If both interest income as well as the return from the risky asset are taxed at the rate t_w we can write final wealth as:

$$
\begin{aligned}
W &= a[1 + x(1 - t_w)] + m[1 + r(1 - t_w)] \\
&= W_0[1 + r(1 - t_w)] + a(x - r)(1 - t_w). \quad (10.9)
\end{aligned}
$$

The wealth-holder wishes to maximize $U(W)$. We can proceed as before. We differentiate U with respect to t_w and set $U'(W)$ equal to zero. Then to get a condition parallel to equation (10.8) we differentiate $U'(\cdot)$ with respect to t_w and set it equal to zero to discover the optimal response of the wealth-holder to a change in t_w.

We discover that:

$$(\partial a/\partial t_w) = \frac{E[U''(W)(x - r)]}{E[U''(W)(x - r)^2]} \frac{Ar}{(1 - t_w)} + \frac{a}{(1 - t_w)}. \quad (10.10)$$

Now, since:

$$(\partial a/\partial W_0) = -[1 + r(1 - t_w)/(1 - t_w)][EU''(W)(x - r)/\{EU''(W)(x - r)^2\}]$$

we substitute into equation (10.10) to get:

$$(\partial a/\partial W) = [W_0 r/(1 + r(1 - t_w))](\partial a/\partial W_0)] + a/(1 - t_w)$$

or, in elasticity form:

$$(\partial a/\partial t_w)(t_w/a) = -\{t_w r/(1 + r(1 - t_w))\}\{(\partial a/\partial W_0)(W_0/a)\} + t_w/(1 - t_w). \quad (10.11)$$

The last term of equation (10.11) is the same as the righthand side of equation (10.8). In addition we now have (the first term on the righthand side of equation (10.11)) an income effect which depends upon the wealth elasticity of holding wealth in the risky asset. This income and the earlier substitution effect are in conflict with each other. However, the substitution effect is likely to dominate the income effect for reasonable values of the parameters.

A special case of the above is the **net tax case** where only the earnings from the risky asset in excess of the return from the safe asset is taxed. Then terminal wealth is:

$$W = a(1 + x) + m(1 + r) - a(x - r)t_w$$
$$= W_0(1 + r) + a(x - r)(1 - t_w). \tag{10.12}$$

Differentiating with respect to t_w we have:

$$E[U'(W)(x - r)(1 - t_w)] = 0 \tag{10.13}$$

and upon differentiating, once again, to find the optimal response to a change in t_w we will get equation (10.8) back again.

If there are many risky assets the results of the net tax case carry over. In other words, if only the returns in excess of the return on the safe asset are taxed, then for the ith risky asset we must have:

$$(\partial a_i/\partial t_{w_i}) = (a_i/(1 - t_i)) \quad \text{and} \quad (\partial a_i/\partial t_{w_j}) = 0 \text{ for } i \neq j \tag{10.14}$$

where a_i is the amount invested in the ith risky asset. This has been demonstrated by Sandmo (1977). No considerations about the joint probability distributions of the returns of assets is necessary. Nothing concrete can be said, however, about the gross taxation case when all assets – risky as well as non-risky – are subject to the same rate of tax.

Other forms of taxation

Suppose that instead of returns from assets, terminal wealth is taxed. Final wealth would then be:

$$W = (W_0(1 + r) + a(x - r))(1 - t_y) \tag{10.15}$$

where t_y is the tax rate on final wealth. The first order condition for final utility maximization can be written as:

$$E[U'(W)(x - r)(1 - t_y)] = 0 \tag{10.16}$$

and upon differentiating once again with respect to t_y we obtain:

$$(\partial a/\partial t_y) = [1/(1 - t_y)]E\{U''(W)W(x - r)\}/\{EU''(W)(x - r)^2(1 - t_y)\}. \tag{10.17}$$

We now assume that the utility function is of the constant elasticity of the marginal utility of wealth form or constant relative risk aversion in the

Arrow–Pratt sense. In that case: $-U''(W)W/(U'(W)) = \alpha$ (a constant). Substituting into equation (10.17) and using (10.16) we will have:

$$(\partial a/\partial t_y) = (1/(1-t_y))[-\alpha E\{U'(W)(x-r)\}]/\{E[U''(W)(x-r)^2(1-t_y)]\} = 0.$$

$$(10.18)$$

Thus, the wealth tax has no effect on the composition of the wealth-holder's portfolio. In cases where constant relative risk aversion does not hold, an increase in the tax will raise (lower) the amount held in the risky asset according to whether relative risk aversion is increasing (decreasing).

10.3   THE MODIGLIANI–MILLER THEOREM AND DECISIONS ON THE FINANCING OF INVESTMENT EXPENDITURE

One major source of risks for households, of course, is the holding of risky assets issued by firms. Unlike the real theory of investment, which we went through in Chapter 9, the financial theory of investment is essentially static. Only very recently have efforts been made to extend it to cover dynamic situations (Merton 1982, for example). From a general viewpoint, one may well argue that it is probably better to study the real theory of investment and its financing at the same time.

The separation of the investment and the financing decisions, which we have implicitly been making, is a reflection of the Modigliani–Miller theorem, hence forth known as MM Modigliani and Miller 1958) which argued that financial policy is irrelevant to determining the present value of the firm's earnings. Since then two strands of the literature have grown up – one that supports the MM result and the other which shows that it does not hold in more general situations.

When financing investment firms have three sources: retained earnings, debt and new equity. The first is referred to as an internal source whereas the latter two are called external sources. Finer classification is possible, for example, long debt and short debt, but we will ignore these.

The MM theorem makes the following assumptions:

(i) Competitive markets for risky assets. Although in our discussion of the Jorgenson model we have assumed perfect foresight, it would be quite opportune to say that firms face a variety of risks. For instance, they may face uncertainty about the demand price, or prices of factors of production and so on. Households that ultimately own all wealth in the economy can reduce risk by holding risk-bearing assets issued by various firms. As will be shown below, the price of risk faced by the firm is determined by an equilibrium in which firm-specific risk is measured as the covariance between the firm's returns with the individual wealth-holder's portfolio income. In the MM theorem, each firm may be characterized by a well-defined risk 'class'. Further, each firm is competitive in that its risk premium is unaffected by the amount of securities it issues.

(ii) The second major assumption of the MM theorem is that firms never become bankrupt. This implies that the contractual interest payable on bonds is certain so that the bondholders earn a safe rate of return on their investments in private bonds. At the same time, households do not go bankrupt and can borrow at a safe rate of interest.

(iii) Neither firms that issue securities nor households who buy them incur transaction costs during these sales/purchases. Firms do not have any inherent advantage over households in issuing securities and the borrowing and lending rates of interest are the same.

(iv) All households have the same information about the future profitability of each firm. Further, households can costlessly monitor the effort undertaken by managers and workers of every firm so that financing considerations are irrelevant when compensating workers or managers for their effort.

(v) There are no taxes.

We are now in a position to prove the MM theorem. The model we choose to study is an old one (Diamond 1967, which is also discussed in Mintz and Purvis 1987) but has been used by other authors in much more recent work. Consider an economy that is populated by N firms indexed by j. Each firm has a capital stock (K_j) a fraction β_j of which is financed by bonds and $(1 - \beta_j)$ by equity. Thus β_j is the debt–capital ratio of the firm. The firm produces during the period and sells its output at the end of the period. It earns uncertain net revenues equal to $R_j(K_j, \sigma)$ where σ is the state of nature, unknown to the households, when investment and financing decisions are made. From these revenues the firm pays bondholders: $r\beta_j K_j$ where r is the rate of interest.

Now, let us consider the budget constraint of each household. Each household (indexed by i) makes portfolio decisions at the beginning of each period, purchasing bonds and equity assets. The initial wealth of the household is A_0^i which includes the value of equity held in firms before the stock market opens. When trading occurs, each individual obtains a share θ_{ij} of the jth firm's equity. The total value of equity in firm j is equal to the amount of financing net of debt issues, required by the firm plus the present value of future profits expected to be earned by the firm. Let us denote the present value of pure profits of the jth firm as H_j and the total amount of equity issued by the firm as $H_j + (1 - \beta_j)K_j$.

At this point we should make the important distinction between the replacement value of the firm's capital (K_j) and the value of the firm which is equal to pure profits plus the replacement value of the capital stock $(H_j + K_j)$. Only when firms earn zero expected future pure profits will the market value of the firm be equal to the replacement value of the capital stock of the firm.

Households use their wealth A_0^i to buy b_i bonds and equity worth $\sum_j \theta_{ij}(H_j + (1 - \beta_j)K_j)$. In equilibrium the sum of all individual purchases must equal total equity, that is,

$\sum_i \theta_{ij} = 1$ (for each firm j) and, further, the total supply of bonds must equal the total demand for bonds so that

$$\sum_i b_i = \sum_j \beta_j K_j.$$

Letting $c_i(\sigma)$ be the consumption of household i in state of the world σ we can write the budget constraint of the household as:

$$c_i(\sigma) = \sum_j \theta_{ij}(R_j(K_j, \ \sigma) - r\beta_j K_j) + rb_i \qquad (10.19)$$

where

$$b_i = A_0^i - \sum_j \theta_{ij}[H_j + (1 - \beta_j)K_j]. \qquad (10.20)$$

The household maximizes expected utility $E_i[U_i(c_i(\sigma))]$ where E_i is the expectations operator conditional on information available to the ith household. The household thus chooses an optimal share of each firm's equity (θ_{ij}) and bonds b_i subject to the budget constraints (10.19) and (10.20). Substituting equation (10.20) into (10.19) we have:

$$c_i(\sigma) = \sum_j \theta_{ij}(R_j(K_j, \ \sigma) - rK_j) + r(A_0^i - \sum_j \theta_{ij}H_j). \qquad (10.21)$$

Note that the debt/capital ratio (β_i) no longer appears in the wealth-holder's budget constraint. This is the famous Modigliani–Miller theorem. The intuition behind this is simply that the wealth-holder negates any financial action undertaken by the firm. If the firm decides to issue an additional dollar's worth of debt, the households will reduce their borrowings (b_i is negative) or increase their ownership of bonds by the same amount.

The role of risk in the Modigliani–Miller theorem

Consider now the optimal choice of θ_{ij} for each household. Using equation (10.21) as the budget constraint in the maximization of household expected utility we can write the first-order condition as:

$$E_i\{(\partial U_i/\partial c_i)[(R_j(K_j, \ \sigma)) - r(K_j + H_j)]\} = 0 \qquad (10.22)$$

where $(\partial U_i/\partial c_i)$ denotes marginal utility of state-contingent consumption. Rewrite equation (10.22) as $E_i(\partial U_i/\partial c_i)R_j = r(K_j + H_j)E_i(\partial U_i/\partial c_i)$. We now add and subtract $E_i R_j$ and rearrange to get:

$$E_i R_j = r(K_j + H_j) - [E_i(\partial U_i/\partial c_i)(R_j - E_i R_j)]/[E_i(\partial U_i/\partial c_i)].$$

By adding and substracting $E_i(\partial U_i/\partial c_i)$ to the last expression we get:

$$\phi_{ij} = -\text{cov}[(\partial U_i/\partial c_i), \ R_j]/[E_i(\partial U_i/\partial c_i)]$$

as a measure of risk premium. In this expression:

$$\text{cov}[(\partial U_i/\partial c_i), \ R_j] = E_i\{(R_j - E_i R_j)((\partial U_i/\partial c_i) - E_i(\partial U_i/\partial c_i))\}.$$

Hence, we have:

$$E_i\{R_j(K_j, \ \sigma)\} - \phi_{ij} = r[K_j + H_j]. \tag{10.23}$$

From the MM theorem we know that $H_j + K_j$ must equal the sum of total bonds and equities issued by firm j. Hence, it must be the case that equation (10.23) says that the discounted value of the expected return to capital, adjusted for risk, is equal to the value of the firm's equity plus debt.

The adjustment for risk depends on the covariance between the marginal utility of state contingent consumption of the ith consumer and the return to capital of the jth firm. One can think of two factors as influencing this covariance. On the one hand the return to capital of the jth firm may be positively correlated with individual *i*'s portfolio of asset returns. On the other hand, the ith investor could be risk averse or risk neutral. If he is risk averse then the marginal utility of consumption is decreasing with higher levels of consumption. In this case the covariance term will be negative if, in addition, there is a positive correlation between the return to capital of the jth firm and individual *i*'s portfolio of asset returns. In case the individual wealth-holder is risk neutral, the marginal utility of his consumption is constant and the risk premium would be zero.

Effects of taxation on the Modigliani–Miller result

What are the effects of taxation on the Modigliani–Miller result? To analyze this problem in its simplest form we abandon uncertainty and work with the model of Miller (1977) and Alvazian and Turnbull (1987). Miller raises the issue of optimal capital structure in a world with personal and corporate taxes. He argues that in the absence of bankruptcy costs, an optimal capital structure would not exist for the individual firm but it would exist for the economy as a whole. Typically, tax laws allow for deductibility of interest paid and tax dividends at the level of the household. Miller argues that the deductibility of interest at the corporate tax level will be exactly offset by increased taxes at the personal level whatever the firm's debt–equity mix. Present value maximizing firms will increase their supply of corporate debt so long as the increase in personal taxes is more than offset by the tax shield to the corporation resulting from interest payment on additional debt. The higher personal tax rates will, in turn, be fully capitalized into higher market yields in equilibrium.

Let i_0 be the yield on tax-free bonds. i_0 is assumed to be constant and exogenously given. Hence, if t_π is the corporate tax rate then firms will pay a rate of return on bonds equal to $i_0/(1 - t_\pi)$. In other words, investors will

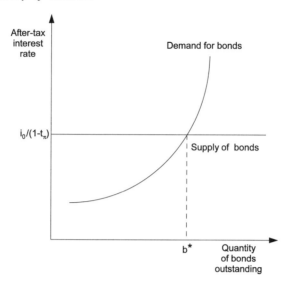

Figure 10.1

be indifferent between buying a tax-free bond and a corporate bond because each gives the same after-tax yield. We analyze this situation in Figure 10.1. In this diagram the demand for bonds is upward sloping as a function of the after-tax interest (negatively sloping with respect to the price of bonds, the reciprocal of the interest rate) and is obtained by summing up individual demand functions. If the tax on bond yields is t_b then individual investors would require a return of $i_0/(1 - t_b)$. The supply curve is horizontal at the rate of interest $i_0/(1 - t_\pi)$ which is what firms must pay. The optimal amount of bonds is b^*. If the tax rate on bonds and the corporate tax rate are different then individuals for whom $t_b < t_\pi$ will get all the surplus generated by the difference between the supply yield $[i_0/(1 - t_\pi)]$ and the minimum demand of investors in the bond market $[i_0/(1 - t_b)]$. All tax-induced surpluses accrue to debt holders and, therefore, capital structure is irrelevant at the individual firm level. The MM theorem is back again.

If dividends were taxed at the rate t_d then Miller's argument would go as follows. By holding a bond an individual gets $i_0/(1 - t_b)$. To be indifferent between holding a bond and an equity the yield on the equity should be $i_0/[(1 - t_d)(1 - t_\pi)]$. Thus, a condition for equilibrium is that:

$$i_0/[(1 - t_d)(1 - t_\pi)] = i_0/(1 - t_b) \tag{10.24}$$

or, that,

$$(1 - t_\pi)(1 - t_d)/(1 - t_b) = 1. \tag{10.25}$$

The present value of the tax shelter associated with debt is:

$$b[1 - (1 - t_\pi)(1 - t_d)/(1 - t_b)]$$

where *b* is the face value of debt outstanding. Firms will issue debt until, in equilibrium, the present value of the tax shelter to any firm is zero. This occurs when equation (10.25) is satisfied. Thus, in equilibrium, capital structure at the level of the firm is irrelevant.

The assumption that there is only one corporate tax rate is crucial to the Miller result. Suppose that there are two corporate tax rates t_π^1 and t_π^2 with $t_\pi^2 > t_\pi^1$. We draw the relevant supply of debt functions in Figure 10.2 – one for each level of the corporate tax rate. Corporations facing the higher corporate tax rate can now effect greater potential tax savings by biasing capital structure in favor of bonds. There are two levels of optimal debt b^* and b^{**} with the higher debt level associated with corporations facing the higher tax rate.

Let us now extend the analysis to consider uncertainty. In this case as the firm issues more debt it increases potential deductions. However, leverage also increases the probability of bankruptcy. An increase in the probability of bankruptcy will lower expected corporate tax shields from the issuance of debt since tax laws in most countries do not permit a complete transfer of unused tax credits and deductions through time or across firms. An increase in leverage will also increase expected direct and indirect bankruptcy costs. De Angelo and Masulis (1980) re-examined Miller's irrelevance argument in a world of uncertainty when there are leverage related costs due to the inability of firms to capitalize on tax deductions in excess of earnings in

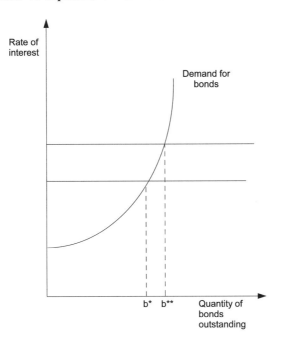

Figure 10.2

bankruptcy states as well as the existence of potential tax shields substitutes for debt. They show that firms will have optimal internal financing mixes. Their model predicts that the level of debt will be inversely related to the ability of the firm to generate tax shields from other sources such as depreciation, contribution to a pension fund and investment tax credits. Ross (1985) has extended the De Angelo and Masulis analysis to show that there is a relationship between the capital structure of the firm – as induced by tax effects – and systematic risk. Bartholdy *et al.* (1985) provide an analysis of corporate capital structure decisions under either partial or full loss offsetting assumptions about the tax code. They derive conditions on the tax rates and other variables for which imperfect loss offsetting in the tax system indicates an internal debt–equity ratio.

We can visualize the analysis under uncertainty in the supply–demand diagram (Figure 10.3). On the supply side, the expected return on corporate debt, $r_s(b)$, will decline with the supply of debt reflecting lower expected corporate tax shields and higher expected bankruptcy costs. As firms issue more debt, the present value of associated tax shelters declines and the present value of associated costs of default rises. Hence, to keep the marginal cost of debt equal to the marginal cost of equity, the pre-tax yield paid by the firm will decline with debt. The demand for debt, $r_d(b)$, will be an increasing function of expected return reflecting higher personal taxes on debt and higher risk discount factors for more risk averse investors. Equilibrium, depicted in Figure 10.3, corresponds to an aggregate level of outstanding debt of $\hat{b}$.

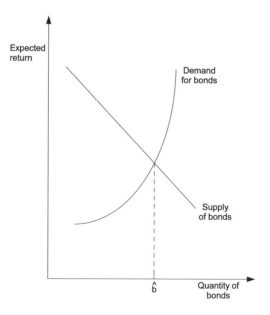

Figure 10.3

One should note, however, that there is no necessary correspondence between investor asset holdings and personal tax rates. Furthermore, corporate debt is relevant not only at the aggregate level but also at the level of the individual firm, since expected bankruptcy costs and loss of tax shields are firm-specific factors.

Uncertainty because of asymmetric information

Uncertainty may also generate asymmetric information problems between the firm and the investors giving rise to agency problems. (Laffont and Tirole 1993). When there are conflicts of interest among various claimants on the firm, viewing the firm's capital structure problem as one of determining the optimal debt–equity mix is too narrow a perspective. The capital structure problem involves determining the whole structure of property rights arrangements on the firm. Jensen and Meckling (1976) define agency costs as including monitoring and bonding expenditures by the principal and the agent respectively, as well as a residual loss reflecting production and investment opportunities foregone as a result of the agency relationship.

Jensen and Meckling (1976) and Myers (1977) examine the role of financial contracts in controlling moral hazard problems. Myers argues that the existence of risky debt claims in the capital structure of a firm with potential growth opportunities may impose an externality on the shareholder-manager's optimal investment strategy. Should the debt mature after the growth opportunities present themselves, bond holders will share in any profitable future investments. Therefore, in certain states of the world, characterized by valuable investment opportunities, stockholders will have the incentive to reject projects with positive net present value since some of the benefits from such projects will accrue to bondholders. The value of such foregone investment opportunities as well as the expenditures incurred in enforcing provisions of the debt contract are part of the agency cost of the debt. Jensen and Meckling argue that even in the absence of any tax advantage to debt, there will be an incentive for the firm to issue debt if the marginal agency costs of debt are less than the marginal agency costs of equity.

Leland and Pyle (1977) and Ross (1977) treat the firm's usage of debt as a signaling device to overcome possible adverse selection problems generated by information asymmetries between managers and shareholders. Shareholders cannot distinguish 'good' managers from 'bad'. Given that managerial compensation depends upon the market value of the firm, managers may use debt to signal to market participants information about managerial quality which they cannot otherwise convey.

Grossman and Hart (1983) argue that leverage may act as a bonding mechanism reducing the scope for opportunistic behavior by management. Leverage increases the risk of bankruptcy and, since bankruptcy is costly for managers, they can use leverage to certify themselves and their favorable prospects to investors and, in effect, lower the cost of capital to the firm.

Agency considerations, once again, lower the empirical validity of Miller's model about the gains from leverage.

Myers (1984) argues that, given the consideration of the costs associated with bankruptcy and financial embarrassments, two general statements can be made about corporate leverage policy. First, there should be an inverse relationship between risk and the amount the firm is willing to borrow (with risk being defined as the variance of the rate of return on the value of the firm's assets). Second, firms holding tangible assets in place having active secondhand markets will be able to borrow more than firms holding specialized, intangible assets or valuable growth opportunities.

The work discussed above thinks of firms as picking leverage to balance the present value of leverage-related costs (bankruptcy costs, agency costs, etc.) against the present value of tax shelters provided by the leverage. Myers (1984) has called this approach the 'static tradeoff hypothesis'. If there are no costs of adjustment then firms should be at their optimal capital structure. However, there may be costs and, therefore, lags in adjusting to the optimum as conditions change. Thus there may be across firms dispersion of debt–equity ratios in a sample of firms. The degree of dispersion will depend upon the magnitude of transactions costs associated with the adjustment process.

10.4　THE EFFECTS OF PROGRESSION ON RISK TAKING

If, for tax purposes, assets are valued at their long-run average value, independent of short-run fluctuations, then the question of the tax effect on risk taking is reduced merely to that on cash returns derived from these assets. We know that with full loss offset of negative income a higher proportional rate of taxation on the returns from a risky asset will lead to more private risk taking. This is because the government serves as a silent partner (or insurer) to both gains and losses, which for a risk-averse individual would increase the certainty equivalent of the project. This is probably true for additional ventures of large corporations which, on the one hand, tend to be subject to proportional corporate taxation in most countries and, on the other, have several ventures running at the same time, so that they can easily set off losses against other incomes. Hence, in such cases reductions in the rate of taxation will reduce risk taking.

The situation is quite different, however, for the individual small entrepreneur venturing into business. If this person has only one source of income he will, in general, have no income against which heavy losses can be offset.[1] Such an entrepreneur is then basically in the situation where the government takes away from his earnings but does not compensate him for losses. In this case as Atkinson and Stiglitz (1980: 112) show higher taxes will reduce risk taking and lower taxation will increase it.[2]

Let us finally consider an income tax on risky returns which takes account of the short-term market valuation of the asset financing a risky venture in the sense of treating increases in the value of this asset as positive and decreases as negative income. In this case as Atkinson and Stiglitz (1980: 106–11) show a lower rate of taxation will lead to an increase in private risk taking if absolute risk aversion is a declining function of wealth. As risk-taking income is likely to be on average high income, the results for a lower rate of taxation carry over to less progressive taxation.

In conclusion we can say that the less progressive tax is likely to increase private risk taking of individuals and small firms, though possibly not that of large corporations. In most cases, the risk taken by large corporations is treated preferentially by government, so that this caveat may not be of much significance.

One can also examine the effect of taxes on the relationship between shareholders (the principal) and managers (the agents). If managers are able to maximize their own utility to a certain extent[3] because they are not fully controlled by shareholders or not subjected to all the competitive pressures of the managerial labor market, then shareholders will have to offer them additional incentive rewards. This would be particularly necessary in cases when shareholders would like managers to take certain risks whereas managers are inclined to play it safe. If the incentive income of managers (for instance, their share in profits) is taxed instead of being untaxed, the incentive effect becomes insufficient. The pre-tax level of these incentives has to be raised that its after-tax level remains the same as the no-tax level. But this would mean that risky projects which also need the control of managers via incentive pay become less profitable for shareholders and some are, hence, not undertaken. More would be undertaken at lower tax rates. As managers have relatively high incomes, this argument about low tax rates carries over to less progressive taxation. It is possible to conclude, then, that less progressive taxation makes it cheaper for shareholders to guide corporate managers towards more risky projects.

If efficiency wages are being paid out[4] then we know that wages are set above market clearing levels in order to ensure that the worker works with full efficiency. In such cases, the relevant wage would be the after-tax wage rate. Thus with lower tax rates, lower pre-tax wages can ensure the same degree of economic efficiency. If it is the case that efficiency wages are paid to middle-income earners, then less progressive taxation at these segments of the wage distribution has the same effect as productivity increases at the lower end of the wage distribution.

It is possible to argue that, in general, lower progressivity in the tax schedule will increase economic efficiency. If, for example, the public imposes a payment on polluters of the environment, a given tax-deductible payment geared to the amount of pollution is more painful at low tax rates than at high rates, for it then reduces after tax returns by more. Thus pollution control by tax-deductible pollution taxes becomes cheaper. This has been shown by Arnott and Stiglitz (1986).[5]

We can conclude then that, in most cases, less progressive taxation will increase economic efficiency.[6] Less progressive taxation may also increase corporate risk taking when this is insufficient without incentive pay for managers.

10.5   CONCLUDING COMMENTS

The effects of taxation on risk taking is a complex issue. In this chapter we have explored some aspects. We began by examining the effects of taxation on optimal portfolio choice of households. Later we realized that these results do not necessarily extend to the case of firms if the Modigliani–Miller theorem holds. If corporate taxes are linear, for example, the Modigliani–Miller result will still hold. This naturally led to a discussion of the conditions under which the Modigliani–Miller theorem may not hold. Among others we considered the existence of uncertainty (partly because of the existence of asymmetric information between shareholders and managers and non-linear corporate taxes). In such cases, the firm's debt–equity composition would once again become relevant and taxation would affect the financing decisions of the firm.

NOTES

1 It is possible, however, that uncorrelated losses over time might be set off against future income.
2 A similar situation arises when comparing safe well-paid jobs with fringe benefits that are untaxed and risky jobs where the remuneration is all in the form of additional monetary benefits, which then get taxed. Higher taxation will lead to a shift away from such socially useful risky jobs and toward the frequently much less useful jobs in the first category.
3 Managers' utility is to be interpreted as their ease and convenience.
4 See, for example, Yellen (1984).
5 Arnott and Stiglitz (1986) also show that if there are only indirect means of public control of moral hazards, the optimal tax problem becomes much more complicated.
6 More precisely, reduce the cost of ensuring efficiency.

ADDITIONAL READING

Two useful treatments of portfolio allocation under risk are Ahsan (1976) and Anderson (1977). The classic work on decision making under risk is Arrow (1970). Recent treatments are available in Blundell (1990, 1992). The literature on the Modigliani–Miller theorem is vast and the references cited in the text of the chapter should serve as a useful introduction.

11 The theory of tax incidence

Key concepts: tax incidence in partial and general equilibrium; output and factor substitution effects; fair wages; rate of return regulation.

11.1 INTRODUCTION

Tax incidence measures the sharing of the tax burden between different groups. When a sales tax is imposed on a commodity, part of the tax may be passed on to consumers so that the burden of the tax is shared by consumers and producers. In this case we say that the incidence of the tax is on producers as well as consumers. If the tax cannot be passed on to consumers then the incidence of the tax would be on producers alone. If a wage tax is imposed and the supply of labor falls, the market clearing wage rate would rise and this would increase the cost of labor to producers. The impact of the wage tax and, hence, the incidence of the wage tax would be on workers as well as employers.

The above two examples illustrate the important point that the measurement of tax incidence is model specific. In the first model, we are essentially carrying out a partial equilibrium exercise as depicted in Figure 11.1. A specific tax is imposed on commodity x. The producer price of the commodity is q and the consumer price is p where

$$p = q + t \tag{11.1}$$

where t is the rate of the specific tax. This is the vertical distance between the pre- and post-tax supply curves in Figure 11.1. The consumer price rises from $p_0 (= q_0)$ to p_1. The producer price is q_1 and we have

$$p_1 = q_1 + t. \tag{11.2}$$

As shown in Figure 11.1, part of the tax burden is borne by the producer and part by the consumer. A moment's thought would tell us that the proportions in which the tax burden is split up between producers and consumers would depend on the elasticities of supply and demand.

In the second example, however, we are admitting **general equilibrium** effects. A wage tax has effects on labor supply which go on to affect the

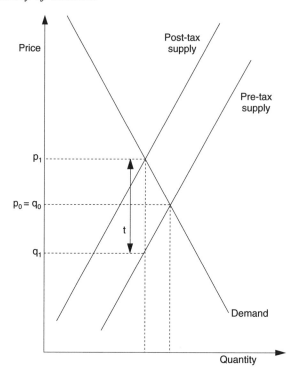

Figure 11.1

wage rate and so on. Hence, the message that the magnitude of tax incidence on any agent is specific to the model we are studying.

In this chapter we will examine alternative models of tax incidence. All these models will be of static general equilibrium. We study tax incidence in dynamic models in Chapter 12. We will begin by considering tax incidence in the full employment general equilibrium model of Chapter 2. This has been studied by a number of authors including Harberger (1965), Mieszkowski (1974) and Atkinson and Stiglitz (1980). We will work out this model in considerable detail. Next we will study tax incidence in a neo-Keynesian model as discussed by Agell and Lundborg (1992). Within the framework of the standard general equilibrium model we introduce some extensions. Finally, we look at tax incidence in a general equilibrium model where there is a rate of return regulation.

11.2 TAX INCIDENCE IN THE TWO-SECTOR MODEL OF GENERAL EQUILIBRIUM

Here we go back to the full employment general equilibrium model of Chapter 2. We first describe the two-sector general equilibrium model without taxes. Then we introduce taxation.

There are two industries X and Y producing output whose amounts are denoted by lower case letters: x and y respectively. Each industry produces output under constant returns to scale and diminishing returns to each factor. There are two factors of production capital K, and labor, L. Each factor of production is smoothly substitutable for the other.

Production conditions are given by the production functions:

$$x = F(K_x, L_x) \tag{11.3}$$

$$\text{and } y = G(K_y, L_y) \tag{11.4}$$

where K_i, L_i are, respectively, the amounts of capital and labor used in industry i $(i = X, Y)$.

We will lay down the structure of the general equilibrium model first without taxes. Then we will perturb the model through taxation and examine the effects on general equilibrium. Differences could, then, be adduced to the tax. We will assume that each commodity is produced under conditions of constant returns to scale. Thus price must equal marginal cost which, in turn, would be independent of output and would depend only upon price of capital (r) and the wage rate (w), both of which are determined in perfectly competitive factor markets.

$$p_x = C_x(r, w) \tag{11.5}$$

$$p_y = C_y(r, w). \tag{11.6}$$

p_i and C_i are, respectively, the price and marginal cost of commodity i $(i = X, Y)$. Since we have constant returns to scale, marginal cost equals average cost and the total cost (TC_i) of producing any level of output must equal marginal cost multiplied by the quantity produced.

$$TC_x = xC_x \tag{11.7}$$

$$TC_y = yC_y. \tag{11.8}$$

Let us now define the following terms:

$$C_{LX} = (\partial C_x / \partial w); \ C_{KX} = (\partial C_x / \partial r)$$
$$C_{KY} = (\partial C_y / \partial r); \quad \text{and} \quad C_{LY} = (\partial C_y / \partial w).$$

Demand for labor in industry X is (xC_{LX}) and in industry Y is (yC_{LY}). Respective demands for capital are (xC_{KX}) and (yC_{KY}).

This is a full-employment general equilibrium model. Total amounts of capital and labor are fixed at K_0 and L_0 respectively and are fully exhausted in producing commodities X and Y. Thus, we have:

$$xC_{KX} + yC_{KY} = K_0 \tag{11.9}$$

$$xC_{LX} + yC_{LY} = L_0. \tag{11.10}$$

Now, totally differentiate equations (11.5) and (11.6) to get:

$$dp_x = C_{KX}dr + C_{LX}dw \tag{11.11}$$

$$dp_y = C_{KY}dr + C_{LY}dw. \tag{11.12}$$

Dividing both sides of equation (11.11) by $p_x = C_x$ and using a hat (^) to denote a rate of change ($\hat{a} = da/a$) we have:

$$\hat{p}_x = (dp_x)/p_x = r(C_{KX}/C_x)(dr/r) + w(C_{LX}/C_x)(dw/w)$$

or

$$\hat{p}_x = r(C_{KX}/C_x)\hat{r} + w(C_{LX}/C_x)\hat{w}. \tag{11.13}$$

In a completely analogous manner we can derive:

$$\hat{p}_y = r(C_{KY}/C_y)\hat{r} + w(C_{LY}/C_y)\hat{w}. \tag{11.14}$$

Let us now define:

$$\beta_{Li} = (wC_{Li})/C_i \text{ (share of labor in industry i)}$$
$$\text{and} \quad \beta_{Ki} = (rC_{Ki})/C_i \text{ (share of capital in industry i).}$$

By Euler's theorem it must be the case that:

$$\beta_{Li} + \beta_{Ki} = 1 \text{ for both industries.}$$

Thus, equation (11.13) can be written as:

$$\hat{p}_x = \beta_{KX}\hat{r} + \beta_{LX}\hat{w} \tag{11.13a}$$

and equation (11.14) as:

$$\hat{p}_y = \beta_{KY}\hat{r} + \beta_{LY}\hat{w}. \tag{11.14a}$$

Subtracting equation (11.14a) from (11.13a) we have:

$$\hat{p}_x - \hat{p}_y = \hat{r}(\beta_{KX} - \beta_{KY}) + \hat{w}(\beta_{LX} - \beta_{LY}). \tag{11.15}$$

This relates changes in relative factor prices to changes in relative output prices and can be rewritten as:

$$\hat{p}_x - \hat{p}_y = (\beta_{LX} - \beta_{LY})(\hat{w} - \hat{r}) \tag{11.15a}$$

(remember that $\beta_{LX} - \beta_{LY} = \beta_{KY} - \beta_{KX}$).

We know that:

$$C_{LX} = C_{LX}(r, w) \tag{11.16a}$$
$$C_{KX} = C_{KX}(r, w) \tag{11.16b}$$
$$C_{LY} = C_{LY}(r, w) \tag{11.16c}$$
$$C_{KY} = C_{KY}(r, w). \tag{11.16d}$$

Totally differentiation of equation (11.16a) yields:

$$dC_{LX} = (\partial C_{LX}/\partial r)dr + (\partial C_{LX}/\partial w)dw.$$

Divide by C_{LX} and multiply and divide both sides conformably to get:

$$(dC_{LX}/C_{LX}) = r(C_{LKX}/C_{LX})(dr/r) + w(C_{LLX}/C_{LX})(dw/w) \tag{11.17}$$

where $C_{LKX} = (\partial C_{LX}/\partial r)$ and $C_{LLX} = (\partial C_{LX}/\partial w)$.

Substituting in equation (11.17) we have:

$$\hat{C}_{LX} = r(C_{LKX}/C_{LX})\hat{r} + w(C_{LLX}/C_{LX})\hat{w}. \tag{11.18}$$

Now, since the production function is homogeneous of degree one, factor demand functions are homogeneous of degree zero. Thus, it must be the case that:

$$wC_{LLX} + rC_{LKX} = 0 \text{ so that } C_{LKX} = -(w/r)C_{LLX}.$$

Substituting in equation (11.18) we have:

$$\begin{aligned}\hat{C}_{LX} &= r[(-w/r)C_{LLX}/C_{LX}]\hat{r} + w(C_{LLX}/C_{LX})\hat{w} \\ &= (\hat{w} - \hat{r})(wC_{LLX}/C_{LX}).\end{aligned} \tag{11.19}$$

Now, multiply and divide the righthand side of this expression by $(-rC_{KX}/C_X)$ to get:

$$\begin{aligned}\hat{C}_{LX} &= -(rC_{KX}/C_X)[-wC_{LLX}C_X/(rC_{LX}C_{KX})](\hat{w} - \hat{r}) \\ &= -\beta_{KX}\sigma_X(\hat{w} - \hat{r})\end{aligned} \tag{11.20}$$

where σ_X (the term inside square brackets [ ]) is the elasticity of substitution between capital and labor in the production of X.

This is a very convenient expression relating changes in labor's contribution to marginal cost to changes in factor prices, the elasticity of substitution and the share of capital. In a completely analogous manner, we can derive:

$$\hat{C}_{LY} = -\beta_{KY}\sigma_Y(\hat{w} - \hat{r}) \tag{11.21}$$

$$\hat{C}_{KX} = \beta_{LX}\sigma_X(\hat{w} - \hat{r}) \tag{11.22}$$

$$\hat{C}_{KY} = \beta_{LY}\sigma_Y(\hat{w} - \hat{r}). \tag{11.23}$$

Now totally differentiate the factor availability equations (11.9) and (11.10) to get:

$$C_{KX}dx + x\,dC_{KX} + C_{KY}\,dy + y\,dC_{KY} = dK_0 = 0 \tag{11.9a}$$

and

$$C_{LX}\,dx + x\,dC_{LX} + C_{LY}\,dy + y\,dC_{Ly} = dL_0 = 0. \tag{11.10a}$$

From equation (11.9a) we derive:

$$\begin{aligned}x(C_{KX})(dx/x) + x(C_{KX})(dC_{KX}/C_{KX}) + y(C_{KY})(dy/y) \\ + y(C_{KY})(dC_{KY}/C_{KY}) = 0\end{aligned}$$

or

$$xC_{KX}\hat{x} + xC_{KX}\hat{C}_{KX} + y(C_{KY})\hat{y} + y(C_{KY})\hat{C}_{KY} = 0;$$

that is

$$xC_{KX}(\hat{x} + \hat{C}_{KX}) + yC_{KY}(\hat{y} + \hat{C}_{KY}) = 0.$$

Dividing by K_0 we have:

$$\lambda_{KX}(\hat{x} + \hat{C}_{KX}) + \lambda_{KY}(\hat{y} + \hat{C}_{KY}) = 0 \qquad (11.24)$$

where λ_{KX} is the proportion of total capital employed in industry X, etc. Now, substituting for $\hat{C}_{KX}$ and $\hat{C}_{KY}$ from equations (11.22) and (11.23) we have:

$$\lambda_{KX}\hat{x} + \lambda_{KY}\hat{y} = -(\hat{w} - \hat{r})[\beta_{LX}\sigma_X\lambda_{KX} + \beta_{LY}\sigma_Y\lambda_{KY}]. \qquad (11.25)$$

In a completely analogous manner we can derive:

$$\lambda_{LX}\hat{x} + \lambda_{LY}\hat{y} = (\hat{w} - \hat{r})[\lambda_{LX}\sigma_X\beta_{KX} + \lambda_{LY}\beta_{LY}\sigma_Y]. \qquad (11.26)$$

Equations (11.25) and (11.26) are very important. They relate output movements to movements in factor prices, technology, and the shares of industry X and industry Y in total employment of capital and labor. Subtracting equation (11.25) from (11.26) we have:

$$(\lambda_{LX} - \lambda_{KX})(\hat{x} - \hat{y}) = (\hat{w} - \hat{r})[\sigma_X(\beta_{KX}\lambda_{LX} + \beta_{LX}\lambda_{KX})$$
$$+ \sigma_Y(\beta_{KY}\lambda_{LY} + \beta_{LY}\lambda_{KY})] = (\hat{w} - \hat{r})(a_X\sigma_X + a_Y\sigma_Y). \qquad (11.26a)$$

Demand side

We now move to the demand side of the general equilibrium model. We will make some simplifying assumptions. We will assume that preferences of society can be represented by an aggregate utility function (hence distributional considerations are not important) U (x,y). Total income is $wL_0 + rK_0 = I$. U is maximized with p_x, p_y and I being treated parametrically. Thus we get Marshallian demand functions:

$$x = x(p_x, p_y, I) \qquad (11.27)$$
$$y = y(p_x, p_y, I). \qquad (11.28)$$

We write the compensated demand functions (with a superscript c) as:

$$x^c = \partial e(p_x, p_y, U)/\partial p_x = x^c(p_x, p_y, U) \qquad (11.29)$$
$$y^c = \partial e(p_x, p_y, U)/\partial p_y = y^c(p_x, p_y, U) \qquad (11.30)$$

where $e(.)$ is the expenditure function and U is the level of utility at which Hicksian compensation is being measured. Totally differentiate equation (11.29) to get:

$$dx^c = (\partial x^c/\partial p_x)dp_x + (\partial x^c/\partial p_y)dp_y + (\partial x^c/\partial U)dU.$$

Dividing through by x^c and rearranging:

$$(dx^c/x^c) = (p_x/x^c)(\partial x^c/\partial p_x)(dp_x/p_x) + (p_y/x^c)(\partial x^c/\partial p_y)(dp_y/p_y)$$
$$+ (I/x^c)(\partial x^c/\partial I)(\partial I/I)(dU/\partial U) \qquad (11.31)$$

$$\text{or} \quad \hat{x} = \hat{x}^c = \epsilon_{xx}\hat{p}_x + \epsilon_{xy}\hat{p}_y + \eta_x(dU/I)e_U$$

where ϵ_{xx} is the compensated own price elasticity of demand for x and ϵ_{xy} is the compensated elasticity of demand for x with respect to p_y, η_x is the income elasticity of demand for x and $e_U = \partial e/\partial U$.

Similarly we can derive:

$$\hat{y} = \hat{y}^c = \epsilon_{yx}\hat{p}_x + \epsilon_{yy}\hat{p}_y + \eta_y(dU/I)e_U. \tag{11.32}$$

Hence we will have:

$$\eta_y\hat{x} - \eta_x\hat{y} = \hat{p}_x[\eta_y\epsilon_{xx} - \eta_x\epsilon_{yx}] + \hat{p}_y[\eta_y\epsilon_{xy} - \eta_x\epsilon_{yy}]. \tag{11.33}$$

From the fact that compensated demand functions are homogeneous of degree zero we will have:

$$\epsilon_{xx} + \epsilon_{xy} = 0 \text{ or } \epsilon_{xx} = -\epsilon_{xy}; \text{ also that } \epsilon_{yy} + \epsilon_{yx} = 0 \text{ or } \epsilon_{yy} = -\epsilon_{yx}.$$

Substituting in equation (11.33) we will get:

$$\eta_y\hat{x} - \eta_x\hat{y} = (\hat{p}_x - \hat{p}_y)(\eta_y\epsilon_{xx} + \eta_x\epsilon_{yy}). \tag{11.34}$$

This is the key demand equation. The term $(\eta_y\epsilon_{xx} + \eta_x\epsilon_{yy})$ is sometimes called the (negative) of the elasticity of substitution in demand in the aggregate $(-\sigma_D)$ so that:

$$\eta_y\hat{x} - \eta_x\hat{y} = -\sigma_D(\hat{p}_x - \hat{p}_y). \tag{11.34a}$$

In this expression if we assume homotheticity, i.e., $\eta_x = \eta_y = 1$ then equation (11.34a) can be written as:

$$(\hat{x} - \hat{y}) = -\sigma_D(\hat{p}_x - \hat{p}_y). \tag{11.35}$$

We will further assume that $\sigma_D > 0$, a sufficient condition for which is that neither good is inferior.

Effects of taxes

What are the effects of taxes in this framework? The way in which the general equilibrium of this economy has been built up, there are three endogenous variables: $(\hat{x} - \hat{y})$, $(\hat{p}_x - \hat{p}_y)$, and $(\hat{w} - \hat{r})$ and three equations (11.15a, 11.35 and 11.26a) to determine them. Let us suppose that there are commodity taxes at the rates t_x and t_y, and sector specific factor taxes: t_{KX}, t_{KY}, t_{LX}, and t_{LY}. We define these taxes in a manner such that in equation (11.35) commodity prices would become: $p_x t_x$ and $p_y t_y$ (and similarly for factor taxes) so that rates of changes of prices would be:

$(\hat{p}_x + \hat{t}_x)$ and $(\hat{p}_y + \hat{t}_y)$ so that equation (11.35), for example, can be written as:

$$(\hat{x} - \hat{y}) + \sigma_D(\hat{p}_x - \hat{p}_y) + \sigma_D(\hat{t}_x - \hat{t}_y) = 0. \tag{11.36}$$

We can first state the following obvious results in Table 11.1 without any proof. Rates of taxes are the same.

Table 11.1

---

t_{KX} and $t_{LX} = t_X$ (a tax on both factors amounts to a tax on the good)
t_{KY} and $t_{LY} = t_y$ (a tax on both factors amounts to a tax on the good)
t_L (a tax on labor in both industries is a general tax on labor)
t_K (a tax on capital in both industries is a general tax on capital).

The literature has singled out for special treatment the issue of a specific factor tax, i.e., a tax on one factor (generally capital) in one industry. Below we analyze the case of a tax on capital in industry X.

A partial factor tax

Suppose that $\hat{t}_{KX} > 0$ and all other taxes are zero. The first important equation (11.35) is unchanged. However, the second important equation (11.26a) can be written as:

$$(\lambda_{LX} - \lambda_{KX})(\hat{x} - \hat{y}) - [a_X\sigma_X + a_Y\sigma_Y](\hat{w} - \hat{r}) + a_X\sigma_X\hat{t}_{KX} = 0 \qquad (11.37)$$

We can then write the last important equation (11.15a) as:

$$(\hat{p}_x - \hat{p}_y) - (\beta_{LX} - \beta_{LY})(\hat{w} - \hat{r}) - \beta_{KX}\hat{t}_{KX} = 0. \qquad (11.38)$$

We can collect these three equations in a matrix framework:

$$\begin{bmatrix} 1 & 0 & \sigma_D \\ (\lambda_{LX} - \lambda_{KX}) & -[a_X\sigma_X + a_Y\sigma_Y] & 0 \\ 0 & -(\beta_{LX} - \beta_{LY}) & 1 \end{bmatrix} \begin{bmatrix} (\hat{x} - \hat{y}) \\ (\hat{w} - \hat{r}) \\ (\hat{p}_x - \hat{p}_y) \end{bmatrix} = \begin{bmatrix} 0 \\ -a_X\sigma_X\hat{t}_{KX} \\ \beta_{KX}\hat{t}_{KX} \end{bmatrix}$$

$$(11.39)$$

To find out the effects of the capital tax on any of the endogenous variables we use Cramer's rule. Thus:

$$(\hat{x} - \hat{y}) = \frac{[a_X\sigma_X\hat{t}_{KX}(\beta_{LX} - \beta_{LY})\sigma_D + \beta_{KX}\hat{t}_{KX}\{\sigma_D(a_X\sigma_X + a_Y\sigma_Y)\}]}{\Delta}$$

$$(11.40)$$

where $\Delta(= [(\lambda_{KX} - \lambda_{LX})\sigma_D(\beta_{LX} - \beta_{LY}) - (a_X\sigma_X + a_Y\sigma_Y)])$ is the determinant of the matrix on the lefthand side of equation (11.39). The effects of the tax on relative output depend in a fairly complicated manner on factor intensities, the share of industry in total employment of capital and labor and elasticities of substitution. We can similarly derive expressions for $(\hat{w} - \hat{r})$ and $(\hat{p}_x - \hat{p}_y)$.

$$(\hat{w} - \hat{r}) = -[a_X\sigma_X\hat{t}_{KX} + (\lambda_{KX} - \lambda_{LX})(\sigma_D\beta_{KX}\hat{t}_{KX}]/\Delta \qquad (11.41)$$

and

$$(\hat{p}_x - \hat{p}_Y) = -[(\beta_{KX}\hat{t}_{KX})(a_X\sigma_x + a_Y\sigma_Y) + (a_X\sigma_X\hat{t}_{KX})(\beta_{LX} - \beta_{LY})]/\Delta.$$

$$(11.42)$$

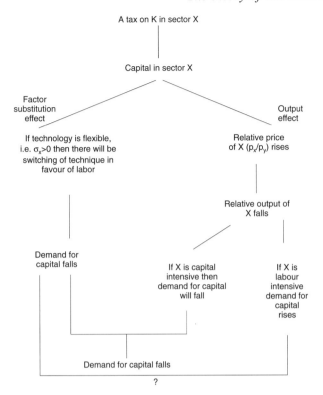

Figure 11.2

As noted by Mieszkowski (1967, 1974) the effects of the partial factor tax on capital can be split up into two effects: **a factor substitution effect** (which depends upon the scope for substitution between factors in the production of X); and **an output effect** (which depends among other things on substitution between the two goods in demand). This is shown in Figure 11.2. If $\sigma_X > 0$ it is possible to substitute labor for capital and the overall demand for capital would fall if X is the capital intensive industry. If X is labor intensive the demand for capital would fall. In either case there would be an effect on relative rates of return to capital and labor. If $\sigma_X = 0$ (we have a Leontief production function) then there is no factor substitution effect. The output effect works in the following manner. Since the tax is imposed on capital in industry X, the cost of production and, hence, the price of X rises relative to Y. The larger the elasticity of substitution in demand (σ_D), the greater would be the shift in demand toward industry Y and the larger the change in relative output.

The effects of other types of taxes can be derived in a manner similar to the above. A matrix equation for this tax would have to be generated along the lines of equation (11.39) and the effects on relative outputs, relative prices, and relative factor rewards solved for using Cramer's rule as above. This then would give us a complete picture of the incidence of the partial factor tax.

11.3 TAX INCIDENCE IN A MODEL OF INVOLUNTARY UNEMPLOYMENT

In an interesting extension of the Harberger–Mieszkowski–Atkinson–Stiglitz model of tax incidence, Agell and Lundborg (1992) have covered involuntary unemployment. In this manner, they are able to articulate the effects of tax policy changes on the rate of unemployment in the economy.

To do this they introduce the notion of efficiency wages in the model of tax incidence. Efficiency wages can be justified on several counts (see Ball and Mankiw 1993). A particularly simple one is the notion of 'fair' wages. If workers feel that they are being paid fair wages (in relation to the return on capital, say) they will put in more effort. In order to induce higher work effort, employers have to pay workers higher wages – higher, particularly, than market-clearing wages. It is argued that it is more cost effective from the point of view of employers to pay existing workers higher wages than to hire additional workers at lower wages and also incur the costs of turnover of the workforce.

In any event, a simple model of effort supply along the above lines can be built up as follows (for details see Shapiro and Stiglitz 1984; Yellen 1984; Stiglitz 1986; Akerlof and Yellen 1987; Ball and Mankiw 1993). Suppose the economy is populated by identical competitive firms. The profit for each firm is given by:

$$(\alpha F(e(w), L) - wL)$$

where e is the effort level per worker, L is the number of employees, w is the wage, $F(.)$ is the production function and α is a demand (shift) parameter. Workers are identical and $e' > 0$. The firm can choose w and L. Once w is chosen, e is determined and given L and α, so are output and profits.

First-order conditions are that:

$$\alpha F'(e'(w)L) - L = 0 \tag{11.43a}$$

$$\text{from which we get } \alpha F'(e'(w)) = 1 \tag{11.43b}$$

and that

$$e(w)\alpha F'(e(w)L) = w \tag{11.43c}$$

so that

$$\alpha F' = w/e(w). \tag{11.43d}$$

Substituting equation (11.43d) into (11.43b) we get:

$$e'(w)w/[e(w)] = 1. \tag{11.44}$$

This is a famous wage-setting condition for such models. It says that the optimal wage is such that the elasticity of effort with respect to the wage rate is unity. Furthermore, from the first-order conditions we also know that firms will hire workers up to the point where marginal product equals the wage rate. It follows that if at this wage aggregate demand for labor falls short of aggregate supply, then there will be involuntary unemployment. Equilibrium shifts in aggregate demand will (shifts in α) will leave the real wage rigid and generate unemployment fluctuations.

Agell and Lundborg postulate that the above effort supply function depends upon two factors: the wage–rental ratio and unemployment (u). Hence the effort function is written as:

$$e = e(w/r, u) \qquad (11.45)$$

with $e_1 > 0$ and $e_2 > 0$ where e_i is the partial derivative of the e(.) function with respect to the ith argument. As the wage rises relative to the return to capital workers feel that they are better treated and supply more effort. As the unemployment rises, workers feel that they will not get a good job if they are fired from the present one and put in more effort.

We now have to distinguish between effective labor supply and physical or 'raw' labor supply. With labor supply at L_X to sector X, for example, effective labor supply is:

$$E_X = e(w/r, u)L_X. \qquad (11.46)$$

Outputs of the two goods are given by the production functions:

$$x = F(E_X, K_X) \qquad (11.47)$$

and

$$y = G(E_Y, K_Y). \qquad (11.48)$$

Production conditions are unchanged from the previous model so that price still equals marginal cost but marginal costs depend upon the 'true' costs of labor and capital. Thus:

$$p_X = C_X(w/e, r) \qquad (11.49a)$$
$$p_Y = C_Y(w/e, r). \qquad (11.49b)$$

The true cost of one unit of labor is w/e. In the previous model we had the special case where $e = 1$. If there are factor taxes such that gross wage in sector X is wt_{LX} and that in sector Y, wt_{LY}, whereas the gross rental paid is rt_{KX} in sector X, and rt_{KY} in sector Y. In that case we would write:

$$p_X = C_X(wt_{LX}/e, rt_{KX}) \qquad (11.50a)$$
$$p_Y = C_Y(wt_{LY}/e, rt_{KY}). \qquad (11.50b)$$

We may now replace C_{LX} with C_{EX} and write:

$$xC_{EX} + yC_{EY} = e(L_o - u) \qquad (11.51)$$

(total effective labor supply is exhausted in sectors X and Y) and:

$$xC_{KX} + yC_{KY} = K_0. \tag{11.52}$$

Capital is fully employed.

Calling the first term within brackets in equation (11.50a) E and totally differentiating we have:

$$dp_x = C_{EX}dE + C_{KX}d(rt_{KX}). \tag{11.53a}$$

Analogously we will get:

$$dp_y = C_{EY}dE + c_{KY}d(rt_{KY}). \tag{11.53b}$$

Dividing equation (11.53a) by p_X, equation (11.53b) by p_Y and rearranging terms we will get:

$$\begin{aligned}\hat{p}_X - \hat{p}_Y &= (1 - \epsilon_1)(\beta_{EX} - \beta_{EY})(\hat{w} - \hat{r}) - \epsilon_2(\beta_{EX} - \beta_{EY})\hat{u} \\ &+ \beta_{EX}\hat{t}_{LX} - \beta_{EY}\hat{t}_{LY} + \beta_{KX}\hat{t}_{KX} - \beta_{KY}\hat{t}_{KY}\end{aligned} \tag{11.54}$$

where ϵ_1 is the elasticity of the effort function with respect to (w/r) and ϵ_2 is the elasticity with respect to unemployment. If there is no problem of 'fair' wages then $\epsilon_1 = \epsilon_2 = 0$ and $E = L$. If, further, there are no taxes then equation (11.54) will collapse to equation (11.15a). In the case of equation (11.54) $\beta_{Ei} = wC_{Ei}/ep_i (i = X, Y)$ is the share of effective labor cost in producing commodity i and $\beta_{Ki} = rC_{Ki}/p_i$ is the share of capital cost in producing commodity i.

Some points are worth noticing here: Relative producer prices are also affected by unemployment. Assume that unemployment increases. Then the second term of equation (11.54) will also increase and the relative price of commodity X will rise if $\beta_{EY} > \beta_{EX}$, i.e., the effective share of labor in Y exceeds that in the X sector. As unemployment rises, work effort rises in both sectors. But since Y is more labor intensive, the favorable effect on the output of Y will be greater than that of X. Hence p_x will rise relative to p_y. The reverse would have been the case had X been the labor intensive industry.

Another point worth noting is that in the first term on the righthand side is multiplied by the elasticity of effort with respect to the wage–rental ratio (ϵ_1). An increase in the wage–rental ratio will increase effort for both sectors. If Y is the more labor intensive industry, the favorable effect on the output of Y will be greater than that of X. Hence p_x will rise relative to p_Y. The opposite would have been true if X was the labor intensive industry.

The demand side of the Agell–Lundborg model is quite close to that of Atkinson–Stiglitz. There exists an aggregate utility function which is maximized with prices etc. being treated as parameters releasing Marshallian demand functions:

$$x = x(p_x T_x, \ p_y T_y, \ I) \tag{11.55a}$$

and

$$y = y(p_x T_x, \ p_y T_y, \ I) \tag{11.55b}$$

where $p_x T_x$ is the post (commodity) tax price of commodity X and $I = w(L_O - u) + rK_0 + T_r$ is total earnings with T_r being a lump-sum transfer.[1]

Thus, in line, with our results in Section 11.2 we can, on assuming homothetic demands, write the demand side as:

$$(\hat{x} - \hat{y}) = -\sigma_D[\hat{p}_x + \hat{t}_x - \hat{p}_y - \hat{t}_y] \tag{11.56}$$

where t_x and t_y represent commodity taxes.

We now work with equations (11.51) and (11.52) to get another equation on the supply side of this model (corresponding to equation 11.26a in Section 11.2).

Totally differentiate equation (11.51) to get:

$$x \, dC_{EX} + C_{EX}dx + y \, dC_{EY} + C_{EY}dy = (L_O - u)de - edu.$$

Rewrite this expression as:

$$C_{EX}x \, (dC_{EX})/C_{EX} + xC_{EX}(dx)/x + C_{EY}y \, (dC_{EY})/C_{EY} + y \, C_{EY}(dy)/y$$
$$= (L_O - u)de - edu.$$

Divide through by $e(L_O - u)$ and, in addition, multiply and divide the last term on the righthand side by u to get:

$$\frac{xC_{EX}\hat{C}_{EX}}{e(L_O - u)} + \frac{xC_{EX}\hat{x}}{e(L_O - u)} + \frac{yC_{EY}\hat{C}_{EY}}{e(L_O - u)} + \frac{yC_{EY}\hat{y}}{e(L_O - u)} = \frac{(L_O - u)de}{e(L_O - u)} - \frac{eduu}{e(L_O - u)u} \tag{11.57}$$

which can be written as:

$$\lambda_{EX}(\hat{C}_{EX} + \hat{x}) + \lambda_{EY}(\hat{C}_{EY} + \hat{y}) = \hat{e} - \hat{u}(u/(L_O - u)) \tag{11.58}$$

where the definitions of the λs is apparent from equation (11.58). In Section 11.2 the righthand side of this equation was zero and $E = L$.

The equation for capital (corresponding to equation (11.24) in section 11.2) can be written as:

$$\lambda_{KX}(\hat{C}_{KX} + \hat{x}) + \lambda_{KY}(\hat{C}_{KY} + \hat{y}) = 0. \tag{11.59}$$

From the fact that the unit cost functions are homogeneous of degree zero in factor prices we will have:

$$\hat{C}_{EX} = -(1 - \epsilon_1)\sigma_X\beta_{KX}(\hat{w} - \hat{r}) + \epsilon_2\sigma_X\beta_{KX}\hat{u} + \sigma_X\beta_{KX}(\hat{t}_{KX} - \hat{t}_{LX}) \tag{11.60}$$

$$\hat{C}_{EY} = -(1 - \epsilon_1)\sigma_Y\beta_{KY}(\hat{w} - \hat{r}) + \epsilon_2\sigma_Y\beta_{KY}\hat{u} + \sigma_Y\beta_{KY}(\hat{t}_{KY} - \hat{t}_{LY}). \tag{11.61}$$

With the tax rates and the ϵs equal to zero equation (11.60) would become identical with equation (11.20) and equation (11.61) with equation (11.21). Substitute from (11.60) and (11.61) for $\hat{C}_{EX}$ and $\hat{C}_{EY}$ respectively into equation (11.58). Also in equation (11.58) use the relation:

$$\hat{e} = \epsilon_1(\hat{w} - \hat{r}) + \epsilon_2\hat{u} \tag{11.62}$$

to get

$$\lambda_{EX}\hat{x} + \lambda_{EY}\hat{y} = [\epsilon_1 + (1 - \epsilon_1)\{\sigma_X\beta_{KX}\lambda_{EX} + \sigma_Y\beta_{KY}\lambda_{EY}\}](\hat{w} - \hat{r})$$
$$+ [\epsilon_2(1 - \sigma_X\beta_{KX}\lambda_{EX} - \sigma_Y\beta_{KY}\lambda_{EY}) - u/(L_O - u)]\hat{u}$$
$$- \lambda_{EX}\sigma_X\beta_{KX}(\hat{t}_{KX} - \hat{t}_{LX}) - \lambda_{EY}\sigma_Y\beta_{KY}(\hat{t}_{KY} - \hat{t}_{LY}). \tag{11.63}$$

In the same way we can derive:

$$\lambda_{KX}\hat{x} + \lambda_{KY}\hat{y} = -(1 - \epsilon_1)(\sigma_X\beta_{EX}\lambda_{KX} + \sigma_Y\beta_{EY}\lambda_{KY})(\hat{w} - \hat{r})$$
$$+ \epsilon_2(\sigma_X\beta_{EX}\lambda_{KX} + \sigma_Y\beta_{EY}\lambda_{KY})\hat{u} + \sigma_X\lambda_{KX}\beta_{EX}(\hat{t}_{KX} - \hat{t}_{LX})$$
$$+ \sigma_Y\lambda_{KY}\beta_{EY}(\hat{t}_{KY} - \hat{t}_{LY}). \tag{11.64}$$

Subtracting equation (11.64) from equation (11.63) and rearranging yields:

$$(\lambda_{EX} - \lambda_{KX})(\hat{x} - \hat{y}) = [(\sigma_X a_X + \sigma_Y a_Y)(1 - \epsilon_1) + \epsilon_1][\hat{w} - \hat{r}]$$
$$+ [\epsilon_2(1 - \sigma_X a_X - \sigma_Y a_Y) - u/(L_O - u)]\hat{u}$$
$$+ a_X\sigma_X(\hat{t}_{LX} - \hat{t}_{KX}) + a_Y\sigma_Y(\hat{t}_{LY} - \hat{t}_{KY}) \tag{11.65}$$

where:

$\lambda_{EX} \equiv C_{EX}x/(e(L_O - u))$, i.e., share of efficiency labor used in X.
$\lambda_{EY} \equiv C_{EY}y/(e(L_O - u))$, i.e., share of efficiency labor used in Y.
$\lambda_{KX} \equiv C_{KX}x/K$, i.e., share of capital used in X.
$\lambda_{KY} \equiv C_{KY}y/K$, i.e., share of capital used in Y.
$\quad \sigma_i \equiv$ elasticity of substitution between capital and labor in efficiency units in sector i.
$a_X \equiv \lambda_{EX}\beta_{KX} + \lambda_{KX}\beta_{EX} (a_X > 0)$ and
$a_Y \equiv \lambda_{EY}\beta_{KY} + \lambda_{KY}\beta_{EY} (a_Y > 0)$.

When $\epsilon_1 = \epsilon_2 = \hat{u} = 0$ then we are back to equation (11.26a) with no difference between labor in efficiency units and natural units. Equation (11.65) is another important equation from the supply side. Finally we look at the effort supply equation $e = e(w'r, u)$. Totally differentiating and rearranging we have:

$$(\hat{w} - \hat{r}) = u(r/w)^2 e_2/e_{11}\hat{u} = h\hat{u} \tag{11.66}$$

where $h < 0$ if e_{11} (the second derivative of e with respect to (w/r)) is negative, which is assumed to be the case.

In this model there are four endogenous variables: $(\hat{x} - \hat{y})$, $(\hat{w} - \hat{r})$, $(\hat{p}_x - \hat{p}_y)$ and $\hat{u}$ and four equations to determine them (11.66, 11.65, 11.56, and 11.54). We can arrange them in a matrix equation just as before:

$$\begin{bmatrix} 1 & \sigma_D & 0 & 0 \\ 0 & 1 & B^1 & B^2 \\ (\lambda_{EX} - \lambda_{KX}) & 0 & B^4 & B^5 \\ 0 & 0 & 1 & -h \end{bmatrix} \begin{bmatrix} \hat{x} - \hat{y} \\ \hat{p}_x - \hat{p}_y \\ \hat{w} - \hat{r} \\ \hat{u} \end{bmatrix} = \begin{bmatrix} -\sigma_D(\hat{t}_x - \hat{t}_Y) \\ B^3 \\ B^6 \\ 0 \end{bmatrix} \tag{11.67}$$

where:

$$B^1 = -(1 - \epsilon_1)(\beta_{EX} - \beta_{EY})$$
$$B^2 = \epsilon_2(\beta_{EX} - \beta_{EY})$$
$$B^3 = \beta_{EX}\hat{t}_{LX} - \beta_{EY}\hat{t}_{LY} + \beta_{KX}\hat{t}_{KX} - \beta_{KY}\hat{t}_{KY}$$
$$B^4 = -[(\sigma_X a_X + \sigma_Y a_Y)(1 - \epsilon_1) + \epsilon_1]$$
$$B^5 = -[\epsilon_2(1 - \sigma_X a_X - \sigma_Y a_Y) - u/(L_0 - u)]$$
$$B^6 = a_X \sigma_X(\hat{t}_{LX} - \hat{t}_{KX}) + a_Y \sigma_Y(\hat{t}_{LY} - \hat{t}_{KY})$$

When $\epsilon_1 = \epsilon_2 = \hat{u} = 0$ then we are back to the model in section 11.2.

To solve for the effects of any of these taxes we use Cramer's rules in equation (11.67). For example if $\hat{t}_X > 0$ and $\hat{t}_y = \hat{t}_{LX} = \hat{t}_{LY} = \hat{t}_{KX} = \hat{t}_{KY} = 0$, then we could solve for:

$$\hat{u} = \sigma_D \hat{t}_X(\lambda_{KX} - \lambda_{EX})/\nabla \qquad (11.68)$$

where ∇ = determinant of the 4×4 matrix on the lefthand side of equation (11.67). Similarly:

$$(\hat{w} - \hat{r}) = -\sigma_D \hat{t}_X\{h(\lambda_{EX} - \lambda_{KX})\}/\nabla \qquad (11.69)$$

$$(\hat{p}_x - \hat{p}_y) = \sigma_D \hat{t}_X\{(\lambda_{EX} - \lambda_{KX})(hB_1 + B_2)\}/\nabla \qquad (11.70)$$

and

$$(\hat{x} - \hat{y}) = \sigma_D \hat{t}_X(hB_4 + B_5)/\nabla. \qquad (11.71)$$

In a similar manner, we can investigate the effects of other taxes on the four endogenous variables here.

The principal payoff from the complication that has been introduced here is that it is possible to ascertain the effects of various types of taxes on the rate of unemployment. This has a feedback effect in that any change in the rate of unemployment would mean a change in the level of effort and, hence, a change in the supply of effective labor to both industries. The only significant generalization that can be made is that the effect of any tax on the rate of unemployment will be the opposite to the effect on the wage–rental ratio. Anything that raises the wage–rental ratio will increase effort and, therefore, increase effort and employment. A demonstration of this can be seen from the example worked out above. Compare equations (11.68) and (11.69). Since $h < 0$ the effect of t_X on $\hat{u}$ is the opposite of the effect on $(\hat{w} - \hat{r})$.

11.4 EXTENSIONS OF THE BASIC MODEL

The competitive model and the competitive model with involuntary unemployment can be thought of as being the basic tools of tax incidence in general equilibrium systems. These two models can be extended in a number of ways to accommodate non-standard, but perhaps more realistic, assumptions. In every case that we mention below the basic equations will be

(11.15a), (11.26a) and (11.35) for the case without unemployment and (11.66), (11.65), (11.56) and (11.54) for the case with involuntary unemployment. Let us consider some cases briefly.

Imperfect factor mobility

Let us first suppose that because of some sort of distortion wage rates across the two sectors are not equalized. Thus wage rate in sector X is w_X and that in sector Y is w_Y. However, there is full employment. The full employment condition will now read:

$$C_{LX}(r, w_X)x + C_{LY}(r, w_Y)y = L_0 \qquad (11.72a)$$

$$C_{KX}(r, w_X)x + C_{KY}(r, w_Y)y = K_0. \qquad (11.72b)$$

With perfect competition in the product market price would still equal marginal cost so that we will have:

$$p_x = C_X(r, w_X) \qquad (11.72c)$$

$$p_y = C_Y(r, w_Y). \qquad (11.72d)$$

The demand side of the model would remain unchanged. To investigate tax incidence we would have to use equations (11.72) on the supply side and the standard equation (11.35) on the demand side. We would have to work through the 3×3 matrix of tax incidence just as before.

This model would be a trifle hard to extend to the case of involuntary unemployment as we would have to think in terms of sector-specific effort supply functions. But, in principle, it could be done. Apart from sector-specific effort functions we would have to alter equation (11.72a) to reflect the exhaustion of total effective labor supply.

Distortions in the product market

Suppose that there exists imperfect competition in industry X so that p_x is not equal to marginal cost but is actually a markup on marginal cost. All other conditions remain unchanged. Thus, the only alteration to the standard model is that:

$$p_x = (1 + \delta)C_X(r, w) \qquad (11.73)$$

where δ is the (fixed) factor of markup. All other equations remain unchanged. The model can then be worked out for the full employment as well as the involuntary unemployment with the pricing equation for sector X amended as above.

11.5   TAX INCIDENCE WITH A RATE OF RETURN REGULATION

Many industries are regulated. This generally happens in the case of industries which, without such regulation, would end up charging monopoly prices. This would include 'natural monopolies' such as public utilities and the like. This regulation usually takes the form of a rate of return regulation where the rate of return to capital in the regulated industry is set below the monopoly rate of return but higher than the competitive rate of return. The study of tax incidence in such a model is an interesting extension of the Harberger model discussed above. This problem was considered in a recent paper by Batra and Beladi (1993).

They consider the same two-sector model as in the Harberger–Atkinson–Stiglitz model. Industry X is the regulated industry whereas industry Y is unregulated. We will let P_x be the (tax inclusive) consumer price of good X and P_y the consumer price of good Y. Thus $P_x(1 - t_x) =$ producer price of X where t_x is the indirect tax on commodity X. Let $w_i(i = x, y)$ be the gross wage paid out be sector i and let t_{ki} be the profit tax rate on sector i where the profit rate for tax calculated as cash flow less payments for labor. The profit for sector Y can, then, be written as:

$$\Pi_y = [P_y(y)(1 - t_y)y - w_y L_y](1 - t_{ky}) - rK_y \qquad (11.74)$$

where P_y is taken as a function of the output of commodity Y. The price of commodity Y depends on the amount produced which is itself a function of capital and labor used. Production conditions are described by:

$$y = y(K_y, L_y) = L_y f(k_y) \text{(assuming constant returns to scale)} \qquad (11.74a)$$

Maximization with respect to L_y yields:

$$P_y(1 - t_y)(\partial y/\partial L_y) - (1 - t_y)y(\partial P_y/\partial y)(\partial y/\partial L_y) = w_y(\text{where } k_y = K_y/L_y)$$

or, upon multiplying and dividing the lefthand side by P_y and letting e_y be (the negative of) the price elasticity of demand:

$$[e_y \equiv (\partial y/\partial p_y)(p_y/y)],$$

we can rewrite this as:

$$P_y(1 - t_y)(1 - 1/e_y)(\partial y/\partial L_y) = w_y. \qquad (11.75)$$

Equation (11.75) says that the marginal revenue product equals the tax inclusive wage rate.

In a similar way maximization of profits with respect to K_y will yield:

$$P_y(1 - t_y)(1 - 1/e_y)(\partial y/\partial K_y)(1 - t_{ky}) = r. \qquad (11.76)$$

This equation says that the rate of return to capital is equated to its after-tax marginal revenue product.

Producers in sector X have a rate of return regulation: after-tax profits as a ratio of K_x should be no greater than some number s. Profits of this sector without the rate of return regulation are:

$$\Pi_x = [P_x(x)(1 - t_x)x - w_x L_x](1 - t_{Kx}) - rK_x. \qquad (11.77)$$

The price of X depends upon the amount produced which itself depends on capital and labor inputs:

$$x = x(K_x, L_x) = L_x g(k_x) \text{(assuming constant returns to scale).} \quad (11.77a)$$

Profit is maximized subject to the constraint:

$$[P_x(x)(1 - t_x)x - w_x L_x](1 - t_{Kx})/K_x \leqslant s(= v + r) \quad (11.78)$$

where it is implied that the maximum rate of return is greater than the market cost of capital by an amount v. The allowed rate of return makes provisions for all taxes.

Equation (11.78) can be rewritten in a more convenient form as:

$$P_x x - w_x L_x - r K_x \leqslant v K_x + t_x P_x x + t_{Kx}[P_x(1 - t_x)x - w_x L_x]$$

so that the Lagrangean can be written (with λ as the Lagrange multiplier) as:

$$\Lambda = [(1 - t_x)P_x(x)x - w_x L_x][(1 - t_{Kx}) - r K_x] - \lambda\{[(1 - t_x)P_x(x)x \\ - w_x L_x](1 - t_{Kx}) - (r + v)K_x\}. \quad (11.79)$$

In a manner exactly analogous to the case of industry Y we derive the following first-order conditions. Differentiation with respect to L_x yields:

$$(1 - \lambda)(1 - t_x)P_x(1 - 1/e_x)(\partial x/\partial L_x) - w_x(1 - \lambda) = 0 \quad (11.80)$$

which we will rewrite as:

$$w_x = T_x P_x a_x(\partial x/\partial L_x) \quad (11.80a)$$

(wage equals marginal revenue product of labor)
where $T_x = (1 - t_x)$ and $a_x = (1 - 1/e_x)$.
Differentiation with respect to K_x yields:

$$(1 - \lambda)[(1 - t_x)P_x(1 - 1/e_x)(1 - t_{Kx})(\partial x/\partial K_x) - r] + \lambda v = 0 \quad (11.81)$$

which we will rewrite as:

$$r = T_x P_x a_x(\partial x/\partial L_x)(1 - t_{Kx}) + v\theta \quad (11.81a)$$

where $\theta = \lambda/(1 - \lambda) > 0$ (It can be shown that $1 > \lambda > 0$ from the second-order conditions). This equation says that the rate of rental equals the marginal revenue product of capital plus an adjustment factor because of the rate of return regulation).

Differentiation with respect to λ gives:

$$(v + r)K_x - [(1 - t_x)P_x(x)x - w_x L_x](1 - t_{Kx}) = 0. \quad (11.82)$$

With labor perfectly mobile across sectors the net wage rate is the same across both sectors. Hence:

$$w_x(1 - t_{Lx}) = w_y(1 - t_{Ly}) = w. \quad (11.83)$$

From equations (11.75), (11.80a) and (11.83) we get the following labor market equilibrium condition:

$$T_x a_x P_x(\partial x/\partial L_x)(1 - t_{Lx}) = T_y a_y(\partial y/\partial L_y) \quad (11.84)$$

In a similar manner from equations (11.76) and (11.81a) we can get the following equilibrium condition for the capital market:

$$T_x a_x P_x (\partial x / \partial K_x)(1 - t_{Kx}) + v\theta = T_y a_y (\partial y / \partial K_y). \tag{11.85}$$

We are assuming that there is full employment of both capital and labor. So, if L_0 and K_0 are the total amounts of capital and labor available then it must be the case that:

$$L_x + L_y = L_0 \tag{11.86}$$

and,

$$L_x k_x + L_y k_y = K_0. \tag{11.87}$$

In equation (11.87) we have assumed that production conditions in both sectors are characterized by constant returns to scale. k_i is the capital–labor ratio in sector $i(i = X, Y)$.

On the demand side the assumption is made that good Y is the numeraire so its price is set equal to 1 so that the relative price of good X is denoted as p_x. If commodity market X is in equilibrium so must be the market for commodity Y. Hence, the commodity market equilibrium condition is written as:

$$x = d_x(p_x, I) \tag{11.88}$$

where I is income in terms of good Y:

$$I = p_x x + y. \tag{11.89}$$

Equations (11.74a), (11.77a), (11.82), (11.84) to (11.89) are nine equations which are enough to solve for the nine variables: $x, y, L_x, L_y, k_x, k_y, p_x, \theta$ and I. In principle, it is possible to solve for these nine variables in terms of the various taxes and assess the impacts of these taxes. To simplify matters, we proceed to present the system as a matrix equation comprising of three endogenous variables in a manner analogous to equation (11.39). We suppose that there is only one wage tax, only one capital tax and only one commodity tax. $t_{Lx} = t_{Ly} = t_L; t_x = t_y = t$ and $t_{Kx} = t_{Ky} = t_K$. If labor is paid its marginal product in both sectors, then it must be the case that:

$$a_x p_x (g - k_g g') = (f - k_y f') \tag{11.90}$$

and that

$$a_x p_x g' + [p_x(1 - a_x)g]/k_x - v/(TT_K) = f' = r. \tag{11.91}$$

Further, that:

$$L_x + L_y = L_0 \tag{11.92}$$

and

$$L_x k_x + L_y k_y = K_0 \tag{11.93}$$

and

$$x = d_x(p_x, p_x x + y) \qquad (11.94)$$

where $T = (1 - t)$, $T_K = (1 - t_K)$ and, in view of constant returns to scale in production, $(f - k_y f')$ is the marginal product of labor in sector Y and $(g - k_x g')$ in sector X etc.

Totally differentiating equation (11.90) we have:

$$(g - k_x g') a_x dp_x + (a_x p_x)[g' dk_x - k_x g'' dk_x - g' dk_x]$$
$$= [f' dk_y - k_y f'' dk_y - f' dk_y]$$

or

$$(g - k_x g') a_x dp_x + a_x p_x(-k_g g'' dk_x) = -k_y f'' dk_y. \qquad (11.95)$$

In this we choose units such that $a_x p_x = 1$ and use the definition of the elasticity of substitution (σ). For example:

$$\sigma_x = -[g'(g - k_x g')]/(k_x g g''). \qquad (11.96)$$

Substituting in equation (11.95) we have:

$$\{g'/(g\sigma_x)\} dk_x - (f'/(f\sigma_y)) dk_y + a_x dp_x = 0. \qquad (11.97)$$

This is our first equation in the three endogenous variables dk_x, dk_y and dp_x.

Now totally differentiate equation (11.91) and substitute for the elasticity of substitution and set $a_x p_x = 1$ and $t = t_K = 0$ initially to get:

$$-[(g'/g) + p_x(1 - a_x)\sigma_x/k_x](\partial x/\partial L_x) dk_x + (\sigma_y f'(\partial y/\partial K_y)/(f k_y)) dk_y$$
$$+ [\sigma_x \sigma_y (g - (\partial x/\partial L_x)/k_x] dp_x = \sigma_x \sigma_y v(dt + dt_k). \qquad (11.98)$$

This is the second major equation determining dk_x, dk_y and dp_x.

Finally we differentiate the demand equation (11.94) to get:

$$dx = (\partial d_x/\partial p_x) dp_x + (\partial d_x/\partial I)[x dp_x + p_x dx + dy]. \qquad (11.99)$$

Define the marginal propensity to consume of good x as:

$$m \equiv (\partial d_x/\partial I) p_x$$

which can then be substituted into (11.99). Then using the definitions of output and the equations relating to total factor supplies we get the last equation with dk_x, dk_y, and dp_x as endogenous variables. This equation is:

$$A dk_x + B dk_y + (k_y - k_x) e_1 x/p_x dp_x = 0 \qquad (11.100)$$
$$\text{with} \quad A = L_x[(1 - a_x m)(\partial x/\partial L_x + k_y g') + (mf/p_x)$$
$$B = L_y[(1 - a_x m)g + (m/p_x)\{(\partial y/\partial L_y) + k_x f'\}.$$

Collecting all three equations (11.97), (11.98) and (11.100), we have:

$$\begin{bmatrix} \sigma_y g'/g & -\sigma_x f'/f & \sigma_x \sigma_y a_x \\ C & \sigma_y f'(\partial y/\partial L_y)/k_y f & \sigma_x \sigma_y (g - (\partial x/\partial L_x))a_x/k_x \\ A & B & (k_y - k_x)e_x x/p_x \end{bmatrix} \begin{bmatrix} dk_x \\ dk_y \\ dp_x \end{bmatrix}$$

$$= \begin{bmatrix} 0 \\ \sigma_x \sigma_y v(dt + dt_K) \\ 0 \end{bmatrix} \tag{11.101}$$

with $C = -[g'/g + \sigma_x p_x(1 - a_x)/k_x]\sigma_x F_L/k_x$.

The determinant of the matrix is on the lefthand side of equation (11.101). It can be shown that $\Delta < 0$ if $k_y > k_x$ or $\sigma_x = 0$; otherwise the sign of Δ is indeterminate. By Cramer's rule we can solve:

$$dk_x = \{[(k_y - k_x)e_x x f'/(p_x f)] + B\sigma_y a_x\}[\sigma_x v(dt + dt_k)/\Delta] \tag{11.102}$$

$$dk_y = \{[(k_y - k_x)e_x x g'/(p_x g)] - A\sigma_x a_x\}[\sigma_y v(dt + dt_K)/\Delta] \tag{11.103}$$

and

$$dp_x = -[(B\sigma_y g'/g) + (A\sigma_x f'/f)][v(dt + dt_K)/\Delta]. \tag{11.104}$$

We can then use these expressions to evaluate the incidence of various taxes.

11.6 CONCLUSIONS

Tax incidence analysis indicates who bears the burden of the tax. As we have seen in this chapter an answer to this question depends on the type of model that we choose. Thus, finding out the effects of taxes on the rate of unemployment will not be possible in a model that assumes full employment.

This chapter has also shown that if we make the models more 'realistic' the analytics get quite messy and unambiguous analytical results may not be possible. Think, for example, of the complexities introduced even in the basic Mieszkowski model of Section 11.2 if variable factor supplies are permitted. In this context we can appreciate the contribution of empirical general equilibrium models which allow for considerable sectoral disaggregation and considerable relaxation of assumptions made. For a review see, for example, Shoven and Whalley (1972, 1984) and Kotlikoff (1987).

NOTES

1 It is being assumed here that all tax revenues are being returned to consumers in a non-distorting, lump-sum manner. We could make the same assumption in the earlier model or we could assume that when the government spends tax revenue it does not affect the economy.

ADDITIONAL READING

Tax incidence analysis has branched out in several directions. As our analysis of even the simplest general equilibrium models indicated, however, qualitative results are hard to come by. Most results are therefore obtained from computable general equilibrium models of the type analyzed by Whalley (1984) and Kotlikoff (1987). Additional useful texts are Aaron (1975), Poterba (1989) and Robertson (1992).

12 Tax incidence in dynamic models

Key concepts: neoclassical model of economic growth; balanced growth path tax incidence; the life-cycle model; tax incidence in monetary growth models; general life-cycle model; incidence of a tax on land.

12.1 INTRODUCTION

In Chapter 11 we have examined some models of tax incidence in static economies. We wish to extend that analysis here to cover some dynamic models of tax incidence. The issue of what constitutes tax incidence can take several forms in such cases. We could look at the effects of taxes on returns to factors of production much as we did in the case of the static model. Or we could consider the effects of different types of taxes on the rate of growth of the economy. We could explore the effects of taxes in the steady state of a growth equilibrium and in transitions to steady state. Various possibilities exist. The basic model to which we address these questions could be different.

Our agenda in this chapter is as follows. First, we shall consider taxation in the neoclassical (Solow) model of economic growth. Second, we shall consider the life-cycle version of the neoclassical growth model. We then consider incidence of taxation in a monetary version of the model. Tax policy in the new version of the life-cycle model due to Blanchard (1986) and others is also studied here. We then take up two specific issues: the incidence of a land tax and the relative attractiveness of bond and tax finance of an increase in government expenditure. The chapter closes with some concluding remarks.

12.2 THE NEOCLASSICAL MODEL OF ECONOMIC GROWTH

In this section we briefly review the neoclassical model of economic growth (the Solow model) without taxation. Later, we will introduce taxation into this model.

The principal elements of Solow's analysis are as follows.

1 Savings can be considered a fixed fraction of national income. However, it is possible to change this fraction through, say, tax changes.

2 We concentrate on the long run of the economy so that short-run issues like unemployment are no longer relevant. We can similarly discard issues relating to demand.

3 Production is defined by an aggregate production function in which capital is smoothly substitutable for labor. Marginal products of both factors are positive and declining. Perfect competition prevails in both product as well as factor markets so that Euler's theorem holds and all output is completely exhausted in payments to factors of production.

4 Labor grows exogenously at the rate n.

We can now specify Solow's model in a little more detail. The production function can be written as:

$$Y = F(K, L) \tag{12.1}$$

where Y is real output and K and L are capital and labor inputs. This production function displays constant returns to scale. Divide through by L to get the 'intensive' production function:

$$Y/L \equiv y = F(K/L, 1) \equiv f(k) \tag{12.2}$$

with $k \equiv K/L$.

The marginal product of capital (f') is the rental of capital whereas labor gets its marginal product or, from Euler's theorem, what is left over after paying capital. Thus the rental rate is (a prime ($'$) denotes a partial derivative):

$$f' = r \tag{12.3a}$$

and the wage rate is

$$f - kf' = w. \tag{12.3b}$$

Total savings are a fixed fraction s of national income: $S = sY$ or savings per capita (there is no difference between per capita and per unit labor magnitudes) are such that:

$$S/L = sf(k). \tag{12.4}$$

Capital formation is gross investment less depreciation:

$$dK/dt \equiv \dot{K} = sY - \gamma K = Lsf(k) - \gamma K \tag{12.5}$$

where γ is the fixed exponential rate of depreciation.
The rate of growth of the capital stock is, therefore:

$$\dot{K}/K = Lsf(k)/K - \gamma. \tag{12.6}$$

The rate of growth of labor is n. Thus:

$$\dot{L}/L = n. \tag{12.7}$$

As can be seen from the above all significant magnitudes are functions of the capital–labor ratio k. Steady state must, therefore, be defined so as to keep this capital–labor ratio unchanged. In other words, we must have in steady state:

$$\dot{k}/k = \dot{K}/K - \dot{L}/L = 0 \text{ or,}$$

$Lsf(k)/K - \gamma - n = 0$ or, since $L/K = 1/k$, we require that:

$$sf(k)/k - \gamma - n = 0 \text{ or } sf(k) - (\gamma + n)k = 0. \tag{12.8}$$

If equation (12.8) is satisfied then the capital–labor ratio of the economy is unchanging. We are, thus, in steady state with unchanging wage rates, rental rates, and output per person. Labor grows at rate *n*. Capital grows at rate $(n + \gamma)$ but the latter part (γ) goes in for depreciation. Hence, the effective growth rate of capital is also *n*. With both capital and labor growing at rate *n* output also grows at rate *n*. The steady-state equilibrium of the economy is depicted in Figure 12.1. The unique steady-state capital ratio is denoted by k^*. From equation (12.8) to the left of k^* we must have $\dot{k} > 0$ and to the right of k^* we must have $\dot{k} < 0$ so that the steady-state capital–labor ratio k^* is (locally) stable.[1]

Effects of taxes

Let us now alter the Solow model a trifle by making the savings propensity a function of the capital–labor ratio and a tax t_k on capital income. We will assume that tax revenues are used by the government to finance exogenous government expenditure. Thus, our steady-state condition now reads:

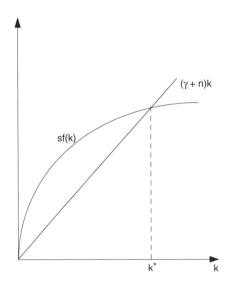

Figure 12.1

$$\dot{k} = s(k, t_k)f(k) - (n + \gamma)k. \tag{12.9}$$

Differentiating equation (12.9) with respect to t_k we have:

$$f(k)[s_k(dk/dt_k)] + sf'(dk/dt_k) + s_{t_k}f - (n + \gamma)(dk/dt_k) = 0$$

from which we can derive:

$$(dk/dt_k)[sf' + fs_k - v] = -s_{t_k}f \tag{12.10}$$

where $v = \gamma + n$.

If the steady state is stable, it can be shown that the coefficient of (dk/dt_k) on the lefthand side of equation (12.10) is negative. Hence the imposition of the capital income tax will make the steady-state capital–labor ratio rise (fall) as s_{t_k} is positive (negative). We depict one case in Figure 12.2. In the diagram the fall in k leads to a rise in the gross returns to capital and a fall in wages. To this extent the tax is 'shifted'. It thus becomes interesting to ask the question: Is it possible for the net return to capital to rise? Writing r for the net return we have:

$$r = (1 - t_k)f'(k)$$
$$dr/dt_k = (1 - t_k)[f''(dk/dt_k)] - f'. \tag{12.11}$$

Using the definition of elasticity of substitution (σ) where $\sigma = f'(f - kf')/(-kff'')$ we have:

$$dr/dt_k = -f'[1 - (1 - t_k)(-s_{t_k})(f - kf')/[(v - sf' - s_kf)k\sigma]]. \tag{12.12}$$

The sign of this expression depends upon the strength of the response of savings (s_{t_k}) as well as on the characteristics of steady state. In order to make further progress, we need to specify the savings process.

We study an example of a society in which there are two classes of people: workers and capitalist with savings propensities s_w and s_r with $1 > s_r > s_w > 0$. We further assume that the underlying production function is of the

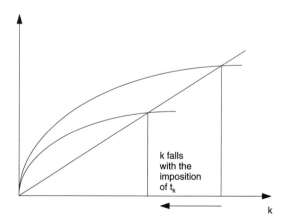

Figure 12.2

Cobb–Douglas type with the share of labor in total product equal to α. The steady state condition would now be written as

$$sf(k) = s_r rk + s_w \alpha f - vk = 0. \tag{12.13}$$

This can be rearranged to give using $r = (1 - t_k)f'$ to yield:

$$r = v/[s_r + \{s_w(\alpha/(1-\alpha))(1-t_k)\}^{-1}]. \tag{12.14}$$

Using a numerical example, take the Cobb–Douglas case with $\alpha = 2/3$, $s_r = 0.5$, $s_w = 0.125$ and a 50 per cent tax causes net return to capital to fall only by a quarter. Hence, there is considerable shifting of the capital tax.

If the tax on capital leads to a fall in k this means that part of the burden of the government expenditure is being shifted. Suppose we now consider an explicitly redistributive tax with the proceeds $T(= t_k f'k)$ being used to finance a lump-sum transfer to workers. Is it possible that this too will be shifted so that the redistributive goal will not be met?

The effect on the level of savings may in the case of the Solow model be represented by:

$$sf(k) = s_r[(1-\alpha)f - T] + s_w(\alpha f + T) \tag{12.15}$$

where, as before, α is the share of output going to workers and $(1-\alpha)$ to capitalists.

Differentiating the condition for steady state growth and using s_a to represent the average savings rate $(s_a = s_w\alpha + s_r(1-\alpha))$ we have

$$[s_a f' + (s_w - s_r)\alpha f' - v](dk/dT) = s_r - s_w \tag{12.16}$$

or

$$P(dk/dT) = s_r - s_w.$$

It can be shown that for stability P must be negative. Hence dk/dT has to be negative. Hence, although the transfer is made to workers, the drop in k will lower the wage rate. We can now investigate the effect on the total income of workers. It can be shown that:

$$d(\alpha f + T)/dT = [s_r f' - v]/P. \tag{12.17}$$

This can be positive or negative. The lower the rate of depreciation and the rate of growth of population and the higher the savings rate of capitalists and the marginal product of capital, the greater the chance that total income of workers will fall.

12.3 BALANCED GROWTH PATH TAX INCIDENCE

Until now we have been discussing the effects of taxes on the capital–labor ratio. Another method of assessing the effects of taxes is to alter some policy measure in addition to the particular tax being considered in order to leave the value of the capital–labor ratio unchanged. This is known as

balanced growth path incidence. Let us suppose that there are two types of assets – equities (which are claims to the existing capital stock) and government bonds. It will be assumed that individual investors are indifferent between holding bonds and equities. This, of course, goes against the spirit of the Ricardian equivalence argument formalized by Barro (1974) and others. The Ricardian equivalence is that if consumers have the welfare of future generations in mind then they will recognize that government bond issues today will have to be paid off by additional taxation on future generations. Hence, they will think of government bonds merely as future tax liabilities and will not regard them as private wealth. We will deal with this issue later in the chapter. For the time being, we think of government bonds as net wealth. In fact from the wealth-holder's point of view, bonds and equities will be regarded as perfect substitutes. We will keep the price of bonds relative to consumer goods fixed (say at one).

Let B stand for bonds, $b = B/L$ be per capita bonds, and T_k be total taxes paid on capital income. Assuming depreciation to be zero the equality of savings and investment per capita requires that:

$$s_r[(1 - \alpha)f + rb - T_k] + s_w(\alpha f + T) = (\dot{K} + \dot{B})/L. \qquad (12.18)$$

In equation (12.18) we are assuming that only capitalists are bondholders and that capitalists pay taxes whereas workers get a transfer. Savings (the lefthand side) are invested in two forms of assets capital (or equities) and bonds. Whenever the government changes taxes, it also alters its debt policy in order to leave the capital–labor ratio unchanged.

Now, we can expand equation (12.18) as follows:

$$(\dot{k}/k) = \dot{K}/K - n = [s_w\alpha + s_r(1 - \alpha)]f/k - n + (s_wT - s_rT_k)/k \\ + (s_r rb/k) - \dot{B}/K. \qquad (12.19)$$

If the capital–labor ratio is to remain unchanged, then the term $(s_wT - s_rT_k)/k + (s_r rb/k) - \dot{B}/K = 0$; then we would be back to the original Solow formulation.

The government's budget constraint can then be written as:

$$\dot{B}/K = (T - T_k)/k + rb/k \qquad (12.20)$$

so that we must have:

$$T - T_k + rb = (s_wT - s_rT_k) + s_r rb \text{ or } T(1 - s_w) = (1 - s_r)(T_k - rb). \qquad (12.21)$$

Moreover, in steady state debt per worker must be constant so that $\dot{b} = 0$ so $\dot{B} = nB$. Substituting in equation (12.20) we have

$$nB/K = (T - T_k)/k + rb/k.$$

Divide through by L to get: $nb/K = (T - T_k)/K + rb/K$ so that, in steady state, we must have:

$$(r - n)b = (T_k - T). \tag{12.22}$$

Combining these results, we get the steady-state transfer as:

$$T = [n(1 - s_r)/\{n(1 - s_w) - r(s_r - s_w)\}]T_k. \tag{12.23}$$

If k is constant then this expression is positive for $1 > s_r > s_w > 0$. Hence, in this case, when T_k goes up so will T. The intuition behind this result is quite straightforward. In the case where k changed in response to the tax then the transfer to workers could drop because the lower value of k would lead to lower wages and higher rentals. However, in the case of balanced growth path incidence, this is ruled out since government debt policy is keeping the capital–labor ratio constant.

Now, this result is strictly contingent on government bonds being considered net wealth. If this is not the case then debt policy could not be used to keep the capital–labor ratio unchanged following an alteration in capital taxes.

12.4 TAXATION IN THE LIFE-CYCLE MODEL

Consider the life-cycle model of savings discussed in Chapter 7. Consider the version of the model without taxation to begin with. Second-period consumption (c_2) will be given by:

$$c_2 = (w - c_1)(1 + r). \tag{12.24}$$

For the generation born in period t the relevant wage is w_t whereas the rate of interest that they receive will be that prevalent for the generation born in the next time period, i.e., r_{t+1}. Hence, we can write first-period consumption for a young person born in generation t as: $c_1(w_t, r_{t+1})$. Hence, per person savings are:

$$S_t(w_t, r_{t+1}) = w_t - c_1(w_t, r_{t+1}). \tag{12.25}$$

We assume that capital lasts only one time period and there are no bonds so that total capital in period $(t + 1)$ is, assuming zero depreciation, the accumulated savings of the young of generation t, i.e.,

$$K_{t+1} = S_t(w_t, r_{t+1})L_t \tag{12.26}$$

where L_t is the size of the labor force in period t. Hence:

$$k_{t+1} = S_t(w_t, r_{t+1})L_t/L_{t+1} = S_t/(1 + n) \tag{12.27}$$

if labor grows at the constant (geometric, since time is discrete here) rate n. Therefore, it must be the case that in steady state:

$$c_1 = w - (1 + n)k \tag{12.28a}$$

and

$$c_2 = (1 + r)(1 + n)k. \tag{12.28b}$$

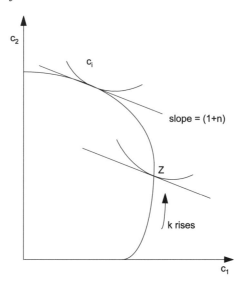

Figure 12.3

By varying k we can trace out the possible steady-state consumption levels. This curve would have the slope:

$$dc_2/dc_1 = [\partial c_2/\partial k][\partial c_1/\partial k] = (1+n)[(1+r) + kf'']/\{-kf'' - (1+n)\}. \tag{12.29}$$

It is plotted in Figure 12.3. As k rises we travel up the c_1c_2 locus in Figure 12.3. At G the slope of the locus is $(1+n)$ which is associated with the golden rule of economic growth[2]. If r is different from n we may be at a point like Z.

Incidence of taxation

We now introduce a tax on capital income which is used to make lump-sum transfers T_1 and T_2 to the two generations (workers and retired persons). The budget constraint of a typical young person is, then,

$$c_1 + c_2/(1+r) = w + T_1 + T_2/(1+r) \tag{12.30}$$

where $r = (1 - t_k)f'(k)$ and the c_1, c_2 frontier is given by:

$$c_1 = w - (1+n)k + T_1 \tag{12.31}$$

$$c_2 = [1 + f'(1 - t_k)](1+n) + T_2. \tag{12.32}$$

Once again, in steady state, the capital stock must equal accumulated savings:

$$(1+n)k = S(w(k), r(k, t_k), T_1, T_2). \tag{12.33}$$

It is implicit in equation (12.33) that w is a function of k and r is a function of k and t_k. Differentiating equation (12.33) totally and collecting terms we can derive:

$$dk[1 + n - S_w(\partial w/\partial k) - S_r(\partial r/\partial k)] = (\partial S/\partial T_1)dT_1$$
$$+ (\partial S/\partial T_2)dT_2 - S_r f' dt_k. \qquad (12.34)$$

If the model is stable then the coefficient of dk on the lefthand side of equation (12.34) is positive. From this we get the obvious result that an increase in t_k raises k if the condition for local stability of the model is satisfied. Hence in this model transfers raise savings.

Balanced growth path incidence

It remains for us to examine the incidence of the capital tax on the balanced growth path of the economy. In this case, again, the government issues debt to neutralize the change in k following an increase in t_k. We assume that equities and debt are perfect substitutes for each other in the investor's portfolio. Thus we write:

$$(1 + n)(k + b) = S(w, r, T_1, T_2) \qquad (12.35)$$

where it is being assumed that all savings are transferred into holdings of capital and government debt. The Ricardian Equivalence criticism will apply in this case as well.

In steady state debt per worker must be constant: $\dot{b} = 0$ so that new issue of debt per period is nb per worker. This, less the interest paid on the debt, must equal the part of the government deficit not covered by taxes. This allows us to write the government budget constraint as:

$$nb = T_1 + T_2/(1 + n) - t_k(k + b)f' + rb. \qquad (12.36)$$

This can be rewritten as:

$$t_k(k + b)f' - T_1 - T_2/(1 + r) = (r - n)[b + T_2/\{(1 + n)(1 + r)\}]. \qquad (12.37)$$

Suppose, now, that we reduce T_2 by dT_2 while increasing T_1 by $dT_2/(1 + r)$ so that the present value is unchanged. Total savings per person would then rise by $dT_2/(1 + r)$. This is equivalent in terms of the effect on total physical capital stock to reducing b by $dT_2/\{(1 + n)(1 + r)\}$ and we can see from equation (12.37) that this would have an equivalent effect on the government budget constraint. Thus government debt policy is equivalent to a lump-sum redistribution between generations.

Finally, we can totally differentiate equation (12.35) and evaluate it at $b = T_1 = T_2 = t_k = 0$ to get:

$$dk[1 + n - S_w(\partial w/\partial k) - S_r(\partial r/\partial k)] = (\partial S/\partial T_1)dT_1$$
$$+ (\partial S/\partial T_2)dT_2 - S_r f' dt_k - (1 + n)db \qquad (12.38)$$

and, therefore:

$$(k + b)f'dt_k - dT_1 - dT_2/(1 + r) = (r - n)[db + dT_2/\{(1 + n)(1 + r)\}].$$
(12.39)

We can then use these equations to judge balanced growth path incidence in the standard manner. Note that at the golden rule the righthand side of equation (12.39) is zero.

12.5   TAX INCIDENCE IN A MONETARY VERSION OF THE SOLOW MODEL

We now wish to inquire into tax incidence in a more general version of the Solow model. We expand it to consider money in the growth model as well as several different forms of taxation. The model we study was used by Jha *et al.* (1990) to study the effects of various types of taxes on the nominal interest rates, but the model can easily be adapted to calculate the effects of different taxes on the capital–labor ratio as well. We will study the effects of a rise in the rate of inflation but any other type of tax could be used just as easily.

The real sector of the model is quite similar to the Solow model that has already been discussed. Labor grows at a constant exponential rate *n* whereas output per unit labor (y) is given as a function of capital per unit labor (k). The paper introduces a notion of optimal capital stock given by:

$$(1 - t_k)f' = (1 - t_k)i + \lambda\pi^e - \pi^e$$
(12.40)

where t_k is, as before, the tax on capital, *i* is the nominal rate of interest, π^e the expected rate of inflation which we set equal to the actual rate of inflation by assuming perfect foresight. λ captures the inflation non-neutralities due to a historic rather than a replacement basis for depreciation, the use of FIFO[3] and the taxation of nominal rather than real capital gains.[4]

Real wealth (W) is composed of real money balances (M/P) and the real value of (corporate) bonds (B/P):

$$W = (M/P) + (B/P).$$
(12.41)

It is assumed that all capital is financed by debt. This is not central to the analysis: equity finance is easily accommodated without changing any of the principal results.

The demand for money grows as the population grows. Any growth in the money supply in excess of population growth will lead to inflation. Thus, we have:

$$\dot{M}/M = \dot{P}/P + n = \pi + n.$$
(12.42)

Since the growth rates of both the money stock as well as the population are exogenously determined, the inflation rate (π) could be treated as a predetermined (or exogenous).

The disposable income of consumers (Y) can be calculated as follows:

$$Y = Lf(k) - T - \pi(M/P). \tag{12.43}$$

Disposable income Y is equal to national income minus both the government's tax receipts T and the fall in the real value of the population's money balance $(\pi(M/P))$. Total taxes are the sum of the capital tax, a personal tax and any residual tax that can be thought of as a lump-sum tax. The government uses these tax receipts plus the increase in money supply $(\dot{M}/P)$ to finance its purchases of goods and services (G). Therefore we can write:

$$Y = Lf(k) - G + \dot{M}/P - \pi(M/P). \tag{12.44}$$

But since $\pi = \dot{M}/M - n$ we can write:

$$Y = Lf(k) - G + nM/P. \tag{12.45}$$

Without any loss of generality we assume that government consumption is a constant fraction (θ) of real national income and that the government maintains a balanced budget. Hence, per capita disposable income Y is:

$$Y = (1 - \theta)f(k) + mn \tag{12.46}$$

where m is per capita real money balances.

Per capita savings (S/L) is a function of after-tax real return to savers (r_s), per capita real wealth, and per capita disposable income:

$$S/L = s(r_s, m + k)y. \tag{12.47}$$

We will assume that $s_r > 0, s_m > 0, s_k < 0$.

$$r_s = (1 - t_p)i - \pi \tag{12.48}$$

where t_p is the marginal personal tax rate.

Steady-state equilibrium requires that:

$$s(r_s, m + k)[(1 - \theta)f(k) + mn] = n(m + k). \tag{12.49}$$

In steady-state equilibrium, saving is just enough to keep per capita real money balances (m) and per capita capital stock (k) constant. Money market equilibrium for this economy is expressed as:

$$m = M[(1 - t_p)i, y], M_i < 0 \text{ and } M_y > 0 \tag{12.50}$$

that is, per capita real money balances equal per capita real money demand which, in turn, depends upon the after-tax nominal rate of interest and real national output.

There are three endogenous variables in this model: i, m, and k. These are determined by the three equations (12.40), (12.49) and (12.50). We totally differentiate these three equations and collect them in (the matrix) equation (12.51) below:

$$\begin{bmatrix} (1-t_k) & 0 & -(1-t_k)f'' \\ s_r(1-t_p)y & s_my-n(1-s) & s_ky+s(1-\theta)f'-n \\ M_i(1-t_p) & M_yn-1 & M_y(1-\theta)f' \end{bmatrix} \begin{bmatrix} di \\ dm \\ dk \end{bmatrix} = \begin{bmatrix} (1-\lambda)d\pi \\ s_ryd\pi \\ 0 \end{bmatrix}$$

$$(12.51)$$

We now want to find the effects of the various taxes on the capital–labor ratio. By Cramer's Rule we can solve:

$$dk/d\pi = A/\Delta \qquad (12.52)$$

where

$$A=(1-\lambda)\{s_r(1-t_p)y(M_yn-1) - M_i(1-t_p)(s_my-n(1-s))\}$$
$$\quad - s_ry\{(1-t_p)(M_yn-1)\}$$
$$\Delta=(1-t_k)\{M_y(1-\theta)f'[s_my-n(1-s)] - [s_ky+s(1-\theta)f'-n](M_yn-1)\}$$
$$\quad - (1-t_k)f''\{s_r(1-t_p)y(M_yn-1)M_i(1-t_p)[s_my-n(1-s)]\}.$$

If the system is stable[5] $s(1-\theta)f' < n$ and Δ, the determinant on the lefthand side of equation (12.51), will be negative. Now, if $\lambda = 0$ and $s_my > n(1-s)$ then the Tobin effect will hold, and $dk/d\pi > 0$, i.e., an increase in inflation will lead an increase in capital intensity. The effects of other taxes could be investigated in a similar manner.

12.6   TAX INCIDENCE IN MORE GENERAL LIFE-CYCLE MODELS

The life-cycle models we have studied so far have been based on the works of Samuelson (1956), Diamond (1965) and Yaari (1965). More recently, the life-cycle model has been extended by Blanchard (1985), Buiter (1988) and Weil (1989). Each individual faces a constant probability of death ϕ just as in the model by Yaari. Hence, unlike the simple life-cycle model discussed above, horizons are not finite but there is a constant probability of death at each point in time.[6]

At every instant of time a new cohort composed of people with constant probability of death ϕ, is born. Each cohort is also assumed to be large enough so that ϕ is also the rate at which the cohort size is decreasing through time. One particularly simple way of normalizing is to set the size of a new cohort equal to ϕ. Thus a cohort born at time v has a size as of time t, of $\phi e^{-\phi(t-v)}$. Thus the size of the population at any time t is equal to:

$$\int_{-\infty}^{t} \phi e^{-(\phi(t-v))}dv = 1. \qquad (12.53)$$

An important characteristic of the new life-cycle model is that, as mentioned above, there is individual but no aggregate uncertainty. Furthermore, no bequest motive is permitted. Hence there is scope for insurance. Insurance companies can offer positive or negative insurance. The representative individual in this model faces the possibility of dying before using all his wealth. He would be better off if he could sell the claim on his wealth in the event he dies, in exchange for command over resources when he is alive.

The insurance company can then make premium payments to the living in exchange for receipts of their estates in the event they die. This is the exact opposite of the 'usual' type of insurance cover.

We will assume that the insurance industry is perfectly competitive so that, in equilibrium, the premium is ϕ and there is no profit or loss. In the absence of a bequest motive individuals will contract to have all their wealth w_t go to the insurance company in the event of their death. In return the insurance company pays them a premium of ϕw_t. The insurance company just balances its books by paying out and receiving ϕw_t per time period.

We denote by $c(v,t)$, $y(v,t)$, $w(v,t)$ and $h(v,t)$ the consumption, labor income, wealth and human capital of an individual of generation v at time t. Since the focus is on individual consumption, the generation indicator v can be omitted. Let $U(c(q))$ be the utility at time q. This individual faces a maximization problem under uncertainty. At time t he would maximize the following:

$$E\left[\int_t U(c(q))e^{-\delta(q-t)}dq\right] \qquad (12.54)$$

where δ is the (fixed) rate of discount and the upper limit of the above integral is uncertain in view of the uncertain time of death. Now, using Yaari's result, and assuming that the utility function is a simple logarithm of consumption, we can write the maximand as:

$$\int_t^\infty \ln c(q)e^{-(\delta+\phi)(q-t)}dq. \qquad (12.55)$$

As in Yaari, the effect of the exponential probability of death assumption is simply to increase the individual's rate of time preference.

If an individual has non-human wealth $a(q)$ at time q, he would receive $r(q)\,a(q)$ in interest where $r(q)$ is the interest rate at time q and $\phi a(q)$ the premium from the insurance company. Thus the individual's intertemporal budget constraint can be written as:

$$da(q)/dq = [r(q) + \phi]a(q) + y(q) - c(q). \qquad (12.56)$$

We have not so far imposed the constraint that the individual's non-human wealth be non-negative. In the absence of any restrictions on borrowing, the solution to the maximization problem is a trivial one. It is for the individual to borrow sufficiently to drive down the marginal utility of consumption to zero which, for the utility function in equation (12.55), amounts to infinite consumption. We therefore need an additional constraint that prevents an individual from choosing a path with an exploding debt. However, we do not want to rule out temporary indebtedness. A constraint that embodies both these aspects is known as the **no Ponzi Game Condition**. For our case this would be written as:

$$\lim_{q \to \infty} e^{-\int_t^q [r(z)+\phi(z)]dz} a(q) = 0. \tag{12.57}$$

If the individual is still alive at time q then satisfaction of equation (12.57) would guarantee that he cannot accumulate debt at a rate higher than the effective rate of interest facing him – the interest rate on the debt plus the insurance premium.

To simplify matters the discount factor is defined as:

$$D(t, q) = e^{-\int_t^q [r(z)+\phi(z)]dz}. \tag{12.58}$$

Using the no Ponzi game condition (12.57) we can integrate equation (12.58) forward to obtain the intertemporal budget constraint:

$$\int_t^\infty c(q)D(t, q)dq = a(t) + h(t) \tag{12.59}$$

where[7]

$$h(t) = \int_t^\infty y(q)D(t, q)dq.$$

The individual maximizes the utility function given in equation (12.55) subject to the budget constraint given in equation (12.59). Performing this maximization problem using the standard Hamiltonian method we get, in addition to the transversality conditions, the following condition characterizing the optimal consumption plan:

$$dc(q)/dq = \{[r(q) + \phi] - (\delta + \phi)\}c(q) = [r(q) - \delta]c(q). \tag{12.60}$$

Thus the individual consumption rises (falls) as the interest rate exceeds (falls short of) the subjective rate of discount. We now integrate equation (12.60) to express $c(z)$ as a function of $c(t)$ and substituting in the budget constraint (equation (12.59)) to get:

$$c(t) = (\delta + \phi)[a(t) + h(t)]. \tag{12.61}$$

Hence individual consumption depends on total individual wealth with propensity to consume $(\delta + \phi)$ which is independent of the rate of interest.[8] Moreover, consumption is independent of age because of the assumption of a constant probability of death.

Aggregate consumption

Let us denote aggregate amounts by upper case letters. Thus $C(t)$, for example, is aggregate consumption. When we are aggregating over generations the generation specific index v will become relevant. Recall further that the size of a generation born $(t - v)$ periods ago is $[\phi e^{-\phi(t-v)}]$. Hence aggregate consumption is given by:

$$C(t) = \int_{-\infty}^{t} c(v, t) e^{[-\phi(t-v)]} dv. \tag{12.62}$$

Similar definitions will apply to aggregate income, aggregate assets, and aggregate human wealth. Using equation (12.61) and (12.62) we write:

$$C(t) = (\phi + \delta)[A(t) + H(t)]. \tag{12.63}$$

We must now derive the dynamic behavior of $A(t)$ and $H(t)$. We know that labor income depends exclusively on human wealth. We will make the assumption that there is retirement so that labor income will eventually decrease with age. Hence, we write:

$$y(v, t) = bY(t) e^{-\alpha(t-v)}, \alpha \geqslant 0 \tag{12.64}$$

and b is a constant which will be determined later. Equation (12.64) implies that the per capita labor income of a member of a given generation is smaller the older the generation.[9] To determine the value of b replace $y(v,t)$ in the expression determining $Y(t)$ and use equation (12.64) to write:[10]

$$b = (\alpha + \phi)/\phi. \tag{12.65}$$

Replacing $y(v,t)$ in the expression for $h(v,t)$ gives:

$$
\begin{aligned}
h(v, t) &= \int_{t}^{\infty} bY(q) e^{-\alpha(q-v)} D(t, q) dq \\
&= b \left\{ \int_{t}^{\infty} Y(q) e^{-\alpha(q-t)} D(t, q) dq \right\} e^{-\alpha(t-v)}
\end{aligned} \tag{12.66}
$$

where the term in braces ($\{.\}$) is independent of time of birth.

We now write aggregate human wealth as:

$$
\begin{aligned}
H(t) &= \int_{-\infty}^{t} h(v, t) e^{-\phi(t-v)} dv \\
&= \int_{-\infty}^{t} \left[b\phi \left\{ \int_{t}^{\infty} Y(q) e^{-\alpha(q-t)} D(t, q) dq \right\} e^{-\alpha(t-v)} e^{-\phi(t-v)} \right] dv.
\end{aligned} \tag{12.67}
$$

Upon rearranging and using the definition of b in equation (12.65) we have:

$$H(t) = \int_{t}^{\infty} Y(q) e^{-\int_{t}^{q} [\alpha + \phi + r(z)] dz} dq. \tag{12.68}$$

Aggregate human wealth is, therefore, the present discounted value of labor income accruing in the future to people alive today discounted at the rate r. This is the same as the present discounted value of labor income discounted at the rate $(\alpha + \phi + r)$. Both interpretations are reasonable.

To arrive at the dynamic behavior of human capital we differentiate equation (12.68) with respect to t to get:

$$dH(t)/dt = [r(t) + \phi + \alpha]H(t) - Y(t) \qquad (12.69)$$

and

$$\lim_{q \to \infty} H(q)e^{-\int_t^q [\alpha + \phi + r(q)]dq} = 0. \qquad (12.69a)$$

Finally, non-human wealth is given by:

$$A(t) = \int_{-\infty}^t a(v, t)e^{-\phi(t-v)}dv$$

which upon differentiation with respect to t yields:

$$dA(t)/dt = \phi a(t, t) - \phi A(t) + \int_{-\infty}^t \left\{ [da(v, t)/dt]\phi e^{-\phi(t-v)} \right\}dv. \qquad (12.70)$$

The first term on the righthand side is the non-human wealth of a new cohort at birth.[11] The second represents the wealth of those who die at time t, and the third is the change in the non-human wealth of the remaining. Using the fact that $a(t, t) = 0$ and equation (12.56) in equation (12.70) we have:

$$dA(t)/dt = r(t)A(t) + Y(t) - C(t). \qquad (12.71)$$

This says that there is an important distinction between the social and private returns to wealth.[12] This difference is very important to the overlapping generations model.

Aggregate behavior

The aggregate equations of this economy can be written as:[13]

$$C = (\phi + \delta)(H + A) \qquad (12.63)$$
$$dA/dt = rA + Y - C \qquad (12.71)$$
$$dH/dt = (r + \phi + \alpha)H - Y \qquad (12.69)$$

$$\lim_{q \to \infty} H(q)e^{-\int_t^q [r(z) + \phi + \alpha]dz} = 0 \qquad (12.69a)$$

In these equations both the propensity to consume and the discount rate for human wealth are increasing functions of the probability of death. The higher is the probability of death, the greater is the propensity to consume and the greater the discounting of future labor income.

An alternative characterization of aggregate behavior goes as follows. Differentiate equation (12.63) with respect to time and use equations (12.69) and (12.71) to eliminate dA/dt and dH/dt to get

$$dC/dt = (r + \alpha - \delta)C - (\phi + \alpha)(\phi + \delta)V \qquad (12.72)$$
$$dA/dt = rA + Y - C. \qquad (12.71)$$

It is typical to analyze this model for two cases – one with constant labor income $(\alpha = 0)$ and the other with declining labor income $(\alpha > 0)$. We consider these two cases here as well. Before we do so, however, we have to close the model by bringing in the production structure.

We have already normalized the population of this economy to equal one. Production conditions are described by a standard neoclassical production function:

$$F(K) = F(K, 1) - \gamma K \qquad (12.73)$$

where γ is the rate of depreciation of this economy. It will be assumed that the only form of non-human wealth is capital so that $A = K$ and, under competitive conditions, the marginal product of capital will equal the interest rate: $r = F'(K)$.

Constant labor income

Using equations (12.71) and (12.72) with r being set equal to F' and α set equal to zero we have:

$$dC/dt = (F'(K) - \delta)C - \phi(\phi + \delta)K \qquad (12.74)$$
$$dK/dt = F(K) - C. \qquad (12.75)$$

These are the two dynamic equations of the system. Once we can solve for C and K in steady state we can solve for all other variables since the latter are all functions of C and K. These two dynamic equations are depicted in Figure 12.4. In this diagram we single out three important levels of the stock of capital. At the point K_n, $F'(K_n) = 0$. Since there is no population growth K_n is the golden rule capital stock. Two other values of the capital stock are denoted in the diagram. At K_1 we have $F' = \delta$ and at K_2 we will have $F' = \phi + \delta$. In Figure 12.4 we also show the $dC/dt = 0$ schedule. The steady state S^* is a saddle point equilibrium.[14]

Important characteristics of the steady-state capital stock (K^*) are as follows:

$$\text{(i)} \quad \delta < F'(K^*) < \delta + \phi. \qquad (12.76)$$

The first inequality follows from equation (12.74) when $dC/dt = 0$. The second inequality can be proved through contradiction. Suppose that contrary to the second inequality we have: $F' = \delta + \phi(1 + \epsilon)$ with $\epsilon > 0$. Then from equation (12.74) with $dC/dt = 0$ we must have: $(1 + \epsilon)C = (\phi + \delta)K^*$. Or, using equation (12.75) we will get: $(1 + \epsilon)F(K^*) = (F' - \delta\epsilon)K^*$.

But since $F(.)$ is a concave function the above equality is impossible because for a concave function we must have $F(K^*) > K^*F'(K^*)$. Hence it must be the case that $F'(K^*) < (\delta + \phi)$.

(ii) A second property of the steady-state equilibrium is that K^* is a decreasing function of the discount rate δ. An increase in the discount rate will shift the $dC/dt = 0$ schedule to the left.

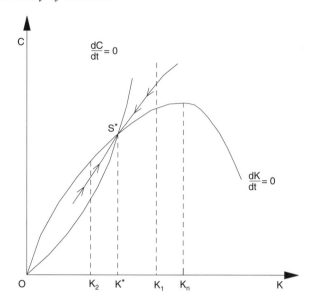

Figure 12.4

These results are important. The market economy yields an equilibrium that is dynamically inefficient. For the equilibrium to be efficient the rate of interest should equal the rate of growth of population – which is zero in this case. Furthermore, the higher the discount rate, the lower the equilibrium capital stock.

Declining labor income

When declining labor income is expected, the individual would like to accumulate more capital in order to satisfy consumption plans later in life when labor income will be low. With given path of interest rate and fixed discount rate this increased capital accumulation will lower the interest rate.

With declining labor income $\alpha > 0$ and the dynamic equations become:

$$dC/dt = [F(k) + \alpha - \delta]C - \phi(\phi + \delta)K \qquad (12.77a)$$

$$dK/dt = F(K) - C. \qquad (12.77b)$$

The $dK/dt = 0$ schedule is the same as in Figure 12.4. Now we define K_4 so that $F'(K_4) = \delta - \alpha$. The $dC/dt = 0$ schedule for C positive is upward sloping, goes through the origin and will reach K_4 asymptotically. Steady-state capital (K^*) in Figure 12.5 is such that $F'(K^*) > \delta - \alpha$.
This is because $(\delta - \alpha)$ can be positive or negative. Hence K may be smaller or larger than the golden rule capital stock K_n.

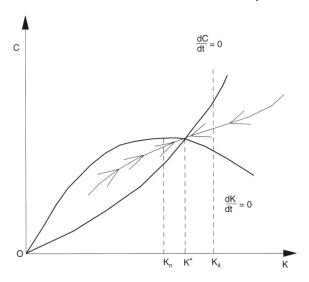

Figure 12.5

An increase in α shifts the $dC/dt = 0$ schedule down which increases the capital stock. Since there is no natural upper bound on α it might be the case that the capital stock is higher than the golden rule level.

Fiscal policy

Let us now introduce taxation and government expenditure into this model. Let government borrowings at time t be $B(t)$ whereas government expenditure is $G(t)$ and taxes are $T(t)$. Hence the government budget constraint can be written as:

$$dB(t) = r(t)B(t) + G(t) - T(t) \qquad (12.78)$$

that is, new borrowings equal total government expenditure.[15] We now confine ourselves to the case where $r > 0$. It should be clear that equation (12.78), by itself, imposes no restraint on the government. We can do so by imposing a no Ponzi game condition on the government. This can be written as:

$$\lim_{q \to \infty} B(q)e^{-\int_t^q r(z)dz} = 0. \qquad (12.79)$$

Integrating equation (12.78) forward subject to (12.79) implies that

$$B(t) = -\int_t^\infty \{[G(q) - T(q)]e^{-\int_t^q [r(z)dz]}\}dq. \qquad (12.80)$$

This is a meaningful intertemporal budget constraint for the government. It implies that the current level of debt must be equal to the present discounted value of primary surpluses.[16] If the government is at this point in time a net debtor then it must plan to run primary surpluses at some point in time. Equation (12.80) does not imply that the debt is necessarily repaid or that it is constant. All that it implies is that the debt ultimately grows at a rate less than the rate of interest.

The government affects aggregate demand in three ways. First, it purchases goods and services to the extent of G and it affects private consumption through taxes,[17] both current and anticipated as well as debt. With the current set up, the principal equations characterizing the economy will become:

$$C(t) = (\phi + \delta)[H(t) + A(t)] \tag{12.81}$$
$$A(t) = B(t) + K(t)$$

$$H(t) = \int_t^\infty [Y(q) - T(q)]e^{-\int_t^q [r(z)+\phi]dz} dq \tag{12.82}$$

$$dA(t)/dt = r(t)A(t) + Y(t) - C(t) - T(t). \tag{12.83}$$

Financial wealth consists of government debt as well as the capital stock. Human wealth is the present discounted value of non-interest income less taxes with $(r + \phi)$ as the rate of discount.

Consider now an intertemporal reallocation of taxes, keeping the path of government expenditure constant. This implies a decrease in taxes at the present time t combined with an increase in taxes at some point in time $(t + s)$. From the government's intertemporal budget constraint we have:

$$dT(t + s) = \{-e^{\int_t^{t+s} r(z)dz}\}dT(t). \tag{12.84}$$

The increase in taxes at time $t + s$ must equal the initial decrease at time t compounded at the rate of interest.

Because $B(t)$ is unchanged at time[18] t, this reallocation has an effect on aggregate demand at time t only to the extent that it affects consumption through its effect on human wealth. From equation (12.82) this effect is:

$$dH(t) = -dT(t) - dT(t + s)e^{\int_t^{t+s} [r(z)+\phi]dz}. \tag{12.85}$$

Using the government budget constraint this can be written as:

$$dH(t) = -dT(t)[1 - e^{-\phi s}]. \tag{12.86}$$

We know that taxes are cut at time t. Hence $dT(t) < 0$. Hence the move to deficit finance will increase $H(t)$ and increase consumption. The larger the time period after which taxes will be raised (s), the greater will be the effect on consumption. The same is true of ϕ. The larger is the probability (ϕ) of death and the utility process coming to an end, the greater will be the effect on consumption.

Recently an extreme case has attracted considerable attention. Suppose $\phi = 0$. This can happen because of two reasons. Either we are working with infinitely lived individuals, or individuals care sufficiently for their progeny so that in effect they are infinitely lived although they have a positive probability of dying at any point in time. In this situation $dH(t) = 0$ and there is no effect on consumption.

This case is now quite popular in the literature and is known as the **Ricardian equivalence theorem** after David Ricardo who first articulated the notion that government bonds are not considered to be net wealth by private consumers. In more recent times this theorem[19] was propounded by Barro (1974).

Effect of debt on the interest rate

An interesting allocative issue that we can study here is the effect of debt on the rate of interest. We will study an illustrative example of this with labor income undiminished by age: $\alpha = 0$. Then we must have:

$$dC/dt = (r - \delta)C - \phi(\phi + \delta)(B + K) \tag{12.87}$$
$$dK/dt = F(K) - C - G \tag{12.88}$$
$$dB/dt = rB + G - T. \tag{12.89}$$

We also know that $F' = r$.

Equation (12.87) says that debt is part of wealth and enters the consumption equation. Government purchases of goods affect the capital accumulation equation (12.88). Given paths for G and T that satisfy the intertemporal government budget constraint we can in principle solve for C and K, given fiscal policy. However, this problem is quite hard to do in practice and we will discuss only the steady state here.

In steady state from equations (12.87) to (12.89) we have:

$$[F'(K^*) - \delta]C^* = \phi(\phi + \delta)(B^* + K^*) \tag{12.90a}$$
$$F(K^*) = C^* + G \tag{12.90b}$$
$$F'(K^*)B^* = T - G \tag{12.90c}$$

with a star (*) denoting steady state values.

In equation (12.90a) we assume that both B^* and K^* are positive hence $r^* > \delta$. Hence, the equilibrium will be inefficient as in the model without government debt.

Suppose now that the government temporarily cuts taxes with expenditure held constant and then later raises taxes in order to satisfy the government budget constraint. Now by substituting (12.90b) into (12.90) we obtain:

$$dK^*/dB^* = \phi(\phi + \delta)/[F''C^* + (r^* - \delta)r^* - \phi(\phi + \delta)].$$

Hence, a change in the steady-state stock of debt with government expenditure held constant will change the capital stock. An overly sufficient condition for the steady-state capital stock to fall is that $r^* < \delta$. Under even more general conditions an increase in the stock of debt will lower the capital stock, i.e, lead to a rise in the rate of interest.

12.7 LAND RENT TAXATION IN AN INTERTEMPORAL ECONOMY

There is another issue that has been quite extensively discussed in the literature. This is the incidence of a tax on land rent. This problem has a special interest because of the immobility of land. We sketch the basic analysis below.

We work with the simple overlapping generations model here except for assuming that the population of the country is constant. In the first period each person works and consumes and in the second they consume, but do not work. The amount of labor supplied per capita is fixed and so is the amount of land per capita. The latter is denoted as T. The amount of capital per capita is k and the amount of labor L. Output per capita is given by the production function $F(L, T, k)$ and, if factors are paid their marginal products, payments to the three factors of production are F_L, F_T and F_k. Remember, however, that the supply of labor and land per capita is fixed and the only variable factor of production is capital. Hence, marginal products will vary only with inputs of k. Naturally, as k rises, F_T and F_L will rise and F_k will fall.

It is precisely through the above relation between k and factor rewards, that a land tax can be shifted. Let us now consider the household's choice problem. In the second period of his life, an individual is retired, consumes an amount c_2 and may, if he pleases, leave behind a bequest (b) for the next generation. Both of these must be financed out of running down of first-period savings in the second time period. The interest rate equals F_k since this is the price producers would be willing to pay for the use of a unit of capital for one time period so that if S is the amount saved when young the second period budget constraint will be:

$$c_2 + b = S(1 + F_k) \text{ or } c_2/(1 + F_k) + b/(1 + F_k) = s.$$

The bequest is received by a child in the first period. Let us now consider steady states, i.e., situations where the amount of capital, factor prices and, hence, all household decisions are the same from one time period to the next. In particular, the amount of bequest received by a household when young, is equal to the amount it eventually pays when old, i.e., b. Each household's income when young is, therefore: $F_L L + b$ so that $S = F_L L + b - c_1 = [c_2 + b]/(1 + F_k)$ or, $c_1 + c_2/(1 + F_k) + b/(1 + F_k) = F_L L + b$ is the lifetime budget constraint.

All saving is carried out by the young who use their savings to purchase assets they can sell in old age. There are two such assets – land and capital. Let the price of land relative to capital (and consumption) be p. In steady state p is constant over time. Then, at the beginning of a period of time, the individuals who have just retired own the capital stock (k per capita) and land worth pT in terms of units of capital per capita which they wish to sell whereas the new young generation with savings of $S = F_L L + b - c_1$ per capita wish to buy the assets. In equilibrium, the demand for assets must equal the supply, or:

$$F_L L + b - c_1 = k + pT. \tag{12.91}$$

Further, households will be willing to hold both land and capital as assets only if the (after-tax) return on each of these is the same. The return per dollar's worth of capital is F_k whereas a unit of land returns F_T to its owner at a cost of p in terms of capital. Thus, in equilibrium, we must have:

$$F_T/p = F_k \text{ or } p = F_T/F_k.$$

Note that p is exactly the present value of the perpetual rent stream F_T discounted at the interest rate F_k.

Let us now examine the effect of a land rent tax in this economy, at a rate t_T. We will assume that the tax proceeds are disposed of by paying them out to old households. To analyze the effect of the tax, let us suppose, at first, that the capital stock and, hence, all factor prices remain unchanged. We can follow through the implications of this assumption and, if all conditions for equilibrium in this economy can still be satisfied, we can conclude that the supposition is correct.

With k fixed, the first point to observe is that the price of land must fall by the present value of future tax payments. This follows from the revised equilibrium condition of equal net returns on land and capital:

$$(1 - t_T)f_T/p' = F_k \quad \text{(where p' is the after} - \text{tax price of land)}$$

$$\text{or that } p' = (1 - t_T)F_T/F_k = F_T/F_k - t_T F_T/F_k. \tag{12.92}$$

The household's budget constraint in the presence of the tax becomes:

$$c_1 + c_2/(1 + F_k) + b/(1 + F_k) = F_L L + b + t_T F_T T/(1 + F_k). \tag{12.93}$$

The last term on the righthand side is the receipt of the government's tax revenue in one's old age. Clearly, if b is unchanged, this will increase lifetime wealth and lead to an increase in consumption in each period, if both c_1 and c_2 are normal goods (which we assume).

Suppose, however, that b changes to b' where $b' = b - t F_T T/F_k$ when the tax is imposed. This means that the lefthand side of equation (12.93) falls by $t F_T T/\{F_k(1 + F_k)\}$ whereas the righthand side falls by $[t F_T T/(F_k)] - [t F_t T/(1 + F_k)]$ because of a reduction in bequests received when young coupled with an increase in future consumption. We can rewrite the change in the righthand side as:

$$[(1 + F_k)t_T F_T T - t_T F_T T F_k]/[F_k(1 + F_k)] = t F_T T/F_k(1 + F_k).$$

Hence lifetime wealth is unchanged and, therefore, c_1 and c_2 are unchanged.

Now consider what happens to asset market equilibrium. If bequests fall to b' then with k and c_1 unchanged, the amount of saving by the young will fall by $tF_T T/F_k$. The total value of assets being sold by the old falls by the same amount because by equation (12.92) the price of land has fallen. Each side of equation (12.91) will, therefore, fall by the same amount so that the asset markets remain in equilibrium.

In sum, then, we have shown that all conditions for equilibrium in the economy continue to hold once a land tax is imposed if:

(a) land values fall by the capitalized value of future taxes;
(b) bequests fall by the same amount;
(c) all other variables in the economy – consumption, capital and all factor prices – remain unchanged. Hence, under these conditions, the land tax is not shifted.

Now suppose that there are no bequests. Then in equation (12.93) lifetime wealth rises by $t_T F_T T (1 + F_k)$. First-period consumption rises by the marginal propensity to consume times (δ) the above change in wealth. If we now look at asset market equilibrium conditions, the price of land must fall as per equation (12.92) to p' in order to preserve equal net rate of return on land and capital. The effect of the tax is, therefore, to disturb the equilibrium condition in equation (12.91) in two ways. Because $b = 0$, lifetime consumption rises by $\delta[t_T F_T T/(1 + F_k)]$. Further, because the price of land falls, the value of assets supplied falls by $(t_T F_T T/F_k)$ both because $\delta < 1$, and $F_k < 1 + F_k$. If c_2 is a normal good then $\delta[t_T F_T T/(1 + F_k)] < (t_T F_T/F_k)$. Hence, the reduction in asset value is greater than the reduction in savings. The asset market can, therefore, not be in equilibrium at pre-tax value of k. Households will wish to save more which will lead to an increase in the stock of capital and a reduction in its marginal product. This is the reasoning behind Feldstein's conclusion that the land tax is shifted (see Feldstein 1977).

12.8   TAX AND DEBT AS REVENUE INSTRUMENTS

In an important paper Feldstein (1985) considers the following question: Suppose that the government can finance its expenditure in two ways: taxation and issuing debt. Suppose that the government decides to increase government expenditure by an infinitesimal amount. How should this additional expenditure be financed?

Feldstein shows that the very formulation of this question depends upon whether the increase in government expenditure is perceived to be temporary or permanent. In both cases he considers a single-sector Solow growth model, amended to incorporate variable supply of labor. Consider first a temporary increase in government expenditure.

At time v there are N_v people in the labor force and each individual supplies an amount of labor equal to l, making the total labor supply

$L_v = lN_v$. Technical progress at the rate μ is occurring. This is Harrod neutral technical progress in order to ensure stability.[20] Under competitive conditions, therefore, the wage rate of labor will also rise at the rate μ. Hence the wage rate at time v can be written as:

$$w_v = (1 + \mu)^{v-1} w_1. \tag{12.94}$$

Taxes are levied at the rate t on wage income so that total tax revenue at time v can be written as T_v where $T_v = tw_v L_v$. There are no taxes on capital income.[21]

Initially the government has a spending plan that calls for an expenditure of G_v in year v. In general, the government budget may not be balanced. Suppose now that the government decides to increase its expenditure in year 1 by the amount dG. In year 2 government expenditure goes back to its planned level. Hence the increase in government expenditure is confined to year 1 alone.

There are two alternative ways of financing this increased expenditure. One way is to increase taxes in time period 1. The other is to issue debt – a perpetuity – and pay interest on this debt. Feldstein considers the question: which of the two is the preferred method of financing the increased expenditure. Feldstein's method consists of comparing the total social cost of the two sources of finance.[22]

Let us consider taxation first. In this case $dT_1 = dG$. Now since $T_1 = tw_1 L_1$ we can write:

$$dT_1 = dG = w_1 L_1 dt + tw_1 (dL/dt)(dt)$$
$$= w_1 L_1 dt + tw_1 (dL_1/d(1-t)w_1)(d(1-t)w_1/dt)dt. \tag{12.95}$$

Let us write: $\epsilon = (dL_1/d(1-t)w_1)((1-t)w_1/L_1)$ for the uncompensated elasticity[23] of labor supply with respect to the disposable wage. Substituting in equation (12.95) we can write:

$$dG = w_1 L_1 [(1 - t - t\epsilon)/(1 - t)]dt. \tag{12.96}$$

Equation (12.96) defines the increase in tax required to finance the additional government spending.

Now this increase in the tax rate implies an increase in the excess burden of the tax. Before this tax increase takes place there was a pre-existing tax at the rate t, the first unit of increased leisure involves an excess burden of tw. As the tax rate rises there is a labor supply effect and the excess burden because of this will be measured as the area of the relevant triangle above the compensated supply curve of labor. Now, the induced change in labor supply because of the increase in tax is $dL_1 = [\gamma L_1/(1-t)]dt$ where γ is the compensated labor supply elasticity. Assuming this supply curve to be linear, the excess burden of increasing the tax rate by dt is, therefore:[24]

$$[\gamma w_1 L_1(t + 0.5dt)/(1 - t)]dt.$$

The total burden of financing the increased expenditure by taxation (B_T) is the sum of dG and the excess burden noted above. In other words:

$$B_T = dG + [\gamma w_1 L_1(t + 0.5dt)/(1 - t)]dt. \tag{12.97}$$

We also know that:

$$dt = dG(1 - t)/(w_1 L_1(1 - t - t\epsilon)).$$

Hence, substituting in equation (12.97) we will have:

$$B_T = dG[1 + \gamma t/(1 - t - t\epsilon) + (1/2)\gamma(dG/(w_1 L_1))(1 - t)/(1 - t - t\epsilon)^2]. \tag{12.98}$$

The first term in this expression is the resource cost of the increased expenditure. The second term is the excess burden because of the preexisting tax[25] and the third term is the excess burden because of the increase in tax.[26] Equation (12.98) then gives the full social cost of the increased government expenditure. This will have to be compared with the burden of debt finance in order to arrive at a judgment about the preferred mode of financing the temporary increase in government expenditure.

To compute the burden of the debt realize that in every time period the interest on the debt will have to be paid. Hence, the decision to finance the increased government expenditure by increasing debt involves raising taxes in every time period to make interest payments. This increase in taxes in any time period will have its own excess burden associated with it which will be added on to the resource cost of paying the interest. Total burden of the debt finance will be the discounted sum of the burden of these interest payments.

To keep things simple, let us assume that the interest rate on the debt is fixed at some $r*$. In time period v the welfare cost of raising taxes to meet the increased interest payment obligation is (from equation (12.98)):

$$B_{D_v} = r^* dG[1 + \gamma t/(1 - t - t\epsilon) +$$
$$(1/2)(\gamma dG)/\{(w_1 L_1(1 + n)^{v-1}(1 + \mu)^{v-1}\}\{(1 - t)/(1 - t - t\epsilon)^2\}]. \tag{12.99}$$

Here the first term is the resource cost of paying the interest.[27] The second term is the excess burden of the pre-existing taxes. The third term is again parallel to that in equation (12.98) except for the fact that we know that as compared to time period 1 both the population as well as the productivity of labor are higher. Labor supply grows at the rate n and the productivity of labor grows at rate μ. Hence the burden of interest payment of the debt taken out in time period is shared among a larger as well as a more productive population. Total cost of debt finance is the discounted sum expressed in equation (12.100):

$$B_D = \sum_{v=2}^{\infty} B_{D_v}(1 - \delta)^{-(v-1)} \tag{12.100}$$

where δ is the social rate of discount. For a meaningful comparison between debt and tax finance, clearly, δ should be[28] less than r. Hence, to find out which method of financing involves lower social cost, the expression in (12.98) has to compared with that in (12.100). There is no obvious winner and qualitative results are possible only in special cases.[29] Feldstein works out some illustrative numerical examples.

Let us now study the case of a permanent increase in government expenditure. If the economy is in steady state equilibrium then the question has to be posed as the choice in financing the increased government expenditure either by increasing taxes or decreasing debt. Suppose the government has a current debt stock of B. So the total government expenditure is the current expenditure (G) plus the interest on the debt, rB, where r is the going rate of interest. This expenditure must be financed by a combination of tax revenue and the issue of new debt ($\dot{B}$). In steady state debt must grow at the same rate as population.[30] Hence, we must have $\dot{B}/B = n$ or $\dot{B} = nB$. Hence the government's budget constraint in steady-state equilibrium is:

$$G + rB = T + nB. \tag{12.101}$$

Dividing both righthand and lefthand sides by the labor force we have:

$$g = \tau - (r - n)b \tag{12.102}$$

where $g = G/N, \tau = T/N$ etc.

If we are at the golden rule then $r = n$ and we must have tax financing. Typically, however, there is a deficiency of the capital stock so that $r > n$. In this case g can go up either if τ goes up or b goes down. If $r < n$ then g can go up if τ goes up or b goes up.[31]

Decreasing the steady-state level of per capita debt requires a period of increasing tax revenues. Thus the real choice when permanently increasing government expenditure is between increasing taxes now by the full amount of the increase in government expenditure or to increase taxes now by more than the increase in government expenditure in order to decrease the current stock of government debt and finance the increased government expenditure. In either case an increase in government spending requires an increase in government tax revenue.

A general qualitative result with respect to this choice is not possible. But Feldstein works out an interesting special case. He tries to find out the preferred method of financing the increased expenditure that imposes the least burden on a representative consumer. He considers a representative consumer who lives for two time periods as per the standard two-period life-cycle model. This consumer's utility function is written as:

$$U = \phi \ln c_1 + (1 - \phi) \ln c_2 + \lambda \ln(1 - l) \tag{12.103}$$

where c_i is consumption in period i ($i = 1, 2$) and ϕ and λ are positive fractions. Writing $(1 - t) = \sigma$ we can write the consumer's budget constraint as:

$$c_2 = (\sigma wl - c_1)(1+r). \tag{12.104}$$

Maximizing the utility subject to the budget constraint we get optimal labor supply and first period consumption as:

$$l = 1/(1+\lambda), c_1 = \phi\sigma wP\phi l. \tag{12.105}$$

Substituting in the utility function (12.103) we can write maximized utility as:

$$U = \Psi + \ln \sigma w + (1-\phi) \ln (1+r) \tag{12.106}$$

where Ψ is a constant.

The government's problem is to maximize this utility function by choosing σ, subject to the government budget constraint and by the process of capital accumulation. Under competitive conditions, the wage rate is $w = f - kf'$ and the interest rate is $r = f'$ where f is the intensive production function.

Now the government budget constraint in per capita terms is:

$$g = (1-\sigma)wl + (f' - n)lk_g. \tag{12.107}$$

g is per capita government expenditure, the first term on the righthand side is government tax revenue whereas the second term is the net return on government capital.[32]

Private capital stock is the accumulated value of last period's savings:

$$K_p = (\sigma wl - c_1)N/(1+n) \tag{12.108}$$

where K_p is private capital stock and N is the size of the population this period. In steady state we will have $\dot{K}_p/K_p = n$. Hence, from equation (12.108) we will have:

$$lk_p = (\sigma wl - c_1)/(1+n) \tag{12.109}$$

or, since $c_1 = \phi\sigma wl$ we will have:

$$lk_p = (1-\phi)\sigma wl/(1+n). \tag{12.110}$$

In steady state both private as well as public capital stock grow at the same rate n. Hence each must be a constant fraction of the capital stock. Let us write $k_g = \beta k$ and $k_p = (1-\beta)k$ where k is the aggregate capital labor ratio and $1 > \beta > 0$.

Therefore, the capital accumulation constraint can now be written as:

$$g - (1-\sigma)wl = ((f' - n)[lk - (1-\phi)\sigma wl/(1+n)]. \tag{12.111}$$

One can solve equation (12.111) for σw as a function of k and this can be substituted back into the utility function (12.106) using $l = 1/(1+\lambda)$ to get:

$$U = \Psi + \ln\{[f - nk - g(1+\lambda)]/[1 + (1-\phi)(f' - n)(1+n)^{-1}]\} \\ + (1-\phi)\ln(1+f'). \tag{12.112}$$

Maximizing this utility function with respect to k we will get as first-order condition:

$$(f' - n)/(f - nk - g(1 + \lambda)) - (1 - \phi)f''/(1 + n) + (1 - \phi)f''/(1 + f') = 0.$$

$$(12.113)$$

This equality will be satisfied at the golden rule when $f' = n$. In this case any permanent increase in government expenditure must be financed by an increase in taxes alone. Clearly this result will not hold generally.

12.9 CONCLUSIONS

Tax incidence in dynamic models depends on model specification. In this chapter we have studied tax incidence in the steady state of some dynamic models. We began with the Solow model and then proceeded to its life-cycle version. Monetary issues were then introduced into the Solow model. Recent versions of the life-cycle model as well as the incidence of a tax on land as well as the question of financing an increase in government expenditure were also taken up.

This chapter, then, does consider a broad range of issues. But we have not dealt with the tricky issue of tax incidence outside of steady state. This is a fairly new area of research. Most results are numerical and analytical conclusions are few and far between. See, for example Chari *et al.* (1994).

NOTES

1 It can also be demonstrated to be globally stable. See Burmeister and Dobell (1970), for example.
2 Suppose the government wanted to choose the savings rate of the economy to maximize per capita consumption in steady state. Since savings per capita are sf(k) consumption per capita must be $(1 - s)f(k)$. In steady state $k = sf(k) - nk = 0$ so that $s = nk/f(k)$ and, hence, $c = (1 - s)f(k) = f(k) - nk$. Maximizing this with respect to s we have $dc/ds = (f' - n)(dk^*/ds) = 0$ where k^* is now the optimum steady-state capital–labor ratio. Hence, at optimum we must have $f' = n$. This is Phelps' famous **golden rule of economic growth** where we maximize per capita consumption in steady state. This analysis easily carries over to the case of discrete time.
3 FIFO stands for first-in, first-out inventory accounting procedures.
4 λ is defined as follows: $\lambda = t_k\mu + g$ where t_k is the tax rate on capital income as above, g is the capital gains tax rate and μ represents the nominal increase in profits per unit of capital due to the effects of inflation on the real value of depreciation allowances and on the after-tax corporate income associated with the taxation of capital gains on inventories. This can be measured as:

$$\mu = [\{CCA + IVA\}/K](1/\pi)$$

where CCA is the capital consumption allowance, IVA is the inventory valuation adjustment and K the capital stock. The derivation of λ is given in Feldstein and Summers (1979)
5 The linearized version of the LM curve is given by

$m = M_0 + M_i(1 - t_p)i + M_y y$ (where M_0 is a constant), or by $(1 - t_p)i = (m - M_0 - M_y y)/M_i$.

Substitute this expression for $(1 - t_p)i$ into the steady-state condition (equation 12.49) and differentiate both respect to k to get the stability condition $s(1 - \theta)f' < n$.

6 It should be understood that although there is uncertainty at the level of the individual consumer, there is no uncertainty in the aggregate as we know with full certainty that a proportion ϕ of the population will die each time period.

7 The assumption here is that labor income depends on human capital alone.

8 This is so because of the assumption of logarithmic utility function.

9 Except, of course, for $\alpha = 0$ in which case per capita labor income is independent of age.

10 Hence for $\alpha = 0$ we must have $b = 1$.

11 This is clearly equal to zero.

12 Individual non-human wealth accumulates at the rate $(r + \phi)$ if an individual remains alive, aggregate wealth accumulates only at the rate r. This is because the amount ϕA is a transfer through insurance companies, from those who die to those who remain alive; but it is not an addition to aggregate net wealth.

13 We have collected terms and ignored the time subscript where this would not cause any confusion.

14 A trivial equilibrium is, of course, the origin.

15 This equals current government expenditure $G(t)$ plus the interest on the accumulated debt $r(t)B(t)$.

16 A primary surplus is the difference between current tax revenue and current expenditure exclusive of the interest on government debt, i.e, $T(q) - G(q)$.

17 It is assumed here that taxes are lump sum.

18 The increase in deficit is a flow and will not instantaneously affect the stock of existing debt.

19 The existence of finite horizons has been cited as the most obvious reason why Ricardian equivalence may fail to hold. Another argument is that individuals are liquidity constrained and a cut in taxes stimulates expenditure.

20 It is well known that in the Solow growth model only labor augmenting technical progress is consistent with stability.

21 This is done merely for the sake of convenience. In any case a distinct tax on capital income would be meaningful only if the savings propensity was variable.

22 The social benefits are the same and equal to the services provided by the increased expenditure dG.

23 Clearly it is being assumed here that an increase in the tax rate leads to an increase in tax revenue.

24 Realize that in the absence of a pre-existing tax $(t = 0)$ this would collapse to the 'usual' excess burden triangle formula: $(0.5 \, \gamma w_1 L_1 (dt)^2)$.

25 This term will be zero if there is no pre-existing tax.

26 This term will not go to zero so long as $dt \neq 0$ even if there is no pre-existing tax.

27 The amount borrowed was dG and the interest on this is $r * dG$.

28 Otherwise the sum in (12.100) will explode without limit.

29 For example when $t = 0$.

30 For the sake of simplicity we assume that the growth of productivity of labor is zero.

31 We will concentrate on the 'usual' case.

32 Government capital stock in per capita terms is k_g. The return on this is f'. However, population grows from one time period to the next by the factor n so that net return on last period's capital today is $f' - n$.

ADDITIONAL READING

The neoclassical model of economic growth in all its variants is well discussed in Burmeister and Dobell (1970) and Romer (1996). Several papers in Friedman and Hahn (1990) are quite relevant to the discussion in this chapter.

13 Some results in commodity taxation

Key concepts: efficient taxation; Corlett–Hague result; inverse elasticity formulae; redistributive indirect taxation; optimal idirect taxation.

13.1 INTRODUCTION

In this chapter we study commodity taxation. It is implicit, therefore, that we take the desirability of commodity taxation for granted. This as well as the thorny issue of the optimal mix of commodity and income taxes are discussed in later chapters. In this chapter we collect and discuss some key results in the theory of commodity taxation. Our analysis here is initially confined to efficiency issues – we think of the best set of taxes to gather a specific amount of tax revenue where 'best' is defined as levying least excess burden on the 'representative' tax payer. We also raise issues of redistribution between consumers but it soon becomes clear that the issue of redistribution is best addressed through direct taxation. Later we discuss, in some detail, a popular indirect tax – the value added tax or VAT.

We will begin with proving three important 'elasticity' type results in optimal commodity taxation. Then we will inquire into the redistributive role of indirect taxes, the desirability (or otherwise) of uniform taxes and value added taxation.

13.2 ELASTICITY TYPE RULES IN COMMODITY TAXATION

There are at least three elasticity type results in optimal commodity taxation. These have been discussed, among others, by Sandmo (1987b). Here we derive each of these results carefully. We are concerned solely with efficiency issues here and all redistributive considerations are eschewed.

There is a representative consumer whose indirect utility function can be written as $V(p_1, \ldots, p_n; y - a)$ where p_i is the price of the ith. commodity (and there are n such commodities). These prices are measured in terms of a numeraire good '0' whose price (p_0) is set equal to 1. y is the consumer's lump-sum income (lump sum because we will be assuming that commodity taxes will not affect the consumer's incentive to work) and *a* stands for direct taxation which may be set equal to zero.

Now write the Slutsky equation for commodity x_i as:

$$(\partial x_i/\partial p_j) = -x_j(\partial x_i/\partial y) + (\partial x_i/\partial p_j)\big|_{dU=0}. \quad (13.1)$$

Multiply through by (p_j/x_i) and also the first term on the righthand side by (y/y):

$$(p_j/x_i)(\partial x_i/\partial p_j) = (-x_i/y)(\partial x_i/\partial y)(y/x_i) + (\partial x_i/\partial p_j)(p_j/x_i)\big|_{dU=0}.$$

Now, multiply through by (-1) to get:

$$\eta_{ij} = \alpha_i E_i + \sigma_{ij} \quad (13.2)$$

or, uncompensated demand elasticity of x_i with respect to p_j, written η_{ij}, is equal to the share of commodity *i* in total income, written E_i, multiplied by the income elasticity of demand for x_i, written α_i, plus the compensated demand elasticity of demand of x_i with respect to p_j, denoted by σ_{ij}.

Let us now introduce commodity taxation into the model. Let p_i be the consumer price and q_i the producer price of commodity *i*. The difference between them is the tax which we take to be specific[1] here:

$$p_i = q_i + t_i. \quad (13.3)$$

Denoting the vector of consumer prices to be *p* we can write the indirect utility of the representative individual as V (p, y) which is maximized subject to a government budget requirement $(p - q)x + a = T$ where *T* is total tax requirement. Setting up the Lagrangean we have:

$$\Lambda = V(p, y) - \mu[T - a - (p - q)x]. \quad (13.4)$$

We will treat $(p_i - q_i)$ as t_i and *a* as a lump-sum tax here. Differentiating equation (13.4) with respect to p_j and *a* we have:

$$-\lambda x_j + \mu\left[\sum_i t_i(\partial x_i/\partial p_j) + x_j\right] = 0 \quad (13.5)$$

$$j = 1, \ldots, n$$

$$-\lambda + \mu\left[\sum_i t_i(\partial x_i/\partial a + 1)\right] = 0, \quad (13.6)$$

where μ is the Lagrange multiplier as defined above and $\lambda = \partial V/\partial y$ is the consumer's marginal utility of income.

Let us now work with equation (13.5). For the term $\partial x_i/\partial p_j$ we substitute the Slutsky equation and rewrite equation (13.5) as:

$$-\lambda x_j + \mu\left[\sum_i t_i\{(\partial x_i/\partial p_j)\big|_{dU=0} - x_j(\partial x_i/\partial y)\} + x_j\right] = 0.$$

Rearrange this to write:

$$\sum_i t_i(\partial x_i/\partial p_j)|_{dU=0} = x_j(\lambda - \mu)/\mu + \sum_i x_j t_i(\partial x_i/\partial y). \qquad (13.7).$$

Divide through by x_j to get:

$$\sum_i (t_i/x_j)(\partial x_i \partial p_j)|_{dU=0} = (\lambda - \mu)/\mu + \sum_i t_i(\partial x_i/\partial y) < 0. \qquad (13.8)$$

Now, we know that the compensated elasticities are symmetric, i.e., if σ_{ij} is the compensated elasticity of x_i with respect to p_j we must have $\sigma_{ji} = \sigma_{ij}$. Hence, we can write the lefthand side of equation (13.8) as:

$$\sum_i (t_i/p_i)(p_i/x_j)(\partial x_i/\partial p_j)|_{dU=0} = \sum_i \theta_i \sigma_{ji}, \text{ where}$$

$\theta_i = t_i/p_i$, so that equation (13.8) can be written as:

$$\sum_i \theta_i \sigma_{ji} = (\lambda - \mu)/\mu + \sum_i t_i(\partial x_i/\partial y) = -\gamma < 0. \qquad (13.9)$$

This is known as the one-person Ramsey rule (Diamond (1975)) and calls for an equal proportionate reduction in demand along the compensated demand curve. This is the first of the three elasticity rules in the theory of optimal commodity taxation. This can be further simplified from equation (13.9) if we assume that all compensated cross-price elasticities are zero. In that case, equation (13.9) will simplify to:

$$\theta_j = -\gamma/\sigma_{jj} \ (j = 1, \ldots, n). \qquad (13.10)$$

This rule says that tax rates should be inversely proportional to the compensated elasticities of demand.

The existence of lump-sum taxation

Up until now we have neglected equation (13.6). Strictly speaking, our results above are optimal only if the possibility of lump-sum taxation can be ruled out. We now introduce the possibility of lump-sum taxation and get a strong result. To proceed multiply equation (13.6) by x_j to get:

$$-\lambda x_j + \mu x_j \left\{ \sum_i t_i(\partial x_i/\partial a) + 1 \right\} = 0.$$

Subtract this from equation (13.5) to get:

$$\mu \left[\left\{ \sum_{i=1}^n t_i(\partial x_i/\partial p_j) + x_j \right\} - x_j \left\{ \sum_{i=1}^n t_i(\partial x_i/\partial a) + 1 \right\} \right] = 0 \qquad (13.11)$$

or, upon cancelling the x_j's:

$$\sum_i t_i(\partial x_i/\partial p_j) - x_j \sum_i t_i(\partial x_i/\partial a) = 0. \tag{13.12}$$

Now, $(\partial x_i/\partial a) = -(\partial x_i/\partial y)$ so, substituting in equation (13.12) we have:

$$\sum_i t_i(\partial x_i/\partial p_j) + x_j \sum_i t_i(\partial x_i/\partial y) = 0.$$

Now, substitute the Slutsky equation to get:

$$\sum_i t_i\{(\partial x_i/\partial p_j)|_{dU=0} - x_j(\partial x_i/\partial y)\} + x_j \sum_i t_i(\partial x_i/\partial y) = 0$$

which yields:

$$\sum_{i=1}^{n} t_i(\partial x_i/\partial p_j)|_{dU=0} = 0 \quad \text{or} \quad \sum_{i=1}^{n} \theta_i \sigma_{ji} = 0. \tag{13.13}$$

In other words, if there is the possibility of a lump-sum tax then all distortionary taxes should be zero. This is another extremely important rule for optimal commodity taxation and is illustrated in Figure 13.1. This shows a two-commodity case (one is commodity X and the other is income, or, all other commodities). The pre-tax budget line is $Z_1 Z_1$. With a distortionary tax on commodity X the budget line becomes $Z_1 Z_2$ and the consumer is able to reach point A on indifference curve I_0. The line BB shows the consumer's budget line with an equal yield lump-sum tax. The consumer is able to reach point C with a higher level of utility I_1. The moral is quite simple here: when a lump-sum tax can be used, there is no additional gain

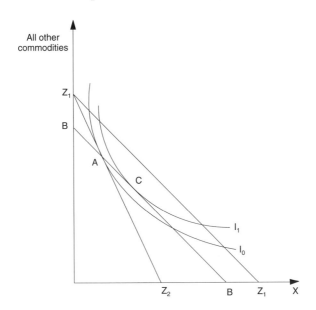

Figure 13.1

to be had from the use of commodity taxes and, in general, their use will diminish welfare.

Now, consider a three good cases – two taxed goods (commodities 1 and 2) and a numeraire. We will assume that lump-sum taxation is not feasible. Then we can write the optimality conditions (equation 13.9) as:

$$\theta_1 \sigma_{11} + \theta_2 \sigma_{12} = -\gamma \tag{13.14}$$

$$\theta_1 \sigma_{21} + \theta_2 \sigma_{22} = -\gamma \tag{13.15}$$

or, as

$$\begin{bmatrix} \sigma_{11} & \sigma_{12} \\ \sigma_{21} & \sigma_{22} \end{bmatrix} \begin{bmatrix} \theta_1 \\ \theta_2 \end{bmatrix} = \begin{bmatrix} -\gamma \\ -\gamma \end{bmatrix} \tag{13.16}$$

so that, by Cramer's rule:

$$\theta_1 = \gamma(\sigma_{12} - \sigma_{22})/\sigma \tag{13.17}$$

$$\theta_2 = \gamma(\sigma_{21} - \sigma_{11})/\sigma \tag{13.18}$$

where σ is the determinant of the matrix on the lefthand side of equation (13.16). We know from the fact that compensated demand functions are homogeneous of degree zero that:

$$\sigma_{10} + \sigma_{11} + \sigma_{12} = 0 \tag{13.19}$$

where '0' stands for the (untaxed) numeraire good. In many cases, this may be leisure. We also see that:

$$\sigma_{12} = -(\sigma_{10} + \sigma_{11}).$$

So, we can rewrite equations (13.17) and (13.18) as:

$$\theta_1 = -(\gamma/\sigma)(\sigma_{11} + \sigma_{22} + \sigma_{10}). \tag{13.20}$$

Similarly:

$$\theta_2 = -(\gamma/\sigma)(\sigma_{11} + \sigma_{22} + \sigma_{20}). \tag{13.21}$$

Hence the difference in the magnitudes of the tax on the goods depends essentially on the relative sizes of σ_{10} and σ_{20} (i.e. the compensated elasticity with respect to the untaxed good). From this follows the **Corlett–Hague** result that the tax rate should be highest on the commodity that is complementary with the numeraire and lowest on the commodity that is a substitute for the numeraire.

In the case where leisure is the numeraire good, the intuition is quite simple. Leisure cannot be taxed directly. If it could have been, and if income is truly lump sum (as we have been assuming) then, it would be optimal to tax all goods at the same rate since this would amount to a lump-sum tax and bring us to the case discussed in Figure 13.1. Now, since leisure cannot be taxed directly, one should make an effort to tax it as much as possible indirectly. Hence we tax goods (such as vacations) that are complementary to leisure at high rates and goods (such as work clothes or monthly bus passes) that are substitutes for leisure at relatively low rates. This result is famous in the literature as the Corlett–Hague result (see Corlett and Hague 1953). This is also the second major elasticity result on optimal commodity taxation that we had to discuss. We now proceed to the third such result.

The third major elasticity result in optimal commodity taxation relates to uncompensated elasticities. Suppose uncompensated demand functions are independent of each other. Working from equation (13.5) we have:

$$\sum_i t_i(\partial x_i/\partial p_j) = (\lambda - \mu)x_j/\mu \text{ or}$$

$$\theta_j = [(\lambda - \mu)/\mu]/e_{jj} = -\alpha/e_{jj} \tag{13.22}$$

where e_{jj} is the uncompensated own price elasticity of demand. This result holds only in the case where uncompensated demand functions are independent of each other. There is another way of seeing this result. In the absence of lump-sum taxation the consumer's budget constraint is written as:

$$\sum_{i=0}^{n} p_i x_i = 0. \tag{13.23}$$

Differentiating this with respect to p_j we have:

$$\sum_{i=0}^{n} p_i(\partial x_i/\partial p_j) + x_j = 0.$$

But, since, cross-price effects are zero by assumption, we can rewrite this as:

$(\partial x_0/\partial p_j) + p_j(\partial x_j/\partial p_j) + x_j$ or, upon substituting e_{jj} for$(\partial x_j/\partial p_j)(p_j/x_j)$ as:

$$e_{jj} = -1 - (1/x_j)(\partial x_0/\partial p_j); \quad j = 1, \ldots, n. \tag{13.24}$$

Substituting from the Slutsky equation we will have:

$$e_{jj} = -1 - (1/x_j)\{-x_j(\partial x_0/\partial y) + (\partial x_0/\partial p_j)|_{dU=0}\}$$
$$= -1 + (\partial x_0/\partial y) - \sigma_{jo}. \tag{13.25}$$

Hence, the inverse elasticity rule can be written as:

$$\theta_j = \alpha/[1 - (\partial x_0/\partial y) + \sigma_{j0}]. \tag{13.26}$$

In this new version of the inverse elasticity rule there are two terms in the denominator. The first term, $(1 - \partial x_0/\partial y)$, which is the same for all goods is the marginal propensity to consume taxed goods. The higher this is, the lower is the optimum level of taxes. Differences between tax rates comes through the second term, σ_{j0}, which is the compensated cross-elasticity with respect to leisure. The result in equation (13.26) relates the inverse elasticity result to both the earlier elasticity rules. Just as in the first rule, the differences in compensated elasticities account for differences in tax rates and, just like the Corlett–Hague result, goods that are most complementary to leisure are taxed at the highest rate.

Each of these three price elasticity formulae has a usefulness of its own. But this usefulness is limited to a particular context.

13.3   UNIFORM COMMODITY TAXATION

Consider a situation where inequality between workers is due to innate productivity differences between individuals – explained more fully in Chapter 14. Suppose that in this economy all individuals have identical utility functions of the form:

$$U = U(l, C(x_1, \ldots, x_n))$$

where l is leisure and x_i is consumption of the ith consumption good. Thus the utility function is weakly separable between leisure and consumption. Now in this type of situation the Corlett–Hague type of complementarity/substitutability of goods with leisure does not arise. Hence the need for differentiated commodity taxation as in the Corlett–Hague example does not occur.

For such an economy Atkinson and Stern (1976) show that a uniform commodity tax is appropriate if either of the following conditions is satisfied: (i) an optimal non-linear income tax is in place; or (ii) all goods have linear Engel curves and an optimal linear income tax is in operation.

The intuition behind this result can easily be appreciated by thinking of cases when differential commodity taxation could usefully supplement the income tax. Three such situations can be visualized:

(a) when the aim is to redistribute income between groups with different consumption patterns (examined above);
(b) when there is only a linear income tax and differentiated commodity taxation could bring in some non-linearities needed for redistribution;
(c) when the higher taxation of some goods can reduce the distortionary burden of the income tax.

Atkinson and Stern rule out case (a) by assuming identical utility functions, and case (b) by requiring that Engel curves be linear when the income tax is linear. Case (c) does not apply because they assume that the utility function is weakly separable between consumption and leisure. Hence we are left with uniform commodity taxation as the optimal choice. It might well be argued that rate of uniform commodity taxation might well be set to zero. This argument we consider in Chapter 14.

Although the Atkinson–Stern result can be seen as providing a case for uniform commodity taxation, one must be aware of the limited circumstances under which it is applicable. In particular, differences in preferences and non-separability of utility functions could introduce significant non-uniformity into the optimal commodity tax structure. Some empirical work along these lines was discussed in Chapter 8.

13.4 REDISTRIBUTIVE INDIRECT TAXATION

In most industrialized countries redistribution is done through the direct tax and transfer system. We will see soon that there is a good reason for this. In many developing countries, however, incomes are too low to make the direct tax and transfer system a viable method of redistribution. In a country such as India, for instance, well over 60 per cent of the tax revenue of the central government comes from central excise taxes alone. If one added other indirect taxes and import tariffs this figure would go well over 80 per cent. Direct taxes (personal and corporate taxes) constitute only a small portion of government revenue. It follows, therefore, that the amount of redistribution that is possible through the direct tax system is very limited. It is not surprising, therefore, that many developing countries try to use indirect taxes for purposes of redistribution. We study this problem now. Our objective now is not to maximize the utility of a representative individual but to maximize a social welfare function where people are differentiated according to their economic position.

We use h to index individuals. There are H individuals in society $(h = 1, \ldots, H)$. The indirect utility function of each individual is written as $V^h(p, y^h)$ where y^h is the income of the hth individual. The social welfare function is written as:

$W[V^1(p, y^1), V^2(p, y^2), \ldots, V^H(p, y^H)]$. Society's aversion to inequality can be expressed in the degree of concavity of the $W[.]$ function. The more concave is this function, the greater would be society's aversion to inequality. We will let x_i^h he the hth individual's consumption of commodity x_i. Specific taxes at the rate of t_i are levied to raise a predesignated amount of revenue, T_0.

Society's maximization problem can be written as maximization of the above social welfare function subject to the realization of the specified amount of revenue. Instruments are the consumer price prices (specific commodity tax rates t_i). Setting up the Lagrangean we have:

$$\Lambda = W[V^1(p, y^1), \ldots, V^H(p, y^H)] + \lambda \left[\sum_{i=1}^{n} t_i \{ \sum_{h=1}^{H} x_i^h \} - T_0 \right]. \quad (13.27)$$

The first-order condition for an internal maximization is:

$$\partial \Lambda / \partial p_i = \sum_i \sum_h (\partial W / \partial V^h)(\partial V^h / \partial p_i) + \lambda [\sum_i t_i \sum_h (\partial x_i^h / \partial p_i)$$
$$+ \sum_h x_i^h (\sum_i \partial t_i / \partial p_i)] = 0. \quad (13.28)$$

Now $\partial V^h/\partial p_i = -\alpha^h x_i^h$ (where α^h is the marginal utility of consumption of the hth person). Further realize that $\partial t_i/\partial p_i = 1$ and that $\partial x_i^h/\partial p_i = \partial x_i^h/\partial t_i$. Hence, we can write equation (13.28) as:

$$\sum_h (\partial W/\partial V^h)\alpha^h x_k^h = \lambda \left[H\bar{x}_k + \sum_i t_i \left\{ \sum_h \partial x_i^h/\partial t_k \right\} \right] \qquad (13.29)$$

for all commodities i and k. $\bar{x}_k = \sum_h x_k^h/H$. Now realize that $(\partial W/\partial V^h)\alpha^h$ (henceforth called β^h) is the **social** marginal valuation of income going to the hth person. We can now use the Slutsky equation for the second term on the righthand side of equation (13.29) to get:

$$\sum_h (\partial W/\partial V^h)\alpha^h x_k^h = \lambda \left[H\bar{x}_k + \sum_i t_i \sum_h \{(\partial x_i^h/\partial t_k)|_{dU=0} - x_k(\partial x_i^h/\partial y^h)\} \right]$$

which can then be rearranged to yield:

$$\sum_i t_i \left\{ \sum_h (\partial x_i^h/\partial t_k) \right\}|_{dU=0} =$$

$$- \left[H\bar{x}_k - \sum_h (\beta^h)/\lambda - \sum_i t_i \left\{ \sum_h x_k^h (\partial x_i^h/\partial y^h) \right\} \right]. \qquad (13.30)$$

In order to help interpret this. let us define:

$$b^h = (\beta^h/\lambda) + \sum_i t_i(\partial x_i^h/\partial y^h) \quad \text{and} \quad \bar{b} = \sum_h b^h/H$$

where b^h is the net social marginal valuation of income measured in terms of government revenue. The gross valuation is β^h/λ. The second term in the definition of b^h is the marginal tax paid by household h upon receiving this extra dollar of income. In this sense, b^h is the net social marginal valuation. $\bar{b}$ is the average of these b^h. Now, we divide through in equation (13.30) by $(H\bar{x}_k)$ to get:

$$\left\{ \sum_i t_i \sum_h (\partial x_i^h/\partial t_k)|_{dU=0} \right\}/\{H\bar{x}_k\} = - \left[1 - \sum_h (b^h/H)(x_k^h)/\bar{x}_k \right] \qquad (13.31)$$

$$k = 1, \ldots, n$$

The lefthand side of equation (13.31) denotes a proportional reduction in consumption along the compensated demand curves. This was the same for all goods in the case of the one-person Ramsey rule. However, the righthand side of equation (13.31) is not the same for all goods. In general, the reduction in demand along the compensated demand curve is smaller:

(a) the more the good is consumed by households with a high social marginal valuation of income (the poor). The greater the proportion of the commodity consumed by the poor, the lower would be the tax.

Hence, the tax would be low on necessities of life and high on luxury items.

(b) the more the commodity in question is consumed by households with a high marginal propensity to consume out of taxed goods.

The analysis of optimal indirect taxation has been advanced in several directions. One area in which the extension has proved particularly useful is in the joint determination of optimal indirect taxes and public sector prices. The realization that indirect taxes and the price of a commodity produced in the public sector should be jointly determined dates back to the seminal work of Diamond and Mirrlees (1971). Since then explicit formulae for the public sector price and rates of indirect taxation have been derived (see, for instance, Feldstein 1972 a,b; Munk 1979); Jha and Murty 1987); Jha *et al.* 1990).

The usual structure of these models is as follows. The public sector is embedded in a general equilibrium competitive framework that is basically the standard one-period model with firms maximizing profits and households maximizing utility which, in turn, is defined over consumption and leisure. Hence, one can derive explicit demand functions for goods produced in the private as well as the public sector. Social welfare is visualized as an aggregate indirect utility function. This is maximized with respect to commodity tax rates and the price of the public good, given an explicit reaction function of the government between public sector prices and indirect taxes. This maximization is constrained by an overall budgetary constraint.

We now describe the basic structure of such models. As before the economy has H individuals indexed by h. There are $(n + 1)$ goods in the economy: the first n is produced in the private sector whereas the $(n + 1)$ st good (an intermediate good in this example) is produced in the public sector. Private sector production is defined by an $(n \times n)$ input–output matrix A and we define b as a $(n \times 1)$ vector representing the requirements of the public sector commodity as an intermediate input. The production function for the public sector good can be written as:

$$x_{n+1} = f(x_1, \ldots, x_n; L_{n+1})$$

where x_i is the amount of the ith good and L_{n+1} is labor input into the production of the public sector commodity. The augmented input–output structure of the economy can be defined by the matrix A* where:

$$A* = \begin{bmatrix} A & x \\ b' & 0 \end{bmatrix}$$

For the private sector, unit (producer price) is equal to cost of production: $q' = p'A + p_{n+1}b' + wL'$ where q is the producer price vector, p is the consumer price vector, L is the per unit labor input requirement vector for goods produced in the private sector and w is the competitively determined wage rate.

The government's overall budget constraint can be written as:

$$\sum_{i=1}^{n} t_i^* x_i + (p_{n+1} - m)x_{n+1} - F = 0$$

where t_i^* is the optimal commodity tax rate on x_i, and m and F are the marginal cost and fixed cost, respectively, of producing good x_{n+1}.

We form the following Lagrangean for society:

$$\Lambda = W(V^1, \ldots, V^H) + \mu \left[\sum t_i^* x_i + (p_{n+1} - m)x_{n+1} - F \right]$$

where μ is an appropriate Lagrange multiplier, V^h is the indirect utility function of the hth consumer and $W(\cdot)$ is the social welfare function that has to be maximized. The above Lagrangean is maximized with respect to t_i^* and p_{n+1}.

Computation of optimal indirect taxes

Computation of optimal indirect taxes with redistributive objectives in mind has proved to be difficult. This is because of the high degree of non-linearity involved in equations such as (13.31). Analytical solutions are almost impossible to arrive at but computational approaches can be tried. One such method, drawing on Jha *et al.* (1990), is discussed below.

This approach begins by supposing that each individual h has a Stone–Geary utility function of the form:

$$U^h = \sum_{i=1}^{n} \alpha_i \ln (x_i - \gamma_i)$$

where $\sum \alpha_i = 1$ and $\alpha_i > 0$ and γ_i is the minimum amount of the commodity i which this individual must have. Only amounts of x_i in excess of γ_i give utility to the consumer. The Stone–Geary utility function is the only utility function that gives rise to the linear expenditure system. The indirect utility function corresponding to the above utility function is:

$$V^h = \left[I^h - \sum \gamma_i P_i \right] / \left[\prod_{i=1}^{n} (P_i)^{\alpha_i} \right].$$

The Ramsey problem of optimal commodity taxation can now be written as:

$$\max_{t_i} W(V^1, \ldots, V^H)$$

subject to the budget constraint

$$\sum_{i=1}^{n} t_i x_i = R$$

where R is the exogenously determined revenue requirement of the government. Following Ahmad and Stern (1984), Jha *et al.* (1990) define λ_i as the marginal social cost of raising a dollar of government revenue with a tax on the ith commodity as:

$$\lambda_i = -(\partial W / \partial t_i) / (\partial R / \partial t_i) \quad (i = 1, \ldots, n).$$

If $\lambda_i \neq \lambda_j$ then social welfare can be improved by reducing taxes on commodities with higher λ_is and increasing taxes on commodities with lower λ_is. The form of the social welfare function chosen is that due to Atkinson (discussed in equation (3.7) of Chapter 3) with varying magnitudes of the inequality aversion parameter. An algorithm is developed which computes λ_is in the above manner and changes these according to the above rule until all the λ_is are equal to each other.

13.5 EXTENT OF REDISTRIBUTION THROUGH COMMODITY TAXATION

We had remarked earlier that the extent of redistribution that can be had through commodity taxation is rather limited. It is time now to substantiate this point. This question was considered in an important paper by Sah (1983). We consider his analysis now.

We have *H* consumers as before and each consumer has an indirect utility function $V^h(p, y^h)$ where *p* is the vector of consumer prices and y^h is lump-sum income. We will let *q* be the vector of producer prices and let *t* be the vector of specific commodity taxes so that:

$$p = q + t. \tag{13.32}$$

We will let the public revenue requirement constraint take the simple form:

$$\sum_h T^h = 0 \tag{13.33}$$

where T^h is the amount of indirect tax collected from the hth individual. In equation (13.33) we are assuming, without any loss of generality, that all indirect taxes are collected for redistribution only.

We define our metric of redistribution as the proportional increase in the real income of the worst-off individual (*l*) due to the change in commodity prices from *q* to *p*. Let Y^l be a hypothetical payment to the individual *l* at the pre-tax price *q* such that *l* is indifferent between receiving Y^l and changing over to the post-tax regime *p*. Thus:

$$Y^l = e^l(q, V^l(p, y^l)) - y^l \tag{13.34}$$

where *e* is the expenditure function. (Y^l / y^l) is, therefore, the proportional increase in real income due to the tax program. This is the metric of redistribution used by Sah.

From the concavity of the expenditure function in prices we know that:

$$y^l + x^l(q - p) \geqslant Y^l + y^l \text{ or } x^l(q - p) \geqslant Y^l \quad \text{or}$$
$$-T^l/y^l \geqslant Y^l/y^l.$$

In other words, the negative of the tax payment is an upper ceiling on the real income gain to the poorest individual from the tax program. The intuition behind this is quite simple. If the welfare of individual l has improved, then he must receive a net subsidy on total purchases, i.e., $-T^l/y^l > 0$. A part of this subsidy goes to meet the deadweight loss and the remainder to increase total income. Hence, our task is to calculate the upper limit of $-T^l/y^l$.

Let $\tau_i = t_i/p_i$ be the *ad valorem* tax rate. As $p_i = q_i + t_i$ and $q_i > 0$ it follows that $\tau_i < 1$ for any finite tax level. Define $\alpha_i^h = x_i^h p_i/y^h$ as the budget share of individual h for good i. Further, let $\alpha_i = x_i p_i/y$ be the average budget share ($y = \sum_h y^h/H$) and assume that $\alpha_i^h > 0$. The public revenue constraint (equation 13.33) can be written as:

$$\sum_i \tau_i \alpha_i = 0. \tag{13.35}$$

Divide the index set of commodities into two groups – one on which there is a tax (J) and the other on which there is a subsidy (K). $\tau_i \geqslant 0$ if $i \in J$ and $\tau_i < 0$ if $i \in K$. From equation (13.35) we have:

$$\sum_{i \in J} \tau_i \alpha_i = - \sum_{i \in K} \tau_i \alpha_i. \tag{13.36}$$

Now, $\sum_{i \in J} \alpha_i > \sum_{i \in K} \tau_i \alpha_i$ because $1 > \tau_i \geqslant 0$ if $i \in J$.
Also, by definition,

$$1 > \sum_{i \in J} \tau_i.$$

Thus $1 > -\sum_{i \in K} \tau_i \alpha_i$ from equation (13.36).
Dividing both sides by $\min_j \{\alpha_j\}$ and because $\alpha_i/\{\min_j (\alpha_j)\} \geqslant 1$ for all i we get:

$$-\sum_{i \in K} \tau_i \alpha_i / \left\{ \min_j (\alpha_j) \right\} \geqslant -\sum_{i \in K} \tau_i \text{ (because } -\tau_i > 0 \text{ for i} \in K).$$

Hence, we get:

$$1 / \left[\min_j (\alpha_j) \right] > -\sum_{i \in K} \tau_i. \tag{13.37}$$

Using the same definitions as above we get:

$$-T^l/y^l = -\sum_i \tau_i \alpha_i^l = -\sum_{i \in J} \tau_i \alpha_i^l - \sum_{i \in K} \tau_i \alpha_i^l. \tag{13.38}$$

The first term on the righthand side is, clearly, negative. Hence, it must be the case that:

$-T^l/y^l < -\sum_{i \in K} \tau_i \alpha_i^l.$ In this expression $(-\tau_i > 0)$ and

$\alpha_i^l \leqslant \max_j \{\alpha_j^l\}$. It, therefore, follows that:

$$-T^l/y^l < \left[-\sum_{i \in K} \tau_i \right] \max_j \{\alpha_j^l\}. \tag{13.39}$$

Substituting equation (13.38) into this we get:

$$-T^l/y^l < \left[\max_j \{\alpha_j^l\} \right] / \left[\min_j \{\alpha_j\} \right]. \tag{13.40}$$

This is a ceiling on the possible redistribution entirely in terms of the budget shares. The proportional real income gain to the worst-off individual is always less than the ratio of the maximum budget share of this person and the minimum average budget share of the economy.

We can consider an example of this limit. Let us suppose that there are only two groups in society rich (r) and poor (p). Their proportions in the population are g^r and g^p. Further, there are only two commodities: necessities and luxuries. The average consumption of commodity i is given as:

$$x_i = \sum_{h=r,p} g^h x_i^h \text{ and the average income is } y = \sum_{h=r,p} g^h y^h.$$

From equation (13.35) we have:

$(\tau_2 - \tau_1)/\tau_2 = 1/\alpha_1$ because $\alpha_2 = 1 - \alpha_1$. Furthermore,

$$-T^p/y^p = -\sum_i \tau_i \alpha_i^p = \tau_2 \{\alpha_1^p[(\tau_2 - \tau_1)/\tau_2] - 1\} \text{ or,}$$

$-T^p/y^p = \tau_2(\alpha_1^p/\alpha_1 - 1)$. Now, if the rich are infinitely richer than the poor so that $y^p/y^r \to 0$ then $\alpha_i = \alpha_i^r$. Hence:

$$-T^p/y^p = \tau_2[\alpha_1^p/\alpha_1^r - 1]. \tag{13.41}$$

If we take good 1 to be the necessity, i.e., $\alpha_1^p > \alpha_1^r$ then it follows that $\tau_2 > 0$. This is as we would expect. The welfare of the poor can be improved only if the luxury is taxed and the necessity is subsidized. Using $1 > \tau_2 > 0$ in equation (13.41) we have:

$$-T^p/y^p < \alpha_1^p/\alpha_1^r - 1. \tag{13.42}$$

To take a numerical example, if the poor spend as much as 80 per cent of their income on necessities and the rich spend 20 per cent on necessities then $-T^p/y^p < 3$.

If income differences are finite (as opposed to the infinite difference assumed in this example) the extent of redistribution is still smaller. The message from Sah's analysis is at once sobering and important. It tells us that commodity taxation cannot be very (or, depending on your aversion to inequality, even sufficiently) redistributive so that direct taxes have to be used. Second, we are well advised to emphasize efficiency in allocation over redistribution in setting commodity tax rates.

13.6   THE VALUE ADDED TAX (VAT)

One of the principal forms that commodity taxation has taken in recent years is that of the value added tax (VAT). It has been used in diverse countries around the globe. The European Community, Canada and New Zealand have had VATs for some time now. Moreover, VAT is on the tax reform agenda for many countries some of which, for example, India, have already adopted modified forms of the VAT and aim to have full-fledged value added tax systems in the near future. In most of these countries the VAT has replaced excise and sales tax structures. Hence, the VAT is a very important commodity tax, indeed the dominant form of commodity taxation, and deserves special study. The literature on VAT is vast and we shall make no attempt to survey it here. However, since the VAT is in use in so many countries around the globe and is generally thought of as being some sort of panacea for problems relating to commodity taxation, it is perhaps more important to study its operational and practical significance.

There are several and, often conflicting, definitions of the VAT. The plain definition of a VAT is a tax levied on businesses on the value they add to their purchases of raw materials and goods and services. Leaving aside the problem of capital and stocks, we can represent this by writing that value added (VA) equals value of output (VO) minus total value of current inputs (VI):

$$VA = VO - VI. \tag{13.43}$$

Now, the difference between value of output and value of input must be the stream of income that is generated by this activity. Let us say that this stream of income consists of wage income (W) and profits (π). Hence, we must have:

$$VA = VO - VI = W + \pi. \tag{13.44}$$

Herein lies a crucial point. VA can be derived by **addition** $(W + \pi)$ or **subtraction** $(VO - VI)$. These are called the addition and subtraction methods of calculating value added (the base of the VAT).

In the theoretical literature VAT is often referred to as a means of collecting tax, which could equally well replace an income tax or a corporation tax. In practice, OECD countries have used VAT to replace other **consumption** taxes, like an excise tax or a sales tax. In Table 13.1 we display some of the principal type of VATs that have been discussed in the literature. In the VAT literature different terminologies have been used and these types are distinguished by bold type in the table.

The net consumption type VAT is the most popular method of calculating the base of the VAT. Within this category the subtraction method is the preferred method of calculating the VAT since there may be ambiguity about the items that may be added (in the addition method). Further, most countries use the indirect method of subtraction. However, the following additional caveats should be added:

1 Countries may disallow deductions for tax on certain business inputs which introduces elements of a gross product type tax (1A) or a net income type tax (1B). For example, Belgium used to not allow deductions of expenses on entertainment.
2 Countries may achieve effects similar to introducing (1A) or (1B) by introducing taxes outside the VAT system. Some of the Scandinavian countries, for example, tax energy use separately.
3 Most countries in moving from (1A) type cascade taxes to (3C) type VAT retained a transitional and declining tax on capital goods which was eventually abolished or is in the process of being abolished.

There is a number of possible types of net consumption value added taxes to choose between. VAT attempts to tax the value added by businesses in the course of their business activities. Value added can be calculated in two ways: it can be built up from its parts (payments such as wages, profits and rents to primary factors of production such as labor, capital and land, shown in method (2A), or it can be derived from the difference between value of the firm's output and its inputs (the subtraction method, 2B). Subtraction methods may be direct or indirect. The direct subtraction method consists of taking the aggregate value of sales and the aggregate value of purchases during a period and taxing the difference between them. The indirect subtraction method requires businesses to collect tax on their individual sales (outputs) and pay tax on their individual purchases (inputs) and hand over to the tax authorities the difference between the tax collected and the tax paid for each tax period.

In the case of the addition method there may be difficulties in defining taxable profits or of making exact border adjustments when dealing with firms operating in more than one country or more than one province in a federal country. Further, it would be hard to administer a VAT with more than one rate of tax under the addition method. The direct subtraction method is the simplest to operate but this tax may also be difficult to apply with more than one tax rate and when some exemptions from the tax are to be granted.

The main advantages of the indirect subtraction method over the addition method or the direct subtraction method are its greater flexibility and

Table 13.1 Possible types of VAT systems

1 Possible coverage of VAT systems		
A	B	C
A tax on all inputs with no deductions at all for business inputs. Called **gross product type VAT**	Deduction for capital goods limited to their depreciation value. Called **net income type VAT**	Deductions for business inputs. Called **net consumption type VAT**

2 Possible methods of operating net consumption type VAT	
A	B
Identification of value added by the summation of all the elements of value added (wages, profit, rents, and interest). Called **addition method**. Sometimes also called **income approach**.	Identification of value added by the difference between inputs and outputs. Called **subtraction method**. Sometimes also called **product approach**.

3 Types of subtraction methods under net consumption type VAT		
A	B	C
Deducting the aggregate tax-exclusive value of purchases from the aggregate tax-exclusive value of sales and taxing the difference between them. Called **direct subtraction method**.	Deducting the aggregate tax-inclusive values of purchases from the aggregate tax-inclusive value of sales and taxing the difference between them. Called **intermediate subtraction method**.	Deducting tax on inputs from tax on sales for each tax period. Called **indirect subtraction method**.

its greater possibility of detecting tax evasion. So far as flexibility is concerned, apart from its use in relieving from tax goods and services such as food, which governments may not wish to tax or tax at a lower rate, the indirect subtraction method is an efficient way of relieving exports of tax under the destination principle. An exporter can claim credit, and a refund, on all his inputs. If he also sells in the domestic market, then he deducts all his credits against the tax he has collected on his output and either receives a refund (if the value of his exports exceeds his home sales) or pays a smaller sum to the tax authorities than if all his sales had been domestic. There is no tracing problem; inputs do not have to be divided into those related to exports and those related to production for the home market. Similarly, this method copes with imports more easily than either the addition or direct subtraction method with its use of chain invoices. The seller and buyer have opposite incentives with regard to tax evasion. This method also offers scope for an audit trail of cross-checking by the tax authorities. No such facility is afforded by the addition method. With the direct subtraction method such cross-checking can be undertaken, but it is not simple, especially if more than one rate is involved.

A comparison of the VAT and the retail sales tax

Several authors, for example, Tait (1988) have argued that a VAT and a retail sales tax (RST) are almost indistinguishable from each other. If this is the case then the analysis of a VAT would be no different from that given in the beginning of this chapter. However, this is only partially true. In this section we make a direct comparison between the RST and the VAT.

The main difference between a single-stage RST and the multi-stage VAT is that the RST is essentially a suspensive system: primary producers, wholesalers, and retailers are generally required to be registered and are accountable for the tax on sales of goods to non-registered persons (usually customers) but may buy and sell goods among themselves without liability to tax, provided that none of these goods is for their own private use. Accordingly, payment of the tax is suspended until the last stage – when the goods are sold by registered traders to unregistered customers. VAT, in contrast, operates an invoice or credit or repayment system and not a suspensive system in that all traders buying goods and services have to pay the tax – irrespective of whether they are registered or not. If they are registered the tax paid is refunded to them. Assuming equal coverage and rates between a VAT and a RST the same amount of tax would be collected under both taxes. In this sense these two taxes are equivalent to each other. However, there are some substantial differences as well. We discuss some of these below.

An important difference between a VAT and a RST is that in the VAT the onus is always on traders to convince tax authorities that their claims for tax credits are justified. In the case of a RST no such effort is required.

VAT credit mechanism obliges traders to keep detailed records of purchases as well as sales, in order to get the rebate on the VAT paid on the inputs; such detailed account-keeping is not required under the RST. However a certain amount of account-keeping is always required to keep a check on trader activity.

Does this mean that administrative costs of a VAT are likely to be higher than those of a RST? The answer is not necessarily so for the following reasons. First, the number of registered traders with which the tax authorities have to deal is unlikely to be very different in the two cases, since even under RST most traders have to be registered. Second, because VAT traders have to record purchases as well as sales, there is likely to be a close tie-up in the information requirement which is absent in the RST case.

Third, and very significantly, possibilities of tax evasion are likely to be higher under the RST. If this is true then it could be argued that if we were comparing taxes with equal yield, the RST may give less revenue. Among the kinds of tax evasion that could take place under both RST and VAT would be concealment by enterprises of transactions through the 'black labor market', e.g. construction workers, car mechanics, etc. Under VAT but not under RST, traders can claim refunds on purchases never made.

Under RST, but not under VAT not-registered users may set up counterfeit registration numbers to obtain tax-free goods. However, with the VAT since both sales and purchases have to be reported, there is a cross-check. Furthermore, it is thought that under RST the whole of the tax is at risk but under the VAT only the tax on value added by the retailer at the last stage is at risk.

So far as services are concerned, there appear to be two reasons why it is easier to accommodate services under VAT than under RST. The first is that the bulk of services to consumers is given by firms which also provide services to firms. The second factor is that mixed-use services for business and private consumption pose far fewer problems under VAT than under RST. Services under VAT rendered to business firms are simply taxed in full. Identification of the purchaser, required under RST if cascading is to be avoided, is unnecessary. Whether or not the purchaser is subsequently entitled to take credit for tax is of no concern to the seller, but a matter between the purchaser and the tax authorities. To take a simple example, consider the purchase of a train ticket for a business trip. The VAT would not require any knowledge by the ticket office of the purpose of the trip. It has been argued that a proper application of the RST would require not only the presentation of an exemption certificate, but also an authentication of the purpose of the trip. This example could be multiplied several-fold in the fields of transportation, communication, advertising and the like. Under the RST, verification of end-use falls on the supplier who cannot know the status of the buyer nor, consequently, the end use; under VAT such verification falls on the purchaser who does know.

So far as producer goods are concerned it is generally agreed to be desirable to relieve them of RST or VAT because the cascading effect of such taxes haphazardly distorts competition. The VAT credit system permits a full credit for taxes paid on purchases of all investment goods and auxiliary supplies used by registered firms. In principle, RST systems permit the same sort of relief for producer goods as VAT but, in practice, this does not work well for mixed-use goods. Under the RST, it is necessary to find out the end use of these goods in order to distinguish between those who should pay the tax and those who should not.

So far as internationally traded goods are concerned, the VAT credit mechanism under which exporters pay tax on their inputs and then have this tax credited against their sales has an advantage over the RST suspensive mechanism under which exporters never pay in that the VAT system is more transparent and allows proper crediting. On the import side, VAT requires importers to pay tax either at the time of importation or soon after, whereas the RST would require that the tax be paid only if the imported commodity is sold to an unregistered user.

There is some truth to these propositions and, perhaps, tax evasion is larger under RST than under VAT. For countries that have undergone the transition from RST to VAT, the experience with tax yields has been somewhat mixed although the empirical evidence itself can be thought to be suspect. In the case of the Swedish transition in 1970 tax revenues did not change very much. However, in the case of the Irish transition during 1972 tax revenues increased from 4.5 per cent of GDP to 5.1 per cent of GDP – a truly significant increase.

On the other hand the two taxes have different compliance costs across different categories of buyers. Since VAT requires traders to record both sales as well as purchases, whereas a RST requires records only of sales, the compliance costs in the aggregate may be lower in the latter case.

13.7 CONCLUSIONS

In this chapter we have studied some aspects of commodity taxation. We recognized that if lump sum taxes are available then it is meaningless to impose any commodity taxes. In the realistic situation that lump-sum taxes are not available, commodity taxes do have a role. We derived key results relating to efficient collection of commodity taxation. We also realized that uniform commodity taxation is not desirable except under special conditions.

We then studied the redistributive role of commodity taxation. We derived the standard Ramsey–Feldstein–Munk formula for optimal redistributive commodity taxation. But we realized, as per the work of Sah, that the extent of redistribution possible through commodity taxation is quite limited. We also studied some operational aspects of a popular form of commodity taxation – the VAT. In the next chapter we broach the important question of the proper mix of direct and indirect taxes.

NOTE

1 A specific tax and an *ad valorem* tax can be shown to be equivalent. It there is an *ad valorem* tax at the rate of τ_i we can write the consumer price as $p_i = q_i(1 + \tau_i)$. For the specific and the *ad valorem* tax to be equivalent $q_i(1 + \tau_i) = q_i + t_i$ or $t_i = q_i\tau_i$.

ADDITIONAL READING

The following additional readings might be of interest to students. Hayek (1979), Kay and King (1990), Wagner (1991), Mulgan and Murray (1993) Giles and Johnson (1994).

14 Aspects of income taxation

Key concepts: optimal direct taxation: linear as well as non-linear; Pareto optimal inter-generational taxation; optimal mix of direct and indirect taxation.

14.1 INTRODUCTION

In this chapter we study income taxation or, more generally, direct taxation. Several aspects have to be considered and it would serve us well to make a list of the issues to be considered. First, we study optimal linear income taxation. Then we move to a study of optimal non-linear taxation. This leads us to consider the role of information in setting optimal income taxes. We then proceed to consider optimal wage and interest income taxation. We realize that in all such models there is only a limited role for indirect taxation. We show, however, that this is true only in models of full certainty. Finally, we offer some concluding comments.

14.2 OPTIMAL LINEAR TAXES

We have already encountered optimal linear taxation in Chapter 8 where we were discussing the effects of taxation on labor supply. In this chapter we consider optimal linear taxation more completely. One part of the basic structure of most optimal income tax models is that there is a trade-off in the imposition of a distortionary tax. In a society where individuals have differing abilities, taxing people with higher skills and, therefore income will lead, ceteris paribus, to higher tax revenues and also reduce income inequalities whereas, at the same time, if labor is variable then the size of the pie to be redistributed will be smaller because more productive labor will reduce labor supply more than proportionately under progressive income taxation. Hence, there is always an implicit trade-off which one has to take account of.

Another aspect of the problem that has to be considered is as follows. The analysis above implicitly assumes absolutely smooth substitution possibilities between different types of labor. Hence if a worker of type a is twice as productive as a worker of type *b* then two workers of type *b* could, in principle, replace one worker of type *a* without any adverse output consequences. In other words, the elasticity of substitution between the two types of labor is infinite. However, there may be less than perfect substitution possibilities between different types of labor. No number of unskilled workers can, for example, replace an accomplished heart surgeon. In this case the elasticity of substitution between different types of labor is finite and the analysis of optimal taxation is somewhat different. All these issues will be considered in this chapter. We begin, however, with an analysis of optimal linear taxation as initially studied by Sandmo (1976) and later by Yaari and others.

An optimal linear income tax

Several individuals exist and they are distinguished by their ability. The cumulative distribution of abilities is given by Φ. This distribution of abilities is common knowledge but the planner does not know the wage of any particular individual. This knowledge is private to the individual alone. It is assumed that, under competitive conditions, the wage of any individual reflects his ability by virtue of the fact that the any worker's wage reflects his marginal product. It is further assumed that the elasticity of substitution between different types of labor is infinite. We normalize the distribution of abilities such that:

$$\int_{w_0}^{\infty} d\Phi = 1 \tag{14.1}$$

where w_0 is the wage of the least able worker. The most able worker will have only finite productivity so that equation (14.1) is always true. Except for differences in abilities, all workers are alike. In particular, they have the same utility function with leisure and consumption as arguments.

Let Y be disposable income, Z pre-tax income and T the tax paid. Then the budget constraint of the individual, under progressive linear taxation can be written as:

$$Y = Z - T = (1 - t) wL + G \tag{14.2}$$

where *t* is the (fixed) marginal tax rate, G the exemption limit of the linear tax, *w* the wage rate and *L* hours worked.

The government has an exogenous revenue requirement of R_0 so that the government's budget constraint in view of equation (14.1) can be written as:

$$G + R_0 = t \int_{w_0}^{\infty} wL d\Phi. \tag{14.3}$$

The government's tax policy attempts to maximize a social welfare function of the form:

$$\int_{w_0}^{\infty} \Psi(U) d\Phi \qquad (14.4)$$

where U is the individual worker's direct utility function. Different assumptions about Ψ would yield different tax rules. For instance, if $\Psi' = 1$ then we have a Benthamite social welfare function.

Forming the Lagrangean for the social planner we have:

$$\Lambda = \int_{w_0}^{\infty} [\Psi + \lambda(twL - G - R_0)]] d\Phi \qquad (14.5)$$

where λ is the Lagrange multiplier. The first-order conditions are that:

$$\int_{w_0}^{\infty} [\Psi'(\partial U/\partial G) + \lambda[tw(\partial L/\partial G) - 1] d\Phi = 0 \qquad (14.6)$$

$$\int_{w_0}^{\infty} [\Psi'(\partial U/\partial t) + \lambda(wL + tw(\partial L/\partial t))] d\Phi = 0 \qquad (14.7)$$

(where a prime ($'$) denotes a partial derivative).

We have no reason to suppose that equations (14.6) and (14.7) will be well behaved. There may be more than one solution to the first-order conditions. In that case, we will have to look at the value of the social welfare function for each such solution and choose the global optimum.

Now, we can write the Slutsky equation for the labor supply as:

$$(\partial L/\partial t) = -w(\partial L/\partial t)|_{dU=0} - wL(\partial L/\partial Z) \qquad (14.8)$$

since labor is an undesirable good. We also know that:

$$(\partial U/\partial t) = -\alpha wL \qquad (14.9)$$

where α is the private marginal utility of income. Substituting in equation (14.6) and (14.7) we have:

$$\int_{w_0}^{\infty} [\Psi'(\alpha/\lambda) + tw(\partial L/\partial Z) - 1] d\Phi = 0 \qquad (14.10)$$

$$\int_{w_0}^{\infty} wL[\Psi'(\alpha/\lambda) + tw(\partial L/\partial Z) - 1 + tw(\partial L/\partial t)|_{dU=0}] d\Psi = 0. \qquad (14.11)$$

Now define b, the social marginal valuation of income, as:

$$b = \Psi'(\alpha/\lambda) + tw(\partial L/\partial Z) \qquad (14.12)$$

and substitute in equation (14.10) to get:

$$\bar{b} = 1 \qquad (14.13)$$

(where $\bar{b}$ is the average b);
and in equation (14.11) to get:

$$\int_{w_0}^{\infty} Z[b - 1 + (tw)/(L)(\partial L/\partial t)|_{dU=0}] d\Phi = 0. \qquad (14.14)$$

Now write $\epsilon_{LL} = \{w(1 - t)/L\}\{(\partial L/\partial t)|_{dU=0}\}$ as the compensated elasticity of labor supply. We can then write equation (14.14) as:

$$\int_{w_0}^{\infty} Z[b - \bar{b} + \{t/(1 - t)\}\{\epsilon_{LL}\}]d\Phi = 0 \qquad (14.15)$$

or,

$$t/(1 - t) = - \text{cov} [b, z]/\left[\int_{w_0}^{\infty} \epsilon_{LL} d\Phi\right]. \qquad (14.16)$$

The conditions (14.13) and (14.16) have a very natural interpretation. $\bar{b}$ is the mean of the bs. Hence, equation (14.13) says that the lump-sum element (G) should be so adjusted as to make the net social marginal valuation of the transfer of one dollar of income measured in terms of government revenue equal, on average, to the cost (one dollar). Equation (14.16) says that the tax rate depends on the compensated labor supply elasticity and the way in which marginal social valuation of income varies with total income. In equation (14.16) $\epsilon_{LL} > 0$ since labor is an undesirable good. The numerator could be positive or negative. Typically, b and Z would be negatively correlated but if leisure becomes an inferior good at high wages, then it is possible that b and Z could be positively correlated.

14.3 OPTIMAL NON-LINEAR INCOME TAXATION (MIRRLEES AND RAMSEY)

The work on optimal non-linear taxation dates back to the classic work of Mirrlees (1971) and, perhaps even earlier, to the path-breaking work of Ramsey (1927). Other important works in this area are Phelps (1973), Mirrlees (1976), Seade (1977), and Auerbach (1987a). Remember, though, that this is a purely **wage income** tax problem and an **atemporal** one at that, and does not include the taxation of other forms of income or problems of taxation over time.

The basic structure common to all purely wage income tax models is the following. People are identical in their tastes but differ in their productivity at work which we index by m. A person with ability m = 1 is only half as productive as a person with ability m = 2. There exists a continuous distribution of people along the this ordinal scale of ability. The cumulative distribution function of abilities is denoted by $\Phi(m)$. The highest and lowest level of abilities are denoted by m_h and m_l respectively.

Apart from these efficiency differences workers are substitutable for each other. Indeed, the elasticity of substitution between different types of labor is infinite so that one labor hour worked by one $m = 3$ worker can be perfectly substituted by three labor hours of $m = 1$ type worker. The labor market is perfectly competitive so that a person with ability m has a gross wage of mw where w is the wage rate of a standard $m = 1$ type worker. Each person has an m-independent utility function:

$$U = U(-L, c) \qquad (14.17)$$

where L is labor (so that -L is leisure) and c is consumption. Leisure and consumption are both desirable goods but one can only be had by sacrificing the other. This utility function is assumed to be strictly quasi-concave and twice continuously differentiable.

The individual's budget constraint is dependent on his m. We choose units such that the wage rate for a person of ability $m = 1$ is simply 1. Thus the (before-tax) earnings of a person with ability m is, simply,

$$Z = Lm \qquad (14.18)$$

and the budget constraint is:

$$Z - T(Z) - c \geqslant 0 \qquad (14.19)$$

where $T(Z)$ is the (possibly non-linear) tax schedule that this individual faces. Setting up the Lagrangean for this person we have:

$$\Lambda = U(-L, c) + \mu[Z - T(Z) - c] \qquad (14.20)$$

where μ is the Lagrange multiplier.

To avoid cluttering up the notation, we write U_i as the partial derivative of the utility function with respect to its ith argument. Thus $U_2 = (\partial U/\partial c)$ and $U_1 = \partial U/\partial L$.

The first-order conditions are that:

$$U_1 = m(1 - T'(.))\mu \qquad (14.21)$$

$$U_2 = \mu \qquad (14.22)$$

$$Z - T(Z) - c = 0. \qquad (14.23)$$

In this set-up, it is assumed that the social planner can observe the distribution of abilities Φ but cannot observe incomes. It is under these conditions that the tax structure has to be set. In setting this tax structure, the government has two requirements. First, it has an exogenous revenue requirement of the amount R_0. Second, it wishes to maximize a social welfare function. The first requirement can be expressed in equation (14.24):

$$\int_{m_l}^{m_h} T(Z)\Phi(m)dm = R_0 \qquad (14.24)$$

where, clearly,

$$T(Z) = Z - c. \qquad (14.25).$$

In specifying the second requirement, together with Mirrlees, we assume that the government wishes to maximize a utiltarian social welfare function. The government's problem can, hence, be written as:

$$\max_{Z, c, T} \int_{m_l}^{m_h} W[U(-L, c)]\Phi(m)dm \qquad (14.26)$$

where W is a social welfare function. This took the utilitarian form in the work of Mirrlees and the Rawlsian maximin form in that of Phelps. This social welfare function is maximized subject to the revenue requirements expressed in equations (14.24) and (14.25) and the utility maximization conditions in equations (14.21) to (14.23). The latter constraints are necessary in view of the fact that individual incomes cannot be observed and, therefore, the tax structure has to be made consistent with rational behavior of individual tax payers.

A solution to this optimal income tax problem proceeds by converting the revenue requirement conditions and the utility maximization conditions as differential equations (in m) so that the resulting problem can then be solved using the methods of optimal control. We first substitute equation (14.25) into equation (14.24) and differentiate with respect to m to get:

$$dR/dm = (Z - c)\Phi(m) \tag{14.27}$$

with

$$R_{m_h} = R_0 \tag{14.28}$$

where R_{m_h} is the cumulative tax revenue until the level of ability m_h.

We now work with the individual utility maximization conditions. Write the indirect utility function as:

$$V_m = \max U(-Z/m, c). \tag{14.29}$$

Differentiate this with respect to m to get:

$$dV_m/dm = -U_1(d/dm)(Z/m) + U_2 dc/dm + U_1 Z/m^2. \tag{14.30}$$

Equation (14.30) characterizes consumer equilibrium in the same sense as equations (14.21) to (14.23) do. Now, when utility has been maximized, its derivative with respect to m must be zero, i.e.,

$$-U_1(d/dm)(Z/m) + U_2(dc/dm) = 0. \tag{14.31}$$

Substituting into equation (14.30) we have:

$$dV_m/dm = U_1 Z/m^2. \tag{14.32}$$

Equation (14.32) expresses fully and completely the constraint that individual rationality places on the social welfare maximization problem.

We have a few more manipulations to carry out before we can make a complete statement of the Mirrlees–Phelps optimal tax problem. In equation (14.29) since U is monotonically declining in L it follows that we can invert this relation. Thus, we write $Z = Z(V, c, m)$. Hence, we eliminate Z as a control variable and include V as a state variable. The final form of this problem is:

$$\max \int_{m_l}^{m_h} W(V)\Phi(m)dm$$

subject to:

$$\text{(i)} \quad dV/dm = U_1[-Z(V, c, m), c)]Z(V, c, m)/m^2$$
$$\text{(ii)} \quad dR/dm = [Z(V, c, m) - c]\Phi(m)$$

and the terminal conditions:

$$R_{m_h} = R_O \text{ and } R_{m_l} = 0.$$

Using Pontryagin's maximization principle (see Kamien and Schwartz 1991) we can write the Hamiltonian for this problem as:

$$H = W(V)\Phi(m) + \theta_1[U_1Z/m^2] + \theta_2[Z - c]\Phi(m) \qquad (14.33)$$

where θ_1 and θ_2 are the costate variables attached to constraints (i) and (ii). In this problem we have one control variable: c and two state variables R and V. Controlling c defines the utility of the individual as well as his contributions to the tax authorities. The necessary conditions for an optimum are:

(a) $(\partial H/\partial c) = 0 = \theta_1(\partial/\partial c)\{U_1Z/m^2\} + \theta_2\{(\partial Z/\partial c) - 1\}\Phi(m)$ (14.34)
(b) $\partial H/\partial V = -(d/dm)\theta_1$ (canonical equation for θ_1)
(c) $\partial H/\partial R = -(d/dm)\theta_2$ (canonical equation for θ_2)

(Realize that θ_1 is a function of m whereas θ_2 is not.)

(d) $\theta_1(m_h) = \theta_1(m_l) = 0$ (transversality conditions)
where $\theta_1(m_h)$ is the value of the costate variable θ_1 at m_h etc.

(e) $R_{m_l} = 0$ and $R_{m_h} = R_0$.

The standard results in optimal tax theory are all derived by interpreting these conditions. Let us first note that:

$$dV_m/dm = U_1Z/m^2 \geqslant 0.$$

In the face of very high marginal tax rates, a person with a high ability always has the option of working less than a person with less ability and enjoying higher leisure. Thus dV_m/dm cannot be negative. A person with high ability must have at least as high utility as a person with low ability. In later work on optimal tax theory, this has been referred to as the **incentive compatibility** or **self-selection** constraint.

It is also easy to see that $T' < 1$ (the marginal tax rate is strictly less than 100 per cent). To see this let us suppose that $T' > 1$. In this interval a person who gives up leisure to work more ends up paying more than 100 per cent of the incremental income in taxes. No rational consumer would target an income in this range of Z.

We now show an important result. In equation (14.34), $\partial Z/\partial c$ is the marginal rate of substitution between income and consumption. From the individual's first-order conditions for utility maximization we know that $\partial Z/\partial c = 1/(1 - T')$ whence, substituting in equation (14.34) we have:

$$T' = -\theta_1[(\partial/\partial c)(U_1 Z/m^2)]/[\theta_2 \Phi(m) - \theta_1\{(\partial/\partial c)(U_1 Z/m^2)\}]. \quad (14.35)$$

This is a highly non-linear form for the optimal marginal tax rate. However, there is one property of the optimal marginal income tax rate that can be established immediately from equation (14.35). Since, from the transversality conditions, $\theta_1 = 0$ at the top and bottom ends of the ability distribution, it must be the case that the optimal marginal income tax rate must be zero at both ends of the ability distribution. We will have more to say about the intuition of this result at a later stage.

A related result is that under the following two conditions the marginal tax rate is non-decreasing ($T' \geqslant 0$). These conditions are:

(i) the cross-partial derivative of the utility function is non-negative: $U_{12} \geqslant 0$ (marginal utility of leisure does not fall when consumption increases);
(ii) the marginal social value of leisure declines with ability, i.e., $d(W_U U_1)/dm \leqslant 0$.

We first show that if condition (ii) holds then $\theta_1 \leqslant 0$. From the canonical equation for θ_1 we have that:

$$\begin{aligned} -(d/dm)\theta_1 &= [W_V + \theta_2 Z_V]\Phi + [(\partial/\partial V)(dV/dm)]\theta_1 \\ &= \beta(m)\theta_2 + \alpha(m). \end{aligned} \quad (14.36)$$

This is a linear differential equation in θ_1 which we can solve to get:

$$-\theta_1(m^*) = \int_{m_1} [\alpha(j)\{e^{\int_{m^*}^{j} \beta(\hat{j})d\hat{j}}\}]dj. \quad (14.37)$$

Since the exponential function is non-negative, the sign of equation (14.37) is given by $\alpha(j)$ alone. It is easy to see that $\alpha(j) \geqslant 0$ whenever $W_U U_1 \geqslant \theta_2$. Now, $W_U U_1$ is monotonically decreasing by assumption and θ_2 is a positive constant, hence we must have $\alpha(j)$ changing sign at most once from positive to negative. Now, from the transversality conditions $\theta_1(m_h) = \theta_1(m_1) = 0$ so that $\theta_1 \leqslant 0$. From equation (14.35) then we will have $T' \geqslant 0$ if $(\partial/\partial c)$ $(U_1 Z/m^2) > 0$. But this derivative equals $[-Z(\partial Z/\partial c)U_{11}/m + ZU_{12} + (\partial Z/\partial c)U_1]/m^2$. Now, $U_{11} < 0$ by concavity of the utility function, $U_{12} > 0$ and $\partial Z/\partial c \geqslant 0$ so that $(\partial/\partial c)(U_1 Z/m^2) > 0$ and hence $T' \geqslant 0$.

If we combine this with the result that T' is zero at the top and bottom ends of the ability distribution, we realize that the marginal tax rate will rise in some ranges of the ability distribution and fall in others. Between the two extremes of m_h and m_1, the marginal tax rate is non-negative whereas at the end points it is zero.

At the qualitative level, not much more can be said about the optimal non-linear tax. To get more precise results, we must do numerical calculations. Mirrlees himself did some calculations using a Cobb–Douglas example. His main conclusions are threefold:

(a) the optimal tax schedule is approximately linear;
(b) the marginal tax rates are rather low;
(c) the income tax is optimally not a very redistributive tax.

Phelps, in his articulation of the optimal tax problem with a Rawlsian social welfare function, came to almost the same conclusions as Mirrlees. As would be expected, however, the Rawls optimum tax schedule is rather more redistributive.

Optimal taxation with many goods

How far can we go (qualitatively) in the case of optimal non-linear taxation with many goods. We pose the problem in a manner completely analogous to the one just discussed.

Labor, apart from efficiency differences, is still substitutable. There are n goods for which taxes must be chosen. The individual's utility function is written as:

$$U = U(-Z/m; c_1, \ldots, c_n) \tag{14.38}$$

where $c_1, \ldots, c_n$ are the amounts of n goods for which tax rates have to be found. The individual's budget constraint is:

$$T(Z) + \sum_j p_j c_j = Z \tag{14.39}$$

where q_j is the producer price of commodity j, $p_j (= q_j + t_j)$ is the producer price and t_j is the specific tax rate on commodity j.

By following the same steps as in the previous section, we can derive maximized utility as a function of optimally chosen leisure and consumption goods:

$$V = \max U(-Z/m; c_1, \ldots, c_n) \tag{14.40}$$

and again we arrive at our familiar envelope condition:

$$dV/dm = U_1 Z/m^2.$$

Mirrlees (1976) has focused on the problem of derivation of an optimal income tax schedule (T) and optimal linear taxes on the n goods. The latter amounts to choosing the consumer prices p_j.

The dual expenditure function for the consumer utility maximization problem can be written as:

$$e = e(p_1, \ldots, p_n; V, -Z/m). \tag{14.41}$$

Hence, we can write the envelope condition as:

$$dV/dm = (Z/m^2) U_1(-Z/m, e_{p_1}, \ldots, e_{p_n}) \tag{14.42}$$

where $e_{p_i} = (\partial e / \partial p_i)$ represents the demand function for commodity i.

The final form of the optimal tax problem can now be written as:

$$\max \int_{m_l}^{m_h} W(V)\Phi(m)dm$$

subject to:

$$dV/dm = (Z/m^2)U_1(-Z/m; e_{p_1}, \ldots, e_{p_n})$$
$$dR/dm = (Z - \Sigma_j p_j e_{p_j})\Phi(m)$$
$$R_{m_l} = 0 \text{ and } R_{m_h} = R_0.$$

The Hamiltonian for this problem can be written as:

$$H = W(V)\Phi(m) + \theta_1(Z/m^2)U_1 + \theta_2(Z - \Sigma p_j e_{p_j})\Phi(m). \tag{14.43}$$

Once again θ_2 is a constant whereas θ_1 is a function of m.
The first-order conditions for an internal maximum are that:

$$\partial H/\partial Z = 0$$
$$-(d/dm)\theta_1 = (\partial H/\partial V) \text{ (canonical equation)}$$
$$-(d/dm)\theta_2 = (\partial H/\partial R) \text{ (canonical equation)}$$
$$\theta_1(m_l) = \theta_1(m_h) = 0 \quad \text{(transverality conditions)}$$
$$R_{m_l} = 0 \text{ and } R_{m_h} = R_0.$$

Results are, on the whole, straightforward extensions of the problem considered in the previous section. It is trivial to show that post-tax utility is a non-decreasing function of ability. Similarly, the result that $T' < 1$ follows easily. The end-point conditions get amended somewhat. The individual's tax liability (τ) can be written as:

$$\tau = T(Z) + \sum t_j e_{p_j}. \tag{14.44}$$

Now increase labor income, Z, by a small amount for some m person on the optimal path. The controls are held constant so that:

$$(\partial \tau/\partial Z) = 1 - \sum q_j(\partial e_{p_j}/\partial Z). \tag{14.45}$$

Now, from the first-order conditions for the maximization of the Hamiltonian we have:

$$0 = (\partial H/\partial Z) = \theta_1(\partial/\partial Z)U_1 + \theta_2[1 - \sum q_j(\partial e_{p_j}/\partial Z)]\Phi. \tag{14.46}$$

Combining equations (14.45) and (14.46) we get:

$$(\partial \tau/\partial Z) = -[\theta_1/(\theta_2\Phi)][(\partial/\partial Z)U_1]. \tag{14.47}$$

At m_l and m_h we have $\theta_1 = 0$, so that, at these and points, $(\partial \tau/\partial Z) = 0$.

An intuitive explanation for this would go as follows. Let us take the higher end of the ability distribution m_h. If the marginal direct plus indirect tax rate is positive here then people with this ability will supply less labor and move, in terms of effective labor supply, to the position of persons whose ability is just less than m_h. The result that the total marginal direct and indirect tax rates should be zero does not, of course, mean that each has to be zero. One of them could be positive and the other negative.

In a similar vein one can establish that $(\partial \tau / \partial Z) \geqslant 0$ so long as:

(i) goods subject to taxation and leisure have non-negative cross partials in the consumer's utility function, i.e.,
     $U_{li} = \partial U_1 / (\partial e_{p_i}) \geqslant 0$;
(ii) the marginal social utility of a dollar is a non-increasing function of utility, i.e., $dW_V \mu / dV \leqslant 0$ (where μ is the Lagrange multiplier associated with the consumer utility maximization problem).

This result, which is left as an exercise for the interested reader, is an exact analog of the result proved for the one good Mirrlees optimal income tax case.

In the Mirrlees framework, then, the existence of several goods is tackled in a relatively simple manner. All taxed goods and untaxed goods (such as leisure) are treated as if they could be aggregated.

14.4 INFORMATION THEORETIC FOUNDATIONS OF OPTIMAL TAX THEORY

Results in optimal tax theory are important because they do not assume observability of incomes. This problem of optimal taxation under conditions of imperfect information has been further analyzed by Stiglitz (1982, 1989) and by several others, for example, Boadway and Keen (1993), Boadway *et al.* (1996).

We start off with the simplest version of this problem and then build it up in complexity. Since imperfection of information is the key issue to be considered, the structure of the model that does not have any bearing on the imperfection of information is kept very simple. We will, for example, collapse the continuous distribution of abilities of the Stiglitz to a situation in which there are only two types of workers – skilled and unskilled. We will begin with the simplest case, that of full information.

Full information case – fixed labor supply

Consider an economy consisting of two types of households (workers): high ability types (type *h*) and low ability types (type *l*). Workers have utility functions: $U^i(c_i, L_i)$ where U^i, c_i, and L_i are the utility function, consumption and labor of a worker of type *i* ($i = l, h$). If there are no taxes, the individual's budget constraint can be written as:

$$c_i = Y_i = w_i L_i \qquad (14.48)$$

where Y_i is gross income and w_i is the competitively determined wage rate. Suppose, to begin with, that labor supplies are fixed so that lump-sum taxes are feasible. The social planner attempts to tax the high-ability persons in order to redistribute income to low-ability people.

With this stipulation, an individual's utility maximization plan can be written as:

$$\max_{c_i} U^i(c_i, \bar{L}_i) \text{ subject to } c_i = w_i\bar{L}_i - T_i.$$

The solution to this problem is:

$$c_i = w_i\bar{L}_i - T_i. \tag{14.48a}$$

The social planner attempts to maximize a social welfare function. Assume that there are N_h number of high-ability workers and N_l number of low-ability workers. Suppose the social welfare function chosen is of the utilitarian type. This is maximized subject to the constraints given in equation (14.48). The Lagrangean for the social planner is:

$$\Lambda = N_h U^h(c_h, L_h) + N_l U^l(c_l, L_l)$$
$$+ \lambda[N_h(w_h\bar{L}_h - T_h - c_h) + N_l(w_l\bar{L}_l - T_l - c_l)]. \tag{14.49}$$

Choosing T_i is tantamount, in this model, to choosing c_i. The first-order conditions are that:

$$N_h(\partial U^h/\partial c_h) - \lambda N_h = 0 \rightarrow \partial U^h/\partial c_h = \lambda \tag{14.50a}$$

$$N_l(\partial U^l/\partial c_l) - \lambda N_l = 0 \rightarrow \partial U^l/\partial c_l = \lambda \tag{14.50b}$$

so that the marginal utilities of the two types of workers are equated. This is depicted in Figure 14.1 where we have drawn a utility possibility frontier between the utility of the two types of workers. Social optimum occurs at point A where the slope of the utility possibility frontier is -1. If, instead, we were working with the Rawlsian social welfare function, utilities would have to be equalized. The social indifference curve would be of the type depicted in Figure 14.2. Optimum occurs at point A.

Essentially, this means that, since there is full information, the government can help solve the individual's utility maximization problem. This would be true even in the case where labor is variable and non-lump-sum taxes have to be used. In this case the first order conditions for utility maximization (when the social welfare function is utilitarian would read):

$$(\partial U^h/\partial c_h) = (\partial U^l/\partial c_l) \tag{14.51a}$$

$$w_i(\partial U^i/\partial c_i) + (\partial U^i/\partial L_i) = 0. \tag{14.51b}$$

It should be noted, however, that if both types of workers have the same utility function and leisure is a normal good then the more able workers will actually be worse off. The utilitarian solution has the property that the high-ability person would prefer the $\{c, L\}$ combination of the low-ability

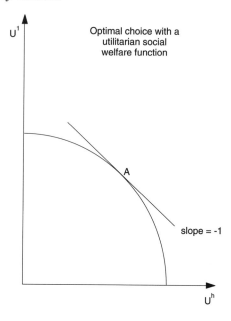

Figure 14.1

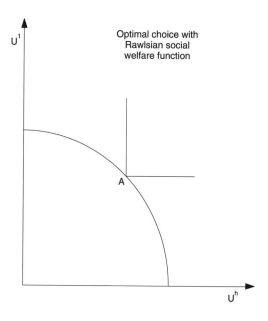

Figure 14.2

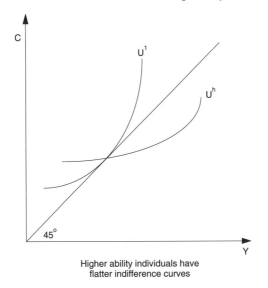

Higher ability individuals have
flatter indifference curves

Figure 14.3

person. This can be seen most easily if the utility function is additively separable (and identical across individuals):

$$U^i = U(c_i) - b(L_i).$$

In this case equation (14.51a) implies that all individuals, regardless of their ability, receive the same level of consumption, but condition (14.51b) requires that those with higher productivity have a higher marginal productivity of work, i.e., they work harder. This is shown in Figure 14.3 where we have drawn indifference curves for the two types of workers in (c, Y) space. In the Rawlsian case, more able workers are not worse off.

Imperfect information case

Suppose now that an individual's labor input and wages are not observable. Hence, the government cannot solve the individual's utility maximization problem so as to achieve a Pareto efficient outcome. Hence, the social planner must redefine the individual's optimization problem in terms of observables. Typically, gross income (Y_i) and consumption (c_i) may be observable. Since $Y_i = w_i L_i$ we can define an individual's utility as V^i where:

$$V^i(c_i, Y_i) \equiv U^i(c_i, w_i L_i / w_i). \tag{14.51}$$

First, let us define the properties of the transformed utility function.
(i) Increase in Y_i decreases utility if c_i is held constant. This is because this would increase work without increasing consumption:

$$(\partial V^i / \partial Y_i)|_{\bar{c}_i} \quad < 0.$$

(ii) More productive individuals will have flatter indifference curves in (c, Y) space. We know that the *mrs* between c_i and Y_i is:

$$(\partial c_i/\partial Y_i)|_{\bar{V}^i} = -(\partial V^i/\partial Y^i)/(\partial V^i/\partial c^i) = -(1/w_i)(\partial U^i/\partial L_i)/[\partial U^i/\partial c_i]. \tag{14.52}$$

More productive individuals have higher w_is and hence $(\partial c_i/\partial Y_i)|_{\bar{V}^i}$ will be lower for such individuals. If leisure is a normal good then, at any given set of values of $\{c, Y\}$, more able persons will work less and, hence, the *mrs* between c and Y will be lower for them.

(iii) We should also note that when individuals maximize their utility, in the absence of taxation, they set the *mrs* between consumption and leisure equal to the wage:

$$(\partial c_i/\partial L_i)|_{\bar{V}} = -[(\partial U^i/\partial L_i)/(\partial U^i/\partial c_i)] = w_i. \tag{14.53}$$

Substituting in equation (14.52) we get:

$$\begin{aligned}(\partial c_i/\partial Y^i)|_{\bar{V}} &= -[(\partial V^i/\partial Y^i)]/[(\partial V^i/\partial c_i)] \\ &= -[(\partial U^i/\partial L_i)/w_i]/[(\partial U^i/\partial c_i)] = w_i/w_i = 1.\end{aligned} \tag{14.54}$$

In the absence of taxation, then, the slope of the indifference curve in $\{c, Y\}$ space is unity.

We already know that in the full information case, the higher ability worker had the incentive to behave like the low-ability worker. It was not possible in that case because of full information. Now that we have admitted the possibility of imperfect information this is a distinct possibility. Hence, any welfare exercise must be consistent with individual incentives, otherwise it is doomed to failure.

We now consider the following Pareto optimizing exercise. We maximize the utility of a representative low-ability worker subject to the constraints imposed by revenue requirement and individual rational behavior. Hence, we consider the following problem:

$$\max V^1(c_1, Y_1) \text{ subject to}$$

(i) $V^h(c_h, Y_h) \geqslant \bar{V}^h$ (standard Pareto constraint)
(ii) $V^l(c_1, Y_1) \geqslant V^l(c_h, Y_h)$ (self-selection constraint on individual l)
(iii) $V^h(c_h, Y_h) \geqslant V^h(c_1, Y_1)$ (self-selection constraint on individual h)
(iv) $R = (Y_1 - c_1)N_1 + (Y_h - c_h)N_h \geqslant R_0$ (revenue requirement).

The self-selection constraints ensure that a high-ability person does not find it in his interest to mimic the behavior of the low-ability worker who, in turn, does not find it profitable to mimic the behavior of the high-ability worker. Setting up the Lagrangean we have:

$$\begin{aligned}\Lambda &= V^l(c_1, Y_1) + \mu V^h(c_h, Y_h) + \lambda_1[V^l(c_1, Y_1) - V^l(c_h, Y_h)] \\ &+ \lambda_h[V^h(c_h, Y_h) - V^h(c_1, Y_1)] + \alpha[(Y_1 - c_1)N_1 + (Y_h - c_h)N_h - R_0]\end{aligned} \tag{14.55}$$

where $\mu, \lambda_l, \lambda_h$ and α are Lagrange multipliers. First-order conditions for an internal optimum are:

$$(\partial\Lambda/\partial c_l) = (\partial V^l/\partial c_l + \lambda_l(\partial V^l/\partial c_l) - \lambda_h(\partial V^h/\partial c_l) - \alpha N_l = 0 \qquad (14.56a)$$

$$(\partial\Lambda/\partial c_h) = \mu(\partial V^h/\partial c_h) - \lambda_l(\partial V^l/\partial c_h) + \lambda_h(\partial V^h/\partial c_h) - \alpha N_h = 0 \qquad (14.56b)$$

$$(\partial\Lambda/\partial Y_l) = (\partial V^l/\partial Y_l) + \lambda_l(\partial V^l/\partial Y_l) - \lambda_h(\partial V^h/\partial Y_l) + \alpha N_l = 0 \qquad (14.56c)$$

$$\begin{aligned}(\partial\Lambda/\partial Y_h) = \mu(\partial V^h/\partial Y_h) - \lambda_l(\partial V^l/\partial Y_h) + \lambda_h(\partial V^h/\partial Y_h) \\ + \alpha N_h = 0.\end{aligned} \qquad (14.56d)$$

These first-order conditions assume that both λ_h and λ_l are strictly positive. In general one or both of the λs may be zero. Let us first consider the case where both λs are zero and study the utilitarian case where $\mu = 1$. This is the case of the **pooling equilibrium** where it is not necessary to distinguish between the two groups of people. From equations (14.56) the *mrs* is then:

$$(\partial c_i/\partial Y_i)|_{\bar{V}} = -(\partial V^i/\partial Y_i)/(\partial V^i/\partial c_i) = 1. \qquad (14.57)$$

This is a result we already know and is depicted in Figure 14.4a.

Let us take the **separating equilibrium** cases now. If $\lambda_l = 0$ then the self-selection constraint on individual of type 1 is binding whereas it is not

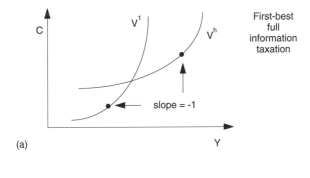

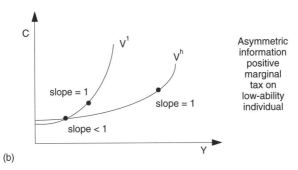

Figure 14.4

binding for workers of type h. Then, from equations (14.56b) and (14.56d) we will have the *mrs* for type *h* as:

$$(\partial c_1/\partial Y_1)|_{\bar{V}1} = \alpha N_h/\alpha N_h = 1.$$

Hence people of type *h* face a zero marginal tax rate. For people of type 1 from equations (14.56a) and (14.56c) we have the *mrs* as:

$$(\partial c_1/\partial Y_1)|_{V-1} = -[\lambda_h(\partial V^h/\partial Y_1) - \alpha N_l]/[\lambda_h(\partial V^h/\partial c_1) + \alpha N_l] < 1 \quad (14.57a)$$

so that people of type 1 face a non-zero marginal tax rate. This is shown in Figure 14.4b. To see this analytically define:

$$\rho^i = -(\partial V^i/\partial Y_1)/(\partial V^i/\partial c_1); \text{ and}$$

$$\delta = \lambda_h(\partial V^h/\partial c_1)/(\alpha N_l).$$

Hence, equation (14.57a) can be written as

$$\rho^l = (1 + \delta\gamma^h)/(1 + \delta) = \alpha^h + (1 - \alpha^h)/(1 + \delta)$$

since $\rho^l > \rho^h$ it follows that $1 > \alpha^l > \alpha^h$.

In an exactly analogous manner it can be shown that if $\lambda_h = 0$ and $\lambda_l > 0$ then the workers of type h will face a non-zero marginal tax rate whereas workers of type l will face a zero marginal tax rate. This is sometimes referred to as the 'normal' case. The high-ability person is strictly better off in his own shoes than mimicking the behavior of the low-ability worker. In this case the marginal tax rate on the high-ability person should be zero. Further, it is easy to show that both λ_h and λ_l cannot be non-zero at the same time.

In the discussion above we have been speaking in terms of a marginal tax rate whereas we have actually been choosing consumption and income. We still have to demonstrate the properties of the optimal tax schedule formally.

If the tax schedule was differentiable, and we have no reason to suppose it is, then we have:

$$T_i = T(Y_i) \text{ and, therefore, } c_i - Y_i - T(Y_i).$$

Now, the individual's first order-condition can be written as:

$$-(\partial V^i/\partial Y_i)/(\partial V^i/\partial c_i) = 1 - T'. \quad (14.58)$$

The lefthand side is the *mrs* and the righthand side is the marginal return to working an extra hour. Although the tax function need not be differentiable we can refer to:

$$1 + (\partial V^i/\partial Y_i)/(\partial V^i/\partial c_i) = 1 + (\partial U^i/\partial L_i)/[w_i(\partial U^i/\partial c_i)] \quad (14.59)$$

as the marginal tax rate. The interpretation of the *mrs* in terms of the marginal tax rates then follows.

It is instructive to visualize the case where persons of high ability face a zero marginal tax rate as in Figure 14.5. The 45-degree ray through the origin is the no-tax line so that the vertical distance between this ray and

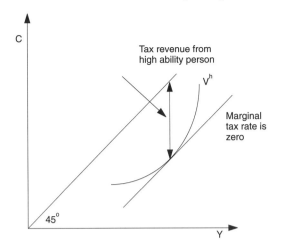

Figure 14.5

any consumer's indifference curve is an indicator of the tax collected from this individual at the margin. So far as the more able individual is concerned, he has self-selected himself into the 'right' category. Hence, society should try to extract as much revenue as possible from this person, at the margin. This will happen when the vertical distance between this individual's optimum and the 45-degree ray is at its maximum, which will be the case when the slope of this individual's indifference curve, at optimum, is the same as that of 45-degree ray. In other words, the slope is 1 and the marginal tax rate on this individual is zero.

Stiglitz then goes on to extend this model to cover a continuous distribution of abilities as in the Mirrlees model. This is sketched out in the Appendix to this chapter. The principal conclusions are as follows:

(i) The marginal tax rate is lower the larger the fraction of the population, ϕ, at a particular income level that pays that marginal tax rate. The tax should not impose large distortions where there are many people.
(ii) The marginal tax rate is lower, the lower is $\theta(w)$, the shadow price of the self-selection constraint. It is zero at both ends of the ability distribution.
(iii) The marginal tax rate is lower, ceteris paribus, the higher the productivity of the group.
(iv) The marginal tax rate is lower, the higher is labor supply response.

14.5 OPTIMAL TAXATION WITH IMPERFECT SUBSTITUTION OF LABOR

An important characteristic of the Mirrlees–Stiglitz framework is that different types of labor are perfect substitutes for each other. If you have enough masons you can replace a brain surgeon.

Clearly, a relevant extension would be to consider the case where no matter how many masons you get you cannot replace a brain surgeon. The elasticity of substitution between different types of labor is finite. This case was considered by Allen (1982).

We assume that there are two types of labor: high ability, h, and low ability, l, labor. But each type of labor is necessary in the production process. Production is given by the standard neoclassical production function:

$$Q = F(N_h L_h, N_l L_l) = L_l N_l f(n) \tag{14.60}$$

where $n \equiv L_h N_h / (L_l N_l)$. $N_i L_i$ is total labor supply by labor of type i and we write the last term on the righthand side of equation (14.60) because we assume constant returns to scale for the production function $F(.)$.

Both types of labor are available in competitive factor markets where they each get their marginal products. Thus:

$$w_h = \partial F / \partial (N_h L_h) = f'(n) \tag{14.61}$$

and

$$w_l = \partial F / \partial (N_l L_l) = f(n) - n f'(n) \equiv g(n). \tag{14.62}$$

We now conduct the same Pareto optimizing exercise. We maximize the utility of a representative worker of type *h*, given the utility of type l workers. This will be subject to three constraints:

(i) There will be a revenue requirement constraint where output less consumption will be set equal to the exogenous revenue requirement R_0.
(ii) There will be a self-selection constraint on type h workers so that they do not find it necessary to mimic the behavior of type l workers.
(iii) There will be a constraint on the wage for the l type workers.

Clearly we could have chosen a different self-selection constraint but the example we are studying here will suffice for illustrative purposes.

Realize that upon substituting for L_i we will get:

$$n = N_h L_h / N_l L_l = N_h Y_h w_l / (N_l Y_l w_h).$$

The Lagrangean for this problem can be written as:

$$\begin{aligned} \Lambda = &V^h + \sigma_1 V^l + \sigma_2 [F(N_l Y_l / w_l, N_h Y_h / w_h) - c_l N_l - c_h N_h - R_0] \\ &+ \sigma_3 [V^h(c_h, Y_h; w_h) - V^h(c_l, Y_l; w_h)] + \sigma_4 [w_l - g(n)] \end{aligned} \tag{14.63}$$

where the σ_is are Lagrange multipliers.

Differentiation yields:

$$(\partial \Lambda / \partial c_h) = (\partial V^h / \partial c_h) - \sigma_2 N_h + \sigma_3 (\partial V^h / \partial c_h) = 0 \tag{14.64a}$$

$$\begin{aligned} (\partial \Lambda / \partial Y_h) = &(\partial V^h / \partial Y^h) + \sigma_2 F_2 (N_h / w_h) + \sigma_3 (\partial V^h / \partial Y_h) \\ &- \sigma_4 g' N_h w_l / (w_h Y_l N_l) = 0 \end{aligned} \tag{14.64b}$$

where F_2 is the marginal product of type h labor. Under competitive conditions this is equal to the wage rate. Hence the second term on the righthand side of equation (14.64b) is simply $\sigma_2 N_h$. Now, let us examine the last term on the righthand side of equation (14.64b). We realize that $(N_h w_l/(w_h Y_l N_l)) = n/Y_h$. Hence, we can write equation (14.64b) as:

$$(\partial \Lambda/\partial Y_h) = (\partial V^h/\partial Y_h) + \sigma_2 N_h - \sigma_4 g'n/Y_h = 0. \tag{14.64b}$$

Dividing equation (14.64b) by (14.64a) we will have:

$$-(\partial V^h/\partial Y_h)/(\partial V^h/\partial c_h) = 1 - \sigma_4 g'n/(Y_h N_h \sigma_2). \tag{14.65}$$

Now, if $f'' = 0$ the last term on the righthand side of equation (14.65) will be zero and the more able person will face a zero marginal tax rate – just as in the Mirrlees model. But $f'' = 0$ corresponds to infinite elasticity of substitution between the two types of labor, which is precisely the point that Allen is making. If $f'' < 0$, as is usually the case, then the more productive individual should work beyond the point where the slope of his indifference curve in $\{c, y\}$ space is unity. In other words, he should face a negative marginal tax rate.

The intuition behind this result is quite straightforward. Since each type of worker is indispensable and, in this example, the self-selection constraint is relevant for type *h* persons, it pays society to induce workers of this type to work more than they would with a zero marginal tax rate. Hence, we have the negative marginal tax rate.

14.6 OPTIMAL WAGE AND INTEREST INCOME TAXATION IN STEADY STATE

An important limitation of the analysis above is that it is static in nature. This is evident both from the atemporal nature of the optimal tax problem as well as from the (implicit) specification of the production function in terms of labor only so that all questions of capital accumulation and the effects of the tax structure on it can be ignored. It is now time to confront this question.

When we move to the question of taxation in intertemporal economies we realize that the problem can be set up in two broad ways. First, we can study the problem of optimal taxation in the steady state of a dynamic economy. The second is to study this problem without reference to any steady state. Clearly, the former method is simpler to work with and we begin with that.

We work with the life-cycle model with which we are familiar and focus on the pathbreaking work of Ordover and Phelps (1979) in this regard. Another reference is Sandmo (1980). At any point in time two generations are alive: the 'young' and the 'old'. Each generation lives for two time periods. In the first period it works and saves and in the second period it is retired and consumes its savings. There are two goods in the model. One good is labor (or leisure) and the other is produced with the help of capital and labor. Capital, itself, is indistinguishable from this commodity. The production function for this commodity is of the constant returns to scale variety. Each consumer has a utility function defined over consumption in both time periods and (first period) leisure. Labor in each period is heterogeneous in the Mirrlees sense and the distribution of abilities stays stable from one time period to the next. In each time period, the social planner imposes a (possibly non-linear) tax on wage and interest income in order to finance exogenous government expenditure. Since this is an intertemporal model it is entirely possible to issue debt.

Let us look at this problem from the vantage point of generation j. Apart from the taxation of savings and wage income, the social planner has two other policy tools available. Each person gets a demogrant G_j when young and H_j when retired. L^m is, as before, the labor supply of a person with ability m. Once again, units are chosen so that the wage of a standard $m = 1$ type of labor is simply 1 so that the earnings, or effective labor supply, of a person with ability m is mL^m. An individual of ability m solves the following optimization problem:

$$\max U(c_1^m, c_2^m, L^m) \tag{14.66a}$$

subject to

$$mL^m + G_j + H_j/F_K - c_1^m - c_2^m/F_K - T_L(mL^m) - T_s(c_2^m - H_j) = S^m \geqslant 0. \tag{14.66b}$$

The budget constraint in equation (14.66b) needs a little explanation. mL^m is wage income and G_j are first period demogrants. H_j are second-period demogrants which have to be discounted back (at the marginal product of capital F_K) to make them comparable with first-period earnings. c_1^m is first-period consumption and c_2^m is second-period consumption which has to be discounted to make it comparable with first-period consumption. $T_L(.)$ is the wage tax schedule and $T_S(.)$ the savings tax schedule. For the sake of simplicity it is assumed that each household has to prepay its savings taxes so that these do not have to be discounted. S^m is net savings which, in the absence of a bequest motive, must equal zero in optimum.

Write down the Lagrangean for this problem as:

$$\Lambda = U(.) + \mu[mL^m + G_j + H_j/F_K - c_1^m - c_2^m/F_K - T_L(.) - T_s(.)] \tag{14.67}$$

where μ is a Lagrange multiplier. We can write the first-order conditions as:

$$(\partial U/\partial c_1^m) - \mu = 0 \tag{14.68a}$$

$$(\partial U/\partial c_2^m) + \mu[-(1/F_K) - T_s'] = 0 \tag{14.68b}$$

$$(\partial U/\partial L^m) + \mu(m - T_L'm) = 0 \tag{14.68c}$$

$$\partial \Lambda/\partial \mu = 0 \tag{14.68d}$$

It is clear from these first-order conditions that the maximized utility of a person with ability m can be written as:

$$V^*(m) = \max U(mL^m + G_j + (H_j - c_2^m)/F_K - T_L(.) - T_S(.); c_2^m, L^m).$$
$$(14.69)$$

In a manner completely analogous to the Mirrlees model (equation (14.32)) we can write the envelope condition:

$$dV(m)/dm = -(\partial U/\partial L^m)mL^m/m^2 \geqslant 0 \qquad (14.70)$$

and we can invert equation (14.69) to get (as a straightforward generalization of the Mirrlees model):

$$c_1^m = Z(V^*(m), c_2^m, L^m). \qquad (14.71)$$

These are the utility envelope conditions to be satisfied by the government of generation j. We could impose a revenue requirement condition for this government of generation j and solve for optimal taxes as do Ordover and Phelps (1979). However, it makes more sense to think of generation j inheriting the debts of the government of generation $(j-1)$, borrowing some and passing on debt to the government of generation $(j+1)$.

The full problem of intra-and inter-generational justice can be looked upon as a two-step exercise. In the first step, each generation solves its own problem of intra-generational justice according to some well-specified norm of justice, for example, the utilitarian or Rawlsian criterion. In the next step, these plans are coordinated and amended to make them conform to society's notion of intergenerational justice.

The government of generation j maximizes the following social welfare function:

$$W^j = \int_{m_1}^{m_h} W^j[U(c_{1'j'}^m, c_{2'j}^m, L_j^m)]d\Phi(m) \qquad (14.72)$$

where $c_{1'j}^m$ is first-period consumption of an m ability person of generation j, etc.

Ordover and Phelps place the following intergenerational restrictions on the maximization of this welfare function. First, there is the question of inter-generational trust. The government of generation j must meet the second-period consumption expectations of the old of generation $(j-1)$. In other words if, as part of their own maximization plans, generation $(j-1)$ gave themselves second-period consumption amounting to $c_2, (j-1)$ then the government of generation j is ethically bound to supply them with this much consumption.

Moreover, the future path of capital and second-period consumption is predetermined, i.e., $K_{j+i}, c_{2, j+i}(i = 1, 2, \ldots)$ is a datum. Why is this justified? Take $c_{2, j+1}$ first. The current generation can always increase its utility by leaving less for future generations' second-period consumption. Inter-generational justice requires that the government of generation j should not be allowed to do so. This would also, of course, imply that the capital stocks for future generations are also predetermined. Thus generation j can choose its capital stock K_j, its second-period consumption $c_{1,j}$ and its labor supply L_j. Maximized utility (V^*) is a state variable and $c_{1,j}$ is a function of V^*. However, notice that since K_{j+i} and $c_{2,j+i}$ $(i = 1, 2, \ldots)$ are given it follows that L_{j+i} is already predetermined. Given the capital stock for any generation and consumption obligations, the labor required to produce this is also predetermined if the labor supply of generation 1 is known. Thus we need to concentrate on the optimal tax program of generation 1 only.

For generation 1, $c_{2'1}^m$ and L_1^m are control variables, V^* is a state variable and $c_{1'1}^m$ is a function of V^* from equation (14.71). Apart from the differential equation (14.70) two other constraints exist for generation 1. First, the second-period consumption expectations of the old of generation 0 must be met. In other words, the second-period consumption of generation 1 cannot be larger than some upper limit $\bar{c}_{2,1}$. Thus we must have:

$$\bar{c}_{2,1} - \int_{m_l}^{m_h} c_{2,1}^m d\Phi(m) \geqslant 0. \tag{14.73}$$

Further, generation 1 must leave a certain minimum capital stock for the young of the next generation:

$$F(K_0, L_1) - \int_{m_l}^{m_h} c_1^m d\Phi(m) - c_{2,0} \geqslant \bar{K}_1. \tag{14.74}$$

$F(K_0, L_1)$ is output produced by the young of generation 1 with its own labor and capital stock inherited from generation 0. The second term on the lefthand side of relation (14.74) is the first-period consumption of generation 1 and the third term is the second-period consumption of the old of generation 0. Thus the lefthand side of relation (14.74) is the saving of the young of generation 1 which will be available as capital stock to the young of the next generation. This must be at least as large as some minimum $\bar{K}_1$.

The Hamilton–Lagrange expression for generation 1 can now be written as:

$$H(m) = V^*(m)d\Phi(m) + \gamma_1[\bar{c}_{2,1} - \int_{m_l}^{m_h} c_{2,1}^m d\Phi(m)]$$

$$+ \gamma_2[-\bar{K}_1 + F(K_0, L_1) - c_{2,0} - \int_{m_l}^{m_h} c_1^m d\Phi(m)] + \theta(m)[-(\partial U/\partial L_m)L_m/m^2]$$

$$\tag{14.75}$$

where γ_1 and γ_2 are Lagrange multipliers for the two inter-generational constraints and θ is, as before, the costate variable on the self-selection constraint. The γs are independent of m whereas θ is a function of m. So far as wage taxation is concerned all the results of the Mirrlees model will hold. Let us now look at interest income taxation.

If $W_1^*(\bar{K}_1, \bar{c}_{2,1})$ is the maximum welfare that generation 1 can attain, given its target $(\bar{K}_1, \bar{c}_{2,1})$ it would follow that:

$$\partial W_1^*/\partial \bar{K}_1 = -\gamma_2 \text{ and } \partial W_1^*/\partial \bar{c}_{2,1} = \gamma_1.$$

Moreover, if we have an internal maximum then both γ_1 as well as γ_2 will be negative. Now, totally differentiate the W_1^* function and write the marginal rate of substitution between capital and second-period consumption as:

$$d\bar{K}_1/d\bar{c}_{2,1} = -(\partial W_1^*/\partial \bar{c}_{2,1})/(\partial W_1^*/\partial \bar{K}_1) = \gamma_1/\gamma_2 > 0. \qquad (14.76)$$

This relation makes sense because it says that if the young of current generation is to leave behind more capital stock for the next generation then it will need to be compensated for that with higher second-period consumption.

Generation 2 inherits K_1 from generation 1 which it (generation 2) can invest at the going rate of interest. Thus, along a contour where W_2^* is constant we must have:

$$(dK_1/dc_{2,1}) = 1/[F_K(K_1, L_2(K_1, c_{2,1}))] \qquad (14.77)$$

where $L_2(.)$ is the predetermined amount of labor supply of generation 2. Equation (14.77) is the *mrs* between K_1 and $c_{2'1}$ for generation 2 and it is implicitly being assumed that capital markets are perfect.

If there is Pareto optimality across generations then the *mrs* between successive generations must be the same. It should be pointed out that Pareto optimality is a requirement in addition to those in equations (14.73) and (14.74) and is not a natural ethical requirement in the same sense that these are. With Pareto optimality, then:

$$\gamma_1/\gamma_2 = 1/[F_K(K_1, L_2(.))] \text{ or } \gamma_1 = \gamma_2/[F_K(K_1, L_2(.))]. \qquad (14.78)$$

Also define r_1^* and $\triangle_1^*$ by:

$$(1 + r_1^*) = F_K(K_1^*, L_2(K_1^*, c_{2,1}^*)) \qquad (14.79)$$

$$\triangle_1^* = (1 + r_1^*)^{-1} c_{2,1}^* - K_1^* \qquad (14.80)$$

where the stars (*) refer to optimal values. Thus equation (14.79) defines the relationship between the rate of interest and the marginal product of capital. Equation (14.80) states that the discounted value of second-period consumption for the old of generation 1 must equal the sum of the capital stock and the face value of the debt ($\triangle$).

Substitute equations (14.79) and (14.80) into the Hamiltonian (equation (14.75)) and use equation (14.78) to rewrite the Hamiltonian for generation 1 as:

$$H_1(m) = V^*(m)d\Phi(m) + \gamma_2[\triangle_1^* - (1 + r_1^*)^{-1}c_{2,1}^m + F(K_0, L_1) - c_1^m \\ - c_{2,0}^m]d\Phi(m) + \theta(m)[-(\partial U/\partial L^m)L^m/m^2]. \qquad (14.81)$$

Differentiating with respect to $c_{2,1}$ we get:

$$(\partial H_1(m)/\partial c_{2,1}) = \gamma_2[-(1 + r_1^*)^{-1} - (\partial c_1^m/\partial c_{2,1}^m)|_{V^*(m)}]d\Phi(m) \\ + \theta(m)(\partial/\partial c_{2,1}^m)\{-(\partial U/\partial L^m)L^m/m^2\} = 0. \qquad (14.82)$$

In practice nothing much can be said about equation (14.82) except at the end points of the ability distribution where, we know, $\theta = 0$. At these end points then:

$$(1 + r_1^*)^{-1} = -(\partial c_1^m / \partial c_{2,1}^m)|_{V^*(m)}. \tag{14.83}$$

Invoking equation (14.79) this implies that the *mrs* between c_1^m and $c_{2,1}^m$ is the same as the mrt. In other words, the marginal tax rate on interest income is zero.

This result is quite important and needs to be put into perspective. First, for a general utility function, the marginal tax rate on savings is zero only at the end points of the ability distribution. Second, Atkinson and Stiglitz (1976) argue that if the utility function is weakly separable in consumption and leisure then the optimal tax rate on savings is **always zero irrespective of the level of ability**. This can be quite easily shown. In equation (14.82), if the utility function is separable then the last term (within braces $\{.\}$) is zero and equation (14.83) will hold. Ordover and Phelps make it clear that for this to hold we need Pareto optimality across generations. Without this requirement, the Atkinson and Stiglitz result does not hold. Jha (1978) reported numerical solutions in favor of this argument.

14.7   THE OPTIMAL MIX OF DIRECT AND INDIRECT TAXES

The result of Atkinson and Stiglitz (1976) discussed above purports to be a general one. Notwithstanding our clarifying the limitations of this argument, there does appear to be a general feeling that when an income tax is available then commodity tax rates are appropriately set equal to zero. To quote from Stiglitz (1987b):

> It can be shown, that if one has a well-designed income tax, adding differential commodity taxation is likely to add little, if anything.
>
> (Stiglitz 1989: 494)

This result is, of course, predicated on the assumption of a utility function that is separable between consumption and leisure. Because of this separability, high- and low-ability individuals have (locally) the same indifference curves between any two ordinary goods (except leisure). This would imply that commodity taxes cannot be used to make the low-ability individual's appealing to the high-ability individual's position less appealing to the higher ability individual than his own. Does this mean that there is no role for commodity taxes in a program of optimal taxation?

This issue was considered in recent papers by Boadway *et al.* (1994) and Cremer and Gahvari (1995). They show that the Atkinson–Stiglitz argument holds only under the special case where there is no uncertainty. When there is uncertainty there is a well-defined role for commodity taxation. Let us examine the analysis of Cremer and Gahvari.

The economy they consider is populated by homogeneous individuals – in order to keep the analysis simple. The economy is subject to shocks which affect the productivity of labor. With a favorable shock the competitive wage rate is w_h and with an adverse shock the wage is w_l where $w_h > w_l$. The (known) probability of a favorable shock is π_h and that of an unfavorable shock $\pi_l = (1 - \pi_h)$. The social planner cannot observe these shocks and, therefore, does not know the post-uncertainty wage or labor supply. He has to design a tax structure which is Pareto efficient which, of course, also requires that there is no incentive for workers to pretend that they have had a low wage realization when, in reality, w_h has been realized. The other self-selection constraint would be less relevant, as before.

The consumer's preferences are given by the following utility function:

$$U = u(b_1, b_2, a_1, a_2) + \alpha(1 - L). \tag{14.84}$$

This individual is assumed to be risk averse. The producer prices of all 'ordinary' goods (a_1, a_2, b_1, b_2) are each set equal to 1 and the amount of time at the worker's disposal is normalized to equal unity. The demand for goods b_1, b_2 have to be precommitted before the resolution of uncertainty whereas the demand for good a_1 and a_2 are determined after the resolution of uncertainty.

Let us now define:

(i) total income $Z = wL$
(ii) $v^i = \alpha(1 - Z/w_i)$ $\quad i = 1, h$
(iii) $u^i = u(b_1, b_2, a_{1i}, a_{2i})$ $\quad i = 1, h.$

The optimal tax mix

Along familiar lines we can define the optimal tax problem as one of maxmizing expected utility subject to the self-selection constraint so that when the high wage is realized there is every incentive to reveal this fact and an exogenous revenue requirement of R_0.

The Lagrangean for this problem can be written as:

$$\Lambda = \pi_l[u^l + v^l(Z_l)] + \pi_h[u^h + v^h(Z_h)] + \mu_1[u^h - v^h(Z_h) - u^l - v^h(Z_l)]$$
$$+ \mu_2[\pi_l(Z_l - a_{1l} - a_{2l}) + \pi_h(Z_h - a_{1h} - a_{2h}) - b_1 - b_2 - R_0]. \tag{14.85}$$

The following first-order conditions can be derived:

$$(\partial\Lambda/\partial b_i) = \pi_l(\partial u^l/\partial b_i) + \pi_h(\partial u^h/\partial b_i) + \mu_1[(\partial u^h/\partial b_i)$$
$$- (\partial u^l/\partial b_i)] - \mu_2 = 0 \quad (i = 1, 2) \tag{14.86a}$$

$$(\partial\Lambda/\partial a_{il}) = \pi_l(\partial u^l/\partial a_{il}) - \mu_1(\partial u^l/\partial a_{il}) - \mu_2\pi_l = 0 \ (i = 1, 2) \tag{14.86b}$$

$$(\partial\Lambda/\partial a_{ih}) = \pi_h(\partial u^h/\partial a_{ih}) + \mu_1(\partial u^h/\partial a_{ih}) - \mu_2\pi_h = 0 \ (i = 1, 2) \tag{14.86c}$$

$$(\partial \Lambda / \partial Z_1) = \pi_1(\partial v^1 / \partial Z_1) - \mu_1(\partial v^1 / \partial Z_1) + \mu_2 \pi_1 = 0 \qquad (14.86d)$$

$$(\partial \Lambda / \partial Z_h) = \pi_h(\partial v^h / \partial Z_h) - \mu_1(\partial v^h / \partial Z_h) + \mu_2 \pi_h = 0. \qquad (14.86e)$$

We now introduce taxation into the picture. Specific taxes on a_is and b_is are, respectively, t_i and τ_i so that consumer prices are $p_i = 1 + t_i$ and $q_i = 1 + \tau_i$. The income tax is represented by the usual function: $T = T(Z)$.

The individual consumer wishes to maximize expected utility (the maximand of the Lagragean in equation (14.85)) subject to the following budget constraint:

$$Z_j - T(Z_j) = \sum_{i=1}^{2} (q_i b_i + p_i a_{ij}), j = 1, h. \qquad (14.87)$$

From the first order conditions for utility maximization in view of equation (14.86) one can write:

(i) In either state, the *mrs* between the goods not precommitted must equal the relative price ratio:

$$(\partial u^1 / \partial a_{11}) / (\partial u^1 / \partial a_{21}) = (\partial u^h / \partial a_{1h}) / (\partial u^h / \partial a_{2h}) = p_1 / p_2. \qquad (14.88a)$$

(ii) The 'expected value' of the *mrs* between the committed goods must equal their relative price ratio:

$$[\pi_1(\partial u^1 / \partial b_1) + \pi_h(\partial u^h / \partial b_1)] / [\pi_1(\partial u^1 / \partial b_2) + \pi_h(\partial u^h / \partial b_2)] = q_1 / q_2. \qquad (14.88b)$$

(iii) The 'expected value' of the *mrs* between committed and non-committed goods must equal the respective relative price:

$$[\pi_1(\partial u^1 / \partial b_i) + \pi_h(\partial u^h / \partial b_i)] / [\pi_1(\partial u^1 / \partial a_{j1}) \\ + \pi_h(\partial u^h / \partial a_{jh})] = q_i / p_j \quad (i, j = 1, 2). \qquad (14.88c)$$

(iv) The *mrs* between leisure and the goods which are not precommitted must equal the relative price:

$$-(\partial v^j / \partial Z_j) / (\partial u^j / \partial a_{ij}) = [1 - T'(Z_j)] / p_i \ (i = 1, 2; j = 1, h). \qquad (14.88d)$$

As before the income tax function $T(.)$ may not be differentiable. However, it is assumed that the tax function is differentiable and write the marginal income tax rate as:

$T' = 1 + p_i(\partial v^j / \partial Z_j) / (\partial u^j / \partial a_{ij}); j = 1,$ h as the marginal tax rate in state j.

Equations (14.86) and (14.88) lead to the following results.

Result 1

In the presence of uncertainty, commodity taxation is essential. Furthermore, the a_is should be taxed differently from the b_is. In particular, the a_is should either go tax free or be subject to a uniform tax whereas the b_is must be taxed and not necessarily at a uniform rate.

Result 2

If the u function is strictly separable between a and b it then follows that the optimal tax rate on the precommitted goods should be smaller than the optimal tax rate on the non-precommitted goods.

Result 3

When the high wage rate is realized the marginal income tax rate is zero but a tax (positive or negative) is imposed on his consumption of precommitted goods.

Result 4

In the low-income state the marginal income tax rate is positive.

14.8 CONCLUSIONS

In this chapter we have examined several aspects of income taxation. The first order of business was to tackle the problem of optimal income taxation when there is imperfect information about the incomes of workers. We considered both optimal linear and non-linear taxation when the elasticity of substitution between different types of workers is infinite. An important result in the non-linear tax case was that, irrespective of the form of the social welfare function chosen, the marginal tax on the upper and lower ends of the ability distribution should be zero. We also considered the case where there is less than perfect substitution possibility between different types of workers. The optimal mix of wage and interest taxation for intra- as well as inter-generational justice was also examined.

These results have two important characteristics. First, with a proper income tax in place there does not seem to be much of a role for commodity taxation. Second, only a few analytical results can be drawn. Most results have to be numerically ascertained.

However, we were able to establish that the first result here is applicable only when we have full certainty. Recent results indicate that with uncertainty a mix of direct and indirect taxes, rather than direct taxes alone, is called for.

ADDITIONAL READING

The following additional texts may be of interest to students: McLure and Thirsk (1975), Ballentine (1980), and Poterba (1992).

APPENDIX

In this appendix we trace out the version of the Stiglitz model which assumes that there exists a distribution of abilities instead of just two ability levels. The formal model is very similar to that of Mirrlees, so that we can be brief. The wage rate is taken as an index of productivity. Wage rates are not observed but the distribution function $\Phi(w)$ of people over wages is common knowledge. Instead of Mirrlees' m, we have Stiglitz's w.

The problem of the government is to maximize the following social welfare function:

$$\int W[U(c(w), Y(w))]d\Phi(w) \qquad (A14.1)$$

subject to the constraint of a revenue requirement which, without loss of generality, can be set equal to zero. This constraint can be written as:

$$\int [c(w) - Y(w)]d\Phi(w) = 0. \qquad (A14.2)$$

The self-selection constraint is the exact parallel of that in the Mirrlees' model (equation 14.32):

$$dU/dw = -U_L y/w^2. \qquad (A14.3)$$

Defining $\phi(w)$ as the density function $d\Phi/dw = \phi(w)$ we can write the Hamiltonian for this problem as:

$$H = [W(U) - \beta(c - Y)]\phi(w) - \theta(dU/dw). \qquad (A14.4)$$

We let U be the state variable and $L(w)$ be the control variable for this problem. Knowing L and U determines $Y(w) = wL(w)$ and $c(w)$ from the equation $U(w) = U[c(w), L(w)]$.

Differentiating H with respective to L we have:

$$(\partial H/\partial L) = \beta[w - (dc/dL)|_{\bar{U}}]\phi(w) + \theta\epsilon^* U_L/w = 0 \qquad (A14.5)$$

where $\epsilon^* = (\partial \ln(dU/dw))/(\partial \ln L)$ and $(dc/dL)|_{\bar{U}} = -U_L/U_c$. Using the same methods as in the Mirrlees model we derive the marginal tax rate as:

$$T'/(1 - T') = U_c\theta(w)\epsilon^*/(\beta\phi(w)) \qquad (A14.6)$$

from which follow the conclusions mentioned in the text of Chapter 14.

15 Topics in the theory of taxation

Key concepts: exogenous and endogenous growth; bracket creep; income tax indexation; Ramsey criterion; time-consistent policy; commitment; tax compliance; underground economy and tax evasion; borrowing constraint and tax compliance.

15.1 INTRODUCTION

In the previous few chapters we have worked on various aspects of optimal commodity and income taxation. In this chapter we want to consider four additional topics in the theory of optimal taxation which have been discussed recently in the literature. We begin with a study of tax policy in a stylized model of endogenous growth. We then consider the problem of income tax indexation in an inflationary economy. We examine the problem of time inconsistency in the context of dynamic tax models. Finally we study a recent model of tax compliance. We should be clear, however, that each of the topics mentioned is a significant area of research in its own right and the exposition here is not meant to be a survey. Our aim is to highlight some important issues that have come up during the course of research in these areas.

15.2 TAXATION IN MODELS OF ENDOGENOUS GROWTH

We have studied tax analysis in dynamic economies in Chapter 12. The growth model studied there has been described as an **exogenous** growth model because the sources of growth can be traced to the accumulation of exogenous factors of production such as capital and labor. In recent years, emphasis has been placed on models of endogenous growth where the source of growth can be traced to the accumulation of human capital. Hence, the amount of resources devoted to education, research and development and the like becomes a crucial determinant of the rate of economic growth. Good expositions of the endogenous growth model can be found in Lucas (1988) and Romer (1990). Tax implications of the endogenous growth model have been discussed in Rebelo (1991), Barro and Sala-I-Martin (1992), Jones *et al.* (1993), Gruner and Heer (1994) and Xu (1994).

In this section we will study a simplified version of the tax with endogenous growth model.[1] The concern here is to examine within the context of the endogenous growth model the impact of taxation on the decisions of the private sector, the size of government, the capital–labor ratio and balanced growth. Two taxes are studied here – an income tax and an inheritance tax.

An important ingredient of the endogenous models of economic growth has been the development of aggregate relations from microeconomic foundations. Consider an individual who lives for one time period but is perfectly altruistic towards his progeny. Each of his descendants behaves in exactly the same way. Hence, the representative individual can be approximated by an infinitely lived agent even though each individual actually lives only one time period. During his lifetime an individual allocates time between work, human capital accumulation and leisure. Growth is generated by human capital accumulation. The government collects taxes to finance a public good. Since inheritances are taxed there is a disincentive to accumulate and leave behind physical capital. By the same token, there is an incentive to accumulate human capital and leave behind human capital as bequests.

The tax rate on inheritance is ϕ. Total time available is J which is allocated between leisure, l_t, education h_t, and work, L_t. Human capital (H_t) accumulation takes place according to the production function:

$$H_t = H(h_t, H_{t-1}) = \alpha h_t H_{t-1} + H_{t-1}. \qquad (15.1)$$

This specification is originally due to Lucas (1990) and suggests that human capital during any time period t is equal to past period human capital (H_{t-1}) and on current allocations of time to human capital accumulation. It is assumed that $\alpha > 0$. Hence, the larger the amount of time allocated to human capital accumulation, the greater is the generation of human capital. Furthermore, the base from which human capital grows (H_{t-1}) is also positively associated with current human capital accumulation.

The individual's labor supply is measured in efficiency units: $H_t L_t$. This person receives a wage (w_t) which is the return to the efficiency labor.[2] Moreover, the individual earns interest income from his stock of physical capital.

This representative individual derives utility from consumption and leisure. Instantaneous utility can be written as:

$$u_t = \Phi_1 \ln c_t + \Phi_2 \ln (J - L_t - h_t). \qquad (15.2)$$

Consider now an individual at time 0. Since he is perfectly altruistic toward his descendants the utility that he maximizes can be written as:

$$U = \sum_{t=0}^{\infty} u_t \delta^t \qquad (15.3)$$

where $1 > \delta > 0$ is the discount factor.

The maximization problem discussed above is subject to two constraints: a time constraint and a flow budget constraint. The time constraint can be written as:

$$J = l_t + L_t + h_t \tag{15.4}$$

The flow budget constraint can be written as:

$$c_t + K_{t+1}/(1 - \phi) = (1 - t_y)w_t L_t H_t + [1 + (1 - t_y)r_t]K_t. \tag{15.5}$$

The first term on the lefthand side is consumption by this consumer. He will leave behind physical capital stock K_{t+1} which will be taxed at the rate ϕ. This explains the lefthand side (the expenditure side) of this budget. On the righthand side we have current earnings which consist of wage income (the first term) and interest income (the second term) with r_t being the contemporaneous interest rate and t_y is the income tax rate. The maximization of the utility function subject to the constraints is done by choosing h_t, L_t, H_t and K_{t+1}.

By repeated substitution the Lagrangean for this problem can be written as:

$$
\begin{aligned}
U/\delta^t = \ldots &+ \mu_1 \ln\{(1 - \phi)w_t H_t L_t + [1 + (1 - t_y)r_t]K_t - (K_{t+1}/(1 - t_y))\} \\
&+ \mu_2 \ln(J - L_t - h_t) + \mu_1 \delta \ln\{(1 - t_y)w_{t+1}H_{t+1}L_{t+1} \\
&+ [1 + (1 - t_y)r_{t+1}]K_{t+1} - K_{t+2}/(1 - \phi)\} + \mu_2 \delta \ln(J - L_{t+1} - h_{t+1}) \\
&+ \ldots + \lambda_t(H_t - \alpha h_t H_{t-1}) + \lambda_{t+1}(H_{t+1} - \alpha h_{t+1}H_t - H_t) + \ldots
\end{aligned}
\tag{15.6}
$$

where the μs and the λs are Lagrange multipliers.

Maximizing this Lagrangean we get the following implications from the first-order necessary conditions:
(i) with respect to h_t

$$\mu_2/l_t = -\lambda_t \alpha H_{t-1} \tag{15.7a}$$

(ii) with respect to h_{t+1}

$$\mu_2 \delta/l_{t+1} = -\lambda_{t+1}\alpha H_t \tag{15.7b}$$

(iii) with respect to c_t

$$[\mu_1/c_t](1 - t_y)w_t H_t = \mu_2/l_t \tag{15.8}$$

(iv) with respect to H_t

$$[\mu_1/c_t](1 - t_y)w_t L_t = -\lambda_t + \lambda_{t+1}(\alpha h_{t+1} + 1) \tag{15.9}$$

(v) with respect to K_{t+1}

$$c_{t+1}/c_t = \delta(1 - t_y)[1 + (1 - t_y)r_{t+1}]. \tag{15.10}$$

The production function is assumed to be Cobb–Douglas with constant returns to scale and can be written as:

$$F(K_t, H_tL_t) = K_t^\beta(H_tL_t)^{1-\beta} \tag{15.11}$$

with $1 > \beta > 0$ and β being the share of capital in output.

Under competitive conditions the rental (interest) rate will be:

$$r_t = \partial F/\partial K_t = \beta(H_tL_t/K_t)^{1-\beta} = \beta k_t^{-(1-\beta)} \tag{15.12}$$

where k_t is the capital effective labor ratio. Similarly the wage rate will be:

$$w_t = (1 - \beta)k_t^\beta. \tag{15.13}$$

This model concentrates on the steady state. In such a situation output, consumption, and human capital all grow at the same rate, say γ. Thus we have:

$$\gamma \equiv H_{t+1}/H_t = \alpha h + 1. \tag{15.14}$$

The time spent on education relative to the time spent on work rises with the productivity of human capital accumulation, α, and falls with the discount factor δ:

$$L = h(1 - \delta) + (1 - \delta)/\alpha. \tag{15.15}$$

From the first-order conditions for utility maximization we can derive:

$$\gamma = \delta(1 - \phi)[1 + (1 - t_y)\beta k^{-(1-\beta)}]. \tag{15.16}$$

Now, from equation (15.14) we will get:

$$h = (\gamma - 1)/\alpha. \tag{15.17}$$

Substituting in equation (15.15) we get:

$$L = (1 - \delta)\gamma/\alpha \tag{15.18}$$

and

$$l = J - L - h = J + (1/\alpha) - [(2 - \delta)/\alpha]\gamma. \tag{15.19}$$

Substituting equation (15.19) and equation (15.8) into the budget constraint (equation 15.5) and dividing by H_tL_t we will get:

$$\begin{aligned}(\mu_1/\mu_2)(1 - t_y)w_t[\{J - ((2 - \delta)/\alpha)\gamma + (1/\alpha)\}/\{((1 - \delta)/\alpha)\gamma\}] \\ + \gamma(k_t/(1 - \phi)) = (1 - t_y)w_t + [1 + (1 - t_y)r_t]k_t.\end{aligned} \tag{15.20}$$

Multiplying this expression by $(1 - \delta)\gamma$ and then dividing by $w_t(1 - t_y)$ and some rearrangement yields:

$$\begin{aligned}(\mu_1/\mu_2)[J\alpha - (2 - \delta)\gamma + 1] = -\{(1 - \delta)/(1 - t_y)\}\{k_t/(w_t(1 - \phi))\}\gamma^2 \\ + (1 - \delta)\gamma + [1 + (1 - t_y)r_t]\{(k_t/w_t)(1 - \delta)/(1 - t_y)\}\gamma\end{aligned}$$

$$\tag{15.21}$$

which can be further rearranged to yield:

$$\gamma^2 - \{[1 + (1 - t_y)r_t](1 - \phi) + [(\mu_1/\mu_2)(2 - \delta)/(1 - \delta)]((1 - t_y)(1 - \phi))$$
$$(w_t/k_t) + (1 - \phi)(1 - t_y)(w_t/k_t)\}\gamma + (\mu_1/\mu_2)(J\alpha + 1)\{(1 - \phi)$$
$$(1 - t_y)(w_t/k_t)\}/(1 - \delta) = 0.$$

(15.22)

Using equations (15.12) and (15.13) in equation (15.22) we can derive:

$$\gamma^2 - \{[1 + (1 - t_y)\beta k^{-(1-\beta)}](1 - \phi) + [(\mu_1/\mu_2)(2 - \delta)/(1 - \delta) + 1]$$
$$(1 - \phi)(1 - t_y)(1 - \beta)k^{-(1-\beta)}\}\gamma + (\mu_1/\mu_2)(J\alpha + 1)[(1 - \phi) \qquad (15.23)$$
$$(1 - t_y)/(1 - \delta)](1 - \beta)k^{-(1-\beta)} = 0.$$

Equations (15.16) and (15.23) are the fundamental equations of the model. We can use them to solve for the equilibrium values of the growth rate (γ) and the capital labor ratio (k) as a function of the various tax rates in the model. Now, since equation (15.23) is a quadratic equation and quite non-linear, analytical solutions for γ and k are well-nigh impossible. One has to resort to numerical methods for this purpose. Gruner and Heer (1994) discuss this point carefully.

To introduce the public good we need a third equation. Let us define a fraction $\theta(1 > \theta > 0)$ as the size of output going for the production of the public good. We can write the resource constraint for the production of the public good as:

$$t_y w_t H_t L_t + t_y r_t K_t + \phi(K_{t+1}/(1 - \phi)) = \theta F(K_t, H_t L_t)$$

or

$$t_y k_t^\beta + [\phi/(1 - \phi)]\gamma k_t = \theta k_t^\beta. \qquad (15.24)$$

This is the equation that is required to study the public goods sector. The numerical results of Gruner and Heer are as follows.[3]

(i) Up to a certain level θ^* of the public sector size, it is best from the point of view of growth to finance the public good with inheritance tax alone.

(ii) For $\theta > \theta^*$ an interior solution is desirable with the value of inheritance tax being very high.

(iii) The growth rate γ depends positively on the rate of inheritance tax and does not depend upon the rate of the income tax.

(iv) The capital–labor ratio is a declining function of both tax rates.

15.3 PROBLEMS OF INCOME TAX INDEXATION

If income tax slabs are set in nominal terms then, in the context of progressive taxation, inflation will drive people into higher and higher income tax brackets without there being any change in their real pre-tax incomes. This phenomenon is sometimes called **bracket creep**. As they move to higher and higher income tax brackets, their tax liabilities under progressive taxation will increase and their real disposable incomes will drop. Hence, an argument has often been made that income tax obligations should be indexed to the rate of inflation so that no one experiences a drop in real disposable income simply because of bracket creep. Income tax indexation is, of course, linked to the problem of wage indexation.

Wage indexation has been studied for a long time.[4] This literature has one strong result. Compared to nominal wage rigidity, wage indexation stabilizes output with respect to demand shocks but makes it more volatile with respect to supply shocks. On the other hand, wage indexation destabilizes prices with respect to both types of shocks.

The first paper to study income tax indexation was Bruce (1981). He studies a closed economy and defines income taxes as being indexed if the real amount of income taxes depends only on real income and not on the price level. Bruce comes to the conclusion that income tax indexation makes output more sensitive to demand shocks but less sensitive to supply shocks – which are exactly the opposite of the results on wage indexation. With income tax indexation, however, prices become more sensitive to both types of shocks. This is in conformity with the results on wage indexation.

Income taxation in an open economy has been studied in two recent papers (Aizenman 1985; Lassila 1995). Our analysis here is suggestive only and based largely on the work of Bruce (1981), although there will be some references to later studies.

Let y^d represent the log of net of tax real income. Now

$$y^d = y - \tau \qquad (15.25)$$

where y is the log of real income and τ is the log of the ratio of gross to net income. As τ increases the average tax rate rises. Consider now the following tax structure:

$$\tau = \rho y + \alpha \rho p \qquad (15.26)$$

where p is the log of the price level, α indicates the degree of tax indexation[5] and ρ indicates the degree of progression of the tax structure.[6]

One can now write down the aggregate demand and supply curves of this economy. Assuming all parameters to be positive one can set the *IS-LM* schedules as:

$$\text{(IS)} \quad y = \gamma_1 y^d - \gamma_2 i \qquad (15.27)$$
$$\text{(LM)} \quad m - p = \lambda_1 y - \lambda_2 i \qquad (15.28)$$

where m is the log of nominal balances and i is one plus the interest rate.

Solving for i from equation (15.28), substituting into equation (15.27) and using the definition of disposable income in equation (15.25) we can derive the aggregate demand schedule:

$$y^d = \sigma_0 - \sigma_1 p \qquad (15.29)$$

where $\sigma_0 = \gamma_2 m / [\{1 - \gamma_1(1 - \rho)\}\lambda_2 + \gamma_2\lambda_1] > 0$, and

$$\sigma_1 = [\gamma_2 + \lambda_2\gamma_1\alpha\rho]/[\{1 - \gamma_1(1 - \rho)\}\lambda_2 + \gamma_2\lambda_1] > 0.$$

On the supply side of the economy it is assumed that there exists an aggregate production function of the form:

$$Y = EF(L) \tag{15.30}$$

where Y is the level of real output, L is the labor input and E is a productivity shock. Perfect competition in the labor market ensures that the marginal product of labor equals the real wage so that the demand for labor (L^d) can be written as:

$$L^d = f(E(W/P)) \text{ with } f' > 0 \text{ and } f'' < 0$$

where W is the nominal wage and P is the price level.

For simplicity it is assumed that demand for labor determines employment. Output supply (Y^s) is then:

$$Y^s = EF[f(E(W/P)]. \tag{15.31}$$

Suppose the total supply of labor is fixed at L_f then full employment level of output is:

$$Y_f = EF(L_f). \tag{15.32}$$

In logarithmic terms we can write the two supply curves (15.31) and (15.32) as:

$$y^s = b + e - \phi\eta(w - p - e) \tag{15.33}$$

$$y_f = b + e + \phi l_f \tag{15.34}$$

where b is a constant, ϕ is the share of labor in value added, η is the elasticity of labor demand (defined to be positive), and the other symbols are logarithms of their upper-case counterparts.

Choose units so that $b = l_f = 0$ so that $y_f = e$ and full employment output is identified with the productivity parameter. Now, let δ be the degree of wage indexation so that $w = (1 - \delta)p$. Hence if $\delta = 0$ we have full wage indexation and the real wage is fixed and if $\delta = 1$ the nominal wage is not indexed at all. Further upon defining $v = \phi\eta$ we can combine equations (15.33) and (15.34) to get one aggregate supply relationship:

$$y^s = (1 + v)y_f + v\delta p. \tag{15.35}$$

The aggregate demand (equation 15.29) and aggregate supply (equation 15.35) can be solved to get equilibrium values of (the logs of) output and the price level:

$$y = \theta\sigma_0 + (1 - \theta)(1 + v)y_f \tag{15.36}$$

$$p = \theta[\sigma_0 - (1 + v)y_f]/(\delta v) \tag{15.37}$$

where $1 > \theta = (\delta v)/(\sigma_1 + \delta v) =$

$$[\delta v]/[\delta v + \{\gamma_2 + \lambda_2\gamma_1\rho\alpha\}/\{\gamma_2\lambda_1 + \lambda_2(1 - \gamma_1(1 - \rho))\}].$$

Equations (15.36) and (15.37) give us considerable information on the effects of indexation on output and the price level. One can see that θ rises as α is decreased (greater tax indexation) but falls as δ is decreased (greater wage indexation). Thus tax indexation has the opposite effects of wage indexation in the stabilization of output around the full employment level. Further, wage indexation makes output less sensitive to demand shocks but more sensitive to productivity shocks (changes in σ_0 and y_f). Price level changes resulting from either demand or supply shocks are amplified by both wage as well as income tax indexation.

15.4   TIME INCONSISTENCY

The problem of time-inconsistent fiscal policy is an area of considerable interest in current research. This debate was initiated in seminal papers by Kydland and Prescott (1977, 1980), and then developed by Calvo (1978), Fischer (1980) and Lucas and Stokey (1983). Currently, the practice of examining whether a given dynamic policy is time consistent, has become almost routine.

The basic time-consistency problem can be described as follows. Policies that are optimal (defined as being derived from an appropriately specified intertemporal optimization model) in period t may no longer be optimal in period $(t + 1)$, even when no structural changes (including taste) have occurred between the periods, and there is no conflict between the objectives of the consumer and those of the government. We turn now to an explanation of these ideas.

Consider a situation in which the optimal tax problem has been solved according to some widely accepted criterion – say the Ramsey criterion. This solution is basically an atemporal one. In an intertemporal context it is probably more useful to think of policies being chosen at each date, with society having no ability to commit itself to future policies. Suppose that we have Ramsey optimality at time t. The solution to the policy choice problem typically does not coincide with the Ramsey policies from that date onward. This problem of dynamic inconsistency has been pointed out by, among others, Kydland and Prescott (1977), Prescott (1977), Calvo (1978), Fischer (1980), and Chari *et al.* (1989).

We now make the more realistic assumption that policy-making at the current point in time does not involve any precommitment. Policy rules must now maximize social welfare at each date given that private agents are behaving rationally. Such policies have been called **sequentially rational**. Similarly, optimality on the part of private agents requires that they forecast future policies as being sequentially rational for society. A sequence of policy rules and private action satisfying these conditions is a **time-consistent equilibrium**. If the Ramsey optimal solution deviates from the time consistent equilibrium then a problem of **time inconsistency** is said to exist.[7] Our discussion will be based on the relatively simple models of

Prescott (1977), Fischer (1980) and Chari *et al.* (1989). We illustrate the basic issues involved with an example due to Fischer (1980) and Chari *et al.* (1989).

Consider an economy with a large number of identical consumers and a government. There is a linear production technology for which the marginal product of capital is a constant, say r where $r > 1$, and the marginal product of labor is[8] 1. There are two time periods in this simple model. Consumers make consumption investment decisions in the first period and consumption labor supply decisions in the second. At the beginning of the first period each consumer has an initial endowment of Ω of the consumption good from which they consume c_1 units and save k. In the second time period they choose to consume c_2 and work l. Labor income is taxed at the rate t_w and capital income is taxed at the rate t_r.

The consumer's utility function is $U(c_1 + c_2, l)$ which is maximized subject to the following constraints:

$$c_1 + k \leqslant \Omega \qquad (15.38a)$$
$$c_2 \leqslant (1 - t_r)rk + (1 - t_w)l. \qquad (15.38b)$$

Clearly, if the tax rate on capital (t_r) is set so that $(1 - t_r)r = 1$ then the consumer is indifferent about the timing of consumption. It will be assumed here that in this case the consumer consumes everything in the second period.

The proportional tax rates, t_r and t_w, are set to finance an exogenously given amount of government spending G. The government's budget constraint is, therefore:

$$G \leqslant t_r rK + t_w L \qquad (15.39)$$

where L is total labor supply. We further assume that $G > r\Omega$, so that even if consumers save their entire endowments and the tax on capital is set equal to one, the government will still need to tax labor.

Let us now consider an economy with commitment. This is defined as a situation in which the social planner sets tax rates before consumers make their decisions. Let $a_1 = (c_1, k)$ and $a_2 = (c_2, l)$ denote an individual consumer's first-and second-stage allocation. Further let $A_1 = (C_1, K)$ and $A_2 = (C_2, L)$ denote the corresponding aggregate allocations. The government policy vector is $\theta = (t_r, t_w)$. It is now possible to define a competitive equilibrium for this economy.

A competitive equilibrium is an individual allocation (a_1, a_2) and an aggregate allocation (A_1, A_2) and a tax policy θ such that:

(i) Given the tax policy the consumer maximizes utility.
(ii) At the aggregate allocation (A_1, A_2) the policy θ satisfies the government budget allocation.
(iii) The individual and the aggregate plans match:[9]

$$(a_1, a_2) = (A_1, A_2).$$

Now let $W(\theta, A(\theta))$ denote the equilibrium value of utility under the policy θ so that:

$$W(\theta, A(\theta)) = U(C_1(\theta) + C_2(\theta), L(\theta)). \qquad (15.40)$$

This is also referred to as the property of **representativeness**. If S denotes the set of policies θ for which an equilibrium exists, then we can define a Ramsey equilibrium (θ, A) which solves:

$$\max_{\theta \in S} W(\theta, A(\theta)).$$

In this set-up if $(1 - t_r)r \geqslant 1$ then consumers will save their entire endowments, while if $(1 - t_r)r < 1$ then all consumption will take place in the first period and nothing will be saved. Consequently, the capital tax acts like a lump-sum tax when it is set at any level less than or equal to $(r - 1)/r$, with all its incentive advantages. Hence, it would be optimal to collect as much revenue as possible from this tax. For this we should set $t_r = (r - 1)/r$. The tax on labor is set to cover the gap between the revenue requirement and the amount collected from labor taxation.

Lack of commitment

We now admit the possibility of lack of commitment on the part of the social planner. The planner does not set tax rates until after consumers have made their first-period decisions. The sequence in which decisions is made is as follows. First, consumers make their first-period decisions, then the planner sets tax rates, finally consumers make their second-stage decisions. Hence, the planner's policy is no longer a set of tax rates but two tax rates as **functions** of first-period decisions of consumers. We call this $\phi(A_1) = (t_r(A_1), t_y(A_1))$. This is referred to as a **policy plan**.

A consumer's second decision depends on the first-stage decision, a_1, the aggregate first-stage decision, A_1, and the tax policy selected. Thus a consumer's second-stage decisions are described by a function d_2 such that:

$d_2(a_1, A_1, \theta) = [c_2(a_1, A_1, \theta), l(a_1, A_1, \theta)]$. This is referred to as a second-stage allocation rule. Similarly the aggregate allocation rule is described by $D_2(A_1, \theta)$.

An equilibrium for such an economy is defined recursively. To begin with second-stage competitive equilibrium is defined, given the history of past decisions by the consumers and the social planner. Then symmetric histories (a_1, A_1, θ) for which individual allocation a_1 equals the aggregate allocation A_1 are considered. This set will constrain policy-making by the social planner. Finally, the first stage competitive equilibrium is defined. Combining all these gives us a **time-consistent equilibrium**.

History is given as (a_1, A_1, θ). Given this history, a competitive equilibrium in the second stage is a set of allocation rules d_2 and D_2 that satisfy:

(i) consumer utility maximization: Given the history (a_1, A_1, θ) the individual allocation rule $d_2(a_1, A_1, \theta)$ solves:

$$\max_{c_2, l} U(c_1 + c_2, l)$$

subject to $c_2 \leqslant (1 - t_r)rk + (1 - t_w)l$.

(ii) representativeness:

$$d_2(a_1, A_1, \theta) = D_2(A_1, \theta).$$

We define this equilibrium for each history and summarize it by the $D_2(.)$ function.

Now consider the problem of the central planner. Given the past aggregate decisions A_1 and knowing that future decisions are selected according to the rule $D_2(A_1, \theta)$, the planner sets a policy $\theta = \phi(A_1)$ that maximizes (aggregate) consumer welfare. The planner's objective function is, therefore:

$$\max W(\phi, D_2; A_1) = U(C_1 + C_2(A_1, \theta), L(A_1, \theta)) \tag{15.41}$$

where $\theta = \phi(A_1)$. Once A_1 and D_2 have been selected we must also check to satisfy the planner's budget constraint:

$$G \leqslant t_r(A_1)rK + t_w(A_1)L(A_1, \phi(A_1)). \tag{15.42}$$

Let $\Psi(D_2, A_1)$ be the set of all policies $\phi(A_1)$ that satisfy equation (15.42). The problem of the social planner is to pick a plan such that for every D_1, $\phi(A_1)$ maximizes utility (equation 15.41) over the set of feasible policies $\Psi(D_2, A_1)$.

Finally, consider the consumer's problem at the first stage. Each consumer chooses an individual allocation for the first stage, $a_1 = (c_1, k)$ together with an allocation rule d_2 for taking actions at the second stage. The consumer takes as given that current aggregate allocation is some A_1, that future policy is set according to the plan ϕ, and that future aggregate allocations are set according to some rule D_2. Under these conditions, the definition of the first-stage competitive equilibrium is analogous to that of the second-stage competitive equilibrium, so that the first-stage competitive equilibrium can be summarized by (ϕ, A_1, D_2).

The above method recursively defines the consumer's and the planner's problem. Combining these gives us an equilibrium with sequential rationality built into it for both the consumers and the social planner. Hence, this equilibrium is time consistent.[10] We can now define a time-consistent equilibrium as a vector (ϕ, A_1, D_2) that satisfies:

(i) sequential rationality by consumers. The vector (ϕ, A_1, D_2) is a first-stage competitive equilibrium. For every history (θ', A_1') the allocation rule $D_2(\theta', A_1')$ is a second-stage competitive equilibrium.

(ii) sequential rationality by the planner. Given D_2, the policy plan ϕ solves the planner's optimization problem for every history A_1'.

We can now show that the time-consistent equilibrium for this economy has first-stage allocations $C_1 = \Omega, K = 0$ and a capital tax plan $t_r(A_1) = 1$. To see this consider first the policy plan ϕ. For any given first-stage aggregate allocation $A_1 = (C_1, K)$, it is obviously optimal for the planner to raise as much revenue as possible from taxing the given amount of capital. By assumption $G > r\Omega$ so even if all the endowments are saved and the resulting capital is fully taxed, the revenues fall short of required public spending. Thus $t_r(A_1) = 1$. Faced with such a tax, it is optimal for consumers to save nothing and consume all their endowments.

At this point we need to ask ourselves the question: what causes the conflict in this example? To answer this question we need to embed the budget constraint of consumers and the government into preferences. Let the preferences of private agents be given by:

$$U(\Omega - k + (1 - t_r)rk + (1 - t_w)l, l) + B(K, L, t_w, t_r)$$

where the *B* function equals zero if its arguments (K, L, t_w, t_r) satisfy the planner's budget constraint, $G \leqslant t_r rK + t_w L$ and *B* equals some large negative number otherwise. At the same time let the planner's preference be:

$$U(\Omega - K + (1 - t_r)rK + (1 - t_w)L, L) + B(K, L, t_r, t_w).$$

Under our assumptions consumers are competitive in the sense that they regard aggregates as being unaffected by their decisions. Hence, the source of the conflict lies in the fact that each consumer cares more about his own utility than what is happening in the aggregate (to other consumers).

Finite repetition of the Fischer model

Suppose now that the above optimization problem is repeated a finite number of times. We make the simplifying assumption that capital cannot be stored between periods. We further assume that there is neither borrowing nor lending between periods, and that government spending is constant.

A competitive equilibrium with commitment is easy to define for this problem. The planner chooses a sequence of tax rates once and for all at the beginning of the problem. A competitive equilibrium would then be a sequence of individual and aggregate allocations that maximize consumer welfare and satisfy the twin conditions of the planner's budget constraint and representativeness. The Ramsey equilibrium in this multi-period model is simply the one-period Ramsey equilibrium repeated finitely many times.

Without commitment, however, the problem is quite complicated. Now all decisions must be sequentially rational. Consumers must forecast how future taxes will be chosen and the planner must forecast how its choices today will affect consumer behavior in the future. We again have to fall back on the notion of history of past decisions. Let h_{1t} represent the history of an individual consumer at the first stage of period t:

$$h_{1t} = (a_v, A_v, \theta_v | v = 0, \dots, t - 1).$$

Aggregate history at the first stage is:

$$H_{1t} = (A_v, \theta_v | v = 0, \dots, t - 1).$$

The aggregate history confronting the government after consumers have made their first-stage decisions in period t is:

$$H_t = (A_v, \theta_v | v = 0, \dots, t - 1) \cup A_{1t}.$$

Correspondingly at the second stage an individual consumer's history is given by:

$$h_{2t} = (h_{1t}, a_{1t}, A_{1t}, \theta_t)$$

and the aggregate history is given by:

$$H_{2t} = (H_{1t}, A_{1t}, \theta_t).$$

Since individual consumers are unable to affect decisions on taxes, aggregate histories do not include individual allocation.

Allocations and policies are defined as functions of the histories. Let $d_t = (d_{1t}, d_{2t})$ denote individual allocation functions that map first- and second-stage individual histories into decisions at the respective stages. Let $D_t = (D_{1t}, D_{2t})$ denote the corresponding aggregate allocation function that maps aggregate histories into aggregate allocations. Let ϕ_t denote the planner's policy function that maps histories H_t into decisions at time t.

In order to define a time-consistent equilibrium, we need to explain how allocations and policy functions induce future changes. Let $d^t = (d_t, d_{t+1}, \dots)$ denote a sequence of individual allocation rules from time t onward. Let D^t and ϕ^t denote the corresponding objects for the aggregate allocation rules and policy plans. Now, given a history h_{1t}, the functions d^t, D^t and ϕ^t induce the following individual histories:

$$h_{2t} = \{h_{1t}, d_{1t}(h_{1t}), D_{1t}(H_{1t}, (\phi_t(H_{1t}, D_{1t}(H_{1t}))\}$$
$$h_{1t+1} = \{h_{2t}, d_{2t}(h_{2t}), D_{2t}(H_{2t})\}$$

and so on. In a similar manner, from any initial aggregate history, say, H_{1t}, the functions D^t and ϕ^t induce future histories:

$$(H_t, H_{2t}, H_{1t+1}).$$

Now consider the first stage of period t. Given some history h_{1t}, an individual consumer chooses a contingency plan d^t. Each consumer is assumed to behave as if future aggregate allocation and policies will evolve according to the histories induced by D^t and ϕ^t.

We can now define a competitive equilibrium at the first stage of t, given a history H_{1t} as a set of contingency plans d^t, D^t and ϕ^t that satisfy:
(i) consumer utility maximization. Given H_{1t}, D^t and ϕ^t the individual allocation rules, d^t, maximize:

$$\sum_{v=t}^{T} \delta^{v-t} U[c_{1v}(h_{1v}) + c_{2v}(h_{2v}) + l_v(h_{2v})]$$

subject to:

(a) $c_{1v}(h_{1v}) \leqslant \Omega - k_v(h_{1v})$

(b) $c_{2v}(h_{2v}) \leqslant [1 - t_{rv}(H_v)]rk_v(h_{1v}) + [1 - t_{wv}(H_v)]l_v(h_{2v})$

where for all $v \geqslant t$, the future histories are induced by d^t, D^t and ϕ^t. Here δ (with $1 > \delta > 0$) is a fixed discount factor and T is the time horizon over which this tax model is repeated. t_{wv} and t_{rv} are, respectively, the tax rate on wage and interest income in period v.

(ii) representativeness, i.e., $d^t = D^t$. Consider the equilibrium pair (ϕ^t, D^t). A competitive equilibrium at the second stage of t, given a history H_{2t} is a set of contingency plans $(d_{2t}, d^{t+1}), (D_{2t}, D^{t+1})$ and ϕ^{t+1} that satisfy usual conditions for representativeness as discussed above. Call this equilibrium $(\phi^{t+1}, D_{2t}, D^{t+1})$.

Consider now the optimization problem of the social planner in period t. Given history H_t and taking as given that future aggregate allocations evolve according to (D_{2t}, D^{t+1}), the planner selects a policy plan ϕ^t that maximizes consumer welfare. The planner's objective function is written as:

$$W_t(\phi^t, D_{2t},\ D^{t+1}, H_t) = U[C_{1t} + C_{2t}(H_{2t}), L_t(H_{2t})]$$
$$+ \sum_{v=t+1}^{T} \delta^{v-1} U[C_{1v}(H_{1v}) + C_{2v}(H_{2v}), L_v(H_{2v})]. \tag{15.43}$$

Given the history H_t and the allocation rules (D_{2t}, D^{t+1}), the planner selects a plan that not only satisfies its current budget constraint:

$G \leqslant t_{rt}(H_t)rK_t + t_{wt}(H_t)L_t(H_{2t})$ as well as the constraint :

$G \leqslant t_{rv}(H_v)rK_v(H_{1v}) + t_{wv}(H_v)L_v(H_{2v})$

for all aggregate histories induced by (D_{2t}, D^{t+1}) and ϕ^t. Let $\Psi_t(D_{2t}, D^{t+1}, H_t)$ be the set of all policy plans ϕ^t that satisfy these budget constraints. The planner's problem is, then, to choose a plan ϕ^t that maximizes consumer welfare as defined in equation (15.43) over the set of all feasible policies: $\Psi_t(D_{2t}, D^{t+1}, H_t)$. Hence we arrive at a type of equilibrium that will not break down as time evolves. This will be true because these policies will be carried out for any possible set of histories.

We can now define a time-consistent equilibrium as a pair (ϕ, D) that satisfies:

(i) sequential rationality by consumers. For every history $H_{1t}, (\phi^t, D^t)$ is a first-stage competitive equilibrium, and for every history H_{2t}, the vector $(\phi^{t+1}, D_{2t}, D^{t+1})$ is a second-stage competitive equilibrium.

(ii) sequential rationality by the planner. For every history H_t, the plan ϕ^t maximizes consumer welfare over the set of feasible plans $\Psi(D_{2t}, D^{t+1}, H_t)$.

Intuitively this process works as follows. At the second stage of the last period, the consumer's decision problem is independent of history and depends only upon current tax rates and the current capital stock. As a consequence, the planner's decision problem depends only upon the current capital stock. Hence the equilibrium in the last period is identical as the single-period problem considered earlier. In particular, it is independent of history. Now consider period $(T-1)$. Obviously, neither the planner's decisions nor private agent's decisions have any effect on outcomes in period T. Hence, the problem in period $(T-1)$ is also static and the outcomes will be identical to those discussed earlier for the single-period case. Repeating this argument convinces us that the time-consistent equilibrium is unique. In particular, it is the sequence of single-period, time-consistent equilibria.

15.5   TAX COMPLIANCE AND TAX EVASION

The problem of tax evasion is of considerable importance in most countries – developed as well as developing. It has been extensively studied in public economics. For a recent survey see Myles (1995: Chapter 12). Our purpose in this section is a relatively modest one – we present a brief overview of the literature and study one model (Andreoni 1992) in some detail.

Early models of tax compliance and tax evasion include Allingham and Sandmo (1973), Srinivasan (1973) and Yitzhaki (1974). The main thrust of this literature[11] was that, in principle, it was possible to ensure full tax compliance simply by setting penalties so high that the expected net gain from cheating is negative. However, as Reinganum and Wilde (1985, 1986), Border and Sobel (1987), Scotchmer (1987), Sanchez and Sobel (1989), Townsend (1979) and Mookherjee and Png (1989) point out, there may be limits to the size of sanctions against tax evaders and enforcing compliance through audits may be a costly affair. Hence, incentives for tax evasion exist. In a dynamic model of tax evasion, Greenberg (1984) assumes perfect capital markets. Imperfect capital markets are introduced in an important paper by Andreoni (1992). In this section we first study the static problem of tax evasion and then Andreoni's dynamic tax evasion model.

Taxation and the underground economy

Underground activity is an important segment of the market in many countries. Economists have dealt with the problem of underground economy from two angles. First, from a theoretical perspective attempts have been made to explain the extent of the underground economy, asking why people work in a clandestine manner, buy and sell goods on the black market and so on. Second, some economists have tried to estimate the extent of the underground economy.[12]

Consider an economy with two broad sectors[13] – the official or legal sector labeled l and the clandestine or underground sector labeled u. There are two types of labor markets and two types of good markets. Hence households and firms interact in four interrelated markets: two goods market (legal and underground) and two labor markets (legal and underground). Both labor and goods are homogeneous across the two sectors except for the different degrees of risk associated with the two sectors. Legal and underground markets differ from each other because of the fact that transactions in official markets are subject to taxes. We suppose that there is a direct income tax for the labor market and an indirect tax for the commodity market. Transactions in the underground market are not subject to tax. If this tax evasion is detected then there is a penalty at rates fixed by the government. The government is assumed to be able to detect tax evasion at fixed probabilities.

The household works L^l and L^u hours respectively in the legal and underground economies. Leisure is denoted by L^e. $L(D)$ denotes the total amount of labor hours supplied by the typical household. The wage rate in the legal economy is w^l and in the underground economy is w^u. We will assume that when working in the legal market, households are subject to a linear income tax with an exemption limit of τ_0 and a marginal rate of τ_1. Hence, the net income of a household from the legal economy is $(w^l L^l (1 - \tau_1) + \tau_0)$. In the underground economy the income is $w^u L^u$. Let p be the probability of being detected to be working in the shadow economy so that $(1 - p)$ is the probability of not being detected. Firms face no penalties for hiring workers in the underground economy.

Table 15.1

Working in the underground economy is not detected (probability $1-p$)

   (i) Disposable income from the labor market is:

      $\tau_0 + (1 - \tau_1)w^l L^l + w^u L^u = Y_1(L^l, L^u)$, where Y_1 is income in this situation.

   (ii) Utility in this situation from the labor market: $U(Y_1, L^l, L^u)$.

   (iii) Utility in this situation from the goods market: $V(d^l, d^u)$ with $Y_1 \geqslant d^l p^l + d^u p^u$ where p^l is the tax inclusive consumer price in the legal market and p^u is the (tax-exclusive) consumer price in the underground market.

Working in the underground economy is detected (probability p)

   (i) Disposable income from the labor market:

      $(1 - \tau_1)w^l L^l + \tau_0 + w^u L^u (1 - \tau_2) = Y_2(L^l, L^u)$.

   (ii) Utility from the labor market:

      $U(Y_2, L^l, L^u)$.

   (iii) Utility from the goods market $V(d^l, d^u)$ with $Y_2 \geqslant d^l p^l + d^u p^u$.

Household commodity demand in the legal market is denoted by d^l and in the underground economy by d^u. The household's choice problem can be depicted as in Table 15.1.

A typical firm has the following choice problem. It may supply an amount s^l for the legal economy and an amount s^u for the underground economy. p^l is the tax inclusive price in the legal market and p^u is the price in the underground economy. The rate of indirect tax is τ_3 and the amount of indirect tax to be paid by the firm per unit sold in the legal market is $\tau_3 P^l$ for a total of $\tau_3 P^l s^l$. If the firm is caught selling goods in the underground economy it has to pay a penalty proportional to its revenue from the underground economy: $\tau_4 p^u s^u$. However, consumers face no penalty for buying goods in the underground economy.

We assume that labor is the only variable cost of production. There is a catch-all fixed cost term labeled *F*. The firm may hire labor in the legal as well as the underground economy. These are denoted l^l and l^u respectively. This literature typically assumes that the legal economy good is produced by labor from the legal labor market alone and underground economy good is produced by labor from the underground economy alone. This separability assumption simplifies the analysis but is a drawback nevertheless. Let the probability of the firm being detected selling in the underground economy be *q*. We can then write the depict the decisions of the firm as in Table 15.2.

The expected utility of the worker is given as by the von Neumann–Morgenstern form:

$$E(U) = (1 - p)U(Y_1, L^l, L^u) + pU(Y_2, L^l, L^u) \qquad (15.44)$$

where $E(.)$ is the expectations operator. This utility function is maximized with respect to L^l and L^u. Y_1 and Y_2 have been defined in Table 15.1. Additional constraints are that:

$$L^l + L^u \leqslant H \qquad (15.45)$$

and $L^l \geqslant 0$ and $L^u \geqslant 0$
where *H* is the total amount of time available with this individual.

Define the dummy variable *D* such that $D = 0$ for $Y = Y_1$ (non-detection) and $D = \tau_2$ for $Y = Y_2$ (detection).

Writing Λ as the Lagrangean and λ for the Lagrange multiplier for the constraint in equation (15.45) for the utility maximization problem of the household, we get as first-order, Kuhn–Tucker conditions:

$$\partial \Lambda / \partial L^l = E[(\partial U / \partial y)]w^l(1 - \tau_1) + E[(\partial U / \partial L^l)] - \lambda \leqslant 0 \qquad (15.46a)$$

$$(\partial \Lambda / \partial L^l) = E[(\partial U / \partial y)w^u(1 - D)] + E[\partial U / \partial L^u] - \lambda \mu \leqslant 0 \qquad (15.46b)$$

$$L^l \geqslant 0, \ L^u \geqslant 0, \ \text{and} \ L^l(\partial \Lambda / \partial L^l) = 0 = L^u(\partial \Lambda / \partial L^u) \qquad (15/46c)$$

$$(\partial \Lambda / \partial \lambda) = H - L^0 - L^u \geqslant 0, \lambda \geqslant 0, \lambda(\partial \Lambda / \partial \lambda) = 0. \qquad (15.46d)$$

Table 15.2

Selling goods in the underground economy undetected (probability $1-q$)

(i) Revenues:

$s^l p^l + s^u p^u$.

(ii) Costs:

$w^l l^l + \tau_3 s^l p^l + w^u l^u + F$.

(iii) Profit:

$(1 - \tau_3)s^l p^l + s^u p^u - w^l l^l - w^u l^u - F$.

Selling goods in the underground economy detected (probability $1-q$)

(i) Revenue:

$s^l p^l + s^u p^u$.

(ii) Cost:

$w^l l^l + \tau_3 s^l p^l + w^u l^u + \tau_4 s^u p^u + F$.

(iii) Profit:

$s^l p^l + (1 - \tau_4)s^u p^u - w^l l^l - \tau_3 s^l p^l - w^u l^u - F$.

Consider the interior solution when labor is positive. In that case $\lambda = 0$; for L^l and $L^u > 0$ and we obtain:

$$E(\partial U/\partial y)w^l(1 - \tau_1) + E(\partial U/\partial L^l) = 0 \qquad (15.47a)$$

and

$$E[(\partial U/\partial y)w^u(1 - D)] + E(\partial U/\partial L^u) = 0. \qquad (15.47b)$$

From equation (15.47a) we get:

$$w^l(1 - \tau_1) = -E[(\partial U/\partial L^u)]/E[(\partial U/\partial y)(1 - D)] \qquad (15.48)$$

which says that the after-tax wage rate for legal work must be equated to the ratio of expected marginal disutility from official work to the expected marginal utility from income obtained both from legal and illegal work. From equation (15.47b) we can derive:

$$w^u = -E[(\partial U/\partial L^u)]/E[(\partial U/\partial y)(1 - D)]. \qquad (15.49)$$

This is a parallel expression for underground work. It says that the wage rate for underground work must be equal to the ratio of the expected marginal disutility from underground work to the expected marginal utility from income obtained both from legal as well as illegal work weighted by the penalty rate to be paid to the tax authorities. This rate is zero if tax evasion is not detected and equal to τ_2 if it is detected. Equations (15.48) and (15.49) determine the implicit labor supply function in the two labor markets:

$$L^l = L^l[w^l, w^u, \tau_0, \tau_1, \tau_2, p] \qquad (15.50a)$$

$$L^u = L^u[w^l, w^u, \tau_0, \tau_1, \tau_2, p] \qquad (15.50b)$$

To facilitate analysis attention is focused on a special functional form of the utility function. In particular it assumed that there are no cross-effects:

$$\partial^2 U/\partial y \partial L^l = \partial^2 U/\partial y \partial L^u = \partial^2 U/\partial L^l \partial L^u = 0.$$

With this assumption we can write the two key conditions (equations (15.48) and (15.49)) in implicit functional form as:

$$\Phi_1(L^l, L^u, p, \tau_0, \tau_1, \tau_2, w^l, w^u) = 0 \qquad (15.51)$$

$$\Phi_2(L^l, L^u, p, \tau_0, \tau_1, \tau_2, w^l, w^u) = 0. \qquad (15.52)$$

These are two equations in two unknowns L^l and L^u. The others are all parameters of the model. Upon total differentiation we can solve for the change in each of these endogenous variables in response to a change in any of these parameters. These effects are summarized in Table 15.3.

Table 15.3

| | *Effects on endogenous variables* | |
	L^l	L^u
Increases in parameter values		
p	+	−
τ_0	−	−
τ_1	?	+
τ_2	+	−
w^l	?	−
w^u	−	?
? = ambiguous sign		

A simplifying aspect of this model is that labor market decisions are separated from goods market decisions.[14] With respect to the goods market, in case income tax evasion is not detected, the household maximizes $V(d^l, d^u)$ with respect to d^l and d^u subject to the conditions

$$Y_1 = w^l L^l (1 - \tau_1) + \tau_0 + w^u L^u \geqslant d^l P^l + d^u P^u \qquad (15.53)$$

with $d^l \geqslant 0$ and $d^u \geqslant 0$.

As long as the household is not satiated with respect to either good, the marginal utilities are positive. Hence the non-negativity constraints are not binding. This, in turn, implies that some of at least one good is consumed and total income, Y_1, is exhausted. The first-order condition for utility maximization can be written as:

$$(\partial V/\partial d^l)/(\partial V/\partial d^u) = P^l/P^u. \qquad (15.54)$$

This implies that the marginal rate of substitution between legal and illegal transactions must be equal to the ratio of their prices.[15] In a manner exactly analogous to the case for labor supply we can write the commodity demand functions, given L^l and L^u, as:

$$d^l = d^l(P^l, P^u, y_1) \tag{15.55}$$

$$d^u = d^u(P^l, P^u, y_1). \tag{15.56}$$

We can then carry out comparative static exercises just as before.

Determination of the firm's underground activities

It is generally assumed that the firm is a risk-neutral decision-maker, choosing simultaneously the demand for labor and the supply of goods (in both legal and illegal markets). The supply of goods is given by a production function with labor alone as arguments. The demand for labor is determined by:

$$l^l = f_1^{-1}(l^l) \tag{15.57}$$

$$l^u = f_2^{-1}(l^u) \tag{15.58}$$

where f_1 and f_2 are the production functions for output in the legal and illegal sectors respectively.

The firm's profit maximization problem can now be written as:

$$\max E(\Pi) = f_1(l^l)P^l(1 - \tau_3)q + f_2(l^u)P^u(1 - q)\tau_4 - w^l l^l - w^u l^u - F \tag{15.59}$$

where Π is profits.

First-order necessary conditions are:

$$q(\partial f_1/\partial l^l)P^l(1 - \tau_3) - w^l \leqslant 0 \tag{15.60a}$$

$$(\partial f_2/\partial l^u)P^u(1 - q)\tau_4 - w^u \leqslant 0 \tag{15.60b}$$

$$l^l \geqslant 0, l^l[\partial E(\Pi)/\partial l^l] = 0, \ l^u \geqslant 0, l^u[\partial E(\Pi)/\partial l^u] = 0. \tag{15.60c}$$

For an internal maximum, marginal product of labor in both markets should be equated to the correctly defined real wage:

$$\partial f_1/\partial l^l = w^l/[P^l(1 - \tau_3)]q \tag{15.61a}$$

$$\partial f_1/\partial l^u = w^u/[P^u(1 - q)\tau_4]. \tag{15.61b}$$

Totally differentiating these conditions we can find out the response of labor demand in the legal and illegal sectors to changes in the parameters. This is depicted in Table 15.4.

The results of this model are to be interpreted as being suggestive. First, The qualitative results have been obtained under very stringent conditions. Second, there is an artificial separation of activities between the labor and commodity markets. Nevertheless, it does point to the key role played by various policy parameters such as the probability of getting caught, the wage rates, the prices and tax rates in influencing producer and consumer behavior about tax evasion.

Table 15.4

	Effects on endogenous variables	
	l^1	l^u
Changes in parameters		
q	0	−
τ_3	−	0
τ_4	0	−
p^l	+	0
p^u	0	+
w^l	−	0
w^u	0	−

15.6 INTERTEMPORAL TAX EVASION: ANDREONI'S MODEL

Each tax payer in Andreoni's model lives for two time periods. In the first time period he receives an income y_1 which is the same for all consumers. This is known to everyone. In the second period each person receives a bequest y_{2h} where h indexes individuals. This bequest is individual specific and, therefore, private information.

Consumer h has a separable utility function between consumption in the two time periods:

$$U^h = u(c_{1h}) + v(c_{2h}).$$

The consumer can transfer income from one time period to the other and hence have a consumption level different from income in either time period by borrowing from banks. Banks know first-period income of each individual but they cannot monitor the bequests of individuals.[16] In addition, first-period income is taxed (at the proportional rate t_y) but bequests are not.[17] In order to get a loan to add to consumption in the second period, an individual has to offer collateral. There is an adverse selection problem here because since the bank does not know the bequest of the person taking out the loan, it is entirely possible that this person will take out a large loan and then default on repayment in the second time period. Faced with this kind of situation, banks would set a limit to the amount of the loan that they would give out. Let us suppose that this is L^* and, without loss of generality, assume that $L^* = 0$.

Now define $m(c_1, c_2) = (\partial u / \partial c_1) / (\partial v / \partial c_2)$ as the marginal rate of substitution between current and future consumption. Consider a level of bequest y_2^* such that $m(y_n, y_2^*) = 1$. Hence this person will consume y_n in the first time period and y_2^* in the second time period. Assuming that the consumer's utility function is concave we will get the result that a consumers with bequests, $y_{2h} < y_2^*$, would have $m(.) < 1$ and this person would like to save (lend). People with $y_{2h} > y_2^*$ would have $m(.) > 1$ and would like to borrow. Hence, the population is split up into three segments. Those with large bequests would like to borrow. Those with small bequests would like to save in order to add to second-period consumption and there is an intermediate range of people who do not borrow or lend.

Now suppose that even first-period income is not observed by banks. In making loan decisions, banks rely on the incomes reported by individuals to the tax authorities. They, in turn, enforce compliance through random audits at the beginning of period 2. The probability that any particular taxpayer will get audited is θ. Hence, there is a time lag between the reporting of income to the tax authorities and the auditing of tax returns. This lag is crucial to Andreoni's model.

In the first period the individual reports income y_{1h}^r so that the amount of underreporting is $u_h^r = y_{1h} - y_{1h}^r$. Hence, for $u_h^r \geqslant 0$ this person will have consumption in period 1 of $c_{1h} = y_{1h} - t_y y_{1h}^r - s_h = y_n + t_y u_h^r - s_h$ where $s_h \geqslant 0$ is the amount saved.

During an audit if a person is caught to have cheated, he has to pay the evaded tax $t_y u_h^r$ plus a penalty which is fixed at Δ for every dollar under-reported. Hence total liabilities when caught are $u_h^r (t_y + \Delta)$. If the tax payer is caught cheating (so that he loses, denoted by the superscript l) his second-period consumption will be $c_{2h}^l = y_{2h} + s_h - (t_y + \Delta) u_h^r$. If, on the other hand, this person is not audited (so that he wins, denoted by the superscript w) then second-period consumption will be $c_{2h}^w = y_{2h} + s_h$. Hence, if a person under-reports a dollar of income, then he will get t_y in the first period, but with probability θ he will lose $t + \Delta$ in the second time period. Hence, the expected value of each dollar of cheating is $\lambda = t_y - \theta(t_y + \Delta)$.

Consumer h then maximizes the following utility function:

$$U_h = u(c_{1h}) + (1 - \theta)v(c_{2h}^w) + \theta v(c_{2h}^l)$$

subject to:

$$0 \leqslant u_h^r \leqslant y_{1h}, s_h \geqslant 0.$$

This maximization is done with respect to u_h^r and s_h.

The first-order conditions for this are as follows:

$$u'(c_{1h})t_y - \theta v'(c_{2h}^l)(t_y + \Delta) \leqslant 0 \tag{15.62}$$

$$- u'(c_{1h}) + (1 - \theta)v'(c_{2h}^w) + \theta v'(c_{2h}^l) \leqslant 0. \tag{15.63}$$

Equation (15.44) holds with equality if $u_h^r > 0$ and equation (15.63) holds with equality if $s_h > 0$. We denote $(\tilde{u}_h^r, \tilde{s}_h)$ as the solutions to equations (15.62) and (15.63).

Let s_h' be the optimal level of savings under full compliance. We get s_h' from equation (15.63) if we constraint u_h^r to be zero. Then a necessary and sufficient condition for $\tilde{u}_h^r$ to be positive is that the lefthand side of equation (15.62) evaluated at $(0, s_h')$ is positive. Rearranging this we have $m(y_n - s_h', y_{2h} + s_h') > \theta(t_y + \Delta)/t_y = 1 - \lambda/t$. However for all h such that $y_{2h} \leqslant y_2^*$ we know that $m(y_n - s_h', y_{2h} + s_h') = 1$ and for all h such that $y_{2h} > y_2^*$ we know that $s_h' = 0$ and $m(y_n, y_{2h}) > 1$. Hence if $\lambda > 0$, then

$1 - \lambda/t < 1$ and everyone will cheat. If $\lambda = 0$ then $1 - \lambda/t = 1$ and only those who face binding borrowing constraints will cheat. Let y^e solve $m(y_n, y^e) = 1 - \lambda/t$. Then if $\lambda < 0$ only those liquidity constrained people with $y_{2h} > y^e$ will cheat.

Hence the existence of imperfect capital markets with the borrowing constraint has a profound implication on tax compliance. If people are liquidity constrained, they may be willing to take unfair risks in order to transfer income from the future to the present. Furthermore, the more severely constrained are people[18] (the greater is their y_{2h}), the lower the λ that they are willing to tolerate. This implies that the tax authorities cannot eliminate cheating by setting enforcement such that $\lambda = 0$. Even if θ is set equal to one so that everyone is audited, we are still not guaranteed full compliance. Someone with a sufficiently high y_{2h} may be willing to pay the penalty in order to increase consumption in period 1.

Cheating to free up the borrowing constraint

Consider cheating in the case where $\lambda < 0$. Restrict $s_h = 0$ and solve equation (15.62) to get optimal u_h^r, say u_h^r. With this we will have:

$$u'(y_n + t_y u_h^r) = v'(y_{2h} - (t_y + \Delta)u_h^r)\theta(t + \Delta)/t_y. \qquad (15.64)$$

For $\tilde{s}_h > 0$ the lefthand side of equation (15.63) should be positive when it is evaluated at $(u_h^r, 0)$. Evaluating (15.63) at this point and substituting from equation (15.64) we get:

$$-u'(y_n + t_y u_h^r) + (1 - \theta)v'(y_{2h}) + \theta v'(y_{2h} - (t_y + \Delta)u_h^r)$$
$$= (1 - \theta)[v'(y_{2h}) - v'(y_{2h} - (t_y + \Delta)u_h^r)] + (\lambda/t_y)v'(y_{2h} - (t_y + \Delta)u_h^r).$$
$$(15.65)$$

We assume that consumers are risk averse. Hence it must be the case that $v'(y_{2h}) \leqslant v'(y_{2h} - (t + \Delta)u_h^r)$. Now since we have assume λ to be negative, it must be the case that equation (15.65) is negative. Hence $(\tilde{u}_h^r, \tilde{s}_h) = (\tilde{u}_h^r, 0)$ for all those with $y_{2h} > y^e$. In other words, if the expected return from cheating is negative, then cheaters will never use their expected taxes to increase savings. If $\lambda < 0$ and a cheater wishes to transfer consumption from the present to the future, then the least-cost way of doing this is to reduce cheating.

If $\lambda > 0$, however, the situation is different. Now equation (15.65) could be positive or negative. Moreover, it will change sign only once. Let y_{2h}^0 be the level[19] of second-period income at which equation (15.65) is zero. In other words:

$$-u'(y_n + t_y u_h^r) + (1 - \theta)v'(y_{2h}^0) + \theta v'(y_{2h}^0 - (t_y + \Delta)u_h^r) = 0.$$

Substituting from equation (15.64) we get:

$$u'(y_n + t_y u_h^r)/v'(y_{2h}^0) = 1 + \lambda/\Delta. \qquad (15.66)$$

Since $u'(y_n) > u'(y_n + t_y u_h^r)$, it must be the case that $m(y_n, y_{2h}^0) > 1$ which, therefore, means that $y_{2h}^0 > y_2^*$. Hence for all persons with $y_{2h} < y_{2h}^0$ savings will be positive. This may include some people who are initially liquidity constrained. Hence, for these people cheating frees up borrowing constrained. However, the most severely liquidity constrained people will remain constrained, even with cheating.

Andreoni shows that his results generalize fairly readily to stochastic incomes. The point that people may evade taxes in order to slacken their borrowing constraint comes out well in this model.

15.7   CONCLUDING COMMENTS

The theory of direct taxation has been the subject of intense research in recent years. In Chapter 14 we studied the foundations and principal results in this area. In this chapter we have studied four areas that have recently occupied the attention of economists as well as policy-makers. These four areas are endogenous growth theory and optimal taxation, the problem of income tax indexation in an inflationary economy, time inconsistency and direct taxation and the problem of tax compliance.

The results collected here are indicative of the work being done at the frontiers in these areas and are not to be construed as exhaustive surveys. However, the basic flavor of the questions asked and key results does come through.

In Chapter 14 and in this chapter we have been concered with optimal taxation. In the next chapter we broach the question of tax reform – an issue that arises when optimal tax rates cannot be achieved in one step.

NOTES

1 Our analysis will be based primarily on the work of Jones *et al.* (1993) and Gruner and Heer (1994).
2 w_t is the wage rate of a standard unit of labor. Hence, the wage income of a person who supplies $H_t L_t$ units of standard units of labor is, simply, $w_t H_t L_t$.
3 These also agree with the results of Jones *et al.* (1993).
4 For a recent statement see Jha (1994: Chapter 4).
5 If $\alpha = 1$ then there is no indexation since a rise in the price level has the same effect on tax livability as a rise in real income. If $\alpha = 0$ then there is perfect indexation, since a rise in price level, by itself, has no effect on tax liability.
6 The higher is ρ the greater the fraction of income taken away as tax and, therefore, the higher the degree of tax progression.
7 Strotz (1955) had shown that time inconsistency may arise if consumer preferences change over time. The time inconsistency problem we are talking about arises even if preferences are unchanged. The basic reason for time inconsistency here, as will become clear soon, is conflict among agents.
8 We keep the production technology simple in order to focus on the key issue of time consistency.
9 Since consumers are all identical we can normalize their size to equal 1.

10 It is easy to verify that utility of consumers in this time-consistent equilibrium is strictly lower than the level in the Ramsey equilibrium.

11 For some amplifications on this point for the case of consumer tax evasion, see Gideon (1995). For tax evasion by firms, see Gideon (1994).

12 In this section we study a simple model of underground activity. Good account of the empirical work on underground activity can be found in Mork (1975), Spicer and Lundstedt (1976), Crane and Nourzad (1987), Poterba (1987) and Schneider and Horfreither (1987).

13 In this section we follow the work of Nayak (1978), Cowell (1985), Isachsen and Strom (1980) and Neck, Schneider and Hofreither (1989).

14 If they were jointly treated meaningful qualitative results would not be possible.

15 Assuming that the utility function is concave, the necessary conditions are also sufficient.

16 A simple reason for this could be that first-period income is the same for everyone whereas second-period bequests vary across individuals.

17 Hence net income in the first time period is $y_n = y_1(1 - t_y)$.

18 The extent of this constraint is defined in terms of the magnitude of second-period income. The larger this income, given that first-period income is the same for everyone, the greater will be the desire to transfer second-period earnings to first-period consumption.

19 This level of income will be unique.

ADDITIONAL READING

A good heuristic explanation of time inconsistency and some other problems in dynamic tax theory can be found in Stern (1991). See also Feldstein (1983), Bosworth (1984) Slemrod (1990b), and Tuomala (1990).

16 Tax reform

Key concepts: tax reform; Diamond–Mirrlees criteria; dynamic tax reform; marginal tax reform; social marginal cost, marginal benefit approach to tax reform; Kay–Panzar–Sadka requirement; the Hatta criterion.

16.1 INTRODUCTION

In real life it is rarely possible to reach optimal tax rates immediately. It is more likely that all the policy-maker is permitted is marginal changes around existing tax rates. Tax reform, loosely speaking, deals with improving welfare by making marginal changes in tax design and structure.

What exactly is tax reform? A moment's consideration will tell us that there is no agreement about this. Contradictory policy measures have been suggested, at different times, under the general rubric of tax reform. For instance, in the 1960s James Callaghan introduced a selective employment tax in the UK and called it tax reform. In the 1970s this tax was replaced with VAT by the then Chancellor of the Exchequer, Anthony Barber, and this move was once again called 'tax reform'. In the 1970s investment tax allowances were introduced in the UK and then abandoned in the 1980s. Both the adoption of the tax allowances as well as their abandonment were called 'tax reform'. Hence, what a tax reform is depends very much on the value systems prevailing at the time. However, not all changes in taxes should be called 'tax reform'. We would do well to reserve this term for 'significant' changes.

Tax reform, so defined, may take a variety of forms. It can cover increases or decreases in tax rates, brackets or thresholds and changes in the tax base; the introduction of new taxes and the abolition of old taxes; and changes in the tax mix. The indexation of a major tax (in the case of an economy experiencing inflation) also constitutes tax reform as does a radical change in administrative practices and procedures.

To be sure current interest in tax reform has been fueled by almost universal tax reforms in the 1980s. The 1980s was truly a decade of world-wide tax reform. Almost all countries of Western Europe would claim to have undergone tax reform during that period. The USA introduced a major Tax Reform Act in 1986. In Canada the Goods and Services Tax (GST) came into place. Japan is undergoing tax reforms. New Zealand has thoroughly revised its tax structures and Australia has made substantial changes to tax laws.

Several developing countries have also undergone or are currently setting up deep tax reforms. These include large developing countries such as India, where the government has appointed a Tax Reforms Committee, and several smaller ones as well. Cnossen (1992) reports, for example, that approximately forty countries in Africa, Asia, and Latin America have a VAT. Twenty-one of the twenty-four OECD countries have a VAT. It is quite surprising to recall that the VAT was almost unknown twenty-five years ago. The phenomenon of tax reform has been truly universal.

Even more interesting than the universality of reforms is the fact that those taking place in different countries have a lot in common. We discuss below some common characteristics, particularly for the developed countries.

(i) An important feature of tax reforms has been reduction in the top rates of income tax. Table 16.1 shows the top rates of personal income tax for a set of OECD countries in 1976 (i.e. before the reforms began); in 1986 (when the reforms program was well under way) and in 1992 (when several countries had finished the bulk of economic reforms).

As Table 16.1 shows the reduction in rates has been quite dramatic for some of the countries. The US and UK top marginal tax rates have been cut

Table 16.1 Top rates of central government personal income tax 1976, 1986, 1992, for selected OECD countries

Country	Top rates per cent			Percentage points reduction 1976 figure minus 1992 figure
	1976	*1986*	*1992*	
Australia	65	57	48	17
Austria	62	62	50	12
Canada	43	34	29	14
Finland	51	51	39	12
France	60	65	57	3
Germany	56	56	53	3
Ireland	77	58	52	25
Italy	72	62	50	22
Japan	75	70	50	25
Netherlands	72	72	60	12
New Zealand	60	57	33	27
Norway	48	40	13	35
Sweden	57	50	20	37
UK	83	60	40	43
USA	70	50	31	39
Unweighted average	**63.4**	**56.3**	**41.7**	**21.7**

Source: Various OECD publications

by more than half. Norway and Sweden have effected deep cuts as well, whereas France and Germany have had smaller cuts. The unweighted average of the top marginal tax rates has also fallen quite sharply.

Coupled with reductions in the top marginal rates were reductions in rates at the lower and middle ranges of the tax schedule, as well as an increase in the exemption limit. In Sweden, for example, after the 1990 reform, there was a single rate of central government income tax of 20 per cent; the lowest rate of tax, hitherto 4 per cent, therefore went up to 20 per cent; but because the exemption limit was increased, the net effect was to reduce the 4 per cent rate to zero.

(ii) Associated with the reduction in tax rates and an increase in the exemption limit was a reduction in the number of slabs in the income tax scale. In the UK the income tax had ten steps in 1976 which came down to three in 1992. At the beginning of the 1980s, New Zealand had nineteen slabs which came down in ten years to just two.

Tax reforms effected were, however, revenue neutral; there was hardly any change in tax revenue as a result of these reforms. How has it been possible to make such marked reductions in income tax while more or less sustaining tax revenue?

This was accomplished:

(a) by broadening the base of the income tax (including tightening up on income-related taxes and/or imposing new income-related taxes);
(b) by changing the tax mix, i.e., raising more from other taxes.

This then leads us to the third and fourth major characteristics of recent tax reforms.

(iii) The third major characteristic of recent tax reforms has been a broadening of the income tax base. This has included reductions and streamlining of different concessions, loopholes, and possible tax shelters.

A particularly important example of this was the taxation of fringe benefits. In New Zealand and Australia, for example, the taxable value of these fringe benefits was raised much closer to their market values and taxed in the hands of the employees.

Another major innovation in this direction was tightening of laws relating to taxing of capital gains. In the USA, for example, capital gains were completely assimilated in the income tax. Similar moves were made in Canada, Australia, Japan and several of the Scandinavian countries.

(iv) Another important characteristic of the tax reform package has been the change in tax mix. Reductions in personal income taxation were partly financed by an increase in other taxes. In most cases this took the form of the introduction of a nationwide VAT. Most European Union (EU) countries have long had the VAT, while New Zealand and Canada introduced it in the guise of a Goods and Services Tax (GST).

Another route taken to compensate for the reduction in tax revenue from personal income taxes was to collect more revenue from corporate taxes. This was generally achieved by broadening the base of the corporate tax (without increasing tax rates). This was done in Canada and the USA.

(v) The broadening of the base of the corporate tax was accompanied by a reduction in the rates. In the UK, for example, from 1984 the 100 per cent first year write-off for plant and equipment was replaced by a 25 per cent depreciation allowance, and provision for stock relief against inflation were withdrawn. In parallel, the rates of corporate tax were cut from 52 per cent to 33 per cent.

Similarly, in the USA the primary rate of corporate tax was cut from 46 to 34 per cent. At the same time, investment incentives were cut. Similar reforms were effected by Canada, Australia, New Zealand, and some of the Scandinavian countries.

(vi) Finally, tax reforms were always accompanied by considerable toning up of tax administration.

Reasons for tax reform

An interesting question to ask at this point is why did such substantial tax reforms take place in so many countries simultaneously. There are several reasons for this:

(a) There was extreme discontent with the existing tax system in most of the countries. This took several forms. On the one hand, it was felt that, high marginal tax rates were having serious disincentive effects on savings, labor supply and entrepreneurship. On the other hand, they were providing considerable avenues for tax avoidance and evasion and considerable energies and resources were being diverted to making up tax shelters. Birnbaum and Murray (1988), for example, provide numerous examples of the extent of tax avoidance by individuals and firms and show why the US Tax Reforms Act of 1986 had become a dire necessity. Similar examples can be found in the experiences of Canada, Japan, Australia and New Zealand.

(b) It was also felt that apart from diverting resources from work and savings to tax avoidance, high marginal tax rates had not achieved the social and economic objectives they had been designed to meet. For instance, there was a widespread perception that high marginal tax rates had failed to reduce or even limit inequalities of income and wealth which was their objective. The rich were best placed to obtain advice on tax shelters and take advantage of tax loopholes. Thus, the effective progression of many tax systems was much less than the nominal progression. It began to be felt that if the tax concessions were reduced or eliminated, the same degree of progression could be achieved, with less horizontal inequity and with lower marginal tax rates.

(c) At the same time there was concern in almost all OECD countries that governments were taxing and spending too much. As Table 16.2 indicates, total tax revenues had climbed up substantially. The 1970s were marked by high inflation which, acting on large unindexed tax systems, perpetrated inequities. (Recall the discussion in Chapter 15.) Those most dependent on tax allowances, which failed to keep pace with prices, were hard hit. Taxpayers climbed into higher tax brackets purely because of inflation, faced higher marginal tax rates and had their real incomes reduced. Interest rates that were not indexed for inflation affected savers. The stagflation that hit major OECD economies (indeed the world economy, generally) in the early 1980s made tax reform more difficult but, at the same time, more necessary. Budget deficits which had grown very large in the 1980s because of higher social sector spending (due to recession) had to be brought under control without undue pain.

The growth in tax revenues across these countries has been achieved, as has been noted above, by reducing marginal tax rates and broadening the tax base. As a result, the shares of various taxes in total tax revenues have

Table 16.2 Growth in total tax revenue (including social security contributions) as a percentage of GDP at market prices, OECD countries, 1965–85

Country	Tax revenue as per cent of GDP		Increase of 1985 over 1965	
	1965	1985	Percentage points	Percentage increase
Australia	23.2	30.0	6.8	29.3
Austria	34.7	43.1	8.4	24.2
Belgium	31.2	47.6	16.4	52.6
Canada	25.4	33.1	7.7	30.3
Denmark	29.9	49.0	19.1	63.9
Finland	29.5	37.0	7.5	25.4
France	34.5	44.5	10.0	29.0
Germany	31.6	38.1	6.5	20.6
Greece	22.0	35.1	13.1	59.5
Iceland	27.8	28.8	1.0	3.6
Italy	25.5	34.4	8.9	34.9
Japan	18.3	27.6	9.3	50.8
Luxembourg	30.6	50.1	19.5	63.7
Netherlands	33.2	44.9	11.7	35.2
New Zealand	24.7	34.1	9.4	38.0
Norway	33.3	47.6	14.3	42.9
Portugal	18.4	31.6	13.2	71.7
Spain	14.3	28.8	14.5	101.4
Sweden	35.2	50.4	15.2	43.2
Switzerland	20.7	32.0	11.3	54.6
Turkey	15.0	19.7	4.7	31.3
UK	30.4	37.9	7.5	24.7
USA	25.9	29.2	3.3	12.7
Unweighted average	**26.7**	**37.2**	**10.5**	**39.3**

Source: *OECD Revenue Statistics*, 1992: 1965–1991

Table 16.3 Shares of various taxes in total tax revenues

	UK	OECD total	OECD Europe	EC
	Taxes on personal income			
1965	29.8	25.9	24.8	20.9
1970	31.4	27.7	26.1	22.2
1975	37.9	30.7	28.8	26.1
1980	29.8	32.0	29.8	27.5
1985	27.1	30.4	27.7	26.5
1988	26.8	30.2	27.9	26.6
1989	27.1	29.3	27.0	25.3
1990	28.6	29.8	27.5	25.9
1991	28.3	29.7	27.6	26.2
1992	28.4	29.7	27.8	26.3
	Taxes on corporate income			
1965	7.1	8.9	6.3	7.0
1970	9.1	8.7	6.4	7.4
1975	6.7	7.5	5.7	6.5
1980	8.3	7.4	6.0	6.6
1985	12.5	7.8	6.9	7.2
1988	10.7	7.7	6.5	7.2
1989	12.1	7.8	6.6	7.4
1990	10.9	7.7	6.7	7.6
1991	8.8	7.3	6.3	7.1
1992	7.6	6.8	5.8	6.7
	Taxes on goods and services			
1965	33.0	38.0	40.1	38.5
1970	28.8	35.8	38.2	36.7
1975	25.4	31.4	33.2	31.5
1980	29.2	30.2	31.9	31.1
1985	30.7	31.0	32.9	31.5
1988	31.3	31.0	32.9	32.5
1989	30.5	30.4	32.2	31.8
1990	30.5	30.0	31.8	31.8
1991	33.3	30.2	31.8	31.8
1992	34.4	30.3	31.9	32.1

Sources: **Revenue statistics of OECD member countries**

not changed much. This is indicated in Table 16.3 for three major heads of taxes: personal taxes, corporate taxes and commodity taxes. This table indicates the broad stability in revenue sources in member countries during periods of intense tax reforms.

The plan of this chapter is as follows. In the next section we examine the welfare foundations of tax reform, then we study tax reforms in a life-cycle context. We move on to a more detailed discussion of tax reform in a dynamic context and articulate the recent marginal cost and marginal benefit approach to tax reform. Finally, there is a section on key conclusions.

16.2   WELFARE FOUNDATIONS OF TAX REFORM

As we have seen, tax reform has often involved quite systemic changes. The important point, however, is that the movement is gradual and proceeds in several directions at the same time. Knowing from second best theory that a move toward Pareto optimality without actually attaining it may not be second-best optimal, we have to inquire into the welfare foundations of tax reform.

Theoretical analysis of tax reforms was first initiated in the classic paper by Diamond and Mirrlees (1971). This work was later developed by several others. A comprehensive treatise on tax reform is Guesnerie (1995). In the following discussion we will adhere to Diamond and Mirrlees and Guesnerie.

The specification of the Diamond–Mirrlees model is as follows. The economy has n private goods indexed by i and H consumers indexed by h. Let us define z_h as the vector of net trade (the excess of consumption over production) of the hth consumer. This individual has a strictly quasi-concave utility function $U^h(z_h, G)$ where G is the amount of a pure public good consumed by this consumer and, hence, by the society.

The consumer price vector is p, the producer price vector is q and the vector of specific commodity taxes is τ where $p = q + \tau$. Let us now define the following terms: $d_h(p, G, S)$ is the solution to the consumer's utility maximization exercise: $\max U(z_h, G)$ subject to the budget constraint $p \cdot z_h \leqslant 0$ where S is a lump-sum transfer. Let Y_v be the vector of private goods produced. The profit-maximizing supply of private goods for producers of private goods is denoted by $\sigma_v(q)$. Thus $\sigma_v(q)$ is the solution to:

$$\max q \cdot y'_v \text{ subject to } y_v \in Y_v$$

where Y_v is the private production set. We assume that the public good producer produces two goods[1] – the pure public good and an input, amounts of which are denoted by G_i. This good is sold as an input (at price vector q) to producers of private goods. Hence for this producer $\sigma_p(G, q)$ is the solution to:

$$\max q \cdot G_i, \text{ such that } G, G_i \in Y_p$$

where Y_p is the production possibility set of this producer.

We can now define a **feasible state** for this economy. This consists of consumption bundles z_h, a private production plan y'_v, intermediate input vector G_i and a public goods production plan G and the price vectors p and q such that the following conditions are satisfied:

(a) $z_h = d_h(p, G, S)$ (16.1)

(b) $y'_v = \sigma_v(q)$ (16.2)

(c) $y''_p = \sigma_p(G, q)$ (16.3)

(d) $\sum_h z_h \leqslant y'_v + G_i.$ (16.4)

In principle, it is possible to aggregate equations (16.2) and (16.3) to get

$$y'' = y'_v + G_i = \sigma(G, q) \qquad (16.5)$$

where $\sigma = \sigma_v + \sigma_p$. Then we can rewrite equation (16.4) as:

$$\sum_h z_h \leqslant y''. \qquad (16.6)$$

When the strict equality holds Guesenrie calls the equilibrium **tight** or **strict**. To define and support this equilibrium we would have to specify the following:

(i) a level of the public good G;
(ii) a vector of specific tax rates. Candidates for this would be a VAT (with different rates, if necessary).

Further, since the producer's profit does not enter the individual demand functions, it is implicitly being assumed that the entire profit of the producers is being taxed away. We could assume that the revenue from this is passed on as lump-sum payment to consumers.

In order to proceed with tax reform we assume full differentiability of all functions above and full rank of the Jacobian so that the above relations can be inverted. Let us denote time by t and think of the problem of tax reform as examining whether there is an improvement in welfare in moving to a neighborhood of the existing (strict) equilibrium. We also define $\dot{S}$ as dS/dt etc and **equilibrium preserving directions of change** $(\dot{p}, \dot{S}, \dot{G}, \dot{q})$ as those for which the following expression holds:

$$(\partial d/\partial p)(\dot{p}) + (\partial d/\partial S)\dot{S} + (\partial d/\partial G)\dot{G} \leqslant (\partial \sigma/\partial G)\dot{G} + (\partial \sigma/\partial q)\dot{q}. \quad (16.7)$$

Expression (16.7) is a basic feasibility condition in that it says that, as a result of the move to a neighboring point, the change in demand should be no greater than the change in supply. It will be strictly equilibrium preserving if the equality holds.

Now, given that the last expression on the righthand side of expression (16.7) is positive, we can write an alternative condition:

$$q(\partial d/\partial p)\dot{p} + q(\partial d/\partial S)\dot{S} + q[(\partial d/\partial G) - (\partial \sigma/\partial G)]\dot{G} \leqslant 0. \qquad (16.8)$$

To simplify the notation we write:

$$\phi_p \equiv q(\partial d/\partial p), \quad \phi_G \equiv q[(\partial d/\partial G) - (\partial \sigma/\partial G)], \quad \phi_S \equiv q(\partial d/\partial S)$$

so that we can rewrite expression (16.8) as:

$$\phi_p \dot{p} + \phi_S \dot{S} + \phi_G \dot{G} \leqslant 0.$$

By the homogeneity of degree zero of the demand function d we must have:

$$\phi_p p + \phi_S S = 0.$$

If expression (16.8) holds as an equality then the move is strictly equilibrium preserving. From those moves that satisfy expression (16.8) we wish to single out those that have certain desirable welfare properties. An obvious candidate for this would be Pareto improving moves. To this end, let us define:

$$C_h(p, S, G) = \begin{bmatrix} \partial U^h[d_h(p, S, G), G]/\partial G \\ \{\partial U^h[d_h(p, S, G), G]/\partial S]\}^{-1} \end{bmatrix}$$

The components of C_h are the willingness to pay for the public good. Hence, for the hth consumer the **welfare improving directions of change** $(\dot{p}, \dot{S}, \dot{G})$ are those that satisfy:

$$-d_h\dot{p} + \dot{S} + C_h\dot{G} > 0. \tag{16.9}$$

An interpretation of this condition would go as follows. Since all goods are normal here the direction of d_h would be the opposite of that of $\dot{p}$; hence the first term on the lefthand side of (16.9) measures the welfare change because of the (consumer) price change. The second term measures the change in lump-sum subsidy to the consumer, and the last term measures the effect of change in the public good. The lefthand side of expression (16.9), then, measures all welfare changes for the hth consumer when there is a tax reform.

A natural extension of this would be **Pareto-improving directions of change**. These are moves for which expression (16.9) is satisfied for all consumers. In other words:

$$-d_h\dot{p} + \dot{S} + C_h\dot{G} > 0 \text{ for all h.}$$

We can then define:

$$\phi \equiv (\phi_p, \phi_S, \phi_G) \text{ and } \Psi_h \equiv (-d_h, 1, C_h).$$

Then we can define a direction of reform $\nabla = (\dot{p}, \dot{S}, \dot{G})$ to be equilibrium preserving and Pareto improving if it satisfies the following two conditions:

$$\text{(i) } \phi \cdot \nabla \leqslant 0 \tag{16.10}$$

and

$$\text{(ii) } \Psi_h \cdot \nabla > 0. \tag{16.11}$$

An important question that arises at this stage is the following: do there exist equilibrium-preserving and Pareto-improving directions of change? This amounts to asking whether the set of directions associated with (16.10) or (16.11) is non-empty. We can, if we wish, confine ourselves to a particular subset of directions B (the set of politically feasible moves?) and ask whether this set of directions includes moves that are equilibrium preserving and Pareto improving.

We are then interested in a direction ∇^B such that:

$$\phi^B \cdot \nabla^B \leqslant 0 \tag{16.12}$$

$$\Psi_h^B \cdot \nabla^B > 0. \tag{16.13}$$

Guesnerie then proves the following important result:
Consider a strict tax equilibrium in which (i) $\phi^B \neq 0$; (ii) the set of Pareto-improving directions of change (within the set B) is non-empty. Then one of the following must be true:

(a) The inequalities $\phi^B \cdot \nabla^B \leqslant 0$ and $\Psi_h^B \cdot \nabla^B > 0$ are incompatible with each other. ϕ^B belongs to the cone generated by the vectors Ψ_h^B.
(b) The inequalities $\phi^B \cdot \nabla^B \geqslant 0$ and $\Psi^B \cdot \nabla^B > 0$ are incompatible with each other. ϕ^B belongs to the cone generated by the vectors $(-\Psi_h^B)$.
(c) The vector ϕ^B belongs to the complement of Ψ_h^B and $(-\Psi_h^B)$ if and only if there exist (in subset B) strict equilibrium-preserving and Pareto-improving directions of change. (Proof: see Guesenrie 1995: 145–6.)

The three cases mentioned above indicate that there are three different possibilities when we are considering tax reforms. In case (a) it is not possible to find a Pareto-improving and equilibrium preserving direction of move. In case (b) it is possible to find a Pareto-improving direction of change but it is not strictly equilibrium preserving. In other words (16.12) holds as a strict inequality. This means that there is a Pareto-improving direction of movement which is feasible but which 'wastes' some resources in the process. Guesenrie shows that this phenomenon can only occur temporarily during a process of tax reform. Hence, he calls these **temporary inefficiencies**. In case (c) the direction of reform is Pareto-improving as well as strictly equilibrium preserving.

A simplified exposition

To better understand the above result let us take the case where there are no public goods nor any lump sum subsidies and focus exclusively on the case of pure tax reforms. Let q^0, p^0 be the initial values of the producer price and the consumer price vectors.

The feasibility condition now takes the following form:

$$\Delta^0 \cdot dp \leqslant 0. \tag{16.14}$$

where $\Delta^0 = q_0(\partial d/\partial p)|_{p^0}$ is a vector of product of the row vector q^0 and the Jacobian matrix of total excess demand. The equality would hold in equation (16.14) if the equilibrium was tight. Hence, starting from (q^0, p^0), neighboring tight equilibrium are of the form $(q^0, p^0 + dp)$ where dp satisfies equation (16.14) as an equality.

As a result of the tax reform the consumer price vector becomes $(p^0 + dp)$ as a consequence of which the net trade vector of household h will change to $z_h^0 \cdot dp$. This will obviously change household welfare only if:

$$z_h^0 \cdot dp < 0. \qquad (16.15)$$

In this case now, an infinitesimal change (dp) that satisfies both equations (16.14) and (16.15) is both feasible as well as Pareto improving. Let us now define the sets:

$$J^0 = \{a \in R^n / \Delta^0 a \leqslant 0\} \text{ and}$$
$$K^0 = \{a \in R^n / z_h^0 a < 0\}.$$

We should note that knowledge of the two sets J^0 and K^0 only requires knowledge of the production prices, the initial trade vectors of all consumers and the elasticities of total demand. In line with Guesenrie's general theorem discussed above we can write the following three cases:

(a) $J^0 \cap K^0 = \phi$ (the intersection of the two sets is null, so that there exists no infinitesimal change which is both feasible as well as Pareto improving).
(b) $J^0 \cap K^0 \neq \phi$ but $K^0 \cap F(J^0) = \phi$.
(c) $K^0 \cap F(J^0) \neq \phi$ (where $F(J^0)$ designates the frontier of J^0). In this case there exist infinitesimal changes that are both feasible and Pareto improving.

Once again in case (b) there are temporary inefficiencies in the process of tax reforms. This would usually happen when the initial specific tax vector is very large (there is a large gap between producer and consumer prices).

Let Z^0 be the cone generated by the vectors z_h^0 and let '$-$' represent symmetry with respect to the origin. Then:

(i) case (a) is equivalent to $\Delta^0 \in -Z^0$;
(ii) case (b) is equivalent to $\Delta^0 \in Z^0$;
(iii) case (c) is equivalent to $\Delta^0 \in [Z^0 \cup -Z^0]$.

We can then develop algorithms of tax reforms. The problem here is to go from the analysis of infinitesimal that give the directions of desirable changes to the analysis of finite changes that are feasible and Pareto improving. The local analysis leads to a differential equation (with a multi-valued righthand side) which has to be integrated to generate an actual tax reform algorithm. In principle, this is the problem of existence and uniqueness of the solution to the differential equation. We also need to study stability in order to examine convergence to the solution.

Our analysis up to now should convince us that even marginal tax reform has formidable data requirements. One would need at least three critical pieces of information:

(i) the impact of the reform on tax revenue;
(ii) the incidence of the reform packet;
(iii) the social welfare weight of each household to be used in aggregating the gains and losses of different households from such tax reform.

In a pioneering paper Ahmad and Stern (1984) showed that the first two data requirements can be met from household expenditure surveys and from a study of the tax system in the aggregate. The third requirement, however, has always posed serious difficulties since it involves complex value judgements.

Typically two approaches have been used to address this third question. Some people have concentrated on Pareto improving tax reforms, thereby circumventing the issue of distributional judgements. The second approach has utilized social welfare function such as the utilitarian or the Rawlsian or Atkinson's measure of social welfare. (Recall the discussion in Chapter 3.)

Recently Mayshar and Yitzhaki (1995) have advocated the use of Dalton's 1920 principle of tax reform. A tax reform is said to be **Dalton improving** if it improves social welfare for all possible social welfare functions that conform to Dalton's principle of transfers. According to this principle, if there exists a prior economic ranking of households, then a transfer is approved if it distributes from high-ranking (rich) to low-ranking (poor) households provided that the ranking itself is not altered.

We immediately realize that Dalton's measure has considerable data requirements. In order to maintain the ordinality of the ranking one has to identify each household in the economy. This may not be required if tax reforms are required to be Pareto improving. Dalton's measure would, therefore, not allow people to remain anonymous whereas in the case of Pareto the principle of anonymity is respected.

In the Dalton scheme of things wealth or income is considered a normal good so that tax payers are always willing to acquire more. It is assumed that the already rich may have the strongest desire to acquire wealth whereas, from the planner's point of view, the poor may be the most deserving. The Dalton approach to tax reform would set a 'deservation' level for a marginal increase in income of the richest household to zero while making this household a strong candidate to give up part of its income (i.e. most deserving marginal decrease). One can normalize the deservingness of a marginal increase or decrease in income to zero for any arbitarily chosen income level (say at the mean or the median or at the poverty level). The scope of tax reforms will then depend upon the choice of this cut-off income level as well as the extent of inequality among households. Mayshar and Yitzhaki use the Dalton measure to evaluate indirect tax reforms for the UK.

16.3 TAX REFORM IN A DYNAMIC CONTEXT

The analysis of Guesnerie presented above deals with tax reform in static economies. One of the important aims of tax reform, in recent years, has been to increase savings and to affect the intergenerational distribution of resources. In this section we study intergenerational transfers and the efficiency of tax reforms. Tax revenues are assumed to be age independently transferred to households. We follow, in the main, the work of Felder (1993).

The framework of the analysis is the standard life-cycle model of savings (with fixed labor) that we have studied in Chapter 7. For a young person at time t we define utility from first- and second-period consumption and write the utility of a representative household as:

$$U_t = U(c_t^1, c_{t+1}^2) \tag{16.16}$$

where the notation is obvious. This worker inelastically supplies one unit of labor in the first time period for which the gross wage is w_t and the net wage is $w_t(1 - \tau_w^t)$ where τ_w^t is the proportional rate of wage tax in time period t. In each period the worker gets a transfer of g and this is assumed to be constant. Thus the consumer's budget constraint with the wage tax is:

$$\begin{aligned} c_t^1 + c_{t+1}^2/(1 + r_{t+1}) &= w_t(1 - \tau_w^t) + g + g/(1 + r_{t+1}) \\ &= w_t(1 - \tau_w^t) + g[2 + r_{t+1}]/(1 + r_{t+1}) \end{aligned} \tag{16.17}$$

where r_{t+1} is the interest rate prevailing in period $(t + 1)$.

If, instead, we had a consumption tax at the rate τ_c^t the budget constraint of the consumer would have been written as:

$$c_t^1/(1 - \tau_c^t) + c_{t+1}^2/[(1 + r_{t+1})(1 - \tau_c^{t+1})] = w_t + g[(2 + r_{t+1})/(1 + r_{t+1})]. \tag{16.18}$$

Finally let us consider an income tax which consists of a wage tax at rate τ_w^t and a savings (or second-period consumption) tax at the rate τ_c^t. In this case we can write the individual's budget constraint as:

$$c_t^1 + c_{t+1}^2/[(1 + r_{t+1})(1 - \tau_c^{t+1})] = w_t(1 - \tau_w^t) + g[(2 + r_{t+1})/(1 + r_{t+1})]. \tag{16.19}$$

Let us assume that the population grows exogenously at the rate n. We further assume that the government transfers all revenues to the households, then the budget constraint of the government can be written in the three cases as:

(a) wage tax case:

$$\tau_w^t w_t = g + g/(1 + n) = g(2 + n)/(1 + n) \tag{16.20}$$

since the relation between population this period and the population last period is $1/(1 + n)$ and this period the government has to make transfers to the young of this period and the old of the last period.

(b) consumption tax case:

$$\tau_c^t[c_t^1 + c_t^2/(1 + n)]/(1 - \tau_c^t) = g(2 + n)/(1 + n). \tag{16.21}$$

The consumption of the young of today is $c_t^1/(1 - \tau_c^t)$. The number of old people from the last generation per young person today is, by virtue of population growth, $1/(1 + n)$. Hence consumption by the old of last period is $c_t^2/(1 + n)/(1 - \tau_c^t)$. This then explains the lefthand side of equation (16.21). The righthand side has already been explained above.

(c) income tax: the budget constraint of the government is now:

$$\tau_w^t w_t + \tau_c^t[c_t^2/(1+n)](1-\tau_c^t) = g(2+n)/(1+n). \tag{16.22}$$

The first term on the lefthand side is the revenue from the wage tax and the second term is the revenue from the consumption tax on the old of the last period who, because of population growth, are fewer than the number of young today.

Now since taxes paid are dependent on age whereas transfers do not depend on age, it follows that there is an intergenerational transfer. This tax-transfer mechanism corresponds to a pay-as-you-go financed public pension scheme. Let us denote $a_t^w w_t$ as the net tax paid (gross tax paid less transfers received) with the wage tax in place. In a similar manner we define $a_t^c w_t$ and $a_t^y w_t$ as the net tax paid under the consumption and income taxes respectively. The net tax paid in each case is linked to the wage rate although wage income is not the base for, say, the consumption tax.

First-period net tax payment with the wage tax on substitution from equation (16.20) is:

$$a_t^w w_t = \tau_w^t w_t - g = \tau_w^t - \tau_w^t w_t(1+n)/(2+n) = \tau_w^t w_t/(2+n). \tag{16.23}$$

For the consumption tax on substitution from equation (16.21) we have:

$$a_t^c w_t = \tau_c^t(c_t^1 - c_t^2)/[(1-\tau_c^t)(2+n)]. \tag{16.24}$$

For the income tax upon substitution from equation (16.22) we will have:

$$a_t^y w_t = [\tau_w^t w_t - \tau_c^t(c_t^2/(1-\tau_c^t))]/(2+n). \tag{16.25}$$

Only the young pay the wage tax whereas both the young and the old pay the consumption and income taxes.

The second-period payments received by old households equals the net tax payments of young households multiplied by the growth factor. For any household, each tax system looks like an intergenerational transfer mechanism to which it contributes $a_t w_t$ when young and receives $a_{t+1} w_{t+1}$ when old. Intergenerational transfers plus the wealth and substitution effects associated with different taxes determine the influence of these respective taxes on the savings decisions of households.

When labor is inelastically supplied, as is being assumed so far, utility is a monotonic function of wealth. Hence, to find out the effects of different taxes we have to examine their effects on lifetime wealth.

In steady state the rate of return on net tax payments in the first period always equals the growth factor so that lifetime wealth W^j under tax regime j ($j = w, c, y$) can be written as:

$$W^j = a^j w(n-r)/(1+r). \tag{16.26}$$

Hence whether wealth increase over one's lifespan would depend upon the sign of a^j which itself depends upon the direction in which intergenerational transfers are going and on the sign of $(n-r)$. When $r < n$ then tax regimes

involving a transfer from the young to the old, for example, will increase
wealth. This is because the net of return on tax paid (n) exceeds that on
productive investment (r). When $r > n$ transfers to the young increase and
transfers to the old would decrease wealth. When we are at the golden rule
$(r = n)$ then there is no opportunity to get a rate of return different from
that given by productive investment and there are no wealth effects.

With a wealth tax a^w is positive and, hence, there is a transfer from the
young to the old. Thus lifetime wealth increases (decreases) with the wage
tax as $r < n(r > n)$. With the consumption tax a^c can take either sign. With
a constant elasticity type of utility function it can be shown that a^c will be
negative so that the young are subsidized by the old. Thus lifetime wealth
decreases (increases) as $r < n(r > n)$. With an income tax at the same rate
on both wage and consumption, the same results as those with wage tax will
hold.

With non-distortionary taxation second-period consumption can be written as:

$$c_{t+1}^2 = s_t(1 + r_{t+1}) + (1 + n)a_{t+1}w_{t+1} \tag{16.27}$$

where s_t represents first-period savings. When the tax changes b will change.
Differentiating s_t with respect to a_t and assuming that $a_t = a_{t+1}$, we will get:

$$ds_t/da_t = [dc_{t+1}^2/da_t - (1 + n)w_{t+1}]/(1 + r_{t+1}). \tag{16.28}$$

The second term within parenthesis is negative. The higher the tax, the
higher the grant and the lower, therefore, the incentive to save. The first
term is also negative if second-period consumption is a normal good. The
higher the a, the lower the net wage and the lower the second-period
consumption. These results are due to the partial equilibrium exercise of
Feldstein (1974) and carry over to general equilibrium provided that it is
unique and stable.

Tax reforms

Tax reforms subject to a balanced budget requirement can easily be analyzed. Since $a^c > a^w$, it follows that when consumption taxes are substituted
for a wage tax savings will increase. This is independent of whether wealth
is rising or falling $(r > n$ or $r < n)$. If preferences are Cobb–Douglas then,
with uniform income tax rates, $a^w > a^y > a^c$. Savings would be highest with
a consumption tax and lowest with a wage tax with the income tax case
falling in between.

Let us now discuss production efficiency. Suppose that production is
carried on with capital and labor as inputs using a standard neoclassical
production function: $f(k_t)$ where k_t is the capital–labor ratio and $f(.)$ is the
intensive production function. Factors are paid their marginal products so
that $r_t = f'$ and $w_t = f - kf'$. Current capital stock is the amortized value of
last period's savings: $k_t = s_{t-1}/(1 + n)$, where s_t denotes savings per worker.

Suppose now that we substitute a consumption tax for the wage tax. Suppose this change occurs at time period $t = 0$. Now, since $a^w > a^c$ there will be a transfer from the old to the young. Hence the old in time period 0 will find their pensions lower by the amount $(a^w - a^c)(1 + n)w$. If $r > n$ then[2] the lifetime wealth of everyone else increases. One can always get more from productive investments than the increased commitments toward the elderly. Hence, savings will also rise. Moreover, since $k_t = s_{t-1}/(1+n)$ it follows that per worker capital stock (k_t^c) will be higher for the consumption tax case as opposed to the wage tax case (k_t^w). This will have the consequence that the rate of return to capital in the consumption tax case (r_t^c) will be lower than that in the wage tax case (r_t^w):

$$r_t^c < r_t^w \text{ for } t = 0, 1, 2, \ldots \tag{16.29}$$

The fact that the capital–labor ratio is higher means that output per worker is higher but it can be shown that this increase in production is not high enough to support an intergenerational transfer mechanism that would improve the welfare of every generation.

Let us now define total consumption per worker c_t as:

$$c_t = c_t^1 + c_t^2/(1+n).$$

In period 0 the change in consumption:

$$\Delta c_0 = c_0^c - c_0^w < 0.$$

This decrease in consumption can be completely offset by an increase in consumption in the subsequent period if:

$$(1 + n)\Delta c_1/(1 + r_1^w) > -\Delta c_0. \tag{16.30}$$

In expression (16.30) Δc_1 is the change in consumption in period 1. Because of the increase in population it will be $(1 + n)$ times this value in time period 0. But the change in consumption will occur in a later period and will, therefore, need to be discounted back. Hence the lefthand side of expression (16.30). If this condition holds then the young can fully compensate the old for their loss. Substituting Δs_0 for $-\Delta c_0$ and rearranging allows us to write (16.30) as:

$$\Delta c_1 > \Delta s_0(1 + r_1^w)/(1 + n). \tag{16.31}$$

Now, the increase in gross output (Δy_t^g) can be written as:
$\Delta y_t^g = \Delta k_t + f'\Delta k_t$ but $f' = r$, because factor markets are competitive. Hence, we will have:

$$\Delta y_1^g = \Delta k_1(1 + \bar{r}_1) = \Delta s_0(1 + \bar{r}_1)/(1 + n) \tag{16.32}$$

where $\bar{r}$ is the average[3] rate of return on capital increase from k^w to k^c. But since $r^w > \bar{r}$ we can write from (16.31) and (16.32) that:

$$\Delta y_1^g < \Delta c_1. \tag{16.33}$$

Hence the increase in consumption in period 1 does not allow the formerly young generation to be compensated adequately. Hence, it can never be efficient to substitute a consumption tax for a wage tax in this sense. Felder (1993) shows that this result easily generalizes to the many period case.

At this point it is worthwhile to allude to the analysis reported in Chapter 7. There we had gone through Summers' (1981) analysis of the so-called 'human wealth effect' where he had shown that in many period life-cycle models savings are very interest elastic. Consequently tax reforms of the above sort can create big changes in the capital stock and result in high steady-state welfare gains. The proposition here shows that a mere increase in the capital stock is not enough to guarantee an increase in welfare.

Summary

Since labor supply is exogenously given in this model, a wage tax is not distortionary. Moreover, a consumption tax is also not distortionary here. Hence the growth path of the economy is dynamically efficient. In this situation the substitution of one tax for another leading to an increase in savings is not necessarily Pareto superior. On the other hand, a policy which reduces savings along such a dynamically efficient path will improve welfare by inducing intergenerational transfers. Examples of such policies are increases in the wealth tax or the substitution of a consumption tax by a wage tax. In the case of the income tax, an excess burden is imposed on the economy because the income tax alters the rate at which the households can exchange present for future consumption. The growth path associated with an income tax is dynamically inefficient as contrasted to the growth path associated with the wage tax or the consumption tax.

However, none of these results will hold when we have an endogenous supply of labor. In that case, a wage tax will also impose an excess burden – indeed each tax will. The theorem of second best tells us that, a priori, we do not know which tax is associated with higher welfare and simulation or computational techniques have to be resorted to.

16.4   THE MARGINAL APPROACH TO TAX REFORM

An influential argument in tax reform theory has been that if, for example, we are substituting one tax for another, then the new tax is an improvement if it involves a lower marginal cost of public funds (MCPF). This is sometimes referred to as the Kay–Panzar–Sadka requirement. This requirement is stated by Mayshar (1990) as:

> A tax reform replacing a tax t_j by t_i at the margin, keeping the total revenues unchanged, is desirable if and only if the marginal cost of public funds measure associated with t_j is higher than the MCPF associated with t_i.

Recently Fullerton (1991) and Ballard and Fullerton (1992) have made important contributions in this area. Schob (1994) has extended this to cover the notion of marginal benefit of public funds (MBPF). In this section we explore this literature somewhat.

Throughout this literature is concerned with efficiency issues and examines the welfare aspects of tax reforms on the utility of the representative household. There are *H* identical individuals in society. The utility function of the representative individual is written as:

$$U = u(x_1, x_2, G) \tag{16.34}$$

where x_1 and x_2 are two commodities consumed by this individual and *G* is the amount of a pure public good. All commodities are measured in terms of leisure[4] (x_0 say) which therefore serves as the numeraire and is untaxed. Producer prices are q_i and consumer prices are p_i. The difference between them is the specific commodity tax t_i. Thus $p_i = q_i + t_i$.

This consumer's budget constraint can be written as:

$$p_1 x_1 + p_2 x_2 = Y^h - T^h = y^h \tag{16.35}$$

where y^h denotes an exogenously given income, T^h is lump-sum tax and y^h is net income for individual *h*. All individuals are identical.

Total consumption of commodity *i* is X_i where

$$X_i = Hx_i \ (i = 1, 2) \quad \text{where } H \text{ is the total number of consumers.}$$

Total lump-sum tax revenue is $T = HT^h$. Now, if $\phi(G)$ (with $\phi' > 0$) of providing the pubic good, the government's budget surplus, *S*, is:

$$S = t_1 X_1 + t_2 X_2 + T - \phi(G). \tag{16.36}$$

Realize also that ϕ' measures the mrt between the numeraire and the public good.

Totally differentiating equation (16.36) with respect to t_1 holding *T* and *S* constant and letting dS_1 represent this change we have:

$$t_1(\partial X_1/\partial t_1)dt_1 + X_1 dt_1 + t_2(\partial X_2/\partial t_1)dt_1 = dS_1, \text{ or}$$

$$X_1[1 + \sum_{i=1}^{2}(t_i/X_1)(\partial X_i/\partial t_1)]dt_1 = dS_1$$

which we write compactly as:

$$X_1[1 + \tau_1]dt_1 = dS_1 \tag{16.37a}$$

with $\tau_1 (= \sum_{i=1}^{2}(t_i/X_1)(\partial X_i/\partial t_1))$ is the own-tax elasticity of good 1 when the cross-price effect is zero.

Similarly differentiating (16.36) with respect to X_2, *T*, and *G seriatim* and letting dS_2 and dG denote the respective changes we have:

$$X_2[1 + \tau_2]dt_2 = dS_2 \tag{16.37b}$$

$$\left[1 - \sum_{i=1}^{2} t_i(\partial X_i/\partial Y)\right]dT = dS_T \tag{16.37c}$$

$$\left[\sum_{i=1}^{2} t_i(\partial X_i/\partial G) - \phi'\right] dG = dS_G. \tag{16.37d}$$

With these definitions we can define describe two types of tax reforms.

(a) **A differential tax reform**: in this case one tax is replaced by another or a marginal public good is financed by increasing a particular tax. An example of such a tax reform would be:

$$dS_1 = -dS_2 > 0. \tag{16.38}$$

(b) **Costs and benefits of a marginal unit of the public good**: in this case we would analyze the costs and benefits of a marginal public goods project. The government wants to increase G and fully finance the additional requirement by increasing a particular tax, say t_2. This reform[5] can be described as:

$$dS_2 = -dS_G > 0. \tag{16.39}$$

This reform is sometimes also called **balanced budget tax reform**. To find out whether differential tax reforms and balanced budget tax reforms are welfare improving we should calculate the MCPF and the MBPF in both cases.

The marginal cost of public funds and tax reform

In the literature two different notions of MCPF in the context of tax reforms have been mentioned. On the one hand Kay (1980), Stuart (1980), and Ballard *et al.* (1985) calculate the **uncompensated marginal cost of public funds ($mcpf^c$)**. On the other hand, authors such as Harberger (1965) and Browning (1976, 1987) have emphasized the importance of the **compensated marginal cost of public funds ($mcpf^c$)**.

Uncompensated measure of excess burden

Consider an individual with an indirect utility function V corresponding to equation (16.34). The utility loss from a change in the tax say t_1 will be $V_1 dt_1$ where V_1 is the partial derivative of the indirect utility function with respect to t_1. Now using Roy's identity we get $du_1/dt_1 = -x_1$ which is the negative of the consumer surplus (CS_1) from a change in tax rate t_1. We know that, at the margin, the CS_1 is equal to the compensating variation CV_1 and the equivalent variation EV. Hence one notion of the excess burden of a marginal variation of t_1 would be:

$$MEB_1^u = H\, CS_1 - dS_1/dt_1 = -\sum_{i=1}^{2} t_i(\partial X_i/\partial t_1) \tag{16.40}$$

so that the uncompensated marginal cost of public funds from changing t_1 ($MCPF_1^u$) is such that:

$$\text{MCPF}_1^u = 1 + \text{MEB}^u/(dS_1/dt_1) = 1/(1 + \tau_1) \quad (16.41)$$

where MEB represents marginal excess burden.

This definition of the marginal cost of public funds measures the social cost of one marginal unit of tax revenue (public funds) raised by an increase of tax t_1. Note that this measure is unit free.

Compensated measure of excess burden

In an analogous manner we can define the compensated measure of marginal excess burden (MEB_1^c) (where the superscript 'c' represents compensated magnitudes) from a variation in t_1:

$\text{MEB}_1^c = \text{H CS}_1 - dS_1^c/dt_1$. Instead of looking at the actual change in marginal tax revenue we are looking at the compensated change in marginal revenue. Hence dS_1^c/dt_1 is defined as:

$$dS_1^c/dt_1 = \left[X_1 + \sum_{i=1}^{2} t_i(\partial X_i/\partial t_1)|_{u=\bar{u}}\right]dt_1 = (1 + \tau_1^c)X_1 dt_1. \quad (16.42)$$

Here $\tau_1^c = \tau_{11}^c + \tau_{12}^c$; is the sum of the partial compensated tax elasticities with $\tau_{ij}^c = \tau_{ji}^c$ and $\tau_{ij}^c = (t_j/x_i)(\partial x_i/\partial t_j)$.

The compensated measure of marginal excess burden can now be written as:

$$\text{MEB}_1^c = -\sum_{i=1}^{2} t_i(\partial X_i/\partial t_1)|_{u=\bar{u}}. \quad (16.43)$$

This is a measure of excess burden that has only the substitution effect at work.[6]

We can then write the compensated marginal cost of public funds (MCPF_1^c) as:

$$\text{MCPF}_1^c = \text{MEB}_1^c/(dS_1/dt) + 1 = -\tau_1^c/(1 + \tau_1^c) + 1$$
$$= \left[1 - \sum_{i=1}^{2} t_i(\partial X_i/\partial Y)\right](1 + \tau_1^c). \quad (16.44)$$

We need to compare the MCPF expressions in equations (16.41) and (16.44). Using equations (16.37) we can see that:

$$\text{MCPF}_1^c = \text{MCPF}_1^u\left[1 - \sum_{i=1}^{2} t_i(\partial X_i/\partial Y)\right] = \text{MCPF}_1^u(dS_T/dT). \quad (16.45)$$

The marginal benefit of public funds

The measures of marginal cost of public funds derived above relate to tax changes. To enable us to apply these to balanced budget analysis we need parallel expressions for the marginal benefit of the tax revenue. The utility change from a marginal unit of the public good can be written as (V_G/V_y) dG where V_G is the partial derivative of the indirect utility function with respect to G etc. From the expression for dS_G in equation (16.37d) we know the amount needed to provide for the additional amount of the public good. The first term $(t_i \sum (\partial X_i/\partial G))$ denotes the feedback effect of public goods provision on tax revenues. This may be interpreted as the **self-financing effects** of the public good.

To define the marginal uncompensated benefits of public funds ($MBPF^u$) we have to express the sum of the marginal rates of substitution (mrs) over all individuals in terms of the marginal expenditure. Thus we have:

$$MBPF^u = H(mrs) / \left[\phi' - \sum_{i=1}^{2} t_i (\partial X_i / \partial G) \right]. \qquad (16.46)$$

The numerator of this expression is clear enough. In the denominator ϕ' represents the marginal rate of transformation (mrt) between the numeraire and the public good. However, as the consumption of the public good expands, so does the consumption of private goods and revenue from commodity taxation goes up by $[\sum_{i=1}^{2} t_i (\partial X_i / \partial G)]$. Hence this reduces the cost of the public good or, equivalently, increases benefits. This explains expression (16.46).

Similarly we can derive an expression for the compensated marginal benefits of public funds ($MBPF^c$). This computation can be split up into two steps. In the first step an increase of t_1 is compensated for by a lump-sum rebate of the same amount. In the second step a lump-sum tax is levied to finance the additional unit of the public good. Hence we must have:

$$MBPF_G^u \left[1 - \sum_{i=1}^{2} t_i (\partial X_i / \partial y) \right] = MBPF^c. \qquad (16.47)$$

Evaluation of tax reforms

Having derived expressions for marginal costs and benefits of public funds we can now investigate the effects of different types of tax reforms. We first consider differential tax reforms and then balanced budget tax reforms.

Consider replacing t_2 by t_1. Define the social welfare function as $Hu(x_1, x_2, G)$. Using Roy's identity the normalized change in welfare $dW^* \equiv dW/V_y = -X_1 dt_1 - X_2 dt_2$. Using equations (16.37 a,b) we have

$$dW^* = [-1/(1 + \tau_1)]dS_1 + [-1/(1 + \tau_2)]dS_2. \qquad (16.48)$$

Dividing through by $dS_1 = -dS_2 > 0$ and using the expressions for $MCPF^u$ we have:

$$dW^*/dS_1 = -MCPF_1^u + MCPF_2^u. \qquad (16.49)$$

Using the Kay–Panzar–Sadka requirement this tax reform is welfare enhancing only if the marginal cost of public funds associated with t_1 is smaller than that with t_2. We have:

$$dW^*/dS_1 \gtreqqless 0 \quad \text{as} \quad MCPF_2^u \gtreqqless MCPF_1^u. \tag{16.50}$$

Let us now consider the second type of reform – the balanced budget tax reform. This tax reform envisages $dS_1 = -dS_G > 0$. The welfare change of this tax reform would be:

$$dW^* = -X_1 dt_1 + \sum_h \text{mrs} \, dG.$$

Working from equation (16.49) we write:

$$dW^*/dS_1 = -MCPF_1^u + MBPF_G^u \tag{16.51}$$

from which it follows that:

$$dW^*/dS_1 \gtreqqless 0 \quad \text{as} \quad MBPF_G^u \gtreqqless MCPF_1^u. \tag{16.52}$$

Additional remarks on tax reforms

An important issue in commodity tax reform has been the uniformity of tax rates. This is reflected in the almost universal movement toward VAT with very few rates. We know, however, that uniform commodity tax rates need not be optimal. But Hatta (1986) and Fukushima and Hatta (1989) have demonstrated both theoretically as well as empirically that the second-best optimum commodity tax structure is close to uniformity. Hence any move toward uniform commodity tax rates with conditions like (16.52) being satisfied along the path of adjustment would be welcome.

16.5 CONCLUSIONS

In this chapter we have examined various aspects of tax reforms. We first remarked on the fact that the meaning of tax reform has been somewhat ambiguous as it has meant different things in different contexts. We have also emphasized the fact that there have been common trends in tax reform in several countries – both developing as well as developed.

Next we considered the standard static approach to tax reform as analyzed in classic papers by Diamond and Mirrlees and Guesnerie. We also considered tax reform in an intertemporal context, as well as some other notions of welfare improvements during tax reform such as reducing the marginal cost of public funds or increasing the marginal benefit of public funds or both.

In conclusion it is worth emphasizing that empirical models of tax reform which actually calculate the desired direction and content of tax reform in a specific context are very important. The analytical results reported in this chapter can act only as broad guidelines to policy, but in doing so they have an important role to play.

NOTES

1 Once can think of two goods or as the same good being put to two different uses.
2 The case $r < n$ is not very interesting since no generation would profit from the shift to consumption taxes.
3 This follows from the mean value theorem of differential calculus where $f'(\bar{k}) = [f(k^c) - f(k^w)]/(k^c - k^w)$ for some $k^c > \bar{k} > k^w$. This f' is called $\bar{r}$ in the text.
4 Implicitly x_0 enters into the utility function and we derive the specification after expressing everything in terms of leisure. Let this original function be written $F(x_0, x_1, x_2, G)$.
5 A third tax reform could increase lump-sum taxes while reducing a commodity tax. This would be written as:

$$dS_T = -dS_G > 0.$$

6 This involves clarifying who is paying the compensation. If the government is paying this consumption by, say, changing some other tax – say the lump-sum tax. This will have its own budgetary impact. Since utility is being held constant here this expression could be interpreted to denote the amount of the compensation required.

ADDITIONAL READING

The following are useful texts on practical aspects of tax reforms: HM Treasury (1986), Hughes (1988), Kay and King (1990), Bennett (1993), Giles and Johnson (1994), Mulgan and Murray (1993) and Wilkinson (1994).

Part IV

Applied problems in public economics

Introduction to Part IV

Part IV consists of four chapters and deals with some applied problems in public economics. It is designed to enable students to understand how theory can help to solve some practical problems.

Chapter 17 deals with public sector pricing. Various facets of this complex problem are studied. We begin by developing the Ramsey–Boiteux linear pricing problem when the public sector price is also to be used as a redistributive measure. We study the properties of marginal cost pricing under constant and increasing returns to scale. Then we examine multi-part tariffs and the limiting case of non-linear pricing. The problem of peakload pricing of utilities is taken up, followed by consideration of the problem of pricing outputs which share fixed costs. Attributable and other methods of allocating costs are discussed. The problem of cross-subsidization is also investigated.

Chapter 18 studies international aspects of tax theory and the adjustments that may have to be made to tax policy in an increasingly integrated world. Bare elements of the theory of tariffs in an open economy are developed. Fiscal coordination among countries for international interest tax harmonization is also considered. The notions of residence-based and source-based taxation are developed. There is an examination of why integration of corporate and personal taxes may not be suitable for an open economy although this is definitely appealing in a closed economy. Finally, there is a discussion of Ramsey taxation in an open economy.

Chapter 19 concerns the rudiments of cost benefit analysis. Criteria for cost benefit analysis such as net present value, benefit cost ratio and the internal rate of return are looked at. There is a discussion of the social rate of discount. First-order and second-order approaches to calculating shadow values are examined. Some illustrations of calculating shadow prices as well as the inadequacies of such calculations are also discussed.

17 Pricing in the public sector

Key concepts: Ramsey–Boiteux linear pricing; marginal cost pricing; second-best pricing; Feldstein redistributive pricing; multi-part tariffs; non-linear pricing; peak-load pricing; allocation of joint costs; fully distributed cost pricing; cross-subsidy free prices.

17.1 INTRODUCTION

In most countries public enterprises exist in the economy. This is certainly true of many developing economies. It is also true of advanced capitalist economies. Whereas in advanced capitalist societies the rationale for the public sector usually involves considerations such as equity or natural monopoly, in developing countries public-sector firms have often been given special importance in the strategy for industrial development. Whatever be the reason for the creation of public-sector firms, their existence has a profound impact on the economy.

In this chapter we focus on the important issue of pricing the output of the public sector. At least four broad aspects of the pricing problem have to have to be considered. These are:

 (i) the Ramsey–Boiteux linear pricing problem;
 (ii) an extension of this problem to cover redistribution as well as non-linear pricing;
 (iii) the problem of peak and off-peak load pricing;
 (iv) the problem of public utility pricing when the public utility produces joint products.

We will consider these problems in the course of this chapter.

17.2 THE RAMSEY–BOITEUX LINEAR PRICING PROBLEM

Attempts to address the problem of public sector pricing can be traced to the work of Ramsey (1927) which we have already discussed in the context of optimal commodity taxation in Chapter 13. Ramsey's work, appropriately interpreted, points to the desirability of determining public-sector prices and optimal commodity taxes at the same time since they occur in a similar fashion in the government budget constraint. In most recent times, the Ramsey model was developed and applied to the problem of public-sector pricing in seminal works by Boiteux (1956, 1971) who, apart from being an excellent economist, was at that time also the manager of the nationalized French electricity industry.

Since that time the Boiteux model has been very popular and has been analyzed and extended in several directions by, among several others, Dreze (1984), Dreze and Marchand (1976), Jha and Murty (1987), and Bos (1986).

The basic Boiteux model can be presented as follows. There is a public enterprise board whose objective is not to maximize net profits from the enterprise but the social welfare generated by the enterprise. This social welfare in accordance with our thinking in the chapter on commodity taxation, can be written as:

$$W = W(V^1, \ldots, V^H) \tag{17.1}$$

where W is an index of social welfare which, in turn, happens to be a function of individual (indirect) utilities V^h which are functions of the price vector (p) and lump-sum income (y^h). There are H such individuals in society and they are indexed by h.

Let $d_i^h(p, y^h)$ be private net demand for the ith good where p is the price vector and y^h is the income of consumer h. $s_i^k(p)$ is the supply of commodity i by producer k and g_i is the net production of good i by the public enterprise. Hence, the constraint that excess demand for commodity i should be equal to zero can be written as:

$$\sum_h d_i^h(p, y^h) - g_i - \sum_j s_i^j(p) = 0 \tag{17.2}$$

$$\text{for } i = 0, 1, \ldots, n$$

Some of the g_i might be zero if these goods are not produced in the public sector. Production conditions for the public sector enterprises can be written as:

$$\gamma_i(g_i) = 0 \tag{17.3}$$

or, in vector form, as:

$$\gamma(g) = 0. \tag{17.4}$$

In making decisions about its prices, the public enterprise board is constrained by a minimum profit or maximum loss constraint which takes the form:

$$\sum_i p_i g_i = \pi(g, p) = \pi^0 \tag{17.5}$$

where the last equality would emerge as a special case when $\partial \pi / \partial g = 0$.

The public enterprise board then chooses its prices (p_g) and net supplies g_i so as to maximize the social welfare function subject to the constraints mentioned above. p_g is the set of prices set by the public enterprise board and, therefore, a subset of all prices. Writing down the Lagrangean we have:

$$\Lambda = W(.) - \sum_i \mu_i \left[\sum_h d_i^h(.) - g_i - \sum_j s_i^j(.) \right] - \delta\gamma(.) - \lambda \left[\pi(.) - \sum_i p_i g_i \right]$$

(17.6)

where μ, δ and λ are Lagrange multipliers.

First-order conditions for an internal maximum are as follows:

$$\sum_h (\partial W/\partial V^h)(\partial V^h/\partial p_g) - \sum_i \mu_i \left[\sum_h (\partial d_i^h/\partial p_g) - \sum_j (\partial s_i^j/\partial p_g) \right] + \lambda g = 0$$

(17.7a)

$$\mu_i - \delta(\partial\gamma/\partial g_i) - \lambda[(\partial\pi/\partial g_i) - p_i] = 0$$

(17.7b)

and that the derivatives with respect to the Lagrange multipliers are equal to zero. p_g is a subset of all prices. If lump-sum income could also be optimally chosen then we would differentiate with respect to y^h as well and write the following additional first-order condition:

$$(\partial W/\partial V^h)(\partial V^h/\partial y^h) - \sum_i \mu_i(\partial d_i^h/\partial y^h) = 0; h = 1, \ldots, H.$$

(17.7c)

The unknown prices, quantities, lump-sum incomes and Lagrange multipliers can be computed from equations (17.7). However, lump-sum income can rarely be chosen and we concentrate on conditions (17.7a) and (17.7b).

Now solve for μ_i from equation (17.7b) and substitute into equation (17.7a) to get:

$$\sum_h (\partial W/\partial V^h)(\partial V^h/\partial p_g) - \sum_i [\delta(\partial\gamma/\partial g_i) + \lambda(\partial\pi/\partial g_i - p_i)]$$

$$\left[\sum_h (\partial d_i^h/\partial p_g) - \sum_j (\partial s_i^j/\partial p_g) \right] + \lambda g = 0.$$

(17.8)

Now divide this equation by $\phi_0 = \delta(\partial\gamma/\partial g_i) > 0.$[1] Define ω^h as $(\partial W/\partial V^h)/\phi_0, \lambda_0 = \lambda/\phi_0$ and $\Phi_i = (\partial\gamma/\partial g_i)/(\partial\gamma/\partial g_0)$. Realize that ω^h is a 'normalized' marginal social welfare of utility of the *h*th individual. λ_0 is a 'normalized' measure of the welfare effects of the size of the public enterprise's deficit. Φ_i is a shadow price that measures the marginal labor costs of publicly producing good *i* (for $g_i > 0$); otherwise it is a partial marginal rate of transformation. It can also be interpreted as marginal cost.

We can now write equation (17.8) as:

$$\sum_h \omega^h(\partial V^h/\partial p_g) - \left[\sum_{i\in g} \Phi_i - \lambda_0 p_i + \lambda_0(\partial\pi/\partial g_i) \right]$$

$$\left[\sum_h (\partial d_i^h/\partial p_g) - \sum_j (\partial s_i^j/\partial p_g) \right] + \lambda_0 g = 0$$

(17.9)

where g is the set of goods produced in the public sector. To arrive at a clearer interpretation of this equation we work with the price marginal cost differential $(p_i - \Phi_i)$ rather than $(\lambda_0 p_i - \Phi_i)$. To do this we add $(1 - \lambda_0)$ $\sum_i p_i / [\sum_h (\partial d_i^h / \partial p_g) - \sum_j (\partial s_i^j / \partial p_g)]$ to both sides of equation (17.9) and rearrange to get:

$$\sum_h \omega^h (\partial V^h / \partial p_g) - (1 - \lambda_0) \sum_i \sum_h p_i (\partial d_i^h / \partial p_g) - \sum_{i \in g} [\Phi_i - p_i + \lambda_0 (\partial \pi / \partial g_i)]$$

$$\left[\sum_h (\partial d_i^h / \partial p_g) - \sum_j (\partial s_i^j / \partial p_g) \right] = -\lambda_0 g - (1 - \lambda_0) \sum_i \sum_j p_i (\partial s_i^j / \partial p_g).$$

$$(17.10)$$

This expression consists of five terms which we can now examine. The first two terms reflect distributional objectives. The first term $\sum_h \omega^h (\partial V^h / \partial p_g)$ is the social valuation of price changes. The absolute value of this is high for necessities and low for luxuries. This becomes transparent when we use Roy's identity:

$$\sum_h \omega^h (\partial V^h / \partial p_g) = - \sum_h \omega^h d_g^h (\partial V^h / \partial y^h) \qquad (17.11)$$

where d_g^h is the net demand for the commodity produced in the public sector by individual h.

Along the lines of the optimal commodity tax literature already discussed in Chapter 13, we define β_e as the distributional characteristic of any good e as the distributionally weighted sum of individual consumption shares:

$$\beta_e = \sum_h \omega^h (\partial V^h / \partial y^h)(d_e^h / d_e) \qquad (17.12)$$

with d_e as the average consumption commodity e.

The second term in equation (17.10) refers to the level of prices and does not include any distributional differentiation between luxuries and necessities. Its absolute value is larger, the smaller is λ_0. A small value of λ_0 could result from a low value of π. Thus the level of prices of a welfare maximizing deficit public enterprise will be lower than that of a profit-maximizing monopolist. Applying the Slutsky equation for $\partial d_i^h / \partial p_g$ and rearranging terms we can write the first two terms of expression (17.10) as:

$$-\beta_e d_e + (1 - \lambda_0) d_e$$

where the first term refers to the distributional effects of the price structure and the second term refers to the price level.

The third and fourth terms in expression (17.10) refer to whether and how far the price of the commodity produced in the public sector should diverge from marginal cost. In recent work, attention has shifted away from first-best pricing rules to second-best ones. In the Boiteux model under consideration second-best constraints are imposed through the profit requirement of π. Hence, we can define an augmented marginal cost $(\lambda_0(\partial\pi/\partial g_i) + \Phi_i) = \Delta_i$. The first term in this expression is the effect on profits of changing sales and the second term is the marginal cost. Hence Δ_i is the augmented marginal cost. The price would equal this in a first-best environment and would depart from it in second-best situations.

The last term in (17.10) reflects the adjustment of public sector pricing to the existence of non-competitive behavior in the private sector. If the private sector follows competitive pricing then profit maximization would lead to the satisfaction of Hotelling's Lemma which says that $\sum_i p_i(\partial s_i^j/\partial p_g) = 0$.

17.3 SOME SIMPLIFIED EXAMPLES

Equation (17.10) presents a general formulation of the optimal public-sector price problem. We now consider some simplified versions.

Let there be just one public-sector undertaking whose operations are subject to a profit constraint. There are $n + 1$ goods in the economy with the first n goods being produced in the private sector and the $n + 1$ st good in the public sector. All individuals have identical utility functions $U^h(d_1^h, d_2^h, \ldots, d_n^h; d_{n+1}^h, L^h)$ where L^h is labor. We will concentrate on efficiency issues and assume that the public enterprise board maximizes the utility of a representative consumer.

We simplify further by assuming that the only costs are labor costs and choosing labor as numeraire we write the profits (π_p) of the private sector as:

$$\pi_p = \sum_{i=1}^{n} p_i g_i - G(d_1, \ldots, d_n) \qquad (17.13)$$

where $G(d_1, \ldots, d_n)$ is the labor requirement by the private sector. If the private sector is perfectly competitive $\pi_p = 0$. Then the prices of the private-sector commodities must equal respective marginal cost:

$$p_i = \partial G/\partial d_i \qquad (i = 1, \ldots, n).$$

Let $Q(d_{n+1})$ be the labor requirement of the public-sector firm. Writing:

$$L = \sum_h L^h$$

as total labor supply, we can write the total labor constraint of the economy as:

$$G(d_1, \ldots, d_n) + Q(d_{n+1}) - L = 0. \qquad (17.14)$$

Let $V(p_1, \ldots, p_n; p_{n+1}, y)$ be the indirect utility function that society attempts to maximize. y is some measure of average income in society. The profit constraint before the public enterprise can then be written as:

$$p_{n+1}d_{n+1} - Q(d_{n+1}) + T \geqslant \pi_0 \qquad (17.15)$$

where T is a pure (poll) subsidy paid by the government and π_0 is the stipulated minimum profit that the public enterprise must earn.

Setting up the Lagrangean for the public enterprise board we have:

$$\Lambda = V(.) + \psi[p_{n+1}d_{n+1} - Q(.) - T]. \qquad (17.16)$$

The first-order condition with respect to p_{n+1} yields:

$$-\alpha d_{n+1} + \psi[d_{n+1} + (p_{n+1} - Q')(\partial d_{n+1}/\partial p_{n+1})] = 0 \qquad (17.17)$$

where a prime ($'$) stands for a first derivative and α is the private marginal utility of income. Now if the lump-sum subsidy can be optimally selected ψ would denote the marginal gain to society of increasing the subsidy by one unit. In other words, ψ would be the marginal utility of income ($= \alpha$). In that case, from equation (17.17) we would have the optimal pricing rule that:

$$p_{n+1} = Q'. \qquad (17.18)$$

In other words that price equals marginal cost. This is just a repudiation of the first-best result that if lump-sum transfers can be optimally selected then price should equal marginal cost for optimality. It should be noted that this pricing rule breaks down if costs are falling. With falling average and marginal costs when price equals marginal cost, the firm will be incurring a loss. This is why we have to go back to equation (17.10) where the effects of the optimal price setting rule on profitability are accommodated. This was done by defining an 'augmented' marginal cost function. If we had redistributive objectives in mind then the first part of equation (17.17) would be $\sum_h(\partial W/\partial V^h)(\partial V^h/\partial p_{n+1})$ and prices would depart from marginal cost in a manner completely analogous to the commodity tax with redistribution problem considered in Chapter 13.

To emphasize the parallel of this problem with the optimal tax consider the following analysis. Let each of the n private-sector goods be taxed. Thus $p_1, \ldots, p_n$ are the consumer prices and $q_1, \ldots, q_n$ are the producer prices. Profits of the private sector are, then:

$$\pi = \sum_{i=1}^{n} p_i d_i - G(.) \qquad (17.19)$$

This profit is taxed at the rate τ and the rest is distributed to the population as a lump-sum payment. Hence, the public sector's budget constraint is:

$$p_{n+1}d_{n+1} - Q(.) + \sum_{i=1}^{n}(p_i - q_i)d_i + \tau\pi = 0. \qquad (17.20)$$

In other words, tax revenue from taxation of profits and private-sector goods plus revenue from selling the commodity produced in the public sector must equal costs. We can make an allowance for a profit here as well.

Setting up the Lagrangean we have:

$$\Lambda = V(p_1, \ldots, p_n; p_{n+1}) + \psi[p_{n+1}d_{n+1} - Q(.) + \sum(p_i - q_i)d_i - \tau\pi].$$

$$(17.21)$$

Differentiating with respect to p_{n+1}, using the Slutsky equation for $(\partial x_{n+1}/\partial p_{n+1})$ and defining β_e as before we can show that:

$$[p_{n+1} - \partial Q/\partial d_{n+1}]/p_{n+1} = \beta_e(d_{n+1} - \partial y/\partial p_{n+1}) \qquad (17.22)$$

and results for optimal commodity taxes can be derived along the lines discussed in Chapter 13. Hence, there is a close parallel between the optimal commodity tax and the optimal price for the public-sector problem.

17.4 THE OPTIMALITY OF MARGINAL COST PRICING

The marginal cost pricing rule which we have obtained in the general case is a challenge to economists because it gives a justification both for public production as well as deficits in the public sector (if marginal costs are falling). It says, in effect, that the public sector must price at marginal cost and suffer the accompanying deficit. Indeed, this is optimal. Empirically this is quite important since most public-sector firms seem to produce under conditions of increasing returns to scale. In the Boiteux framework this problem is addressed by assuming that it is possible to have lump-sum transfers. This, of course, is a gross oversimplification although it is formally correct. Many economists have wondered, however, about the usefulness of this arrangement. A typical concern is whether following the marginal cost rule will mean negative income for ever. Some have suggested that the pricing formula be changed to a **two-part tariff**. Here the pricing formula consists of two parts. The enterprise follows a marginal cost pricing rule. This is the first part of the pricing formula. The difference between total cost and total revenue (at this price) is then apportioned among all consumers as the second part of the pricing formula (see Beato 1982).

Others have argued that marginal cost pricing may not be optimal. If the production possibilities are non-convex (increasing returns to scale), marginal cost equilibria may fail to be Pareto optimal. This literature tries to find conditions under which at least one equilibrium is Pareto efficient. However, there exist examples showing that even in very simple cases such conditions cannot be found. We give one example, due to Brown–Heal (1979), in Figure 17.1.

Consider a two-consumer, one-producer economy. The production possibilities for this non-convex economy are shown by the steps in Figure 17.1. The Scitovsky social indifference curve through point A is denoted as I_A. If endowments and the relative price change, the social indifference curve changes from I_A to I_B. This means that the new equilibrium is at point B. Both A and B are equilibria since they satisfy the first-order conditions but

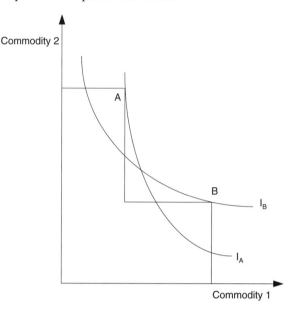

Figure 17.1

neither is Pareto optimal because the indifference curves intersect. The practical importance of such examples depends upon endowments of consumers because these affect the social indifference curves and the possibility of their intersecting.

Hence, we are faced with the question: when, in the presence of increasing returns to scale, is marginal cost pricing optimal? This was clarified by Milleron (1972) and Dierker (1986). Consider a particularly simple example. Let the commodity produced by the public sector (d_g) be related to an input s through an increasing return to scale technology so that:

$$d_g \leqslant |s|^\alpha \qquad (17.23)$$

with $\alpha > 1$ describes the production process. α is assumed to be fixed, hence we are assuming equation (17.23) to represent the envelope of a one-parameter family of short-run production functions geometrically represented by the tangents of $d_g = |s|^\alpha$ in Figure 17.2. A typical tangent intersects the input axis at a point $-z < 0$ with z indicating fixed costs measured in terms of the input commodity.

In a well-known paper Baumol *et al.* (1982) argue that z should be associated with public goods. After investing a fixed amount z in these public goods the economy has a linear technology at its disposal as in Figure 17.2. Economic agents have to fix a certain level of fixed costs (investment in public goods) and to finance it. Given this investment, economic agents have a simple production problem involving one input and one output and a linear technology.

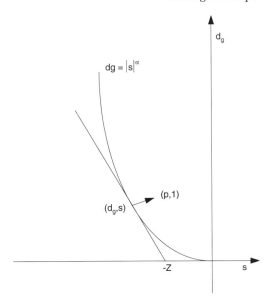

Figure 17.2

Consider now the production plan (d_g, s) with $d_g > 0$ and $s < 0$. The tangent to the technology at (d_g, s) has a normal vector (at right angles to it). We measure price (p) in terms of the input commodity and call this normal vector (p, 1) where:

$$(p, 1) = [(1/\alpha)|s|^{1-\alpha}, 1]. \tag{17.24}$$

The tangent to the technology will intersect the s axis at $-z = (1 - 1/\alpha)s$. Thus p, the price of output, is optimally set equal to the marginal cost.

With this pricing rule in effect the value of the output $(pd_g \equiv v)$ as well as the implied amount of the public good are proportional to the amount of the input. Hence a production allocation for this economy is the triple (v, s, z) where:

$$(v, s, z) = [(1/\alpha)|s|, s, (1 - (1/\alpha))|s|] \tag{17.25}$$

The first two elements of this triple are private goods and the third is an (aggregated) public good. All three elements of the triple are expressed in value terms (in terms of units of the input s). The relative price of output is $(1/\alpha)|s|^{1-\alpha}$ which when multiplied by the production $(|s|^\alpha)$ yields $p.d_g$.

Moreover, the total production set to the left of $d_g = |s|^\alpha$ can be thought of as the union of all short-run production curves or tangents of $d_g = |s|^\alpha$. Consider the tangent intersecting the s axis at $-\bar{z}$. Let $(p(\bar{z}), 1)$ be the corresponding normal price vector. The equation for this tangent is $(p(\bar{z}), 1)(d_g, s) = -\bar{z}$ or, this tangent satisfies the equation:

$$p(\bar{z}) \cdot d_g + s + \bar{z} = 0 \text{ or } v + s + \bar{z} = 0.$$

In this simple case the marginal rate of substitution between the public good z and the private (numeraire) good s is one. This reflects the fact that the numeraire commodity serves both as a fixed cost as well as a variable cost. Hence, an increasing returns to scale technology has been transformed into a simple linear technology.

We now have to transform the consumer's preferences from the original two-commodity case to the transformed three-commodity case. Observe that the triple (v,s,z) in value terms contains enough information to determine uniquely a commodity bundle (d_g, s). Information about the fixed cost z amounts to knowledge of the short-run production function associated with z. This short-run production function is linear and is characterized by the normal price vector $(p,1)$ where

$$p = (1/z)[1 - (1/\alpha)]^{\alpha-1}z^{1-\alpha}. \tag{17.26}$$

Now let consumers be indexed by h and let their preferences in the two-commodity case be represented by $U^h(.)$ a quasi-concave function. The equivalent utility functions for the three-commodity case can be defined as $\tilde{U}^h$ which can be written as:

$$\tilde{U}^h(v_h, s_h, z) = U^h[\alpha(1 - (1/\alpha))^{1-\alpha}s^{\alpha-1} \cdot v_h, s_h]. \tag{17.27}$$

The first argument of $U^h(.)$ is, simply, d_g.

The new public good economy has the advantage of exhibiting constant returns to scale instead of the original increasing returns to scale. However, realize that the preference relation $\tilde{U}^h$ need not be quasi-concave any longer. This is the price that one has to pay for achieving this simplification.

We can now define a **marginal cost price equilibrium** (MCP). An MCP equilibrium is a vector $[(d_{gh}, s_h), (d_g, s), p]$ consisting of consumption plans, a production plan, and a price p such that:

$$p = (1/\alpha)|s|^{1-\alpha}, \sum_h d_{gh} = d_g, \sum_h s_h = s + w$$

where $(0, w)$ denotes initial total endowments of the output and input. The wealth y_h of each consumer is given by a lump-sum distribution of the total wealth y:

$$y = pd_g + s + w \tag{17.28}$$

among the consumers and consumer h's consumption bundle (d_{gh}, s_i) is demanded at the price vector $(p, 1)$ and wealth $y_h(p)$.

Given the above MCP equilibrium, we can prove that the associated allocation in the transformed public good economy given by:

$$(v_h, s_h, z) = (pd_{gh}, s_h, \alpha^{1/(1-\alpha)}(1 - 1/\alpha)p^{1/(1-\alpha)}$$

satisfies Samuelson's condition $(\sum mrs = mrt)$ for optimal supply of the public good. (In this economy $mrt = 1$).

From the definition of $\tilde{U}^h$ we have that:

$$\sum_h (\partial U^h / \partial z) = \sum_h (\partial / \partial d_g) U^h [\alpha (1 - (1/\alpha))^{1-\alpha} z^{\alpha-1} \cdot v_h, s_i]$$

$$[\alpha (1 - (1/\alpha))^{1-\alpha} (\alpha - 1) z^{\alpha-2} v_h]. \tag{17.29}$$

Hence, the sum of the *mrs* is:

$$\text{sum of mrs} = \left[\sum_h \{\partial \tilde{U}^h / \partial z\} / \{\partial \tilde{U}^h / \partial s_h\} \right]$$

$$= p\alpha \left[1 - (1/\alpha)^{1-\alpha} (\alpha - 1) z^{(\alpha-2)} \sum_h v_h \right]$$

since $p = \{\partial U^h / \partial v_h\} / \{\partial U^h / \partial s_h\}$.
Using now the definitions of p $(= (1/\alpha)|s|1^{1-\alpha})$ and $z (= [1 - (1/\alpha)]|s|)$ we get:

$$\sum_h \text{mrs} = [z/(pd_g)] \left(\sum_h v_h \right) / z = 1. \tag{17.30}$$

Hence $\sum \text{mrs} = \text{mrt}$ and the claim that marginal cost pricing leads to Pareto optimal supply of the public good is verified.[2]

The first-order condition $\sum \text{mrs} = \text{mrt}$ would satisfy Pareto optimality if $\tilde{U}^h$ was quasi-concave. However, we know that this need not be the case. Under these circumstances the first-order conditions may be satisfied but the associated equilibrium need not be a Lindahl equilibrium. If the Lindahl equilibrium does not exist then an efficient outcome is ruled out.

We know from the second optimality theorem of Chapter 2 that Pareto optimality requires not only that prices equal marginal cost but also that wealth be properly adjusted. If this second condition is not satisfied then marginal cost pricing may be incompatible with efficiency. An important problem at this juncture is: under what conditions, for a transformed economy of the type that we are studying, can satisfaction of the first-order conditions also mean the attainment of a Lindahl equilibrium?

Let us examine the following Cobb–Douglas utility function: $U^h(d_{gh}, s_h) = d_{gh} s_h$, so that the transformed utility function becomes $\tilde{U}^h(v_h, s_h, z) = \alpha(1 - (1/\alpha)) d_{gh}^\alpha s_h z^{\alpha-1}$ with $\alpha > 1$. Now, under what conditions will $\tilde{U}^h$ retain its quasi-concavity? If it is quasi-concave then the optimality of the MCP equilibrium can be guaranteed.

Let us consider an MCP equilibrium $[(\bar{d}_{gh}, \bar{s}_h), (\bar{d}_g, \bar{s})]$ and let the utility associated with this be $\bar{U}^h$. Now consider the set of allocations B that are better than this in the sense that utility is no lower. This set is defined by:

$$B = \left\{ \left[\sum v_h, \sum s_h, z \right], \quad \text{such that for all } h : \tilde{U}^h(v_h, s_h, z) \geqslant \bar{U}^h \right\}.$$

In order to see when B is convex consider (d_{gh}, s_h) such that for all h $U^h(d_{gh}, s_h) = \bar{U}^h$ and the total derivative (dU^h) is a positive multiple of some price system $(p,1)$. Substitute $v_h = pd_{gh}$, $\bar{v}_h = \bar{p}\bar{d}_{gh}$, $z = \alpha^{1/(1-\alpha)}$ $p^{1/(1-\alpha)}$ and $\bar{z} = \alpha^{1/(1-\alpha)}(1 - (1/\alpha))\bar{p}^{1/(1-\alpha)}$. We would like to know when:

$$[(1/2)\left(\sum_h (v_h + \bar{v}_h)\right), (1/2)\left(\sum (s_h + \bar{s}_h)\right), (1/2)(z + \bar{z})] \in B.$$

Since we have assumed U^h to be quasi-concave, the above will be true when

$$(1/2)\sum(v_h + \bar{v}_h)[(1/2)(p^{1/(1-\alpha)} + \bar{p}^{1/(1-\alpha)})]^{\alpha-1} \geqslant (1/2)\sum(d_{gh} + \bar{d}_{gh}).$$
$$(17.31)$$

It can be shown that if $2 > \alpha > 1$ then expression (17.31) will hold if

$$\sum(pd_{gh}/\bar{p} + \bar{p}\bar{d}_{gh}/p) \geqslant \sum(d_{gh} + \bar{d}_{gh}).$$

If we assume that $p > \bar{p}$ then the requirement is simply that:

$$\sum(pd_{gh} - \bar{p}\bar{d}_{gh}) \geqslant 0.$$

In other words, the higher price must be associated with the higher value of Hicksian (compensated) demand.

Hence, under certain conditions for a Cobb–Douglas utility function it is possible to show that satisfaction of the Samuelson condition will be associated with the Lindahl equilibrium. In fact it is possible to be a bit more general (see Dierker 1986).

17.5   SECOND-BEST RAMSEY–BOITEUX PRICING ONCE AGAIN

Although it is theoretically possible to defend marginal cost pricing under certain conditions, it would appear that we are well advised to go beyond it; indeed to go beyond first-best pricing. To do this we now go back to the original Ramsey problem. Suppose we make the following assumptions:

(i) Only the prices of publicly produced goods are to be set.
(ii) The private sector is perfectly competitive.
(iii) The distribution of lump-sum incomes is optimally chosen; hence we can deal with compensated demand.
(iv) The public enterprise is restricted by an exogenously fixed deficit or profit level π_0.

In this case the optimal pricing formula (17.10) can be shown to reduce to:

$$\sum_{i \in g}(p_i - \Phi_i)(\partial d_i^h/\partial p_g) = -\lambda_0 g \qquad (17.32)$$

with $\lambda_0 \neq 0$. For the most relevant case where π_0 exceeds the unconstrained (first-best) optimum it will be the case that $0 < \lambda_0 < 1$. Hence, price will exceed marginal cost.

This Ramsey rule is characterized by a kind of trade-off between the level and structure of prices. The **level** of prices is primarily influenced by the value of π_0 chosen. Ramsey pricing can, therefore, stand for high prices (low prices) depending on the profit target (admissible loss). All or some prices can fall below marginal cost to bring about a deficit π_0.

So far as the **structure** of prices is concerned, recall that the public sector has to observe a revenue constraint and meet all demand. Hence, the public enterprise board must consider the price elasticities of demand for different goods. If redistribution is not an objective, the more price inelastic the demand for a commodity is, the more easily can its price be raised in order to achieve π_0. The enterprise board will not raise the prices of goods with elastic demands very much. Of course, cross-price elasticities may affect this pattern. If, however, we ignore these cross-price elasticities then we would have the result that the price–cost margin of a commodity should be higher the smaller the absolute value of the price elasticity.[3] The structure of Ramsey optimal prices is, then, quite like that of Ramsey optimal commodity taxes discussed in Chapter 13 and the results derived there basically carry over.

In order to avoid repetition we pose the problem slightly differently from the optimal commodity tax problem. Let us suppose that there are n goods each with demand function $d_i(p_1, \ldots, p_n)$ and that the aim of the planner is to maximize the sum of consumer and producer surplus subject to, say, a break-even constraint.

The consumer surplus (CS) can be written as:

$$CS = \int_p^\infty \sum_{i=1}^n d_i(p_1, \ldots, p_n) dp_i = U(d_1, \ldots, d_n) - \sum p_i d_i. \qquad (17.33)$$

Similarly we can write the producer's surplus (PS) as:

$$PS = \sum_{i=1}^n p_i d_i(p_1, \ldots, p_n) - C(d_1(.), \ldots, d_n(.)) \qquad (17.34)$$

where $C(.)$ is some joint cost function. Consumer surplus plus producer surplus can, hence, be written as:

$$CS + PS = \int_p^\infty \sum_{i=1}^n d_i(p_1, \ldots, p_n) dp_i + \sum_{i=1}^n p_i d_i(p_1, \ldots, p_n) - C(.) \qquad (17.35)$$

If there was no other constraint we would obtain efficient prices by maximizing expression (17.35) with respect to the prices $p = (p_1, \ldots, p_n)$. Straightforward differentiation says that the optimum price vector $p^*(= p_1^*, \ldots, p_n^*)$ is given by the following condition:

$$\partial(CS + PS)/\partial p_i|_{p=p^*} = \sum_{j=1}^n [p_i - (\partial C/\partial d_j)](\partial d_j/\partial p_i)|_{p=p^*} = 0. \qquad (17.36)$$

If the maximum is unique then we get from equation (17.36)

$$p_j^* = \partial C / \partial d_j,$$

or price equals marginal cost.

Now let us impose a profit constraint, say a break-even constraint that $\sum_{i=1}^n p_i d_i = C(.)$. Forming the Lagrangean we have (with ϑ as a Lagrange multiplier):

$$\Lambda = \int_p^\infty \sum_{i=1}^n d_i dp_i + (\vartheta + 1) \left[\sum_{i=1}^n p_i d_i - C \right]. \qquad (17.37)$$

We have to choose prices $p_1, \ldots, p_n$ to maximize the above expression.

The first-order conditions can be arranged to yield:

$$\sum_{j=1}^n \{ [p_j - \partial C / \partial d_j]/p_j \} \epsilon_{ji} p_j q_j / (p_i q_i) = \vartheta/(1 + \vartheta), i = 1, \ldots, n \qquad (17.38a)$$

(where $\epsilon_{ji} = -(\partial d_j / \partial p_i)(p_i / d_j)$ is the cross-price elasticity of demand)

$$\sum_{i=1}^n p_i d_i - C = 0. \qquad (17.38b)$$

If demands are independent (so that $\epsilon_{ji} = 0$ for $i \neq j$ and $\epsilon_{ii} \neq 0$) we will have:

$$\vartheta d_i + (\vartheta + 1)[p_i - (\partial C / \partial d_i)](\partial d_i / \partial p_i) = 0$$

or

$$[\{p_i - (\partial C / \partial d_i)\}/p_i] = \vartheta/[(1 + \vartheta)\epsilon_{ii}]. \qquad (17.39)$$

Hence the price–marginal cost margin depends upon the inverse of the own price elasticity of demand.

In the general case when $\epsilon_{ji} \neq 0$ we can write the first-order condition as (following Rohlfs 1979):

$$(\vartheta/(1 + \vartheta)) = [\{p_i - (\partial C / \partial d_i)\}/p_i]S_i = [\{p_k - (\partial C / \partial d_k)\}/p_k]S_k \qquad (17.40)$$

where i and k are two products and S_i is the **super elasticity** of d_i. This is given by:

$$S_i = 1 / \left[\sum_{j=1}^n r_{ji} \kappa_{ji} \right], \quad r_{ji} = p_j d_j / (p_i d_i) \text{ and } \kappa_{ji}$$

is the elasticity of the inverse demand function $p_j(d_i, \ldots, d_n)$ with respect to $d_j : \kappa_{ji} \equiv (\partial p_j / \partial d_i)(d_i / p_j)$ is also referred to as the 'flexibility' of d_j with respect to p_i.

Yet another way to write the Ramsey optimal price formula is to work with the utility function in equation (17.33). The appropriate Lagrangean is now (with ϑ_1 as the Lagrange multiplier):

$$\Lambda = U(d_1, \ldots, d_n) - C(d_1, \ldots, d_n) + \vartheta_1 \left[\sum_{i=1}^{n} p_i d_i - C(.) \right] \qquad (17.41)$$

where $p_i = p_i(d_1, \ldots, d_n)$ is the inverse demand function. We maximize the Lagrangean with respect to d_i to get:

$$(\partial \Lambda / \partial d_i) = (\partial U / \partial d_i) - (\partial C / \partial d_i) + \vartheta_1 [MR_i - MC_i] = 0 \qquad (17.42)$$

where

$$MR_i \equiv [\partial / (\partial d_i)] \left\{ \sum_{i=1}^{n} p_i d_i \right\} \text{ and } MC_i \equiv \partial C / \partial d_i.$$

From the utility maximization of the individual consumer $(\partial U / \partial d_i) = p_i$ so $p_i - MC_i + \vartheta_1 [MR_i - MC_i] = 0$
or, for any two outputs, *i* and *k* we must have:

$$(p_i - MC_i)/(MC_i - MR_i) = (p_k - MC_i)/(MC_k - MR_i) = \vartheta_1. \qquad (17.43)$$

This is a much more complicated set of results than the simple inverse elasticity rule in the case of independent demands. However, the flavor of the argument is the same. Instead of the simple own price elasticity term we have the super elasticity terms (remember that $MR_i = p_i[1 + \sum_{j=1}^{n} r_{ji} \kappa_{ji}]$) which include correctional terms depending upon the cross-price elasticities. Markets are assigned high markups where the effect of a small change in price is to perturb consumption a relatively small mount in relation to where they would be under marginal cost pricing. The effect of cross-elasticities is that even if the own price elasticity in a market is quite low, when a rise in that price exerts a large distortionary effect in other markets, then a low price is required.

17.6 REDISTRIBUTIVE RAMSEY (FELDSTEIN) PRICING – THE GENERAL CASE

We wish now to extend the analysis for the case when public-sector pricing has distributional objectives as well. This is sometimes known as **Feldstein pricing**. We have already discussed a simplified example.

We assume that only prices of publicly produced goods are controlled and there is perfect competition in the private sector. Further, all lump-sum incomes are given so that we are dealing with uncompensated demand schedules and there is a minimum profit or maximum loss requirement of π_0.

Since we are dealing with redistributive pricing there is no point in having optimal lump-sum incomes. If we had optimal lump-sum incomes, public-sector prices would not have to perform a redistributive function.

As redistributional pricing is applied revenue will tend to fall – perhaps below costs, because any internal subsidization of the poor is limited by the possibility that the rich leave the market. The poor consume goods with low elasticities of demand in higher proportion than the rich. Hence, the prices of precisely those goods that should be high on efficiency grounds are to be lowered. Similarly, the rich consume goods that have high elasticity of demand in higher proportion than the poor. The prices of these goods, which should be lowered on grounds of efficiency, are to be raised. These two facts imply that redistributive pricing will lead to financial strain.

These financial difficulties would become even worse if private competitors were allowed to enter public enterprise markets. We will not broach this issue here; for details see Bos (1987).

With this assumption we can write the pricing formula in equation (17.10) as:

$$\sum(p_i - \Delta_i)(\partial d_g^u / \partial p_g) = -(1 - \beta_g)g \qquad (17.44)$$

where β_g is the distributional characteristic of the commodity produced in the public sector as defined in equation (17.12) and d_g^u denotes uncompensated demand.

The distributional characteristic of any good is higher, the larger is its share in the consumption of low-income people. Hence β_g will be higher for necessities than for luxuries. Thus Feldstein pricing would tend to reduce the price of necessities and increase those of luxuries.

17.7 MULTI-PART TARIFFS

Sometimes it is possible to increase the efficiency of a pricing mechanism if we move from a single price to more than one price. This allows the firm to distinguish between consumers on the basis of the volume of their demand. We have seen an example of this in Chapter 4. The discussion in this section is based on, among others, the work of Brown and Sibley (1986).

To clarify this point let us suppose that consumer demand can be represented in the following manner:

$$q = f(p, \theta) \qquad (17.45)$$

where q is the demand vector, p is the vector of marginal prices and θ is a taste parameter.

Preferences can be said to satisfy **weak monotonicity** when a person with high value of θ (great taste for this commodity) enjoys greater surplus from consuming this commodity than persons with lower values of θ. Preferences are said to satisfy **strong monotonicity** if higher θ is associated with higher demand.

The relationship between weak monotonicity and strong monotonicity is shown by Figures 17.3 and 17.4. In Figure 17.3 at the price p_1 the person with a high value of θ has a higher consumer surplus than a person with a low value of θ. This illustrates weak monotonicity. In Figure 17.4 a person with a high value of θ has higher demand at price p_1. This illustrates strong monotonicity.

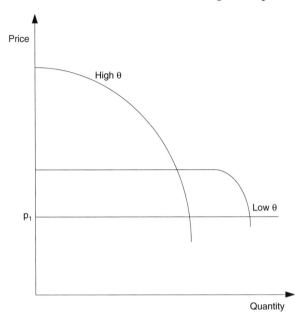

Figure 17.3

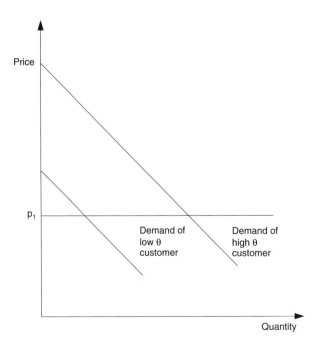

Figure 17.4

Most of the literature on public-sector pricing assumes strong monotonicity. However, it is hard actually to measure the taste parameter, θ. In any event it may not be necessary actually to measure an individual's θ. All that is really required is the distribution of θ – which is a much weaker requirement.

Given that consumers differ in their tastes (and hence willingness to pay) the response of the firm will depend upon how much it knows about consumers' tastes. If it broadly knows the distribution of tastes across the population of consumers, the firm can set a non-uniform or multi-part price schedule with different prices for consumers in different segments of the distribution of θ. Let us examine how this may be done.

We study an example whereby there are three segments to the distribution of θ as in Figure 17.5. Suppose the demand for the commodity that we are discussing is given by:

$$f(p, \theta) = (a - p)\theta$$

where a is a constant and p is the price. Suppose now that the following tariff structure is offered. There is an entry fee of E and then the fee structure is as follows:

$$p_1 = b \quad \text{for} \quad 0 \leqslant f(\,) \leqslant B \quad \text{and}$$
$$p_2 = c \quad \text{for} \quad f(\,) > B$$

where $c < b$ and B is a known level of demand.

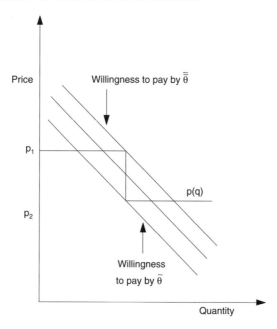

Figure 17.5

Since for given θ the demand curve is a straight line, potential consumer surplus at any given price is a triangle with area equal to

$$(a - p)^2 \theta / 2.$$

Assume that at θ_0, the consumer who is indifferent between consuming a small amount and not consuming at all, buys on the first rate block. The value of θ_0 is given by setting consumer surplus equal to zero with an entry fee of E. In other words:

$$(a - p)^2 \theta_0 / 2 - E = 0 \quad \text{or} \quad \theta_0 = 2E/(a - p)^2.$$

Now when demand is equal to B the willingness to pay off the next group of consumers (with taste parameter θ_1) will be $B = (a - c)\theta_1$. Knowing this we can solve for $\theta_1 = B/(a - c)$.

In terms of Figure 17.5 the taste levels $\tilde{\theta}$ and $\tilde{\tilde{\theta}}$ are found by solving the following two equations:

$$B = (a - p_1)\tilde{\theta} \text{ and } B = (a - p_2)\tilde{\tilde{\theta}} \text{ so that } \tilde{\theta} = B/(a - p_1) \text{ and } \tilde{\tilde{\theta}} = B/(a - p_2)$$

so that demands with price p_1 and p_2 are respectively $(a - p_1)\theta_1$ and $(a - p_2)\theta_1$. If the distribution of θ was lognormal, say the distribution of θ and that of demand would be as in Figures 17.6 and 17.7.

We can now formally define a multi-part (m part) tariff structure as a non-uniform price schedule with a finite number m ($\geqslant 2$) of rate steps. It consists of an entry fee E and a marginal price schedule as follows (with d indicating demand):

$$p(q) = p_1 \text{ for } 0 \leqslant q \leqslant q^1$$
$$= p_2 \text{ for } q^1 \leqslant q \leqslant q^2$$
$$\cdots \cdots$$
$$= p_m \text{ for } q^{m-1} \leqslant q.$$

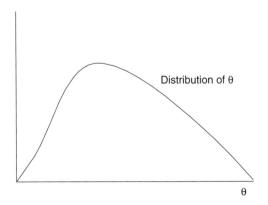

Distribution of θ

θ

Figure 17.6

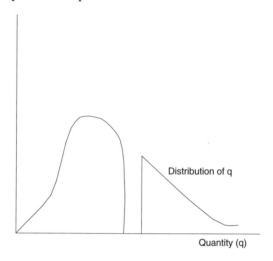

Figure 17.7

Corresponding revenues will be:

$$R(q) = E + p_1 q \text{ for } q < q^1$$
$$= E + p_1 q^1 + (p_2 - p_1)q \text{ for } q^1 \leqslant q \leqslant q^2$$

....

$$= E + \sum_{i=1}^{m-1} p_i q_i + p_m(q - q^{m-1}) \text{ for } q \geqslant q^{m-1}.$$

In an important paper Faulhaber and Panzar (1978) pointed out a link between two-part tariffs and multi-part tariffs which points to the way in which multi-part tariffs help to sort out consumers according to their tastes. Suppose that we have a five-part tariff as in Figure 17.8 given by the revenue function $E_1 J_1 J_2 J_3$. It gives rise to the declining block price structure as in the lower panel of Figure 17.8. Hence, we can think of the single multi-part tariff as consisting of four two-part tariffs (E_1, p_1), (E_2, p_2), (E_3, p_3) and (E_4, p_4) with entry fees E_1, E_2, E_3 and E_4 such that $E_4 > E_3 > E_2 > E_1$ and marginal prices p_1, p_2, p_3, and p_4 such that $p_4 < p_3 < p_2 < p_1$. Clearly, when these two-part tariffs are juxtaposed as in Figure 17.8 consumers will only select portions of them which are in the lower envelope of the set, which is $E_1 J_1 J_2 J_3$. Thus when a multi-part tariff shows quantity discounts, it can be viewed as the lower envelope of a set of two-part tariffs from which consumer choose their optimal consumption plans. It is for this reason that such tariffs are called the **self-selecting** set of two-part tariffs.

From Figure 17.8 it is easy to see why a multi-part tariff will achieve finer sorting than a single price or a two-part tariff. It is the equivalent of offering heterogeneous consumers a wider variety of tariff packages from

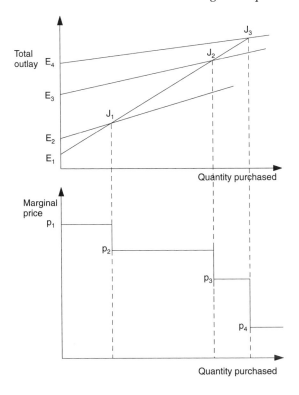

Figure 17.8

which they can select, some of which will be better tuned to the needs of
more different consumers than any single uniform price or two-part tariff
could be.

Faulhaber and Panzar (1978) proved another important result which
follows naturally from the above. They show that if θ has a continuous
distribution then, under an optimal set of selecting two-part tariffs, the
lowest usage charge will exceed the marginal cost. With a multiple tariff
structure, the usage cost lies closer to marginal cost than in the previous
case. One can indeed show that the optimal $(m + 1)$ part tariff is at least as
efficient as the optimal m part tariff.

Derivation of optimal non-uniform prices (multi-part tariffs)

We now discuss a straightforward method of deriving the optimal non-
uniform price schedule under the condition that the distribution of θ is
continuous. Let the willingness to pay be described by $w(q, \theta)$ where q is
quantity consumed, with $(\partial w / \partial q) < 0$ (willingness to pay more declines as
consumption rises) and $(\partial w / \partial \theta) > 0$ (which follows from the assumption
of strict monotonicity).

The marginal consumer group at q, θ_0, is defined by the self-selection constraint:

$$w(q, \theta_0) = p(q). \tag{17.46}$$

Hence:

$$\partial\theta/\partial p(\theta) = 1/w_\theta > 0.$$

We assume that the marginal cost of production is constant – say Φ. Consumer surplus up to a taste level θ_1 can be written as

$$\int_{\theta_0}^{\theta_1} [w(q, \theta) - p(q)]\psi(\theta)dq \tag{17.47}$$

where ψ is the distribution function of θ. Similarly, producer surplus is given by:

$$\int_{\theta_0}^{\theta_1} [p(q) - \Phi]\psi(\theta)d\theta = (1 - \psi(\theta))(p(q) - \Phi) \tag{17.48}$$

so that consumer surplus plus producer surplus is obtained by adding up expressions (17.47) and (17.48).

The break-even constraint is given by:

$$\int_0^\infty (1 - \Psi(\theta))(p(q) - \Phi)dq = F \tag{17.49}$$

where F is the fixed cost.

We use ϑ_2 as the Lagrange multiplier and form the Lagrangean

$$\Lambda = \int_0^\infty [\int_{\theta_0}^{\theta_1} \{w(q, \theta) - p(q)\}\psi(\theta)d\theta + (1 - \Psi(\theta))(p(q) - \Phi)]dq$$

$$+ \vartheta_2[\int_0^\infty (1 - \Psi(\theta))(p(q) - \Phi)dq] - (1 + \vartheta_2)F. \tag{17.50}$$

The necessary condition for optimality is given by setting the total derivative $\delta\Lambda = 0$ for any variation δp. Now:

$$\delta\Lambda = \int_0^\infty [\{-(w(q, \theta_0) + p(q)\}\psi(\theta_0)(\partial\theta_0/\partial p) - (1 - \Psi(\theta_0))$$

$$+ (1 - \Psi(\theta_0)) - \psi(\theta_0)(p(q) - \Phi)(\partial\theta_0/\partial p)]\delta p \, dq$$

$$+ \vartheta_2 \int_0^\infty [-\psi(\theta_0)(\partial\theta_0/\partial p)(p(q) - \Phi) + (1 - \Psi(\theta_0))]\delta p \, dq = 0. \tag{17.51}$$

Because $w(q, \theta_0) = p(q)$ expression (17.51) reduces to

$$\int_0^\infty [-(1 + \vartheta_2)(p(q) - \Phi)\psi(\theta_0)(\partial\theta_0/\partial p) + \vartheta_2(1 - \Psi(\theta_0))]\delta p \, dq = 0 \tag{17.52}$$

so that for the variation $\delta\Lambda$ to vanish for any variation δp, the quantity inside the square brackets in equation (17.52) must vanish.

Rewriting this we have:

$$(p(q) - \Phi)/p(q) = (\vartheta_2/(1 + \vartheta_2))(1 - \Psi(\theta_0))[p(q)\psi(\theta_0)(\partial\theta_0/\partial p)]$$
$$= (\vartheta_2/(1 + \vartheta_2))\{[-\partial\ln(1 - \Psi(\theta_0))]/[\partial\ln p(q)]\}$$
$$= [\vartheta_2/(1 + \vartheta_2)][1/\epsilon(q, p(q))] \tag{17.53}$$

where ϵ is the price elasticity in a given q market. This formulation of the non-uniform pricing problem is appealing because it has a link with the optimal Ramsey price derived earlier. The quantity $(1 - \Psi(\theta_0))$ is the demand in a given dq market. Hence, equation (17.53) says that the optimal price–marginal cost mark-up in any particular market segment is inversely related to the elasticity of demand, ceteris paribus. This is the essential message from the Ramsey pricing problem as well.

Some remarks on non-linear pricing

Our analysis of multiple tariffs extends quite naturally to the case of **non-linear pricing**. This refers to different types of consumers being charged different prices for the same publicly provided commodity. In the case of multiple tariffs, analyzed above, the emphasis is on efficient pricing. It could well have been redisributive pricing with the publicly operated firm trying to maximize some kind of social welfare index.

The maximization problem could, hence, be written as:

$$\max \int_{\theta_0}^{\theta_m} w(q, \theta)\Phi(\theta)d\theta$$

where θ_m is the upper limit of the distribution of θ. One could then write an individual's constraint in terms of the price paid by each θ type $(p(q(\theta))$. The ensuing problem then is completely analogous to the optimal non-linear tax problem analyzed in Chapter 14 and the same broad results would follow. Formal analyses can be found in Spence (1977), Roberts (1978), and Walsh (1978).

17.8   PEAK LOAD PRICING

The peak load pricing problem has been dealt with in considerable detail by several authors. We present here a simplified version of the analysis due to Williamson (1966) and Platts (1981). Central to this work is the notion of **effective demand for capacity**.

Suppose that a public utility (say a firm generating electricity) has two relevant production periods. We have the peak period defined as one in which all of the productive capacity of the firm is utilized. In the off-peak period the full capacity of the firm is not utilized. Williamson's approach consists of adopting the whole cycle as the uniform time for which output is consumed or produced. Hence the demand for electricity is basically the price for 1KW for 24 hours (1KW-day) and costs of production are in terms of the same unit of output. Let α_j be the proportion of the cycle taken up by period j with $\sum \alpha_j = 1$. Suppose that there are only two periods of 9 hours and 15 hours. So $\alpha_1 = 3/8$ and $\alpha_2 = 5/8$.

Every possible short-run capacity has a fixed maximum output, however, up to that limit, the running cost per unit is constant. Hence, each short-run marginal cost curve (SMC) has a backward-L shape. It is further assumed that there are constant returns to scale and that new capacity is completely divisible. The marginal variable cost of production is (fixed at) γ per 1KW-day, so that the running cost of producing 1KW for the portion α_j of the time cycle is $\alpha_j \gamma$. The least daily equivalent capital cost is Γ per 1KW extra generating capacity. Then long-run marginal cost (LMC) $= \gamma + \Gamma$ per KW-day. In Figure 17.9 two LMC curves are drawn, corresponding to a higher (Γ_h) and a lower (Γ_1) level of capital costs. We want to determine optimal prices in the two periods.

Let us move on now to demand. We have to define period demand prices in the same terms to be consistent. Let p_j be the price that people would have paid per KW-day if the level of demand in period j had persisted over the whole 24-hour cycle instead of just for the fraction α_j. If people are willing to pay p_j^0 for q^0 KW-days of electricity if the level of demand in period j had continued for 24 hours. Hence the true period demand is such that people will pay $\alpha_j p_j^0$ for q^0KW of electricity for the duration

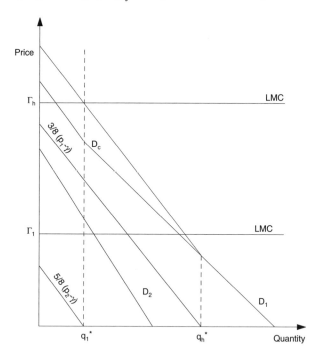

Figure 17.9

of the period itself. Hence $(\alpha_j p_j^0, q^0)$ is a point on the period demand curve.

From this we have Williamson's result that each period's demand could be shown in either of two ways:

(i) The period demand curve with points $(q, \alpha_j p_j)$ where q is the number of KW consumed for portion α_j of the day.
(ii) Following Williamson, we could, from the period demand curve, construct a schedule which shows the equivalent price–quantity relation that would have materialized if demand for period j had actually persisted over the whole 24-hour cycle. This has been called the **cycle equivalent** period demand curve. It would have points (q, p_j) where q is the number of KW-days.

It is standard to adopt this (ii) approach so that the unit of quantity in both cost and demand curves is the KW-day. In Figure 17.9 D_1 and D_2 are the cycle equivalent period demand curves for the peak and off-peak periods respectively.

The demand for capacity can be defined in the following manner. In any period the price paid for any level of output must be high enough to cover running costs. Moreover, it would make sense to add to the capacity of the plant only if the extra output can be priced high enough to cover not only the running costs but also make some contribution to the cost of adding to capacity. Hence, the requirement for the demand in any period to contribute to the demand for capacity is that $\alpha_j p_j > \alpha_j \gamma$ or simply[4] that $p_j > \gamma$. Assuming this condition to be met we have the result that in period j consumers will contribute $\alpha_j(p_j - \gamma)$ to the capital cost of an additional unit of capacity. Hence, the total[5] contribution to the marginal unit of capacity addition would be[6] $\sum_j \alpha_j(p_j - \gamma)$. In Figure 17.9, for any particular unit of capacity that may be added to the capacity of the plant, this sum is the vertical summation over j of $\alpha_j(p_j - \gamma)$ with $p_j > \gamma$. With this, the logical conclusion is that a unit increase in capacity is warranted only if:

$$\sum_j \alpha_j(p_j - \gamma) \geqslant \Gamma. \tag{17.54}$$

At optimum capacity expression (17.54) must hold as an equality. From this we get:

$$\gamma + \sum \alpha_j(p_j - \gamma) = \gamma + \Gamma \text{(LMC)}. \tag{17.54a}$$

Since $\gamma = \sum \alpha_j \gamma$ the expression $\gamma + \sum \alpha_j(p_j - \gamma)$ reduces simply to $\sum \alpha_j p_j$. Diagrammatically this would be the vertical summation of the two demand curves, except for the stipulation that $p_j > \gamma$. Hence, $\gamma + \sum \alpha_j(p_j - \gamma)$, with $p_j > \gamma$ may be interpreted as the effective demand for capacity price. This must be equated to LMC for optimum capacity, at the margin. This is shown as D_c in Figure 17.9. Optimum capacity is high (q_h^*) for the low level of marginal cost and low (q_1^*) for the high level of marginal cost.

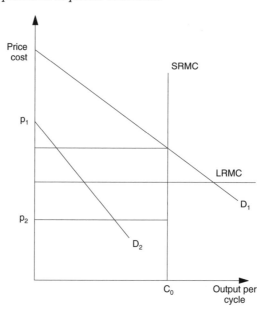

Figure 17.10

To discuss optimal pricing during the two periods we consider the special case where marginal benefit is equated to marginal cost in each period. In Figure 17.10 we show fluctuating demand between the peak and off-peak periods and consider the special case where the benefit of the new capacity accrues only to peak users. In Figure 17.10 the demand curve for the peak period (D_1) is the same as in Figure 17.9, similarly for the demand curve for the off-peak period (D_2). In conformity with this, the horizontal axis shows output per cycle rather than output per period.

At price p_1 the existing capacity of C_0 would just be rationed off among consumers during the peak period (fraction α_1 of the day). Thus total demand during the peak period is $\alpha_1 C_0$. Suppose during the off-peak period the price $p_2(=\gamma)$ has been chosen.[7] Then this will just cover marginal variable cost during this phase of the cycle of demand. Total demand during the off-peak period would be, then, $\alpha_2 C_2$.

For the peak users the marginal benefit is $MB = \alpha_1 p_1$. For the non-peak users the marginal benefit is $\alpha_2 p_2$. The marginal cost of expanding the capacity is the fixed cost Γ and the marginal running cost γ which is incurred for a fraction α_1 of the day by peak-period users. Hence marginal cost of expanding capacity is $MC = \alpha_1 \gamma + \Gamma$. Equating this to MB for peak users we have:

$MC = \alpha\gamma + \Gamma = \alpha P_1$ so that optimal peak period price (p^*) is such that
$$p_1^* = \Gamma/\alpha + \gamma.$$

Hence, optimal peak period price exceeds marginal cost.

We can show that with this pricing arrangement total revenue will equal total cost and the utility will just break even. Total cost (TC) equals $\Gamma C_0 + \alpha_1 \gamma C_0 + \alpha_2 \gamma C_2$. On the other hand, total revenue (TR) equals the sum of revenue from each period. $TR = p_1 \alpha_1 C_0 + p_2 \alpha_2 C_2 = (\gamma + \Gamma/\alpha_1)\alpha_1 C_0 + \gamma \alpha_2 C_2$. Thus total revenue equals total cost and the utility will break even.

This last result is contingent upon a non-varying cost of addition to capacity. If this cost was falling then there would be a loss with optimal prices. We would be back to the problem of funding deficits of public enterprises that are levying optimal prices (equal to marginal cost) and incurring losses.

17.9 PRICING OF JOINT PRODUCTS – ALLOCATION OF COMMON COSTS

In many instances public enterprises provide many services simultaneously and these have significant joint costs which are very hard to allocate. Several examples of this can be found. One of the most common is postal services. The Post Office provides many services and these have many common costs. Yet these services must be priced separately. Telephone pricing or pricing of different classes of travel by train are all examples of this phenomenon.

In this section we discuss three different approaches to the allocation of fixed costs. The first method is known as the **fully distributed cost pricing** method. The second approach uses concepts from the theory of **cooperative games**, whereas the third is sometimes known as the **axiomatic method** to cost allocation. The point here is to start by specifying reasonable properties that an allocation mechanism should satisfy and then deduce what price structures are consistent with these axioms.

Fully distributed cost (FDC) pricing

The FDC method proceeds in the following manner. It first separates the part of the cost that can easily be ascribed to service i. This is called the **attributable cost**. Then it selects a fraction δ_i of common costs which can be attributed to service i. Thus the FDC of service i (written FDC$_i$) is:

$$FDC_i = \text{attributable cost of } i + \delta_i * (\text{common cost}). \qquad (17.55)$$

Three different approaches to estimating δ_i are common. Suppose n services are being provided jointly. The output of service i is q_i and the associated revenue is R_i. Then:

$$\delta_i = q_i / \left(\sum_{i=1}^{n} q_i \right) \text{ (under the relative output or ROM method)}$$

$$\delta_i = R_i / \left(\sum_{i=1}^{n} R_i \right) \text{ (under the relative revenue or RRM method)}$$

δ_i = (attributable cost of service *i*) / (total attributable cost) (under the attributable cost or ACM method).

In practice, FDC also involves numerous conventions regarding depreciation rates, valuation of assets, work in progress and so on. But we shall ignore these and simply think of the fixed cost, *F*, as the joint cost.

Recently some regulatory agencies have begun using price elasticities of demand in setting FDC prices. Let us examine this in the context of the ROM. Assume that demands are independent. Denote the attributable cost of service *i* in period *t* by AC_{it}. Using data from year *t* the unit price for service *i* is computed using the following formula in period $(t+1)$:

$$p_{i, t+1} = \left[AC_{it} + \left\{ q_{it} / \left(\sum_{i=1}^{n} q_{it} \right) \right\} F \right] / q_{it} \qquad (17.56)$$

whereas the demand-compatible prices would have $AC_{i,t+1}$ and $q_{i,t+1}$ in the above formula. So there is no guarantee of compatibility between the two sets of prices.

Breautigam (1980) has shown that if the public firm is constrained to break even then the RRM and the ACM give identical results. To see this let us write the price under the ACM:

$$p_i = (AC_i/q_i) * \left[1 + F / \left(\sum_{i=1}^{n} AC_i \right) \right]. \qquad (17.57)$$

Under the RRM the price is: $p_i = [AC_i + F.R_i/R]/q_i = [AC_i/q_i][R/(R-F)]$ where *R* is total revenue and *F* is fixed cost. With zero profit it must be the case that:

$$R = \sum_{i=1}^{n} AC_i + F.$$

Hence, substituting $(R-F)$ for $\sum AC_i$ in equation (17.57) we get for the price under the ACM: $p_i = (AC_i/q_i)[1 + F/(R-F)] = (AC_i/q_i)[R/(R-F)]$ which is the price under the RRM.

The principal difficulty which some economists have with FDC methods is the arbitrariness with which joint costs are allocated among the services. They argue that there does not seem to be any economic rationale for this and no optimality properties can be claimed for such prices. However, we shall soon see that FDC prices are not entirely without merit.

The game theoretic method to allocating costs

Many public services that are jointly provided often have a large component of joint costs that is hard to allocate. When prices are set without firm theoretical foundations there may be complaints of **cross-subsidization**. This implies that some services are being deliberately 'overpriced' in order to subsidize others. Thus first-class travel on trains may be overpriced in order to charge lower prices to second-class passengers.

This complaint can be made operational in the following manner. Suppose some service (*i*) is cross-subsidizing some other service (*j*). If the extent of the cross-subsidy is large enough then it might become profitable for another agency to supply service *i* alone and on its own. In this sense we can think of the original arrangement where all *n* services are provided jointly as a **grand coalition**. The reason for forming this coalition is that, ceteris paribus, costs are lower for each service separately as well as for any smaller coalition in the grand coalition than they would be otherwise. However, if cross-subsidization is being practised then there would be an incentive for the services providing the subsidy to defect from this coalition.

The operational problem then is the following: What is the set of prices for these *n* services such that no service, either singly or jointly in coalitions smaller than the grand coalition, has the incentive to leave the grand coalition? This problem in the theory of cooperative games was solved by Faulhaber (1975).

To analyze Faulhaber's result assume that demands are price inelastic so that outputs are fixed. Let the cost function with a coalition of *J* players be C(J) (also known as the 'stand-alone' cost of *J* services) so that the cost function for the grand coalition is C(n). Denote by s_i the price paid by any service (cross-subsidy paid out) to belong to the grand coalition. To prevent *J* services from defecting from the grand coalition it must be the case that:

$$\sum_{i \in J} s_i \leqslant C(J). \tag{17.58}$$

This must be true for each possible sub-coalition *J* which can be formed from the grand coalition. In addition the grand coalition must break even:

$$\sum_{i=1}^{n} s_i = C(n). \tag{17.59}$$

If conditions (17.58) and (17.59) are satisfied for all *J* then there would be no incentive to break the grand coalition. Another interpretation of these conditions is possible and more insightful. Consider a subset *J* for which condition (17.58) is being satisfied. All other services $(n - J)$ must also pay no more than their stand-alone cost $C(n - J)$. Substitute into equation (17.59) to get:

$$\sum_{i \in n} s_i = \sum_{i \in (n-J)} s_i + \sum_{i \in J} s_i = C(n) \text{ which implies that}$$

$$\sum_{i \in J} s_i > C(n) - C(n - J).$$

All groups in *J*, therefore, must bring in to the grand coalition their incremental cost. This must be true for all *J*. Thus we know that, in order for there to be no desertions from the grand coalition, (the prices charged to belong to the core of the game) two conditions must be satisfied:

(i) no group of services must pay more than its stand-alone costs;
(ii) each group of services must pay at least its incremental cost.

We have been talking of breaking coalitions in terms of the costs. It is straightforward to extend this to cover benefit. This requires that the benefits (b_i) from staying in the coalition must at least outweigh subsidy paid out:

$$s_i \leqslant b_i \tag{17.60}$$

When this condition is met as well as conditions (17.58) and (17.59) then the prices charged do certainly belong to the core. Such prices are also referred to as **subsidy-free prices**.

It is possible to compare the prices consistent with equations (17.58) to (17.60) with the prices under the fully distributed cost (FDC) method already discussed. Under the FDC method price for service i is:

$$R_i = AC_i + \delta_i F \text{ with } \delta_i < 1. \quad \text{Thus}$$

$$\sum_{i \in J} R_i = \sum_{i \in J} (AC_i + \delta_i F) \leqslant \sum_{i \in J} (AC_i + F) \quad \text{for} \quad J \leqslant n.$$

and

$$\sum_{i=1}^{n} (R_i - AC_i) - F = 0.$$

Hence, when the cost function takes the form of an attributable cost and a joint fixed cost, the FDC approach gives subsidy-free prices. Therefore, we come to two conclusions. First, since any FDC method is subsidy free, prices calculated according to these methods cannot be used to test for cross-subsidy. Second, since each of the FDC methods does have the property of being cross-subsidy free, there are some merits to FDC methods.

The axiomatic approach to allocating fixed costs

This approach begins by trying to articulate the desirable properties of any allocation scheme. These desirable properties are considered as axioms.

The precise nature of these axioms depends, in part, upon what costs are fixed in the long run. It is sometimes argued that in the long run all costs are variable. Mirman and Taubman (1982), Billera and Health (1982) and Samet and Tauman (1982) discuss these axioms for the case in which all costs are variable in the long run. In the short run, however, some costs will be fixed and axioms for this case are discussed in Mirman et al. (1983). They present six axioms for the case in which the cost function is not assumed to represent the long-run efficient technology for the given level of output and where a fixed cost is present.

Consider the following cost function:

$$C = F + V(q_1, \ldots, q_n) \qquad (17.61)$$

where $V(.)$ is the variable cost of output. The six axioms for efficient pricing with this cost function are:

Axiom 1: cost sharing

The prices chosen must be such that costs for the implied vector of output are fully covered. This simply requires that the firm break even.

Axiom 2: rescaling

If the scales of measurement of the quantities of services are changed, the prices should change accordingly. This axiom seems harmless enough.

Axiom 3: consistency

Services with the same marginal cost should be priced the same. This is required, irrespective of the price elasticities of demands of these services. This is a major departure, then, from Ramsey pricing which, as we know, requires prices to be inversely related to elasticity of demand, ceteris paribus.

Axiom 4: positivity

Consider two alternative total cost functions C_0 and C_1 such that for zero output costs under C_0 are larger than those under C_1. Further, as output rises the (positive) difference between the costs between C_0 and C_1 keeps rising. In this case, a reasonable pricing mechanism will have higher prices under cost function C_0 than under C_1. In this particular case marginal costs are higher under C_0 than under C_1 and this axiom requires that the higher marginal cost is associated with the higher price.

Axiom 5: additivity of allocations

Suppose that the variable costs associated with a given vector of output $(q_1^0, \ldots, q_n^0)$ can be split up into m stages each with its own variable cost. Hence:

$$V(q^0) = v_1(q^0) + \ldots + v_m(q^0).$$

This is often possible with production involving more than one stage. In this case the pricing mechanism should allocate a fraction $\delta_j (j = 1, \ldots, m)$ of the fixed cost to each stage's variable cost. Further, total revenue for the output vector q^0 should be expressed as the sum of the costs of each stage. In other words:

$$\text{Total revenue} = \sum_{j=1}^{m} [v_j(q^0) + \delta_j F].$$

Thus this axiom is saying that common costs are to be 'added on' to allocable/variable costs.

Axiom 6: correlation

With reference to Axiom 6, if the variable cost for any stage k is greater than for another stage h $(v_k(q^0) > v_h(q^0))$ then the fixed cost allocated to stage k must also be greater than that allocated to stage h.

Mirman *et al.* (1983) consider these axioms as being reasonable and on that basis prove an important result. Their result is related to the notion of an **Aumann–Shapley price** after Aumann and Shapley (1974). We refer to Figure 17.11 where two outputs (q_1 and q_2) are considered. Current output is labeled (q_1^0, q_2^0) in the diagram. At each point along the ray from the origin to (q_1^0, q_2^0) we compute the marginal cost of an additional unit of each service and then average each of these marginal costs. This averaged marginal cost is referred to as the Aumann–Shapley price for service i and is labeled ASP_i. Mirman *et al.* show that the only price that is consistent with the above six axioms is:

$$p_i = (\text{ASP}_i/q_i)[1 + F/V(q_1, \ldots, q_n)]. \tag{17.62}$$

With this definition revenue (R_i) from service i is:

$$R_i = \text{ASP}_i[1 + F/V]. \tag{17.63}$$

Hence costs are covered with this price.

To get further intuition into this price consider the following restricted variable cost function:

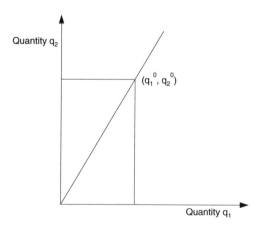

Figure 17.11

$$V(q_1, \ldots, q_n) = \sum_{i=1}^{n} V_i(q_i).$$

In this case $ASP_i = V_i(q_i)$ and

$$R_i = V_i(q_i)[1 + F/\sum_{i=1}^{n} V_i(q_i)].$$

But this is the same revenue that is given by the attributable cost method (ACM) discussed in connection with the FDC method.

17.10 CONCLUSIONS

This has been a long chapter and yet it has only presented the very basics of the problem of public-sector pricing. Several issues have not been covered. However, important results with regard to both first-best and second-best pricing, efficient pricing and marginal-cost pricing, peak-load pricing and pricing under joint production have been derived and interpreted. Issues neglected include price reform – in parallel to tax reforms. When price optimality cannot be guaranteed welfare improving price changes need to be considered. Considerations of this sort will take us too far afield into the area of public-sector pricing. If nothing else, this chapter should have introduced students to optimal pricing issues and formula and made them more appreciative of the enormous complexities associated with public sector pricing.

NOTES

1 Dreze and Marchand (1976) show the following. If we differentiate the Lagrangean with respect to initial endowments of labor d_0 and s_0 it is straightforward to prove that $\phi_0 > 0$ and $\mu_0 > 0$.
2 In this case we had lump-sum income (taxation). In case we had distortionary taxation then the amended Samuelson conditions would be satisfied with marginal cost pricing.
3 If we can choose optimal lump-sum incomes the demand schedules are compensated and if the concerned commodities are normal then the own price elasticity will be negative.
4 $\alpha_j p_j$ is the price consumers will pay for an extra KW of electricity for the duration of period j and $\alpha_j \gamma$ is the additional variable cost of producing it.
5 Across peak and off-peak periods.
6 Assuming, of course, that $p_j > \gamma$.
7 This would be a natural way to proceed since this would equated marginal benefit and marginal cost during the off-peak period.

ADDITIONAL READING

The survey article by Bos (1987) and subsequent work by him provide excellent surveys of the field of public sector pricing. The works of Feldstein and Munk referred to deal with redistributive pricing. The reference for axioms relating to fully distributed cost pricing is Billera and Heath (1982).

18 International aspects of taxation

Key concepts: tariffs in an open economy; terms of trade; optimum tariff; international fiscal coordination; second-best taxation; tax integration; Ramsey optimal taxation.

18.1 INTRODUCTION

Traditionally, public economics has been the subject for a closed economy. Open economy considerations were thought to be in the domain of international economics. However, the theory of international economics had a considerable amount to say about tariffs and quotas but relatively little about corporate and personal taxes in the open economy.

Over the last few years this has changed considerably and has been partly due to the rapid growth of international transactions. The globalization of domestic economies has meant that issues of international taxation cannot be ignored. Several important discussions on the subject are now available. Dixit (1987) provided a pioneering survey article. Other important contributions include Frenkel *et al.* (1991), Boadway and Bruce (1992), Tanzi (1994), and Giovannini *et al.* (1993). Needless to say, this area is expanding very rapidly. In this chapter we do not intend to provide a comprehensive survey of the research in this area but confine ourselves to studying some selected problems in the theory of international taxation.

We begin with an analysis of some standard problems in the theory of taxation in an open economy, followed by a study of tax coordination. In doing this we draw on the work of Frenkel *et al.* (1991) and Boadway and Bruce (1992). Then we examine the issue of integration of direct taxes in an open economy. Finally, we consider some issues related to optimal tariffs.

18.2 THE THEORY OF TARIFFS IN AN OPEN ECONOMY

We first study the rudiments of the theory of tariffs in an open economy. We will use for this the 'dual' approach to international trade popularized, among others, by Dixit and Norman (1980). The basic Dixit–Norman model is quite similar to the model of tax incidence in a static general equilibrium model studied at length in Chapter 11.

Consider the static general equilibrium model from Chapter 11. Let a_{ij} $(i = K, L; j = X, Y)$ denote the quantity of factor i required to produce one unit of commodity j. Then we have:

$$a_{LX}X + a_{LY}Y = L \tag{18.1a}$$

$$a_{KX}X + a_{KY}Y = K \tag{18.1b}$$

$$a_{LX}w + a_{KX}r = p_X \tag{18.1c}$$

$$a_{LY}w + a_{KY}r = p_Y \tag{18.1d}$$

where w and r are the price per unit of labor, L, and capital, K, respectively and p_X and p_Y are the prices of commodities X and Y respectively.

These equations emphasize the dual relations between factor endowments and commodity outputs (first two equations) and between commodity prices and facto prices in the presence of constant returns to scale (last two equations) from Chapter 11. Further, with constant returns to scale, the input coefficients depend solely upon the ratio of factor prices:

$$a_{ij} = a_{ij}(w/r), \ i = K, L; j = X, Y. \tag{18.2a -- --18.2d}$$

The eight equations in (18.1) and (18.2) describe the production side of the model and make it possible to determine the eight unknowns a_{ij}, X, Y, w, r given the four parameters L, K, p_x, p_y. Totally differentiating equations (18.1) we have:

$$Xda_{LX} + a_{LX}dX + Yda_{LY} + a_{LY}dY = dL \tag{18.3a}$$

$$Xda_{KX} + a_{KX}dX + Yda_{KY} + a_{KY}dY = dK \tag{18.3b}$$

$$wda_{LX} + a_{LX}dw + rda_{KX} + a_{KX}dr = dp_X \tag{18.3c}$$

$$wda_{LY} + a_{LY}dw + rda_{KY} + a_{KY}dr = dp_Y. \tag{18.3d}$$

Letting a rate of change be denoted by a hat ($\wedge$) such that $\hat{s} \equiv ds/s$ we get:

$$\lambda_{LX}\hat{X} + \lambda_{LY}\hat{Y} = \hat{L} - (\lambda_{LX}\hat{a}_{LX} + \lambda_{LY}\hat{a}_{LY}) \tag{18.4a}$$

$$\lambda_{KX}\hat{X} + \lambda_{KY}\hat{Y} = \hat{K} - (\lambda_{KX}\hat{a}_{KX} + \lambda_{KY}\hat{a}_{KY}) \tag{18.4b}$$

$$\theta_{LX}\hat{w} + \theta_{KX}\hat{r} = \hat{p}_X - (\theta_{LX}\hat{a}_{LX} + \theta_{KX}\hat{a}_{KX}) \tag{18.4c}$$

$$\theta_{LY}\hat{w} + \theta_{KY}\hat{r} = \hat{p}_Y - (\theta_{LY}\hat{a}_{LY} + \theta_{KY}\hat{a}_{KY}) \tag{18.4d}$$

where $\lambda_{LX} \equiv a_{LX}X/L$, $\lambda_{LY} = a_{LY}Y/L$ denote the fractions of the labor force used in sector X and Y respectively with, clearly, $\lambda_{LX} + \lambda_{LY} = 1$. Similarly $\lambda_{KX} \equiv a_{KX}X/K$, $\lambda_{KY} \equiv a_{KY}Y/K$ and $\lambda_{KX} + \lambda_{KY} = 1$. The θs denote the factor shares in each sector with, for example, $\theta_{LX} = a_{LX}w/p_X$. Clearly $\theta_{LX} + \theta_{KX} = 1$ and $\theta_{LY} + \theta_{KY} = 1$.

At this point we can derive an important result about the general equilibrium effects of a tariff. From equations (18.4c) and (18.4d) we will have:

$$\hat{w} = (\theta_{KY}\hat{p}_X - \theta_{KX}\hat{p}_Y)/(\theta_{LX}\theta_{KY} - \theta_{LY}\theta_{KX}) \qquad (18.5a)$$

$$\hat{r} = (\theta_{LX}\hat{p}_Y - \theta_{LY}\hat{p}_X)/(\theta_{LX}\theta_{KY} - \theta_{LY}\theta_{KX}). \qquad (18.5b)$$

Suppose the economy is open and commodity X is the numeraire good so that $\hat{p}_X = 0$. A positive (negative) value of $\hat{p}_Y$ therefore means an increase (decrease) in the relative price p_Y/p_X due to, say, the increase (decrease) of a tariff on commodity Y (which can be thought of as the import). Similarly a positive (negative) value of $\hat{w}$ means an increase (decrease) in the unit real reward of labor (in terms of the numeraire).

Suppose now that the commodity Y is labor intensive and that the relative price of this commodity increases (say because of a tariff). Given the definitions of the θs, the greater relative labor intensity of Y amounts to the inequality $\theta_{LY}/\theta_{KY} > \theta_{LX}/\theta_{KX}$ and, therefore, the denominator of the expressions on the righthand side in equation (18.5) is negative. As we have supposed that $\hat{p}_Y > 0$, it follows that $\hat{w} > 0$ and $\hat{r} < 0$. The increase in the unit real reward of the factor used intensively in the industry producing the commodity with the relative price increase is proved. This is known as the **Stolper–Samuelson theorem**, initially proved by Stolper and Samuelson (1941). Thus if, following the Heckscher–Ohlin factor proportions theory, a capital intensive country is exporting capital intensive goods and importing labor intensive goods, then the imposition of an import tariff will improve the earnings of domestic labor at the expense of domestic capital.

Tariffs, terms of trade and domestic relative prices

Suppose we live in a world of two countries: country 1 and country 2. Suppose that country 1 imports commodity X and exports commodity Y while the opposite holds for country 2. Define $p \equiv p_Y/p_X$ as the relative price with commodity X taken as numeraire. Also define $X^d(I_X, p)$ as the demand for commodity X in terms of the income in terms of commodity X called I_X, and the relative price. Further let $E_{iX}(p)$ be the excess demand for commodity X in country i. Consider now the excess demand for commodities X and Y in country 1 and the budget constraint:

$$E_{1X}(p) = X_1^d(I_{1X}, p) - X_1(p). \qquad (18.6a)$$

Excess demand for commodity X is defined as the demand less the supply. (The supply of X depends on the relative price, p.)

$$E_{1Y}(p) = Y_1^d(I_{1X}, p) - Y_1(p). \qquad (18.6b)$$

Excess demand for commodity Y is demand less the supply.

$$E_{1X}(p) + pE_{1Y}(p) = 0. \qquad (18.6c)$$

Sum of the excess demand is equal to zero (Walaras' Law).
(It is left as a simple exercise for the student to show that I_{1X} is a function of p alone, under competitive conditions. Hint: realize that factor rewards are

equal to the respective marginal products.) If the economy is closed then the equilibrium conditions would require that $E_{1X} = E_{1Y} = 0$. However, with international trade we have, for country 2:

$$E_{2X}(p) = X_2^d(I_{2X}, p) - X_2(p) \tag{18.7a}$$

$$E_{2Y}(p) = Y_2^d(I_{2X}, p) - Y_2(p) \tag{18.7b}$$

$$E_{2X}(p) + pE_{2Y}(p) = 0. \tag{18.7c}$$

International equilibrium requires that the world demands for the two commodities are equal to the respective world supplies, namely:

$$E_{1X}(p) + E_{2X}(p) = 0 \tag{18.8a}$$

$$E_{1Y}(p) + E_{2Y}(p) = 0. \tag{18.8b}$$

These conditions are not independent because either can be derived from the other given the two countries' budget constraints. By using these constraints, international equilibrium can also be expressed as:

$$E_{1X}(p) = pE_{2Y}(p) \tag{18.9a}$$

$$pE_{1Y}(p) = E_{2X}(p) \tag{18.9b}$$

where, of course, either one depends on the other.

If we assume that country 1 imports commodity X and imports commodity Y while the opposite holds for country 2, international equilibrium is defined as:

$$E_{2Y} + E_{1Y}(p) = 0 \tag{18.10a}$$

or, as

$$E_{2Y}(p) = -E_{1Y}(p) \tag{18.10b}$$

that is, excess demand for commodity Y by country 2 (country 2's demand for imports) is equal in absolute to the excess supply of this commodity by country 1 (country 1's supply of exports).

In the case that a country, say country 2, levies a tariff, the domestic relative price of that country – to which its economic agents respond – is no longer p but $p_{\tau d} = p(1 + \tau)$ where τ is the rate of *ad valorem* duty. Therefore E_{2Y} will be a function of p_τ instead of p. Moreover, we must introduce the spending of the revenue by the government, which in real terms is dE_{2Y}. We assume that the government spends a fraction α, $(0 < \alpha < 1)$, of this revenue to purchase commodity Y and the remaining fraction $(1 - \alpha)$ to purchase commodity X. Hence, country 2's total (private + government) demand for imports will be $(1 + \alpha\tau)E_{2Y}$.

Hence we have the relations:

$$(1 + \alpha\tau)E_{2Y}(p_\tau) + E_{1Y}(p) = 0 \tag{18.11a}$$

$$p_\tau - p(1 + \tau) = 0. \tag{18.11b}$$

Equations (18.11) constitute a set of two implicit functions in three variables (p_τ, p, τ). Therefore, provided that the Jacobian of these functions with respect to p_τ and p is different from zero at the equilibrium point, by the implicit function theorem we can express p_τ and p as differentiable functions of τ in a neighborhood of the equilibrium point and conduct exercises in comparative statics. In particular, we are interested in the effects on p and p_τ of the introduction of a tariff.

The Jacobian of equations (18.11) is:

$$J = \begin{vmatrix} (1 + \alpha\tau)E'_{2Y} & E'_1 \\ 1 & -(1 + \tau) \end{vmatrix} = -(1 + \alpha\tau)(1 + \tau)E'_{2Y} - E'_{1Y} \qquad (18.12)$$

where a prime ($'$) denotes a partial derivative. At the initial free trade point (where $\tau = 0$) this Jacobian is:

$$J = -(E'_{2Y} + E'_{1Y}). \qquad (18.13)$$

Multiplying and dividing by E_{2Y}/p we get:

$$J = -(E_{2Y}/p)[E'_{2Y}p/E_{2Y} + E'_{1Y}p/E_{2Y}] \qquad (18.14)$$

and, since $E_{2Y} = -E_{1Y}$ in the initial equilibrium situation we have:

$$J = -(E_{2Y}/p)[E'_{2Y}p/E_{2Y} - E'_{1Y}p/E_{1Y}] \qquad (18.15)$$

which can be rewritten as:

$$J = -(E_{2Y}/p)[\xi_2 - \epsilon_1] \qquad (18.16)$$

where ξ_2 and ϵ_1 are elasticities whose magnitudes are defined in equation (18.15). It is easy to show that $\epsilon_1 = -(1 + \xi_1)$ where ξ_1 is conformably defined. Substituting in equation (18.16) we have:

$$J = -(E_{2Y}/p)(1 + \xi_1 + \xi_2). \qquad (18.17)$$

It can be shown that for stability we must have $(1 + \xi_1 + \xi_2) < 0$ so that $J > 0$.

We now calculate p'_τ and p' the derivatives of p_τ and p with respect to τ. Totally differentiating equations (18.11) with respect to τ we have:

$$\alpha E_{2Y} + (1 + \alpha\tau)E'_{2Y}p'_\tau + E'_{1Y}p' = 0 \qquad (18.18a)$$

$$p'_\tau - p'(1 + \tau) - p = 0. \qquad (18.18b)$$

Now, by using the fact that the derivatives are computed at the initial free-trade equilibrium situation ($\tau = 0$), and rearranging terms we have:

$$E'_{2Y}p'_\tau + E'_{1Y}p' = -\alpha E_{2Y} \qquad (18.19a)$$

$$p'_\tau - p' = p. \qquad (18.19b)$$

From these we can solve for p'_τ and p' to get:

$$p'_\tau = (\alpha E_{2Y} - E'_{1Y}p)/J \qquad (18.20a)$$

$$p' = (\alpha E_{2Y} + E'_{2Y}p)/J. \qquad (18.20b)$$

By replacing J with the expression in (18.17) we have:

$$p'_\tau = -(p/E_{2Y})[\alpha E_{2Y} - E'_{1Y}p]/(1 + \xi_1 + \xi_2) = -p(\alpha + \epsilon_1)/(1 + \xi_1 + \xi_2).$$
(18.21)

Similarly we can obtain:

$$p' = -p[\alpha + \xi_2]/(1 + \xi_1 + \xi_2).$$
(18.22)

Given the $(1 + \xi_1 + \xi_2) < 0$ the signs of (18.21) and (18.22) depend only upon the numerators of the two expressions.

Suppose now that country 2 imposes a tariff on its imports – commodity Y. Typically, its domestic terms of trade (p_Y/p_X) should increase. However, there is an interesting special case called the **Metzler Paradox** where the terms of trade decrease. In this case we require that $p'_\tau < 0$, i.e., $\alpha + \epsilon_1 < 0$. But since $\epsilon_1 = -(1 + \xi_1)$ (a fact that is easy to show and left as an exercise for the reader) we have:

$$\alpha - \xi_1 - 1 < 0 \text{ or that } \alpha - \xi_1 < 1. \tag{18.23}$$

In the normal good case the elasticity $\xi_1 < 0$ so that the condition for Metzler's case to occur is that the sum of the fraction α and the absolute value of the elasticity of the rest-of-the-world's demand for imports should be smaller than one. This is equivalent to saying that the rest-of-the-world's import demand must be sufficiently inelastic. If, on the other hand, we have an abnormal case (for example commodity X is an inferior good for country 1), the elasticity $\xi_1 > 0$ and condition (18.23) is satisfied for any non-negative α.

Another interesting case is **Lerner's**. This occurs when after the imposition of the tariff, the terms of trade are higher, instead of being lower than in the initial free trade situation. In formal terms this requires that $p' > 0$; i.e., given (18.22), $\alpha + \xi_2 > 0$ or:

$$-\xi_2 < \alpha. \tag{18.24}$$

As before, two cases ought to be distinguished. In the normal case the elasticity ξ_2 is negative, so that the condition for Lerner's result to occur is that the tariff imposing country's demand for imports is sufficiently rigid, with an elasticity in absolute value smaller than the fraction α. In the abnormal cases (for example, when commodity Y is an inferior good for country 2), the elasticity ξ_2 is positive and equation (18.24) holds for any non-negative α.

The optimum tariff

As a final topic in the theory of tariffs in open economies, we examine the argument for an **optimum tariff**. If we denote W as the social welfare function having the quantities demanded (consumed) of the two commodities as arguments, we have for country 2:

$$W = W(X_2^d, Y_2^d) = W(X_2 + E_{2X}, Y_2 + E_{2Y}). \qquad (18.25)$$

We have to maximize this welfare function. From the transformation function for country 2 we write $X_2 = \Phi(Y_2)$. We also know that $E_{2Y} = -E_{1Y}$ and that $E_{2X} = -E_{1X} = pE_{1Y}$. We thus have to maximize:

$$W = W[\Phi(Y_2) + pE_{1Y}(p), \; Y_2 - E_{1Y}(p)] \qquad (18.26)$$

with respect to Y_2 and p. The first-order conditions are that:

$$\partial W/\partial Y_2 = (\partial W/\partial X)(\partial \Phi/\partial Y_2) + (\partial W/\partial Y_2) = 0 \qquad (18.27a)$$

$$\partial W/\partial p = (\partial W/\partial X)(E_{1Y} + E'_{1Y}p) - (\partial W/\partial Y_2)E'_{1Y} = 0. \qquad (18.27b)$$

From the first, we get:

$$(\partial W/\partial Y_2)/(\partial W/\partial X) = -\partial \Phi/\partial Y_2 \qquad (18.28a)$$

and from (18.27a) after some manipulation:

$$E_{1Y}[(\partial W/\partial X)\{1 + E'_{1Y}(p/E_{1Y})\} - (\partial W/\partial Y_2)(1/p)E'_{1Y}(p/E_{1Y})] = 0. \qquad (18.28b)$$

Using the definition of ϵ_1 and rearranging terms we have:

$$(\partial W/\partial Y_2)/(\partial W/\partial X) = p(1 + \epsilon_1)/\epsilon_1. \qquad (18.29)$$

We also know that:

$$-\Phi' = p(1 + \epsilon_1)/\epsilon_1$$

It is also the case that in equilibrium the marginal rate of transformation (*mrt*) equals country 2's domestic relative price, which in turn equals the terms of trade plus tariff. Hence, we have:

$$p(1 + \tau) = p(1 + \epsilon_1)/\epsilon_1$$

so that, in optimum, we must have:

$$\tau = 1/\epsilon_1. \qquad (18.30)$$

Thus we have the result that optimum tariff for country 2 equals the reciprocal of the elasticity of country 1's supply of exports.

There are several other results in taxation in open economies but the discussion here has given a sample. Interested readers should read Dixit (1987) and Dixit and Norman (1980).

18.3   INTERNATIONAL FISCAL COORDINATION: INTEREST TAXATION

We now move to studying international coordination when capital and goods markets are fully integrated. What does this imply for coordination with respect to direct and indirect taxation?

Two principles have been advanced for taxing income in an international context. These are the **residence** principle and the **source** principle. According to the residence principle residents of a country are taxed on their worldwide income uniformly, regardless of the source of their income (domestic or foreign). Hence, incomes of non-residents are not taxed. According to the source principle all incomes generated within the geographical boundaries of the country are taxed. Hence, incomes of non-residents generated within the country are taxed whereas the foreign incomes of residents are taxed.

Since capital markets are assumed to be integrated residents of a country are able to invest in other countries. Hence there will be international tax arbitrage. Such arbitrage has important implications for the viability of equilibrium in the capital markets of both countries.

To see this consider a two-country example – the home country and the foreign country. All foreign magnitudes are denoted by a star (∗). The home interest rate is r and the foreign interest rate is r^*. The literature then distinguishes between three different effective tax rates applying to interest income:

(i) tax rate levied on residents on domestic source income labeled t_{rd};
(ii) effective rate of additional tax levied on residents on foreign source income (over and above the tax paid in the foreign country), labeled t_{ra};
(iii) tax rate levied on the income of non-residents, labeled t_{rn}.

For the foreign country we have the corresponding magnitudes t_{rd}^*, t_{ra}^* and t_{rn}^*. It is assumed that these taxes are applied in both the home and foreign countries symmetrically on both interest income as well as interest expenses.[1]

In equilibrium an investor in the home country must be indifferent between investing in the home and the foreign countries. Abstracting from exchange rate fluctuations, then, international interest tax arbitrage will imply that the net rates of return in the two countries be equalized for the home investor:

$$r(1 - t_{rd}) = r^*(1 - t_{rn}^* - t_{ra}). \tag{18.31}$$

Similarly for the foreign investor we can write:

$$r^*(1 - t_{rd}^*) = r(1 - t_{rn} - t_{ra}^*). \tag{18.32}$$

since equations (18.31) and (18.32) must hold simultaneously and are, hence, linearly dependent. Thus we can write:

$$(1 - t_{rd})(1 - t_{rd}^*) = (1 - t_{rn} - t_{ra}^*)(1 - t_{rn}^* - t_{ra}). \tag{18.33}$$

Equation (18.33) implies that even though home and foreign countries may not explicitly coordinate their tax policies, international arbitrage would require that coordination takes place. To see this suppose that both countries adopt the residence principle of taxation. Then we would have:

$$t_{rd} = t_{ra} + t_{rn}^*, \ t_{rd}^* = t_{ra}^* + t_{rn}, \ t_{rn} = t_{rn}^* = 0 \tag{18.34}$$

whereas with the source principle we would have:

$$t_{rd} = t_{rn}, \; t_{rd}^* = t_{rn}^*, \; t_{ra} = t_{ra}^* = 0. \tag{18.35}$$

In both cases equation (18.33) is satisfied. However, if one country uses the source principle, whereas the other uses the residence principle, then equation (18.33) will not be satisfied and a viable capital market equilibrium may not exist.

Note further that if both countries follow the residence principle so that equation (18.34) holds then from equation (18.34) we must have $r = r^*$ (gross rates of return on capital in both countries are equalized). This would lead to a Pareto optimal international allocation[2] of capital. However, if $t_{rd} \neq t_{rd}^*$ then the net rates of return to capital are not equalized: $r(1 - t_{rd}) \neq r^*(1 - t_{rd}^*)$ even though the gross rates of return to capital are equalized.

If both countries use the source principle then, from equation (18.35), it must be the case that the net rates of return to capital are equalized: $r(1 - t_{rd}) = r^*(1 - t_{rd}^*)$. However, if the tax rates are not the same $(t_{rd} \neq t_{rd}^*)$, then the gross rates of return are not equalized. In either case international capital market equilibrium will exist.

Indirect taxation

Let us now look at the problem of indirect tax coordination. This is most easily studied in the case of a single rate VAT. According to the destination principle of VAT in an open economy, a good or service purchased by a resident is taxed irrespective of whether this commodity is domestically produced or imported. In other words, exports are tax exempt whereas imports are taxed. According to the source principle all goods produced within the country pay the VAT irrespective of whether these items are meant for domestic or foreign consumption. Hence, exports are not exempt from VAT in this case. Now let:

(i) t_d be the tax rate levied on the good if produced and sold domestically;
(ii) t_x tax rate levied on exports of the good;
(iii) t_z effective tax rate levied on the imports of the good (in addition to the tax levied abroad);
(iv) q is the producer price of the home good in the home country.

Then international commodity market equilibrium for the home country would require that:

$$q(1 + t_d) = q^*(1 + t_x^* + t_z) \tag{18.36}$$

whereas for the foreign country we would require that:

$$q^*(1 + t_d^*) = q(1 + t_x + t_z^*). \tag{18.37}$$

Once again, in the face of international commodity arbitrage, equations (18.36) and (18.37) will not be independent of each other. For full international equilibrium we will have to satisfy:

$$(1 + t_d)(1 + t_d^*) = (1 + t_x^* + t_z)(1 + t_x + t_z^*). \qquad (18.38)$$

It is straightforward to see that if both countries adopted the source criterion or the destination criterion then equation (18.38) will be satisfied. However, if one country uses the source criterion and the other uses the destination criterion then equation (18.38) will not be satisfied and commodity market equilibrium may not exist.

Second-best taxation

Suppose capital is free to move across international boundaries and the principle of residence based taxation of interest income is applied. We know that this would lead to the equality of the domestic interest rate with the world interest rate and, hence, to the satisfaction of Pareto optimality conditions with respect to the capital market. An important question to ask at this stage is the following: Should we persist in satisfying this condition for Pareto optimality even though other conditions may not be satisfied?

Frenkel *et al.* (1991) use a slightly amended two-period, life-cycle model of optimum taxation to address this question. In the first period there exists an initial endowment of the composite good for each household. Households are free to choose how much of this initial endowment to consume and how much to save in the first period. This saving is allocated to home and foreign investment and income from these is taxed according to the residence principle.

Hence the first-period budget constraint can be written as:

$$c_{1h} + K_h^d + K_h^f = \Omega_h \qquad (18.39)$$

where c_{1h} is first-period consumption, K_h^d and K_h^f are, respectively, savings in the home and foreign capital markets and Ω_h is the initial endowment of household h.

In the second period, output produced by capital and labor[3] and the income from foreign investment earnings is allocated between private consumption (c_{2h}) and a public good amounts of which are denoted by G. The government employs taxes on labor, and on income from domestic and foreign investments in order to finance the public good as well as a uniform lump-sum subsidy for purposes of redistribution. Hence, the second-period budget constraint of the household can be written as:

$$c_{2h} = K_h^d[1 + r(1 - t_{rd})] + K_h^f[1 + r^f(1 - t_{ra})] + (1 - t_w)wL_h + D \qquad (18.40)$$

where t_{rd} is the tax on capital income from domestic sources, t_{ra} is the tax on capital income from foreign sources, t_w is the wage tax, D is the lump-sum subsidy (demogrant) given in the second period and r^f is the return on foreign capital after all foreign taxes.

There are H households. The utility function of consumer h is written as:

$$U^h(c_{1h},\ c_{2h},\ L_h,\ G). \tag{18.41}$$

Consider the case where the country under question is a capital exporter, i.e., $K_h^f \geqslant 0$.

International capital market arbitrage will require[4] that:

$$r(1 - t_{rd}) = r^f(1 - t_{ra}). \tag{18.42}$$

Now, households are completely indifferent between investing in the home economy or the foreign economy. Hence the budget constraints for the two periods can be consolidated into one:

$$c_{1h} + p_{c2}c_{2h} = \Omega_h + w_L L_h + D' \tag{18.43}$$

where $p_{c2} = [1 + (1 - t_{rd})r]^{-1}$ is the after tax price of second-period consumption, w_L is the after tax wage rate and $D' = Dp_{c2}$ is the present value of the demogrant.

Maximizing the utility function subject to the budget constraints yields consumption and labor supply in the second period in terms of the variables that are exogenous to consumer h. Thus we write:

$$c_{2h} = c_{2h}(p_{c2}, w_L, \Omega_h + D', G) \tag{18.44}$$

and

$$L_h = L_h(p_{c2}, w_L, \Omega_h + D', G) \tag{18.45}$$

which when plugged into the utility function (equation 18.11) yields the indirect utility function:

$$V^h(p_{c2}, w_L, \Omega_h + D', G). \tag{18.46}$$

Production in the second time period is described by a standard neoclassical production function:

$$Y = F(K, L) \tag{18.47}$$

where Y is the amount of the composite output. Clearly $K = \sum_h K_h^d$ and $L_h = \sum_h L_h$. Competitive factor markets ensure that factor rewards equal respective marginal products:

$$r = \partial F / \partial K \text{ and } w = \partial F / \partial L. \tag{18.48}$$

In the first time period the aggregate resource constraint can be written as:

$$\sum_h \Omega_h = \sum_h c_{1h} + \sum_h K_h^d + \sum_h K_h^f. \tag{18.49}$$

The second period aggregate resource constraint can be written as:

$$Y + (1 + r^f) \sum_h K_h^f + \sum_h K_h^d = \sum_h c_{2h} + G. \tag{18.50}$$

Now substitute (18.39), (18.44), (18.45), (18.47) and (18.49) into equation (18.50) to get the overall constraint:

$$F\left[\sum_h \Omega_h - \sum_h c_{1h}(p_{c2}, w_L, \Omega_h + D') - \sum_h K_h^f, \sum_h L_h(p_{c2}, w_L, \Omega_h + D', G)\right]$$
$$+ (1 + r^f) \sum_h K_h^f + \sum_h \Omega_h - \sum_h c_{1h}(p_{c2}, w_L, \Omega_h + D', G) - \sum_h K_g^f$$
$$- \sum_h c_{2h}(p_{c2}, w_L, \Omega_h + D', G) - G = 0. \tag{18.51}$$

The government's second-best optimal tax problem is then to maximize the social welfare function:

$$W = W(V^1(p_{c2}, w_L, \Omega_1 + D'), \ldots, V^H(p_{c2}, w_L, \Omega_H + D')) \tag{18.52}$$

subject to the overall constraint expressed by equation (18.51). The control variables are p_{c2} and w_L which are actually controlled by changing the tax rates t_{rd} and t_w.

From the first-order conditions it is easy to check that:

$$r = r^f. \tag{18.53}$$

This will hold only if capital moves freely across international boundaries and the residence principle of taxation is followed. In other words $t_{rd} = t_{ra}$. The intuition behind this result is that if capital is freely mobile across international boundaries and labor is completely immobile, source-based capital taxes are completely shifted to labor and it is better then to tax labor directly rather than indirectly through capital.

18.4 INTEGRATING PERSONAL AND CORPORATE TAXATION IN AN OPEN ECONOMY

It is generally argued that integration of personal and corporate income for purposes of comprehensive income taxation as per the Haig–Simons criterion[5] is desirable. One obvious example of the advantages to be had from such integration is that corporate income will not be taxed twice.[6] Second, it removes the tax disadvantage for making distributions to shareholders in the form of dividends rather than share redemptions. Third, it removes a bias in the choice of investment finance – debt vs equities. Moreover, in an unintegrated set-up the corporation tax acts like a partial factor tax.[7] Some economists argue that as a tax on capital income it probably reduces the incentive to save and invest. On equity grounds, the corporate income tax violates horizontal equity since taxpayers who receive greater capital income would be taxed at a higher rate. In the USA, for example, non-capital income up to $15,000 a year is exempt from income taxes. But if someone had $15,000 as capital income – say from pensions – she would be taxed. Thus, it would appear that integration of corporate and income taxes would be welfare improving. Integration would involve the lumping together of corporate and all other incomes for purposes of direct taxation.

In an important paper Boadway and Bruce (1992) show that such integration is not unambiguously desirable in an open economy.[8] Let us study this result in the context of a simplified version of the Boadway–Bruce model.

There are two time periods in this model. At the end of the second time period all wealth is transferred to households. Households and firms are heterogeneous in the Boadway–Bruce model. Householders (or shareholders) can be classified according to whether they are acquiring or divesting equity. In a closed economy this has to be domestic shares whereas in an open economy this could be domestic or foreign shares. Firms could be mature (in which case they pay dividends in the first time period) or immature (in which case they pay dividends only in the second time period). Firms can also be classified according to whether they are capital importing or capital exporting.

There are three types of taxes in this model: t_y is the tax rate on household income (including dividend income); t_θ is the tax rate on capital gains on a realization basis[9] and t_π is the rate of corporate tax. In addition, there is an investment tax credit[10] at the rate α. Hence, the effective tax rate on dividends received by the shareholder is $\tau = (t_y - \alpha)/(1 - \alpha)$.

Capital is fully mobile internationally but labor is not. In the first time period domestic capital stock for the firm (K_1^d) and ownership of foreign shares (K_1^f) are known. The firm has to decide upon the extent of domestic investment $(K_2^d - K_1^d)$ and foreign investment $(K_2^f - K_1^f) \cdot K_1^d$ and K_1^f are predetermined. In the first period the dividend per share $(\delta_1 \geq 0)$ is also announced. Let P^d and S^d be respectively the purchases and sales of shares by domestic shareholders and let P^f be the purchases of shares by foreign shareholders. Thus $P_2^f - P_1^f$ will be net acquisitions of domestic shares by foreigners in period 2. Hence the net change in share holdings between period 2 and period 1 can be written as $(P^d - S^d + P_2^f - P_1^f)$. If V_1 is the value of a share redeemed at time 1 then we can write the cash flow constraint of the firm as:

$$V_1(P^d - S^d + P_2^f - P_1^f) + Q_1(1 - t_\pi) + r_x^* K_1^f - \delta_1(P_1^d + P_1^f)$$
$$= K_2^d - K_1^d + K_2^f - K_1^f. \tag{18.54}$$

The first term on the lefthand side measures the earnings from shares, $Q_1(1 - t_\pi)$ is the earnings from domestic investment after corporate taxes. r_x^* is the fixed rate of return on foreign shares so $r_x^* K_1^f$ is earnings from foreign shares. $\delta_1(\geq 0)$ is the dividend paid out in the first period so that $\delta_1(P_1^d + P_1^f)$ is the value of shares paid out. Hence, the lefthand side of equation (18.54) represents the net earnings by firms. This is expended on domestic and foreign investment (righthand side).

Shareholders derive utility from first- and second-period consumption (C_1 and C_2 respectively). First- and second-period consumption can, in turn, be written as:

$$C_1 = W_1 + \delta_1(1-\tau)P_1^d - V_1(P^d - S^d) - t_\theta(V_1 - V_0)S^d \qquad (18.55)$$

$$C_2 = W_2 + [V_2 + \delta_2(1-\tau)](P_1^d + P^d - S^d) - t_\theta[(V_2 - V_0)(P_1^d - S^d)P^d]. \qquad (18.56)$$

$W_i (i = 1, 2)$ is exogenous wage income in period i. Taking equation (18.55) first, the second term on the righthand side is after tax earnings from domestic shares. The third term represents the net value of earnings forgone because of selling shares. The last term is the capital gains tax paid on change in asset value between period 0 and period 1. Now, examining equation (18.56), the second term on the righthand side can be interpreted as follows. V_2 is the value of shares redeemed, $\delta_2(1-\tau)$ is the dividend earned so this second term represents earnings from shares. The last term represents capital gains taxes paid out.

In addition, the following firm valuation constrains must obtain:

$$(i) V_0(P_1^d + P_1^f) = K_1^d + K_1^f. \qquad (18.57)$$

This says that the investment in capital – whether domestic or foreign – in time period 1 must be financed by earnings evaluated at the value of shares during time period 0.

$$(ii)(V_1 + \delta_1 - V_0)(P_1^d + P_1^f) = Q_1(1 - t_\pi) + r_x^* K_1^f. \qquad (18.58)$$

On the righthand side of this expression we have earnings of the firm during time period 1. This consists of domestic earnings after taxes (the first term) and foreign earnings (the second term). This is expended in share purchases and dividends paid less share sales which is the expenditure of the firm noted on the lefthand side of equation (18.58).

$$(iii)(V_2 + \delta_2 - V_1)(P_1^d + P^d - S^d + P_2^f) = Q_2(1 - t_\pi) + r_x^* K_2^f. \qquad (18.59)$$

Equation (18.59) states that earnings during the second time period (the righthand side) must equal expenditures (the lefthand side).

In addition, if domestic corporations must attract foreign capital, $P_2^f > 0$ then they must pay a sufficiently high rate of return. This is expressed by the constraint given in (18.60):

$$V_2 - V_1 + \delta_2 = r_m^* V_1 \qquad (18.60)$$

where r_m^* denotes the rate of return that must be paid in order to attract foreign capital. Typically $r_m^* > r_x^*$ unless both countries exempt foreign income of corporations from taxation.

The firm tries to maximize the utility of the household which is given by a twice continuously differentiable utility function $U(C_1, C_2)$ with C_1 and C_2

being given by equations (18.55) and (18.56). This maximization is subject to the constraints given by equations (18.58) and (18.59) and some non-negativity constraints.

The Lagrangean expression is written as:

$$\begin{aligned}
\Lambda = {} & U(C_1, C_2) + \lambda_1[V_1(P^d - S^d + P_2^f - P_1^f) + Q_1(1 - t_\pi) - K_2^f - K_2^d \\
& - \delta_1(P_1^d + P_1^f)] + \lambda_2[(V_1 + \delta_1 - V_0)(P_1^d + P_1^f) - Q_1(1 - t_\pi)] \\
& + \lambda_3[(V_2 + \delta_2 - V_1)(P_1^d + P^d - S^d + P_1^f) - Q(K_2^d)(1 - t_\pi) - r_x{}^*K_2^f] \\
& + \lambda_4\delta_1 + \lambda_5\delta_2 + \lambda_6V_2 + \lambda_7P^d + \lambda_8S^d + \lambda_9K_2^f + \lambda_{10}P_2^f.
\end{aligned}$$

$$(18.61)$$

The first-order conditions for an internal maximum are given by:
(i) with respect to δ_1:

$$(\partial U/\partial C_1)(1 - \tau)P_1^d + (\lambda_2 - \lambda_1)(P_1^d + P_2^d) + \lambda_4 = 0. \qquad (18.62a)$$

(ii) with respect to δ_2:

$$(\partial U/\partial C_2)(1 - \tau)(P_1^d + P^d - S^d) + \lambda_3(P_1^d + P^d - S^d + P_2^f) + \lambda_5 = 0.$$

$$(18.62b)$$

(iii) with respect to V_1:

$$\begin{aligned}
& (\partial U/\partial C_1)(1 - t_\theta)S^d - \{(\partial U/\partial C_1) - t_\theta(\partial U/\partial C_2)\}P^d + (\lambda_2 - \lambda_3)(P_1^d + P_1^f) \\
& + (\lambda_1 - \lambda_3)(P^d - S^d + P_2^f + P_1^f) = 0.
\end{aligned}$$

$$(18.62c)$$

(iv) with respect to V_2:

$$(\partial U/\partial C_2)(1 - t_\theta)[P_1^d + P^d - S^d] + \lambda_3(P_1^d + P^d - S^d + P_2^f) + \lambda_6 = 0.$$

$$(18.62d)$$

(v) with respect to P^d:

$$\begin{aligned}
& [-(\partial U/\partial C_1) + t_\theta(\partial U/\partial C_2) + \lambda_1 - \lambda_3]V_1 + [(\partial U/\partial C_2)(1 - t_\theta) + \lambda_3]V_2 \\
& + [(\partial U/\partial C_2)(1 - \tau) + \lambda_3]\delta_2 + \lambda_7 = 0.
\end{aligned}$$

$$(18.62e)$$

(vi) with respect to K_2^d:

$$-\lambda_1 - \lambda_3(\partial Q/\partial K_2^d)(1 - t_\pi) = 0. \qquad (18.62f)$$

(vii) with respect to K_2^f:

$$-\lambda_1 - \lambda_3r_x{}^* + \lambda_9 = 0. \qquad (18.62g)$$

(viii) with respect to P_2^f:

$$(\lambda_1 - \lambda_3)V_1 + \lambda_3(V_2 + \delta_2) + \lambda_{10} = 0. \qquad (18.62h)$$

These first-order conditions are different across closed and open economies. For closed economies $K_2^f = P_1^f = P_2^f = 0$. To simplify further we set $\delta_2 = \lambda_6 = 0$ to get for the immature[11] firm:

$$(\partial U/\partial C_1)/(\partial U/\partial C_2) - 1 = (1 - \tau)(\partial Q/\partial K_2^d)(1 - t_\pi).$$

Unintegrated tax systems in a closed economy will impose several distortions on the investment and financing decisions of firms. The presence of both personal and corporate taxation will impose a 'double distortion' on investment financed with equity. Marginal investment by immature firms, for example, will bear both the personal tax rate as well as the corporate tax rate. Further the effect of the tax structure will depend on the mode of finance of investment. Clearly, unincorporated businesses are favored over incorporated businesses since the former bear only the personal tax whereas the latter face both the personal as well as the corporate tax.

With full integration the equilibrium levels of savings and investment are defined by:

$$(\partial U/\partial C_1) - 1 = (1 - t_y)(\partial Q/\partial K_2^d). \tag{18.63}$$

This will be satisfied if corporate income is imputed to the shareholders and they are then taxed at the rate t_y. In the case of the open economy for a capital importing country, for example,[12] we will have:

$$(\partial Q/\partial K_2^d)(1 - t_y) = r_m^*. \tag{18.64}$$

As in the case of the closed economy an unintegrated income tax system creates a distortion between saving and investment because of the combined corporate and personal (when marginal saving consists of acquiring new shares) tax rates on equity income. However, because of the independence between the saving and investment decisions in an open economy, investment decisions will be affected only by the corporate tax rate and saving decisions will be affected by the personal income tax rate alone. The unintegrated income tax system also discriminates between new share purchases and retained earnings. However, this differential arises from the personal tax system alone and, therefore, affects savings alone – not the investment decision.

Further, because of this separation the incidence of the corporate tax is not on corporate income. The corporate tax causes investment to fall. As a consequence of this the pre-tax rate of return rises such that the after-tax rate of return is unchanged. Hence, non-capital factors of production bear the burden of the corporate tax.

18.5 RAMSEY OPTIMAL TAXATION IN AN OPEN ECONOMY

Dixit (1987) has extended the Ramsey framework of optimal taxation to an open economy. The social welfare function is defined as:

$$W = W(U^1(C^1), \ldots, U^H(C^H))$$

where there are H individuals in society. The constraints for this maximization are written as:

$$\sum_h C^h \leqslant \sum_h \omega^h + \sum_j y_j + z - x \qquad (18.65)$$

where ω^h is initial endowment of individual h, y_j is production of the jth commodity, z is imports and x exports. In addition, we will have the following constraints:

$$F_j(y_j) \leqslant 0 \text{ (production constraint for jth unit)} \qquad (18.66)$$

$$G(z) \leqslant 0 \text{ (imports constraint).} \qquad (18.67)$$

The solution to this problem will yield the first-best solution, if incomes can be arbitrarily chosen. The first-best conditions will imply: DRS = DRT = FRT where DRS is the marginal rates of substitution in consumption in the home country, DRT is the domestic marginal rate of transformation in production, and FRT is the marginal rate of transformation achievable through foreign trade. This is the usual set of conditions implying the optimality of free trade. If the country has some degree of market power in international trade then the appropriate condition would read DRS = DRT = MFRT where MFRT stands for the marginal foreign rate of transformation.

If optimal lump-sum transfers across consumers are not possible, then we have to solve the second-best Ramsey problem in the context of an open economy. Let $V^h(p, 0)$ be the indirect utility function of the hth consumer with p as the consumer price vector. For the sake of simplicity, units have been chosen so that the consumer's income is zero. The social welfare function is, then, $W(V^1(.), \ldots, V^H(.))$ and the material balance condition can be written as:

$$\sum_h C^h(p, 0) \leqslant \sum_h \omega^h + \sum_j y_j + z - x. \qquad (18.68)$$

The first-order conditions here will parallel the optimum commodity tax conditions derived in Chapter 13. Domestic equilibrium conditions will be as derived in Chapter 13. So far as the foreign sector is concerned we will still have DRT = FRT. Only the monopoly argument can justify the imposition of a tariff.

Other topics covered by Dixit include tax and tariff reforms as well as optimal taxation in a situation with non-traded goods. Some aspects of international investment and taxation have been covered by Giovannini *et al.* (1993).

18.6   CONCLUDING REMARKS

With increasing globalization occurring in the world economy the international aspects of public economics have become increasingly important. In this chapter we have studied some problems in this area. We first spelt out some well-known results in the theory of taxation in an open economy. Then we examined the implications of integrated capital markets for interest taxation and an open economy for the VAT were also worked out. We then took a brief overview of the proposition that direct tax integration, while desirable in a closed economy, loses its appeal in an open economy. Finally, we examined some aspects of the familiar Ramsey problem in an open economy.

The international aspects of public economics are subjects of intense research. Some important developments and references in this area were mentioned.

NOTES

1 In other words full interest expenditure deductibility is allowed.
2 Assuming that all other conditions for Pareto optimality are satisfied.
3 People are assumed to work only during the second period.
4 If capital flows are restricted then equation (18.12) need not hold. In that case there will be an infra-marginal profit on foreign investment resulting from the net interest rate differential. We assume that this profit is fully taxed away by the government so that equation (18.12) holds in effect.
5 The Haig–Simons defines all increments to gross wealth (human as well as non-human) during a year as the base for income taxation during that year. Thus all income earned during the year from all sources will be included in the base of the tax.
6 In the absence of such integration corporate income is typically taxed twice – once as corporate profits tax at the level of the firm and the second as income tax on dividends at the level of the individual tax payer.
7 We know this from Chapter 11.
8 As we shall see an important reason for this is the breakdown of the link between savings and investment in an open economy. However, empirically there is much to be said for carrying on with the recommendations of the closed economy model to the open economy in view of the so-called Feldstein–Horioka puzzle. See Feldstein and Horoika (1980). They argue that even in an open economy there is strong correlation between domestic savings and investment.
9 An important distinction is made between taxation of capital gains on accrual basis and on realization. If capital gains are taxed when these gains accrue then asset holders may have considerable difficulties in paying this tax. Hence, capital gains are usually taxed on realization. When a wealth holder actually sells his asset and makes the capital gain he is liable for the capital gains tax.
10 This dividend tax credit is available only to domestic shareholders and only to earnings from domestic corporations.
11 One can similarly derive optimal conditions for the mature firm. See Boadway and Bruce (1992). Our purpose here is merely expository and we need not concern ourselves with all cases.
12 It is relatively straightforward to check that for acquiring shareholders we will have:

$$(\partial U/\partial C_1)/(\partial U/\partial C_2) - 1 = (1 - \tau)r_m^*$$
$$(\partial U/\partial C_1)/(\partial U/\partial C_2) - 1 = (1 - \theta)r_m^*.$$

ADDITIONAL READING

For a lucid introduction to the theory of international trade see Gandolfo (1994); see also Dixit and Norman (1980).

19 Cost-benefit analysis

Key concepts: net present value, internal rate of return, benefit–cost ratio; social rate of discount; shadow prices; first- and second-order approximations; Little–Mirrlees and UNIDO criteria.

19.1 INTRODUCTION

In its most general form cost-benefit analysis refers to changes in the allocation of resources brought about by a project. Thus cost-benefit analysis is, in principle, a straightforward matter. One looks at the allocation of resources before and after the installation of a project. Given some norm of calculating social welfare, one can compare it in the two situations. If social welfare is higher after the project is installed, then the project is worthwhile, otherwise it is not.

In practice, however, cost-benefit analysis[1] turns out to be quite a complex matter. We will encounter and try to come to grips with these difficulties later in this chapter, but some can be mentioned here as well. Let us assume that we live in the simple world of the second optimality theorem of welfare economics studied in Chapter 2. Suppose, then, that we have both perfect competition as well as Pareto optimality. Consider a project which is a marginal investment decision on the part of the government.

The output from this project can be easily priced and we know that this price will reflect the true social opportunity cost of output. Similarly, the inputs can be priced in a satisfactory manner. If the project is going to yield benefits over a period of time or/and require inputs over a period of time, we know that the real rate of interest (which in equilibrium equals the marginal product of capital) will be the proper discount rate for discounting the stream of future benefits and costs. It is in this kind of world that cost-benefit analysis is a straightforward matter.

In the real world, however, things are nowhere as simple. It is in such situations that cost-benefit analysis becomes difficult as well as interesting. Consider the case of a malaria control program in a poor country with imperfect and, in some cases, non-existent markets. This program clearly has profound external effects. Many lives would be saved and the good health of many people would be maintained. A large number of enterprises and, indeed, society as a whole are going to gain from this. But the difficulty here is that many of these effects are intangible. The benefits cannot be accurately measured since markets may not exist. It would be hard, indeed, to find a perfect market for the future health of the citizens of any country, let alone a poor country.

Even if markets exist it would be unrealistic to expect them to be perfect. Tax distortions, quotas, regulations, etc. have the effect of making prices depart from true social opportunity costs even if external effects are not present. The presence of import quotas and exchange regulations might indicate an 'overvalued' exchange rate, for example. A related but distinct problem is that the project being considered might trigger off distortions in some other sector of the economy.

Yet another set of problems arises if the project under consideration involves increasing returns to scale technology. In this case, as we know from Chapter 17, marginal cost pricing would involve perpetual losses and the market profitability criterion would break down. There would be additional problems if two or more projects with increasing returns to scale technology compete for the same resources, for example, the same strip of land or the same source of funds.

When the project involves benefits and costs spread over a period of time additional complications arise. One set of complications relates to the fact that if there are distortions in the capital market, the market rate of interest may not be the appropriate rate of discount. Moreover, it has been argued that the current generation will undervalue the benefits that future generations may get from the project and will, therefore, save too little. When a member of the current generation saves more resources then these are, in principle, made available to all members of future generations. Hence, there is a public good aspect to current saving in an intertemporal framework. In less developed countries this problem is compounded by the fact that capital markets, where they exist, may provide a rather inadequate framework to predict the future. Moreover, with widespread poverty there might be an overwhelming desire to postpone or avoid saving. In other words, the social rate of discount is lower than the private rate of discount. An additional problem is the treatment of risk and uncertainty associated with future benefits and costs. In recent times, this risk and uncertainty component has taken sinister turns in the case of, say, accidents at Three Mile Island, Chernobyl and Bhopal, pointing to the need for a corresponding **risk-benefit analysis**.

In this chapter we study some aspects of the problem of cost-benefit analysis. We examine elementary notions of costs, benefits and rates of discounts and the notion of shadow price and the first-order and second-order approaches to measuring these. Some difficulties in such measurement are also pointed out. The chapter closes with a concluding section.

19.2 CRITERIA FOR COST-BENEFIT ANALYSIS

Suppose that we have been able to measure costs and benefits of a project accurately.[2] How do we go about comparing them in order to decide whether the project is worth undertaking? The literature typically distinguishes between three different criteria:

(i) Net Present Value (NPV)

Let B_t be the return from the project in period t (and benefits last until period T_0), C_t be the cost attributable to the project in period t (and costs last until period T_1) and δ be the appropriate social rate of discount. The net present value of the project is, then:

$$NPV = \sum_{t=0}^{T_0} B_t/(1+\delta)^t - \sum_{t=0}^{T_1} C_t/(1+\delta)^t. \tag{19.1}$$

It is implicitly assumed here that costs, benefits, their time spans and the social discount rate[3] are all accurately measured. A simple criterion would be, then, that a project should be pursued if it has a positive NPV.[4]

(ii) Internal Rate of Return (IRR)

The internal rate of return (labeled λ) of a project is defined as the rate of discount which, when applied to the stream of benefits and costs, would make the NPV so calculated just equal to zero. Thus, we have:

$$\sum_{t=0}^{T_0} (B_t - C_t)/(1+\lambda)^t = 0 \tag{19.2}$$

where T_0 is the common horizon over which benefits and costs accrue. We have to solve for λ from equation (19.2) and then compare it with some market rate of interest. Two practical problems arise right here. First, equation (19.2) is a fairly high order polynomial in λ. A unique solution is ruled out[5] and, indeed, several roots of equation (19.2) may not be real.[6] Second, there is the problem of choice of the market rate of return to compare λ with. If one uses the market rate of interest then we are implying that, if the IRR is larger than this rate of interest, then the project has a net yield which is larger than those from available alternatives. When there are many projects with λs larger than the market rate of interest, we could rank these projects according to their IIRs and go down the list until the total budget for public projects is exhausted.

Although the NPV has a definite intuitive meaning, the IRR is a less clear guide. Consider, for example, the example in Table 19.1.

In Table 19.1 we consider two projects yielding returns over two time periods: 1 and 2. Each costs $1. The pattern of returns from these projects is

Table 19.1 Rankings of two projects according to NPV and IRR criteria

	Cost ($)	Return in period 1 ($)	Return in period 2 ($)	λ	NPV with δ = 0 ($)	NPV with δ = 1 ($)
Project I	1	0	4	1	3	0
Project II	1	2	1	1.414	2	0.25

as shown in the table. We work with two discount rates $δ = 0$ and $δ = 1$. Project I has a higher NPV but lower IRR than Project II with $δ = 0$. With $δ = 1$, the NPV of Project I is zero whereas that of Project II is 0.25. If $δ$ is interpreted as the market rate of interest, then with $δ = 0$ Project I is superior to Project II according to the NPV criterion and with $δ = 1$ Project II is better. However, with the IRR Project II is always better than Project I. Hence, the prescriptions of the NPV and the IRR criteria may not coincide. The NPV is an intuitively straightforward criterion to understand and would, under such circumstances, be preferred to the IRR. The IRR has the further problem that it neglects the time profile of benefits and costs associated with the project. Consider a project which has losses for some time but large surpluses afterwards. If the discount rate is low NPV may be high but as the discount rate rises, NPV tends to drop off. Through all this the IRR remains unchanged.

(iii)   Benefit Cost Ratio (BCR)

This is defined simply as the ratio of the present value of benefits to the present value of costs. Letting $β$ denote BCR we have:

$$β = \sum_{t=0}^{T_0}(B_t/(1 + δ)^t)/\sum_{t=0}^{T_0}C_t/(1 + δ)^t. \qquad (19.3)$$

Thus $β \gtrless 1$ as NPV $\gtrless 0$. In this sense there is a clear link-up between the BCR and the NPV criteria. However, the BCR has the drawback that, by concentrating on the ratio of benefits to costs, it ignores the scale of the project. Take a numerical example. Project I has benefits and costs with present value $400 and $200 respectively and the corresponding magnitudes for Project II are $340 and $160. The values of $β$ for the two projects are 2 and 2.125 respectively. Hence, according to the BCR criterion, Project II is superior to Project I. But, clearly, according to the NPV criterion Project I is superior.

The gist of the arguments so far is that the BCR and IRR have some difficulties when it comes to the scale of a project and its optimal timing. The NPV criterion might also have some difficulties if projects are lumpy and funds scarce. Thus, choosing the appropriate criterion for cost-benefit analysis is no simple matter. But these difficulties pale into insignificance when we consider the difficulties associated with measuring benefits and costs and choosing the 'right' rate of discount. To these we now turn.

19.3 THE SOCIAL RATE OF DISCOUNT

What is the 'right' rate of discount to use for the stream of benefits and costs from a project? Suppose we live in an economy with identical individuals. Suppose, further, that all markets are perfect and the project being considered is a marginal one, i.e., it does not have any effect on the structure of costs and prices in the rest of the economy. In such an economy suppose that all individuals discount the future at the real rate of interest r. Should the social rate of discount also be r?

At first sight, the answer to this question would appear to be 'yes'. However, this is correct only under certain additional assumptions. In particular, some value judgments will have to be made. The projects undertaken today have an effect on the resource/production position in the future. Decisions on a project today will affect future generations, either because the life span of a project is longer than the life span of a generation, or because the structure of projects today affects the type and nature of projects that can be undertaken by future generations. Only if we ignore these effects can we claim that the social rate of discount is equal to the private rate of discount being used by the current generation.

There is yet another reason why the private discount rate cannot be used as the social rate of discount. This is because even a perfect market today neglects the external effect that the welfare of future generations has on savings today. Suppose society consists of H identical individuals with the private rate of discount equal to the (perfect) real rate of interest, r. Suppose a typical individual values one dollar transferred as assets to his inheritors as b dollars and one dollar transferred to the inheritors of others as a dollars. Suppose a fraction θ of his lifetime earnings goes to his inheritors so that $(1 - \theta)$ goes to the inheritors of others. Hence the individual in formulating his optimal saving decision will equate the marginal cost of saving one dollar (which is one dollar) to private marginal benefit which is $(\theta b + (1 - \theta)a)(1 + r)$. Hence the private discount rate is equal to:

$$r = 1/[\theta b + (1 - \theta)a] - 1. \qquad (19.4)$$

The social benefit from saving one dollar is higher since the private saving of every individual has a beneficial effect on (H-1) individuals. The social benefits of one dollar saved are:

(i) private benefit of the saver:

$$\theta b + (1 - \theta)a.$$

(ii) benefits to the current generation from consumption of the savers' heirs, i.e., $(H - 1)\theta a$.

(iii) benefits to the current generation from their own heirs' consumption, i.e., $(1 - \theta)b$.

(iv) benefits to the current generation from the consumption of heirs other than those of the saver, i.e., $(H - 2)(1 - \theta)a$.

Total social benefit is, therefore, $b + a(H - 1)$. Hence, the true social rate of discount will be r_s, where:

$$r_s = 1/[b + a(H - 1)] - 1. \qquad (19.5)$$

Only under very special circumstances will r_s equal r. Usually, $r_s < r$. By that token, it is also clear that with the discount rate set at r, savings will be less than optimal.

Another reason why one might not want to use the market interest rate as the social discount rate is because there might be intergenerational inequities associated with the working of the market mechanism. Bequests may not be optimal because the present generation derives too little utility from the welfare of its inheritors. In other words, the present generation might take up a larger than socially optimal share of capital resources of the economy. There is an effect working in the opposite direction as well. If the economy is going through a phase of technical progress, then there might be a case for transferring resources from the future to the present.

Under these circumstances the rate at which the market permits transformation between present and future consumption may not be the ideal rate of discount to use in cost-benefit analysis. To see this suppose that we have a social welfare function that spans the consumption levels of different generations. We write it as:

$$W = W(C_0, \ldots, C_T, \ldots) \qquad (19.6)$$

where C_i is the consumption level of generation i. To make it more specific we make it the discounted[7] sum of utilities:

$$W = \sum_{t=0}^{T} U(C_t)/(1 + \lambda)^t.$$

Upon total differentiation we have:

$$dW/W_0 = dC_0 + (1 + \lambda)^{-1}(U_1/U_0)dC_1 + \ldots + (1 + \lambda)^{-t}(U_t/U_0)dC_t + \ldots \qquad (19.7)$$

where U_i is $\partial U/\partial C_i$ (the marginal utility of consumption in the ith period).

A much studied utility function in this context is one where marginal utility takes the special form:

$$U_i = \alpha C_i^{-\eta} \qquad (19.8)$$

where α and η are positive parameters. Now consider the discount factor applied to period t. It is:

$$(1+\lambda)^{-t}U_t/U_0 = (1+\lambda)^{-t}(C_t/C_0)^{-\eta} = (1+\lambda)^{-t}(1+g)^{-\eta t}$$
$$= (1+\lambda+g\eta)^{-t} \tag{19.9}$$

where g is the (assumed constant) rate of growth of consumption each period. Hence, the proper discount rate is $(\lambda+g\eta)$ where λ is the discount rate applied to utility and the second term reflects the fact that consumption is going to grow exogenously over time so that future consumption can be discounted at a higher rate. There is no reason whatsoever why $(\lambda+g\eta)$ should bear any resemblance to the market rate of interest. One can think of circumstances where the social discount rate should be less than the rate of interest.[8] Suffice it to say here that there are no hard and fast rules for selecting the social discount rate and much will depend on the value judgment of the planner.

19.4   EVALUATING BENEFITS AND COSTS – SHADOW PRICES

We now come to the problem of evaluating the benefits and costs of a public project. These measurements are often carried out using the notion of a shadow price.

Let the vector of net output of the public sector be G with G_g indicating the net output of good g. This net output is defined as total production less the input of commodity g demanded by the public sector. Hence G_g is the net amount of the publicly produced good g which is available to private consumers.

When a new public project comes along it is referred to as ΔG, i.e., an increment in the net production vector of the public sector. We now have to evaluate this change and decide whether it is worth the while of society. Let this valuation function[9] be denoted by $V(\Delta G)$. Once we have been able to fix this valuation function we would also be able to decide whether the value attached to Project I is higher than that to Project II: $V(\Delta G^I) > V(\Delta G^{II})$.

Let us make the assumption here that the V function is differentiable and the project ΔG is marginal. Then we may write a first-order approximation to $V(\Delta G)$ as:

$$V(\Delta G) = V'(0)\Delta G \tag{19.10}$$

where $V'(0)$ is the derivative of the V function at zero net output of the public sector. $V'(0)$ is often referred to as the vector of **shadow prices**, s. Hence a project is desirable only if $s\Delta G > 0$. The problem, then, is to devise good methods of measuring this vector of shadow prices.

Little and Mirrlees (1968, 1974) have advocated the use of actual border prices as shadow prices for goods that are internationally traded. This can be shown to be a special case of a more general rule, of using as shadow prices the prices for private producers that would obtain in an economy with optimal commodity taxes as derived in Diamond and Mirrlees (1971,

1976). If the government is using optimal taxes – both direct and indirect – then there is no question that this method would give the right results. However, there is no reason to suppose that at any point in time taxes will be set optimally. Hence it becomes necessary to go beyond the Little–Mirrlees framework.

To evaluate the benefits and costs of a project – the shadow prices – one has to devise a method of measuring the effects of a project on the consumers of society. This has to be in terms of money. We will develop such a measure – first for a representative agent model and then for a heterogeneous agent model. The analysis here is based on the work of Boadway and Bruce (1984) and Hammond (1988).

For the representative consumer, let U be the utility function, p be the consumer price vector, y be the vector of goods bought[10] and I be the amount of transfers received.[11] The superscript 'b' refers to the situation before the project is introduced and the superscript 'a' refers to the situation after the project is installed. Hence, it is being assumed here that the project is going to affect the consumer indirectly through changes in p, y and I.

From our analysis of the expenditure function (denoted by E here) in Chapter 1 we know that the change in utility ΔU of this consumer can be written as:

$$\Delta U = E(p^b, y^a) - I^b = E(p^b, y^a) - E(p^b, y^b). \tag{19.11}$$

The price vector p includes price gross of any tax paid for commodities purchased by the consumer and net of taxes paid for commodities – including labor.

We are assuming here that $I^b = E(p^b, y^b)$ which is standard practice in consumer demand theory. To know the value of ΔU one has to know or estimate the expenditure function.[12] In cost-benefit analysis, however, one tries to circumvent this problem by making approximations to equation (19.11).

If the consumer maximizes utility after the introduction of the project then it must be the case that $I^a = E(p^a, y^a)$ so that equation (19.11) can be written as:

$$\begin{aligned} \Delta U &= E(p^b, y^a) - I^a = E(p^b, y^a) - E(p^a, y^a) + I^b - I^a \\ &= [E(p^b, y^a) - E(p^a, y^a)] + \Delta I \end{aligned} \tag{19.12}$$

where the term in square brackets is the equivalent variation for the price change alone.

From the theory of expenditure function we know that:

$$E(p, y^a) \leqslant py^a \tag{19.13}$$

and the equality holds only when $p = p^a$. Further, $p = p^a$ is a global maximum of the function:

$$F(p) = E(p, y^a) - py^a \tag{19.14}$$

because F (p) is zero at $p = p^a$ and negative everywhere else. The first-order condition for a maximum of F(.) is that:

$$\partial F/\partial p = \partial E/\partial p - y^a = 0 \qquad (19.15)$$

where the ∂s are to be interpreted as the gradient functions. Hence at the optimal consumption basket the gradient of the expenditure function is equal to the net demand function, y^a.

Hence we have the first-order approximation

$$E(p^b, y^a) - E(p^a, y^a) = (p^b - p^a)y^a = -\Delta p \cdot y^a. \qquad (19.16)$$

Substituting this into equation (19.12) we have:

$$\Delta U(1) = \Delta I - \Delta p \cdot y^a \qquad (19.17)$$

where $\Delta U(1)$ stands for the first-order change in the utility of the consumer. On equation (19.17) we can impose the consumer's budget constraint: $I^a = p^a y^a, I^b = p^b - y^b$ to get:

$$\Delta U(1) = p^a y^a - p^b y^b - (p^a - p^b)y^a = p^a(y^b - y^a) = p^b \Delta y. \qquad (19.18)$$

This term is often used in cost-benefit analysis. However, clearly this rule will not be very useful when $p^b \Delta y = 0$. In this case we have to rely not on first-order but on second-order approximations.

Second-order approximations

We take a second-order Taylor series expansion of expression (19.16) to get:

$$E(p^b, y^a) - E(p^a, y^a) = -\Delta p \cdot y^a + (1/2)\Delta p \cdot H \cdot \Delta p \qquad (19.19)$$

where *H* denotes the second-order Hessian matrix of second-order partial derivatives: $\partial^2 E/(\partial p_i \partial p_j)$ where $\partial E/\partial p_i = y_i$ for each good *i*. Hence this Hessian matrix is also the Jacobian matrix *J* with elements y_p^a where $y_p^a = y_p(p^a, y^a)$ which expresses net demands for each commodity as a function of the price vector *p*, evaluated at p^a, holding fixed the level of income.

In this case the second-order approximation can be written as:

$$\Delta U(2) = p^b \Delta y + (1/2)p^a[\Delta y - y_I^b(p^b, \Delta y)] \qquad (19.20)$$

where y_I^b is the vector of demand responses $\partial G_g/\partial I$ for each good *g* at (p^b, I^b) and $\Delta U(2)$ is the second-order approximation to the welfare change.

We can easily extend the analysis here to the case of heterogeneous consumers. Let consumers be indexed by *h* and let *H* be the (finite) set of all consumers. Each consumer has a net demand vector y_h, but faces the common price vector *p*. In this case each individual *h* experiences a net gain of welfare, based on *h*'s own expenditure function E_h. This gain in net welfare is:

$$\Delta U_h = E_h(p^b, y_h^a) - E_h(p^b, y_h^b) \tag{19.21}$$

and the first-order approximation is:

$$\Delta U_h(1) = p^b \Delta y_h \tag{19.22}$$

and the second-order approximation is:

$$\Delta U_h(2) = p^b \Delta y_h + (1/2)[p^a - (p^a, y_{I_h}^b)p^b]\Delta y_h \tag{19.23}$$

where I_h is the earned income of the hth consumer. Now if a project produces changes such that $\Delta U_h(1)$ and $\Delta U_h(2) > 0$ for all $h \in H$ then, clearly, this project is Pareto improving in nature and should be undertaken. Generally, however, a project may benefit some consumers and hurt others. In such case we will have to resort to evaluating welfare changes according to some sort of social welfare function. What kind of social welfare function should be used for this purpose?

Some economists advocate the use of the utilitarian criterion. Thus they would calculate $\sum_h \Delta U_h(1)$ or $\sum_h \Delta U_h(2)$. If the decision rule $\sum_h \Delta U_h(1)$ gives an unambiguous answer then they would choose a project for which this sum was positive and reject those for which this sum was negative. If the first-order approximation does not give an unequivocal answer then one may have to go to the second-order approximation.

If we recall our discussion of Chapter 3, we realize that the use of the utilitarian criterion may mean that projects which primarily benefit the poor may not get selected. In such cases, it may be necessary to use concave sums: $\sum_h \beta_h \Delta U_h(1)$ and/or $\sum_h \beta_h \Delta U_h(2)$ where the weights β_h are high for poor consumers and low for rich consumers. We have seen examples of this in the case of the problem of public-sector pricing discussed in Chapter 17.

No matter which criterion is used for evaluating the effects of the public project, one needs to estimate Δy_h, Δp and ΔI_h. So far we have been treating these as being exogenous, which is not quite satisfactory.

Suppose that private producers face the producer price vector q so that their supply decisions are represented by $S(q)$ where $S(q)$ is the supply function. Let the *ad valorem* tax vector be τ so that $p_g = (1 + \tau_g)q_g$. Now write z for the vector of net outputs of the public sector, including the project(s) being evaluated. The public project(s) can then be regarded as a change Δz in this vector. If s is a suitable shadow price vector, one can write $s\Delta z \gtrless 0$ according as the project $\epsilon \Delta z$ is favorable or unfavorable for small $\epsilon > 0$.

Market equilibrium conditions can be written as:

$$\sum_h y_h(p(q), I_h) = S(q) + z. \tag{19.24}$$

On the lefthand side we have consumer demand that is a function of consumer prices which, in turn for a given vector of commodity taxes, is a function of the producer price vector, and consumer unearned incomes I_h. On the righthand side we have supply which consists of the supply by private producers, $S(q)$, and the net supply of the public projects.

If equation (19.24) is satisfied then it must be the case that $p(q)\sum_h y_h p(q), I_h) = p(q)[S(q) + z]$. However, we also know from the fact that individual budgets are exhausted in equilibrium that $p(q)y_h(p(q), I_h) = I_h$ for each consumer h. Hence, q can be solved as a function of $q(z)$ only if:

$$\sum_h I_h = p(q(z))[S(q(z)) + z]. \tag{19.25}$$

Given I_h, now the righthand side of equation (19.25) has to be a constant, independent of z, which is unlikely. Realize that equation (19.25) represents the aggregate budget equation of the economy. Since we are assuming that consumers are exactly meeting their budget constraints, equation (19.25) requires that the government must also balance its budget and that firms must pay out their net profits $qS(q)$ as dividends. The government's net budget surplus[13] can be written as:

$$-\left[\sum_h I_h - qS(q)\right] + pz + (p - q)S(q). \tag{19.26}$$

The first term (within square brackets) determines the consumer's net income from government transfers (unearned income minus dividends). The second term is revenue from sale of output of the public project and the last term is the revenue from indirect taxation.

z must be treated as exogenous in cost-benefit analysis, precisely because the aim is to evaluate specified changes in z. Hence, the government needs a **balancing policy** which maintains equation (19.25) even as z is allowed to change parametrically. Since the government can determine I_h and $p(q)$, these in reduced form will become functions of z. Moreover, I_h should also be a function of q in order to ensure that the firm's profits are distributed. Hence, equation (19.24) can now be written in the form:

$$\sum_h y_h(p(q, z), I_h(q, z)) = S(q) + z \tag{19.27}$$

$$\text{with } \sum_h I_h(q, z) = p(q, z)[S(q) + z]. \tag{19.28}$$

Because of equation (19.28) the number of equations in (19.27) is one less than the number of variables to be solved for. Hence, all solutions must be in terms of the output vector of the public project (s): z. Thus these computations are valid in some neighborhood of the initial output vector.

Proceeding along these lines, now, we totally differentiate equation (19.27) to get:

$$\sum_h [y_{ph}^b(p_q^b dq + p_z^b dz) + y_{I_h}^b(I_{qh}^b dq + I_{zh}^b dz)] = S_q^b dq + dz. \tag{19.29}$$

Here $y_{ph}^b, q_p^b, p_z^b \cdot S_q^b$ denote the Jacobian matrices of partial derivatives evaluated at the original equilibrium, $y_{I_h}^b$ is the vector of responses to change in consumer incomes, and (I_{qh}^b, I_{zh}^b) is the gradient vector of I_h evaluated at (q^b, z^b). Choosing one commodity as the numeraire and solving we have:

$$dq = \left[\sum_h (y_{ph}^b p_q^b + y_{I_h}^b I_{qh}^b) - S_q^b \right]^{-1} [(ID) - \sum_h (y_{ph}^b p_z^b + y_{I_h}^b I_{zh}^b)] dz \quad (19.30)$$

where (ID) stands for the identity matrix. This equation has a solution provided that the inverse in the first part of the righthand side exists. Equation (19.30) can be substituted into the differential expressions for dp and dI_h to get:

$$dp = p_q^b dq + p_z^b dz = \tilde{p}_z^b dz \quad (19.31)$$

$$dI_h = I_{qh}^b dq + I_{zh}^b dz = \tilde{y}_{zh}^b dz \quad (19.32)$$

where the tilda ($\tilde{\ }$) refers to the total effect of the project. It must also be the case that:

$$dy_h = y_{ph}^b dp + y_{I_h}^b = \tilde{y}_{zh}^b dz. \quad (19.33)$$

From this we can derive the following differential measure of each individual's net gain in money metric utility:

$$dU_h = p^b dy_h + dI_h - dp \cdot y_h = U_{zh}^b = s_h dz \quad (19.34)$$

where s_h is the shadow price for the net benefit to the hth consumer. So that from equations (19.31), (19.32) and (19.33) we get:

$$y_h = U_{zh}^b = p^b y_{zh} = I_{zh}^b - p_z^b y_h. \quad (19.35)$$

The first-order expression for individual hth's net benefit is, then,

$$\Delta U_h(1) = s_h \Delta z. \quad (19.36)$$

For society as a whole we get the first-order change in welfare, $\Delta W(1)$, as:

$$\Delta W(1) = \sum_h \beta_h^b \Delta U_h(1) = \sum_h \beta_h^b (s_h \Delta z) = s \Delta z$$

where $s = \sum_h \beta_h s_h$ is the shadow price vector, a welfare weighted sum of the individual shadow price vectors. Generally, s is sensitive to the welfare weights β_h except in the special case when all the vectors s_h are proportional.

It is important to note that each component of each shadow price vector (s_h) and s may be completely unrelated to the producer price vector, q, and the consumer price vector, p. Indeed some of the components of s_h may be negative.

In the Diamond–Mirrlees framework with optimal commodity tax rates, producer prices will reflect true social scarcities. These producer prices could then be used as shadow prices in the calculation of costs and benefits. In the special case when the country in question is a small open economy, international trade in goods can be regarded as the activity of a firm facing border prices. The border prices are the producer prices of this firm. Hence, the equality between shadow prices and producer prices translates itself onto equality between shadow prices and border prices.

An important precondition for this argument to hold true is that commodity taxes be optimal both before and after the installation of the project. In the absence of optimal taxes after the project, Dasgupta and Stiglitz (1974) and Blitzer *et al.* (1981) have demonstrated that the planner's policy responses would make the appropriate shadow price vector different from the border price vector. Bruce and Harris (1982) and Diewert (1983) are the other significant contributions in this area.[14]

Some examples

(i)   *The shadow price of labor*

Evaluation of costs and benefits – even when using the methods outlined above – is a major problem when markets do not exist or are distorted because of taxes, quotas and the like. We can illustrate the issues involved while considering the problem of arriving at the shadow price of labor. Labor markets are often quite distorted. For example, there might be involuntary unemployment[15] so that the going wage rate does not reflect the true scarcity of labor. Another example would be that in developing countries the minimum wage paid in the urban sector may be higher than the prevailing wage in the rural/unorganized sector. This latter wage is, clearly, the opportunity cost[16] to society of transferring a worker from the unorganized to the organized sector.

The project evaluator takes these distortions as a fact of life. He still has to determine the social opportunity cost of labor to society. Additional labor for the project may come from three sources: workers previously employed elsewhere at the market wage rate; workers involuntarily unemployed; and workers voluntarily employed. The shadow wage rate is a weighted average of the wage rate for each type of labor. For workers employed elsewhere, the opportunity cost of using them in the project is the gross of tax wage (assuming that they are being paid their marginal product) which they are getting. For workers who are voluntarily unemployed it is the net of tax wage that they must be paid in order to induce them to work. The wage rate for involuntarily unemployed workers is a bit tricky. These workers may be willing to work at less than the going wage rate but surely the opportunity cost of employing them is greater than zero.[17] In practice, several different numbers may be tried.

(ii)   The shadow price of foreign exchange

Another interesting example is the measurement of the shadow price of foreign exchange. Many projects may directly or indirectly use tradeable inputs. Or the output of a project may be traded or this output may be an input into some other industry whose output is traded. It is important, then, for the project evaluator to have a good idea of the social opportunity cost of foreign exchange. If we are dealing with a small open economy in the sense that it cannot affect world prices or interest rates and there are no tariff or non-tariff barriers to international trade and we live in a fully flexible exchange rate regime then we can use the exchange rate itself as the appropriate opportunity cost foreign currency. In practice, however, there are many distortions in foreign trade so that shadow prices have to be used.

Consider the following example. We have a small open economy with a common tariff rate (at rate τ) on all imports. Thus all imports can be treated as a composite good and imports and exports can be denominated in terms of foreign exchange. The supply curve of foreign exchange from the sales of exports is upward sloping because, given the world price of exports and the price (e) of foreign exchange, the higher will be the price received in terms of domestic currency for these exports and, hence, more exports will be offered. Imports involve a demand for foreign exchange and the price is equal to the international price plus the tariff. Hence, the shadow price of foreign exchange (p_e) can be written as:

$$p_e = e(dX/dG) - e(1 + \tau)(dZ/dG)$$

where dX (dZ) is the change in exports (imports) consequent to a change in the project, dG.

This analysis can easily be extended to cover many imports with different tariff rates. Thus if there are n imports ($Z_i, i = 1, \ldots, n$) with n different tariff rates (τ_i) we can easily derive:

$$p_e = e(dX/dG) - \sum_{i=1}^{n} e(1 + \tau_i)(dZ_i/dG).$$

The technique discussed above converts foreign prices into domestic prices. In the face of tariff distortions this will create wrong incentives. Thus, with import tariffs and an overvalued exchange rate, resources would be diverted to the export sector and there would be an incentive to economize on imports. As noted above, Little and Mirrless have advocated a system whereby all domestic prices are converted into foreign price equivalents. This raises problems when one comes to non-traded goods – say electricity. In this case Little and Mirrlees advocate going to an earlier stage of production – say the technology and equipment for power generation from thermal units. These goods are sold in the international market and these prices could be used. While this logic does take us some distance, it cannot solve all our problems since certain goods are neither traded nor have traded goods as inputs. An obvious example of this would be labor.

(iii) The shadow value of public money

Many projects are not self-financing. This may be because of economies of scale or because the project has benefits in the distant future or for some other reason. Currently, however, the deficit must be financed. One must also find out the opportunity cost of financing since this diverts resources from the private sector.

If we were to follow the method of Feldstein (1985) we would calculate this cost of finance as the resource cost plus the deadweight loss of distortionary taxation used to finance the project. This cost depends upon the method of financing. In Chapter 12 we have considered tax versus bond financing and these same formulae could be used to ascertain the cost of financing the value of public money used in the project.

Another approach that has sometimes been used in the literature is due to Feldstein (1972). Consider the problem of financing the deficit associated with a public project. This diverts resources from the private sector. Let us suppose that a fraction α of this would have been invested and the fraction $(1 - \alpha)$ consumed. We know that α depends on the method of financing.

Currently a dollar's worth of consumption is valued at one dollar. Consider now investment. Suppose that the IRR on private investment is i_p. We might expect i_p to exceed the social rate of discount δ because of corporate income taxation and other factors. A dollar's worth of investment yields a perpetual stream of consumption of size i_p/δ. Hence the opportunity cost p_g of a dollar diverted from the private sector is:

$$p_g = (1 - \alpha) + \alpha i_p/\delta.$$

This formulation can be further complicated by assuming that part of i_p is invested and will yield a further income stream which will have to be considered in the formulation of opportunity cost.

Feldstein argues that if D_t is the deficit in year t then net present value of the project should be defined as:

$$V = \sum_t [B_t - C_t - (p_g - 1)D_t]/(1 + \delta)^t$$

where p_g is the opportunity cost of public funds as defined above and $(p_g - 1)D_t$ is the additional opportunity cost incurred in the financing of the losses from the project over and above that incurred by a non-distortionary transfer of funds. It is clear that p_g and D_t may vary from one time period to the next.

19.5   SOME DIFFICULTIES IN THE MEASUREMENT OF BENEFITS AND COSTS

The approach to the measurement of benefits and costs discussed above relies basically upon the compensated demand curves. However, there are certain elements of benefits and costs that are very hard to measure using these methods. Consider, for example, the construction of a new highway. It is believed that this project will improve road safety, reduce wear and tear on vehicles and save travel time. These will be the benefits of the project.

Now these benefits are not readily tangible and reducible to monetary terms and some ingenuity may be called for. For example, one may try to impute the benefits of improved road safety by adding up the medical costs associated with them and the cost of lost work during treatment. However, the benefit of saving lives is somewhat more controversial. How does one put a monetary value on human life? One method is to assume that the person whose life has been saved is being paid her marginal product. The discounted value of all her future earnings is the value of the life saved. There are some difficulties with this reasoning. What, for example, is the value of the life of an unemployed or retired person? Is the value of the life of a high earner greater than that of a low earner? Moreover, any existing discrimination against women and racial minorities can get built into these calculations.

An alternative method that is used to value human life is the required compensation approach. With this method individuals are asked questions of the form: how much would you pay to have the risk to your life reduced?[18] This method also has problems associated with it. In almost all cases individuals do not have enough information to make a reasoned judgment about such issues. What about the value of one's life to one's dependents and so on. Once all such elements are factored in, the value of a human life would probably be higher than the amount of human capital embodied in the person. There are no easy answers to such questions. Much depends upon the project in question and on the value judgments of the planner.

The remaining benefits of the highway are simpler to obtain. Reduced wear and tear on vehicles can be evaluated through using engineering and cost data. Finally, the saving of travel time can be evaluated at the wage rate reflecting the current leisure/labor trade-off.

In addition to these elements we have to consider the indirect benefits and costs of the project. A new airport, for example, will involve noise pollution, which is a negative externality, as well as the creation of new jobs in the area of the airport (which would then be a positive externality).

19.6   CONCLUSIONS

In this chapter we have studied some aspects of the problem of cost-benefit analysis. We studied elementary notions of costs, benefits and rates of discounts. We also discussed the notion of shadow price and the first-order and second-order approaches to its measurement. Some difficulties in such measurement were also pointed out.

Our analysis in this chapter has by no means been exhaustive. However, it does point out some of the key concerns of social cost-benefit planners.

NOTES

1 In the jargon of economics, cost-benefit analysis is part of the set of policy choices gathered under the umbrella of 'project appraisal'. For a broader treatment of cost-benefit analysis see Boadway and Bruce (1984) or Dreze and Stern (1987).
2 We will address this issue in some detail a little later on in this chapter.
3 If capital markets were perfect the discount rate would coincide with the rate of interest. But this may not be the case. We will consider this issue later in this chapter.
4 It is usual to simplify the NPV formula so that both benefits as well as costs accrue over the same horizon.
5 When this happens it is common to choose the highest real value of λ as the IRR.
6 In some instances, the problem may be less severe than it appears at first glance. The number of roots depends on the number of times $(B_t - C_t)$ changes sign. This may happen only infrequently in the case of a typical project. In many instances $B_t - C_t$ is negative to begin with and then later becomes positive.
7 Ramsey (1928) had forcefully argued that λ should equal zero. A positive λ would indicate myopia and would, therefore, not be suitable as an intertemporal social welfare function for society. Here λ is different from the internal rate of return discussed earlier.
8 Indeed we have discussed some reasons for this.
9 This subsumes, therefore, both the benefits as well as the costs of the project.
10 To be sure, goods may be bought and sold at different points in time. These are called different goods in the consumption vector. y.
11 All input by this consumer is counted as negative consumption. This would include labor services. Hence I includes transfers or unearned income.
12 For a review of the empirical work on the estimation of the expenditure function see Blundell (1990).
13 Which should be equal to zero.
14 Hammond (1986) and (1989) has demonstrated that under some conditions even in the absence of optimal commodity taxes, the Diamond–Mirrlees intuition of having shadow prices determined by border prices for traded goods may be right for outputs and inputs that are internationally traded. For outputs and inputs that are not traded the shadow prices derived earlier in this chapter will continue to be relevant.
15 The unemployment is involuntary in the sense that workers are willing to work at the going wage rate but are unable to find jobs.
16 One should add, of course, travel and transactions costs.
17 A similar problem arises with respect to 'disguised' unemployment in the case of developing countries; see Sen (1967), for instance.
18 Implicitly, then, what is the value you attach to reducing the risk to your life by using the better safer highway?

ADDITIONAL READING

Interesting works on cost-benefit analysis include Harberger (1978), Haveman and Margolis (1983) and Gramlich (1990).

Part V
Fiscal federalism

Introduction to Part V

Part V deals with some aspects of public policy-making in a federal economy and consists of two chapters. We begin Chapter 20 with a discussion of criteria for efficiency and equity in a federal economy. The efficiency and equity aspects discussed deal with the internal common market, the provision of local public goods, interjurisdictional tax and expenditure spillovers and tax harmonization between levels of government. We then review the arguments for and against subcentral provision of local public goods. Tax exporting and tax competition are also discussed here. We end the chapter with an examination of Gordon's well-known work on the benefits of centralization.

Chapter 21 is concerned with grants and taxes within the federal framework. It begins with a discussion of various forms of grants (including equalization, revenue sharing, grants to correct for fiscal imbalances and conditional grants) and their objectives. We examine the effects of grants in traditional models as well as the newer models incorporating different assumptions about the behavior of bureaucrats. We then study tax assignment in federal structures. Problems of tax coordination and harmonization across jurisdictional boundaries are discussed. Reasons for allocating individual taxes to one or more than one level of government are also considered here.

20 Issues in fiscal federalism

Key concepts: devolution of tax and expenditure authority; efficiency and equity in a federal economy; local public goods and externalties; interjurisdictional spillovers; tax harmonization; subcentral provision of local public goods; centralization versus decentralization; optimal size of local jurisdictions; impure public goods.

20.1 INTRODUCTION AND BACKGROUND

Economic analysis with several layers of government has had a long and distinguished tradition in public economics.[1] One of the most significant issues addressed in the literature is that of the proper devolution of tax/expenditure authority between different levels of government. It is typically argued that the level of government which is legislatively superior should have the mandate, in some sense, to treat the lower levels of government as equals. Moreover, it is argued, that there are economies of scale in collecting taxes. If states, for example, were to impose income taxes there would be considerable difficulties in the treatment of the incomes of tax-payers who migrate across state boundaries. Moreover, it would be difficult to apply any notion of equity on a national scale. Similarly, the bulk of commodity taxation is best carried out by the central government. It is not entirely improbable that state governments, left on their own, would opt for increasing their own tax revenues even at the risk of causing considerable allocative damage at the national level. On the other hand, it is argued that decentralization of tax and expenditure authority has innate advantages. Local governments would be more responsive to local needs. Moreover, local governments can be held accountable by residents in an easier and more transparent manner than higher level governments. This kind of reasoning, of course, does not preclude the possibility that the degrees of decentralization in tax and expenditure authority may be different. In particular if, as the above argument indicates, expenditure responsibilities are decentralized to a greater extent than tax authority we would be setting up the rationale for fiscal transfers from higher to lower levels of government.

In this chapter and the next we address some broad issues of fiscal federalism. We examine the pros and cons of decentralization as well as considerations involved in defining the optimal size of a jurisdiction. An optimal tax approach to decentralization due to Gordon (1983) is also considered (in the Appendix). In the next chapter we consider tax, expenditure and related functions of lower level governments.

20.2   EFFICIENCY AND EQUITY IN A FEDERAL ECONOMY

The conditions under which the market performs satisfactorily are well recognized and well appreciated. Under conditions explored in some detail in Chapter 2 the market mechanism leads to the attainment of Pareto optimality. We have also discussed the conditions under which interference with the operation of the market mechanism may be justified. These could be broadly classified as the inefficiency and inequity associated with the market mechanism. Our discussion was in terms of a unitary form of government. What are the parallel conditions in a country with several levels of government?

In a federal economy the notions of efficiency and equity have several more dimensions than the three[2] associated with the Paretian criterion. A list of some of the important elements is as follows:

(a) The internal common market

If goods, services and factors of production can flow unimpeded within a country unencumbered by the geographical boundaries of lower levels of government, an internal common market may be said to obtain with all the attendant advantages. When barriers to such movement occur either because of taxes and/or quantitative restrictions the efficiency of the common market arrangement is compromised. To be sure, there are natural impediments to completely free movements such as language and transport costs, but we are here concerned with conscious policy measures designed to restrict free flow of goods, services and factors of production. If several jurisdictions impose such restrictions overall economic activity may decline significantly and all jurisdictions may be worse off. To be sure, there is a body of literature in public choice theory which suggests that interjurisdictional competition to woo factors of production and goods and services may be a good thing since it encourages local governments to be more and more efficient and induces them to work in the best interests of their residents.[3]

(b) Local public goods and externalities

A strong argument for decentralization is that many public goods are purely local in nature and are ideally supplied at the local level. Efficiency in a federation requires that the level of local public goods in each locality be determined by the benefits of the residents being served. A decentralized federation has the benefit that each local government is able to provide the type and mix of public services that its local residents prefer. Furthermore, if residents are relatively mobile, they should be free to move to the jurisdiction that best satisfies their tastes for public goods. The Tiebout model, which we have already studied, has stressed the benefits of free migration combined with decentralized decision-making in a federation in which some public goods are local in nature and persons have different preferences.

(c) Interjurisdictional spillovers

A problem with the above argument for decentralization is that the benefits of different local public goods may not be limited to the geographical boundary of the locality providing them. In such cases there are interjurisdictional spillovers. Local governments will typically not have an incentive to consider the beneficial effects to other jurisdictions of local public goods supplied by them. In such cases, from a macro perspective, there will be an undersupply of local public goods. Such instance would require interventions from a higher level of government.

(d) Tax harmonization

Local governments typically have some liberty to set their tax rates and structures. If this is done in an uncoordinated fashion, inefficiencies will creep in because distortions will differ across jurisdictions. This can be a result of differential tax rates on capital and labor income, or different tax rates for goods and services across jurisdictions such that production and/or consumption decisions get distorted. These distortions can be minimized if tax rates are chosen across jurisdictions in a coordinated and harmonized manner. Such harmonization can occur either at the instance of cooperation among lower level jurisdictions, or at the instance of a higher level of government. It can be argued that tax harmonization is most important for capital and income taxes and less so for indirect taxes. But this does not imply that there are no costs to not harmonizing the indirect tax structure.

20.3 EQUITY CONSIDERATIONS WITH LAYERS OF GOVERNMENTS

With layers of government an important issue that has to be addressed is: which level of government is responsible for vertical equity in a society? On the one hand, there is the argument that, since the concept of vertical equity applies to all citizens of a country, it is ideal for the central government to tackle the issue of vertical equity. On the other hand, economists who prefer a smaller amount of redistribution typically see the central government engaging in too much redistribution. They argue that the task of redistribution should be entrusted to lower levels of government. This together with interjurisdictional competition, it is argued, would reduce the amount of redistribution that occurs and would provide a mix of local public goods and taxes that is consistent with maximization of the welfare of the representative resident taxpayer. Similar arguments would apply for the case of horizontal equity. But a large majority of economists would agree that the issue of equity is appropriately addressed at the central level.

The brief overview above tends to indicate that a determination of the ideal degree of decentralization remains an elusive goal. Many factors are at work here and much depends upon value judgments and empirical consequence which are hard to verify. In many cases, even though a better assignment of functions to levels of government is known, it is hard to move toward it. In countries that run the immediate risk of disintegration, a higher degree of decentralization, although desirable, may be impractical and fraught with too much danger. The extent of decentralization also depends, to some extent, upon the desired magnitude of the role of the government in the economy. Typically economists who prefer a smaller role for the government would also favor more decentralization. As would be expected, it is not possible to resolve these issues in a definitive manner. What one can do, however, is to outline the considerations that might be useful in approaching this question.

20.4 RATIONALE FOR THE EXISTENCE OF SUBCENTRAL AUTHORITIES

In Chapter 6 we learnt about local public goods. The existence of such goods provides perhaps the most salutary rationale for the existence of local/state governments. The simplest example of this would be the case when for technological reasons the benefits from the public good must necessarily be confined to a particular area, say, for example, a flood control program for a river which regularly inundates its banks in a particular area. However, even here there could be spillover effects onto other areas. An item like defense is probably a purely national public good but even here there may be local effects: a country's defense services would be unable to protect, say, some remote islands that belong to it.

The upshot of this is that determining which jurisdiction should provide any public good or service is an issue that merits detailed consideration in every case. Two types of decisions have to be made:

(i) One must decide whether central or subcentral authorities should provide the public good.
(ii) It must then be decided what level of subcentral authority is required. The public good could be supplied by the state government or the town council or the county government and so on.

Clearly an important factor in deciding the level of government which must supply the public good is the level of benefits that this public good will confer on citizens who do not live within the geographical boundaries of this jurisdiction. The greater the proportion of benefits that accrue to citizens who are not residents of the jurisdiction in question, the stronger would be the argument for providing this public good at a more centralized level.

Another factor that may affect the extent of centralization is the technical nature of the public good being provided. In the case of street lighting and sewerage facilities to citizens, the need for maintaining certain uniform standards across the country would mean that there could be several jurisdictions each with responsibility for its own services. In the case of national defense, on the other hand, coordination is generally handled by a central authority and centralized provision makes more sense.

Arguments in favor of subcentral provision of public goods

The most common argument in favor of subcentral provision of public goods is that local authorities can better supply public goods whose quantity and quality vary according to the requirements and preferences of residents. If these were provided by the central government then, in all probability, there would be uniformity of services.

A simplified version of this argument is illustrated in Figure 20.1 where we have drawn preferences for local public goods by five different localities. The central government is likely to create uniform provision in all areas. This will make for administrative simplicity. Moreover, the central government would finance this public good by levying a uniform tax across the country. In Figure 20.1 with central provision of the public good the nationwide provision of this public good would be Q_3. However, if we had five different jurisdictions, each would get its most preferred level of the public good. Each jurisdiction would have its own public goods/tax packet to suit the needs of its residents. Clearly, it need not be the case that each jurisdiction would have its own unique public goods level. In Figure 20.1 it might be the case that residents of more than one jurisdiction prefer public goods level Q_1, and/or Q_2 and so on. Thus, there might be bunching of jurisdictions around levels of public good supply. However, so long as there is some heterogeneity of tastes, providing this public good locally would be preferable to central provision.

Another important argument in favor of decentralization is that it brings better democratic control over public officials. Local officials and bureaucrats would be more accountable to the residents of a locality than central bureaucrats. A related argument made by Jones (1975) is that when there is overlap between the powers of different tiers then the authorities of one tier of government would have to learn to cooperate with officials of the other tiers. In such cases if one tier does not seem to heed the wishes of the

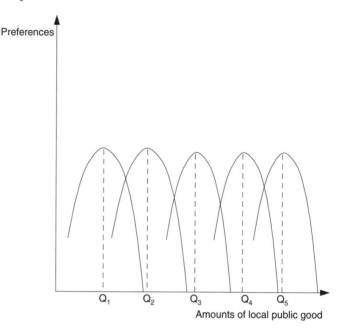

Figure 20.1

residents then they can apply pressure not only directly but also indirectly through officials of other tiers.

Oates (1972) has pointed out that subcentral provision may lead to people becoming more aware of the costs and benefits of public goods and, hence, making better choices about public goods. Suppose a local public good is to be provided by a subcentral authority and this is to be financed by a local tax. Both the public goods project as well as the tax can be put to the vote and residents will be better aware of the costs of a project than they would if it was financed by, say, revenues from a nation-wide income tax. Oates makes the point that decentralization will result in more experimentation and innovation in the supply of local public goods. If, for example, a novel recycling project were to come up, it would be more likely that a local government would try it than the central government.

Arguments against subcentral provision of public goods

There are several arguments against subcentral provision of public goods. An important one is the phenomenon of **tax exporting**. This happens when local governments levy taxes on non-residents. An obvious example of this is to levy taxes on restaurants and entertainment in tourist areas frequented by non-residents. Under these conditions, if residents insist on a public goods supply such that marginal benefit equals marginal cost, then, since marginal cost has been lowered by tax exporting, there might be excessive expenditure on the part of the local authority and an excessive supply of public services. Hogan and Shelton (1973) point out, however, that residents of any particular jurisdiction might also be paying taxes to other areas so that there will be some check on this excessive expenditure. Another method by which taxes may be exported is to levy taxes on businesses. Typically these do not have much of a say in deciding the public goods/tax package. However, to the extent that the incidence of business taxes is on residents, this will lead to an increase in costs. To the extent that the incidence of these business taxes is on residents, local costs will not rise. One point is clear, however; tax exporting can lead to considerable misallocation of resources in the country as a whole.

Another way of exporting taxes is through deducting local taxes paid from tax liability to the central government. In several countries taxes paid to state governments, for example, are set against federal tax liabilities. McLure (1967) estimated that in 1962 on average 20 to 25 per cent of state taxes were being exported in the USA. In certain states this figure was as high as 40 per cent.

In an important contribution McLure demonstrated how a local tax on an exported commodity could raise its equilibrium price. This depends on the elasticity of net demand facing the jurisdiction. This phenomenon can be illustrated using a partial equilibrium demand supply framework. We let the subscripts l and n refer to local and non-local respectively. Suppose the price of a good nationally is p and a per unit tax of τ is imposed on suppliers in a jurisdiction. In this case one can write the condition for equilibrium in the market for this commodity (with D and S representing demand and supply respectively):

$$D_1(p) + D_n(p) - S_1(p - \tau) - S_n(p) = 0. \tag{20.1}$$

This equation determines p as a function of τ. Let s_1^D, s_1^S denote the local share in total supply and demand (e.g. $s_1^D = D_1/(D_1 + D_n)$). Further let ϵ_1^S and ϵ_1^S denote local and non-local demand and supply elasticities, then straightforward differentiation of equation (20.1) yields:

$$\begin{aligned}
dp/d\tau = &-[p(s_1^S \epsilon_1^S)/(p - \tau)]/[s_1^D \epsilon_1^D + (1 - s_1^D)\epsilon_n^D \\
&- \{p/(p - \tau)\}s_1^S \epsilon_1^S - (1 - s_1^S)\epsilon_n^S].
\end{aligned} \tag{20.2}$$

Hence $dp/d\tau = 0$ and the equilibrium price is not affected at all if the elasticity of local supply is zero ($\epsilon_1^S = 0$) or if any other demand or supply elasticities are infinite. However if $dp/d\tau > 0$ then it is possible that some of the tax burden will be shifted onto non-residents.[4] The essential point of this argument is as follows. Following an incremental increase $d\tau$ the loss in welfare to local residents is $D_1(dp/d\tau)$ and the loss to local producers is $[-S_1\{d(p - \tau)/d\tau\}]$. The increase in tax revenue is $[S_1 + \tau S_1'\{d(p - \tau)/d\tau\}]$

where S_1' is the derivative of local supply with respect to p. Adding up we get the net gain to the local jurisdiction as:

$$\tau S_1' d(p - \tau)/d\tau + (S_1 - D_1)dp/d\tau. \tag{20.3}$$

For $\tau > 0$ the first term is negative.[5] The second term is positive if the local jurisdiction can affect the equilibrium price for the good. For τ sufficiently small, the second term will dominate the first and an imposition of the tax will improve local welfare.

From this it should be clear that jurisdictions definitely have incentives to use taxes which are clearly non-optimal from the national perspective. The analysis here has assumed that local tax revenues are returned lump sum to local residents. This would usually take the form of land tax reductions for residents to offset the increased revenue from taxing local exports. The principal point remains. Tax exporting can reduce welfare.

If, as is often alleged, businesses are more attracted to a tax locality by tax concession than by the level of services provided, then in an effort to attract such businesses some local governments may underprovide services. This will set up a trend toward **tax competition** among subcentral governments. This tendency could be arrested if local authorities were allowed to impose only those taxes that did not affect businesses very much.

It is also possible that if subcentral authorities are not obliged to meet certain budgetary balances and can bank upon receiving grants from the central government, then they may issue inordinately high amounts of debt. Thus budgets of state and local governments may be persistently and deeply in the red which they cover by issuing bonds. There is some evidence that the median voter model works reasonably well in the context of decisions on local public goods. Suppose the subcentral government attempts to satisfy the needs of the median voter. Also suppose that this median voter recognizes that he/she may leave this locality before the costs of public expenditure are met. Then there will be a tendency to spend too much on public services and cover this with new debt issue since the median voter will not feel liable for the expenditures involved.

Arnott and Grieson (1981) have presented a useful formal analysis of the general equilibrium effects of tax exporting and tax competition. We eschew distributional issues and consider a representative resident. Let $x = (x_1, \ldots, x_n)$ be a net consumption bundle of traded and non-traded goods for this individual.[6] The producer price vector for this good, q, is assumed fixed. Consumer prices are $q + \tau$ where τ is the vector of specific tax rates. We assume that there are no profits or lump-sum incomes. The consumer's indirect utility function is $V(q + t; G)$ where G is a vector of public goods. The locally optimal tax policy, conditional on the given vector of public goods G being produced is found by maximizing the consumer's indirect utility subject to the revenue constraint:

$$\tau X = C(G) \tag{20.4}$$

where X is the vector of taxable net consumer demand, including both local demand x and non-local demand x' where $X = x' + x$ and C (G) is the cost function of the public good. We use a Lagrange multiplier λ for the revenue constraint in equation (20.4). Then maximizing indirect utility subject to the constraint in (20.4) and using Roy's identity, we have:

$$-V_i x_i + \lambda[X_i + \tau(\partial X/\partial \tau_i)] = 0 \qquad (20.5)$$

for all taxable commodities[7] i.

Equation (20.5) says that the local real income loss per dollar's worth of incremental tax revenue collected from an increase in the tax rate is equated across all taxed goods i and j. In other words:

$$x_i/[X_i + \tau(\partial X/\partial \tau_i)] = x_j/[X_j + \tau(\partial X/\partial \tau_j)] = \alpha. \qquad (20.6)$$

Except for cross-price effects, equation (20.6) says[8] that the rate of tax on a commodity is higher, the greater the fraction of non-local demand and the lower the demand elasticity. This last part is familiar to us from our discussion of optimal commodity taxes in Chapter 13. We can rewrite this in another familiar form. Suppose all cross-effects are zero ($\partial X_k/\partial t_i = 0$ for all $k \neq i$ and for all i). Let $\epsilon_i = (\partial \ln X_i/\partial \ln(q_i + \tau_i))$ denote the total demand elasticity for commodity i and let $s_i = x_i/X_i$ be the local share of total demand for commodity i. Further define $\gamma_i = \tau_i/(q_i + \tau_i)$ as the proportionate tax rate on commodity i. Then equation (20.6) can be written as:

$$\gamma_i/\gamma_j = (\epsilon_j/\epsilon_i)(1 - \alpha s_i)/(1 - \alpha s_j). \qquad (20.7)$$

This is just the inverse elasticity rule altered to show that tax rates also depend on local consumption shares.

The Arnott–Grieson results discussed above show that optimal taxation from the point of view of the local jurisdiction will lead to non-zero tax rates for both traded as well as non-traded goods. The optimal tax formulae emphasize the importance of cross-price effects. There is a balancing of the revenue gains against the local real income loss. Further, tax exporting allows taxes to be shifted more heavily in favor of goods with a high component of non-resident demand.

Another problem with subcentral provision of public goods as noted by Peacock (1977) is that the scale of operation may not be large enough for all economies of scale to be exhausted. In that case costs are likely to be higher than they could be. Against this we have the argument that if the size of jurisdictions gets very large then the purpose of catering to divergent tastes is defeated. Finally, we have the criticism that subcentral governments ignore spillover effects of their decisions on public goods supply.

A rebuttal to some of the arguments made above would be that the operation of the Tiebout mechanism would ultimately lead to an optimal allocation of public goods and attendant taxes across jurisdictions. This argument, as we know from the discussion in Chapter 6, is only partly true. The Tiebout mechanism has inefficiencies of its own and there is reason to suppose that the amount of migration implied by the this process may not be possible. For various reasons people may simply not be as mobile as Tiebout suggests they are.

Starrett (1980a,b, 1982) and Boadway (1982) have evaluated the welfare effects of an increment in public expenditure in a jurisdiction on the individuals initially residing there. This argument can easily be understood within the context of a two-class economy. The two classes are rentiers (r) who get income solely from the ownership of land. The other class is that of workers (w). Landowners are immobile because of the land whereas workers are freely mobile. Suppose that jurisdiction i imposes a land tax at the rate of τ_{ir} and also imposes a head tax of τ_{ih}. Each class has an initial endowment of cash equal to $\omega^k (k = r, w)$. The rentiers living in jurisdiction i have an indirect utility function with returns, tax rates and amounts of the locally supplied public good, G_i, as arguments.

Since workers are free to move anywhere in the economy the local authority is constrained to keep their utility equal to some exogenously given level $\bar{V}^w$ which is the level of utility available to workers elsewhere. In other words local policy cannot affect the utility of workers. Hence one might as well make the assumption that local policy is chosen by the immobile households. The activities of the local government, however, are restricted by a budget constraint:

$$\tau_{ir} T_i + \tau_{ih}(n_i^w + 1) = C_i(n_i^w + 1, G_i) \qquad (20.8)$$

where we have normalized the number of rentiers to equal 1, n_i^w is the number of workers in this locality and T_i is the base of the land tax in jurisdiction i. C_i is the cost function of the public good and the first argument in C_i denotes congestion in the availability of the public good.

It can then be shown that the locality will choose the efficient level of the public good so long as the congestion effects are internalized at the margin. If this is not the case then the locality will have an incentive either to attract or repel migrant workers. Hence the problems of locational efficiency and expenditure efficiency are linked together.

20.5   OTHER ROLES OF SUBCENTRAL AUTHORITIES

Subcentral authorities have a relatively minor role to play in the redistributive functions of government. There is widespread agreement that horizontal and vertical equity are best served by centralized taxation and spending policies. See, for example, Oates (1972) and Musgrave and Musgrave (1976).

There is still less scope for subcentral authorities in designing stabilization policies. If monetary and/or fiscal policies were carried out by subcentral authorities the very purpose of stabilization would be belied.

However, these authorities have a role to play in regional development policies. In many countries the unemployment rate, for example, may differ widely across regions. One way out of this problem would be to make the region with high unemployment rates more attractive for industry to locate. If subcentral authorities are made entirely responsible for regional development policies then it would follow that their rate of unemployment in particular and level of development in general could be made a factor in disbursing central grants to lower level governments.

In such situations it is quite likely that tax competition among jurisdictions may emerge. Different local governments would vie with each other in offering tax concessions to industry to locate within their jurisdiction. This low level of taxation may then result in low levels of services being provided.

At this juncture it is important to point out that we have been implicitly assuming that the aforementioned low levels of taxation and consequent low levels of public services are in the interest of both the officials of the jurisdiction as well as the residents. It might well be the case that 'low' tax rates are prescribed by local officials in order to attract more business whereas the residents of the jurisdiction would prefer more services notwithstanding the fact that this may involve larger taxes. In such cases it would be important to ensure that local officials better reflect the preferences of residents.

The upshot of this argument is that although subcentral authorities have a role to play in fostering regional development, they should not be made entirely responsible for it. There is a significant role both for the residents of local jurisdictions as well as the central government to play in fostering regional development and regulating the functions of subcentral authorities.

20.6 THE OPTIMAL SIZE OF LOCAL JURISDICTIONS

Assuming that it is advisable to decentralize, a natural question that arises is: what is the optimal size of the local jurisdiction? In this section we will try to make an attempt to answer this quite vexed question.[9] We should first note that there are several ways of defining size with perhaps the most popular being population and geographical area.

Several variants of this question will be considered. In the simplest version an attempt is made to define optimal size in terms of population size. This assumes, of course, that this population is stationary and does not migrate across jurisdictions. In another version we shall bring in interjurisdictional mobility.

Suppose that we are defining the optimal size of the population to enjoy a local public good. We assume that all citizens are homogeneous with respect to tastes and incomes and that there is only one local public good. Governments do not coordinate efforts, nor do they face any administrative costs. There are no congestion costs.

Now as the size of jurisdiction supplying the public good rises, two types of economies set in. First, there are economies of scale in the production of this public good. Second, as size increases externalities are internalized and costs fall. However, the benefits from the public good are a declining function of the tax price – if the public good has declining marginal benefits as a function of tax price.

This is shown in Figure 20.2. In Figure 20.2a we show an individual tax payer's demand for the public good as a function of the tax price. In Figure 20.2b we show present value of gains to society (measured as the sum of the relevant area under demand curves such as in Figure 20.2a) under the assumption that the marginal benefits keep falling continuously whereas costs fall and then rise. Optimal size of the authority is given at S* where the present value of gains from the public good is maximized. So with homogeneous population and a single local public good there will be N/S* (where N is the size of the total population of the country) identical local jurisdictions each of size S*.

Suppose now that we introduce one of the principal reasons for decentralization – heterogeneity of tastes – into this very simple picture. Suppose that there are two types of consumers – types *A* and *B*. Our analysis is conducted in Figures 20.3a and 20.3b which show public goods demand by these two types of consumers if they had to live in jurisdictions of the sort

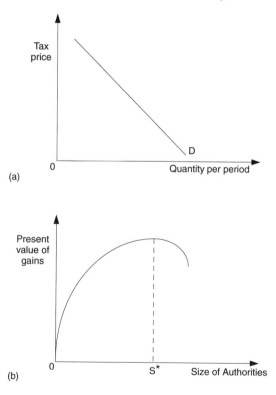

Figure 20.2

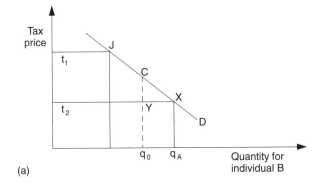

(a)

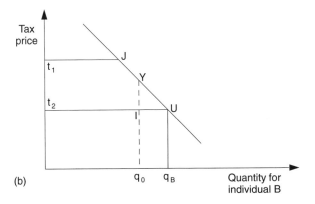

(b)

Figure 20.3

discussed just above. In both these diagrams the tax price of the public good is t_2. At this price the public good demand by an individual of type A is q_A whereas individuals of type B want q_B units. By the very nature of a public good both types of individuals have to consume the full amount of the public good which is, say, q_0 in this case. Hence consumer surplus for type A individuals is $JCYt_2$ which is CYX smaller than the amount that consumer surplus would have been had the optimal amount of the public good from this person's point of view been supplied. For type B individuals this is $JYIt_2$ which is smaller by the amount YIU than what it would have been had this individual been able to consume the amount of the public good that he wants at the tax price t_2.

Now in calculating the net present value of gains from the public good these losses would have to be deducted. In Figure 20.4 we show the case when these losses rise with population size. We have drawn the same present value schedule as in Figure 20.2 and added the loss function LL. Two results follow from this. First, the net gain is now going to be smaller. Second, if LL rises with population size the optimal size of the jurisdiction

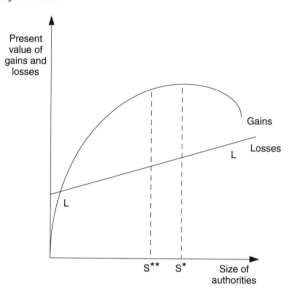

Figure 20.4

will fall from S* to S**. The optimal size may still be S* provided *LL* is horizontal. In general, however, we would expect the optimal size to be smaller.

Resident mobility

Suppose now that we introduce resident mobility into the analysis. Once migration is permitted and is responsive to differences in public services/tax packages, this would create a problem for the above analysis. Citizens might want to move for two reasons. First, they might move from poor areas to rich areas in search of jobs and better living conditions, for example. They might migrate in search of tax/public goods packages that better suit their preferences – the Tiebout type of migration. We will rule out the former by supposing that there exist equalizing grants in place. These grants ensure broad levels of uniformity in tax/public goods packages across jurisdictions. It is assumed that as a consequence of this, only Tiebout-type migration occurs.

While this type of migration is going on, clearly it is not possible to articulate what one means by an optimum size of jurisdictions. However, it is possible to characterize the optimal size once this migration has run its course and come to a halt.

We illustrate this in Figure 20.5 where we redraw Figure 20.4. The line *LL* represents the loss function before any migration has taken place. Once Tiebout-type migration has been permitted it is likely that jurisdictions and individuals will be better matched and the loss function will be lower at *L'L'*.

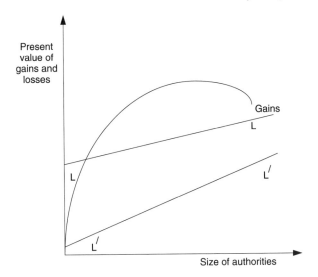

Figure 20.5

Clearly what is relevant to determining the optimal size of the jurisdiction in this case is the relative slopes of the *LL* and L'L' schedules. If the latter is steeper than the optimal size, the jurisdiction will be smaller. However, there is no compelling reason for any particular relation between the slopes of these schedules. In practice, then, it is hard to say whether Tiebout-type migration leads to larger or smaller sized jurisdictions.

Impure public goods

Our analysis, so far, has concentrated on pure public goods. Suppose, however, that the local public good we are considering is impure. To take a particular example let us suppose that the public good we are considering is fire protection. There is a fire station in the town. However, the closer your home is to the fire station, the greater the amount of effective fire protection you enjoy. However, everyone pays the same amount for fire services. In this particular case it is possible to argue that this fact will be reflected in property values. Homes closer to the fire station will, ceteris paribus, have higher property values than those further away. With given property tax rates, homes close to the fire station will attract higher absolute values of taxes. Hence, the effective price paid for fire protection by home owners close to the fire station will be higher than those living further away. Although formally correct, this argument presupposes that the housing market is perfect.

Our analysis has so far assumed that there is only one local public good or that there are many public goods which can effectively be aggregated into one public good. If that is not the case then we are faced with the problem of defining optimal jurisdiction size with multiple public goods. The literature on this issue is rather sparse.[10] Some general considerations can be advanced. It might be the case that the optimal size associated with different public goods is different. Hence there might be a multiplicity of types of subcentral authorities – from state governments to village councils with responsibility for different types of public goods. In such cases we would also have to include administration and coordination costs among different levels of governments. If only one level of subcentral authority[11] can be permitted then we would have to define an optimal sized population keeping in mind the net gain from all public goods. The optimal sized jurisdiction would be one which would maximize the net gains from all public goods taken together.[12]

20.7 CONCLUSIONS

In this chapter we have studied some aspects of fiscal federalism. We have recognized that complex considerations are involved in deciding when to decentralize and how much to decentralize. There are some important empirical factors to be taken into account but these are hard to quantify in practice. Hence, in many cases the value judgments of economists and policy planners are likely to be as important as 'objective' considerations.

NOTES

1 For an excellent review see King and Fullerton (1983). Our analysis in the chapter follows this work as well as several others that are listed in the text.
2 To remind students in the context of a unitary form of government these are efficiency in production, efficiency in exchange and overall efficiency.
3 We will have more to say on this later in the chapter.
4 This argument is an old one in the theory of international trade and is known as the **optimum tariff argument**. If a country (jurisdiction in our case) has some market power as expressed in the form of the supply elasticities mentioned in the text, then it would be welfare improving for the local residents to impose a tax. There is an optimum level of this tax which maximizes local welfare and this is known as the optimum tariff.
5 Because $d(p - \tau)/d\tau < 0$.
6 Non-traded goods could include labor, for example.
7 In the special case where $X_i = 0$ equation (20.5) simply becomes the formula for collecting maximal tax revenue from non residents. This tax is such that $x_i' + \tau(\partial x'/\partial \tau_i) = 0$.
8 α = marginal utility of income.
9 In the Appendix to Chapter 20 we detail an approach to the determination of the Pareto optimal size of a jurisdiction along the lines of Buchanan and Wagner (1970) and Wildasin (1986).
10 An example is Foster *et al.* (1980).
11 For, say, constitutional reasons.
12 As mentioned in the chapter, the literature on these issues is relatively sparse. An interesting question to ask would be the following: Under what conditions is the welfare (of the same population) associated with just one level of subcentral

authority permitted, higher than that associated with the larger number of subcentral authorities?

ADDITIONAL READING

Apart from the texts referred to in the chapter, the following additional readings may be of interest to students: Stigler (1965), Break (1984), Fisher (1988).

APPENDIX

The inefficiency of decentralized decision-making

What are the inefficiencies associated with decentralized decision-making when subcentral authorities care only for the welfare of their residents and disregard the external effects imposed on other jurisdictions? An answer to this question was attempted in a well-known paper by Gordon (1983). We will now study his results.

In his work Gordon seeks to answer two questions.

1 Is decentralized taxation inefficient?
2 If the answer to the first question is yes, what corrective measures can be adopted to restore efficiency?

Gordon argues that independent tax decisions by local governments will generate various types of externalities leading to a misallocation of resources at the national level. He then argues that these problems can be eliminated through suitable coordination by the central government – in effect an internalization of these external effects.

Gordon considers a polar case where there is no coordination between local governments and a hierarchical social welfare function which for each government differs only in respect of its geographical domain. In addition he makes the assumption that when the central government begins to coordinate the efforts of local government, no coordination costs are involved.

Gordon considers a fairly general model of fiscal federalism with local jurisdictions able to tax both goods and factors of production. Each jurisdiction tries to maximize a utilitarian social welfare function with its own residents' welfare as arguments.

There are K subcentral authorities[1] and these are indexed by k. Commodities are indexed by i. Producer prices are written q_{ik} which is the price received for a unit of commodity i by a firm in jurisdiction k. The corresponding consumer price is p_{ik}. Factors of production are indexed by j. r_{jk} is the price paid for factor j by a firm in jurisdiction k whereas w_{jk} is the reward actually received by this factor. The difference in both cases is the specific tax imposed. Thus we can write:

$$p_{ik} - q_{ik} = t_{ik} \qquad \text{(A20.1)}$$

where t_{ik} is the specific tax imposed on the ith commodity by the kth jurisdiction. Similarly:

$$r_{jk} - w_{jk} = \delta_{jk} \qquad \text{(A20.2)}$$

where δ_{jk} is the specific tax imposed on the jth factor by the kth locality. The vector of prices and taxes in community k is denoted by upper-case letters: $P_k, Q_k, R_k W_k, T_k$ and Δ_k. The extended vector of all prices has a star: $(P^*, Q^*, R^*, W^*, T^*, \Delta^*)$.

Firms must hire all factors of production within their own jurisdiction but they can sell their output anywhere. Hence firms in jurisdiction k face producer prices Q^* and produce output $Y^*{}_k$. However, their factor prices are jurisdiction specific[2] (R_k). This firm is assumed to face a constant returns to scale technology and be a perfect competitor in both product and factor markets. Thus it treats factor and producer prices to be given parametrically and chooses output (Y_k^*) and input (X_k) vectors to maximize profits which can be written as: $Q^* Y_k^* - R_k X_k$ where output and input are related by the implicit production function $\phi_k(Y_k^*, X_k) = 0$. Total output (Y^s) sold in jurisdiction s can be written as the sales by firms of all jurisdictions in locality s:

$$Y^s = \sum_k Y_k^s \qquad \text{(A20.3)}$$

where Y_k^s is the amount of sales by firms of jurisdiction k in jurisdiction s.

Consumers are heterogeneous and their types are indexed by h. The utility function of an individual of type h living in jurisdiction k is written as U_k^h. Since it is assumed that there are many types of individuals spread over many communities, it is possible to regard U_k^h as a continuous variable with one individual's utility having no effect on that of any other.

Each individual in jurisdiction k faces the vector of consumer prices P_k^* and the vector of after-tax factor rewards W_k^*. In addition each individual can get benefits from a vector of public services Z^* where Z_{jk} is the level of the jth service available in jurisdiction k.

Different types of individuals are imperfect substitutes for each other in the production process. This is necessary, along the lines of the Berglas model developed in Chapter 6, to allow for heterogeneity of communities. The specific human capital of an individual of type h is written as G_h where G_h is a vector of length equal to the number of individuals with zero in all entries except the hth. Individuals may also own non-human capital in various communities. Let the vector of human and non-human wealth be G_h^*. Individuals are assumed to be adversely affected by congestion costs which are c_k for jurisdiction k. Hence the indirect utility function V_k^h of a resident of jurisdiction k can be written as:

$$V_k^h = V_h(P^*, W^*, G_h^*, c_k, Z^*, k). \qquad (A20.4)$$

The index of the community appears specifically in the indirect utility function because the attractiveness of purchasing and selling goods in any community depends on the community in which individual h lives. One can take account of transport costs in this manner as well. Migration of individuals across jurisdictions ensures that the individual will settle in that locality where V_k^h is the highest.

From the theory of duality we know that:

$$(\partial V_k^h / \partial p_{jm}) = -\alpha_{hk} y_{jm}^{hk} \qquad (A20.5)$$

where α_{hk} is the marginal utility of income of the hth person living in the kth jurisdiction[3] and y_{jm}^{hk} is the demand of the hth person living in the kth jurisdiction for the jth good sold in the mth jurisdiction.

Tax revenues for local community k are labeled T_k and can be written as $T_k = \sum_i t_{ik} Y_k^* + \sum_j \delta_{jk} X_k^*$. These tax revenues are assumed to be used to buy a vector of factors of production (b_k) for community k at the prices that prevail in this community in order to produce the local public goods. Hence the total expenditure would be $b_k W_k$. There would also be an implicit production function linking amounts of the public good produced and the inputs of factors of production. To close this model it has been assumed that factor and output markets (in the economy as a whole) clear.

Let n^{ik} be the number of people of type i that choose to locate themselves in locality k. Further suppose that the central government places a weight of β_i on the welfare of the ith individual irrespective of the locality in which she lives. With centralized decision-making, the maximand would be:

$$W = \sum_i \beta_i \sum_k n^{ik} V^i$$

which would be maximized with respect to the vector of commodity and factor taxes, factor amounts devoted to the production of the public good and the aggregate amount of production of the public good and subject to the aggregate budget constraint of the central government which reads:

$\sum_k (T_k Y_k + \Delta_k - W_k b_k) = 0$ and the implicit production function for the production of the public good.

With decentralized decision-making local government k would maximize $\sum_i \beta_i n^{ik} V^{ik}$ with respect to its own commodity tax rates, factor tax rates, amounts of factors devoted to public goods production and the amount of public goods production subject to its own budget constraint which reads: $T_k Y_k + \Delta_k - W_k b_k = 0$ and the implicit production function for producing public goods in this jurisdiction: $\phi = 0$.

The essential difference between the two maximization problems is the set of external effects neglected by the decentralized decision-making process but fully captured in the process of centralized decision-making. This list of effects external to jurisdiction k but internal to the whole economy is as follows:

(a) People non-resident in this jurisdiction pay some of its taxes.
(b) Non-residents may receive some of the benefits of the public services provided by this jurisdiction.
(c) Congestion costs faced by non-residents may change.
(d) Tax revenues received in other communities may change due to the spillover of economic activity.
(e) Output and factor prices change may favor residents over non-residents.
(f) Distributional effects among non-residents would be ignored.

In some cases the external effects may tend to cancel each other out. For example, if someone moves from one area to another he will reduce congestion in the community he is leaving and add to the congestion of the community to which he is moving. However, in general the net effects of all external effects would not be zero.

An evaluation of the Gordon model

Gordon's work is an important contribution to the theory of tax assignments and, therefore, deserves close scrutiny. Gordon has made the important point that coordination between local authorities is necessary to ensure efficiency. We have seen this earlier in the chapter and will see it again in Chapter 21 in the context of grant giving by a higher level government. Gordon has made this point with reference to tax devolution as well.

Clearly, however, his is an extreme case. Local governments may co-operate with each other in setting tax rates and, therefore, the external effects that exist in Gordon's model may be less severe. Similarly, there may exist substantial coordination costs for the central government. If both these factors are true, as well may be the case, then the inefficiency of taxation by local authorities is by no means obvious.

Resource costs of coordination include obtaining and processing information, establishing and maintaining the necessary administrative and legal infrastructure, and the costs of decision in a milieu of conflicting intergovernmental interests. Resource costs of different coordination policies may vary but each make some demand on a community's resources.

Welfare costs of non-voluntary coordination may manifest themselves in many forms. As a consequence of coordination, the political system of a federation becomes more centralized. Coordination takes the form of reassignment of property rights in decision-making among the different levels of government. Thus the property rights in taxation of the local government are partially transferred to the central government. This may cause welfare losses for two reasons. First, restriction on local fiscal decisions may lead to loss in desired heterogeneity. Moreover, people may feel a loss in welfare because of the political and decision-making process itself becoming more centralized. Gordon's model fails to capture this type of welfare loss because he has defined utility functions in such a manner as to exclude any preference for decentralization as such.

Furthermore, if major taxes get centralized then local governments have to use less efficient forms of taxation in order to meet revenue needs. Similarly, revenue sharing may create inefficiencies of its own. By breaking the link between the benefits and costs of public policies, revenue sharing has sometimes led to inefficient fiscal behavior on the part of the recipient governments. This has been documented for India by Grewal (1975) and for Australia by Matthews (1980).

Notes

1 Only two levels of authorities are considered. Gordon mentions that his results would survive if we had more than two levels of authorities.
2 This is because of local taxes.
3 Mirrlees (1972) makes the important point that whereas the utility of the hth type of individual will be the same across all jurisdictions after migration has ceased, the marginal utilities of the same type of persons need not be equalized.

21 Grants and taxes in federal countries

Key concepts: revenue sharing grants; equalization grants; grants to internalize externalities; grantor preference for merit goods; fiscal imbalances; conditional grants; lump-sum grants; new models of effects of grants; tax assignment; tax harmonization; tax coordination; excess burdens and administrative costs.

21.1 INTRODUCTION

In Chapter 20 we have discussed various factors that determine the optimal size of a jurisdiction. Suppose that decisions have been made to allocate some functions to local jurisdictions. It now behooves us to explain the finances of these jurisdictions. These can be put into two categories:

(i) those received as grants from a higher level of government;[1]
(ii) revenue collected directly through taxes and charges.

In this chapter we want to outline the major types of grants and their effects. We also consider issues of taxation by subcentral governments. Our analysis follows the work of King and Fullerton (1984) and others.

In Tables *21.1* and *21.2* we cite evidence from the USA of the magnitude of grants that flow from the federal to lower levels of government. Table 21.1 shows taxes and expenditures per capita of selected US states whereas Table 21.2 does this for some major US cities. It is apparent that federal grants play an extremely important role in the finance of lower levels of government.

There are two important policy issues in formulating a good system of grants. First, one has to decide the purpose for which the grant is to be given and, second, one has to decide upon the precise type of the grant to be given.

21.2 PURPOSES OF GRANTS

Why are grants given out by higher level governments to lower level governments? The literature has distinguished four reasons. First, the higher

Table 21.1 State government expenditures and taxes, selected states, fiscal 1990

State	Tax per capita $	Expenditure per capita $	Taxes as a percentage of personal income of the state %
Alabama	945	2,006	6.8
California	1,459	2,650	7.5
Delaware	1,696	3,195	9.1
Florida	1,027	1,697	5.9
Indiana	1,101	1,878	6.9
Michigan	1,220	2,485	7.0
Missouri	965	1,627	5.9
New Hampshire	537	1,778	2.7
New York	1,591	3,287	7.6
Texas	866	1,532	5.5
All states	1,211	2,305	6.9

Source: US Department of Commerce, Bureau of the Census, *State Government Finances in 1990*, Washington DC, US Government Printing Office, 1991: Tables 26, 17 and 29

Table 21.2 Taxes and Expenditures per capita, Fiscal 1990, Selected Cities with populations of 75,000 or More

City	Tax per capita $	Expenditure per capita $
Montgomery, Alabama	349	453
Los Angeles, California	519	963
Hartford, Connecticut	1,376	3,537
Gainesville, Florida	204	1,092
Decatur, Illinois	254	422
Indianapolis, Indiana	533	1,237
Boston, Massachusetts	996	2,593
Albuquerque, New Mexico	318	1,307
New York, New York	2,063	4,256
Austin, Texas	366	1,164

Source: US Department of Commerce, Bureau of the Census, *City Government Finances in 1989–90*, Washington DC; US Government Printing Office, 1991: Table 6

level government may be interested in persuading the lower level government to take account of the external effects generated by its actions (for other jurisdictions). Second, grants may be given to enforce grantor preferences. Third, there are **revenue sharing grants** which are given out to correct fiscal imbalances between various local jurisdictions. Finally there are **equalization grants**.

At a broad level the first two objectives of grants are best tackled through conditional grants whereas the latter two objectives could be served with general grants.[2] We discuss the four objectives of grants below.

Grants to internalize externalities

Consider an economy with local jurisdictions and two goods – a private good X and a local public good G. If there are no external effects across jurisdictions and financing for the public good is available through lump-sum taxes, then the following Samuelson condition should be satisfied for each jurisdiction k:

$$\mathrm{mrt}_{x,G}^{k} = \sum \mathrm{mrs}_{x,G}^{k} \tag{21.1}$$

where the summation runs over the population of the jurisdiction. We can simplify matters still further by assuming that the *mrt* and *mrs* are the same across jurisdictions.

If indeed there were no external effects from one jurisdiction to another then equation (21.1) would lead to a Pareto optimal supply of the public good. Now let us relax this assumption. Suppose there are two areas A and B and when either raises its consumption of the public good then, without lowering its own benefits from the public goods, it generates beneficial effects for the other jurisdiction. To make matters more concrete let us assume that if A increases its consumption of the public good by one unit, then the consumption of the public good by B goes up by a fraction β and if B if increases his consumption of the public good by one unit then A's consumption goes up by a fraction α. Suppose the population of A is n_A and that of B, n_B. Then the revised Pareto optimum conditions in the two localities will be:

$$\mathrm{mrt}_{xG} = \sum^{n_A} \mathrm{mrs}_{x,G}^{A} + \beta \sum^{n_B} \mathrm{mrs}_{x,G}^{B} \tag{21.2}$$

$$\mathrm{mrt}_{xG} = \sum^{n_B} \mathrm{mrs}_{x,G}^{B} + \alpha \sum^{n_A} \mathrm{mrs}_{x,G}^{A}. \tag{21.3}$$

To simplify matters, and without any loss of generality, we are assuming that each jurisdiction has the same *mrt*.

Now each area is interested in the welfare of its own citizens hence, in the absence of any persuasion from the central government, the government of each area will satisfy equation (21.1). Hence, there will be a Pareto inferior supply of the public good in each locality.

The role of the central transfer is to reduce the mrt of each area so that public goods production will be increased and equations (21.2) and (21.3) are satisfied. Suppose a grant of T_A is given to jurisdiction A and T_B to jurisdiction B. Hence, with the grant the jurisdictions will satisfy:

$$\mathrm{mrt}_{xG} - T_A = \sum^{n_A} \mathrm{mrs}_{x,G}^{A} \tag{21.4}$$

$$\mathrm{mrt}_{xG} - T_B = \sum^{n_B} \mathrm{mrs}_{x,G}^{B} \tag{21.5}$$

Now multiply equation (21.3) by β and subtract from equation (21.2) to get:

$$\text{mrt}_{xG}(1 - \beta) = \sum^{n_A} \text{mrs}^A_{x,G}(1 - \alpha\beta). \tag{21.6}$$

Similarly multiply equation (21.2) by α and subtract it from equation (21.3) to get:

$$\text{mrt}_{xG}(1 - \alpha) = \sum^{n_B} \text{mrs}_{x,G}(1 - \alpha\beta). \tag{21.7}$$

Now from equation (21.4) we have:

$$T_A = \text{mrt}_{xG} - \sum^{n_A} \text{mrs}^A_{x,G}. \tag{21.4'}$$

Now from equation (21.6) we have:

$$\sum^{n_A} \text{mrs}^A_{x,G} = \text{mrt}_{xG}(1 - \beta)/(1 - \alpha\beta).$$

Substituting this for $\sum \text{mrs}^A_{x,G}$ in equation (21.4') we get:

$$T_A = \text{mrt}_{xG}(1 - (1 - \beta)/(1 - \alpha\beta)) = \text{mrt}_{xG}[\beta(1 - \alpha)/(1 - \alpha\beta)]. \tag{21.8}$$

In an exactly parallel manner we can derive:

$$T_B = \text{mrt}_{xG}[\alpha(1 - \beta)/(1 - \alpha\beta)]. \tag{21.9}$$

These are the solutions to the optimal transfers to the jurisdictions.[3] The grant to any jurisdiction is higher the greater is the spillover from its public good to the other jurisdiction. These simple formulae make considerable intuitive sense.[4]

Grants to enforce grantor preference for merit goods

Often local authorities may not have enough funds to provide certain services at an efficient level. Musgrave and Musgrave (1976) suggest that almost all subcentral services are viewed as merit goods by the central government. In such cases grants may be used to supplement local jurisdiction efforts to provide these services at an efficient level.

At one level, these grants would be viewed as being beneficial by the local jurisdictions. However, it should be remembered that they will be financed by taxes on the same residents which these merit goods are supposed to benefit. The net beneficial effect of this grant, then, should take into account the effects of the taxes used for financing.

A typical situation could be of the type shown in Figure 21.1. In this we show the effect of a matching grant to a local jurisdiction. Initially the jurisdiction faces the budget line $B_1 B_1$ and comes to equilibrium at the point E_1 on the community indifference curve I. Now suppose the central government gives a specific[5] and matching grant to the local jurisdiction in order to persuade it to consume more of the merit good. The effect of this grant would be to lower the effective price of the merit good and the community

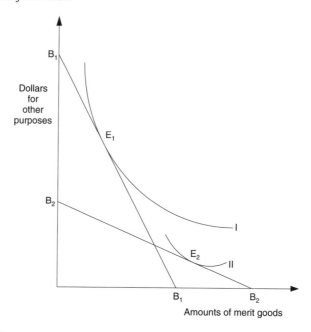

Figure 21.1

budget line, on this count, would twist in an anti-clockwise direction. However, the fact that this grant will be financed by taxation will mean that the budget line will also move toward the origin. The new budget line will be B_2B_2 where the community comes to equilibrium at the point E_2 on indifference curve II. This equilibrium is purposely drawn in such a way that it could intersect the old budget line B_1B_1. Hence the grant could be thought of as reducing the utility of residents.

The question that naturally arises is, then, why should such grants be given? Musgrave and Musgrave (1976) address this point in detail. They argue that residents of local jurisdictions may be ignorant of the true worth of the merit good in question. As they get more exposed to it, they may form better preferences for this merit good. Second, such grants could be used to finance goods which are important but which voters typically undervalue. A classic example is school education. Adult voters may undervalue the importance of children's education and there may be underprovision. A matching specific grant would protect the interests of children who are non-voting residents of the jurisdiction.

Another point which Musgrave and Musgrave emphasize is that matching grants may be given to fund services which help only a minority of the population. For example, suppose there is a community with a river flowing through it. A program of flood control may benefit only the people who live along the banks of this river. If matters were left solely to the local government then flood control may be severely underfunded.

Grants to correct for fiscal imbalances

Another important reason for grants to exist is to compensate local governments for any mismatch between their receipts and expenditures. This has been called a **vertical fiscal imbalance**. It is 'vertical' because it refers to the role of one level of government with respect to another.

This vertical fiscal imbalance is likely to arise in practice if taxes are collected largely by higher level authorities[6] and expenditure decisions are considerably more decentralized in order to better reflect local preferences.[7]

Equalization grants

These grants are extremely important in several major federations. Their principal aim is to reduce the extent to which some subcentral authorities might be able to offer their residents more attractive fiscal packages than others. An important argument in favor of equalization grants is horizontal equity considerations. This is important for three reasons. First, some jurisdictions might have higher per capita tax bases than others and so be able to raise equal per capita amounts of revenue at lower tax rates. Second, some areas might need more units of public services per head than others to provide similar standards of services. A classic example of this is schooling in a country with large variations in population density across jurisdictions. A sparsely populated jurisdiction might need higher grants for schooling per child, ceteris paribus, than thickly populated ones. Third, the costs of unit services might be higher in some areas than others. In remote areas of a country, for example, transportation and infrastructural costs may be higher.

In operational terms, almost all equalization schemes address the first of these problems and some address the second. But there are hardly any that address the third problem.

Sometimes a case for equalization grants is also made on grounds of efficiency. It is argued that if there were substantial horizontal inequities across jurisdictions then there would be considerable migration from worse off to better off jurisdictions. This would place considerable strain on the infrastructural facilities of the jurisdiction to which the migration was taking place. To forestall such migration, it is argued, equalization grants should be made.

Although the discussion above provides some good reasons for equalization grants, there are some caveats as well which we should take into account. First, if there is horizontal inequality across regions, then this fact would get capitalized in the housing market. As people migrate from areas with low fiscal residuum[8] to high fiscal residuum property values change. Land prices fall in the former and rise in the latter. Housing rentals would behave in a similar manner. In this manner, people would pay more to live in areas with better fiscal conditions and this would, of itself, tend to reduce horizontal inequality. However, Hamilton (1976) has argued that the fear that a reduction in the tax base per head would result in capital losses could make residents of a jurisdiction reluctant to allow construction of new dwellings which would attract new migrants and lead to the loss in capital value. For example, if an income tax is being levied by jurisdictions then there would be widespread opposition to housing being developed for lower income individuals.[9] In such situations equalization grants clearly do have a role to play. For further details see King (1984).

A second argument against equalization grants comes from the possibility of **benefit taxation**. Suppose jurisdictions are able to finance their services with taxes that corresponded to the amount of benefits[10] that people receive from these services. If this was possible then equalization payments may not have much of a role to play. From our study of the Lindahl–Wicksell mechanism we know that this is in principle possible. However, we also know that the main difficulty with this is that people will usually understate their preference for public goods. Hence, there will still be a need for equalization grants.

The proponents of benefit taxation would argue that, in the face of the free-rider problem, one should design prices with reference not to actual demands for the public good but some 'average' demand. The aggregate benefit of a public service is related to the total cost of providing it and this aggregate is then divided among the beneficiaries in proportion to their consumption levels. To take an example, suppose that we have a service being provided by the central government, then it could be deemed that all citizens get an equal amount of benefit from it and the cost could be divided equally among them.

However, this argument would not work very well in the case of sub-central authorities. For instance, police protection would be more acutely needed by high crime areas rather than low crime areas. With benefit pricing the residents of the high crime area pay a larger share of the costs of police protection rather than residents of low crime areas. Hence this would lead to horizontal inequity. It would appear that if such benefit taxation was pursued, one would need equalization grants to get horizontal equity. Hence, benefit taxation does not obviate the necessity for equalization grants.

A final objection to equalization grants comes from the fact that these could be replaced with a system of taxation by the central government whereby the rates of these taxes varied from area to area with low rates for poor areas and high rates for rich areas. Buchanan (1950) has suggested that one advantage of such a switch would be that less central taxes would have to be collected. This would be welcome at a time when people are skeptical of the virtues of 'big government'. However, this method would work well only if there was an increase in the total yield of subcentral taxes. In particular poorer areas would have to tax more in order to replace revenues that would be lost with the abolition of equalization grants. However, Oates (1972) has pointed out that in the case of this inverse tax option, low resource and high need local jurisdictions will have much greater fiscal independence. Hence, discriminatory taxation could, in principle, substitute for equalization grants. But again, as Oates points out, discriminatory taxation is ruled out in practice because of constitutional provisions.

A diagrammatic analysis of equalization grants

Since equalization grants are so important in practice, it might be useful to look at their role in promoting horizontal equity across regions of a country. We do this in Figure 21.2.

Consider two jurisdictions – one with high tax base B_h and the other with low tax base B_1. We may regard the base of the tax as income or we may assume that income is a suitable proxy. In Figure 21.2 tax base is on the vertical axis and expenditure on G on the horizontal axis. Since both axes are in terms of dollars, initial budget lines have a slope of minus 1. The rich jurisdiction faces the constraint $B_h^0 B_h^1$ and we suppose it elects to give up $B_h^0 K$ income to get G_h^0 of the public good. The ray from the origin, R_h, is the reciprocal of the tax rate: the steeper the ray, the lower the rate of the tax. The poorer government has the budget line $B_1^0 B_1^1$. If the poorer subcentral government levied the same rate of tax, it would sacrifice $B_1^0 a$ income to secure only G_1^0 of the public good. To obtain the public good level G_h^0 it would have to move along the ray R_1 levying tax at the (higher) rate of $B_1^0 c / OB_1^0$ where 0 is the origin.

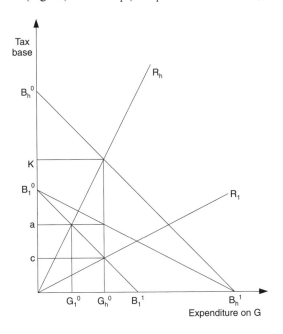

Figure 21.2

Base equalization schemes envisage the richer local jurisdiction stepping in as residual tax payer. This implies that the budget line of the poorer local jurisdiction swings to become $B_1^0 B_h^1$. If the poorer government levies tax at the old rate $B_1^0 a / OB_1^0$ it will get the old amount of the public good G_1^0 on its own whereas the equalization grant would provide the amount ac which would lead to an increase in the public good supply by $G_1^0 G_h^0$. Hence, poorer jurisdiction would end up consuming the same amount of the public good as the richer jurisdiction.

21.3 TYPES OF GRANTS

In a typical federal country there are several types of grants – some of which we have discussed. In Figure 21.3 we present a taxonomy of these grants. The first distinction made is between conditional/specific grants and general/unconditional grants. In the first category of grant the higher level government decides the specific purpose for which the grant has to be given. Since conditions are attached to the way in which the funds may be spent, such grants are called 'conditional'. The second major category is the one in which grants are given without any specification on how the funds may be spent. As shown in Figure 21.3, general grants can be fixed in amount or they may depend upon the actions of the lower level government.

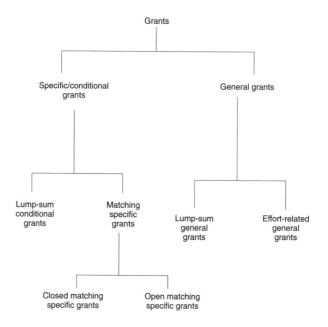

Figure 21.3

Conditional grants can be subdivided into lump-sum grants and matching grants. In the former case, the lower level government receives a fixed amount to spend on the designated service. In the latter case the amount of funds is variable and depends upon how much funds the lower level government is able to collect on its own.

21.4   THE EFFECTS OF VARIOUS TYPES OF GRANTS – TRADITIONAL MODELS

Before we can devise a grant to suit a purpose it is important to understand the effects of grants on the receiver. In particular it is necessary to assess the impact of the grant on the expenditure of the grant-receiving jurisdiction.

The literature on the effects of a grant can be split up into two broad areas: 'traditional' models and 'new' models. We will first study the effects of grants in traditional models and then examine some aspects of the new models.

Good reviews of traditional models can be found in Wilde (1971), Oates (1972), King (1980), Romer and Rosenthal (1980), Boadway and Wildasin (1984) and Wildasin (1986). The analysis in these traditional models makes some stringent assumptions. It is assumed that community preferences can be summarized in a standard indifference map,[11] that local jurisdictions are unable to export taxes, that each jurisdiction takes the reactions of other jurisdictions to the grant scheme as given and that prices of all grantee functions are unaffected by the grant.

Lump-sum grants

With these assumptions let us study the effects of a lump-sum grant to a local authority. We discuss this in Figure 21.4. On the x axis we measure units of the public service provided by this jurisdiction and on the y axis we have funds for all other purposes. Before the lump-sum grant is given, the budget line of the jurisdiction is A_0A_1 and the jurisdiction comes to equilibrium at E_1. Suppose now that a general lump-sum grant of the amount A_0B_0 is given by the central government. This would shift the budget line to B_0B_1 and since, by assumption, relative prices are not affected, there is a pure income effect. The community comes to equilibrium at point E_2.

Suppose now that we have a matching grant. With this the central government gives a grant equal to the cost of the amount of G provided by the local government at the old equilibrium point E_1. Hence the budget line of the local government becomes A_0CB_1. The equilibrium for the local government is still unaltered at E_2 if E_2 is still available. This will be the case if E_2 is to the right of C in Figure 21.5. Hence, in this particular case, there is no difference between the effects of a general grant and a matching grant. Clearly this would not have been the case had E_2 been to the left of C (as shown in Figure 21.5) on the line B_0B_1. In this case the matching lump-sum grant will involve an equilibrium at C in Figure 21.5 and the level of community welfare would be lower.

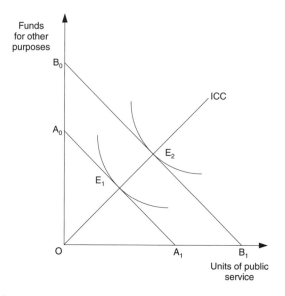

Figure 21.4

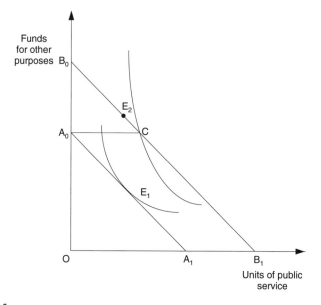

Figure 21.5

Conditional grants

Suppose now that we have an open matching specific grant. We examine the effects of this in Figure 21.6. The budget line before the grant is A_0A_1 and the initial equilibrium is at E_1. Now suppose that the central government

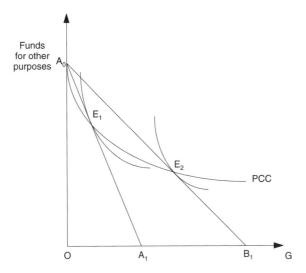

Figure 21.6

proposes to pay a fraction B_1A_1/OB_1 of the cost. This has the effect of lowering the relative price of G to the jurisdiction. Hence its effective budget line of the community becomes A_0B_1 and equilibrium is at point E_2. Successive increases in funding will trace out the price consumption curve (PCC) as in the diagram.

We can compare this matching grant with a lump-sum grant as in Figure 21.7 which basically redraws Figure 21.6. With the conditional grant, equilibrium is at E_2. The distance A_1B_1 is the value of the grant given (in terms of G). If this was given as a lump-sum amount then the budget line would become $C_0E_2C_1$ and the community could come to equilibrium at E_3 on a higher indifference curve.

We can now study a **closed conditional** grant. This is a conditional grant that is subject to an upper limit. We examine one case in Figure 21.8. Suppose the central government promises to pay a fraction A_1F_1/OF_1 of the cost of the service G subject to an upper limit. If there was no upper limit then the jurisdiction's budget line would have been A_0F_1 – a case we have already analyzed – and would come to an equilibrium at point E_1 where the price consumption curve (PCC) cuts the budget line. Suppose, however, that the upper limit to the amount of the grant that can be given is the amount A_1B_1. Hence the effective budget line becomes A_0ZB_1 and has, therefore, a kink. Another possibility examined in Figure 21.8 is one where the limit of the grant is larger – say A_1D_1. Then the effective budget line for the local jurisdiction again has a kink and is A_0JD_1. In the latter case equilibrium E_1 is permissible but this is not possible in the former case. In this case equilibrium would be where the ICC cuts A_0ZB_1. This is because the closed grant does not change relative price of G in the effective range

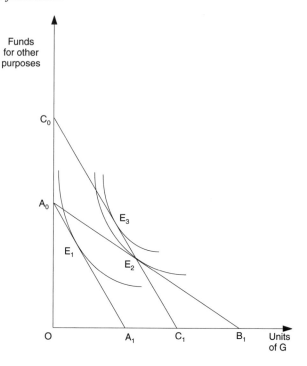

Figure 21.7

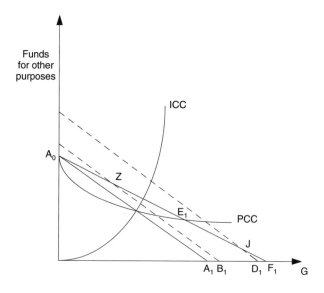

Figure 21.8

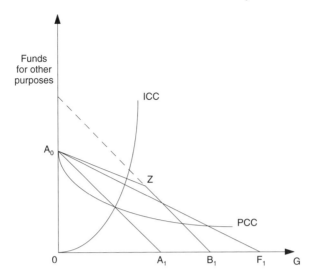

Figure 21.9

and is to be looked upon as a pure income expansion. Another possibility not examined in the diagram is one where the point Z lies to the right of the point where the ICC cuts the budget line.

As a last possibility consider the case where the budget line has a kink at Z as in Figure 21.9. It is easy to show here that the equilibrium would be at point Z itself. The reason for this is that there is no solution along the range A_0Z since all (unkinked) budget lines starting at A_0 have tangencies on the PCC which does not cut A_0Z. Similarly there will be no solution along the segment ZB_1 since all budget lines parallel to A_0A_1 have tangencies on ICC. which does not intersect ZB_1. Hence the equilibrium must reflect a corner solution. The point Z represents the highest indifference curve that can be reached – even though it is a corner solution.

The gist of the analysis here is the not surprising conclusion that local jurisdictions would prefer lump-sum conditional grants to other conditional grants and lump-sum general grants even more. On the other hand the higher level government would prefer open matching conditional grants as the most reliable way of ensuring an increase in the consumption of *G*.

So far we have been assuming that funds for the granting government are not collected from the local jurisdiction. This, of course, is not true. Funds which are later distributed as grants will actually be collected as taxes from residents of local jurisdictions. It is relevant, therefore, to examine the effects of such taxation.

If tax payments precisely match grant receipts in the area then the equilibrium with the lump-sum general grant after the tax will be in precisely the same place as the one before the grant. Hence the grant will have no effect on jurisdictional equilibrium in this case. The inward shift of the budget line is exactly matched by the outward shift in response to the grant. So far as lump specific grants are concerned, these too will have no effect unless they are able to bias consumption, by changing relative prices, in favor of commodity G. The same would be true of an open matching conditional grant since this would also encourage consumption of G by altering the relative price. Conditional matching specific grants may have no effect at all but, if they do, they will only encourage the consumption of G.

21.5   THE NEW MODELS OF THE EFFECTS OF GRANTS

Niskanen (1971) and Breton and Wintrobe (1975) argue that what have been alleged to be the preferences of the local residents are actually the preferences of the bureaucrats in the local government. The bureaucrats are supposed to know the preferences of their citizens. They manage the production of G for a subcentral authority. We consider their behavior in Figure 21.10. The average cost of production of G rises along the line AC in Figure 21.10. AV and MV denote the average valuation and marginal

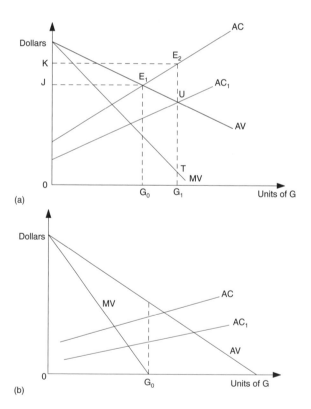

Figure 21.10

valuation of the commodity G by residents of the subcentral authority. Suppose this jurisdiction now receives an open matching conditional grant which reduces the per unit cost of G by some fraction. The new average cost schedule is shown as AC_1. Niskanen assumes that the bureaucrats are not crude profit maximizers. They want to maximize their influence by expanding the size of their budget subject, of course, to their breaking even. Thus, in Figure 21.10a, output would be G_0 before the grant and G_1 after the grant. The budget rises from OJE_1G_0 to OKE_2G_1. Total benefits increase by $G_0E_1UG_1$. Tax revenue rises and the budget rises by more than the amount of the grant. In Figure 21.10b the AC cuts AV when MV would become zero. Hence the grant induces no increase in output from G_0. The budget rises but output stays constant. This would imply increasing X-inefficiency on the part of the local government.[12]

A related work is that of Romer and Rosenthal (1980). Here jurisdictions are assumed to budget maximizers and no particular distinction is made between bureaucrats and politicians. There is a reversion level of expenditure and the local authority has to choose that unless there is a referendum in which the residents opt for a level of expenditure different from the reversion level. This reversion level could be last year's expenditure or some average expenditure.

In this referendum the preferences of the median voter will prevail. In Figure 21.11, G_0 is the reversion level of the commodity G. We have also drawn in this diagram the indifference curve of the median voter. Suppose that level G_2 was put to the vote in the referendum because the bureaucrat wants to maximize the budget. In this case the reversal level G_0 would win. However, if level G_1 were put up in the referendum against the reversal level

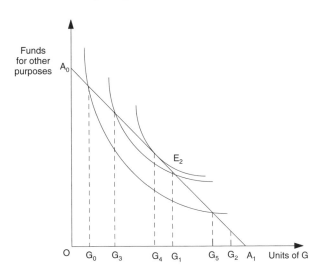

Figure 21.11

G_0 then this would win. The median voter would gain in utility and the bureaucrat would get a higher budget to work with. However, if the reversal level was G_3 then the only option that would win in a referendum would be the utility maximizing one, i.e., G_4. But that would mean a lower budget for the bureaucrat. Hence, in the Romer–Rosenthal model the bureaucrat would have a preference for a low reversal level whereas the median resident would be better off if there was a larger value of G as the reversal level.

In an interesting model Oates (1979a, b) supposes that the bureaucrat is not trying to maximize the budget but to maximize the welfare of the median voter. However, the median voter is imperfectly informed about the grant so that it is possible for the bureaucrat to deceive the median voter into accepting a larger budget than is optimal. The intuition behind this is as follows. Suppose that the tax price of G has been fixed by the local authority and the quantity of this commodity produced is then determined by the demand by the median voter. Suppose now that a grant is given to the local authority but the median voter is unaware of it. In that case, the income of the median voter increases as does his demand for G. At the old price a higher budget for the service can be supported.

An alternative would be for the jurisdiction simply to pass on the grant from the central government as a transfer payment to residents so that the demand would go up and the bureaucrats would end up with a larger budget. This has been analyzed in Figure 21.12. The effect of the transfer payment to the residents is to give them a lower tax price for the commodity G. The schedule $S_0 S_1$ is the schedule denoting the supply price of this commodity. The higher the transfer payment to the residents, the lower the supply price. Given the demand schedule of the median voter, produc-

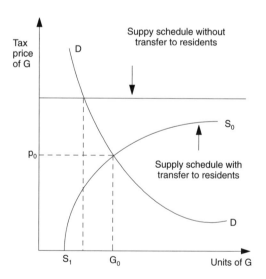

Figure 21.12

tion is G_0 and the tax price is p_0 in Figure 21.12. If price elasticity of demand is non-zero then the drop in price would raise the output and the budget. If the absolute value of the price elasticity exceeds one then tax payments would also rise.

The crucial difference between the new models and the old models is that in the new models it is made explicit that the voter who counts is the median voter and further that the identity of this voter does not change when transfers are made. This is not the case in the old models.

21.6 TAX ASSIGNMENT IN FEDERAL COUNTRIES

So far we have laid out the rationale for the existence of several tiers of government and for grants from higher to lower level governments. A natural question that arises at this stage is how should local governments finance the rest of their expenditures. The literature distinguishes between three broad categories of revenues for the lower level government. These are: (a) taxes; (b) charges; (c) loans. We will confine ourselves to taxation.

When designing tax structures for lower level governments emphasis is laid on the twin concepts of **tax harmonization** and **tax coordination**. We will discuss each of these in turn now.

Tax harmonization

This refers primarily to the adjustment of tax systems in different jurisdictions in the pursuit of a common policy objective. In this context, the main goals of tax harmonization are to eliminate barriers to trade, remove tax distortions, and bring about a more efficient allocation of resources so that businesses and individuals across jurisdictions experience similar tax burdens. Tax harmonization can be both **vertical** and **horizontal**.

This working definition seems to emphasize that horizontal equity is an important ingredient of tax harmonization. To achieve horizontal harmonization, governments at the same level that share a particular tax base would apply a similar tax rate on a uniform tax base and/or use a similar definition and formula in calculating the amounts owing. Similarly, with vertical harmonization, governments that occupy the same tax base could either piggyback (tax on the same base) or allocate separate tax revenue sources for each level of government.

Unless we have horizontal tax harmonization we would, no doubt, have horizontal inequity across jurisdictions. In turn, this inequity could stimulate migration from one jurisdiction to another. This would consume resources and may have an adverse effect on output levels as well. It might be argued that the prevalence of non-uniform tax structures in different jurisdictions would enable people to vote with their feet for their preferred jurisdiction/tax package. However, with no harmonized tax structures the chances of non-optimal location with a non-uniform tax package would go up considerably. In a complex federal country with several levels of governments and tax benefit packages, the link between the taxes paid by the individual and the benefit package received could become very weak and the relevance of the voting with the feet model could be questioned. A further argument for a harmonized tax structure would be that, in the absence of such a system, jurisdictions would have to worry too much about the reactions of others. With a common, near-uniform program of tax and public goods package, reactions of other jurisdictions would become less relevant. With a non-harmonized tax structure in place, if a jurisdiction started taxing at a higher rate it might lose rich residents. If the tax structure favors residents the higher tax need not outweigh the costs of moving and the rich residents might not move. An additional reason for tax harmonization is in the context of local jurisdictions having more than one tax. Tax harmonization in this context would mean that these subcentral governments should not only use the same set of taxes, but also that they should set the same relative rates. Widely disparate tax rates might well arise if each jurisdiction chose to rely on the small group of taxes that involved the least welfare loss for its median voter and this median voter varied considerably from one jurisdiction to the next.

In principle, then, tax harmonization is desirable. But in a federal framework it may face considerable difficulties. The biggest challenge is to convince a sufficiently large number of policy-makers at various levels of government of the need to move toward a harmonized tax structure.[13]

Tax coordination

Hence, an essential element of tax harmonization is the need for tax coordination between different levels of government.[14] An additional reason for tax coordination would be that this would lead to less tax exporting and tax competition across jurisdictions.

It would be reasonable to argue that a precondition for tax coordination would be a clear enunciation of the taxing powers of different levels of government. This has been called the tax assignment problem by Musgrave and Musgrave (1972). Once this assignment problem has been addressed, they argue, the problem of tax coordination will be simpler.

Suppose that a given set of central, state and local jurisdictions are confronting the process of forming a federation. Available taxes are the personal income tax, corporation profits tax, destination type consumption tax (retail sales tax or VAT), and property tax. Musgrave and Musgrave (1972) argue that in assigning taxes one should try to minimize the extent of spillover (in the form of external effects, tax exporting or tax competition) from one jurisdiction to another. Within this framework the following set of assignment rules is advocated.

(i) State and, particularly, local governments should tax bases that have low mobility. Thus, for example, landed property is immobile and is almost universally taxed by local authorities. In addition, the federation as a whole will be concerned with efficiency in the entire federation. The most efficient way to do this is to require uniform taxes across jurisdictions. This is usually the case, for example, in federations which use the VAT where the rates of the VAT across different states are almost the same. Clearly local level consumption taxes are inappropriate because of the high mobility of goods.

(ii) Personal taxes should be administered by the level of government responsible for overall fiscal efficiency in the economy. This is principally because individuals are quite mobile and some economy-wide notion of equity is involved in such cases. Similarly, corporate incomes are hard to conceive of at the subnational level and are best taxed at a central level.

(iii) A third principle espoused by Musgrave and Musgrave (1972) is that taxes that are meant for redistribution should be administered centrally. This must be true because the concept of redistribution does not make much sense at the subnational level.

(iv) Countercyclical fiscal policy should be centrally administered whereas subnational tax rates should be cyclically neutral. Aggregate demand control through appropriate countercyclical tax policy, for example, is best left to the central government. This is primarily but not exclusively because countercyclical fiscal policy at the subnational level will be subject to considerable leakages. If, in response to excessive aggregate demand, a local government increased taxes, factors of production would move to another jurisdiction. This kind of leakage would reduce the effectiveness of countercyclical fiscal policy. Moreover, the central government has superior powers of credit and debt policy and local governments would like their revenues to be fairly stable over the business cycle. Again it appears that income and profits taxes are more suitable for the central government, whereas consumption and real estate taxes are more suitable at the middle and local levels.

(v) Suppose there are some tax bases that are distributed highly unequally across local jurisdictions. A classic example of this would be natural resources which may be concentrated in few parts of a large federation. If taxation of natural resources by local jurisdictions is permitted then the resource-rich jurisdictions might be able to provide services at a low price compared to resource poor states. Hence, resources would be attracted to the former jurisdictions and, given the small size of these jurisdictions, this migration would be on an inefficient scale. In other words, business would move in because of better tax prices but the local demand would not be enough to enable the businesses to produce on the minimum point of their cost curves.

(vi) Benefit taxes and user charges are useful at all levels of government. The significance of these instruments at various levels of government depends upon the nature of the public service, i.e., whether the benefits these services bestow are general or applicable to particular groups of people. If the former is the case, then local charges would be more useful.

It would appear, then, that a good tax for subcentral authorities would be one that has a base that is widely and evenly distributed across the country. Several reasons are generally advanced in favor of this argument. First, if tax bases for local jurisdictions are unevenly distributed then, to the extent that grant payments have conditions[15] attached to them, these will also be unequal. Second, if local tax bases are highly unequal then a system of equalization grants may involve negative grants for some areas. Negative grants are likely to be highly unpopular and, hence, it is best to assign tax bases to local jurisdictions so that such grants are rarely necessary.

Furthermore, with evenly distributed tax bases the need for equalization grants is reduced. In most cases the design of equalization grant formulae and the methods used to define 'needs', 'resources' and 'tax effort' of jurisdictions are subjects of considerable controversy. If equalization grants are small in magnitude then these controversies are less important. Additionally, equalization grants transfer resources from high tax base areas to low tax base areas. Thus unless subcentral authorities also rely on an income tax, this transfer need not be from high income to low income areas. For reasons mentioned above, it is best to leave income taxation to the central or, at most, state governments. In this situation, the smaller the equalization grant, the greater the chance that the transfer is being made from high to low income areas as well.

Another important consideration concerning yields of taxes is the **elasticity** or **buoyancy** of the tax. At least two different definitions of this term have been used. Sometimes an elastic tax is defined as one whose yield tends to rise at least as fast as costs and incomes without the need for a change in the rate of the tax. In other words, the yield from the tax is required to keep pace with inflation. Another definition of an elastic tax is one whose yield tends to rise at least as fast as disposable income without the need for a change in the tax rate. Hence this definition would require that yields go up automatically with real incomes as well as with inflation.

Consider now a situation in which there is inflation but real incomes are stagnant. Now if the structure of income taxes is progressive, and tax bands are held fixed in nominal terms, as nominal pre-tax incomes rise[16] people move into higher income tax brackets where they face higher marginal tax rates. Hence tax revenues from the income tax will go up and the income tax is an elastic source of tax revenue. With corporate profit taxes or VAT imposed on an *ad valorem* basis constant tax rates will mean that tax yields will rise roughly in proportion to the rise in price. Hence these taxes have an inflation elasticity equal to unity. To the extent that taxes are specific rather than *ad valorem*, the yields from such taxes will fall with inflation and, therefore, such taxes are not inflation elastic.

Let us now take the opposite case of zero inflation and rising real incomes. Income tax payers will be moving into higher tax bands and will, therefore, be facing higher marginal tax rates. Consequently, the income tax is elastic with respect to income changes as well. With a payroll tax or VAT or any other tax with a constant *ad valorem* rate, higher real incomes will mean higher expenditures and higher tax yields. It is easy to see that such taxes will have unitary elasticity with respect to changes in real income if the income elasticity of demand of these goods was unity.

Administrative costs and excess burdens

All taxes leave consumers worse off. Those that are distortionary[17] in addition inflict excess burdens of taxpayers. Hence total burdens of tax imposed may be usefully split up into two categories: (a) resource costs broadly defined to include administrative costs as well as costs of compliance; (b) excess burden of the tax.

Administrative and compliance costs depend on the particular types of taxes that are being levied. It is probably the case that costs of collection of any particular tax in relation to its yield will fall as the yield increases. On that count, it is probably better to have a few high yielding taxes as opposed to a large number of low yield taxes. Income and corporate taxes with a nationwide reach will clearly have lower administrative costs than those which vary from region to region. For such taxes there are probably economies of scale in tax collection.

So far as the excess burden of taxation is concerned, it is possible that problems will rise if different areas use different taxes or use the same taxes but have very different rates. Tax harmonization would tend to reduce the magnitude of this excess burden but cannot eliminate it. For example, even with harmonized taxes if per capita tax bases varied across the country there would be differences in public services which would induce migration. This migration would in turn consume resources. As discussed earlier a system of equalization grants could help reduce this migration.

Taxes assigned to more than one level of government

Notwithstanding the considerations spelt out above, there may still be some taxes which may be assigned to more than one level of government. It has been argued that the same tax should not be levied by more than one level of government. If this is the case then the tax has a **cascading effect**. However, there is no intrinsic a priori argument against the multiple use of a tax. One should not tax the same base excessively. However, if there are good reasons for more than one level of government using the same tax base, then a properly coordinated tax structure across these levels of government could actually be welfare improving. Different levels of government cross-checking with each other could, for example, reduce the extent of tax evasion.

Taxes that could be levied at both state and national level could include the VAT as well as an income tax. Tax overlap between local and central governments and between local and state governments will be less likely.

The allocation of tax yields to different authorities

An important issue in tax coordination is the proper assignment of tax revenues exacted from each taxpayer whether the tax is based on the taxpayer's income, expenditure, or property. This is obviously very simple in the case of the property tax since the tax will be paid to the authority where the property is located. If the income tax is paid only to the central government, then again there will be no difficulty. If, however, income taxes are also paid to state governments then the use of the above residence principle might involve some difficulty in the case of persons who maintain more than one residence or work in one state and live in another. In such cases proper apportionment rules have to be devised.

21.7 CONCLUSIONS

The assignment of taxes in a federal structure is a complex matter. Issues concerning horizontal as well as vertical imbalances come up and have to be evaluated carefully in an operational program of tax assignment. This chapter has studied some of these problems.

We have also studied issues relating to the structure of grants from higher to lower level governments. Once again, difficult issues came up: should we use specific grants or general grants, conditional or unconditional grants and the like.

In this chapter we have sketched out some of the principal considerations that would be involved in making such choices. These considerations are helpful if incomplete guides to the actual design of tax/grant structures in federal countries.

NOTES

1　Grants are usually paid by a higher tier authority to a lower tier authority, for example, grants from the central government to state/local governments. The reason for this harks back to the argument put forward in Chapter 20 that there may exist economies of scale in tax collection and, therefore, it is more appropriate to let most taxes be collected by higher level governments.
2　See Section 21.3 on Types of Grants.
3　It is important to note that we have so far been assuming that the transfers to the jurisdictions are financed by lump-sum taxes. If these are instead financed by distortionary taxes then the formula for the optimal supply of the public good will have to be amended to include the excess burden of such taxation along the lines suggested in Chapter 6.
4　Subject, of course, to the consideration that each jurisdiction must put in maximal effort to raise resources on its own.
5　For a fuller discussion of specific or conditional grants see Section 21.3.
6　To take advantage of the economies of scale or for equity reasons as discussed in Chapter 20.
7　We had discussed in Chapter 20 that this sets up an important rationale for fiscal devolution from higher to lower levels of government.

8 The expression 'fiscal residuum' is due to Buchanan and is interpreted to mean benefits less taxes paid.

9 Hamilton argues that in such situations a poll tax will be poor friendly since it will not meet the same opposition from the rich as an income tax.

10 Bendfit pricing traces its intellectual origins to the Lindahl–Wicksell mechanism for public goods discussed in Chapters 5 and 6.

11 An important question that arises here is: whose indifference map is it? Typically it is taken to be the indifference map of the median voter and reference is made to the median voter theorem to claim that this person's preferences will win.

12 The notion of X inefficiency refers to administrative and managerial inefficiency. It owes its origin to a work by Leibenstein (1966).

13 This problem may become quite acute, particularly if there is lack of unanimity about the structure of harmonized taxes and if different political parties are in power at different levels of government.

14 It should be mentioned here that any exercise in tax coordination between different levels of governments absorbs scarce resources – both tangible as well as intangible. Hence, there are limits to tax coordination as well as its professed aim of tax harmonization.

15 Like a matching grant.

16 We are assuming that real pre-tax incomes are constant.

17 This includes almost all taxes except the much maligned poll tax.

ADDITIONAL READING

The following texts will be of interest to students: Oates (1972) and Rubinfeld (1987), Clotfelter and Cook (1990), Kenyon and Kincaid (1991).

Problems

In this section problems are arranged by broad sections of the text rather than individual chapters.

CONSUMER DEMAND THEORY

1. The following is referred to as a constant elasticity of substitution utility function:

$$U(x_1, x_2) = [\beta_1 x_1^\delta + \beta_2 x_2^\delta]^{1/\delta} \text{ where } \beta_1, \beta_2 \text{ and } \delta \text{ are parameters.}$$

(a) Show that the elasticity of substitution between x_1 and x_2 is constant. What is the value of this elasticity?

(b) Show that as:

  (i) $\delta \to 0$, we get the Cobb–Douglas utility function $U(.) = x_1^{\beta_1} x_2^{\beta_2}$;

  (ii) $\delta = 1$, the indifference curves between x_1 and x_2 become flat;

  (iii) $\delta \to -\infty$, the indifference curves become right-angle, Leontief-type utility functions.

2. Now consider the Stone–Geary utility function (the only utility function that is associated with the linear expenditure system):

$$\ln U(x_1, x_2) = \alpha_1 \ln(x_1 - \gamma_1) + \alpha_2 \ln(x_2 - \gamma_2) + \alpha_3 \ln(x_3 - \gamma_3)$$

where γ_1 is the 'minimum' amount of good i ($i = 1, 2, 3$) that has to be consumed and $\alpha_i > 0 (i = 1, 2, 3)$.

(a) Show that without loss of generality we can assume:

$$\alpha_1 + \alpha_2 + \alpha_3 = 1.$$

(b) Carry out the utility maximization exercise and derive the expenditure function and the indirect utility function. This utility function has also been referred to in Chapter 13.

3. Consider the additive separable utility function:

$$U(x_1, \ldots, x_n) = \sum_{i=1}^{n} U_i(x_i).$$

(a) Show that additive separability is a cardinal property and is preserved only under linear transformations of the utility function.
(b) Show that if the U_i are strictly concave then the Walrasian and Hicksian demand functions admit no inferior goods.
(c) Suppose that all the U_i are identical and twice differentiable.

Let $\tilde{U}(.) = U(.)$. Show that if $-[\theta\{\partial^2\tilde{U}(\theta)/\partial\theta^2\}/(\partial\tilde{U}(\theta)/\partial\theta)] < 1$ for all θ, then the Walrasian demand function $x(.)$ has the property of *gross substitution*, i.e., $\partial x_i(.)/\partial p_j > 0$ for all i and $i \neq j$.

4. Suppose there are two groups of commodities, x_1 and x_2 with corresponding prices p_1 and p_2. The utility function of the consumer is $U(x_1, x_2)$ and net income is $I > 0$. Suppose that prices for goods x_2 always vary in proportion to one another, so that we can write $p_1 = \rho p_0$. For any number $\gamma \geqslant 0$ define the function:

$$\hat{U}(x_2, \gamma) = \max_{x_1} U(x_1, x_2) \text{ subject to } p_0 \cdot x_2 \leqslant \gamma.$$

(a) Show that if we now postulate that there are two goods in the economy x_1 and a single composite good γ, that $\hat{U}(x, \gamma)$ is the consumer's utility function and that ρ is the price of this composite commodity, then the solution to the maximization problem: $\hat{U}(x_1, \gamma)$ subject to $p_1 x_1 + \rho\gamma \leqslant I$ will give the actual levels of x_1 and $\gamma = p_0 x_2$.
(b) Show that the properties of the Walrasian and Hicksian demand functions are retained intact.

WELFARE ECONOMICS AND THE THEORY OF PUBLIC EXPENDITURE

1. Consider an economy with H consumers and three goods. Two of the goods (x and y) are private goods and the third is a pure public good, G. A typical consumer, indexed by h, has the following additive separable utility function:

$$U^h(x^h, y^h, G) = x^h + 2\log y^h + \log G$$

where the notation is obvious.

Good x is the only good available in the economy as a primary resource. Let $x_w^h(> 2)$ be the endowment of good x with consumer h. Production conditions for the good y are described by:

$y = (x_i)^{0.5}$ where x_i is the input of commodity x in the production of good y. Production conditions for the public good are given by

$G = x_I$ where x_I is the input of commodity x in the production of the public good.

(a) Consider the objective function denoted by $\sum_h U^h(.)$ subject to the technological constraints and the scarcity constraints. Consider the maxima of this objective function which are associated with a positive consumption of good x. Show that the amount of the public good consumed is the same in each of these optima.

(b) Assume that each consumer is entitled to $(1/H)$ of the firms' profits. Now the government can achieve any one of the optima calculated in part (a) as a competitive equilibrium in the market for private goods. To accomplish this the government

   (i) sets the output of the public good;
   (ii) establishes prices for the private goods;
   (iii) imposes lump-sum taxes on the consumers.

Calculate the prices established. Show that the sum of the lump-sum taxes is equal to the cost of financing of the public good.

(c) Now suppose that it is impossible to levy a lump-sum tax. Instead the government taxes good 2 to finance the production of the public good with τ being the specific tax. Calculate the value of τ that would suffice to finance the amount of the public good given in part (a).

(d) How does this tax generate a social loss? Explain carefully.

(e) Why does the second-best optimum require a level of the public good different from that in part (a)?

2.   A competitive industry draws its workers from a pool of existing workers whose alternative wage is w. The productivity of these workers can be improved by worker training schemes. The greater the resources put into the scheme, the higher the productivity of the workers. Once trained, a worker's skills are the same no matter which firm in the industry employs the worker. However, skills are specific to this industry so the worker's alternative wage rate in other industries continues to be w. Suppose that a given proportion of workers move from one firm to another within the industry each period.

(a) Compare the optimal allocation with the allocation that would result if all training were done independently by the firms.

(b) Discuss alternative ways in which, in theory, the optimal allocation could be attained.

(c) How would your answers to parts (a) and (b) change if these skills were not specific to the industry?

3.   Consider a two-person economy consisting of a public good, G, and a private good, x. Both persons have the same utility function $U(x_i, G) = x_i G^{0.5}$ where x_i is the consumption of the private good by person i ($i = 1, 2$) and G is the amount of the public good. The production possibility curve of the economy is given by the transformation function $\phi(x, G) = 0$.

(a) Describe the Pareto-efficient allocations of resources that could be achieved in this economy. Depict your answer diagrammatically.

(b) Which allocation would be chosen by a social welfare maximizing government which used a maximin social welfare function? A utilitarian social welfare function? Why?

(c) Describe the allocations that would be achieved by a system of voluntary contributions.

(d) How would your answer change if the transformation function was linear?

4   Consider a two-person economy consisting of a public good, G, and a private good, x. The utility function for both individuals (A and B) is: $U(x_i, G) = \ln x_i + \alpha \ln G$ where α is positive. The production possibility curve of the economy is described by $x_A + x_B + G = C$ where C is a constant and corresponds with the value of resources in the economy. For a fixed value of α:

(a) Describe the Pareto-efficient allocations of resources that could be achieved in this economy. Depict your answer diagrammatically.

(b) Which allocations would be chosen by a social welfare maximizing government which used a utilitarian social welfare function? Why?

(c) Explain why voluntary provision of the public good will not lead to a Pareto-efficient allocation of resources.

(d) Explain how your answers would change as α varies.

5.   Lake L_c is freely accessed by fishermen. The cost of sending a boat out on the lake is $\alpha > 0$. When b boats are sent out onto the lake, $f(b)$ fish are caught in total so that each boat catches $f(b)/b$. We assume $(\partial f / \partial b) > 0$ and $(\partial^2 f / \partial b^2) < 0$ for all $b \geqslant 0$. The price of fish is $p > 0$, which is unaffected by the level of the catch from lake L_c.

(a) Derive an expression for the optimal number of boats to be sent out onto the lake.

(b) Derive an expression for the equilibrium number of boats to be sent out onto the lake. How does this compare to the answer in part (a).

(c) Characterize the per boat tax that would restore efficiency.

(d) Suppose that this lake is owned by a single individual who can choose how many boats are to be sent out. What level would this individual choose? Why?

6.   Suppose the government is considering building a public project. The cost is C. This would benefit n individuals indexed by i. Individual i's privately known benefit from the project is $b_i > 0$. The government's objective is to maximize the expected value of aggregate surplus. Derive the Groves–Clark mechanism for this case. Can you construct a scheme that will balance the government's budget on average (over all realization of the b_i's)?

7.   A firm faces fixed input prices $\bar{q}$ and has a cost function $c(Q, e)$ where Q is the output level. This output is sold at the price $p > 0$. e is a level of negative externality generated by the firm. This externality affects a single consumer whose indirect utility function is $\Phi(e) + \bar{q}$. The actions of the firm and consumer do not affect any market prices.

(a) Derive the first-order condition for the firm's choice of Q and *e*.
(b) Derive the Pareto optimal conditions for Q and *e*.
(c) Show that a tax on the firm's output will not restore efficiency and that a tax on the externality itself will.
(d) Show that if the externality is produced in fixed proportion with output ($e = \delta Q$, with $\delta > 0$) then a tax on output can lead to the Pareto optimal outcome.

8. Is it possible for a policy to affect the allocation of resources without altering the distribution of income? If so, give an example of such a policy. If not, explain why.

9. Suppose that there are two persons in society – two 'hawks' who want more government expenditure on defense and one 'dove' who derives negative benefits from expenditure on defense. What is the optimal quantity of defense in this case? Show algebraically as well as with a diagram. Is there any way that the government could finance this efficient quantity that would benefit all three people? What happens to this optimum solution if (a) the number of hawks increases; and (b) the number of doves increases?

10. How is the size of an externality related to the importance of undertaking corrective policy?

11. What is rational voter ignorance? Does its presence lead voters to prefer larger or smaller government budgets than they would if they understood completely the effects of government policies?

12. Provide an explanation in terms of logrolling of why House and Senate Committees (in the USA) and Parliamentary Committees (in the UK) dealing with spending programs hear more pro-spending witnesses.

INCENTIVE EFFECTS OF TAXES

1. In a two-asset world, one risky and one not, replacing an income tax with a tax on the return to the risky asset alone will reduce risk taking. Evaluate. How would your answer change if the risk-free asset paid a positive (fixed) return?

2. Imposing a general income tax to pay off some of the government debt will reduce savings whereas imposing a sales tax for the same purpose will have no effect on savings. True or false? Evaluate.

3. Consider an overlapping generations model of the sort used by Summers (1981) and discussed in Chapter 7. Labor productivity is growing at the rate γ whereas the population is declining at the same rate γ. The government is contemplating introducing an unfunded system of public pensions.

(a) Compare the short- and the long-run effects of financing the pension benefits using a wage tax, a consumption tax and an income tax.

(b) Discuss how your answer to part (a) would change if: (i) labor supply was fixed; (ii) retirement age were variable.
(c) Explain how the results would be affected by the presence of:
(i) intended bequests; (ii) unintended bequests.

4. Consider a household that lives for two periods of equal lengths. In the first period, this household receives fixed earnings of $200. No earnings are received in period 2. Capital markets are perfect and the interest rate facing the household is 9%. The households's utility function is:

$$U = 1.2\ln C_1 + 0.5\ln C_2$$

where C_1 and C_2 are consumption levels in the two periods.

(a) How much saving is done by the household in the absence of taxes?
(b) Suppose the government levies a wage tax of 15%. What is the effect on saving? (Assume the revenues from the tax are used for some purpose which does not directly affect household utility.)
(c) The government is now contemplating replacing the wage tax on the household with a different tax yielding the same present value of tax revenue from the household. For each of the following taxes, determine the tax rate required and the effect on personal and total (personal plus public) saving as well as the excess burden associated with the tax:

(i) a consumption tax;
(ii) an income tax.

(d) Explain qualitatively how your answer would change if the household had some earnings in the second period.
(e) Suppose now that the household has the utility function:

$$U = 1.2\ln C_1 + \alpha\ln L + 0.5\ln C_2$$

where L is first-period leisure and $\alpha(> 0)$ is the weight given to leisure. The wage rate is $200 per time period. How would your answer to parts (b), (c) and (d) change? What would be the effect of the household increasing/decreasing α? Discuss carefully.

5. Suppose that the probability of the household being alive in the second period is 1/2. (The probability of being alive in the first period is 1.) Suppose also that the household maximizes expected utility over its lifetime. (The utility if not alive is 0.)

(a) In the model with fixed labor what would saving be in the absence of taxes? What would average per capita bequests be if all households were identical?
(b) What would happen to household saving if the government were to introduce an actuarially fair annuity system with a premium of 10 in the first period? What would average per capita bequests be in this case?
(c) How would answers change if labor supply was variable?

6. Go back to the household of Problem 4 with fixed labor supply. Suppose the economy consists of overlapping generations of such households. The population growth rate is 3 per cent. The economy is a small open one so that the interest rate and the wage rate (and thus the amount of earnings) are exogenously fixed. The economy is currently under a 15 per cent wage tax system.

(a) Determine the effect on saving, consumption, GNP and lifetime welfare of a switch to a consumption tax system yielding the same stream of revenues per period to the government. Do the calculation for the steady states only, but discuss the transition from one steady state to another.

(b) Repeat part (a) for a switch to an income tax system.

(c) Describe qualitatively the effect on your answer of each of the following changes in assumptions:

   (i) the economy is a closed one so that the wage rate and the interest rate are endogenous;

   (ii) earnings are obtained in the second period of the life cycle;

   (iii) households care about the level of welfare of the next generation.

(d) Imagine there being an intergenerational social welfare function denoted $W(U_t, U_{t+1}, U_{t+2}, \ldots)$ where U_t is the utility of cohort t. Suppose you are in the wage tax equilibrium to begin with. Discuss what tax policies you might recommend to a far-sighted planner if the social welfare function were each of the following types:

   (i) Maximin: $W = U_{min}$ where U_{min} is the utility of the worst-off generation.

   (ii) Utilitarian: $W = \Sigma U_t$.

(e) How would your answers change if the rate of growth of the population was negative?

7. Suppose the corporate sector of an economy has a production function of the type:

$$Y_t = K_t^\alpha$$

so that the elasticity of output with respect to capital is $\alpha(> 0)$. The relative price of capital goods and consumption goods are fixed, but nominal prices are all rising at a rate of 6 per cent. Capital goods are measured in units such that the relative price of capital goods in terms of final output is unity. Capital can be accumulated or decumulated instantly and capital depreciates at a rate of 10 per cent. The debt equity ratio of the firm is 0.6. There are no personal taxes on capital income. There is a corporation income tax at the rate of 40 per cent. The base for this tax consists of total revenues less nominal interest payments less depreciation. For tax purposes the depreciation rate is 20 per cent. There is also an investment tax credit of 10 per cent on gross investment. The investment tax credit is subtracted from the book value of the capital stock for depreciation purposes. The firms operate in an economy which faces fixed world real interest rate of 4 per cent. For a fixed value of α:

(a) Calculate the equilibrium stock of capital and the marginal effective tax rate facing the corporate sector.
(b) Explain why the marginal effective tax rate differs from the statutory corporate tax rate.
(c) Determine the effect of each of the following tax changes (undertaken separately starting from the above equilibrium) on the marginal effective tax rate:

   (i) the tax system is indexed for inflation;
   (ii) the investment tax credit is replaced with a scheme of accelerated depreciation which allows firms to write off their investment over two years in equal amounts each year (i.e. using straight-line depreciation);
   (iii) the investment tax credit is no longer deducted from the book value of capital for depreciation purposes.

(d) Suppose the tax system is as described above except that the tax depreciation rate is the true depreciation rate (10 per cent in the above example). Explain whether such a system would favor or discriminate against long-lived investments. (You have to assume that different firms have different types of capital now.)
(e) Suppose that the above firm is just starting up and the first few years of operation it sustains have negative taxable income. Suppose the tax system does not give refunds for negative tax liabilities but instead allows the firm to carry forward its tax losses to deduct against positive tax liabilities in future years. Explain, qualitatively, how the absence of symmetric treatment of positive and negative tax liabilities will affect the path of accumulation of capital by the firm.
(f) What reforms would be needed to turn this tax system into a neutral one?
(g) How would your answers change as α varied?

8. A single household lives for two time periods and obtains utility from consumption in each period according to the utility function:

$$U(C_1, C_2) = \ln C_1 + \operatorname{Ln} C_2.$$

The government levies an income tax to pay for public expenditures which do not affect the utility the consumer attains from consumption. Earnings of the household are I_1 in the first period and I_2 in the second. The interest rate is r and the capital markets are perfect. Compare the effects of income taxation on the decisions taken by the household in each of the following circumstances:

   (i) $I_1 > 0, I_2 = 0$;
   (ii) $I_1 = I_2 > 0$;

(iii) $I_1 > I_2 > 0$;

(iv) $I_2 > I_1 > 0$;

(v) Earnings are endogenous and given by an earnings transformation function $F(I_1, I_2) = 0$ with $\partial F/\partial I_i > 0$ and $\partial^2 F/\partial I^2 < 0$.

(vi) $I_1 > 0$ and $I_2 = 0$ and the household can invest some of their savings in an asset with a stochastic rate of return $\in$.

9. Can the welfare cost of a tax caused by labor supply effects be greater than the revenue collected by the tax? Illustrate using a diagram.

10. Why are tax rate reductions for the wealthy less likely to reduce the tax revenue collected than are tax rate reductions for middle income taxpayers? What are the arguments for favoring a tax cut favoring the rich?

PROBLEMS ON TAX INCIDENCE

1. Consider the standard two-sector general equilibrium model. Discuss the incidence effects of the following tax changes:

(a) a substitution of a tax on industry X for a tax on capital in industry X;

(b) the imposition of a tax on labor when the labor supply is variable;

(c) excise taxes at the same rate on both industries when labor supply is variable;

(d) an excise tax on industry Y when the economy is a small open one (facing fixed world prices of output);

(e) the imposition of a tax on capital in industry X when industry X uses capital and labor in fixed proportions.

2. Discuss the effect each of the following would have on the magnitude of the distortion imposed by taxes on capital markets:

(a) an increase in the tax rate imposed on corporations;

(b) the elimination of the tax on capital gains;

(c) indexing the corporate and personal tax system;

(d) an increase in the dividend tax credit rate (the tax credit given to shareholders on the receipt of dividends from the corporation);

(e) an increase in the rate of inflation.

3. Consider the two-sector static general equilibrium model of tax incidence. Suppose that the economy is an open one so that the relative price of Y for X is given to the economy by world markets. Suppose the government has to raise a given amount of revenue and is considering the alternative ways of doing this. Compare the effects on the production side of the economy of a tax on labor income in both industries, a tax on the output of the X industry, and a tax on capital in the Y industry for economies with the following sets of production technologies:

(i) Industry X: $L_X^{0.5}K_X^{0.5}$, Industry Y: $L_Y^{0.5}K_Y^{0.5}$;

(ii) Industry X: $L_X^{0.5}K_X^{0.5}$, Industry Y: $L_Y^{0.75}K_Y^{0.25}$;
(iii) Industry X: $L_X^{0.5}K_X^{0.5}$, Industry Y: $\min(L_Y, K_Y)$;
(iv) Industry X: $L_X^{0.75}K_X^{0.25}$, Industry Y: $L_Y + K_Y$.

4. Explain why it is not inconsistent to hold that excise taxes are shifted forward to consumers in the form of higher prices, as well as to say that a general sales tax may not lead to higher product prices but instead to lower input prices.

5. Why does an excise tax produce a welfare cost? Describe the welfare cost. Would there be an equivalent welfare cost if the excise tax were placed on an industry with external costs?

6. Successive equal increments in a per unit excise tax imply smaller and smaller percentage increases in the tax. Hence, the additional welfare cost of each increment gets smaller and smaller. Do you agree? Explain fully.

PROBLEMS ON OPTIMAL TAXATION

1. Consider a society with two types of worker: skilled and unskilled. The planner can observe total income and consumption but neither the hours worked nor the wages of workers. The planner has to design an optimal non-linear tax structure.

(a) Show that a 'self-selection' equilibrium in which the workers sort themselves into appropriate ability types is preferable to a 'pooling' equilibrium in which such sorting need not occur.
(b) Characterize a tax structure that would support such an equilibrium.
(c) Show that if the elasticity of substitution between labor types is infinite, the optimal marginal tax on skilled labor is zero.
(d) Show that if the elasticity of substitution between labor types is finite then the optimal marginal tax on skilled labor is negative.

2. In the case of one-person Ramsey optimal taxation discuss the relation between the rule that commodity tax rates should be inversely proportional to the uncompensated elasticities of demand and the Corlett–Hague result.

3. Consider an economy in which there are two types of workers, high-ability types and low-ability types. There is an equal number of each. Each household starts with an endowment of time only, but the two types have different abilities to transform time into labor on the market as reflected in their wage rates, $w_h > w_l$. All households have the same utility function, whose arguments are consumption and leisure. Compare the structure of the optimal tax transfer system under a utilitarian and a maximin social welfare function for each of the following cases:

(i) labor supplies are fixed;
(ii) labor supplies are variable; the government can observe wage rates;

(iii) labor supplies are variable; the government cannot observe wage rates and is constrained to use lump-sum taxes only;
(iv) labor supplies are variable; the government cannot observe wage rates and uses non-linear income taxes;
 (v) labor supplies are variable; the government cannot observe wage rates and uses linear income taxes only.

4. The utility of an agent depends upon his consumption of good x according to the function: $U(x) = \log x$. The agent's income I depends on his innate ability m (which is an unobservable) and his level of education e according to the formula: $I = me$. The cost (measured in units of the consumption good) of acquiring education is:

$$\phi(e) = e^{1+\gamma}/(1+\gamma), \gamma > 0.$$

In the absence of an income tax, the consumption behavior of an agent with ability m who has attained an education level e is given by: $c(m, e) = me - \phi(e)$.

Each agent chooses an optimal level of education. There exists a large number of agents whose abilities are represented by the following alternative distributions:

(i) $\Psi(m) = \delta \underline{m}^{\delta}/m^{1+\delta}, \delta > 1, \underline{m} > 0$
$\quad m > \underline{m}$
$\quad \delta\gamma - \gamma - 1 > 0;$
(ii) a Pareto distribution;
(iii) a lognormal distribution.

(a) In each case the government wants to redistribute income using the Rawlsian maximin principle. Suppose m is observable. What is the optimal income tax as a function of m.
(b) Now suppose that m is not observable but me $(= I)$ is. Suppose the tax function is given by the progressive linear tax:

$$T(I) = -\alpha + (1 - t_y)I$$

where α is the exemption limit and t_y is the marginal tax rate. Derive the values of α and t_y in each case.

5. Why do many economists favor the closing of tax loopholes? What are the advantages of a more comprehensive base for income taxation?

6. It is widely held that sales and excise taxes are regressive. Do you agree with this view? Explain. Is this true of a VAT as well?

7. Explain the welfare costs of a VAT.

8. A tax on income is fairer than a tax on consumption because income is a broader measure of the taxpayer's ability to pay. Do you agree? Why?

PROBLEM ON PRICING

1. Consider an economy with three goods: x,y,z. x is electricity use during the day, y is electricity use during the night, and z is 'all other goods' and also serves as the numeraire. The utility function of a representative consumer is given by the additive form: $U(x, y, z) = \alpha_1 \log x + \alpha_2 \log y + z$ with $\alpha_1, \alpha_2 > 0$. Let $\phi(I)$ be a uniform density function over the interval $[\underline{I}, \bar{I}]$ where $\underline{I}$ and $\bar{I}$ are the lower and upper bounds of income. Suppose that $\bar{I} - \underline{I} = 1$ (for convenience).

Suppose that the consumer must pay an initial installation charge of S and then a per unit price of p during the day and a unit price q during the night for electricity.

The optimization problem for the consumer with income I is written as:

$$\text{Max } \alpha_1 \log x + \alpha_2 \log y + z$$

subject to $px + qy + z = I - S$.

(a) Derive the individual demand functions for electricity and the aggregate functions $X(p)$ and $Y(q)$. Suppose that $\underline{I}$ is large enough so that all consumers will buy electricity.

Electricity production entails an investment in capacity of K for which the marginal cost is constant at β. K must satisfy: $K \geqslant X, K \geqslant Y$. Further the marginal maintenance cost is b for electricity use both during the day as well as the night. Assume that the utility producing electricity is bound by a zero profit constraint.

(b) Show that this constraint can be written as

$$S + (p - b - \beta)X(p) + (q - b)Y(q) = 0$$

when we assume that the day period is the peak period.

(c) Write the indirect utility function for a consumer with income I, i.e., $V(p, q, I - S)$. Derive the optimal pricing schedule (p^*, q^*, S^*) for a utilitarian planner constrained to balance the budget. Discuss the result.

PROBLEMS ON FISCAL FEDERALISM

1. Explain carefully the principles that should be taken into account when deciding whether a particular government function is best handled by the federal, state, or local governments. For each of the following economic activities explain which level of government should ideally carry it out: police protection; national intelligence service; fire protection; highway maintenance; college education; unemployment compensation; and welfare payments.

2. Suppose that a locality decides to increase property taxes and to use the revenue to increase spending on public schools. What effect would you expect this to have on the locational decisions of households?

3. Explain carefully the implications of tax exporting, tax competition and benefit spillovers on the budgets of local governments.

4. Suppose the federal government gives the following kind of matching grant for a project (costing $50 million) of the local government. The federal government covers 50 per cent of the cost of the project and promises only $10 million beyond that. What are the implications for the budget of the local government?

5. Is there an economic justification for both the federal as well as the state government providing subsidies to local governments for public schooling?

Bibliography

Aaron, H. (1966) 'The social insurance paradox', *Canadian Journal of Economics and Political Science*, vol. 32, pp. 371–374.

Aaron, H. (1975) *Who Pays the Property Tax?*, Washington DC: The Brookings Institution.

Aaron, H. (1976) *Inflation and the Income Tax*, Washington DC: The Brookings Institution.

Aaron, H. (1982) *Economic Effects of Social Security*, Washington DC: The Brookings Institution.

Aaron, H. and Boksin, M. (eds) (1980) *The Economics of Taxation*, Washington DC: The Brookings Institution.

Aaron, H. and McGuire, M. (1969) 'Efficiency and equity in the optimal supply of a public good', *Review of Economics and Statistics*, vol. 51, pp. 31–39.

Aaron, H. and McGuire, M. (1970) 'Public goods and income distribution', *Econometrica*, vol. 38, pp. 907–920.

Abe, K. (1992) 'Tariff reform in a small open economy with public production', *International Economic Review*, vol. 33, pp. 209–222.

Abel, A. (1978) *Investment and the Value of Capital*, PhD thesis, Department of Economics, MIT.

Abel, A. (1979) *Investment and the Value of Capital*, New York: Garland.

Abel, A. (1981) 'Taxation, inflation and the durability of capital', *Journal of Political Economy*, vol. 89, pp. 548–560.

Abel, A. (1986a) 'Capital accumulation and uncertain lifetimes with adverse selection', *Econometrica*, vol. 54, pp. 1079–1097.

Abel, A. (1986b) 'The failure of Ricardian equivalence under progressive taxation', *Journal of Public Economics*, vol. 30, pp. 117–128.

Abbott, M. and Ashenfelter, M. (1976) 'Labor supply, commodity demand and the allocation of time', *Review of Economic Studies*, vol. 43, pp. 389–412.

Agell, J. and Lundborg, P. (1992) 'Fair wages, involuntary unemployment and tax policies in the simple general equilibrium model', *Journal of Public Economics*, vol. 47, pp. 299–320.

Ahmad, E. and Stern, N. (1984) 'The theory of reform and Indian indirect taxes', *Journal of Public Economics*, vol. 25, pp. 259–298.

Ahsan, S. (1974) 'Progression and risk taking', *Oxford Economic Papers*, vol. 26, pp. 318–328.

Ahsan, S. (1976) 'Taxation in a two period temporal model of consumption and portfolio allocation', *Journal of Public Economics*, vol. 5, pp. 337–352.

Aizenman, J. (1985) 'Wage flexibility and openness', *Quarterly Journal of Economics*, pp. 539–550.

Aizenman, J. and Frenkel, J. (1985) 'Optimal wage indexation, foreign exchange intervention and monetary policy', *American Economic Review*, vol. 75 pp 402–42.

Akerlof, G. (1970) 'The market for lemons: quality uncertainty and the market mechanism', *Quarterly Journal of Economics*, vol. 84, pp. 488–500.

Akerlof, G. (1978) 'The economics of "Tagging"' *American Economic Review*, vol. 68, pp. 8–19.

Akerlof, G. and Yellen, J. (1987) 'Rational models of irrational behavior', *American Economic Review*, vol. 77, pp. 137–142.

Allan, C. (1971) *The Theory of Taxation*, London: Penguin Books.

Allen, F. (1982) 'Optimal linear taxation with general equilibrium effects on wages', *Journal of Public Economics*, vol. 17, pp. 135–143.

Allingham, M. and Sandmo, A. (1973) 'Income tax evasion: a theoretical analysis', *Journal of Public Economics*, vol. 1, pp. 323–338.

Alm, J. and Beck, W. (1990) 'Tax amenities and tax revenues', *Public Finance Quarterly*, vol. 18, pp. 433–454.

Altman, E. (1984) 'A further investigation of the bankruptcy cost question', *Journal of Finance*, vol. 39, pp. 1067–1090.

Alvazian, V. and Turnbull, S. (1987) 'Taxation and capital structure: a selected review', in J. M. Mintz and D. Purvis (eds) *Taxation and Business Activity*, Kingston: John Deutsch Institute, Department of Economics, Queen's University.

Anderson, P. (1977) 'Tax evasion and labor supply', *Scandinavian Journal of Economics*, vol. 79, pp. 375–383.

Andreoni, J. (1992) 'IRS as loan shark: tax compliance with borrowing constraints', *Journal of Public Economics*, vol. 49, pp. 35–46.

Aoki, M. (1971) 'Marshallian external economies and optimal tax-subsidy literature', *Econometrica*, vol. 39, pp. 35–53.

Archibald, G. and Donaldson, D. (1976) 'Non-paternalism and the basic theorems of welfare economics', *Canadian Journal of Economics*, vol. 84, pp. 492–507.

Arnott, R. and Grieson, R. (1981) 'Optimal fiscal policy for a state or local government', *Journal of Urban Economics*, vol. 9, pp. 210–224.

Arnott, R. and Stiglitz, J. (1986) 'Moral hazard and optimal commodity taxation', *Journal of Public Economics*, vol. 29, pp. 1–24.

Arrow, K. (1951) 'An extension of the basic theorems of welfare economics', in J. Neyman (ed.) *Proceedings of the Second Berkeley Symposium on Mathematical Statistics and Probability*, Berkeley: University of California Press.

Arrow, K. (1963a) *Social Choice and Individual Values*, 2nd edn, New York: John Wiley.

Arrow, K. (1963b) 'The role of securities in the optimal allocation of risk bearing', *Review of Economic Studies*, vol. 31, pp. 91–96.

Arrow, K. (1965) *Aspects of the Theory of Risk Bearing*, Helsinki: Yrjo Jahnssonin Saatio.

Arrow, K. (1970) *Essays in the Theory of Risk Bearing*, Amsterdam: North Holland.

Arrow, K. (1977) 'The property rights doctrine', Harvard University Economics Department Discussion Paper.

Arrow, K. (1973) 'Some ordinalist-utilitarian notes on Rawls' theory of justice' *Journal of Philosophy*, vol. 70, pp. 245–263.

Arrow, K. and Hahn, F. (1971) *General Competitive Analysis*, Edinburgh: Oliver and Boyd.

Arrow, K. and Lind, R. (1970) 'Uncertainty and the evaluation of public investment decisions', *American Economic Review*, vol. 60, pp. 364–378.

Atkinson, A. (1970) 'On the measurement of inequality', *Journal of Economic Theory*, vol. 2., pp. 244–263.

Atkinson, A. (1973) 'How progressive should income tax be?', in M. Parkin and A. Nobay (eds) *Essays in Modern Economics*, London: Longman.

Atkinson, A. (1979) 'Horizontal equity and the distribution of the tax burden', in H. Aaron and M. Boskin (eds) *The Economics of Taxation*, Washington DC: The Brookings Institution.

Atkinson, A. (1987) 'On the measurement of poverty', *Econometrica*, vol. 55, pp. 749–764.

Atkinson, A. (1971) 'Capital taxes, the redistribution of wealth and individual savings', *Review of Economic Studies*, vol. 38, pp. 209–228.

Atkinson, A. and Harrison, A. (1978) *The Distribution of Personal Wealth in Britain*, Cambridge: Cambridge University Press.

Atkinson, A. and Sandmo, A. (1980) 'Welfare implications of taxation of savings', *Economic Journal*, vol. 90, pp. 529–549.

Atkinson, A. and Stern, N. (1976) 'Pigou, taxation and public goods', *Review of Economic Studies*, vol. 41, pp. 119–128.

Atkinson, A. and Stern, N. (1980) 'On the switch from direct to indirect taxation', *Journal of Public Economics*, vol. 14, pp. 195–224.

Atkinson, A. and Stiglitz, J. (1972) 'The structure of indirect taxes and economic efficiency', *Journal of Public Economics*, vol. 1, pp. 97–119.

Atkinson, A. and Stiglitz, J. (1976) 'The design of tax structure: direct vs. indirect taxes', *Journal of Public Economics*, vol. 6, pp. 55–75.

Atkinson, A. and Stiglitz, J. (1980) *Lectures on Public Economics*, London: McGraw Hill.

Auerbach, A. (1979a) 'Wealth maximization and the cost of capital', *Quarterly Journal of Economics*, vol. 93, pp. 433–446.

Auerbach, A. (1979b) 'Inflation and the choice of asset life', *Journal of Political Economy*, vol. 87, pp.621–638.

Auerbach, A. (1983) 'Corporate taxation in the United States', *Brookings Papers on Economic Activity*, vol. 2, pp. 451–505.

Auerbach, A. (1987) 'The theory of excess burden and optimal taxation', in A. Auerbach and M. Feldstein (eds) *Handbook of Public Economics*, Amsterdam: North Holland, pp. 61–128.

Auerbach, A. and Hines, J. (1987) 'Anticipated tax changes and the timing of investment', in M. Feldstein (ed.) *The Effects of Taxation on Capital Accumulation*, Chicago: University of Chicago Press for the NBER.

Auerbach, A, and King, D. (1983) 'Taxation, portfolio choice and debt-Equity ratios: a general equilibrium approach', *Quarterly Journal of Economics*, vol. 47, pp. 587–609.

Auerbach, A. and King, M. (1982) 'Corporate financial policy with personal and institutional investors', *Journal of Public Economics*, vol. 17, pp. 259–285.

Auerbach, A., Kotlikoff, L. and Skinner, J. (1983) 'The efficiency gains from dynamic tax reform', *International Economic Review*, vol. 24, pp. 81–100.

Auerbach, A. and Kotlikoff, L. (1987) *Dynamic Fiscal Policy*, Cambridge: Cambridge University Press.

Aumann, R. (1964) 'Markets with a continuum of traders', *Econometrica*, vol. 34, pp. 1–17.

Aumann, R. and Shapley, L. (1974) *Values of Non-atomic Games*, Princeton NJ: Princeton University Press.

Averch, H. and Johnson, L. (1962) 'Behavior of the firm under regulatory constraint', *American Economic Review*, vol. 52, pp. 1052–1069.

Axelrod, R. (1981) 'The emergence of cooperation among egoists', *American Political Science Review*, vol. 75, pp. 306–318.

Bailey, E. (1973) *Economic Theory of Regulatory Constraint*, Lexington MA: Lexington Books.

Balasko, Y. and Shell, K. (1980) 'The overlapping generations model I: the case of pure exchange without money', *Journal of Economic Theory*, vol. 23, pp. 281–306.

Balasko, Y. and Shell, K. (1981) 'The overlapping generations model II: the case of pure exchange with money', *Journal of Economic Theory*, vol. 24, pp. 112–142.

Balcer, Y. (1980) 'Taxation of externalities: direct vs. indirect', *Journal of Public Economics*, vol. 13, pp. 121–129.

Baldry, J. (1979) 'Tax evasion and labor supply', *Economics Letters*, vol. 3, pp. 53–56.

Ball, L. and Mankiw, G. (1993) 'Relative price changes as aggregate supply shocks', Federal Reserve Bank of Philadelphia Working Paper.

Ballard, C. (1990) 'Marginal welfare cost calculations: differential analysis vs. balanced budget analysis', *Journal of Public Economics*, vol. 41, pp. 263–276.

Ballard, C. and Fullerton, D. (1992) 'Distortionary taxes and the provision of public goods', *Journal of Economic Perspectives*, vol. 6, pp. 117–131.

Ballard, C., Shoven, J. and Whalley, J. (1985) 'The total welfare cost of the US tax system: a general equilibrium approach', *National Tax Journal*, vol. 38, pp. 125–140.

Ballentine, J. (1980) *Equity, Efficiency and the US Corporation Income Tax*, Washington DC: American Enterprise Institute.

Ballentine, J. and Eris, I. (1975) 'On the general equilibrium analysis of tax incidence', *Journal of Political Economy*, vol. 83, pp. 633–644.

Barlow, R. and Sparks, G. (1964) 'A note on progression and leisure', *American Economic Review*, vol. 54, pp. 372–377.

Barnett, R. and Topham, N. (1980) 'A critique of equalizing grants to local governments', *Scottish Journal of Political Economy*, vol. 27, pp. 235–249.

Baron, D. and Myerson, R. (1982) 'Regulating a monopoly with unknown costs', *Econometrica*, vol. 50, pp. 911–930.

Barro, R. (1974) 'Are government bonds net wealth?', *Journal of Political Economy*, vol. 82, pp. 1095–1117.

Barro, R. (1990) 'Government spending in a simple model of endogenous growth', *Journal of Political Economy*, vol. 98, pp. 103–125.

Barro, R. and Gordon, D. (1983) 'Rules, discretion and reputation in a monetary economy', *Journal of Monetary Economics*, vol. 12, pp. 101–121.

Barro, R. and MacDonald, G. (1979) 'Social security and consumer spending in an international cross-section', *Journal of Public Economics*, vol. 11, pp. 275–290.

Barro, R. and Sala-I-Martin, X. (1992) 'Public finance in models of endogenous growth', *Review of Economic Studies*, vol. 59, pp. 645–661.

Bartholdy, A.G. Fisher and Mintz, J. (1985) 'An empirical study of the impact of corporate taxation on the debt policy of Canadian firms', Discussion Paper, Department of Economics, Queen's University, Canada

Bates, R. (ed.) (1988) *Toward a Political Economy of Development*, Berkeley: University of California Press.

Batra, R. (1975) 'A general equilibrium model of the incidence of the corporation income tax under uncertainty', *Journal of Public Economics*, vol. 8, pp. 101–114.

Batra, R. and Beladi, H. (1993) 'Regulation and the theory of tax incidence', *Public Finance*, vol. 48, pp. 329–349.

Baumol, W. (1964) 'External economies and the second order conditions', *American Economic Review*, vol. 54, pp. 358–371.

Baumol, W. (1965) *Welfare Economics and the Theory of the State*, Cambridge MA: Harvard University Press.

Baumol, W. (1977) 'On the proper cost tests for natural monopoly in a multiproduct industry', *American Economic Review*, vol. 67, pp. 809–822.

Baumol, W. (1972) 'On taxation and the control of externalites', *American Economic Review*, vol. 62, pp. 307–322.

Baumol, W. and Bradford, D. (1970) 'Optimal departures from marginal cost pricing', *American Economic Review*, vol. 60, pp. 265–283.

Baumol, W. and Malkiel, B. (1967) 'The firm's optimal debt-equity combination and the cost of capital', *Quarterly Journal of Economics*, vol. 18, pp. 547–578.

Baumol, W. and Oates, W. (1975) *The Theory of Environmental Policy*, Engelwood Cliffs NJ: Prentice Hall.

Baumol, W. and Willig, R. (1977) 'Weak invisible hand theorems on pricing and entry in a multiproduct natural monopoly', *American Economic Review*, vol. 67, pp. 350–365.

Baumol, W., Panzar, C. and Willig, R. (1982) *Contestable Markets and the Theory of Industrial Structure*, New York: Harcourt, Brace and Jovanovich.

Beato, P. (1982) 'The existence of marginal cost pricing equilibria with increasing returns', *Quarterly Journal of Economics*, vol. 97, pp. 669–688.

Becker, G. (1983) 'A theory of competition among pressure groups for political influence', *Quarterly Journal of Economics*, vol. 98, pp. 371–400.

Bennett, R. (1982) *Central Grants to Local Governments: The Political and Economic Impact of the Rate Support Grant in England and Wales*, Cambridge: Cambridge University Press.

Bennett, E. and Conn, D. (1976) 'The group incentive properties of mechanisms for the provision of public goods', *Public Choice*, vol. 29, pp. 95–102.

Bennett, F. (1993) *Social Insurance: Reform or Abolition*, London: Institute for Policy Research, The Commission on Social Justice.

Bennett, R. and Johnson, M. (1980) 'Tax reduction without sacrifice: private sector production of public services', *Public Finance Quarterly*, vol. 8, pp. 363–396.

Bentham, J. (1791) *Principles of Morals and Legislation*, London: Doubleday.

Berglas, E. (1976) 'On the theory of clubs', *American Economic Review Papers and Proceedings*, vol. 66, pp. 116–121.

Bergson, A. (1938) 'A reformulation of certain aspects of welfare economics', *Quarterly Journal of Economics*, vol. 52, pp. 314–344.

Bergson, A. (1976) 'Social choice and welfare economics under representative government', *Journal of Public Economics*, vol. 6, pp. 171–190.

Bergstrom, T. (1973) 'A note on efficient taxation', *Journal of Political Economy*, vol. 81, pp. 187–191.

Bergstrom, T. (1979) 'Why does majority rule supply public goods efficiency?', *Scandinavian Journal of Economics*, vol. 81, pp. 216–226.

Bergstrom, T., Blume, L. and Varian, H. (1986) 'On the private provision of public goods', *Journal of Public Economics*, vol. 29, pp. 25–49.

Bergstrom, T. and Cornes, R. (1983) 'Independence of allocative efficiency from distribution in the theory of public goods', *Econometrica*, vol. 51, pp. 1753–1765.

Bergstrom, T. and Goodman, R. (1973) 'Private demands for public goods', *American Economic Review*, vol. 63, pp. 280–296.

Bernanke, B. (1983) 'The determinants of investment: another look', *American Economic Review*, vol. 73, pp. 71–75.

Bernheim, D. (1987) 'Ricardian equivalence: an evaluation of theory and evidence', *NBER Macroeconomics Annual*, vol. 2, pp. 263–303.

Besanko, D. and Sappington, D. (1987) *Designing Regulatory Policy with Limited Information*, London: Harwood Academic Press.

Bewley, T. (1981) 'A critique of Tiebout's theory of local public expenditures', *Econometrica*, vol. 49, pp. 713–740.

Bhagwati, J. (1980) 'Lobbying and welfare', *Journal of Public Economics*, vol. 14, pp. 355–364.

Bhagwati, J. (1982) 'Directly unproductive, profit-seeking activities', *Journal of Political Economy*, vol. 90, pp. 988–1002.

Bhatia, K. (1979) 'Corporate taxation, retained earnings, and capital formation', *Journal of Public Economics*, vol. 11, pp. 123–134.

Bhatia, K. (1986) 'Taxes, intermediate goods, and relative prices: the case of variable coefficients', *Journal of Public Economics*, vol. 19, pp. 197–213.

Billera, A. and Heath, D. (1982) 'A unique procedure for allocating common costs for a production process', *Journal of Accounting Research*, vol. 19, pp. 185–196.

Bird, R. (1976) *Charging for Public Services: A New Look at an Old Idea*, Toronto: Canadian Tax Foundation.

Bird, R. and Head, J. (eds) (1972) *Modern Fiscal Issues: Essays in Honor of Carl Shoup*, Toronto: University of Toronto Press.

Birnbaum, J. and Murray, A. (1988) *Showdown at Gucci Gulch*, New York: Random House.

Biswal, B. (1996) *Optimal Provision of Education in Developing Countries*, Delhi: Commonwealth Publishers.

Black, D. (1958) *The Theory of Committees and Elections*, Cambridge: Cambridge University Press.

Blackorby, C. and Donaldson, D. (1978) 'Measures of inequality and their meaning in terms of social welfare', *Journal of Economic Theory*, vol. 18, pp. 59–80.

Blair, D. and Pollak, R. (1982) 'Acyclic collective choice rules', *Econometrica*, vol. 50, pp. 931–943.

Blanchard, O. (1984) 'Current and anticipated deficits, interest rates and economic activity', *European Economic Review*, vol. 25, pp. 7–27.

Blanchard, O. (1985) 'Debt, deficits and finite horizons', *Journal of Political Economy*, vol. 93, pp. 223–247.

Blanchard, O. (1986) 'Hysteresis and the European unemployment problem', *NBER Macroeconomics Annual 1986*, Cambridge MA: MIT Press.

Blanchard, O. and Fischer, S. (1991) *Lectures on Macroeconomics*, Cambridge MA and London: MIT Press.

Blinder, A. (1975) 'Distribution effects and the aggregate consumption function', *Journal of Political Economy*, vol. 83, pp. 447–475.

Blitzer, C., Dasgupta, P. and Stiglitz, J. (1981) 'Project appraisal and foreign exchange constraint', *Economic Journal*, vol. 91, pp. 58–74.

Blomquist, N. (1983) 'The effect of income taxation on the labor supply of married men in Sweden', *Journal of Public Economics*, vol. 22, pp. 169–197.

Blundell, R. (1990) 'Consumer behaviour: theory and empirical evidence', *Economic Journal*, vol. 100, pp. 1–50.

Blundell, R. (1992) 'Labor supply and taxation: a survey', *Fiscal Studies*, vol. 13, pp. 15–40.

Blundell, R. and Meghir, C. (1986) 'Selection criteria for a micro economic model of labor supply', *Journal of Applied Econometrics*, vol. 1, pp. 55–81.

Blundell, R. and Ray, R. (1984) 'Testing for linear Engel curves and additive separable preferences using a new flexible demand system', *Economic Journal*, vol. 94, pp. 800–811.

Blundell, R. and Walker, I. (1982) 'Modeling the joint determination of household labor supplies and commodity demands', *Economic Journal*, vol. 92, pp. 351–364.

Blundell, R. and Walker, I. (1986) 'A life cycle consistent empirical model of family labor supply using cross section data', *Review of Economic Studies*, vol. 53, pp. 239–558.

Boadway, R. (1974) 'The welfare foundations of cost-benefit analysis', *Economic Journal*, vol. 84, pp. 926–939.

Boadway, R. (1976) 'Integrating equity and efficiency in applied welfare economics', *Quarterly Journal of Economics*, vol. 90, pp. 541–556.

Boadway, R. (1978) 'Public investment decision rules in a neoclassical growing economy', *International Economic Review*, vol. 19, pp. 265–287.

Boadway, R. (1979) *Public Sector Economics*, Boston: Winthrop.

Boadway, R. (1982) 'Equalization in a federal state', mimeo, Queen's University, Canada.

Boadway, R. and Bruce, N. (1979) 'Depreciation and interest deductions and the effect of corporation income tax on investment', *Journal of Public Economics*, vol. 11, pp. 93–105.

Boadway, R. and Bruce, N. (1984) *Welfare Economics*, Oxford: Basil Blackwell.

Boadway, R. and Wildasin, D. (1984) *Public Sector Economics*, Boston: Little Brown.

Boadway, R. and Bruce, N. (1992) 'Problems with integrating corporate and personal income taxes in an open economy', *Journal of Public Economics*, vol. 48, pp. 39–66.

Boadway, R., Bruce, N., McKenzie, K. and Mintz, J. (1982) 'Marginal effective tax Rates for capital in the Canadian mining industry', *Canadian Journal of Economics*, vol. 20, pp. 1–16.

Boadway, R., Bruce, N. and Mintz, J. (1982) 'Corporate taxation and the cost of holding inventories', *Canadian Journal of Economics*, vol. 15, pp. 278–293.

Boadway, R., Bruce, N. and Mintz, J. (1986) *The Taxation of Capital Income in Canada: Theory and Policy*, Toronto: Canadian Tax Foundation.

Boadway, R. and Harris, R. (1977) 'A characterization of piecemeal second best policy', *Journal of Public Economics*, vol. 8, pp. 169–190.

Boadway, R., Horiba, I. and Jha, R. (1996) 'Financing and the optimal provision of public expenditure with decentralized agencies', Working Paper 472, Department of Economics, University of Warwick.

Boadway, R. and Keen, M. (1993) 'Public goods, self-selection and optimal income taxation', *International Economic Review*, vol. 34, pp. 463–478.

Boadway, R., Marchand, M. and Pestieau, P. (1994) 'Toward a theory of the direct-indirect tax mix', *Journal of Public Economics*, vol. 55, pp. 271–288.

Boadway, R. and Wildasin, D. (1989) 'A median voter model of social security', *International Economic Review*, vol. 30, pp. 307–328.

Boiteux, M. (1956) 'Sur la gestion des monopoles publics a l'equilibre budgetaire, *Econometrica*, vol. 24, pp. 22–40.

Boiteux, M. (1971) (English translation) 'On the management of public monopolies subject to a budget constraint', *Journal of Economic Theory*, vol. 3, pp. 219–240.

Borcherding, T. (1977) 'The sources of growth in public expenditures in the United States 1902–1970', in T. Borcherding (ed.) *Budgets and Bureaucrats: The Sources of Government Growth*, Durham NC: Duke University Press.

Borcherding, T. and Deacon, R. (1972) 'The demand for the services of non-federal governments', *American Economic Review*, vol. 62, pp. 891–901.

Border, K. and Sobel, J. (1987) 'Samurai accountant: a theory of audit and plunder', *Review of Economic Studies*, vol. 54, pp. 525–540.

Bos, D. (1986) *Public Sector Economics*, Amsterdam: North Holland.

Bos, D. (1987) 'Public sector pricing', in A. Auerbach and M. Feldstein (eds) *Handbook of Public Economics*, Amsterdam: North Holland, pp. 129–212.

Boskin, M. (1967) 'The negative income tax and the supply of work effort', *National Tax Journal*, vol. 20, pp. 353–367.

Boskin, M. (1973a) 'Local government tax and product competition and the optimal provision of public goods', *Journal of Political Economy*, vol. 81, pp. 203–210.

Boskin, M. (1973b) 'The economics of labor supply', in G. Cain and H. Watts (eds) *Income Maintenance and Labor Supply*, Chicago: Rand McNally.

Boskin, M. (1975) 'Efficiency aspects of differential tax treatment of of market and household economic activity', *Journal of Public Economics*, vol. 4, pp. 1–25.

Boskin, M. (1977) 'Social security and retirement decisions', *Economic Inquiry*, vol. 15, pp. 1–25.

Boskin, M. (1978) 'Taxation, saving and the rate of interest', *Journal of Political Economy*, vol. 86, pp. S3–S27.

Boskin, M. (1988) 'Tax policy and economic growth: lessons from the 1980s', *Journal of Economic Perspectives*, vol. 2, pp. 71–97.

Boskin, M. and Lau, L. (1978) 'Taxation, social security and aggregate factor supply in the U.S.', mimeo, Stanford University.

Boskin, M. and Sheshinski, E. (1978) 'Optimal income redistribution when individual welfare depends on relative income', *Quarterly Journal of Economics*, vol. 92, pp. 589–602.

Bosworth, B. (1984) *Tax Incentives and Economic Growth*, Washington DC: The Brookings Institution.

Bovenberg, L. (1986) 'Capital income taxation in growing open economies', *Journal of Public Economics*, vol. 31, pp. 347–377.

Bradford, D. and Fullerton, D. (1981) 'Pitfalls in the construction and use of effective tax rates', in C. R. Hulten (ed) *Depreciation, Inflation, and the Taxation of Income from Capital*, Washington DC: The Urban Institute.

Bradford, D. and Oates, W. (1971a) 'Towards a predictive theory of intergovernmental grants', *American Economic Review Papers and Proceedings*, vol. 61, pp. 440–448.

Bradford, D. and Oates, W. (1971b) 'The analysis of revenue sharing in a new approach to collective fiscal decisions', *Quarterly Journal of Economics*, vol. 85, pp. 416–439.

Braeutigam, R. (1979) 'Optimal pricing with intermodal competition', *American Economic Review*, vol. 69, pp. 38–49.

Braeutigam, R. (1980) 'An analysis of the fully distributed cost pricing in regulated industries', *Bell Journal of Economics*, vol. 11, pp. 182–196.

Break, G. (1967) *Intergovernmental Fiscal Problems in the United States*, Washington DC: The Brookings Institution.

Break, G. (1974) 'Relationship between the corporate and individual income taxes', *National Tax Journal*, vol. 28, pp. 341–350.

Break, G. (1980) *Financing Government in a Federal System I*, Washington DC: The Brookings Institution.

Break, G. (1984) *Financing Government in a Federal System II*, Washington DC: The Brookings Institution.

Brems, H. (1983) *Fiscal Theory*, Lexington MA: Lexington Books.

Brennan, H. and Buchanan, J. (1979) 'The logic of tax limits: alternative constitutional constraints on the power to tax', *National Tax Journal*, vol. 32, pp. 11–22.

Breton, A. (1977) 'The theory of local government finance and the debt regulation of local governments', *Public Finance*, vol. 32, pp. 16–28.

Breton, A. and Scott, A. (1978) *The Economic Constitution of Federal States*, Canberra: Australian National University Press.

Breton, A. and Scott, A. (1980) *The Design of Federations*, Montreal: Institute for Research on Public Policy.

Breyer, F. (1989) 'On the intergenerational Pareto efficiency of a pay-as-you-go financed pension system', *Journal of Institutional and Theoretical Economics*, vol. 145, pp. 643–658.

Breyer, F. and Straub, M. (1993) 'Welfare effects of unfunded pension systems when labor supply is endogenous', *Journal of Public Economics*, vol. 50, pp. 77–91.

Brown, D. and Heal, G. (1980) 'Two part tariffs, marginal cost pricing and increasing returns in a general equilibrium framework', *Journal of Public Economics*, vol. 13, pp. 25–49.

Brown, D. and Heal, G. (1983) 'The optimality of regulated pricing: a general equilibrium analysis', in Aliprantis, Burkinshaw and Rothman (eds) *Lecture Notes in Economics and Mathematical Systems*, vol. 244, Berlin: Springer Verlag.

Brown, C., Levin, E., Rosa, E., Ruffell, P. and Ulph, D. (1986) 'Payment system demand constraints and their implications for research into labor supply', in R. Blundell and L. Walker (eds) *Unemployment, Search, and Labor Supply*, Cambridge: Cambridge University Press.

Brown, S. and Sibley, D. (1986) *The Theory of Public Utility Pricing*, Cambridge: Cambridge University Press.

Brown-Heal, G. (1979) 'Equity, efficiency and increasing returns', *Review of Economic Studies*, vol. 46, pp. 571–585.

Browning, E. (1976) 'The marginal cost of public funds', *Journal of Political Economy*, vol. 84, pp. 283–298.

Browning, E. (1987) 'Marginal welfare cost of taxation', *American Economic Review*, vol. 77, pp. 11–22.

Browning, E. (1993) 'Subsidies financed with distorting taxes', *National Tax Journal*, vol. 46.

Browning, M. (1982) 'Savings and pensions: some U. K. evidence', *Economic Journal*, vol. 92, pp. 954–963.

Bruce, N. (1981) 'Some macroeconomic implications of income tax indexation', *Journal of Monetary Economics*, vol. 8, pp. 271–275.

Bruce, N. (1985) 'Some macroeconomic effects of income tax indexation', *Journal of Monetary Economics*, vol. 8, pp. 271–275.

Bruce, N. and Harris, R. (1982) 'Cost-benefit criteria and the compensation principle in evaluating small projects', *Journal of Political Economy*, vol. 90, pp. 755–776.

Bruce, N. and Purvis, D. (1984) 'The structure of goods and factor markets in open economy macro models', in R. Jones and P. Kenen (eds) *Handbook of International Economics*, Amsterdam: North Holland.

Brueckner, J. and Lee, K. (1991) 'Economics of scope and multiproduct clubs', *Public Finance Quarterly*, vol. 19, pp. 193–208.

Buchanan, J. (1950) 'Federalism and fiscal equity', *American Economic Review*, vol. 40, pp. 583–599.

Buchanan, J. (1963) 'The economics of earmarked taxes', *Journal of Political Economy*, vol. 71, pp. 457–469.

Buchanan, J. (1965) 'An economic theory of clubs', *Economica*, vol. 32, pp. 1–14.

Buchanan, J. (1967) *Public Finances in Democratic Process*, Chapel Hill, NC: University of North Carolina Press.

Buchanan, J. (1968) *The Demand and Supply of Public Goods*, Shokie, Ill: Rand McNally.

Buchanan, J. (1969) 'External diseconomies, corrective taxes and market structure', *American Economic Review*, vol. 59, pp. 174–177.

Buchanan, J. and Goetz, C. (1972) 'Efficiency limits of federal mobility: an assessment of the Tiebout hypothesis', *Journal of Public Economics*, vol. 1, pp. 25–43.

Buchanan, J. and Tullock, G. (1962) *The Calculus of Consent*, Ann Arbor, Michigan: University of Michigan Press.

Buchanan. J. and Wagner, R. (1970) 'An efficient basis for federal fiscal equalization', in J. Margolis (ed.) *Analysis of Public Output*, New York: Columbia University Press/NBER.

Buchanan, J. (1975) *The Limits of Liberty*, Chicago: University of Chicago Press.

Buchanan, J. (1976a) 'Barro and the Ricardian equivalence theorem', *Journal of Political Economy*, vol. 84, pp. 337–342.

Buchanan, J. (1976b) 'A Hobbesian interpretation of the Rawlsian difference principle', *Kyklos*, vol. 29, pp. 5–25.

Buchanan, J. (ed.) (1980) *Toward a Theory of the Rent Seeking Society*, College Station: Texas A&M University Press.

Buiter, W. (1988) 'Death, birth, productivity growth and debt neutrality', *Economic Journal*, vol. 89, pp. 279–293.

Bulow, J and Summers, L. (1984) 'The taxation of risky assets', *Journal of Political Economy*, vol. 92, pp. 20–39.

Burmeister, E. (1971) 'The degree of joint production,' *International Economic Review*, vol. 12, pp. 99–105.

Burmeister, E. and Dobell, R. (1970) *Mathematical Theories of Economic Growth*, New York: Macmillan

Burtless, G. and Hausman, J. (1978) 'The effect of taxation on the labor supply: evaluating the gory negative income tax experiment', *Journal of Political Economy*, vol. 86, pp. 1103–1130.

Calvo, G. (1978) 'On the time consistency of optimal policy in a model of monetary policy', *Econometrica*, vol. 46, pp. 1411–1428.

Cass, D. (1972) 'On capital overaccumulation in the aggregate, neoclassical model of economic growth', *Journal of Economic Theory*, vol. 4, pp. 200–223.

Cebula, R. (1979) 'A survey of the literature on the migration impact of state and local governments', *Public Finance*, vol. 34, pp. 69–84.

Chamley, C. (1981) 'The welfare cost of capital income taxation in a growing economy', *Journal of Political Economy*, vol. 89, pp. 468–496.

Chamley, C. (1986) 'Optimal taxation of capital income in a general equilibrium model with infinite lives', *Econometrica*, vol. 54, pp. 607–622.

Chari, V., Christiano, L. and Kehoe, P. (1994) 'Optimal fiscal policy in a business cycle model', *Journal of Political Economy*, vol. 102, pp. 617–652.

Chari, V., Kehoe, P. and Prescott, E. (1989) 'Time consistency and policy', in R. Barro (ed.) *Modern Business Cycle Theory*, Oxford: Basil Blackwell.

Chesher, A. and Irish, M. (1987) 'Residual analysis in the grouped and censored normal linear model', *Journal of Econometrics*, vol. 34, pp. 33–61.

Chipman, J. and Moore, J. (1980) 'Compensating variation, consumer surplus and welfare', *American Economic Review*, vol. 70, pp. 933–949.

Christensen, L. and Lau, L. (1973) 'Transcendental logarithmic utility functions', *American Economic Review*, vol. 65, pp. 367–380.

Christiansen, V. (1980) 'Two comments on tax evasion', *Journal of Public Economics*, vol. 13, pp. 389–393.

Clotfelter, C (1983) 'Tax evasion and tax rates: an analysis of individual returns', *Review of Economics and Statistics*, vol. 65, pp. 363–373.

Clotfelter, C. and Cook, P. (1990) 'On the economics of state lotteries', *Journal of Economic Perspectives*, vol. 4, pp. 105–119.

Crossen, S. (1992) 'Misunderstanding VAT: a comment', *Australian Tax Forum*, vol. 9, pp. 271–276.

Coase, R. (1960) 'The problem of social cost', *Journal of Law and Economics*, vol. 3, pp. 1–44.

Cohen, L. (1979) 'Cyclical sets in multidimensional voting models', *Journal of Economic Theory*, vol. 20, pp. 1–12.

Cooter, R. (1982) 'The cost of Coase', *Journal of Legal Studies*, vol. 11, pp. 1–33.

Corlett, W. and Hague, D. (1953) 'Complementarity and the excess burden of taxation', *Review of Economic Studies*, vol. 21, pp. 21–30.

Cornes, R. and Sandler, T. (1984) 'The theory of public goods: non-Nash behavior', *Journal of Public Economics*, vol. 23, pp. 381–390.

Cornes, R. and Sandler, T. (1986) *The Theory of Externalities, Public Goods and Club Goods*, New York: Cambridge University Press.

Courant, P. and Rubinfeld, D. (1981) 'On the welfare effects of tax limitation', *Journal of Public Economics*, vol. 16, pp. 289–316.

Cowell, F. (1981) 'Taxation and labor supply with risk activities', *Economica*, vol. 48, pp. 365–379.

Cowell, F. (1985) 'Tax evasion with labor income', *Journal of Public Economics*, vol. 26, pp. 19–34.

Cowell, F. (1989) *Cheating the Government: The Economics of Evasion*, Cambridge MA: MIT Press.

Cowell, F. and Gordon, J. (1988) 'Unwillingness to pay: tax evasion and public goods provision', *Journal of Public Economics*, vol. 36, pp. 305–321.

Crane, S. and Nourzad, F. (1985) 'Time value of money and income tax evasion under risk-averse behavior', *Public Finance*, vol. 40, pp. 381–394.

Crane, S. and Nourzad, F. (1986) 'Inflation and tax evasion: an empirical analysis', *Review of Economics and Statistics*, vol. 68, pp. 217–223.

Crane, S. and Nourzad, F. (1987) 'On the treatment of income tax rates in empirical analysis of tax evasion', *Kyklos*, vol. 40, pp. 338–348.

Cremer, H. and Gahvari, F. (1995) 'Uncertainty, optimal taxation and the direct versus indirect tax controversy', *Economic Journal*, vol. 105, pp. 1165–1179.

Cross, R. and Shaw, G. (1982) 'On the economics of tax aversion', *Public Finance*, vol. 37, pp. 36–47.

Dalton, H. (1920) 'The measurement of the inequality of income', *Economic Journal*, vol. 30(119), pp. 348–361.

Daly, G. (1969) 'The burden of the debt and future generations in local finance', *Southern Economic Journal*, vol. 36, pp. 44–51.

Dardanoni, V. (1988) 'Optimal choices under uncertainty: the case of two-argument utility functions', *Economic Journal*, vol. 98, pp. 429–450.

Dasgupta, P., Marglin, S. and Sen, A. (1972) *Guidelines for Project Evaluation*, New York: United Nations.

Dasgupta, P., Sen, A. and Starrett, D. (1973) 'Notes on the measurement of inequality', *Journal of Economic Theory*, vol. 6, pp. 180–187.

Dasgupta, P. and Stiglitz, J. (1974) 'Benefit cost analysis and trade policies', *Journal of Political Economy*, vol. 82, pp. 1–33.

Davies, J., Whalley, J. and Hamilton, B. (1989) 'Capital income taxation in a two commodity life-cycle model: the role of factor intensity and asset capitalization effects', *Journal of Public Economics*, vol. 39, pp. 101–126.

Davis, O. and Whinston, A. (1965) 'Welfare economics and the theory of the second best', *Review of Economic Studies*, vol. 32, pp. 1–14.

Deacon, R. and Shapiro, P. (1975) 'Private preferences for public goods revealed through voting on references', *American Economic Review*, vol. 65, pp. 943–955.

De Angelo, H. and Masulis, R. (1980) 'Leverage and dividend irrelevance under corporate and personal taxation', *Journal of Finance*, vol. 35, pp. 453–464.

Deaton, A. (1974) 'A reconsideration of the empirical implications of additive preferences', *Economic Journal*, vol. 84, pp. 338–345.

Deaton, A. and Irish, M. (1984) 'Statistical models for zero expenditures in household budgets', *Journal of Public Economics*, vol. 23, pp. 59–80.

Deaton, A. and Muellbauer, J. (1980) *Economics and Consumer Behavior*, Cambridge: Cambridge University Press.

Debreu, G. (1959) *The Theory of Value*, New Haven: Yale University, Cowles Commission for Research in Economics.

Demsetz, H. (1970) 'The private provision of public goods', *Journal of Law and Economics*, vol. 13, pp. 292–306.

Diamond, P. (1965) 'National debt in a neoclassical growth model', *American Economic Review*, vol. 55, pp. 1126–1150.

Diamond, P. (1967) 'The role of the stock market in a general equilibrium model with technological uncertainty', *American Economic Review*, vol. 57, pp. 759–776.

Diamond, P. (1973) 'Taxation and public production in a growth setting', in J. Mirrlees and N. Stern (eds) *Models of Economic Growth*, London: Macmillan.

Diamond, P. (1975) 'A many-person Ramsey tax rule', *Journal of Public Economics*, vol. 4, pp. 227–244.

Diamond, P. and McFadden, D. (1974) 'Some uses of the expenditure functions in public finance', *Journal of Public Economics*, vol. 3, pp. 3–21.

Diamond, P. and Mirrlees, J. (1971) 'Optimal taxation and public production I–II', *American Economic Review*, vol. 61, pp. 8–27, 261–278.

Diamond, P. and Mirrlees, J. (1976) 'Private constant returns and public shadow prices', *Review of Economic Studies*, vol. 43, pp. 41–47.

Dicks-Mireaux, L. and King, M. (1984) 'Pension wealth and household saving', *Journal of Public Economics*, vol. 23, pp. 115–139.

Dierker, E. (1986) 'Why does marginal cost pricing lead to Pareto efficiency?', *Zetschrift fur Nationalokonomie*, vol. 21, pp. 41–66.

Dierker, E., Guesneries, R. and Neuefeind, W. (1985) 'General equilibrium when some firms follow special pricing rules', *Econometrica*, vol. 53, pp. 1369–1393.

Diewert, E. (1982) 'Duality approaches in microeconomic theory', in K. Arrow and M. Intriligator (eds) *Handbook of Mathematical Economics*, vol. II, Amsterdam: North Holland, pp. 535–599.

Diewert, W. (1983) 'Cost benefit analysis and project evaluation: a comparison of alternative approaches', *Journal of Public Economics*, vol. 22, pp. 265–302.

Dixit, A. (1987) 'Tax policy in open economies', in A. Auerbach and M. Feldstein (eds) *Handbook of Public Economics*, Amsterdam: North Holland, pp. 314–374.

Dixit, A. and Norman, V. (1980) *Theory of International Trade*, Cambridge: Cambridge University Press.

Dobb, M. (1937) *Papers on Capitalism, Development and Planning*, London: Macmillan.

Dreze, J. (1984) 'Second-best analysis with markets in disequilibrium: public sector pricing in a Keynesian regime', in M. Marchand, P. Pestieau and H. Tulkens (eds) *The Performance of Public Enterprises*, Amsterdam: North Holland, pp. 45–79.

Dreze, J. and Marchand, M. (1976) 'Pricing, spending, and gambling rules for non-profit organizations', in R. Grieson (ed.) *Public and Urban Economics: Essays in Honor of William S. Vickrey*, Lexington, Mass: Heath, pp. 59–89.

Dreze, Jean and Stern, N. (1987) 'The theory of cost benefit analysis', in A. Auerbach and M. Feldstein (eds) *Handbook of Public Economics*, Amsterdam: North Holland.

Easterly, P. and Sergio, R. (1993) *Fiscal Policy and Economic Growth: An Empirical Investigation*, Washington DC: The World Bank.

Farquharson, R. (1969) *Theory of Voting*, New Haven: Yale University Press.

Faulhaber, G. (1975) 'Cross subsidization: pricing in public enterprises', *American Economic Review*, vol. 65, pp. 966–977.

Faulhaber, G. and Panzar, J. (1978) 'Pricing in natural monopolies', mimeo, Bell Labs.

Felder, S. (1993) 'The welfare effects of tax reforms in a life cycle model: an analytical approach', *Public Finance*, vol. 48, pp. 210–224.

Feldstein, M. (1972a) 'Distributional equity and the optimal structure of public sector prices', *American Economic Review*, vol. 62, pp. 32–36.

Feldstein, M. (1972b) 'The inadequacy of weighted discount rates', in R. Layard (ed.) *Cost Benefit Analysis*, Harmondsworth: Penguin Books, pp. 311–332.

Feldstein, M. (1973) 'On the optimal progressivity of the income tax', *Journal of Public Economics*, vol. 2, pp. 236–276.

Feldstein, M. (1974a) 'Social security, induced retirement, and aggregate capital accumulation', *Journal of Political Economy*, vol. 82, pp. 905–926.

Feldstein, M. (1974b) 'Incidence of a capital income taxation in a growing economy with variable savings rates', *Review of Economic Studies*, vol. 44, pp. 505–513.

Feldstein, M. (1976) 'On the theory of tax reform', *Journal of Public Economics*, vol. 6, pp. 77–104.

Feldstein, M. (1977) 'Does the United States save too little?', *American Economic Review Papers and Proceedings*, vol. 67, pp. 116–121.

Feldstein, M. (1978) 'The welfare cost of capital income taxation', *Journal of Political Economy*, vol. 86, pp. S29–S51.

Feldstein, M. (1983) *Capital Taxation*, Cambridge, MA: Harvard University Press.

Feldstein, M. (1985) 'Debt and taxes in the theory of public finance', *Journal of Public Economics*, vol. 28, pp. 233–245.

Feldstein, M. and Horioka, C. (1980) 'Domestic savings and international capital flows', *Economic Journal*, vol. 90, pp. 314–328.

Feldstein, M., Poterba, J. and Dicks-Mireaux, L. (1983) 'The effective tax rate and the pre tax rate of return', *Journal of Public Economics*, vol. 21, pp. 129–158.

Feldstein, M. and Summers, L. (1979) 'Inflation and the taxation of capital income in the corporate sector', *National Tax Journal*, vol. 32, pp. 445–470.

Fishburn, P. (1973) *The Theory of Social Choice*, Princeton: Princeton University Press.

Fisher, I. (1930) *The Theory of Interest*, New York: Macmillan.

Fisher, R. (1988) *State and Local Public Finance*, Glenview, Ill.: Scott Foresman.

Fischer, S. (1980) 'Dynamic inconsistency, cooperation and the benevolent dissembling government', *Journal of Economic Dynamics and Control*, vol. 2, pp. 93–107.

Flatters, F., Henderson, V. and Mieskowski, P. (1974) 'Public goods, efficiency, and regional fiscal equalization', *Journal of Public Economics*, vol. 3, pp. 99–112.

Foley, D. (1967) 'Resource allocation and the public sector', *Yale Economic Essays*, vol. 7, pp. 45–98.

Follain, J. (1979) 'Grant impacts on local fiscal behavior: full information maximum likelihood estimates', *Public Finance Quarterly*, vol. 7, pp. 479–500.

Foster, C., Jackman, R. and Perlman, M. (1980) *Government Finance in a Unitary State*, London: Allen and Unwin.

Frenkel, J., Razin, A. and Sadka, E. (1991) *International Taxation in an Integrated World*, Cambridge MA: MIT Press.

Frey, B. and Pommerehne, W. (1984) 'The hidden economy: state and prospects for measurement', *Review of Income and Wealth*, vol. 30, pp. 1–23.

Friedman, B. and Hahn, F. (1990) *Handbook of Monetary Economics*, vols 1–3, Amsterdam: North Holland.

Friedman, M. and Friedman, R. (1980) *Free to Choose*, New York: Harcourt Brace Jovanovich.

Fukushima, T. and Hatta, T. (1989) 'Why not tax uniformly rather than optimally?', *Economic Studies Quarterly*, vol. 40, pp. 220–238.

Fullerton, D. (1991) 'Reconciling recent estimates of the marginal welfare cost of taxation', *American Economic Review*, vol. 81, pp. 302–308.

Fullerton, D., King, A. Shoven, J. and Whalley, J. (1981) 'Tax integration in the U.S.: a general equilibrium approach', *American Economic Review*, vol. 71, pp. 677–691.

Fullerton, D. and Rogers, D. (1993) *Who Bears the Lifetime Tax Burden?*, Washington DC: The Brookings Institution.

Gaertner, W. and Wenig, A. (eds) (1985) *The Economics of the Shadow Economy*, Heldelberg: Springer Verlag.

Gandolfo, G. (1994) *International Economics*, Berlin: Springer-Verlag.

Geeroms, H. and Wilmots, H. (1985) 'An empirical model of tax evasion and tax avoidance', *Public Finance*, vol. 40, pp. 190–209.

Gerard, M. (1994) 'Cost of capital, investment location and marginal effective tax rate: methodology and application', in H. Motamen (ed.) *Fiscal Policy in an Integrating World*, London: Butterworth.

Gersovitz, M. (1985) 'The effects of domestic taxes on foreign private investment', in N. Stern and D. Newberry (eds) *Taxation in Developing Countries*, Washington DC: The World Bank.

Gibbard, A. (1969) 'Social choice and Arrow Conditions', mimeo.

Gibbard, A. (1973) 'Manipulation of voting schemes: a general result', *Econometrica*, vol. 41, pp. 587–602.

Gideon, Y. (1994) 'Tax evasion and the income tax rate', *Public Finance*, vol. 49, pp. 107–112.

Gideon, Y. (1995) 'A note on the tax evading firm,' *National Tax Journal*, vol. 48, pp. 113–120.

Giles, C. and Johnson, P. (1994) 'Tax reform in the UK and changes in the progressivity of the tax system, 1985–95', *Fiscal Studies*, vol. 15, pp. 64–86.

Gillespie, W. (1965) 'Effect of public expenditures on the distribution of income', in R. Musgrave (ed.) *Essays in Fiscal Federalism*, Washington DC: The Brookings Institution, pp. 122–186.

Giovannini, A., Hubbard, R. and Slemrod, J. (eds) (1993) *Studies in International Taxation*, Chicago: University of Chicago Press for the National Bureau of Economic Research.

Goldstein, G. and Pauly, M. (1981) 'Tiebout bias on the demand for local public goods', *Journal of Public Economics*, vol. 16, pp. 131–144.

Gordon, H. (1954) 'The economic theory of a common property resource: the fishery', *Journal of Political Economy*, vol. 62, pp. 124–142.

Gordon, R. (1983) 'An optimal taxation approach to fiscal federalism', *Quarterly Journal of Economics*, vol. 89, pp. 567–586.

Gordon, R. (1985) 'Taxation of corporate capital income: tax revenues versus tax distortions', *Quarterly Journal of Economics*, vol. 100, pp. 1–27.

Gordon, R. (1986) 'Taxation of investment and savings in a world economy', *American Economic Review*, vol. 76, pp. 1087–1102.

Gosskopf, S. and Yaisawarang, S. (1990) 'Economics of scope in the provisions of local services,' *National Tax Journal*, vol. 43, pp. 61–74.

Gould, J. (1968) 'Adjustment costs in the theory of investment of the firm', *Review of Economic Studies*, vol. 35, pp. 47–55.

Graaf, T. (1957) *Theoretical Welfare Economics*, Cambridge: Cambridge University Press.

Gramlich, E. (1990) *Benefit-Cost Analysis of Government Programs*, 2nd edn, Englewood Cliffs NJ: Prentice Hall.

Gramlich, E. and Rubinfield, D. (1982) 'Micro estimates of public spending demand and tests of the Tiebout and median voter hypotheses', *Journal of Political Economy*, vol. 90, pp. 536–560.

Green, J. (1973) 'Public decisions', mimeo Harvard University.

Green, J. (1981) 'The effects of taxation on savings', Harvard University Discussion Paper.

Green, J. and Laffont, J. (1979) *Incentives in Public Decision Making*, Amsterdam: North Holland.

Greenberg, J. (1984) 'Avoiding tax avoidance: a (repeated) game-theoretic approach', *Journal of Economic Theory*, vol. 32, pp. 1–13.

Grewal, B. (1975) 'Equalization techniques for school finance', Department of Economics, Australian National University Working Paper.

Grewal, B., Brennan, H. and Matthews, R. (eds) (1980) *The Economics of Federalism*, Canberra: ANU Press.

Grossman, G. and Helpman, E. (1991) *Innovation and Growth in the Global Economy*, Cambridge MA: MIT Press.

Grossman, S. and Hart, O. (1983) 'An analysis of the principal-agent problem', *Econometrica*, vol. 51, pp. 7–45.

Grossman, S. and Stilglitz, J. (1980) 'Stockholder unanimity in making production and financial decisions', *Quarterly Journal of Economics*, vol. 94, pp. 543–566.

Groves, T. (1973) 'Incentives in teams', *Econometrica*, vol. 43, pp. 617–631.

Groves, T. and Ledyard, J. (1977) 'Optimal allocation of public goods: a solution to the free rider problem', *Econometrica*, vol. 45, pp. 783–809.

Groves, T. and Loeb, M. (1975) 'Incentives and public inputs', *Journal of Public Economics*, vol. 4, pp. 211–226.

Gruner, H. and Heer, B. (1994) 'Taxation of income and wealth in a model of endogenous growth', *Public Finance*, vol. 49, pp. 358–372.

Guesnerie, R. (1975) 'Pareto optimality in non-convex economies', *Econometrica*, vol. 43, pp. 1–30.

Guesnerie, R. (1977) 'On the direction of tax reform', *Journal of Public Economics*, vol. 7, pp. 179–202.

Guesnerie, R. (1995) *A Contribution to the Pure Theory of Taxation*, Cambridge: Cambridge University Press.

Gwartney, J. and Wagner, R. (ed.) (1988) *Public Choice and Constitutional Economics*, Greenwich, Conn.: JAI Press.

Hahn, F. (1973) 'On optimum taxation', *Journal of Economic Theory*, vol. 6, pp. 96–106.

Ham, J. (1982) 'Estimation of a labor supply model with censoring due to unemployment and underemployment', *Review of Economic Studies*, vol. 49, pp. 335–354.

Ham, J. (1986) 'On the interpretation of unemployment in empirical labor supply analysis', in R. Blundell and I. Walker (eds) *Unemployment, Search and the Labor Supply*, Cambridge: Cambridge University Press.

Hamilton, B. (1976) 'Capitalization of intrajurisdictional differences in local tax practices', *American Economic Review*, vol. 66, pp. 743–753.

Hamilton, J. (1987) 'Optimal wage and income taxation with wage uncertainty', *International Economic Review*, vol. 28, pp. 373–388.

Hammond, P. (1979) 'Straightforward individual incentive compatibility in large economies', *Review of Economic Studies*, vol. 46, pp. 263–282.

Hammond, P. (1980) 'Cost benefit analysis as planning procedure', in D.A. Currie and W. Peters (eds) *Contemporary Economic Analysis*, London: Croom Helm, pp. 221–250.

Hammond, P. (1983) 'Approximate measures of the social welfare benefits of large projects', Stanford University, IMSSS Technical Report no. 410.

Hammond, P. (1985) 'Welfare economics', in G. Feiwei (ed.) *Issues in Contemporary Microeconomics and Welfare*, London: Macmillan, pp. 405–434.

Hammond, P. (1986) 'Project evaluation by potential tax reform', *Journal of Public Economics*.

Hammond, P. (1989) 'Principles for evaluating public sector projects', in P. Hare (ed.) *Surveys in public Sector Economics*, Oxford: Basil Blackwell, pp. 15–44.

Harberger, A. (1965) 'The incidence of the corporation income tax', *Journal of Political Economy*, vol. 70, pp. 215–240.

Harberger, A. (1971) 'Three basic postulates for applied welfare economics: an interpretive essay', *Journal of Economic Literature*, vol. 9, pp. 785–797.

Harberger, A. (1978) 'On the use of distributional weights in social cost-benefit analysis', *Journal of Political Economy*, vol. 86, pp. S87–120.

Harsanyi, J. (1953) 'Cardinal utility in welfare economics and in the theory of risk taking', *Journal of Political Economy*, vol. 61, pp. 434–435.

Harsanyi, J. (1955) 'Cardinal welfare, individualistic ethics and interpersonal comparisons of utility', *Journal of Political Economy*, vol. 73, pp. 309–321.

Harsanyi, J. (1975) 'Can the maximin principle serve as a basis for morality? A critique of John Rawls's theory of justice', *The American Political Science Review*, vol. 69, pp. 594–606.

Hatta, T. (1979) 'A theory of piecemeal policy recommendations', *Review of Economic Studies*, vol. 44, pp. 1–22.

Hatta, T. (1986) 'Welfare effects of changing commodity tax rates toward uniformity', *Journal of Public Economics*, vol. 29, pp. 99–112.

Hausman, J. (1978) 'Specification tests in econometrics', *Econometrica*, vol. 46, pp. 1251–1257.

Hausman, J. (1979) 'The effects of wages, taxes and fixed costs of women's labor force participation', *Journal of Political Economy*, vol. 14, pp. 161–194.

Hausman, J. (1981) 'Exact consumer's surplus and deadweight loss', *American Economic Review*, vol. 71, pp. 662–676.

Hausman, J. (1985) 'The econometrics of nonlinear budget sets', *Econometrica*, vol. 6, pp. 1255–1283.

Hausman, J. and Rudd, P. (1984) 'Family labor supply with taxes', *American Economic Review*, vol. 74, pp. 242–248.

Haveman, R. and Margolis, J. (1983) *Public Expenditure and Policy Analysis*, 3rd edn, Boston: Houghton Mifflin.

Hayashi, F. (1982) 'Tobin's marginal q and average q: a neoclassical interpretation', *Econometrica*, vol. 50, pp. 213–224.

Hayek, F. (1960) *The Constitution of Liberty*, Chicago: University of Chicago Press.

Hayek, F. (1979) *Law, Legislation and Liberty*, London: Routledge and Kegan Paul.

Head, J. (1974) 'Public goods and public policy', in S. Baker and C. Elliott (eds) *Readings in Public Sector Economics*, Lexington MA: D.C. Heath and Company, pp. 23–34.

Heckman, J. (1974) 'Shadow prices, market wages and labor supply', *Econometrica*, vol. 42, pp. 679–694.

Heckman, J. (1978) 'Dummy endogenous variables in a simultaneous equation system', *Econometrica*, vol. 46, pp. 931–959.

Heckman, J. (1979) 'Sample selection bias as a specification error', *Econometrica*, vol. 47, pp. 153–162.

Hellwig, M. (1986) 'The optimal linear income tax revisited', *Journal of Public Economics*, vol. 31, pp. 163–179.

Hemming, D. and Harvey, R. (1983) 'Occupational pension scheme membership and retirement saving', *Economic Journal*, vol. 93, pp. 128–144.

Hicks, J. (1939) 'The foundations of welfare economics', *Economic Journal*, vol. 49, pp. 696–712.

Hicks, J. (1940) 'The valuation of the social income', *Economica*, vol. 7, pp. 105–124.

Hicks, J. (1981) *Wealth and Welfare*, Cambridge MA: Harvard University Press.

Hirschleifer, J. and Riley, J. (1979) 'The analytics of uncertainty and information: an expository survey', *Journal of Economic Literature*, vol. 17, pp. 1375–1421.

HM Treasury (1986) *The Reform of Personal Taxation*, Cmnd 9756, London: HMSO.

Hochman, H. and Rodgers, J. (1969) 'Pareto optimal redistribution', *American Economic Review*, vol. 59, pp. 542–557.

Hogan, T. and Shelton, R. (1973) 'Interstate tax exportation and states' fiscal structures', *National Tax Journal*, vol. 20, pp. 49–77.

Homburg, S. (1990) 'The efficiency of unfunded pension schemes', *Journal of Institutional and Theoretical Economics*, vol. 146, pp. 640–647.

Hubbard, G. and Slemrod, J. (1993) *Studies in International Taxation*, New York: Columbia University Press.

Hughes, D. (1988) 'Tax expenditures for local governments', *Public Budgeting and Finance*, vol. 8, pp. 68–73.

Hurwicz, L. (1973) 'The design of mechanisms for resource allocation', *American Economic Review*, vol. 63, pp. 1–30.

Hurwicz, L. (1979a) 'Outcome functions yielding Walrasian and Lindahl allocations at Nash equilibrium points', *Review of Economic Studies*, vol. 46, pp. 217–225.

Hurwicz, L. (1979b) 'On allocation attainable through Nash equilibria', *Journal of Economic Theory*, vol. 21, pp. 140–165.

Ilhori, T. (1987) 'Tax reform and intergenerational incidence', *Journal of Public Economics*, vol. 33, pp. 377–387.

Inman, R. (1977) 'Macro-fiscal planning in the regional economy: a general equilibrium approach', *Journal of Public Economics*, vol. 7, pp. 237–260.

Inman, R. (1987) 'Markets, governments, and the 'New' political economy', in A. Auerbach and M. Feldstein (eds) *Handbook of Public Economics*, vol. II, pp. 647–777.

Ippolito, R. (1985) 'Income tax policy and lifetime labor supply', *Journal of Public Economics*, vol. 26, pp. 327–347.

Isachsen, A. and Strom, S. (1980) 'The hidden economy: the labor market and tax evasion', *Scandinavian Journal of Economics*, vol. 82, pp. 304–311.

Jacobsson, U. (1976) 'On the measurement of the degree of progression', *Journal of Public Economics*, vol. 5, pp. 161–168.

Jaffee, D. and Russell, R. (1976) 'Imperfect information, uncertainty and credit rationing', *Quarterly Journal of Economics*, vol. 90, pp. 651–666.

Jensen, M. and Meckling, W. (1976) 'Theory of the firm: managerial behavior, agency costs and ownership structure', *Journal of Financial Economics*, vol. 3, pp. 305–360.

Jha, R. (1978) *Essays in Economic Theory*, Ph. D. dissertation, Department of Economics, Columbia University.

Jha, R. (1986) 'Optimal labor supply and the accumulation of human and financial capital with capital market imperfections', *Indian Economic Review*, vol. 21, pp. 21–39.

Jha, R. (1987) *Modern Theory of Public Finance*, New Delhi: Wiley Eastern.

Jha, R. (1994) *Macroeconomics for Developing Countries*, London and New York: Routledge.

Jha, R. and Lachler, U. (1981) 'Optimum taxation and public production in a dynamic Harris-Todaro world', *Journal of Development Economics*, vol. 9, pp. 357–373.

Jha, R. and Lachler, U. (1983) 'Inflation and economic growth in a competitive economy with exhaustible resources', *Journal of Economic Behavior and Organization*, vol. 4, pp. 113–129.

Jha, R. and Mittal, S. (1990) 'Saving, investment and marginal effective tax rates in India', *International Journal of Development Banking*, vol. 8, pp. 3–13.

Jha, R., Mohanty, M. and Chatterjee, S. (1995) *Fiscal efficiency in the Indian federation*, Bombay: Reserve Bank of India, Development Research Group Study No.11.

Jha, R. and Murty, M. (1986) 'Optimal non-linear taxation with interdependent utilities', *Journal of Quantitative Economics*, vol. 2, pp. 213–220.

Jha, R. and Murty, M. (1987) 'Distributional equity and optimal structure of prices for the public sector: the flexible coefficients case', *Energy Economics*, vol. 9, pp. 46–54.

Jha, R., Murty, M. and Ray, R. (1990) 'Dual pricing, rationing and Ramsey commodity taxation: theory and an illustration', *The Developing Economies*, vol. 28, pp. 229–239.

Jha, R. and Sahni, B. (1993) *Industrial Efficiency: An Indian Perspective*, New Delhi: Wiley Eastern.

Jha, R. and Sahu, A. (1997) 'Tax policy and human capital accumulation in a resource constrained, growing dual economy,' *Public Finance Quarterly*, (vol. 25, pp 58–82).

Jha, R. Sahu, A. and Meyer, L. (1990) 'The Fisher equation controversy: a reconciliation of contradictory results', *Southern Economic Journal*, vol. 57, pp. 106–113.

Jha, R. and Wadhwa, N. (1990) 'A note on private corporate taxation and effective tax rates', *Public Finance Quarterly*, vol. 18, pp. 454–464.

Jones, L. (1975) *The Value of Life – an Economic Analysis*, Chicago: Chicago University Press.

Jones, L., Manuelli, R. and Rossi, P. (1993) 'Optimal taxation in models of endogenous growth', *Journal of Political Economy*, vol. 101, pp. 485–515.

Jorgenson, D. (1963) 'Capital theory and investment behavior', *American Economic Review*, vol. 53, pp. 247–259.

Just, R., Hueth, D. and Schmitz, A. (1982) *Applied Welfare Economics and Public Policy*, Englewood Cliffs NJ: Prentice Hall.

Kaldor, N. (1939) 'Welfare propositions and interpersonal comparisons of utility', *Economic Journal*, vol. 49, pp. 549–552.

Kaldor, N. (1955) *An Expenditure Tax*, London: Allen and Unwin.

Kamien, M. and Schwartz, N. (1991) *Dynamic Optimization*, 2nd edn, Amsterdam: North Holland.

Kay, J. (1972) 'Social discount rates', *Journal of Public Economics*, vol. 1, pp. 359–378.

Kay, J. (1980) 'The deadweight loss from a tax system', *Journal of Public Economics*, vol. 13, pp. 111–119.

Kay, J., Keen, M. and Morris, C. (1984) 'Estimating consumption from expenditure data', *Journal of Public Economics*, vol. 23, pp. 169–181.

Kay, J. and King, M. (1983) *The British Tax System*, Oxford: Oxford University Press.

Kay, J. and King, M. (1990) *The British Tax System*, 5th edn, Oxford: Oxford University Press.

Keen, M. (1986) 'Zero expenditures and the estimation of Engel curves', *Journal of Applied Econometrics*, vol. 3, pp. 277–286.

Kelly, J. (1976) *Arrow Impossibility Theorems*, New York: Academic Press.

Kenyon, D. and Kincaid, J. (eds) (1991) *Competition Among State and Local Governments*, Washington DC: Urban Institute Press.

Kihlstrom, R. and Laffont, L. (1983) 'Taxation and risk-taking in general equilibrium models with free entry', *Journal of Public Economics*, vol. 21, pp. 159–181.

King, D. (1980) *Fiscal Tiers: The Economics of Multi-layer Government*, London: Allen and Unwin.

King, M. (1980) 'Savings and taxation', in G. Hughes and G. Neal (eds) *Public Policy and the Tax System*, London: Allen and Unwin.

King, M. (1983) 'Welfare analysis of tax reforms using household data', *Journal of Public Economics*, vol. 21, pp. 183–214.

King, M. and Fullerton, D. (eds) (1983) *The Taxation of Income From Capital: A Comparative Study of the United States, the United Kingdom, Sweden, and West Germany*, Chicago: University of Chicago Press for NBER.

King, R. and Rebelo, S. (1990) 'Public policy and economic growth: developing neoclassical implications', *Journal of Political Economy*, vol. 98, pp. 126–150.

Kolm, S. (1973) 'A note on optimum tax evasion', *Journal of Public Economics*, vol. 2, pp. 265–270.

Kolm, S. (1976) 'Unequal inequalities I and II', *Journal of Economic Theory*, vol. 12, pp. 416–442; vol. 13, pp. 82–111.

Koopmans, T. (1957) *Three Essays on the State of Economic Science*, New York: McGraw Hill.

Koskela, E. (1983) 'On the shape of the tax schedules, the probability of detection, and the penalty schemes as deterrents to tax evasion', *Public Finance*, vol. 38, pp. 70–80.

Kotlikoff, L. (1979) 'Testing the theory of social security and life cycle accumulation', *American Economic Review*, vol. 69, pp. 396–410.

Kotlikoff, L. (1987) 'The theory and measurement of effective tax rates: comment', in J. Mintz and D. Purvis (eds) *The Impact of Taxation on Business Activity*, John Deutsch Institute, Queen's University, Canada.

Kreps, M. (1990) *A Course in Microeconomic Theory*, New York: Prentice Hall.

Krueger, A. (1974) 'The political economy of the rent-seeking society', *American Economic Review*, vol. 64, pp. 291–303.

Kurz, M. (1981) 'The life-cycle hypothesis and the effects of social security and private pension on family saving', Institute of Mathematical Studies in the Social Sciences Working Paper, Stanford University.

Kydland, F. and Prescott, E. (1977) 'Rules rather then discretion: the inconsistency of optimal plans', *Journal of Political Economy*, vol. 85, pp. 473–491.

Kydland, F. and Prescott, E. (1980) 'Dynamic optimal taxation, rational expectations and optimal control', *Journal of Economic Dynamics and Control*, vol. 2, pp. 79–91.

Laffont, J. (1987) 'Incentives and the allocation of public goods', in A. Auerbach and M. Feldstein (eds) *Handbook of Public Economics*, Amsterdam: North Holland, pp. 537–569.

Laffont, J. (1994) 'The new economics of regulation ten years after', *Econometrica*, vol. 62, pp. 507–537.

Laffont, J. and Tirole, J. (1993) *The Theory of Incentives in Procurement and Regulation*, Cambridge MA: MIT Press.

Lassila, J. (1995) 'Income tax indexation in an open economy', *Journal of Money, Credit and Banking*, vol. 27, pp. 389–403.

Layard, R. (ed.) (1972) *Cost Benefit Analysis: Selected Readings*, Harmondsworth: Penguin Books.

Lee, L. and Pitt, M. (1986) 'Microeconomic demand systems with binding non-negativity constraints: the dual approach', *Econometrica*, vol. 54, pp. 1237–1242.

Leibenstein, H. (1966) 'Allocative efficiency vs. "X- efficiency"' *American Economic Review*, vol. 56, pp. 392–415.

Leibenstein, H. (1969) 'Organizational or frictional equilibria, X-efficiency, and the rate of innovation', *Quarterly Journal of Economics*, vol. 83, pp. 600–623.

Leibenstein, H. (1976) *Beyond Economic Man*, Cambridge MA: Harvard University Press.

Leland, H. and Pyle, D. (1977) 'Informational asymmetries, financial structure and financial intermediation', *Journal of Finance*, vol. 52, pp. 371–387.

Lindahl, E. (1967) 'Just taxation – a positive solution', in R. Musgrave and A. Peacock (eds) *Classics in the Theory of Public Finance*, New York: St. Martin's Press, pp. 168–176.

Lindsey, L. (1990) *The Growth Experiment*, New York: Basic Books.

Lipnovsky, I. and Maital, S. (1983) 'Voluntary provision of a pure public good as the game of "chicken"', *Journal of Public Economics*, vol. 20, pp. 1–44.

Lipsey, R. and Lancaster, K. (1957) 'The general theorem of second best', *Review of Economic Studies*, vol. 24, pp. 11–32.

Little, I. (1957) *A Critique of Welfare Economics*, 2nd. edn, Oxford: Clarendon Press.

Little, I. and Mirrlees, J. (1968) *Project Appraisal for Planning*, Paris: OECD.

Little, I. and Mirrlees, J. (1974) *Project Appraisal and Planning for Developing Countries*, London: Heinemann.

Lord, W. (1989) 'The transition from payroll to consumption receipts with endogenous human capital', *Journal of Public Economics*, vol. 38, pp. 53–73.

Lucas, R. (1976) 'Econometric policy evaluation: a critique', *Carnegie Rochester Conference Series on Public Policy*, vol. 1, pp. 19–46.

Lucas, R. (1988) 'On the mechanics of economic development', *Journal of Monetary Economics*, vol. 22, pp. 3–42.

Lucas, R. (1990) 'Supply-side economics: an analytical review', *Oxford Economic Papers*, vol. 42, pp. 2–42.

Lucas, R. and Stokey, N. (1983) 'Optimal fiscal and monetary policy in an economy without capital', *Journal of Monetary Economics*, vol. 12, pp. 55–93.

Luce, R. and Raiffa, H. (1957) *Games and Decisions*, New York: John Wiley.

Luce, R. and Suppes, P. (1965) 'Preference utility and subjective probability', in R. Luce, R. Bush, and E. Gallanter (eds) *Handbook of Mathematical Psychology*, New York: John Wiley.

McCaleb, T. (1976) 'Tax evasion and the differential taxation of labor and capital income', *Public Finance*, vol. 31, pp. 287–294.

McFadden, D. (1969) 'A simple remark on the second best Pareto optimality of market equilibria', *Journal of Economic Theory*, vol. 1, pp. 26–38.

McLure, C. (1967) 'The interstate exporting of state and local taxes: estimates for 1962', *National Tax Journal*, vol. 20, pp. 49–77.

McLure, C. (1979) *Must Corporate Income be Taxed Twice?*, Washington DC: The Brookings Institution.

McLure, C. (1981) 'The elusive incidence of the corporate income tax: the state case', *Public Finance Quarterly*, vol. 9.

McLure, C. and Thirsk, W. (1975) 'A simplified exposition of the Harberger model, I: tax incidence', *National Tax Journal*, vol. 28, pp. 1–28.

McNutt, P. (1996) *The Economics of Public Choice*, Cheltenham: Edward Elgar.

Mankiw, G. and Summers, L. (1986) 'Money demand and the effects of fiscal policies', *Journal of Money, Credit and Banking*, vol. 18, pp. 415–429.

Marglin, S. (1963) 'The social rate of discount and the optimal rate of investment', *Quarterly Journal of Economics*, vol. 77, pp. 95–112.

Mas-Collel, A., Whinston, M. and Green, J. (1995) *Microeconomic Theory*, New York: Oxford University Press.

Maskin, E. (1978) 'A theorem on utilitarianism', *Review of Economic Studies*, vol. 45, pp. 93–96.

Matthews, R. (ed.) *State and Local Taxation*, Canberra, ANU Press.

Mayshar, J. (1990) 'On measures of excess burden and their applications', *Journal of Public Economics*, vol. 43, pp. 263–289

Mayshar, J. and Yitzhaki, S. (1995) 'Dalton-improving indirect tax reform', *American Economic Review*, vol. 85, no. 4, pp. 793–807.

Merton, R. (1978) 'On the price of contingent claims and the Modigliani Miller theorem', *Journal of Financial Economics*, vol. 5, pp. 241–249.

Merton, R. (1982) 'On the microeconomic theory of investment under uncertainty', in K. Arrow and M. Intrilligator (eds) *Handbook of Mathematical Economics*, Amsterdam: North Holland, pp. 601–669.

Mieszkowski, P. (1967) 'On the theory of tax incidence', *American Economic Review*, vol. 75, pp. 250–262.

Mieszkowski, P. (1969) 'Tax incidence theory: the effects of taxes on the distribution of income', *Journal of Economic Literature*, vol. 7, pp. 1103–1124.

Mieszkowski, P. (1974) 'Integration of the corporate and personal income tax: the bogus issue', *Finanzarchiv*, vol. 31, pp. 286–297.

Mieszkowski, P. (1978) 'The choice of tax base: consumption versus income taxation', in M. Boskin (ed.) *Federal Tax Reform*, San Francisco: Institute for Contemporary Studies, pp. 27–53.

Mikami, K. (1993) 'Providing public goods with distortionary taxes', *Public Finance*, vol. 48, pp. 76–91.

Miller, J. (1977) 'The transactions demand for money in a three asset economy', *International Economic Review*, vol. 18, pp. 345–366.

Milleron, J. (1972) 'Theory of value with public goods: a survey article', *Journal of Economic Theory*, vol. 5, pp. 419–477.

Mintz, J. and Purvis, D. (eds) (1987) *The Impact of Taxation on Business Activity*, Kingston, Canada: John Deutsch Institute for the Study of Economic Policy, Queen's University.

Mintz, J. and Tulkens, H. (1986) 'Commodity tax competition between member states of a federation: equilibrium and efficiency', *Journal of Public Economics*, vol. 29, pp. 133–172.

Mirman, L., Samet, D. and Taubman, Y. (1983) 'Axiomatic approach to the allocation of a fixed cost through prices', *Bell Journal of Economics*, vol. 14, pp. 139–151.

Mirman, L. and Sibley, D. (1980) 'Optimal non-linear prices for multiproduct monopolies', *Bell Journal of Economics*, vol. 11. pp. 659–670.

Mirman, L. and Taubman, Y. (1982) 'Demand compatible, equitable, cost sharing prices', *Mathematics of Operations Research*, pp. 40–66.

Mirrlees, J. (1971) 'An exploration in the theory of optimal taxation', *Review of Economic Studies*, vol. 38, pp. 175–208.

Mirrlees, J. (1972) 'On producer taxation', *Review of Economic Studies*, vol. 39, pp. 105–111.

Mirrlees, J. (1975) 'Optimal commodity taxation in a two class economy', *Journal of Public Economics*, vol. 4, pp. 27–33.

Mirrlees, J. (1976) 'Optimum tax theory: a synthesis', *Journal of Public Economics*, vol. 6, pp. 327–358.

Mirrlees, J. (1986) 'The theory of optimal taxation', in K. Arrow and M. Intrilligator (eds) *Handbook of Mathematical Economics*, Amsterdam: North Holland.

Mirrlees, J. (1990) 'Taxing uncertain incomes', *Oxford Economic Papers*, vol. 42, pp. 34–45.

Mishan, E. (1971) 'The postwar literature on externalities: an interpretive essay', *Journal of Economic Literature*, vol. 9, pp. 1–28.

Modigliani, F. and Miller, M. (1958) 'The cost of capital, corporation finance and the theory of investment', *American Economic Review*, vol. 48, pp. 261–297.

Mookherjee, D. and Png, I. (1989) 'Optimal auditing, insurance and redistribution', *Quarterly Journal of Economics*, vol. 54, pp. 399–416.

Mookherjee, D. and Png, I. (1992) 'Monitoring vis-à-vis investigation in enforcement of law', *American Economic Review*, vol. 82, pp. 101–114.

Mork, K. (1975) 'Income tax evasion: some empirical evidence', *Public Finance*, vol. 30, pp. 70–76.

Mueller, D. (1973) 'Constitutional democracy and social welfare,' *Quarterly Journal of Economics*, vol. 87, pp. 60–80.

Mueller, D. (1979) *Public Choice*, Cambridge: Cambridge University Press.

Mueller, D. (1989) *Public Choice I*, Cambridge: Cambridge University Press.

Mueller, D. (1995) *Public Choice II*, Cambridge: Cambridge University Press.

Mulgan, G. and Murray, R. (1993) *Reconnecting Taxation*, London: Demos.

Munk, J. (1979) 'Optimal public sector pricing taking the distributive aspect into account', *Quarterly Journal of Economics*, vol. 91, pp. 639–650.

Munnell, A. (1976) 'Private provision and saving: new evidence', *Journal of Political Economy*, vol. 84, pp. 1013–1032.

Murray, C. (1988) *In Pursuit of Happiness and Good Government*, New York: Simon and Schuster.

Musgrave, R. (1959) *The Theory of Public Finance*, New York: McGraw Hill.

Musgrave, R. (1971) 'The postwar literature on externalities: an interpretive essay', *Journal of Economic Literature*, vol. 9, pp. 1–28.

Musgrave, R. and Musgrave, P. (1972) 'International equity', in R. Bird and J. Head (eds) *Modern Fiscal Issues: Essays in Honor of Carl Shoup*, Toronto: University of Toronto Press.

Musgrave, R. and Musgrave, P. (1976) *Public Finance in Theory and Practice*, New York: McGraw Hill.

Musgrave, R. and Musgrave, P. (1982) *Public Finance in Theory and Practice*, 3rd ed, New York: McGraw Hill.

Myers, S. (1974) 'Interactions of corporate financing and investment decisions – implications for capital budgeting', *Journal of Finance*, vol. 29, pp. 1–25.

Myers, S. (1977) 'Determinants of corporate borrowing', *Journal of Financial Economics*, vol. 5, pp. 147–175.

Myers, S. (1984) 'The capital structure puzzle', *Journal of Finance*, vol. 39, pp. 575–592.

Myles, G. (1995) *Public Economics*, Cambridge: Cambridge University Press.

Nayak, P. (1978) 'Optimal income tax evasion and regressive taxes', *Public Finance*, vol. 33, pp. 358–366.

Neck, R., Schneider, F. and Hofreither, M. (1989) 'The consequences of progressive income taxation for the shadow economy', in D. Bos and B. Felderer (eds) *The Political Economy of Progressive Taxation*, Berlin: Springer Verlag.

Ng, Y. (1975) 'Bentham or Bergson? Finite sensibility, utility functions and social welfare economics', *Review of Economic Studies*, vol. 42, pp. 545–569.

Ng, Y. (1979) *Welfare Economics: Introduction and Development of Basic Concepts*, London: Macmillan.

Niskanen, W. (1971) *Bureaucracy and Representative Government*, Chicago: Aldine.

Oakland, W. (1972) 'Congestion, public goods and welfare', *Journal of Public Economics*, vol. 1, pp. 339–357.

Oakland, W. (1974) 'Public goods, perfect competition and underproduction', *Journal of Political Economy*, vol. 82, pp. 927–939.

Oakland, W. (1987) 'The theory of public goods', in A. Auerbach and M. Feldstein (eds) *Handbook of Public Economics*, Amsterdam: North Holland, pp. 485–535.

Oates, W. (1972) *Fiscal Federalism*, New York: Harcourt, Brace Jovanovich.

Oates, W. (1979a) 'Intergovernmental grants and revenue sharing: theory and evidence', Discussion Paper, University of Leicester.

Oates, W. (1979b) 'Lump sum government expenditures have price effects', in P. Mieszkowski and W. Oakland (eds) *Fiscal Federalism and Grants in Aid*, Washington DC: The Urban Institute.

Olmsted, G. (1985) 'Tiebout and the demand for local public goods', mimeo, Department of Economics, University of Ohio.

Olson, M. (1968) *The Logic of Collective Action*, Cambridge: Harvard University Press.

Olson, M. (1969) 'The principle of fiscal equivalence', *American Economic Review Papers and Proceedings*, vol. 59, pp. 479–487.

Ordover, J. (1976) 'Distributive justice and optimal taxation of wages and interest in a growing economy', *Journal of Public Economics*, vol. 5, pp. 139–160.

Ordover, J. and Panzar, J. (1980) 'On the non existence of Pareto superior outlay schedules', *Bell Journal of Economics*, vol. 11, pp. 351–354.

Ordover, J. and Panzar, J. (1982) 'On the non-linear pricing of inputs', *International Economic Review*, vol. 23, pp. 659–676.

Ordover, J. and Phelps, E. (1975) 'Linear taxation of wealth and wages for intra-generational lifetime justice: some steady-state cases', *American Economic Review*, vol. 65, pp. 660–673.

Ordover, J. and Phelps, E. (1979) 'The concept of optimal taxation in the overlapping generations model of capital and wealth', *Journal of Public Economics*, vol. 12, pp. 1–26.

Ordover, J. and Willig, R. (1979) 'The role of information in designing socially optimal policies toward externalities', *Journal of Public Economics*, vol. 12, pp. 215–233.

Panzar, A. and Schmeidler, D. (1974) 'A difficulty in the concept of fairness', *Review of Economic Studies*, vol. 41, pp. 441–443.

Panzar, A. and Schmeidler, D. (1978) 'Egalitarian equivalent allocations: a new concept of economic equity', *Quarterly Journal of Economics*, vol. 92, pp. 671–687.

Pardo, J. and Schneider, F. (eds) (1996) *Current Issues in Public Choice*, Cheltenham: Edward Elgar.

Pattanaik, P. (1971) *Voting and Collective Choice*, Cambridge: Cambridge University Press.

Payne, J. (1993) *Costly Returns: The Burdens of the US Tax System*, San Francisco: Institute of Contemporary Studies.

Peacock, A. (1977) *The Economic Analysis of Government and Related Themes*, London: Robertson.

Peacock, A. and Shaw, G. (1982) 'Tax evasion and tax revenue loss', *Public Finance*, vol. 37, pp. 269–278.

Pedersen, K. (1995) 'Rent seeking, political influence and inequality: a simple analytical example', *Public Choice*, vol. 82, pp. 281–305.

Pencavel, J. (1979) 'A note on income tax evasion, labor supply and non-linear tax schedules', *Journal of Public Economics*, vol. 12, pp. 115–124.

Penrose, E. (1963) *The Theory of the Growth of the Firm*, Oxford: Oxford University Press.

Phelps, E. (1961) 'The golden rule of accumulation: a fable for growthmen', *American Economic Review*, vol. 51, pp. 638–643.

Phelps, E. (1973) 'The taxation of wage income for economic justice', *Quarterly Journal of Economics*, vol. 87, pp. 331–354.

Phelps, E. (1977) 'Linear "maximin" taxation of wage and property income on a "maximin" growth path', in B. Balassa and R. Nelson (eds) *Economic Progress, Private Values and Public Policy*, Amsterdam: North Holland.

Phelps, E. and Riley, J. (1978) 'Rawlsian growth: dynamic programming of capital and wealth for intergenerational "maximin" justice', *Review of Economic Studies*, vol. 45, pp. 103–120.

Pigou, A. (1947) *A Study in Public Finance*, 3rd ed, London: Macmillan.

Platts, A. (1981) 'Traditional peakload pricing theory: a synthesis', *Journal of Economic Studies*, vol. 8, pp. 47–51.

Plott, C. (1967) 'A notion of equilibrium and its possibility under majority rule', *American Economic Review*, vol. 57, pp. 787–806.

Plott, C. (1976) 'Axiomatic social choice theory: an overview and interpretation', *American Journal of Political Science*, vol. 20, pp. 511–596.

Poterba, J. (1987) 'Tax evasion and capital gains taxation', *American Economic Review*, vol. 77, pp. 234–239.

Poterba, J. (1989) 'Lifetime incidence and the distributional burden of excise taxes', *American Economic Review*, vol. 79, pp. 325–330.

Poterba, J. (1992) 'Tax burdens on owner occupied housing in US and Canada', in J. Shoven and J. Whalley (eds) *Canada, US Tax Comparisons*, Chicago: University of Chicago Press, pp. 23–42.

Poterba, J. and Summers, L. (1984) 'New evidence that taxes affect the valuation of dividends', *Journal of Finance*, vol. 39, pp. 1397–1415.

Pratt, J. (1964) 'Risk aversion in the small and the large', *Econometrica*, vol. 32, pp. 122–136.

Prescott, E. (1977) 'Should control theory be used for economic stabilization', *Journal of Monetary Economics*, special issue, vol. 7, pp. 101–102.

Purvis, D. (1976) 'The neoclassical theory of the firm: a note on production and investment decisions', *Canadian Journal of Economics*, vol. 9, pp. 331–341.

Radner, R. (1980) 'Collusive behavior in non-cooperative epsilon equilibria of oligopolies with long but finite lives', *Journal of Economic Theory*, vol. 22, pp. 136–154.

Ramsey, F. (1927) 'A contribution to the theory of taxation', *Economic Journal*, vol. 37, pp. 47–61.

Ramsey, F. (1928) 'A mathematical theory of savings', *Economic Journal*, vol. 38, pp. 543–559.

Rawls, J. (1971) *A Theory of Justice*, Cambridge MA: Harvard University Press.

Rebelo, S. (1991) 'Long-run policy analysis and long-run Growth', *Journal of Political Economy*, vol. 99, pp. 500–521.

Reinganum, J. and Wilde, L. (1985) 'Income tax compliance in a principal-agent framework', *Journal of Public Economics*, vol. 26, pp. 1–18.

Reinganum, J. and Wilde, L. (1986) 'Equilibrium verification and reporting policies in a model of tax compliance', *International Economic Review*, vol. 27, pp. 739–760.

Roberts, K. (1977) 'Voting over income tax schedules', *Journal of Public Economics*, vol. 8, pp. 329–340.

Roberts, K. (1978) 'Welfare considerations of nonlinear pricing', *Economic Journal*, vol. 89, pp. 66–83.

Roberts, K. (1980) 'Possibility theorems with interpersonally comparable welfare levels', *Review of Economic Studies*, vol. 47, pp. 409–420.

Robertson, H. (1992) *Social Security: What Every Taxpayer Should Know*, Washington DC: Retirement Policy Institute.

Rogerson, W. (1985) 'The first-order approach to the principal-agent problem', *Econometrica*, vol. 53, pp. 1357–1368.

Rohlfs, J. (1974) 'A theory of interdependent demands for a communication service', *Bell Journal of Economics and Management*, vol. 5, pp. 16–37.

Rohlfs, J. (1976) 'Evaluation of changes in a sub-optimal economy', *Review of Economic Studies*, vol. 43, pp. 359–362.

Rohlfs, J. (1979) *Economically-efficient Bell system pricing*, Bell Laboratories Economics Discussion Paper, no. 138.

Romer, C. (1990) 'The Great Crash and the Onset of the Great Depression', *Quarterly Journal of Economics*, vol. 105, pp. 597–624.

Romer, D. (1996) *Advanced Macroeconomics*, New York: McGraw Hill.

Romer, T. and Rosenthal, H. (1978) 'Political resource allocation, controlled agendas, and the status quo', *Public Choice*, vol. 33, pp. 27–43.

Romer, T. and Rosenthal, H. (1980) 'An institutional theory of the effects of intergovernmental grants', *National Tax Journal*, vol. 24, pp. 143–155.

Ross, P. (1977) 'A view of tax reform', *Bulletin for International Fiscal Documentation*, vol. 31, pp. 107–114.

Ross, P. (1985) 'The new view of tax reform', mimeo, Tel Aviv University.

Rothschild, M. and Stiglitz, J. (1970) 'Increasing risk I: a definition', *Journal of Economic Theory*, vol. 2, pp. 225–243.

Rubinfeld, D. (1987) 'The economics of the local public sector', in A. Auerbach and M. Feldstein (eds) *Handbook of Public Economics*, vol. 2, Amsterdam: North Holland, pp. 571–645.

Sadka, E. (1976) 'On income distribution, incentive effects and optimal income taxation', *Review of Economic Studies*, vol. 43, pp. 261–267.

Sah, R. (1983) 'How much redistribution is possible through commodity taxes?', *Journal of Public Economics*, vol. 20, pp. 89–101.

Samet, D. and Atuman, P. (1982) 'Sharing costs', Bell Laboratories Working Paper.

Samuelson, P. (1947) *Foundations of Economic Analysis*, Cambridge MA: Harvard University Press.

Samuelson, P. (1954) 'A pure theory of public expenditure', *Review of Economics and Statistics*, vol. 36, pp. 387–389.

Samuelson, P. (1955) 'Diagrammatic exposition of a theory of public expenditure', *Review of Economics and Statistics*, vol. 37, pp. 350–356.

Samuelson, P. (1956) 'Social indifference curves', *Quarterly Journal of Economics*, vol. 70, pp. 1–22.

Samuelson, P. (1958) 'An exact consumption loan model of interest with or without the contrivance of money', *Journal of Political Economy*, vol. 66, pp. 467–482.

Samuelson, P. (1968) 'The two-part golden rule deduced as the asymptotic turnpike of catenary motions', *Western Economic Journal*, vol. 6, pp. 85–89.

Samuelson, P. (1974) 'Complementarity: an essay on the 40th anniversary of the Hicks-Allen revolution in demand theory', *Journal of Economic Theory*, vol. 12, pp. 1255–1289.

Samuelson, P. (1975) 'Optimum social security in a life cycle growth model', *International Economic Review*, vol. 16, pp. 539–544.

Sanchez, I. and Sobel, J. (1989) 'Hierarchical design and enforcement in income tax policies', University of California at San Diego discussion paper.

Sandler, T. and Tschirhart, J. (1980) 'The economic theory of clubs: an evaluative survey', *Journal of Economic Literature*, vol. 18, pp. 1481–1521.

Sandler, T. and Tschirhart, J. (1993) 'Multiproduct clubs: membership and sustainability', *Public Finance*, vol. 48, pp. 153–170.

Sandmo, A. (1972) 'Discount rates for public investment under uncertainty', *International Economic Review*, vol. 13, pp. 287–302.

Sandmo, A. (1973) 'Public goods and the technology of consumption', *Review of Economic Studies*, vol. 49, pp. 517–528.

Sandmo, A. (1974) 'A note on the structure of optimal taxation', *American Economic Review*, vol. 64, pp. 701–706.

Sandmo, A. (1975) 'Optimal taxation in the presence of externalities', *Swedish Journal of Economics*, vol. 77, pp. 86–98.

Sandmo, A. (1976) 'Optimal taxation – an introduction to the literature', *Journal of Public Economics*, vol. 6, pp. 37–54.

Sandmo, A. (1977) 'Portfolio theory, asset demand and taxation: comparative statics with many assets', *Review of Economic Studies*, vol. 49, pp. 517–528.

Sandmo, A. (1980) 'The rate of return and personal savings', *Economic Journal*, vol. 91, pp. 536–540.

Sandmo, A. (1981) 'Income tax evasion, labor supply, and the equity-efficiency tradeoff', *Journal of Public Economics*, vol. 16, pp. 265–288.

Sandmo, A. (1983) 'Progressive taxation, redistribution and labor supply', *Scandinavian Journal of Economics*, vol. 85, pp. 311–323.

Sandmo, A. (1987a) 'The effect of taxation on savings and risk-taking', in A. Auerbach and M. Feldstein (eds) *Handbook of Public Economics*, Amsterdam: North Holland, pp. 265–311.

Sandmo, A. (1987b) 'A reinterpretation of elasticity formula in optimum tax theory', *Economica*, vol. 54, pp. 89–96.

Scarf, H. (1973) *The Computation of Economic Equilibria*, Cowles Commission, Yale University.

Schneider, F. and Horfreither, M. (1987) 'Aspects of tax evasion', mimeo, Tel Aviv University.

Schob, R. (1994) 'On marginal cost and marginal benefit of public funds', *Public Finance*, vol. 49, pp. 87–106.

Scitovsky, T. (1941) 'A note on welfare propositions in economics', *Review of Economic Studies*, vol. 9, pp. 77–88.

Scitovsky, T. (1951) 'The state of welfare economics,' *American Economic Review*, vol. 41, pp. 303–315.

Scotchmer, S. (1987) 'Audit classes and tax enforcement policy,' *American Economic Review Papers and Proceedings*, vol. 77, pp. 229–239.

Seade, J. (1977) 'On the shape of optimal tax schedules,' *Journal of Public Economics*, vol. 7, pp. 203–236.

Seade, J. (1982) 'On the sign of the optimum marginal income tax', *Review of Economic Studies*, vol. 49, pp. 637–643.

Seidman, L. (1980) 'The personal consumption tax and social welfare', *Challenge*, vol. 23, pp. 10–16.

Seidman, L. (1984) 'Conversion to a consumption tax: the transition in a life cycle growth model', *Journal of Political Economy*, vol. 92, pp. 247–267.

Sen, A. (1961) 'On optimizing the rate of saving', *Economic Journal*, vol. 71, pp. 479–496.

Sen, A. (1967) 'Isolation, assurance and the social rate of discount', *Quarterly Journal of Economics*, vol. 81, pp. 112–124.

Sen, A. (1970a) *Collective Choice and Social Welfare*, San Francisco: Holden Day.

Sen, A. (1970b) 'The impossibility of a Paretian liberal', *Journal of Political Economy*, vol. 78, pp. 152–157.

Sen, A. (1972) 'Control areas and accounting prices: an approach to economic evaluation', *Economic Journal*, vol. 82 (supplement), pp. 486–501.

Sen, A. (1973) *On Economic Inequality*, Oxford: Clarendon Press.

Sen, A. (1976) 'Real national income', *Review of Economic Studies*, vol. 43, pp. 19–39.

Sen, A. (1977) 'Social choice theory: a reexamination', *Econometrica*, vol. 45, pp. 53–89.

Sen, A. (1979a) 'The welfare basis of real income comparisons: a survey', *Journal of Economic Literature*, vol. 17, pp. 1–45.

Sen, A. (1979b) 'Personal utilities and public judgments: or what's wrong with welfare economics?', *Economic Journal*, vol. 89, pp. 537–558.

Shapiro, C. and Stiglitz, J. (1984) 'Equilibrium unemployment as a worker discipline device', *American Economic Review*, vol. 74, pp. 433–444.

Sheshinksi, E. (1972) 'The optimal linear income tax', *Review of Economic Studies*, vol. 39, pp. 98–100.

Sheshinski, E. (1978) 'A model of social security and retirement decisions', *Journal of Public Economics*, vol. 10, pp. 337–360.

Sheshinski, E. and Weiss, Y. (1981) 'Uncertainty and optimal social security systems', *Quarterly Journal of Economics*, vol. 96, pp. 189–206.

Shorrocks, A. (1983) 'Ranking income distributions', *Economica*, vol. 50, pp. 3–17.

Shoven, J. and Whalley, J. (1972) 'A general equilibrium calculation of the effects of differential taxation of income from capital in the U.S.', *Journal of Public Economics*, vol. 1, pp. 281–321.

Shoven, J. and Whalley, J. (1984) 'Applied general equilibrium models of taxation and international trade: an introduction and survey', *Journal of Economic Literature*, vol. 22, pp. 1007–1051.

Singh, B. (1973) 'Making honesty the best policy', *Journal of Public Economics*, vol. 2, pp. 257–263.

Slemrod, J. (1988) 'Effects of taxation with international capital mobility', in H. Aaron and J. Pechman (eds) *Uneasy Compromise: Problems of a Hybrid Income-Consumption Tax*, Washington DC: The Brookings Institution.

Slemrod, J. (1990a) 'Optimal taxation and optimal tax systems', *Journal of Economic Perspectives*, vol. 4, pp. 157–178.

Slemrod, J. (1990b) *Do Taxes Matter?*, Cambridge MA: MIT Press.

Slemrod, J. and Yitzhaki, S. (1987) 'The optimal size of a tax collection agency', *Scandinavian Journal of Economics*, vol. 89, pp. 183–192.

Smale, S. (1980) 'The Prisoner's Dilemma and dynamical Systems associated to non-cooperative games', *Econometrica*, vol. 48, pp. 1617–1634.

Spence, M. (1977) 'Nonlinear prices and welfare', *Journal of Public Economics*, vol. 8, pp. 1–18.

Spence, M. and Zeckhauser, R. (1971) 'Insurance, information, and individual action', *American Economic Review Papers and Proceedings*, vol. 61, pp. 380–387.

Spicer, M. and Hero, R. (1985) 'Tax evasion and heuristics: a research note', *Journal of Public Economics*, vol. 26, pp. 263–267.

Spicer, M. and Lundstedt, S. (1976) 'Understanding tax evasion', *Public Finance*, vol. 31, pp. 295–305.

Sproule, R. (1985) 'Tax evasion and labor supply under imperfect information about individual parameters of the tax system', *Public Finance*, vol. 40, pp. 441–456.

Sproule, R., Komus, D. and Tsang, E. (1980) 'Optimal tax evasion: risk neutral behavior under a negative income tax', *Public Finance*, vol. 35, pp. 309–317.

Srinivasan, T. (1973) 'Tax evasion: a model', *Journal of Public Economics*, vol. 2, pp. 339–346.

Starrett, D. (1980a) 'On the method of taxation and the provision of local public goods', *American Economic Review*, vol. 70, pp. 380–392.

Starrett, D. (1980b) 'Measuring the externalities and second best distortions in the theory of local public goods', *Econometrica*, vol. 48, pp. 627–642.

Starrett, D. (1982) 'On the method of taxation and the provision of local public goods: reply', *American Economic Review*, vol. 72, pp. 852–853.

Stern, N. (1976) 'On the specification of models of optimum income taxation', *Journal of Public Economics*, vol. 6, pp. 123–162.

Stern, N. (1987) 'The effects of taxation, price control and government contracts in oligopoly and monopolistic competition', *Journal of Public Economics*, vol. 32, pp. 133–158.

Stern, N. (1991) 'The economics of development: a survey', in A. Oswald (ed.) *Surveys in Economics*, Oxford: Blackwell.

Stern, N. (1992) 'From the static to the dynamic: some problems in the theory of taxation', *Journal of Public Economics*, vol. 47, pp. 273–297.

Stigler, G. (1965) 'The tenable range of the functions of local government', in E. Phelps (ed.) *Private Wants and Public Needs*, New York: W.W. Norton, pp. 167–176.

Stiglitz, J. (1969a) 'The effects of income, wealth and capital gains taxation on risk-taking', *Quarterly Journal of Economics*, vol. 83, pp. 262–283.

Stiglitz, J. (1969b) 'A reexamination of the Modigliani-Miller theorem', *American Economic Review*, vol. 59, pp. 784–793.

Stiglitz, J. (1973) 'Taxation, corporate financial policy, and the cost of capital', *Journal of Public Economics*, vol. 2, pp. 1–34.

Stiglitz, J. (1974) 'On the irrelevance of corporate financial policy', *American Economic Review*, vol. 64, pp. 851–866.

Stiglitz, J. (1976) 'The corporation tax', *Journal of Public Economics*, vol. 5, pp. 303–311.

Stiglitz, J. (1982) 'Self-selection and Pareto efficient taxation', *Journal of Public Economics*, vol. 17, pp. 181–211.

Stiglitz, J. (1986) *Economics of the Public Sector*, New York: W.W. Norton.

Stiglitz, J. (1987) 'The theory of Pareto efficient and optimal redistributive taxation', in P. G. Hare (ed.) *Surveys in Public Sector Economics*, Oxford: Blackwell, pp. 71–114.

Stiglitz, J. (1989) 'The new, new welfare economics and Pareto optimal taxation', in A. Auerbach and M. Feldstein (eds) *Handbook of Public Economics*, Amsterdam: North Holland.

Stiglitz, J. and Weiss, A. (1979) 'Credit rationing in markets with imperfect information', *American Economic Review*, vol. 71, pp. 393–410.

Stolper, W. and Samuelson, P. (1941) 'Protection and real wages', *Review of Economic Studies*, vol. 9, pp. 50–73.

Streissler, E. (1986) 'The international consequences of less progressive taxation', in D. Bos and B. Felderer (eds) *The Political Economy of Progressive Taxation*, Berlin: Springer Verlag.

Strotz, R. (1955) 'Myopia and inconsistency in dynamic utility maximization', *Review of Economic Studies*, vol. 23, pp. 165–180.

Stuart, C. (1980), 'Evaluating the federal aid reform option', *National Tax Journal*, vol. 34, pp. 329–333.

Summers, L. (1981) 'Taxation and capital accumulation in a life cycle growth model', *American Economic Review*, vol. 71, pp. 533–544.

Summers, L. (1988) 'Tax policy and international competitiveness', in J. Frenkel (ed.) *International Aspects of Fiscal Policy*, Chicago: University of Chicago Press.

Tait, A. (1988) *Value Added Tax: International Practice and Problems*, Washington DC: International Monetary Fund.

Takayama, A. (1985) *Mathematical Economics*, Cambridge: Cambridge University Press.

Tanzi, V. (1994) *Taxation in an Integrating World*, Washington DC: The Brookings Institution.

Tiebout, C. (1956) 'A pure theory of local expenditure', *Journal of Political Economy*, vol. 64, pp. 416–424.

Townsend, R. (1979) 'Optimal contracts and competitive markets with costly state verification', *Journal of Economic Theory*, vol. 21, pp. 265–293.

Tulkens, H. (1978) 'Dynamic processes for public goods: an institution oriented survey', *Journal of Public Economics*, vol. 9, pp. 163–201.

Tuomala, S. (1990) *Optimal Income Tax and Redistribution*, Oxford: Clarendon Press.

Turvey, R. (1968) 'Peak load pricing', *Journal of Political Economy*, pp. 101–113.

Turvey, R. (1971) *Economic Analysis and Public Enterprises*, London: Allen and Unwin.

Turvey, R. and Anderson, D. (1977) *Electricity Economics*, Baltimore: Johns Hopkins University Press.

Usher, D. (1983) 'The welfare economics of the socialization of commodities', *Journal of Public Economics*, vol. 20, pp. 347–356.

Uzawa, H. (1969) 'Time preference and the Penrose effect in a two class model of economic growth', *Journal of Political Economy*, vol. 77, pp. 628–652.

Varian, H. (1980) 'Redistributive taxation as social insurance', *Journal of Public Economics*, vol. 14, pp. 49–68.

Varian, H. (1984) 'Price discrimination and social welfare', *American Economic Review*, vol. 75, pp. 870–875.

VicKreg, W. (1947) *Agenda for Progressive Taxation*, New York: Ronald Press.

Virmani, A. (1989) 'Indirect tax evasion and production efficiency', *Journal of Public Economics*, vol. 39, pp. 223–237.

Wagner, G. (ed.) (1991) *Labor Market Dynamics in Present day Germany*, London and Boulder: Westview Press.

Wales, T. and Woodland, A. (1979) 'Labor supply and progressive taxes', *Review of Economic Studies*, vol. 46, pp. 83–95.

Walsh, A. (1978) *The Public's Business*, Cambridge MA: MIT Press.

Watson, H. (1985) 'Tax evasion and labor markets', *Journal of Public Economics*, vol. 27, pp. 231–246.

Weil, P. (1989) 'The equity premium puzzle and the risk-free rate puzzle', *Journal of Monetary Economics*, vol. 24, pp. 401–421.

van Welthoven, B. (1989) *The Endogenization of Government Behavior in Macroeconomic Models* Berlin: Springer Verlag.

Whalley, J. (1984) 'Basis linkage in international tax treatment of goods and capital income', *National Tax Journal*, vol. 37, pp. 195–200.

Wildasin, D. (1977) 'Public good provision with optimal and non optimal commodity taxation: the single consumer case', *Economics Letters*, vol. 4, pp. 59–64.

Wildasin, D. (1984) 'On public goods provision with distortionary taxation', *Economic Inquiry*, vol. 22, pp. 227–243.

Wildasin, D. (1986) *Urban Public Finance*, London, Paris and New York: Harwood.

Wilde, J. (1971) 'Grant in aid: the analytics of design and response', *National Tax Journal*, vol. 24, pp. 143–155.

Wilkinson, M. (1994) 'Paying for public spending: is there a role for earmarked taxes?', *Fiscal Studies*, vol. 15, pp. 119–135.

Williamson, O. (1966) 'Peak-load pricing and optimal capacity under indivisibility constraints', *American Economic Review*, vol. 56, pp. 810–827.

Williamson, O. (1974) 'Peak-load pricing: some further remarks', *Bell Journal of Economics*, vol. 5, pp. 223–228.

Willig, R. (1976) 'Consumer's surplus without apology', *American Economic Review*, vol. 66, pp. 589–597.

Wilson, J. (1991a) 'Optimal public good provision in the Ramsey tax model: a generalization', *Economics Letters*, vol. 35, pp. 57–61.

Wilson, J. (1991b) 'Optimal public good provision with limited lump sum taxation', *American Economic Review*, vol. 81, pp. 153–166.

van Winden, F. (1983) *On the Interaction between the State and the Private Sector*, Amsterdam: North Holland.

Wright, C. (1969) 'Saving and the rate of interest', in A. Harberger and M. Bailey (eds) *The Taxation of Income from Capital*, Washington DC: The Brookings Institution.

Wyckoff, P. (1990) 'The simple analytics of slack-maximizing bureacracy', *Public Choice*, vol. 67. pp. 35–47.

Xu, B. (1994) 'Tax policy implications in endogenous growth models', IMF Discussion Paper.

Yaari, M. (1965) 'Uncertain lifetime, life insurance, and the theory of the consumer', *Review of Economic Studies*, vol. 32, pp. 137–150.

Yellen, J. (1984) 'Efficiency wage models of unemployment', *American Economic Review*, vol. 74, pp. 200–205.

Yitzhaki, S. (1974) 'A note on income tax evasion: a theoretical analysis', *Journal of Public Economics*, vol. 3, pp. 201–202.

Young, D. (1982) 'Voluntary purchase of public goods', *Public Choice*, vol. 38, pp. 73–86.

Zabalza, J. and Arrufat, J. (1986) 'Female labor supply and taxation: random preferences and optimization', *National Tax Journal*, vol. 28, pp. 341–350.

Zee, H. (1994) 'Time consistent optimal intertemporal taxation in externally-indebted economies', *Public Finance*, vol. 40, pp. 113–125.

Name Index

Subject Index